Managing your Home

A former associate editor of the *Sunday Mirror Magazine*, Liz Vercoe has written for the *Sunday Times Magazine*, *You*, *House Beautiful* and *Woman's Own*. She has also renovated and furnished three houses built between 1720 and 1920 and created home comforts for a 32-foot sailing boat. Liz currently works for *Radio Times* and lives on the banks of the Thames with her journalist husband and their baby, Adam.

Managing your Home

EDITOR

LIZ VERCOE

BLOOMSBURY

For my late mother, Elise Latta, who had a very special talent for home-making.

First published in 1995 by Bloomsbury Publishing Plc, 2 Soho Square, London W I V 6HB

Copyright © 1995 Bloomsbury Publishing Plc
The moral right of the authors has been asserted

A CIP catalogue entry is available on request from the British Library

ISBN 0 7475 1989 7

10 9 8 7 6 5 4 3 2 1

Compiled, edited, designed and typeset by Karen Sullivan, Simon Bell and Sylvie Rabbe
for Book Creation Services Ltd,
21 Carnaby Street,
London W I V I PH

Illustrations by Val Hill

Printed in Britain by Clays Ltd, St Ives Plc, Bungay, Suffolk

Contents

CHAPTER SEVEN **Basic car maintenance**
Maria Young

CHAPTER EIGHT **Gardening**
Hazel Evans

CHAPTER NINE **Pets**
Claire Bessant

Introduction

This book is very much a "if only I'd known then what I know now" piece of work. If I'd had such a compendium when I first left home it might have saved me from learning the hard way that cooking oil self-ignites if you keep heating it, that a fridge door which opens the wrong way for the kitchen layout requires you to be a contortionist (this has to be weighed up against the fridge's cheapness, of course), that keeping money in the wrong account is like throwing money in the dustbin each month, and that a bargain carpet which on close inspection reveals more backing than tufts is no bargain. It wasn't much fun, either, sticking a screwdriver into a live socket (disguised as an extension lead but I was being dumb). Thank heavens for circuit breakers (see page 68).

From the day I first moved into a student flat, aged 18 (just) with a repertoire of two recipes (fish pie and potato cakes, both requiring phone calls home to double check), the ability to sew on a button but not much more, and no thought that I would ever have to look inside a plug let alone a socket, I could only but learn. And the most important lesson was that the more you know about something the less likely you are to be taken for a ride, sold a dud, or make a bad choice.

The pages which follow are a gathering together of all that might be useful to someone setting up or, indeed, simply leaving home for the first time. They're full of the sorts of things parents wished their children knew before fleeing the nest and, maybe, things children wished their parents had known in the first place. With this book you can tackle furnishing a flat or house with items which won't turn out to be a waste of money (and discover how to keep them in tip-top order), find your way through a cookery book without it seeming a foreign language, know your rights as a consumer and at work and pick the best car for your budget and the perfect plant for that bare spot in the garden.

You can be quite a handy man/woman, too, with the help of the sections on DIY, sewing and car care. There's no doubt that if you have both the time and the inclination, and I speak with two self-renovated houses behind me and a series of beloved cars aged from 18 down, it is totally rewarding to make or fix something yourself. But if you are one of the GSI (Get Someone In) persuasion, which with another house I was, the sections will also help you know when you are being spun an incompetent or expensive yarn by your so-called expert.

We haven't forgotten family and friends, either – from babies to budgies and partners to pooches there's advice on keeping them healthy and content. For humans you'll find tips on a balanced diet, an A to Z of common illnesses and tips for staying fit; for the furry and feathered you'll get all the advice you need on picking the pet which will make you happy and how to keep it a happy pet.

And that's really the gist of it all. This book aims to help you get it right, then you can get on with enjoying your life. We all wish you every happiness in your new home.

Liz Vercoe

CHAPTER ONE **A new home**

Sonia Roberts

Long-established contributor to leading trade and consumer publications in the field of home furnishing and decor. She also writes about antiques and garden design.

Unless you are fortunate enough to have enough money to equip and furnish your new home straightaway, it is worth sorting out the essentials you'll need to get started. This will allow you to spread your budget around the home. You'll find there is a relatively short list of essentials for each room of the house. However, now is also the time to work out what you will want in the future so that you don't make life difficult for yourself later by not leaving sufficient space for an item or forgetting to install necessary electrical or plumbing connections. The following checklists will help you identify what you need around the home **Now, Soon** and **Sometime**. They'll also help you draw up a wedding list, if that's needed.
The checklists are followed by a buyers' guide, to make sure you select the right items for you.

Bedroom

When things are really tight most people start from the bedroom and expand from there – rather like creating your own bed-sitting room. If you have furnished your bedroom, you have somewhere to sit, somewhere to sleep, somewhere to work and relax. Then you can move on to creating a living room and fitting out your kitchen. (see pp. 161-71).

Now
- ☞ Bed
- ☞ Sheets, duvet cover and pillowcases – enough for one in use, one in the wash
- ☞ Curtains
- ☞ Duvet or blankets
- ☞ Pillows
- ☞ Hanging rail
- ☞ Full length mirror
- ☞ Shelves or drawers

Soon
- ☞ Additional sheets and pillows plus valance or valance sheets if a divan bed
- ☞ Bedside tables and lights
- ☞ Radio alarm clock

Sometime
- ☞ Telephone

Choosing . . . a bed

A third of your life is spent asleep and a good night's rest is essential to health and wellbeing. So if your budget is tight, whatever else you economise on, don't skimp when buying a bed. Get the very best you can afford.

Prices of beds in standard manufacturers' ranges vary dramatically, but it should be possible to acquire a reasonable quality double bed, capable of giving eight to ten years' good service, for somewhere between £500 and £800.

> **Never feel tempted by the low cost to consider a secondhand mattress. No matter how cheap, it won't be a bargain and could create health problems.**

Beds come as **divans** with independent removable headboards, or as **bedsteads** with the head- and foot-boards a permanent part of the bed-base frame.

Padded headboards covered in fabrics like Dralon velvet can look attractive but may well quickly get marked or faded and need replacing sooner than a wooden or metal headboard.

Size

When buying a bed think big, for generally speaking the bigger the bed the greater the comfort.

As standard ranges British beds come in the following sizes:

75 cm	**x**	**190 cm**
2 ft 6 in	**x**	**6 ft 3 in**
90 cm	**x**	**190 cm**
3 ft	**x**	**6 ft 3 in**
120 cm	**x**	**190 cm**
4 ft	**x**	**6 ft 3 in**
135 cm	**x**	**190 cm**
4 ft 6 in	**x**	**6 ft 6 in**
150 cm	**x**	**200 cm**
5 ft	**x**	**6 ft 6 in**
180 cm	**x**	**200 cm**
6 ft	**x**	**6 ft 6 in**

The biggest standard size doubles were sometimes sold as queen size (150 cm x 200 cm) and king size (180 cm x 200 cm) but these terms have now been largely dropped because they were also applied by some manufacturers to describe their de luxe and top-of-the-range models, regardless of size.

Most manufacturers are happier to make bigger than standard beds by special order

and will also produce fancy shapes, of which ovals and rounds are the most popular. But it is worth remembering that non-standard size and shape beds will also require special sheets and these, like the beds themselves, will be more expensive.

Ideally a double bed should be at least 15 cm (6 in) longer than the tallest sleeper and a single bed for an adult should be 90 cm (3 ft) wide.

All beds come in two parts, **base** and **mattress**, but both sections need to be bought at the same time. Correct support and comfort depends on the interaction between the two sections.

Bases

The various types of base are:

Sprung edge: In a sprung-edge base the spring unit sits on top of a frame. The advantage is even springing over the total area and, in conjunction with a correctly chosen mattress, the sprung-edge base acts as a giant shock absorber as the sleepers twist and turn, which in an average night they will do at least sixty times. The sprung edge is the most durable but also the most expensive type of base.

Firm edge: In the firm-edge base – a type of construction most commonly found in single divan-style beds – the spring section is set into the frame. The firm edge usually has fewer springs than the sprung-edge base and is generally, though not necessarily, less expensive.

Platform (sometimes also described as solid or padded bases): Often preferred by those who like their beds firm, they are cheaper than either sprung-edge or firm edge construction. But because it is the mattress rather than combination of mattress and base which takes the strain of the sleepers' weight and movement, the mattress is likely to wear out much faster than the base.

Slatted: Slatted bases are more common in bedsteads than in divans, with slats that are either rigid or sprung. The more expensive types of sprung slatted beds can often be adjusted to vary the degree of firmness at hip level where the concentration of weight is greatest.

In Britain slatted base beds are often bought for use in conjunction with a **futon** or by sleepers with back problems who need an ultra firm bed.

A **futon** is the wadded cotton mattress traditional to Japan, where it is placed directly on the floor. In its Westernised form it is used on a bed-base and this combination of base and mattress is often described as a futon.

In Japan the futon is rolled and stowed in a cupboard during the day. In Europe in daytime it is more likely to be folded up as part of a sofa or settee.

The quality of a futon mattress depends on the number of layers of cotton wadding beneath the cover. There should be at least three but luxury quality futons can have as many as nine. And in Westernised futon beds, other materials – wool, felt or polyester – may well be substituted for cotton.

Futons represent good value for money but because of the constant rolling and unrolling will wear out quicker than more conventional European mattresses, which normally come as **pocketed sprung**, **open spring**, **latex**, **foam** and **fibre**.

Mattresses

Pocketed sprung mattresses consist of individual springs, each enclosed in a separate canvas pocket which reacts individually to pressure. In double beds an advantage of this system is that the movement of one of the sleepers is less likely to disturb the other. But because of the amount of handwork which goes into their construction pocketed-sprung mattresses can never be cheap – prices start at around £400 for a 135 cm (4 ft 6 in) double.

Open spring: In this type the spring section takes the form of a mesh of interlocking coils constructed as a single component, making the mattress much cheaper than the pocketed-sprung type. Its quality depends on the number of springs used. British Standards insist on a minimum of 288 in a 135 cm (4 ft 6 in) mattress, though most reputable manufacturers are much more generous.

Latex or **foam** mattresses achieve resilience through the sponginess of the moulded component beneath the cover, which can be of natural or synthetic rubber or of polyurethane foam. In days gone by latex mattresses had the reputation of being too hot for comfortable sleep but this fault has been largely cured by improvements in the composition of the latex itself.

Fibre, one of the newest types of mattress, derives bounce-back qualities not from metal springs or the air bubbles trapped in sponge rubber or polyurethane foam but from millions of curled, hollow, manmade fibres with, sandwiched at their core, a firm central core to provide additional support.

Polyester fibres incidentally allow body moisture to evaporate quickly, helping to keep a bed dry – an important factor since every healthy adult exudes at least a pint of sweat each night.

Whatever the mattress, but particularly in the case of springs, there will be a layer of padding immediately beneath the cover (technically referred to as the tick). Traditionally this was made of coir (coconut fibre), felt, sisal, wool or animal hair (usually horse hair). Today it is just as likely to be a manmade material, usually a polyester foam, secured to the outside by stitching.

This finishing touch is an important feature, anchoring the padding to prevent movement and adding a decorative effect to the outer cover. There are four main methods of stitching: **tufting, micro- (or multi-) quilting, diamond-quilting** (also known as deep stitch) and **smooth top**. Tufting is most often used for pocketed sprung mattresses; micro-quilting is currently the most fashionable finish and therefore the most frequently seen; diamond-quilting is the most traditional, and smooth top, with padding secured only round the edge, is the simplest process at the factory stage and therefore the cheapest at retail level.

As a general rule the heavier the sleeper the firmer the mattress needed for correct support. But personal taste plays an important role. Most manufacturers now grade mattresses on a scale of one to eight – the higher the number the firmer the mattress. However, standards are not consistent which is yet another reason for never buying a bed without first trying it in-store.

So don't be bashful when buying a bed. Don't just sit shyly on the edge of the showroom model. Be prepared not only to bounce up and down but to stretch out full length and test its comfort lying on your back, your side and your front. If, when lying on your back, there is a gap at your waist, the mattress may be too firm for your weight.

When buying a double, always take your partner along, remembering that for couples of very disparate weights and sizes two separate units with differing degrees of firmness which can be linked with a zip are often a much better buy than a conventional double.

So if you are working to a tight budget put your money where it counts – on the interior – and settle for a simple plain cover of nylon or non-woven fabric.

When the bed arrives . . .

Remove the plastic film cover which has been put on at the works to keep the bed clean en route. If this is left on the result will be condensation on the plastic and mould on the mattress.

It does make sense to put a protective cover made from a breathable fabric over the mattress itself (similar covers are now also being made for pillows and duvets) to protect them from staining or accidental spills.

Any salesman should be prepared to explain why one bed is worth more than another but if you want to do your homework before going out to shop contact:

**the NATIONAL BED FEDERATION
251 Brompton Road,
London SW3 2EZ,**

not forgetting to enclose a large stamped self-addressed envelope.

Bed care

When you get up in the morning throw back the bed clothes and leave the bed open for at least twenty minutes before remaking.

Turn a spring-interior mattress over and reverse the head and foot at least once a week for the first month and thereafter at three monthly intervals. This helps the upholstery fillings to settle evenly.

Never bend a spring mattress; it can damage the springs.

Every few months both the mattress and the upholstered base should be cleaned with a soft brush to remove dust and fluff. Avoid pulling on mattress tufts or buttons as they hold the filling in place – like the machine stitching on the mattress surface.

If a liquid is spilled on the bed, immediately blot up as much as possible with an old terry towel or kitchen paper.

If the culprit is a leaking hot water bottle a hair dryer is the quickest and simplest way to dry up the damp.

Choosing . . . bed linen

Though we still talk of bed linen it is many a long day since 'linen', fibres obtained from flax, played a dominant role. In the 1990s the choice is usually between 100 per cent cotton or a blend of cotton and a manmade fibre for sheets, pillowcases and duvet covers.

Cotton is pleasantly crisp to the touch and can be dyed to any colour, as well as providing a perfect base for interesting floral or abstract printed designs.

Unless cotton is guaranteed colour-fast and sold with precise washing instructions be wary of very deep dye shades which are often not as colour-fast as pastel tints and can sometimes bleed colour on to other items in the washing machine. Crimson, scarlet, navy and black are the most likely culprits.

The finest quality is the cotton percale sheet, distinguished by a very dense weave which lends an ultra smooth finish to the fabric as well as greater tensile strength and durability.

The disadvantage of pure cotton is that to achieve a crisp finish, sheets and pillowcases will need ironing each time they are laundered.

The addition of a manmade fibre, usually polyester in a 50/50 blend, makes for easier laundering. Sheets dry quicker, require only minimal ironing and have a very similar feel to pure cotton.

Types and sizes

Sheets come in two types: fitted and loose.

Fitted bottom sheets are labour savers, cutting down on the time it takes to make a bed in the morning. And they stay comfortably smooth longer because they are less likely to be rumpled by even the most restless sleeper.

But often fitted sheets, particularly the cheaper kind, don't last as long as flat sheets since the elastic threads which shape the sheet's corners don't stand up to laundering as well.

If you choose flat sheets they should be at least a foot longer and two feet wider than the dimensions of the bed to allow for folding down and tucking in.

The size of both sheets and pillowcases also varies according to their country of origin.

In continental Europe, for instance, pillows are usually square in shape rather than oblong and are mostly 65 cm (26 in) square.

However, sizes vary from nation to nation and manufacturer to manufacturer so always take the trouble to check that pillowcases fit your pillows if an imported design takes your fancy.

Americans tend to think bigger than the British on both bed and bedding sizes.

Choosing . . . pillows

Pillows come with two types of filling – manmade or natural. Pillows with synthetic fillings suit those who like firm support; natural-fill pillows mould more easily to the shape of the sleeper's head.

In **natural fill** pillows the choice is between chicken feathers – usually referred to as curled feather because the manufacturers put an artificial curl into the feather to soften it and make the pillow easier to plump up – duck feathers, goose feathers and down.

Chicken feather is the cheapest but often the softening process is only partially successful and the pillow feels hard and scrunchy because the contents consist mainly of chopped quill, or merely feather dust.

Both **duck** and **goose** feathers make a softer, fluffier filling because the individual feathers themselves are smaller and fluffier. They are, however, more expensive.

Down is reckoned to be the finest natural filling but produces a pillow which is too soft for some tastes. A down pillow will be lighter in weight than other natural fill types and is more expensive but should last longer. A good down pillow which will probably cost £40 plus (1995 prices) should have at least a ten-year life span.

Synthetic fill pillows are a wiser choice for the allergy prone.

When pillows are dry cleaned by normal methods, the solvent used in the cleaning process can get trapped in the filling. Some cleaners are now getting round this problem by the use of ultra violet light instead of conventional solvents. Check before leaving your pillows at the cleaners.

Polyester is the most common filling for **synthetic** pillows, most of which have at their core a slab or roll of polyester fibre which is surrounded by tiny filaments of polyester which have been hollowed out to make the pillow easier to plump up.

There is however another type of polyester filling, which consists of tiny balls of polyester fibre. Such pillows feel more like natural feather – more pliable and softer than conventional synthetic fillings.

Whatever filling you choose it is important to check the cover **fabric**. This needs to be closely woven and well stitched or there is a risk of the filling escaping through the tiny gaps between the threads which make up the fabric and join seams.

Care

Your pillows need a good daily shake and, in the case of down or feather pillows, an occasional airing in the sunlight.

Since moisture as well as dust tends to accumulate in pillows it is a good idea to give them an occasional wash – always taking care to check the manufacturers' instructions which should be attached to any good branded product.

Incidentally, natural fill pillows wash as well – sometimes better – than those with synthetic content.

Choosing . . . a duvet, eiderdown and blankets

Keeping warm

The difference between a duvet and the old-fashioned English eiderdown is that the duvet is the complete bed covering, a feather or synthetic fibre-filled quilt or sac contained within a removable cover, whereas the decorative cover of an eiderdown is permanently sewn to the quilt.

Like pillows, duvets come with both natural and synthetic fillings and here again the most expensive is down.

Down is considered the connoisseur's choice because its high tog rating – its degree of warmth – can be combined with light weight. Duvets suited to the coldest conditions have the highest numerical rating on the tog scale – 13 is usually considered the most suitable for the British winter and 3 for summer.

Polyester-filled duvets are just as warm as **feather-filled** types and come with a similar range of tog ratings but are generally heavier in weight.

Duvets are variously fastened into their removable covers by tie strings, press studs, zip fasteners and Velcro strips.

Technically, an **eiderdown** is only truly an eiderdown when it is filled with down taken from the breast or the arctic nest of the eider duck. In spring this species pulls out its own breast feathers to provide a cosy lining for the ground-based nest in which it rears its family.

Over the years however the term has become generic for any form of permanently covered padded quilt designed to be used over blankets. There is also the all-over American lightly quilted cover (bedspread) which is only suitable for warmer climates or permanent central heating unless accompanied by blankets.

> As a precaution against moth damage wool blankets should always be stored in a tightly closed plastic bag when not in use.

Traditional blankets are usually made of wool, a blend of wool and manmade fibre or occasionally, at the very top end of the market, cashmere yarns. After weaving, traditional blanket cloth is heat treated to produce a felted surface and sometimes 'teased' or brushed to give a soft fluffy handle.

Cellular weaves give warmth without weight. Today they are especially popular as cot blankets which require frequent laundering and are often made from acrylic yarns which are easier to wash and quicker to dry than wool. **Acrylic blankets** also have the virtue of being moth proof. Cellular cot blankets are commonly made of cotton.

The linen cupboard

As well as bedding, the check list for a well stocked linen cupboard should include:

Now

- ☞ Three bath towels and three hand towels for each member of the family.
- ☞ Two kitchen towels and six tea towels – even if you have a dishwasher, cloths will be needed for jobs like polishing delicate glassware.

Sometime

- ☞ Additional sheets, pillow cases and duvet covers.
- ☞ Towels for the guests.
- ☞ A tablecloth for dinner party entertaining with matching table napkins.
- ☞ More tea towels.

Carpets

Getting the best wear out of your carpet means choosing the right quality for each area. Bedrooms for instance get less wear than living rooms while hallways and stairs get the heaviest wear in the house.

Tufted or woven?

Woven carpets

Woven carpets are made by two methods both bearing the names of the West Country town where these techniques were first developed: Axminster and Wilton.

Axminster carpets are woven with the pile forming a series of U-shaped tufts which are then attached to a backing.

Wilton carpets are produced with the pile and back interwoven, a process which results in a thick carpet with a velvetry surface.

Tufted carpets

The tufts are inserted into a backing and secured there by a layer of latex which may form the actual underside of the carpet or be concealed by another layer of fabric.

Their low price brought the possibility of all-over-the-house carpet to a wider range of buyers.

A good tufted can hold its own for quality and performance with the best of the traditionals and are included as an alternative choice in the ranges of all the leading manufacturers of traditional woven carpets.

> **When choosing a carpet for its hard-wearing properties don't be taken in by apparent thickness. Many tricks of the trade are employed by manufacturers to make carpet pile seem denser than it actually is but if you bend a small section of a carpet sample till the back shows through you'll get clearer idea of the actual quality.**

Carpet manufacturers grade
their wares from A to F so look
for the code on the label:

A indicates a contract quality
which is the hardest wearing
of all but usually sold only to
hotels or for public buildings.
B is suitable for halls and stairs.
C and **D** qualities are sensible
living room choices.
E is ideal for rooms not in
regular use – guests' or formal
dining areas in houses where
most everyday meals are
eaten in the kitchen.
F is bedroom grade.

Carpets are also described by the type of pile:
Saxony carpets come in two types, long
and short pile. The long-pile type is luxurious
under foot and makes a good bedroom
carpet but wears less well than short-pile
Saxony, which is a better choice for living
rooms. **Cut and loop** pile is also a good
living room selection and in its most
hardwearing grades is suitable for halls.

Berber on the other hand, although its
tweedy looks suggests toughness, wears less
well than other types and therefore is best
used in light footfall areas.

What's it made of?

All-wool carpets are the connoisseur's
choice for appearance, underfoot texture and
flame resistance. They are not however the
most hardwearing and have been overtaken
in the popular market by 80 per cent wool
20 per cent nylon blends.

Nylon is also a component of carpets
which appears under a variety of other
names, of which one of the most frequently
used in the carpet trade is Antron. Today
however polypropylene is presenting a real
challenge to nylon as a partner for wool while
polypropylene on its own is making major
headway in the all-synthetic fibre carpet
market.

Today **fitted carpet** is the most popular
choice but a continuing advantage of
choosing unfitted carpet is that it can be
picked up and turned round from time to
time so that it wears more evenly and
therefore last longer.

Unfitted carpets are easier to clean –
the vacuum cleaner can go right to the edge
so they may be a better choice where
hygiene is of primary importance as, for
instance, in a nursery.

Most **woven carpets** will need to be laid
by a professional fitter which like the cost of
underlay has to be taken into account when
budgeting for the overall cost of floor
covering.

Budget-quality rubber-backed carpet can
however be cut with scissors and can be
more easily laid by the amateur. Also useful
cost-cutting alternatives to carpet which do
not require to be permanently fixed to the
floor but can be loose laid are **sisal**, **coir**,
and **rush mattings**.

Carpet care

Forget the old wives' tale that new carpets
should not be vacuumed for three months
until they have 'settled' and cease to lose fluff.

Carpets should be cared for from the day
they are laid. Allowing dust to work its way
into the pile for eight to ten weeks is only
storing up trouble for the future.

While the surplus fluff or 'nap' is still
working its way to the surface – a process
which should be complete in about three
months – twice weekly vacuuming should be
sufficient.

**Carpet can be used all over the
house and today special qualities
are made for both bathrooms
and kitchens. Bathroom carpet
is rubber backed to make it
impervious to water and kitchen
carpets are usually sold in the
form of tiles so that the almost
inevitable grease stains can be
replaced without having to re-
carpet the whole floor.**

If you decide on a long-pile carpet you'll need a vacuum cleaner which combines suction to remove the dirt with a rotary brush which restores the pile depressed by constant walking across its surface or by pressure from furniture.

Lighting

The correct choice of lighting depends first on deciding the activities for which a room will be most often used:

In living rooms **wall lights** tend to light the room more attractively than a centre light and **uplighters**, which cast a soft glow on the ceiling and are either wall-mounted or free-standing, are ideal for TV viewing.

A desk or bureau used as a home office or for children to do their homework should be fitted with a jointed arm, or flexible spring, **table lamp** which can focus directly on the work surface. Beware of too bright or white a bulb, however, as this can cause glare from the page and eyestrain.

Spotlights, either wall-mounted or on a track, focus attention on particular areas and are ideal for highlighting ornaments. Focusing direct light on valuable pictures, particularly watercolours which can fade, is not a good idea.

A **pendant light** over the centre of the table which can be raised or lowered – high and out of the way for informal family meals, closer to the table as a sole source of light for intimate tête à tête – is a good dining room choice.

Dimmer switches (see also page 66) can be used in conjunction with normal light (they don't work with fluorescent bulbs) to vary light levels. These are very useful in the nursery.

Try to think of light as you would paint and colour when decorating a room. With a combination of spotlights. Table lamps and general lighting on dimmer switches you can create different looks for day, evening, parties and TV watching.

Use **spotlights** or wall-mounted **fluorescent bars** to get maximum illumination for kitchen chores. Most central ceiling lights are virtually useless in a kitchen but can be extended by a lead which loops across the ceiling taking the light where it's more needed.

In the bedroom you need light to dress by – normally a central ceiling light – light for hair, makeup and grooming – (either a table lamp on the dressing table or a wall light by a mirror) and bedside lights. It's tempting to choose rather dim lights here but they are not good for reading. You need a 60-watt bulb. You may also want striplighting in the wardrobe so you can select clothes easily.

For the bathroom, you can buy **combined shaver points and light** to site above a mirror.

When planning lighting don't forget the **outdoors**. A porch light which can be switched on from the outside as well as inside will save hours of fumbling for keys on a dark night. Alternatively fit one with a PIR sensor which automatically lights as you approach. Good for deterring vandals, too.

Porch lights in combination with a door peephole also provide an opportunity to check on who is calling unexpectedly at a late hour without having to open the door first.

If you are rewiring, install a separate 3amp circuit for table lamps worked by a light switch at the door. Then your room gets the look you want instantly, without going round switching on lights individually.

For right-handed folk the source of light should be behind their left shoulder, for left handers it should be to their right.

Curtains

Whether for the bedroom, living room or any other part of the house the basic rules for curtain buying remain the same.

Whether buying curtain fabric or ready-made curtains you will need the width and height of your windows and the length of the curtain track if one is not already in place.

Curtain tracks are usually longer than the width of the actual window so that when the curtains are open they hang on either side of the window, letting in the maximum amount of light.

When buying curtain track pick a type suitable to carry the weight of your curtains – a particularly important factor where lined curtains in heavy materials such as velvet or brocade are the choice.

Tracks or poles?

Curtain poles, in metal, wood or plastic, are more suitable for rooms in either genuine or reproduction Georgian, Regency or Victorian style.

Both curtain poles and track are available with pull-cord closure systems. These are initially more expensive than a system in which the curtains are drawn manually but the curtains last longer because there's less wear and tear and less risk of soiling the curtain fabric. If you can afford to shop at the luxury end of the market there are electrically powered systems which incorporate a time switch mechanism. That way, even if you are away from home the curtains will close as usual at twilight – and not advertise to burglars the fact that the premises are unoccupied.

Curtain track these days is almost always made of plastic and several excellent branded systems of track and runners are available as complete curtain kits from leading department and DIY store groups. For the new home owner such compendium packs – the smallest generally contains 120 cm (4 ft) of track plus all the necessary fixings – may well represent better value than unbranded track in cut lengths with all the other components having to be bought separately. Their biggest advantage, though, is that they come with fixing instructions.

Plastic track systems are cheaper than poles and if required can easily be disguised by fancy headings to the curtains themselves; by solid or fabric pelmets or by independently fitted swathes, swags or curtain frills.

Curtain lengths

When measuring up for curtains, measure the drop (the curtain length) from the top of the track to where you want your curtains to finish.

Short curtains are usually made either to skim the windowsill or to hang approximately 24 cm (9 in) below sill level. Short curtains make narrow windows seem wider and are the best choice for small, cottage style or corner windows

Floor-length curtains should finish approximately an inch above carpet level. They increase the apparent depth of a window, helping to create the illusion of added height in a low-ceilinged room.

Curtain widths

To give a proper impression of fullness in the finished curtains you will need between one-and-a-half and three times the actual window size (see page 140), depending on the style of curtain you choose.

Choosing the fabric

Remember: the wider and fuller the curtain the more expensive the process of dressing the window will be. However, for the best results, it is always better to choose wider curtains in a cheaper fabric which you can hang generously, rather than selecting narrower ones in an expensive fabric which folds skimpily.

The choice of fabrics is virtually infinite. Take your pick from silks, plain, slubbed or with woven-in patterns; imitations of these in manmade fibres or rayon; velvets made from silk or cotton; wool tapestries or folk weaves; linens plain, printed or blended with cotton, and glazed or matt-finish cottons.

Meanwhile sheer net curtains are available in a variety of manmade fibres, 100 per cent cotton, cotton and manmade mixes, and in easy-care 100 per cent manmade fibres.

For instructions on how to make your own curtains, see pp. 140-4.

Curtain care

Silk looks lovely but is obviously one of the most expensive fabrics and when soiled will almost certainly have to be professionally dry cleaned.

Professional dry cleaning is also generally recommended for all types of velvet or woollen curtains, not so much because they won't withstand home washing but because of their extremely heavy weight, especially when wet, and the length of time it takes to dry them thoroughly.

Cotton or cotton blended fabrics are probably the most practical choice both from the viewpoint of cost and wash and wear.

Lining

Lined curtains gather more richly, keep out unwanted light at night and protect the face fabric from fading and rotting through exposure to bright sunlight.

Lined curtains are initially more expensive but can reduce heating bills and draughts, particularly if the lining has thermal insulating properties.

Heavy-weight lined curtains made sufficiently full to give an overlap when drawn are great draught excluders – an important

factor when you consider that as much as 10 per cent of a room's warmth can escape through ill-fitting and inefficiently curtained windows.

Where the radiator is already built under the window, either build out the window sill slightly and hang your curtains to that length so that hot air is not lost behind them, or fit 'false' full-length curtains which never close, plus a blind to give privacy and cover the window itself at night.

Blinds

> **When thinking energy saving don't hang curtains or put solid furniture in front of a central heating radiator or you will lose much of the value of your heating.**

Blinds come in four distinct types: drop blinds such as Austrian, festoon and Roman blinds, roller blinds, Venetians and verticals. They can be made of paper, canvas, fabric, wool, plastic or metal.

> **Venetian blinds, favoured in hot climates, with slats made of wood give more protection against heat loss than metal, but all slatted blinds fail to keep in as much warm air as solid blinds.**

Austrian or **festoon** blinds (see also page 144) are usually made of sheer fabrics ruched so that they can be raised or lowered in sections to create fancy shapes. **Roman blinds** rise and fall in crisp horizontal pleats. The aim is to choose the blind to suit your style of home.

Roller blinds are the simplest and most traditional type, raised or lowered by a central pull cord or by side-sited continuous plastic chains. In steaming kitchens or bathrooms the plastic chain is a better bet than a spring-action metal mechanism which could well rust and start to stick.

Venetian blinds consisting of horizontal bars have the advantage of offering varying levels of light entry according to the time of day by means of a simple pull action on the cords which control the angle of the slats. **Vertical** slatted blinds work in the same manner as classic Venetians but as the name suggests the slats run vertically rather than horizontally. They are more usually to be found in offices or large public buildings.

The living room

Now
- ☞ Settee
- ☞ Chairs
- ☞ Rugs or carpet
- ☞ Television
- ☞ Music centre
- ☞ Telephone

Soon
- ☞ Side or occasional tables
- ☞ Table lamps
- ☞ Bookshelves or bookcase
- ☞ Video recorder
- ☞ Cassette and CD storage
- ☞ Telephone answering machine

The one thing most first-time home buyers are likely to have is something to play music on. So while a music centre may not seem essential, it's included in the list because it's probably already there! If you are moving on from sitting on the bed, watching TV or playing tapes or CDs, living room furniture seems totally luxurious. This soon becomes the room where guests are entertained and most of your relaxation time is spent, so invest wisely.

Furniture

Remember that most furniture showrooms are a good deal more spacious than the average living room and tend to make items like settees, armchairs and dining suites look smaller than they really are.

Never trust merely to eye and memory but take accurate measurements of the space available in the room to be furnished and take with you not only a list of these measurements but a tape measure to check the precise size of the pieces which interest you.

Your list of home measurements should also include the dimensions of any door through which the furniture has to pass, not forgetting headroom on the stairs when buying furniture destined for the first or second floor.

Take care when buying secondhand anywhere but in a shop or sale-room – the furniture may not be governed by the current fire regulations for low flammability. Furniture sold in shops or sale-rooms must by law be up to date on this. The same rules apply to beds.

Choosing . . . seating

As with beds there's only one failsafe way to check the 'easiness' of an armchair – by personal trial, which means perseverence in the showroom. For instance when testing a sofa for comfort don't simply perch on the edge, sit well back and remain sitting for a minimum of ten minutes.

Seating for the living room comes in almost as many shapes and sizes as the people who will use it. So although traditionally the three-piece suite has been the way to furnish a living room there's a case for letting every member of the household choose the form of chair most suited to their weight, height and posture rather than buying a set piece suite on which no one is 100 per cent comfortable.

Hard or soft?

Sofa cushions filled with foam or polyester fibre are firmer and need plumping up less often than feather, although all cushions will have to plumped from time to time.

Quality checks

When buying upholstered furniture you have to a large extent to take on trust the manufacturers' and retailers' word that the components beneath the cover are of a standard compatible with the asking price, because obviously you can't pull upholstered furniture apart to see how it is made. But there are quality checks you can make.

Ask the shop assistant to tip up a chair or

settee so that you can get a look at the frame. In cheap suites the frame is usually made of stapled chipboard. In better-quality seating the frame will be made of hardwood and screwed or dowelled.

If the furniture comes with a patterned cover check that the motifs match up correctly, particularly in the case of wide stripes.

Check the seat cushions. They should fit snugly with no gaps between the edge of the cushion and the chair arm.

> **Do consider having your upholstered furniture given a treatment, such as the Scotchguard process, which gives protection against spills and staining, before it leaves the store for your home. The cost of such treatments will vary according to the type of fabric selected and the size and shape of the suite being treated but reckon on spending up to 10 per cent of the purchase cost for this facility. You can also spray the smaller pieces of upholstery yourself using aerosol cans.**

Feel the padding on the back and arms of a sofa or armchair. If you can feel the frame – forget it.

Coverings

Leather looks luxurious and is long lasting. But light shades may not be the best choice for a family with boisterous young children or pets.

Fabric choices are very wide. Brocades, damasks, velvets, cut moquettes, linen union and a huge range of cotton and manmade fabrics are available in upholstery qualities, and most retailers will be happy to give advice on relative durability and on care.

> **When ordering fabric to make fitted or loose covers for easy chairs or settees, never be tempted to use curtain or dress material because these are cheaper than similar looking fabrics sold in the upholstery section. They won't stand the strain of being constantly sat upon nor will they satisfy the legal requirements of non-flammability now demanded of fabrics designed for covering furniture.**

Choosing . . .wooden furniture

Many people setting up home for the first time settle for secondhand wooden furniture. It is basically so durable that if you like the design, the table and chairs will be perfectly servicable. Do check for woodworm, however, by looking for small holes, as if a pin has been driven in many times, in the unpolished surfaces of the wood (the underside of a table, the bottom and sides of drawers, the back of cabinets or wardrobes or the underside of wooden seats or seat frames). Even if you find the holes, all is not lost (see page 37).

When buying old furniture do check how well fixed together it still is: old glue perishes and joints open up. You might find that lovely-looking table and chair is decidedly rickety when you try to move it. So do sit on all the chairs and lean against the table.

> **Green Tip** **Buying second-hand tables and chairs helps preserve the world's timber.**

You may want to buy new furniture made from **old wood**. Many shops specialise in this, most commonly using reclaimed pine. The quality can vary enormously, from very soft white pine which has been stained to dense mellow pine from church pews or old floorboards. Soft pine marks very easily, for instance through writing paper, and the stain might mark with spills from wine or warm drinks.

The quality of construction also varies. Price may be a guide but you would do best to take a close look at the joints to see how well fitting they are, how much excess glue is to be seen and how sturdy the piece feels. By shopping around you can develop an eye for a real bargain.

Choosing . . . storage and display

Shelving

Shelves to take books, videos and music cassettes or to display ornaments are other living room essentials. And before putting up shelves always remember to measure the space needed for the items to be stored – it's easy to misjudge (see also page 38).

Where the shelving needs to accommodate a few very large books it saves space to make the shelf itself wider and lay the books flat rather than have very wide gaps between shelves.

Glass shelves for display chinaware, trophies or collections are attractive but for safety's sake should be at least 6 mm ($\frac{1}{4}$ in) thick and supported by brackets not more than 40 cm (16 in) apart. Go to the expense of getting the edges of the glass polished to avoid cuts.

 Green Tip **Add a recycling container for newspapers to your 'Now' list for the living room.**

Choosing . . . televisions

The advantage of hire is the promise made by most of the major companies that should the set malfunction they will get a repairman round in twenty-four hours and provide a replacement if the set has to be removed for repair. However many extended guarantees on new sets offer a similar service. The problem can arise if you own an older set – getting repairs can take longer.

Shop around: the electronics field has become a buyers' market with retail chains competing fiercely to offer the best deals. If hiring, for instance, there may be sizable discounts available if you pay by direct debit or pay a year in advance.

There are also schemes which offer what seems to be hire for a two- to three-year period (with the service advantage of hire), after which the set becomes your property. It is however a form of purchase on credit, the main advantage being that after a certain point you can simply return the set with no embarrassment if you can't keep up the payments.

Are you sitting comfortably?
For comfortable viewing – with no strain on the eyesight of even most ardent viewer – the size of TV should relate to the size of the room.

Know your frequencies?
For the clearest, trouble-free picture you need to be tuned to the transmitter nearest to your home.

There are now forty transmitters responsible for sending out signals for four nationally obtainable channels, each of which uses a different frequency. The frequencies are identified by a numerical code numbered from 21 to 69 by the broadcasting authority.

To find the location of your local transmitter and its channel numbers apply in writing to the BBC's ENGINEERING INFORMATION DEPARTMENT Broadcasting House, London W1A 1AA,

or to your LOCAL INDEPENDENT TELEVISION STATION whose name and address you will find in the Yellow Pages.

As a general rule assume that correct viewing distance will be between three and five times the screen size, remembering that the quoted size of a screen is measured diagonally across the face of the tube.

Screen size	How far away?
34 cm	1 to 1.6 m
14 in	3 ft 3 in to 5 ft 4 in
41 cm	1.2 to 2 m
17 in	4 ft to 6 ft 6 in
51 cm	1.5 to 2.5 m
21 in	5 ft to 8 ft 6 in
59 cm	1.8 to 2.8 m
25 in	6 ft to 9 ft
66 cm	2 to 3.2 m
28 in	6 ft 6 in to 10 ft 6 in

Choosing . . . video recorders

A high percentage of TV programmes are now being transmitted in Nicam stereo, and nearly all the titles available for rent in video shops are already recorded in stereo. So if you want good sound quality and already possess either a Nicam TV or hi-fi system plus a realistic stereo effect, buy or hire a VCR with Nicam Hi Fi Stereo.

You get the best sound by connecting the Nicam VCR to the hi-fi system with the speakers a couple of metres apart on either side of the television.

When it comes actually to recording programmes the options currently available include manual keying-in of dates, times and channels, sometimes weeks in advance – which many people find confusing – and video programming by Teletext, known as VPT, which allows you to call up the TV listings on screen and move a cursor against the programmes you want to record. The VCR then automatically sets itself.

Choosing . . . telephones

Prices start at less than £20 as long as you have modern plug-in sockets. Alternatively BT will rent you a telephone if you want to see what use you get from a variety of functions such as memory, last-number redial and call waiting. Gone too are the days when you had to dash into the hall to pick up the phone. Today you can buy a cordless for about £60 (1995 prices).

Cordless phones may not be the answer if you have a large home with many rooms. Pipes in walls interrupt the reception, which make them less practical for some old British homes.

Many phones have special facilities like a **memory** which allows you to program in numbers which you can then dial by the touch of a button, or a system which saves you picking up the receiver to dial – you only lift the handset when the number comes through. One model relays the call through a **loudspeaker** and saves you picking up the handset at all, others have clocks, timed calls and digital displays.

The dining room

Now

- ☞ Table and chairs
- ☞ Protective place mats

Soon

- ☞ Best cutlery, crockery and linen
- ☞ Candle holders

Dimensions for dining

Today the usual height for a dining table is 76 cm (30 in) and the space beneath the table top which allow diners' leg room is 35 cm (14 in). While six people can sit at a 120 by 60 cm (4 ft by 2 ft) table there may not be much room for glasses, serving dishes, flowers or candles. Extra table width, rather then length, can give more comfortable eating and serving. A round table is attractive and encourages exchange of conversation by the whole party, but is harder to add to when you have extra guests.

Dining chairs with arms (carvers) usually cost more but some people find them more comfortable so the usual solution is for a set of six dining chairs to feature four single chairs and two carvers.

In many families the dining room is reserved for special occasions, and breakfast, especially, is eaten sitting up at a counter. For comfortable eating a counter top must be a minimum of 20 cm (8 in) wide with the seats of the stools between 25 cm (10 to 12 in) lower than the counter top.

> **When buying a dining table choose a design which incorporates a leaf or leaves, giving scope for seating an expanding family or extended entertaining.**

Care for living and dining room furniture

- ☞ Don't put hot plates or dishes on a polished surface without the protection of a mat or coaster.

- ☞ Don't allow cold water spills (i.e., from an over-filled flower vase).
- ☞ Don't spill alcoholic drinks, perfume, toilet water or hair lacquer on a polished surface.
- ☞ Don't stand polished wood furniture directly in front of a radiator and remember that constant exposure to central heating can shrink wood and ultimately result in cracking. Period or antique furniture is particularly prone to this type of damage and where valuable antiques have to co-exist with central heating the installation of a humidifier to reduce the dryness of the atmosphere may be essential.
- ☞ Most finishes on cabinet (wooden) furniture needs less maintenance than most people imagine. It's a fallacy for instance that wax polishing is essential to 'feed' the wood. Most polished furniture needs no more than cleaning to remove fingermarks or smears and this can easily be achieved with a damp cloth and a little household detergent.

 **Green Tip** **Choose lamps which take low-voltage bulbs to save electricity.**

- ☞ Don't site upholstered furniture in strong sunlight which fades the colours of the covers.
- ☞ Don't pull at loose threads. Cut them off cleanly with a sharp pair of scissors.
- ☞ Regular vacuuming will help preserve the fabric of easy chairs and settees.

Cutlery

For most people 'silver' cutlery amounts to a few teaspoons from Granny or christenings and the rest silver plate – new or hand-me-downs. The designs tend to be classic, for example you'll find the 'King's' pattern in most ranges. These classic designs are also available in stainless steel as well as contemporary patterns. In the long term, silver plate adds more 'sparkle' to your table, but it does need polishing. And don't let stainless steel items touch silver or silver plate in the dishwasher or you'll speed up discoloration.

SILVER PLATE GUARANTEES AFFECT THE PRICE

• **Indefinite guarantee – spoons, forks and knife handles made from high grade 10 per cent nickel silver will be silver plated to between 35 and 40 microns.**
• **35-year guarantee – plated to between 22 and 25 microns.**
• **25-year guarantee – between 12 and 15 microns.**

The bathroom

In most new homes the design of the bathroom is a *fait accompli*, the fixtures being selected by the builder and their price included in the overall price of the house. In such situations the criteria for choice may well rest more on the level of profit they afford the seller than the future convenience of the customers.

Similarly the placement of the units: bath, basin, loo and possibly also shower and bidet, may well have been decided by ease of installation for the plumber rather than aesthetics, space saving or even common sense.

However if as a first-time homemaker you do have a chance to choose how your bathroom will look and function, these are checks you should make before signing a cheque at the builders merchants: Is the

bathroom suite a colour you will continue to like for a long time and a shade that you would be happy to have greet you early in the morning every day? If in doubt about a colour it is always better to opt for plain white and build in contrast with the soft furnishings of the bathroom, carpets, curtains and bath towels.

Some of the prettiest bathroom fitments – and certainly the most avant garde modern designs in bathroom ceramics – are imports, especially from Italy. However, take care they don't use different bore size plumbing from the UK as it may be difficult to find suitable taps (unless these are included).

Don't assume a corner bath is a space saver. Often they are more greedy of space than the conventional shapes, so always measure the area available very carefully and draw out the alternatives on a piece of graph paper before embarking on a bathroom conversion. Is the bath comfortable? Some are too narrow, others don't support your back.

The bath

Baths come in **cast iron**, **vitreous enamel over steel**, **sanitary ceramics** and **manmade** materials, usually acrylic.

Cast-iron baths are the most durable but the most expensive. Victorian cast-iron baths can sometimes be bought from architectural scrap merchants, but need to be checked carefully for rust damage and holes. The principal disadvantage of cast iron is its weight. Such baths are incredibly heavy to man-handle into position and even heavier when full. So check the soundness of the floor joists beneath the bath – there are tales of cases where the bath, the bath water and its occupants have unexpectedly descended into the room below.

Vitreous enamel over steel is a popular modern alternative. Its advantages are that it looks like cast iron; it remains rigid when you get in without the creaks and movement of plastic baths, so it less likely to pull from the wall tiles, and it cleans well. Its disadvantages are that it is cold to lean back against and can chip if you drop anything hard on it.

Ceramic baths, popular in the USA, share

most of the vices and virtues of cast iron which they largely replaced in the early years of the century. Here ceramics tend to be left to the basin, bidet and loo.

Acrylic baths first became widely available in the 1960s and because of their comparitively low price – today you can buy a bath of this type in a discount DIY store for under £100 – transformed the market, allowing the average family to think about bathroom revamps. Acrylic baths are light in weight and therefore easier for the amateur to install. Their disadvantages are that they can easily be scratched and they flex which can cause a seal problem around the edges – normally overcome by using flexible sealant rather than tile grout. Some are made from thicker acrylic (7mm instead of 5mm) which firms things up.

The wash basins

These come in such a wide variety of shapes and sizes that they can be fitted into almost any available space. However before deciding on dimensions, think about what kind of washing will regularly take place. For instance, a mini-basin which projects just 15 cm (6 in) from the wall might be quite adequate for a downstairs cloakroom, but if you going to wash your hair over the basin the minimum sensible size would be 60 x 40 cm (24 x 16 in).

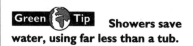 **Green Tip** **Showers save water, using far less than a tub.**

Most pedestal basins have a standard height of around 80 cm (32 in). If you want it higher, you either need to raise it on a plinth or save one built into a vanity unit – the only solution if you need a lower basin. In the toss up between acrylic and ceramic, ceramic usually wins for durability and prolonged good looks.

The lavatory

To comply with legal regulations about ventilation as well as to avoid expensive re-routing of pipes, take the advice of a reputable plumber before thinking of moving the position of the loo. If you are choosing a new one, its worth knowing that while the ones with slimline plastic cisterns appear to be space-saving, there are fully ceramic classic designs shorter from front to back (giving you more knee room). So check measurements. Also, loos vary in comfort. If you can stand the embarrassment, sit on a few in the showroom!

The shower

The elements of the shower are the shower head, the tray, and something to keep the water from going everywhere.

The head can be an extension of your bath taps. Fine if the water pressure is good and you have standing height room at the end of the bath. If water pressure is low you might need to fit a pump or a separate electric shower unit.

The shower tray will be a choice of plastic, ceramic or tiled with waterproof grouting. The last one requires the most skill to ensure it's waterproof. The pros and cons of plastic and ceramic are the same as for baths.

Keeping the water on you and off the rest of the room can be as simple as a shower curtain on a spring adjusted pole, a glass screen fixed to the wall or a hinged screen. There are also purpose-built shower cabinets designed to be installed in one piece.

Security

Many burglaries are committed by amateurs seeking easy pickings. They need a fast way in – and out. Show them a businesslike lock and they will probably move on. And you'll keep your insurance premiums down.

There are dozens of different types of lock on the market, most of which will do an excellent job. But your insurance company may specify particular makes so check the small print in your policy – or get them to supply you with a list. Their specifications won't be cheap but they may save you a lot of grief later on.

To work out the best protection for your house call the local police crime prevention officer who will advise you and provide the literature you need.

Windows

Fit locks on all ground floor windows and near any a flat roof or drainpipe whch would give a thief easy access.

For any window hidden from public view and glazed exterior doors it's worth considering laminated glass – glass strengthened with a layer of plastic. Wired glass is not much help: it's too easy to cut.

Doors

- ☞ A cheap cylinder lock on your front and back doors is an invitation to an experienced thief.
- ☞ Fit a mortise deadlock which can only be opened with a key – a five-lever model gives best protection.
- ☞ Make sure your front and back doors are genuine exterior doors, about 45 cm (1¼ cm) thick, and that the door frame is sound – if it's rotten have it replaced.

Burglar alarms

The most popular type is the **whole-house system** which sets off an alarm when someone tries to break in. Magnetic switches are fitted to doors and windows and connected to a central control unit.

SECURITY TIPS
If you are away always make your home look lived-in.

- ☞ **Cancel milk and papers.**

- ☞ **Get a neighbour to check that post isn't visible.**

- ☞ **In winter get your neighbour to make footprints in any snow.**

- ☞ **Consider engaging a telephone answering service to avoid giving thieves a clue that the house is empty.**

- ☞ **Tell the local police you will be away – they will keep an eye on the house.**

- ☞ **If you return home to find it broken into, do not enter. Go to a neighbour's and call the police.**

- ☞ **If you walk in on a burglar don't get belligerent: let him get away but immediately call the police with as detailed a description as possible.**

Pressure pads, fitted under the carpet by your front door, and/or elsewhere in the house, trigger an alarm when someone walks on it, but they become unreliable with age and need to be checked.

An inexpensive **door alarm** can be fitted to go off when the door is opened. It works on batteries without the need for electrical connections.

An **acoustic alarm** is sparked off by a noise such as splintering glass or wood. It is cheap, compact and easy to install.

> **An enterprising burglar is always on the lookout for tools to help him break in – a garden spade, for instance, will open many windows. So keep your garden shed and garage secure and padlock any ladders to wall hooks. If you have a coal chute make sure it is sealed – it can provide a means of entry.**

An **ultrasonic alarm** sends out continuous sound waves which trigger an alarm if they are broken by a burglar walking past or a door being opened.

The **infra-red alarm** detects body heat and sets off a siren which can only be turned off by a key. Several rooms can be connected to a central unit.

A **panic button** fitted by your bed or the front door can be operated if anyone tries to break in.

Other precautions

While you are away you can make your house look lived in by using **time switches** (available from a DIY or hardware store) which turn lights, radio and television on and off.

A **sunset switch** is light sensitive and switches on as daylight fades.

An **automatic outdoor light** will switch on after dusk when anyone gets within range – it will turn off again after a few minutes (see lighting).

What the insurers say

In today's crime-ridden era, insurance companies expect house owners, and the tenants of rented property, to take sensible precautions against burglary and here again, unless their rules are adhered to, may refuse to pay out.

Until recently every insurance company had its own favourite security system, which could be confusing. At last however the Association of British Insurers has laid down guidelines which it has advised insurance companies to specify in their home contents policies. So find out what type of lock is specified and be certain to ask for a British Standards Institute (BSI) approved model – and sleep peacefully at night. Here are the basics ...

Front door

Fit a British Standard 3621 approved cylinder rim lock, and for added safety when you are indoors a deadlock (a bolt) to the same standard.

Back door

Your existing lock, usually a mortice, should be a British Standard approved model plus two key-operated security bolts and, if the door opens outward, two hinge bolts as the hinges can be tampered with on an outwards-opening door.

Windows

Most burglars enter a house this way so all ground floor and basement windows need special attention. Any window accessible without a ladder should be secured by a key-operated window lock or a lockable window handle.

How safe is your home?

☞ Don't have electric flexes trailing across walkways or try to run a dozen appliances from one plug point by using adapters.

☞ Don't plug shavers or electric irons into light sockets or use anything other than specially fitted appliances in bathrooms – bathrooms of course should only have pull cord light switches.

☞ Don't run appliances on fuses other than those recommended by the manufacturers and when installing a new appliance do check that you have the correct loading of fuse in the plug (see page 62).

☞ It's all right to be houseproud, but not to the point where a polished floor performs like a skating rink and rugs slide away beneath the family's feet. It makes sense to fit loose rugs with anti slip tape as a safety precaution.

Childproofing your home

When a twosome becomes a family, homes as well as lifestyles have to be amended to ensure that the natural inquisitiveness of the lively toddler or under-five doesn't lead to damage, danger or disaster.

☞ Ensure that the bathroom cabinet is at adult level and equipped with a secure lock.

☞ If the sideboard contains alcoholic drinks, condiments or even such apparently harmless substances as a bowl of sugar or dish of jam, make sure that it too locks firmly.

☞ Move detergents, scouring powers and especially disinfectants from the under-sink cupboard to an adults-only height shelf.

☞ Have gates fitted to the top and bottom of the stairs to prevent toddler climbs and tumbles.

☞ Even in a house with only adults make sure the stair area is adequately lit and that grab rails and bannister are firmly fixed.

☞ Watch out for loose carpeting on stairs, another very common cause of accidents for family members of all ages but especially the very young and the elderly.

☞ See that all open, electric or gas fires are fitted with fire guards firmly secured to the wall so that they can't be pulled over or away from the fire.

☞ Never, never feel tempted to air laundry on the edge of a fire guard rail.

In the garden shed, workroom or indeed anywhere around the home never re-use lemonade or pop bottles for non-potable liquids and particularly not for disinfectants, paraffin or weed killers which to a small child may look very similar to a favourite soft drink.

☞ In the kitchen, make certain all saucepan handles and kettle spouts are turned inward to the center of the stove rather than outward where they might well be reached and their scalding contents poured out. Better still, get the stove fitted with a saucepan guard which will lock the handles into place.

☞ For garden safety, see page 389.

☞ Fit a child lock to the fridge and the freezer and if you are exchanging your old fridge or freezer for new, make certain the outgoing model goes directly to the dump.

☞ Tidy away all plastic bags the moment clothes return from the dry cleaners or you take your shopping out of the supermarket carriers. Plastic, particularly the lightweight films used to protect clothes awaiting collection, can be lethal if used as playthings.

Remember a smoke alarm is only as efficient as the batteries which power it, so make regular checks – at least once every three months – that the device is still in working condition.

Danger signs

Fire is one of the greatest hazards in the home, which is why an efficient smoke alarm which costs only a few pounds to buy and only pennies to operate could be the best investment of a lifetime – literally a life-saver. If in doubt about the model best suited for your home, have a word with the local fire brigade who will also be able to advise where they should be sited.

If you live in an apartment block or, even more important, in a converted Victorian or Edwardian home broken into a series of flats or bedsitters, the fire prevention officer at the local station can tell you whether there are sufficient fire doors and escape ladders, whether they should be installed and whose responsibility it would normally be to pay for any building work necessary to render the building safe.

FIRE PRECAUTIONS

☞ **Always turn off the TV before going to bed and take the plug out of the socket.**

☞ **If sparks or a smell of burning come from an electrical socket turn off the main switch at the fusebox and get an expert to check the problem. If it is the plug causing the smell, replace it, checking the wires of the appliance are sound and the correct fuse fitted (see page 62).**

☞ **If the frying pan catches fire, immediately turn off the cooker and cover the pan with a large lid, plate or thick damp (not wet) towel. Better still, keep the purpose-made fire blanket always at hand in the kitchen.**

☞ **Ensure all your furniture meets the current flammability regulations.**

☞ **If an electrical appliance catches fire, never throw water on the blaze while the power is still on – you could be electrocuted. Water, however, is the right way to extinguish an oil heater blaze, but don't get too close to the flames – stand at least 2 m (7 ft) away.**

☞ **If you must smoke, don't smoke in bed or when you are tired sitting in front of the television and make certain cigarettes are properly extinguished.**

☞ **Fit smoke alarms!**

Dealing with service engineers and contractors

When you need help with major structural work such as plumbing, wiring or roofing, or a relatively minor repair to a household appliance, try to get a recommendation from neighbours or friends.

If it is a substantial job check that your contractor is a member of his trade association, which will give you someone to complain to if anything goes wrong. Builders can also be members of the Federation of Master Builders which will give you some judge of their expertise. For qualified gas and plumbing work look for a CORGI member.

Never start the work without discussing price. Ask for as much detail as possible in a written estimate (which is not legally binding) and then get a quote (which is). If you can get more than one estimate, so much the better, but remember that price isn't everything. Standard of work is important so try to get a look at previous jobs carried out by the contractors.

If it is a big job draw up a contract stating start and finishing dates and materials to be used. It might be useful to hire a surveyor to check the work and materials at various stages – if they are not up to scratch the contractor is obliged to do it again.

A contract should also specify at what stage payments should be made to cover materials and work up to that point – which will also encourage the contractor to accept the contract.

For repair work to appliances you need to shop around comparing call-out charges and repair charges and what they cover. Some only cover the first 10 minutes' work. An independent repairer may be more competitive but before you enter into an agreement make sure he knows about your brand of equipment and the model, and that he holds spares.

Remember that if the job is going to be costly and the machinery is old it might be cheaper to buy a new model.

Two addresses to keep in your diary in case of breakdowns. Both will supply lists of their members in your area:

☞ **NATIONAL ASSOCIATION OF PLUMBING, HEATING AND MECHANICAL SERVICES CONTRACTORS, 14-15 Ensign House, Ensign Business Centre, Westwood Way, Coventry CV4 8JA (Tel: 0203 470626)**

☞ **ELECTRICAL CONTRACTORS ASSOCIATION, Membership Services Department, 34 Palace Court, London W2 4HY (Tel: 0171 229 1266)**

Moving on

At best moving home is exhausting. At worst it can be a nightmare. Either way advance planning will take some of the strain.

First find a **removal company**. Get a recommendation from friends or contact the British Association of Removers who will provide names in your area. Then get estimates from several and make sure the price covers the entire job, including insurance, so that you you don't get any nasty surprises at the finish. And don't forget to add on VAT, currently £17.50 on every £100.

☞ Let the **telephone**, **gas**, **electricity** and **water** companies know you are leaving and arriving – make sure they read the outgoing householder's meters on the day they leave so your bills start from the day you move in.

☞ Don't forget to notify the **local councils** so that they can remove/add you to their rating list and at least five days before the move get a form from the post office to have any **mail redirected** for a small fee.

☞ Notify your **bank** and/or **building society**, any **finance companies**, **insurance company**, the **Inland Revenue**, any companies in which you have shares, any **sports** or **social clubs**, your **doctor**, **dentist**, **newsagent** and **dairy** if you have deliveries, and your **TV** or **video rental company**.

☞ And don't forget to tell all your friends!

Chapter Two **Basic DIY**

David Holloway

Former editor of Handyman Which?, the Consumers' Association do-it-yourself magazine. Now an independent consultant, he has written and edited several books and is a regular contributor to home improvement and DIY magazines such as Ideal Home, Homes and Ideas, HomeStyle, Practical Householder and Creating Your Home.

Even if you are not – and do not intend to be – a DIY enthusiast, you will need a certain number of tools for running repairs in and around the home.
Specialists can be expensive and the more basic jobs you can do yourself, the better. In this chapter there are explanations of how to deal with common emergencies, such as blocked sinks, leaking pipes and broken windows. There is a description of how central heating systems and plumbing work (pp. 53-60) and how domestic electrical systems work (pp. 61-70). There is advice on lighting your home (pp. 72-74), as well as decorating (pp. 75-93) and tiling (pp. 94-96).

Basic tools

Making holes

You need some kind of tool for making holes – mainly in wood, but perhaps also in metal and in brick walls for putting in wall plugs.

A good tool to start with is a battery-operated **cordless electric drill**. This has the advantage over a mains-powered electric drill, because it can be used anywhere (including up a ladder, in the garden, on a boat or caravan) and at any time, including when the electricity is turned off.

Cordless drills, although not as powerful as mains-powered electric drills, are light and easy to handle and can also be used effectively as a powered screwdriver, taking the strain out of undoing or doing up screws; some have hammer action which means they are quicker at drilling holes in masonry. The price varies with the power – for most uses, a 7.2V drill is ideal. This comes with its own charger (charging the batteries takes between one and four hours).

To go with your cordless drill, you'll need two kinds of drill bits – high-speed steel **twist drills**, which are used for making holes in wood and metal, and tungsten carbide-tipped **masonry drills** which are used to make holes in brick walls to take the wall plugs for screws to hold up cupboards, shelves and anything heavier than a picture.

Electrical tools

The main everyday electrical tasks are fitting plugs and changing fuses. To fit a plug, you will need at least one, and preferably two, **screwdrivers** (see 34), plus **wire cutters** and **wire strippers** (sometimes combined in the same tool) and a **trimming knife**. With most plugs, the wires need to be cut to different lengths (and you should always remove the bright soldered bits left on the ends of wires on new appliances).

Remove outer sheathing of the flex using the trimming knife, lay the flex in the plug to see how long to cut each wire and then strip off around 10 mm ($\frac{1}{2}$ in) of the wire insulation before connecting the wires to the correct terminals – brown to L, blue to N and green/yellow to E.

A trimming knife is useful for lots of other jobs, too – choose the kind with a retractable blade.

You will also need one or more screwdrivers, and perhaps wire cutters to mend or replace a fuse.

Plumbing tools

At least two (adjustable) **spanners** are useful for everyday plumbing jobs – such as tightening the nuts on a compression joint to stop a leak. You will also need a spanner to re-washer a tap and unscrew a drain valve.

Cutting tools

It's difficult to get by without at least two **saws** – a **hacksaw** for cutting metal or plastic such as curtain rails or protruding screws and bolts (to start with, buy a small 'junior' hacksaw) and a **tenon saw** for cutting wood.

Screwdrivers

You need at least three **screwdrivers** in your 'running repairs' tool kit – one **medium size screwdriver** (say, 12.5 cm [5 in] long) for general use, one small **electrician's screwdriver** for the fiddly screws in plugs, etc., and one **cross-head screwdriver** for the increasing number of cross-head screws (screws with a cross in the head rather than one ridge). If you are only working on wood screws, go for a No. 2 Pozidriv screwdriver (which also fits Supadriv screws); if you might need to work on machinery (including cars), go for a No. 2 Phillips which can also be used on Pozidriv/Supadriv screws (but not vice versa!).

Screws, etc.

It helps to have a small selection of **wood screws** to replace ones which rust or break. The most useful sizes are probably 25 mm (1 in), 38 mm (1½ in) and 50 mm (2 in), No. 8 and No. 10 – you can buy others separately if you need them.

Have a pack of **wall plugs** handy – choose the plastic kind which can take a range of screw sizes – and have a box of miscellaneous metal washers which always come in handy.

Hammers and nails

For your first **hammer**, buy a **claw hammer**, one part of which is for putting in nails, the other for pulling them out (and also useful for levering things apart).

Nails are cheap to buy, but it is as well to have some 25 mm (1 in) **panel pins**, some 50 mm (2 in) **oval wire nails**, some 50 mm (2 in) **wire nails** and some 50 mm (2 in) **floorboard brads** handy.

General tools

You will not get far without a pair of **pliers** – to start with choose the combination type, which can double as **wire cutters** and which generally can be used for gripping and turning things or for straightening out bent bits of wire.

Measuring and marking

For measuring up around the home – whether for carpet, curtains or shelves – you need a **steel tape measure** (don't rely on using a cloth dressmaking tape measure). A 2m (6 ft 6 in) tape is a good length to start with – all tape measures have both millimetre and inch marking on them, so they provide a useful instant conversion table.

How to deal with...

Dripping loo overflow pipe

An overflow pipe is deliberately positioned so that it will annoy you when it drips. There could be three reasons why it is dripping:

☞ water level inside cistern too high – bend or adjust the arm of the float-operated valve;

☞ dirt or debris inside float-operated valve – dismantle or clean;

☞ failed valve washer – dismantle or clean.

▶ **Connect the ball valve to the cistern with its two nuts and washers and fit a tap connector for the main connection.**

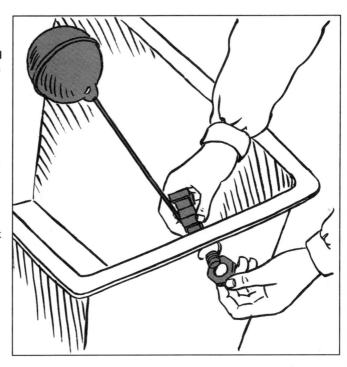

For the first repair, you only have to lift the lid of the cistern; for the second or third, you need to turn off the water (at the mains if it is mains-fed or at the gate valve (see page 52) by the cold water cistern if it is cistern-fed), flush the cistern and then use spanners and a screwdriver to remove and dismantle the float-operated valve. If the cistern fills noisily, it is better to replace the valve with a modern 'quiet' type, available at a DIY shop, or plumber's supply.

Blocked sink

Sinks get blocked with vegetable matter, tea leaves, grease and all kinds of unmentionable things. You can prevent blockages by pouring a solution of washing soda down the sink at regular intervals, but if a blockage does occur, the first thing to try is the old-fashioned sink plunger – a rubber cup on the end of a wooden handle. This is held over the open plug-hole and the handle pumped up and down; use a little Vaseline or liquid soap smeared around the rubber cup to ensure a good seal and cover the overflow with a cloth. A hand-operated force pump is even more effective.

Fit a 'balloon' made from chicken wire into the top of downpipes to stop birds nesting there.

If plunging does not work, try wiggling' out the blockage with a length of flexible wire – a net curtain support wire is ideal fitted with a hook on the far end. And if this does not work, place a bucket under the trap (the bottom side of the plug-hole, under the sink) and unscrew the trap. The blockage may be in the trap itself or you will be able to 'wiggle' further along the waste pipe. Do not pour the contents of the bucket back into the sink until you have re-fitted the trap!

Radiators won't heat up

There could be an airlock. Using a radiator key and starting at the top of the house, turn the nut found at the end of each radiator until you hear hissing. A soon as water trickles out, tighten the nut again. Work your way down the house until the airlock is cleared.

Blocked gutters

Gutters mainly get blocked with leaves (though the odd tennis ball has been known to find its way in, too!), so the best thing to do is to clear all gutters in the autumn after

▲ **Use roof and gutter sealant for leaky roofs and guttering.**

▼ **Use small wire brushes on your electric drill to remove all traces of root before priming and repainting.**

the leaves have fallen. If you have a blocked gutter at any other time of the year, though (perhaps caused by a bird's nest), it must be dealt with right away.

Standing on a well-supported ladder, use a garden trowel to clear out the debris from the gutter and finish by running the water in from a hosepipe to check that it is working correctly. If the downpipe is blocked, you may be able to use some bent wire to pull the blockage out upwards, or a set of hired drain rods to push it out downwards.

If gutters are leaking it could be that the joints have failed, the gutter has cracked or a support bracket is allowing the gutter to sag. Failed joints, cracks and splits in plastic gutters are easy to repair with a gutter repair sealant (or replacing the rubber gasket in a failed joint); cast-iron gutters are more difficult to repair and if the joints have gone and the gutters are splitting and rusting, it might be time to think about changing them for modern plastic ones. A plumber can help you here, or get some advice from your local DIY shop.

Rust

Rust is mainly a problem with old-fashioned cast iron downpipes and gutters and with wrought iron garden gates and railings. You

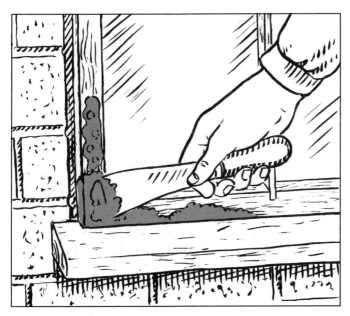

◀ **Fill the affected areas and holes with wood filler, and allow it to dry before sanding. Rub down the rest of the window frame to achieve a smooth finish.**

can remove rust with a hand-held wire brush, or with a circular wire brush fitted into the chuck of an electric drill. If you can get back to clean metal, use a rust-inhibiting primer before repainting; otherwise use a rust-killing primer or rust-killing paint, which you can put on over the rust.

You can get separate rust-killers for use on things where you do not want to use a wire brush – a rusty steel rule or chisel, for example.

Woodworm in furniture

The trouble with woodworm is that you can't see it – the tell-tale holes are made by the adult beetle leaving the wood and you do not know if there are more larvae inside waiting to grow up and eating away at the wood in the meantime.

If the wood is bare (the back of a dressing table, for example) you can 'paint' on woodworm fluid directly. Do this outside

> **Brown shoe polish can also be brushed into areas of wood that have become bleached by the woodworm fluid, or plugged with wood filler.**

the house and do not bring the furniture back in for at least twenty-four hours. If the surface is finished with polish or wax, buy a woodworm fluid container which has a nozzle, so that you can inject the fluid directly into the flight holes.

Once the woodworm fluid has dried (and for serious attacks, two treatments are necessary), fill the flight holes with wood filler (if necessary, dyed to match the surrounding wood) before re-finishing.

Rot in window frames

Where water collects at the bottom of window frames and sills and the paint has failed, the wood can suffer from wet rot. This is fairly easy to repair using a rot-repair kit.

First of all, cut out all the soft timber with a sharp knife or chisel, going back until you have reached solid wood. Then paint on the wood hardener and allow this to dry (at least six hours). Fill the hollow with the special exterior wood filler and allow this to set before sanding it down level and re-painting or re-varnishing.

Some repair kits have a preservative in the wood hardener; others provide preservative pellets which you put into the holes drilled in the sound wood (filling the holes afterwards). Both will prevent further attacks.

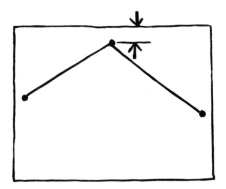

◀ **When hanging your picture on something fixed to the wall, the key measurement is from the top of the picture to the apex.**

▼ **Use tape on the wall to avoid damaging plaster when hanging a picture.**

Hanging pictures

When hanging groups of pictures, you will want them to look right as a group, which means that the spacing between the pictures is important (and should usually be equal) and that pictures in a row should line up either at the top or bottom.

Pictures can be hung in one of two ways – by the old-fashioned hook over a picture rail with a long hanging cord or with a short hanging cord over something screwed or hammered into the wall.

When using something fixed into the wall, the important measurement is the distance from the top of the picture down to the apex of the hanging cord or wire when this is pulled taut. If you then mark the position of the sides and top of the picture you can correctly work out where the hanging point should be.

There is a choice of pins and hooks you can use:

☞ Picture pins – for light pictures
☞ Masonry nails – for heavier pictures into solid walls
☞ Picture hooks – for medium-weight pictures
☞ Screws into wall plugs – for heavy pictures.

Make sure you use the correct type of wall plug, especially on hollow walls (see *Putting up shelves*).

> **You need two people to hang pictures – one to hold the pictures on the wall and the other to stand back to see if they are in the right position.**

Putting up shelves

Putting up one or more shelves is probably the first do-it-yourself job that most of us attempt.

A single shelf can be put up on individual brackets, which range from the functional to the ornate, while a rack of shelves, one above the other, can be put up using brackets which slot into vertical uprights screwed to the wall. The basic method, for which a **spirit level** is essential, is the same.

Start by putting up one bracket at the height you want the shelf to be – or one vertical upright covering a range of shelf heights. With an upright, start by putting in one screw and then use the spirit level to get the upright vertical before marking the positions of the other screws.

Now place a shelf on the bracket (fit one bracket to the upright on the wall), place the spirit level on top of the shelf, hold another bracket (or bracket and upright) against the

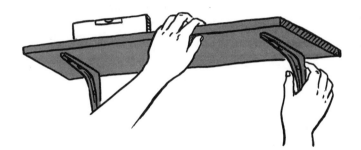

◀ **Fix one bracket, then, with the spirit level on the shelf, fix the other.**

other end of the shelf and mark the positions for the screw holes when the spirit level shows the shelf is horizontal. With an upright-and-bracket (adjustable) system, once you have got one shelf level, the others will be, too. For shelves carrying more than a very light load (ornaments, say), you will want to be sure that the brackets and uprights are well secured to the wall. On solid walls, this is no problem (using plastic wall plugs and long screws), but on hollow walls (a timber framework covered in plasterboard) do not rely on using hollow-wall fixings for supporting shelves. Instead, find the positions of the timber uprights (by tapping, probing with a sharp point or using a joist and batten detector (available at any DIY or hardware shop) and then use even longer screws directly through into the timber uprights. This will mean using more brackets and uprights than normal.

The recommended maximum spacing between shelf brackets is:

Material	Space between brackets	
15 mm (½ in) chipboard	40 cm	(16 in)
19 mm (¾ in) solid timber	60 cm	(2 ft)
25 mm (1 in) solid timber	1 m	(3 ft)

Where just two brackets are used, they should be spaced two-ninths of the overall shelf length in from either end. This minimises bending of the shelf.

Fixing light things to walls and doors

For shelves, you definitely need proper screws into wall plugs or directly into the timber framework of a hollow wall. But for lighter things, such as spice racks, loo-roll holders, coat hooks or toothbrush holders you may be able to get away with one of the following:

- ☞ double-side adhesive tape
- ☞ self-adhesive Velcro fasteners
- ☞ panel adhesive
- ☞ hot-melt glue (from a glue gun)
- ☞ masonry nails (into solid walls)
- ☞ picture pins
- ☞ hollow-wall fixings
- ☞ hollow-door fixings (for doors faced in hardboard).

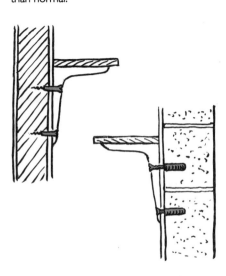

Left: use wall plugs in a masonry wall.

Right: a partition wall requires only screw-in studs.

Re-wiring a table lamp

If the flex of a table lamp has become damaged you may want to replace it. Similarly, if you stumble across an unwired antique lamp, it's fairly easy to wire it yourself.

First of all, choose a flex which is the correct size for the job. For table lamps, this is 0.5 sq mm flex and you can choose either two-core flex or three-core flex, depending on whether the lamp has any exposed metal – if it has, three-core flex with a separate earth wire is essential.

▶ **Wiring a metal**   **neutral**   **live**
pendant lampholder.

earth

At the plug end, the flex is stripped and connected to the terminals as described on pp. 33-4. (with two-core flex only the brown and blue wires are connected to the L and N terminals). The flex then needs to be threaded through the lamp until it can be wired to the lamp-holder (normally this is screwed to the top of the lamp with the flex going down inside, so start by unscrewing the lamp-holder and withdrawing the old flex. Here, the sheathing of the flex needs to be removed as for the plug, but the two wires will be cut to the same length before their ends are stripped off.

It does not matter which way round the two wires are connected to the two terminals on the lamp-holder – what does matter is that the earth (E) wire is securely attached to its little brass screw (if required) and that there are no loose bits of wire sticking out. Re-assemble the lamp holder and secure it back on to the table lamp before re-fitting the shade and light bulb.

Re-glazing a window

When the glass in a window cracks or breaks you want to replace it as soon as possible – not only will the window now let heat out and the weather in, but it is an obvious security risk.

For most **windows** in the home, you need 4 mm ($\frac{1}{6}$ in) glass; with very small windows you may get away with 3 mm ($\frac{1}{8}$ in) glass; large windows could need 6 mm ($\frac{1}{4}$ in) or even 10 mm ($\frac{1}{2}$ in) glass. Choose the same size as the glass already in the window.

For **'high-risk'** areas – such as low-level glazing, large 'picture' windows, glass doors and panels next to glass doors – you should always use **safety glass**, either toughened or laminated. Toughened (heat-treated) glass is five times stronger than normal glass and if it does break, it shatters in tiny harmless fragments. Laminated glass has a thin sheet of plastic sandwiched between two sheets of normal glass and in the event of impact holds the pieces of glass together. This makes it virtually impossible to break though, which could be an important security consideration.

> **To avoid breaking the new glass, slide the head of your hammer along the surface of the glass – or, better, use the flat side of a firmer chisel to do the hammering.**

To re-glaze a normal window:
1. Start by taking out the old glass. If it is only cracked, run a glass cutter round the edge of the pane on the outside and then knock the glass inwards on to a large sheet of paper on the floor.
2. Wearing gloves, pick out the 'shards' of glass from all round the frame and use an old chisel to remove all the old putty, and a pair of pincers or pliers to remove the glazing sprigs or the clips (on metal windows).
3. Measure the height and width of the opening in at least three places and subtract 3 mm ($\frac{1}{8}$ in) from the largest measurement.

4. Take the measurements to a glass merchant and ask them to cut the glass to the exact size – if you can, take the window frame itself.

5. You will also need some putty suitable for the type of frame (metal or wood) and some glazing sprigs (clips for metal frames).

6. Before fitting the glass, work some putty in your hands and apply a 'bead', 3 mm ($^1\!/_8$ in) thick, all round the recess in the frame, squeezing the putty between your thumb and forefinger.

7. Lift the glass in place and press it down on to the putty – never press in the middle, only at the edges. This should force putty out on the inside of the frame – if not, you have not put a large enough bead in.

8. Once the glass is in place, hammer in the sprigs or put the clips in place on a metal window frame.

9. Now apply a second 'bead' of putty, larger than the last (around 5 mm) around the edges of the glass. Use a putty knife to smooth this into a nice triangular shape, taking special care at the corners – if the knife sticks, dip it in water.

10. Clean the glass with white spirit and leave the putty for ten to fourteen days before painting it. Allow the paint to spread just over the edge of the putty on to the glass, which will help prevent the putty drying out.

▼ **Using a hammer and chisel chop out the old putty.**

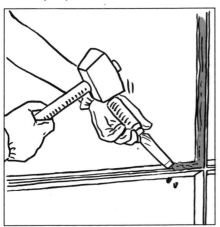

▼ **New putty can be passed into the window recess.**

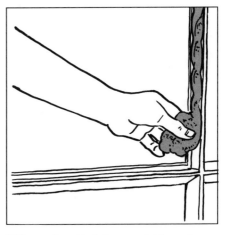

▼ **Glazing sprigs or clips can be hammered or tapped into place.**

▼ **Smooth putty into a neat triangular shape.**

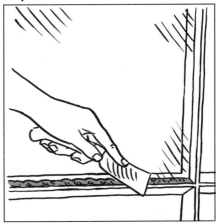

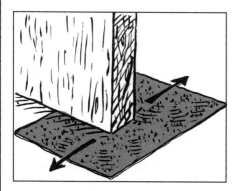

Curing sticking doors

Before adopting a cure for a sticking door, you need to know what is causing it to stick; it could be:

- ☞ swelling due to damp (on exterior doors)
- ☞ too much paint
- ☞ a thicker floorcovering
- ☞ problems with the hinges.

Problem	Likely cause	Cure
Sticks at top	Damp swelling	Sand/plane
Sticks at bottom	Thicker carpet	Trim door
	Damp swelling	Sand/plane
	Loose hinges	Repair
Sticks on handle edge	Damp swelling	Sand/plane
	Too much paint	Sand/plane
	Loose hinges	Repair
Binds on hinge edge	Too much paint	Sand/plane
	Hinge problems	Repair

Sanding and planing

Where a door is sticking because paint has built up over the years, or the door has swollen due to damp, it can be planed or sanded down. Often this can be done with the door in place, but sometimes it may be necessary to remove the door and, if you are working on the lock side, to remove the door lock. Painting the tops and bottoms of external doors (something which is not often done) will help keep the moisture out, which causes them to swell.

For the sake of appearance, it is better to sand or plane the whole of the side of a door

◄ **If the door is sticking at the bottom, tape some sandpaper down to the floor under the sticking bit and force the door backwards and forwards.**

before repainting it, taking most off the bit which is sticking. For sanding, use sandpaper wrapped around a cork or wooden block; for planing, use a bench plane along the side and a block plane for top and bottom, always working from the sides towards the centre to avoid splitting the wood.

Trimming doors

Where a new floorcovering has been fitted inside the house, the bottom of your doors may need to be trimmed. This is something professional carpet layers and floorcovering contractors can do for you, using a special saw without taking the door off its hinges. If you do it yourself, you will need to remove the door and support it while you cut along a straight marked line with a panel saw or electric-powered saw (circular saw or jigsaw); if using a powered saw, clamp a wooden batten to the door to guide the edge of the saw's soleplate – note that this batten will be spaced some way from the cutting line and correct positioning is vital.

Hinge problems

If the screws in hinges become loose, the door can sag and catch on the floor or the frame. Try tightening the screws first, but if they can't be tightened because the hole has worn, remove the existing screws and replace with longer ones of the same size. Alternatively, try packing the holes with matchsticks glued into place. If too large a screw has been used, its head will stick up above the surface of the hinge, causing the hinge to bind – replace as above.

If the door is sticking or binding, it could be that the hinge recess has been incorrectly cut – it should be exactly the same depth as the thickness of one half of the hinge. If the recess is not deep enough (causing sticking), remove the door and deepen the recess with a chisel. If it is too deep (causing the door to bind), cut a piece of cardboard to the same size as the recess and slip it under the hinge before replacing the screws.

▼ **You can plane sticking doors fairly easily. Make sure it is supported, then plane from one side to the centre, turn the door and repeat on the other side.**

new piece in place, clamping it while the glue sets. Try out the drawer and, if necessary, plane it down until it runs smoothly. Where a drawer slides on **side runners** (which fit into slots on either side of the drawer), it is usually possible to replace each side runner with a new piece of hardwood of the correct size. If, however, the slot in the drawer is also worn, this may have to be enlarged with a chisel (if you have one, a router is the ideal tool) before fitting larger size hardwood runners.

Before finally re-fitting the drawer, rub the sliding surfaces with a candle to make the drawer run smoothly.

Sticking drawers

A wooden drawer normally sticks because of wear on the **drawer runners** or on the drawer itself (**drawers without runners**). Many drawers (especially in chests of drawers) have no runners, but rely simply on the bottom of the drawer to provide a guide. When this has become worn, you will have to remove the misshapen portion of the wood and replace it with a new piece of the same thickness.

By measuring the height of the drawer at the front or the back, you will be able to work out how much wood to remove in order to accommodate the new piece. Buy the new wood and use it to draw a line on the edge of the drawer. Then cut out the old wood with a saw and/or a plane and glue the

▼ **When mending a stiff drawer, mark a line as close as possible to the bottom edge and cut along the drawer.**

Fixing a door latch

A door latch should operate smoothly when you turn the handle to open the door, and automatically when the door is closed.

If you have a **ball-operated catch** (no turning door handle), this can wear, or become dirty and stick. You could try lubricating it to make it work more smoothly, but the best answer is usually to replace it with an identical catch. Replacement ball catches are inexpensive and easy to fit into existing holes, needing only a screwdriver.

The more usual type of **handle-operated latch** (sometimes incorporating a **key-operated lock**) can also stick and again you could try lubricating it: graphite lubricant or WD40 is better than oil as oil can encourage dirt to collect inside and jam the mechanism.

Sometimes slight movement of the door can cause a lock or latch to stop working properly. The reasons for this are varied:

- ☞ the hinges have loosened
- ☞ the door has swollen due to damp (see *Curing sticking doors*, pp. 42-3)
- ☞ the door has warped slightly so that the door and latch no longer line up.

It is possible to correct a warp in a door by using wedges to force it to bow the other

way and leaving it for a few days, but generally it is easier to cope with the problem in hand and deal with the latch or lock. The latch or lock itself in the door should not be touched – what you re-position is the 'keeper' in the door frame.

It will not be difficult to work out if the keeper needs to be moved up or down – by looking closely into the gap as the door is closed, you should be able to see if the latch or lock is catching on the keeper plate, or you could mark where they meet the frame and compare this with the actual position of the keeper.

Working out if the keeper needs moving to one side is more complicated:

- ☞ With the door shut, measure the thickness of any gap between the door and the door stop (the piece of wood it closes against) – a one pence coin is 1.5 mm thick ($\frac{1}{15}$ in), two pence is 2 mm ($\frac{1}{12}$ in), fifty pence is 2.5 mm ($\frac{1}{10}$ in) and one pound is 3 mm ($\frac{1}{8}$ in).
- ☞ Measure from the closing edge of the door to the closest edge of the latch or lock bolts and transfer this measurement plus the thickness of the gap to the side of the rebate where the keeper is. This will tell you whether the keeper needs to be moved and, if so by how much.
- ☞ Moving a keeper will mean enlarging at least one side of the hole in which the box sits and adjusting the size of the recess for the foreplate (some latches and locks have only a foreplate and no box). When putting the keeper in its new position, it will help if you pack out the recess with cardboard or thin slivers of wood to prevent it sliding back into its old position. Use a bradawl to start new screw holes as far as possible away from the existing screw holes.

▼ **Cut out the hole for the striking plate, and screw in the plate so it is flush with the frame.**

Damage limitation: leaks, drips and floods

Water in the wrong place in the home is a menace. It can cause wet rot and dry rot in timber, provide the right conditions for woodworm attack and can create the ideal environment for mould to grow.

Dampness in the home can be caused by a number of things:

☞ leaking pipes or joints
☞ rising damp
☞ penetrating damp (often associated with a fault in guttering or downpipes outside)
☞ leaking roof coverings
☞ gaps around door and window frames
☞ condensation.

You should be on the outlook for all of these things – and if you have a flood causing severe dampness, you may need to hire or buy a dehumidifier to dry out the house.

Leaking pipes and joints

Generally pipes only leak when they have burst following freezing in very cold weather. The first step of damage limitation is to put a container under the leaking water. The next is to stop the water supply (see page 53). It is vital to know where your water supply taps are.

A temporary repair can be made using a burst-pipe repair clamp, but a more permanent solution is to cut out the affected length of pipe and to replace it. You can get special burst-pipe repair 'kits' with a short length of pipe and two push-fit fittings to make this job easier. You will make much neater cuts in pipes using proper pipe cutters (where you 'wind' a blade round the pipe until it is cut through) rather than trying to use a hacksaw.

Joints on the other hand can and do leak – especially in hot water pipes and central heating pipes where the pipes are continually expanding and contracting as they heat up and cool down, which puts strain on the joints. A leaking compression joint can usually be cured by tightening one or both nuts – use one spanner on the nut and a second to

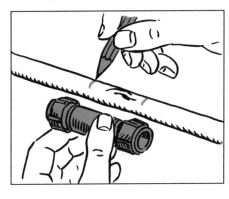

▲ **With a new connector, mark the area of burst or damaged pipe to be cut away.**

prevent the fitting turning. This compresses a metal 'olive' which bulges and so seals the pipe. If this doesn't work, you will have to drain the pipe and remake the fitting, using a replacement olive – the small brass ring which makes the seal. If necessary, saw off the old olive with a junior hacksaw, but make sure you do not cut into the pipe.

Leaking capillary joints (where the seal is made by hold solder creeping into any gaps) are more difficult to deal with. In order to re-make the joint you will have to drain the pipe and unsolder the present joint, using a blow lamp, and then clean up the pipe before soldering a new one in its place. For a straight coupler joining two lengths of pipe, it would be easier to cut the joint out and replace using a burst pipe repair kit with push-fit fittings.

▼ **Use two spanners to tighten the joints one on the nut and the other on the fitting.**

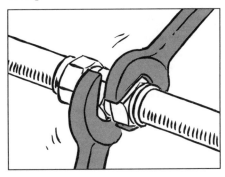

Rising damp

Where a brick or block wall is in contact with the ground, water will naturally rise up though the pores in the bricks until it reaches quite a high level. To prevent this, house walls are built with a damp-proof course (DPC) low down – typically 15 cm (6 in) above the ground – which is usually made from bitumised felt or, in older houses, slate.

Damp-proof courses (especially older slate ones) can fail in time and allow the water to rise, but there are other ways in which damp can rise which should be checked out first.

The symptom of rising damp is a 'tidemark' along ground floor walls, causing staining of the painted or papered walls. This will be present all the time, not just after it has rained.

The most common cause of rising damp is **'bridging'** of the damp-proof course – often caused either by cement rendering on the outside or plaster on the inside, allowing the rising damp to by-pass the DPC. This can be cured by hacking off the offending rendering or plaster. The DPC can also be bridged by earth being piled up in flowerbeds outside the house or by a path or patio being built too close to the DPC, allowing rainwater to splash up the wall. Again all of these are easy to cure.

Installing a new physical (solid) DPC is a major undertaking and requires a specialist firm, but there are several firms who can install a chemical DPC by drilling holes in the walls and injecting a silicone solution. You would not want to do this yourself for a whole house, but if there is just a localised area which has failed, you can hire all the equipment necessary to inject a chemical DPC.

> **There may be faults in cavity walls which allow damp to get across the cavity, such as wall ties sloping upwards to the outside rather than downwards or poor bricklaying practice allowing mortar to collect on wall ties or at the base of the wall.**

> **Note that all airbricks should be entirely clear – their (important) job is to allow a free flow of air underneath suspended timber ground floors to keep the timbers dry.**

Where damp has been rising for some time, the plaster inside will often have become damaged and will need to be hacked off and replaced with special damp-resisting plaster which will allow the wall to dry out without damaging any new internal decorations.

Penetrating damp

Where water passes through the walls of a house, it is known as penetrating damp. The resultant damp patches are often worse after a spell of rain.

The majority of houses (and certainly those built since the 1930s) have double thickness (cavity) wall with an air gap to prevent penetrating damp, but older houses with solid walls can suffer, especially if exposed to **driving rain**.

The way to deal with penetrating damp caused by driving rain is to 'paint' a colourless silicone water repellent on to the outer surface of the wall – a job you could do yourself.

Often penetrating damp is the result of a plumbing problem outside, such as a **dripping overflow** (see page 34) or damaged rainwater downpipes or gutters. Most cracks and splits in gutters or downpipes can be dealt with by using gutter repair tape or a gutter sealant piped out of a cartridge, but older cast-iron gutters are more difficult to repair and if they're leaking or sagging or have rusted, it would be better to think about having them replaced. A sagging plastic gutter can usually be dealt with by replacing the support bracket. See also *Blocked gutters*, pp. 35-6.

Leaking roof coverings

Both pitched and flat roofs can develop leaks which show up as damp patches in the rafters or ceilings underneath – not always directly underneath the leak, however.

Pitched roofs

On a pitched roof, the leak is often caused by one or more slates or tiles slipping. With slates, this is often the result of 'nail sickness', where one or both nails holding the slate in place has broken; with tiles, it can often be the effect of wind lifting the tile, but sometimes the 'nibs' on the back of a tile which hold it in place may have broken off. You can replace accessible slipped slates and tiles yourself, but if a large number have gone or if there is damage to the ridge tiles at the top of the roof, you will want to hire a roofing contractor who has the necessary equipment and expertise. There are also firms who will spray a coating over the inside of the roof which will stop the leaks, secure the roof covering and provide a high degree of insulation.

▼ **Slide the slate ripper under the slate and pull it loose.**

▼ **The nails broken, damaged slates are easy to remove.**

▼ **A 'tingle' (see page 48) should be hammered between the exposed slates.**

▼ **Carefully line up the new slate with the existing slates and bend the tingle to hold it in place.**

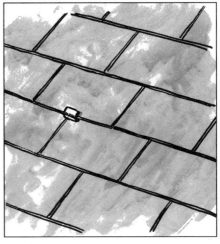

A single slipped tile can often simply be slid back into place by easing up the surrounding tiles and re-hooking the tile into place. To replace a slate – or a tile which has lost its 'nibs' – you will need a short length of lead, zinc or copper (around 23 cm (8 in) long and 2.5 cm (1 in) wide), known as a 'tingle'. This is nailed down into place underneath the slate or tile. The tile or slate is then pushed into place and the bottom of the tingle is then bent up to secure it.

Where just one nail holding a tile has broken, you will need to hire a slate ripper to remove the other nail. Slide it up underneath the slate and then yank it downwards to break through the nail.

The other main problem with pitched roofs is failure of the **flashing** – the join between the chimney stack and the remainder of the roof. Ideally, this should be made from lead, but many builders use cement mortar instead, which dries, cracks and lets in water. Have it replaced with a proper flashing.

Flat roofs

Flat roofs on extensions and attached garages are notorious for leaking – often as a result of the poor-quality felt which has been used to cover them. The life of felt is only about ten years.

There are much better coverings available for flat roofs and if yours has seriously gone, it would be worth considering having it replaced. You can, however, repair cracks, splits and blisters in flat roofs using **bitumen adhesives and sealants** and waterproof the entire covering by adding a 'liquid rubber' compound. All of these jobs are fairly straightforward, if messy to undertake. Any chippings on the roof should be removed first and then replaced – they do an essential job in reflecting the sun's rays to keep the roof cool.

Where a flat roof joins the main house, water can get in through the join. As with the join between a chimney stack and a pitched roof, a proper flashing should have been used here, but if a mortar flashing has been used and has failed, you can repair it using a self-adhesive flashing tape, which is pressed down into place after the surface has been cleaned, and then primed using the special primer supplied with the flashing tape.

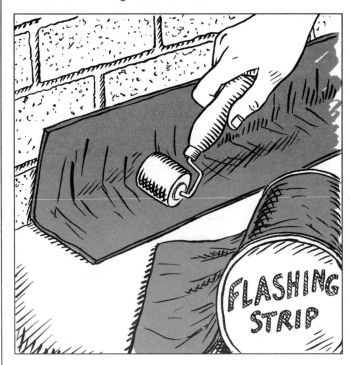

◀ **A strip of self-adhesive flashing can be cut and rolled into place with a roller.**

◀ **Use a canking gun to apply silicone sealant or non-setting mastic around door and window frames.**

Gaps around door and window frames

There must be a gap between door and window frames and the surrounding wall to allow for the differential movement of the two materials (wood and masonry) as the temperature and humidity changes. Builders often fill these gaps with putty or cement mortar, both of which will dry, crack and fall out, allowing water in which can produce rot in the frame.

The answer is to scrape out all the old material, allow the timber to dry and then to fill the gap with either **silicone sealant** or with **non-setting mastic**. These will effectively seal the gaps but will allow for the materials to move. Both are applied using a **'caulking' gun,** which is readily available and easy to use – note that there are two sizes of gun and two sizes of cartridge to fit them.

Condensation

Generally considered to be one of the biggest problems in today's houses, condensation is caused by warm moist air meeting a cold surface. Cold air can hold less water vapour than warm air and the excess is deposited on the surface as water droplets – familiar as the misting-up of windows first thing in the morning.

Condensation is a particular problem in houses which have been thoroughly draughtproofed (and in loft spaces which have been well insulated) and there are three basic methods of solving it:

☞ to produce less moisture (or to get rid of it or restrict it to certain areas of the house)
☞ to insulate (and so warm up) the cold surfaces
☞ to improve ventilation.

Less moisture

You can't do much about one of the main causes of moisture in the home – people breathing – but you can do something about many of the others. For example, do not dry clothes indoors; fit a venting kit to a tumble dryer and keep lids on saucepans.

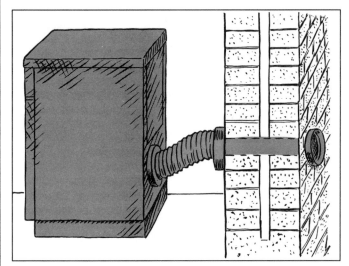

◀ **Fit a venting kit to your tumble dryer to avoid a build-up of condensation from drying clothes.**

It will also help if you fit draught excluders around kitchen and bathroom doors and to keep them closed while you are creating moisture inside, but a better measure is to fit extractor fans in both bathrooms and kitchens (plus a cooker hood in a kitchen) to remove as much moisture as possible at source.

Paraffin and stand-alone LPG heaters should be avoided at all cost – although convenient and cheap to operate, they produce huge amounts of water vapour as well as being a safety hazard. Stick to heaters which do not produce moisture.

Warmer surfaces

Cavity walls can be warmed up considerably by having cavity-wall insulation professionally installed (this will pay for itself in three to five years in reduced fuel bills), but all walls can be warmed up by applying a thin layer of expanded polystyrene underneath the wallcoverings. This has the disadvantage that it is easily dented, but will raise the inside temperature of the wall enough to prevent condensation, although the thin material has little insulating effect.

Similarly, windows can be warmed up by double glazing – even the cheapest DIY methods of double glazing will be effective at reducing condensation.

It is always a good idea to give the house a good 'airing' at least once a day by opening windows, even if it is raining outside. Do not worry about heat loss – very little will be lost in the five minutes or so necessary to air the house.

Ventilation

A good flow of air around the house is essential to prevent condensation. This is particularly important in lofts, where there should be a gap all round the edge of the loft to allow air in (and special ventilators fitted if necessary), but also in fitted wardrobes where clothes can get musty (if necessary, drill ventilation holes at the top and bottom).

Boilers connected to conventional chimneys need their own supply of fresh air (ideally a ventilator fitted in the wall close to the boiler).

Coping with a flood

The most likely cause of a flood inside your house are a disaster with the washing machine, a burst pipe following freezing and a burst water main outside the house allowing water to come in.

The steps necessary to prevent pipes freezing (and then bursting as they thaw out) are given on pp. 53-4: they should not be a problem in houses which are occupied, but can make a terrible mess if they do occur. A washing machine flood is usually localised and is difficult to prevent if the cause is a fault in the washing machine, Not leaving washing machines unattended is the only answer – and mopping up the flood quickly if and when it does happen.

A burst water main outside your home is completely out of your control, though you can find out where the nearest water main is and whether you would be in the flooded area if it were to burst. Large water mains produce a lot of water in the long time it takes to turn them off and the result can typically be 15 to 23 cm (6 to 9 in) of water in your home. You and your neighbours will know fairly quickly when the main has burst and there will be a period of some hours during which you can limit the damage. For a start, you could lift all the manhole covers around your home to allow a route for the water to escape – but place a large pole in

each one so that no one (a visiting fireman, for example) falls down them when they are covered in water (we're talking serious flooding here). Next remove as much furniture as possible to the second floor of your house, plus any valuable rugs: taking up fitted carpet will much more difficult. Good-quality doors can be unscrewed from their hinges and taken upstairs, too. Remove the plinth fascias from underneath kitchen cupboards: if the cupboards are on adjustable legs, they may escape; if they sit directly on the floor, they will get ruined if water enters the house. It is extremely unlikely that you'll need to sandbag the bottom of doors (assuming that the firebrigade or water company come round delivering sandbags). Water will get in through air bricks and simply though the saturated soil (remember water always finds its own level) and come up though the floorboards!

Damage from floods is covered by your contents and by your buildings insurance (so make sure you are fully covered and paid up!): you will never get back the full cost of what needs replacing (though you may well end up with new carpet, kitchen units and decorations) and you will have been expected to limit the damage as far as possible.

▼ **Stopvalves are fitted where the water is at mains pressure.**

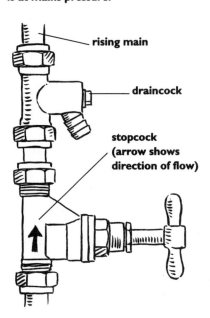

rising main

draincock

stopcock
(arrow shows
direction of flow)

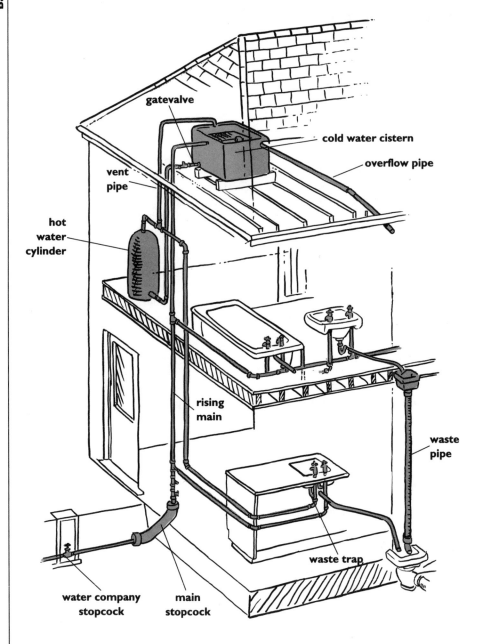

▲ Indirect cold water supply – in most houses all cold taps
(except kitchen and garden) are fed from the cistern.

Plumbing and central heating – how it works

Most of the plumbing in a house is hidden – in the walls, under the floorboards, inside the airing cupboard and in the loft. And as long as it works, with water coming out of the taps properly and the radiators heating up at the right time, that's fine. But when pipes get blocked, spring a leak or something else goes wrong, it helps to know what kind of system you have got and how it works.

The plumbing/heating of a house divides up into five main parts:
- ☞ the cold-water supply
- ☞ the hot-water supply
- ☞ the central-heating radiator circuit
- ☞ the central-heating hot-water circuit
- ☞ the drainage system

Cold water supply

Cold water is brought to your house via a branch pipe from the nearest water main. This is fitted with a **stopvalve** outside your property (usually under a small metal cover in the pavement) so that the water company can turn it off. If you have the correct key, you can also turn the water off here.

From the water company stopvalve, the **service pipe** leads into the house and there is a second **householder's stopvalve** for you to turn off your water. This is usually under the kitchen sink, but may be under the floorboards – find it, label it and make sure it works!

Immediately above the householder's stopvalve is a drainvalve, and a pipe then rises all the way to the top of the house to the main **cold water cistern** – a large open tank in the loft, containing around 227 litres (50 gallons) of water. This pipe is known as the **rising main**.

To provide a supply of fresh (i.e., not stored) water at the kitchen sink for drinking and cooking, a branch pipe leads off the rising main to the kitchen sink cold tap. This pipe may also feed a washing machine and a garden tap.

In some homes, other cold taps (and WCs) around the house are also fed from the rising main (in what is known as a 'direct' cold-water system), but most homes will have an 'indirect' system where all cold taps are fed from a pipe leading out of the bottom of the cold water cistern. A float-operated valve ('ballvalve') allows more water into the cistern as water is drawn off from the bottom: the pipe leading out of the cistern is fitted with a red- or orange- handled gatevalve, so that the supply to the cold taps and WCs can be turned off. The cistern will also be fitted with an overflow pipe.

Note that with the usual indirect system, only the kitchen cold tap has fresh drinking water. All the other cold taps have stored water – and if you look at the inside of your cold water cistern, you may have second thoughts about drinking the water in it.

Direct vs indirect

The two methods of cold water supply each have their pros and cons.

Direct (all cold taps and WCs fed with mains water)

For
- ☞ drinking water at all taps
- ☞ no need for cold-water cistern in the loft (unless needed for supply to hot water cylinder)

Against
- ☞ no reserve supply if main cold water fails
- ☞ not permitted by all water companies

Indirect (kitchen tap fed from rising main, all others from cold water cistern)

For
- ☞ reserve supply (in cistern) if water cut off
- ☞ cistern available to feed hot water cylinder

Against
- ☞ cold-water cistern (and pipes) in loft could freeze in winter
- ☞ drinking water only at kitchen tap

Burst and frozen pipes

Pipes and cisterns should not freeze (or burst) in houses which are occupied (and heated) during the winter. But if a house is left unattended, they can be a serious problem – especially in lofts, under ground floors and in outhouses.

The problem in the loft and in other places can be solved by fitting **pipe-warming cables** around the pipes, but otherwise if you are leaving a house for extended periods (say two or three weeks) in the winter, you should drain down the cold water system, by turning off the main stopvalve and opening all the cold taps. Do not drain the central-heating circuit – add special anti-freeze to the water, instead.

For a weekend break, you do not need to drain the system: instead, leave the heating on 24-hour operation on its lowest setting and prop the loft hatch open.

Hot-water supply

There are two main ways of providing hot water in the home – from a hot-water cylinder and from an instantaneous heater.

Hot-water cylinder

Here, a copper cylinder (which should be well-insulated) is supplied with cold water from the main cold water cistern via a pipe leading out of the bottom of the cistern and going into the bottom of the cylinder. This, too, has a red- or orange-handled gatevalve, but this will normally be positioned close to the cylinder (in the airing cupboard) rather than close to the cistern.

If the house has a 'direct' cold water supply (see above), the cistern needs only feed the hot water cylinder and can be

smaller – it may well be positioned in the airing cupboard above the cylinder rather than in the loft.

The water stored in the cylinder is heated up and kept hot by one of two methods. The simplest is an electric **immersion heater** (rather like a large kettle element), fitted with a thermostat, which heats up the water (to the temperature set on the thermostat) when it is switched on. The second is by having a coil of pipe inside the cylinder through which water heated by the central-heating boiler circulates (there are two extra connections on the side of the cylinder for the flow and return pipe to the boiler). This is explained in more detail in *Hot-water heating circuit* (see pp. 57-8).

From the top of the hot-water cylinder a pipe – the **safety open vent pipe** – rises

▼ **An immersion heater heats water only when it is switched on.**

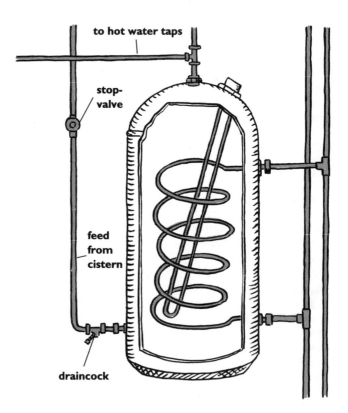

to hot water taps

stop-valve

feed from cistern

draincock

up to the loft and is bent over the top of the cold-water cistern. This pipe allows any steam or air to escape if the system should overheat, but connected to it is the pipe which takes water to the hot taps around the home. Note that as the hot water comes out of the *top* of the cylinder, you cannot drain a hot water cylinder by opening the hot taps – there should be a drainvalve (to which you attach a hosepipe) fitted on the cold water supply pipe coming into the *bottom* of the cylinder.

Instantaneous heater

This is a powerful heater which heats up cold water (from the rising main) as it passes through to provide hot water. You can have small gas instantaneous heaters fitted over the kitchen sink or an electric heater to provide a shower in a bathroom. Or there could be a large **multi-point** gas heater in the kitchen or bathroom which supplies hot water to the whole house. In some homes a combination boiler will provide instantaneous hot water as well as heating up the radiators – see *Hot-water heating circuit*, pp. 57-8.

Cylinder versus instantaneous heating

Each method has its pros and cons and one may suit your lifestyle better than the other.
Cylinder heating
For
☞ provides a good flow of water from the taps
☞ reliable
☞ can be used with either electricity or gas

Against
☞ long wait for water to heat up (unless a high-recovery hot-water cylinder is fitted)
☞ costs more (as stored hot water will lose heat)
☞ needs a cistern

Instantaneous heating
For
☞ hot water always available
☞ cheap to run (no heat lost)
☞ needs no cistern

Against
☞ slow flow rate of water
☞ needs gas supply (except electric shower)
☞ suffers from scale build-up in hard water areas

Scale

Familiar as the 'furring' inside kettles, scale is produced by magnesium and calcium salts in hard water which 'precipitate' out at water temperatures above 70°C (160°F). It can be controlled in hot-water cylinders by keeping the temperature of the water below 70°C (160°F), and is not a problem in central-heating systems – see *Central-heating radiator circuit*, below. But it is a problem with gas and electric instantaneous water heaters in hard water areas. The problem can be solved by fitting a **water softener** or a **scale reducer** to the system.

Central-heating radiator circuit

Some homes may be heated by electric-storage heaters, which take in heat at night and give it out during the day (see *Electricity – how it works*, page 61) and some may have gas-convector heaters attached to the outside walls to heat the whole house, but most homes will have radiators fed with hot water from a boiler.

Water is usually supplied to the circuit from a smaller cistern in the loft, called the **feed-and-expansion cistern**. Like the main cold-water cistern, this has an overflow pipe and is connected to the rising main via a float-operated valve, but the level of water in the cistern when the heating system is cold is much lower, to allow for the inevitable expansion of water which takes place when the system heats up. The cistern is there only to make up for water losses from the system, due to leaks and evaporation – basically the same water goes round and round all the time, which means that even in hard-water areas scale is not a problem.

Two pipes are connected to the boiler – the flow and return pipes – which carry heated water to and from the radiators. Each radiator has one connection to the flow pipe and another to the return pipe. Water is

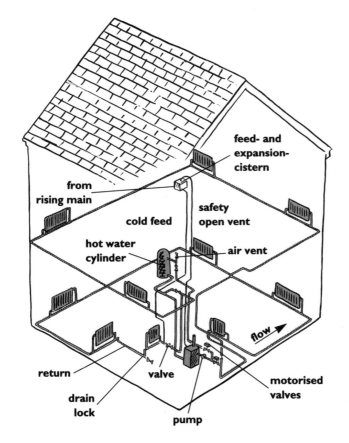

from rising main

feed- and expansion-cistern

cold feed

safety open vent

hot water cylinder

air vent

return

valve

drain lock

pump

motorised valves

flow

▲ **A wet central-heating system.**

driven round the circuit by a **pump** and there are two other pipes connected to the system:

☞ the **cold feed** pipe which runs from the bottom of the feed-and-expansion cistern

☞ the **safety open vent pipe** which allows air and steam to escape which rise up to the feed-and-expansion cistern and loops over the top.

At each radiator, there are two valves fitted. On the flow pipe into the radiator (the one which heats up first) is a handwheel valve which you can use to turn the radiator down or off altogether. On each return pipe is the lockshield valve, which does not have a handle and usually needs a spanner to turn. This is used to set the amount of water

flowing though the radiator (a process known as 'balancing' and should not normally be touched. If you do need to close it (to remove a radiator, for example), count how many turns it takes and then open it by the same amount when the radiator is re-fitted.

To provide precise temperature control in a particular room (and to save on heating costs), the handwheel valve can be replaced by a **thermostatic radiator valve** which you can adjust so that the temperature in the room is kept lower. As the air around the valve heats up, it closes, shutting off the flow of water to the radiator. To 'bleed' a radiator to remove an air lock, see page 35.

The whole system is controlled (brought on and turned off) by two devices – a timer (or programmer) and a room thermostat.

You set the **timer** with the times you want the heating to come on and go off. For some systems, you need only a simple timer: a **programmer** will control both the radiator and hot-water heating circuits, sometimes independently.

The **room thermostat** measures the air temperature around it (usually in the hall or on the landing) and turns the boiler and pump on when the temperature falls, turning them off when it rises. It will operate only during programmed 'ON' times.

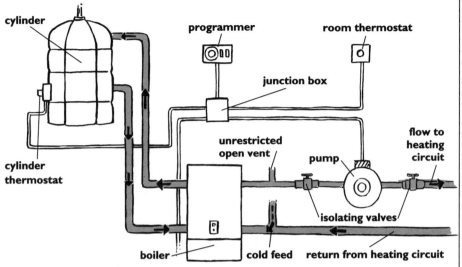

cylinder

programmer

room thermostat

junction box

cylinder thermostat

unrestricted open vent

pump

flow to heating circuit

isolating valves

boiler

cold feed

return from heating circuit

▲ **Gas or oil-fired central-heating, relying partially on gravity.**

Sealed systems

Some modern homes will have a sealed central-heating system. This does away with the feed-and-expansion cistern (and associated cold feed and safety-opening vent pipes), but is fitted with other devices:

- ☞ an **overlimit thermostat** (on the boiler) prevents the system overheating
- ☞ an **expansion vessel** provides a space in which the heated water can expand
- ☞ a **fill unit** allows water to be added to the system.

Hot-water heating circuit

Where the central-heating boiler also heats the hot water in a hot-water cylinder, there will be two extra flow and return pipes going to the cylinder.

In a **gravity** system, these pipes are connected to the boiler and circulation relies on the fact that hot water is lighter than cold so the hot water rises and the cold water falls. In a **fully pumped** system, the central-heating pump also drives the water round the hot-water circuit and the hot-water circuit flow pipe is connected to the main flow pipe

at a **three-way motorised valve**. This valve, which is wired to both the room thermostat and the **hot-water thermostat** which is strapped to the side of the hot-water cylinder allows water to flow to the radiator circuit or to the hot-water heating circuit (and, sometimes, to both) depending on which circuit needs heat.

Gravity versus fully pumped

Gravity
For
- ☞ simple to install

Against
- ☞ cylinder takes a long time to heat up
- ☞ water temperature uncontrolled – eventually reaching temperature of water leaving boiler

Fully pumped
For
- ☞ water in cylinder quicker to heat up
- ☞ water temperature controlled (by cylinder thermostat)

Against
- ☞ more complicated and expensive to install

About boilers

Boilers can be gas-fired, oil-fired or coal-fired. Gas is the most common, oil is the cheapest but needs room for the oil storage tank, solid fuel needs space for storing the fuel and a lot of time emptying and re-filling the boiler.

☞ Gas or oil boilers come in versions which are either wall-mounted or floor-mounted and are either for attaching to a conventional chimney or to a balanced flue (allowing fresh air in as well as exhaust gases out).

☞ A **fan-assisted** boiler can be mounted on an internal wall with a duct leading to a balanced flue outlet on an external wall.

☞ The most efficient type of boiler (mainly gas) is a **condensing** boiler, which extracts heat out of the exhaust gases; a **combination** boiler provides whole-house instantaneous hot water as well as heating up the radiator circuit.

☞ Boilers have different capacities, measured in British Thermal Units (BTU), calculated according to the number of radiators, the home's insulation and the hot water requirements.

The drainage system

The purpose of the drainage system is to take dirty water out of the house into the main sewer – there will also be a separate system

▼ A P-trap type of trap makes it possible to empty the trap of debris if it gets blocked.

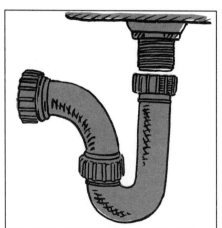

for collecting rainwater from the roof and taking it away either to the main sewer or to a separate water drain or to a soakaway.

The drainage system for the house is divided into three parts:
☞ waste pipes
☞ soil pipes
☞ underground drains.

Waste pipes

Each bath, basin, shower tray and sink in the house is fitted with a **waste outlet** (plug hole) to which is connected a trap. The purpose of the **trap** (which is always full of water) is to keep drain smells and insects from getting into the house. From the trap, a short length of pipe leads to the soil pipe.

Soil pipes

Some older houses have two soil pipes outside the house: one is just for the waste from the WC, the other takes the waste from baths and basins via a 'hopper head' with the kitchen sink waste going directly to a gully

▼ A single soil pipe is common in most houses.

TROUBLE-SHOOTING

Problem	Cause	Remedy
Blocked sink or basin	• Dirt, hair or grease in the trap or in the waste pipe • Waste pipe frozen	• Remove blockage with a plunger (or force pump) – if necessary, remove and clean trap • Thaw with hot towels
Cistern slow to fill	• Dirt in ballvalve • Wrong type of ballvalve fitted	• Dismantle and clean • Use HP valves on mains supplies and LP on stored supplies
Dirty water from taps	• Dirt in cold-water cistern	• Drain and clean. Fit lid
Drains blocked	• Dirt and debris in underground drains • Tree roots growing into drains	• Hire drain rods and clear • Consult drain expert
Hot tap won't work	• Airlock in pipes	• Attach hosepipe to hot tap and cold tap and turn both on
Hot water overhot	• Failed immersion heater thermostat • Gravity hot-water heating system	• Replace • Convert to fully pumped operation
Cistern leaking	• Failure of galvanised metal	• Replace with plastic cistern
Noisy cistern filling	• Old-fashioned ballvalve	• Replace with modern type
Noisy heating system	• Pipes rubbing against surfaces as they expand and contract • Corrosion debris in boiler	• Fit insulation around pipes where they cross joists • Add corrosion inhibitor to system
Noisy cold-water pipes	• Usually water hammer	• Replace tap washers, close main stopvalve slightly or replace ballvalve
Overflow pipe dripping	• Faulty ballvalve	• Repair, clean, adjust or replace
Pipe leaking	• Failed joint • Pipe burst (rare)	• Re-make or replace joint • Cut out and replace ruptured pipe
Radiators cold all over – at top – at bottom	• Failed (or closed) valve • Air build-up • Corrosion sludge build-up	• Replace (or open) valve • Bleed radiator by opening air vent • Drain and clean system before adding corrosion inhibitor
Shower blocked	• Scale build-up	• Dismantle and clean showerhead
Stopvalve won't turn	• Lack of use	• Apply gentle heat until free: close half turn from fully open
Tap dripping from spout	• Failed tap washer • Scored tap seat	• Rewasher • Hire and use tap re-seating tool
Tap leaking from top	• Failed packing or 'O' ring	• Dismantle and replace
WC blocked	• Waste material in trap	• Use WC plunger
WC won't flush	• Broken link • Failed flap washer	• Replace • Drain, dismantle and replace

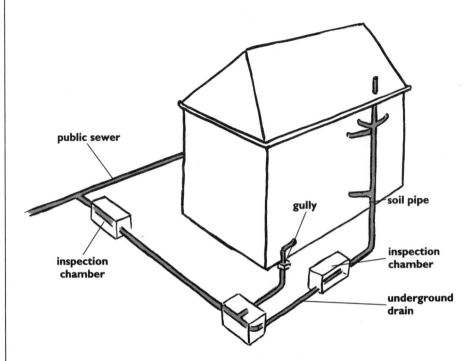

public sewer

gully

soil pipe

inspection chamber

inspection chamber

underground drain

(usually at the bottom of the bath/basin soil pipe).

Modern houses have just one soil pipe, to which all the wastes are connected – sometimes this will be inside rather than outside the house.

Underground drains

The soil pipe or pipes are connected to the underground drain which in turn connects to the main sewer – or, in some rural properties to a septic tank or cesspool. Wherever a soil pipe joins the drains or wherever the underground clay or plastic pipe changes direction, there is an **inspection chamber** (fitted with a cover) which allows you to clean the drains and also to deal with any blockages.

Plumbing materials

The material used for making pipes has undergone several changes over the years.

☞ **Lead** was used widely for both supply and waste pipes. It is no longer permitted (as dissolved lead in pipes can be a health hazard), and has largely been replaced.

▲ **Single house drainage; underground drains lead to the public main sewer system.**

☞ **Copper** is the universal material for supply pipes and central-heating pipes. It is relatively cheap and widely available and familiar to all plumbers.

☞ **Stainless steel** enjoyed a short vogue (when copper prices rose a few years ago) but is not common as it is difficult to work with.

☞ **Cast iron** was widely used for soil pipes (and many houses still have cast-iron soil pipes) but has now been replaced by plastic.

☞ **Plastic** is now universal for waste pipes and soil pipes and is common for underground drainage, but plastic is now more widely used for water-supply pipes and central heating. Here, it has the advantage that it can be bent around gentle corners and comes in long lengths, so needing fewer fittings, but the disadvantage is that it can sag and needs more room for expansion and contraction.

Electricity – how it works

Electricity is vital for modern living – but its provision in houses is often inadequate, with too few sockets, not enough lighting points and usually not enough circuits (or allowance for extra circuits).

It helps to understand how your electricity works so that you can cope with problems when they occur and know what is possible in the way of alterations and additions, but on the whole it is best to leave the wiring alone. **ELECTRICITY CAN KILL** and you should not mess about with it unless you have some experience. **NEVER** work on the wiring without first turning off at the mains and never work on an appliance without first unplugging it.

Watts, volts and amps

All these are measures of electricity and are named after famous physicists.

☞ The amount of electricity flowing along a wire or around a circuit is measured in **amps** – the more amps, the more electricity.

☞ You do not need to worry so much about **volts**: the voltage is a measure of the 'pressure' of the circuit, but virtually all homes run at a standard 240V, though there may be some low-voltage

▶ **Remove the fuse carrier from the fuse box (consumer unit) and replace either the wire or cartridge and return to the box.**

circuits (typically 12V or 24V) for lighting or for powering garden equipment such as pumps for pools.

☞ The rate at which electricity is used is measured in **watts** – for example a 100W light bulb is brighter and uses more electricity than a 60W one. For more powerful appliances, kilowatts are used – one kilowatt (1kW) equals one thousand watts (1000W).

Remember that

Watts = Volts X Amps

so if you want to work out how much current something is using, simply divide its wattage by 240 (or, to do it roughly in your head, multiply the wattage by four and then divide by 1000).

The basic system

Electricity is supplied via a single cable to your home, which goes first to a large single fusebox owned (and sealed) by the electricity company. This fuse protects their equipment in the event of a major fault or of you using

too much electricity at any one time and if it 'blows' you must get them to come and repair it. From the electricity company fusebox, the supply is taken to the **meter**, which measures how much electricity you use and then to your fusebox or consumer unit.

Older houses may have several **fuseboxes** (one for each circuit in the house); modern homes will have a **consumer unit** which contains all the fuses (or miniature circuit breakers) for the house. From the consumer unit, cables go around the house to provide the different circuits, of which there will usually be a minimum of six:

- ☞ downstairs lighting
- ☞ upstairs lighting
- ☞ downstairs socket outlets
- ☞ upstairs socket outlets
- ☞ immersion heater
- ☞ cooker

There may also be extra circuits needed now or in the future. For example,

- ☞ electric shower
- ☞ outside (shed/garage/garden)
- ☞ kitchen socket outlets
- ☞ low-voltage lighting
- ☞ additional socket outlets

Each circuit cable contains three wires:

- ☞ the live wire (coloured red in cable and brown in flex)
- ☞ the neutral wire (coloured black in cable and blue in flex)
- ☞ the earth wire (bare, but covered in green/yellow sleeving where exposed) in cable and green or green/yellow in flex.

It helps to think of the electricity flowing down the live wire and then back along the neutral (which is why all fuses and switches are fitted to the 'live' side). The earth wire is there for safety – if the metal casing of an appliance becomes 'live' due to a fault, the current will flow quickly down the earth wire (which is connected to the casing) blowing the fuse in the process and preventing you getting a shock if you were to touch the casing.

▶ **Top: cartridge fuses have in most homes replaced those that need wiring (bottom).**

Fuses

The purpose of a fuse is to protect the wiring beyond it. It is a deliberate 'weak link' in the circuit and will 'blow' if too much electricity flows for the rating of the fuse.

Electricity causes wiring to heat up and if too much flows the wiring could overheat and start a fire. So the fuses in the consumer unit protect the electric cable which makes up the circuits around the house while the fuse in individual plugs protects the electric flex from the plug to the electrical appliance to which it is connected. There may be an additional fuse inside the appliance as well to protect its wiring.

Fuses in consumer units can be one of two types – re-wireable or cartridge (like fuses in plugs, but bigger). Modern homes will have miniature circuit breakers (MCBs) which perform the same function but either flip a switch or pop out a button so are simple to re-set when they trip.

Re-wireable fuse

For
- ☞ cheap

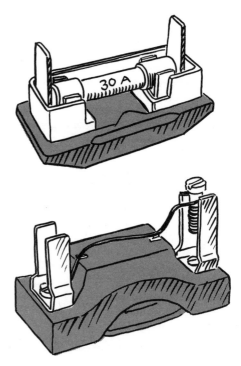

Against

- ☞ fiddly to repair
- ☞ need to keep a stock of fuse wire
- ☞ needs twice-rated current to blow
- ☞ has to be removed to isolate circuit

Replaceable (cartridge fuses)

For

- ☞ easy to replace

Against

- ☞ need to keep stock of replacements
- ☞ needs three times rated current to blow
- ☞ has to be removed to isolate circuit

Miniature circuit breakers (mcbs)

For

- ☞ easy to re-set
- ☞ can be switched off to isolate circuit
- ☞ blows at rated current

Against

- ☞ expensive

Lighting circuits

- ☞ A lighting circuit is rated at five or six amps (5A or 6A) and can have up to twelve lighting points on it.
- ☞ From the consumer unit, a single cable (the size is 1 sq mm or 1.5 sq mm) goes to the first lighting point (in, say, the living room) and then a second cable goes on to the next lighting point (say in the dining room) and so on to the last lighting point (usually in the hall or on the landing). At each lighting point there is an extra cable which goes to the light switch.
- ☞ There are two methods for lighting wiring – junction box and loop-in – and you need to know which you have got for a particular light if you want to make any alterations. Older houses tend to have junction-box wiring and new houses loop-in wiring, but this is not always the case and some houses may have both systems at the same time.

Junction-box wiring

Here, the 'circuit' links a number of junction boxes – one for each light fitting for each room. So each junction box has one cable

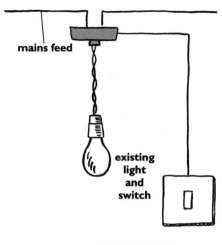

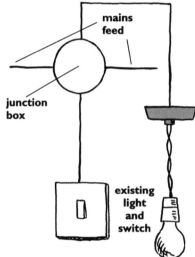

▲ **Top: an existing light wired into a lighting circuit.**
Bottom: an existing light wired on the junction box system.

coming in from the previous junction box (or the consumer unit for the first junction box) and one cable going out to the next junction box (except the last junction box in the circuit).

Two other cables are connected: one to the light switch and one to the light fitting (or light fittings if more than one is controlled by the same switch). Usually this cable will go to a ceiling rose in the room concerned to which the light fitting is then connected.

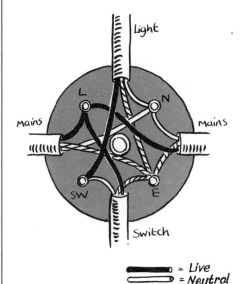

= Live
= Neutral
= Earth

▲ **A lighting circuit junction box, where the lighting circuit is wired to the box.**

Inside the junction box

There are four terminals – live, switch live, neutral and earth.

☞ The **live** terminal takes the red wires from the IN and OUT mains cables plus the red wire of the cable going to the SWITCH.

☞ The **neutral** terminal takes the black wires from the IN and OUT cables and the black wire of the cable going to the LIGHT.

☞ The **switch live** terminal takes the black wire of the SWITCH cable (as this is 'live' when the switch is 'ON', a piece of red insulating tape is usually wound round this wire).

☞ The **earth** terminal takes all the earth wires (covered in green/yellow sleeving).

Inside the switch

The switch has only two terminals – one for the red wire and one for the black wire. It does not matter which way round the wires are connected, but it does matter which way round the switch is fitted into this box to enure the rocker is down when the switch is on. Often two-way switches are used, which have three terminals.

All three are needed for two-way switching (see below) but for normal one way switching (one switch controlling one or more lights) only two terminals (C and L2) are used.

Inside the ceiling rose

The earth wire (covered in green/yellow sleeving) goes to the earth terminal, while the red and black wires of the LIGHT cable go to the two outer terminals where the flex of the light fitting is connected (brown flex wire to red cable wire, blue flex wire to black cable wire).

▼ **The inside of a tumbler light switch. Ensuring the power is turned off at the mains, it can be quite easily replaced.**

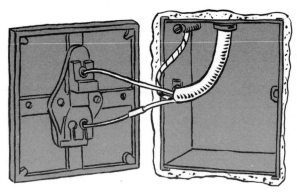
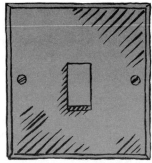

Loop-in wiring

Here, all the cables for a single light fitting (IN, OUT and SWITCH) go into the ceiling rose which has an earth terminal and three other 'banks' of terminals. As before, all bare earth wires (covered in green/yellow sleeving) are connected to the earth terminal, for the other terminals, the wiring is as follows:

☞ The **switch live** terminal bank takes the black wire from the SWITCH cable and the brown wire of the flex.

☞ The **live terminal** bank takes the red wires of the IN, OUT and SWITCH cables.

☞ The **neutral terminal** bank takes the black wires of the IN and OUT cables and the blue wire of the flex.

Junction box vs loop-in

Junction box

For
☞ uses less cable
☞ makes adding extra lights simpler
☞ can be used for wall lights or ceiling-mounted non-pendant lights

Against
☞ junction box needs to be wired from above
☞ needs more connections and more components

Loop-in

For
☞ simpler to wire
☞ wiring connection can be made from underneath
☞ good for pendant ceiling lights

Against
☞ not suitable for all types of light
☞ difficult to add extra lights
☞ uses more cable

Low-voltage lighting

A low-voltage lighting fitting is run at just twelve volts (12V). The fittings themselves are very elegant and compact and take tiny light bulbs which produce a clear clean light. The advantages over normal 240V lighting

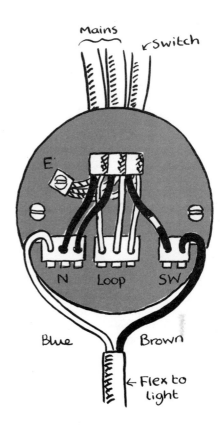

▲ **The loop-in system with three cables.**

(apart from the neatness of the fitting) are that the bulb runs cool, lasts longer and is cheaper to run.

The voltage is 'stepped down' from 240V to 12V in a transformer. They can either be fitted within the light fitting (which means the light fitting can replace an existing fitting) or can be installed at the beginning of the circuit with new (and much larger) cables run to the low-voltage light fittings.

Some garden lighting is also low-voltage, run from a transformer fitted inside the house or in the garage or garden shed.

Two-way switching

Normally a single switch controls just one light (or, perhaps two wall lights). A second switch can be installed so that the light (or lights) are controlled for two places – perhaps by the door and over the bed in a

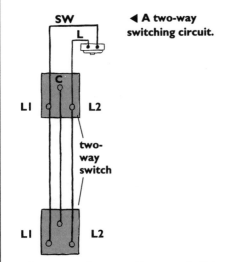

SW

L

C

L1   L2

two-
way
switch

L1   L2

◀ **A two-way
switching circuit.**

bedroom or at the top and bottom of a flight of stairs.

The wiring is as shown in the drawings: the cable to the existing switch is connected to the L1 and L2 terminals (rather than to the C and L2 terminals) and a new length of 3-core and earth cable is fitted between the existing switch and the new switch (both of which must be two-way switches). When either switch is operated, the light comes on.

Dimmer switches/security light switches

Both of these can be fitted to replace an existing light switch with no other changes in the wiring.

A **dimmer switch** reduces or increases the light level gradually rather than simply turning it on or off; a **security** light switch can be programmed to bring on an internal (or, more usually, an external) light at pre-set times.

Wall lights

Many people find wall lights more interesting and more restful than central pendant or ceiling lights. The main problem with fitting them is running the cable down to the light fitting, otherwise the wiring is the same as for a ceiling light using junction box wiring.

Socket outlet circuits

A socket outlet circuit is usually rated at thirty amps (30A) and can have any number of sockets on it – the limitation is only the floor area it can serve.

There are three main socket outlets in use. By far the most common is the 'ring' circuit, where two cables are joined at the fuseway or MCB in the consumer unit. Each socket outlet (which can be a single or double unit) has two cables connected to it, linking it to the previous and the next socket outlet, so forming a complete 'ring'. In addition, each socket can have a third cable connected into the L (live), N (neutral) and E (earth) terminals at the back which goes off to feed an additional 'spur' socket outlet. Rings are used for the main socket outlet circuits in the house – downstairs, upstairs and, sometimes, kitchen.

There are also 'radial' circuits, where a single cable is connected to the consumer unit fuseway and goes to the first socket outlet, with a second cable going to the next outlet and so on to the last where just the one cable is connected. There are two sizes of radial circuit, depending on the cable size used. The smaller one could suit a garage or loft conversion; the larger one a kitchen.

▼ **This diagram shows a ring circuit. Each spur is connected to the main ring and can serve either a single appliance or a single or double socket.**

spur from junction box

spur
from
socket

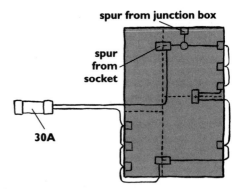

30A

THE CIRCUITS IN DETAIL		
Circuit type	Fuse rating	Cable Area size served
Ring	(MCB)	30A 2.5 sq mm 100 sq m
Radial	20A	2.5 sq mm 20 sq m
Radial	30A [1]	4.0 sq mm 50 sq m

[1] Must be cartridge fuse or MCB – i.e., not a re-wirable fuse

Excluding fused connection units, the minimum recommended number of sockets is

Kitchen	8
Living room	12
Dining room	6
Double bedroom	8
Single bedroom	6/8
Landing/hall	4
Garage	4
Store/workroom	2

(All sockets to be installed as double units – e.g., minimum four double socket outlets in a kitchen).

In addition to socket outlets (to take plugs) socket outlet circuits also contain fused connection units for wiring fixed appliances, such as an extractor fan, a central-heating boiler, a wall heater, a water disposal unit and so on. These contain a fuse (and may be switched or unswitched, with or without a neon warning light) and the flex leading to the appliance is wired directly into the unit rather than being connected via a plug.

▼ It is quite simple to convert a single socket to a double.

Adding socket outlets

The simplest way of increasing the normally inadequate number of socket outlets in a house is to covert all the existing single sockets to double (or even triple) sockets. This is not difficult to do, especially if the sockets are mounted on the wall surface rather than being recessed into it.

Additional spurs can also be run from the back of existing sockets which do not already have spurs added (perhaps to a new socket next to the existing one or on the other side of an internal wall) and socket 'tracks' can be fitted where a lot of sockets are needed in

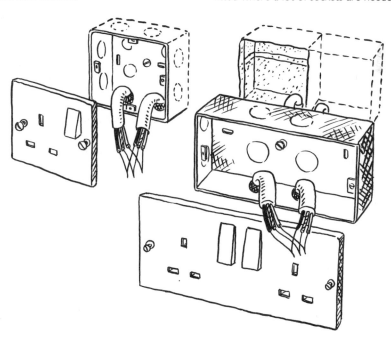

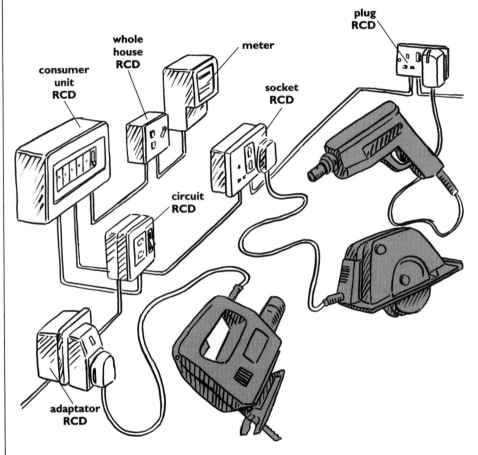

consumer
unit
RCD

whole
house
RCD

meter

plug
RCD

socket
RCD

circuit
RCD

adaptator
RCD

▲ **A residual current device (RCD) can prevent you receiving a fatal electric shock.**

one locality – for a computer or hi-fi set-up, for example.

Plug-in adapters and trailing flexes should be avoided (they both get hot and could cause a fire), but trailing adapters can also be useful – one of these can be plugged into a single socket outlet to give four outlets (but note that the total load is restricted to 13A – that is, 3120 volts).

Residual current devices

Fuses, remember, protect cables and flex from overheating while earthing protects you from shock only if you touch something

metallic which has become live. There is nothing built into a house's electrical system which protects you from the shock you could get if you drill into an electric cable buried in the wall or cut through the cable of an electric lawnmower.

This protection (particularly important when using equipment outside the house where it could be wet) can be provided by a residual current device – or RCD for short.

An RCD monitors the currents flowing in the live and neutral wires and will trip very quickly, shutting off the electricity flow, if it detects even a tiny difference – which could happen if the electricity were flowing through you.

An RCD can be fitted in one of six places:
☞ Between the meter and the consumer unit to give whole-house protection.

- ☞ In the consumer unit to protect particular circuits (usually the socket outlet, garden and electric shower circuits).
- ☞ After the consumer unit to protect the whole of a single circuit.
- ☞ In the socket outlet to protect anything plugged into that outlet.
- ☞ In an adapter, fitted between the plug and socket outlet to protect anything plugged into the adapter.
- ☞ In the plug of a single appliance (i.e., a lawnmower) to protect that appliance whichever socket outlet it is plugged into.

Immersion heater circuit

Although some house builders will use a socket outlet to power an immersion heater, it should have its own circuit, rated at 15 or 20A, run in 2.5 sq mm cable all the way from the consumer unit to a fused connection unit mounted on the wall next to the hot-water cylinder. If an immersion heater timer is fitted, this should be wired between the fused connection unit and the immersion heater; an Economy 7 controller is fitted in place of the fused connection unit.

Cooker circuit

An electric cooker can draw a lot of current and needs its own separate circuit. Depending on the size of cooker, this can be a 30A, 40A or a 45A circuit – the way to find out is to check the overall rating (in kW) of the cooker and multiply that by 4 to get the approximate maximum current use – e.g., a 12kW cooker could use 48A.

- ☞ Take the first 10A at 100 per cent and the remainder at 30 per cent (to allow for the fact that you will never use everything at once) plus 5A for a possible socket in the cooker control panel – so the 12kW cooker rating is 10 plus 30 per cent of 38 plus 5 = 10 + 11.4 + 5 = 26.4, so a 30A circuit will do, though many people argue that installing the maximum (45A) size of cooker circuit is good practice.

The circuit is run all the way from the consumer unit to the cooker control panel and the size of cable used depends on the

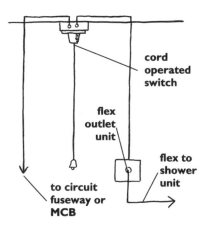

cord operated switch

flex outlet unit

flex to shower unit

to circuit fuseway or MCB

▲ **Circuit wiring for an electric shower unit.**

circuit rating, the length of cable run and the type of fuse used.

For cable runs up to 20 m (65 ft), the following sizes of cable should be used:

Method of fusing	30A	40A/45A
Rewirable fuse	6 sq mm	10 sq mm
Replaceable fuse/MCB	4 sq mm	6 sq mm

For cable runs of more than 20m, you must go up a size – 4 to 6, 6 to 10 or 10 to 16 sq mm.

Electric shower circuits

An electric shower also needs its own circuit, run all the way from the consumer unit to the shower and protected with an RCD (residual current device). The fuse rating for the circuit and the size of cable used, depends on the rating of the shower, the length of cable run and the type of fuse used.

Up to shower ratings of 7.2 kW, a 30A circuit can be used, from 7.2 kW up to 9.6 kW a 40A circuit and above 9.6 kW a 45A circuit. The cable sizes are then the same as for cookers.

Outside circuits

It is very useful to have socket outlets and lighting in sheds, in the garden and in detached garages (attached garages can have electricity brought through from the house). For sheds and garages, the normal answer is to have a 20A radial circuit (see *Socket outlet circuits*, page 66), which is then connected to a two-way consumer unit in the shed or garage – a 5A fuse feeding the shed/garage lighting and a 15A fuse feeding one or more socket outlets.

The problem is getting the power from the house to the shed or garage. There are two ways to do this: overhead or underground.

☞ With overhead wiring, you can use normal cable (in this case 2.5 sq mm) provided it is at least 3.6 m (12 ft) above the ground (5.2 m [17 ft] if over a driveway). For cable runs of more than 3 m (10 ft), the cable must be supported on a 'catenary' wire, strung between supports at the house and the shed/garage ends and supporting the cable with rubber loops.

☞ For underground wiring, normal cable must be protected by running it in rigid PVC conduit or special armoured cable must be used, both in a trench at least 50 cm (20 in) deep to avoid damage from digging. If you are taking a trench to a garden shed, it is worth making it deeper (75 cm [30 in] – the maximum depth for frost) and running a water pipe in it as well for a tap down the garden.

Off-peak tariffs

Where you use electricity for night storage heating or for heating hot water in an immersion heater, it is worth being on one of the off-peak tariffs offered by electricity companies, the best-known of which is the Economy 7 tariff. Under this, you pay slightly more for daytime electricity (and slightly more in standing charges), but less than half the daytime rate for any electricity used at night. No extra wiring is needed to install an off-peak meter (which is installed free); you will, however, need a second consumer unit for storage heaters, timed so that it only comes on during the economy period) and an Economy 7 controller or simple timeswitch to control the operation of the immersion heater.

Bathroom electrics

Because the combination of electricity and water is potentially dangerous, there are special rules about using electricity in bathrooms. These include:

☞ No rocker switches (light switches, double-pole switches or switched fused connection units within reach of the bath or shower (although ceiling-mounted pull-cord switches are allowed).

☞ No socket outlets in bathrooms, except special shaver sockets.

☞ No portable electrical appliances to be taken into bathrooms, (though fixed appliances, such as extractor fans and heated towel rails are OK).

☞ No pendant lights unless fitted with a special 'skirt' to prevent the terminals ever being touched.

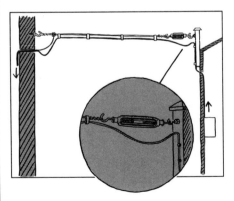

◀ **An overhead cable for outdoor wiring is supported by a timber post and attached to a catenary wire.**

DIY – When to get an expert

It is essential to know your own limitations as a DIYer, and to know when you can tackle something yourself and when you should call in an expert who has both the skill and knowledge necessary to complete the job safely and properly.

Skill and knowledge

Some DIY jobs – for example, basic plumbing and electricity – require surprisingly little skill. The use of DIY kits, semi-flexible plastic pipe and push-fit fittings has made plumbing very simple these days, while much electrical work is more about making holes in walls and floors to run the cable than it is to do with the actual wiring. But both have safety elements – electricity in particular, can kill you, but many people think plumbing is more risky than electrical work because of the possibility of flooding the house. Both, however, require a degree of expertise which only comes with experience and knowledge. The scope of this book doesn't allow for full explanations of electrical wiring and plumbing, etc. (see pp. 53-70), but there are a number of very good books devoted solely to these subjects and certainly an absolute beginner can learn to undertake much of what needs to be done around the house.

By contrast, however, you can read as many books as you like on **plastering** and still not be able to do it. Unlike many other DIY skills (woodwork, for example), you cannot take your time over plastering: it has to be done at the professional speed which can produce dire results for the unskilled beginner.

Any work involving work on the **roof** of your house is something definitely best left to the professionals. They will have the confidence necessary to work on the roof and will know how to get across the roof without damaging it. They'll also have the proper access equipment – roof ladders and, if necessary, scaffolding.

For anything involving **structural alterations** to the house, you should always employ professional help. Not only could what you propose be dangerous, but it may contravene building regulations or local planning laws. And, of course, you should always seek help if you have structural problems (rot, woodworm attack or suspected subsidence, for example), where you will be unable to assess the extent or the severity of the attack yourself.

Most of the contractors and advisors you might want to use will belong to a **trade association** or professional institution.

Safety

Apart from the obvious risks in doing your own home electrics, there are safety aspects to any DIY job, which mean not only that you must know what you are doing, but also that you must have the correct equipment, including appropriate safety wear.

◄ **Undertaking any DIY work sensibly means wearing the correct protective equipment: eyes, skin, ears and mouth must always be appropriately protected.**

71

Working with ladders is a common cause of injury. It is essential that all ladders are put up on a firm base – and, in the case of long extension ladders, firmly secured to the house. When using a ladder, you should never lean sideways and there should never be more than two people on the ladder at the same time. The base of an extension ladder should be 1 m (40 in) away from the wall for every 4 m (160 in) the top of the ladder is up the wall.

Working with **chemicals** requires care, too – especially paint strippers, brush cleaners and preservatives used in decorating. Good rubber **gloves** are an essential when using them, as are the correct type of **eye protector** where there is a risk of splashing. If you do get chemicals in your eye, the first response should normally be to put your head under the nearest tap and to rinse as much as possible out before seeking medical attention, if necessary.

A lot of DIY accidents involve the use of **tools**. Trimming knives, with their very sharp blades, are a particularly hazard and you should make sure that the line of cut is always outside your body and not directed towards your other hand.

It is essential to keep cutting tools sharp – you are much more likely to injure yourself forcing a blunt tool (such as a chisel) than you are when working with a really sharp one.

Stout gloves are often necessary when working with this kind of tool – and **eye protectors**, **a face mask** and sometimes **ear defenders** when working with power tools such as sanders, grinders and circular saws.

Which light bulb where?

There are three things to think about when choosing a light bulb:
- ☞ how long the light bulb is going to last
- ☞ how much it is going to cost to run
- ☞ the appearance of the light – or, rather, the effect the light bulb has on the things which it is illuminating (particularly important when it comes to things like food).

Incandescent lighting

The most common type of light bulb is the 'incandescent' type with a tungsten filament which glows brightly. This produces a 'warm' effect, but the bulbs do not last very long (typically 1000 to 2000 hours) and are expensive to run as they produce much more heat than they do light.

The most familiar is the **GLS (General Lighting Service)** bulb, available in a wide range of brightness (watts), in different shapes (pear, mushroom, round, candle and pygmy, for example) and with different finishes (clear, pearl or coloured). This type of bulb can be used anywhere and is found mainly in pendant light fittings, wall lights, standard lamps and table lamps.

There is a range of **reflector bulbs** which are internally silvered to produce a more concentrated beam of light. These cost more to buy than normal light bulbs, but last no longer and are no more efficient. They are found mainly in ceiling fittings – such as downlighters and recessed 'eyeball' spotlights and in wall- and track-mounted spotlights. One type – the **PAR (parabolic aluminised reflector)** lamp – is commonly used for outside spotlights and floodlights as it is particularly resistant to temperature changes; another – the **CS (crown-silvered)** lamp – gives a particularly well-defined beam.

Also used outside are **tungsten halogen** bulbs which produce a very strong white beam of light ideal for floodlighting.

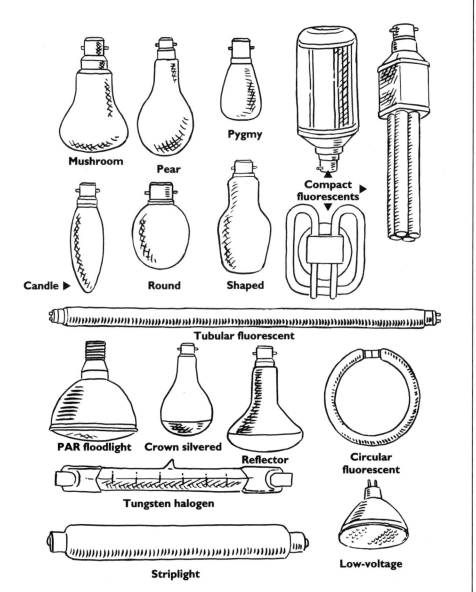

Mushroom

Pear

Pygmy

Compact ▶ fluorescents ▼

Candle ▶

Round

Shaped

Tubular fluorescent

PAR floodlight **Crown silvered**

Reflector

Circular fluorescent

Tungsten halogen

Striplight

Low-voltage

Fluorescent lighting

▲ **The variety of lamps (bulbs) used in light fittings.**

A fluorescent light does not have an element, but relies on the glow produced by an electrical discharge within the 'bulb' – which for most fluorescent fittings is a long tube. The big advantages of fluorescent lighting are that it is much cheaper to run (very much more energy is converted into light than with a tungsten light) and that the tubes last longer – five to six times more on average than a light bulb. Life is shortened by constant

switching on and off, so it is better to leave this type of light on in any room you are using constantly.

The disadvantage of fluorescent lighting is that the light the tubes produce is cold and unflattering – both to food and to human skin. They are widely used for lighting kitchens and offices, though most people prefer the warmth of tungsten lighting in living rooms and bedrooms. You can, however, get 'warmer' versions, though these are not always held in stock by electrical suppliers.

Most fluorescent lights need a special fitting – either a long one on the ceiling or a shorter one for a light mounted underneath a kitchen wall cupboard. But the last few years has seen the introduction of compact fluorescent lamps – so-called **'low-energy' lamps**, which can be fitted in place of normal light bulbs. None looks like a normal light bulb and they come in funny shapes – a large inverted 'jam jar', a series of upward-facing tubes or a circular ring, for example – but they are much cheaper to run. Although they cost very much more than a normal light bulb, the fact that they last up to six times longer and use only 20 to 25 per cent of the electricity mean that over their lifetime, they cost only a quarter as much as a normal bulb.

Low-voltage lighting

These small compact lights save energy, too, because they run at a much lower voltage and more of their energy goes into light production than heat production. They produce a very clear pure light in a concentrated beam, which makes them ideal for task lighting (the light over a desk, say) with the added bonus that the fittings give out very little heat. They are also good for unobtrusive general lighting (tiny spotlights set into the ceiling, for example) and for highlighting features such as pictures or ornaments.

You need a **transformer** to run low-voltage lighting. Some fittings come with the transformer built in, so can be used to replace a normal light, while some have a plug-in transformer which goes into a socket outlet to power a table or desk light. For running a whole circuit of low-voltage lights, you will need a separate transformer – see page 65 for details.

Fitting light bulbs

Fluorescent tubes, **tungsten striplights**, **tungsten halogen** light and **low-voltage** lights each have their own unique connectors

designed to go into their individual fittings. **Light bulbs**, however, can have one of four different fittings and it is essential to know which one you want and to check on the packaging when you buy to ensure you have got the correct sort.

Most normal light bulbs use a **Bayonet Cap (BC)** fitting. There are two contacts on the end of the bulb and two pins sticking out from the side. To insert the bulb into the fitting you first push (to depress the spring loaded contacts in the fitting) and then twist (to lock the pins into slots in the side of the fitting). Some bulbs (candle bulbs, for example) have a smaller version – **Small Bayonet Cap (SBC) –** which operates in the same way, but the two fittings are not interchangeable.

Many reflector bulbs (and some other bulbs) use a different type of fitting – the **Edison Screw (ES)** cap – where you turn the light bulb a couple of times to secure it. In this case the bulb has only one contact on the end, the other one being the side of the cap. Again, there is a smaller, non-interchangeable version called **Small Edison Screw (SES)**.

Designing lighting

When considering how to light a room, you must think of how the room is going to be used.

All rooms need general lighting, although this does not always have to be on all the time. You may also want background lighting (wall lamps and uplighters on the wall, for example) and task lighting for reading, sewing, preparing food, etc. In some rooms, feature lighting will be important if you have pictures or ornaments you want to illuminate (sometimes the lighting can be fitted inside a display cupboard). Looking at home improvement magazines and lighting catalogues will give you ideas of what is possible: you do not have to be restricted by the unimaginative lighting fittings provided by the builder of the house!

Decorating – what's easy, what's not

Economics dictate that most home-owners will need to do some if not all of their own home decoration – painting, wallpapering, exterior decoration, tiling and, perhaps, floor covering. Some of this is easier to do than others.

Easy – recommended for beginners

☞ painting internal walls in good condition

Fairly easy – needs time and patience

☞ painting internal walls in poor condition (i.e., needing preparation)
☞ painting internal woodwork in good condition

Less easy, needing some skill

☞ wallpapering internal walls
☞ painting exterior walls
☞ tiling flat surfaces
☞ painting internal woodwork in poor condition
☞ laying floor coverings on a flat floor

Fairly difficult, for the more experienced

☞ putting up washable wallpaper
☞ wallpapering ceilings and stairwells
☞ painting exterior woodwork in good condition
☞ painting exterior walls in poor condition
☞ tiling shaped or uneven surfaces
☞ laying floor coverings on an uneven floor

Very difficult – best left to a professional

☞ re-plastering internal walls before decoration
☞ painting exterior woodwork in poor condition
☞ hanging exotic wallcoverings (hessian or silk, for example)
☞ laying new carpet

Painting

Putting paint on to internal surfaces – walls and woodwork, doors, skirtings and architraves, etc. – is probably one of the first DIY jobs anyone attempts. If the existing surfaces are in good condition – and all you want to do is to change the colour or the style of finish – the job is easy to do, especially if you use one of the modern convenience paints. But if the surfaces are in poor condition, so that you have to strip and fill them, the job becomes much harder and takes much longer.

Be sure of one thing: preparation is the key to all decorating jobs – if you skimp on the preparatory work, the finish will never be good.

Later on, you will want to get on to painting exterior walls and woodwork, where the function of the paint is now to protect as well as to decorate. Different products are needed – and, sometimes, different tools and techniques.

Measuring up

It helps to have a rough idea of the surface areas you are painting, and it will be easiest if you measure in metres as the spreading capacity of paint is quoted in square metres on the can.

Multiply the width of each wall by its height. This will give you the square metre measurement of the wall. Add together all the walls you want in the same colour. You will need at least two coats of most paints for a really professional finish.

When measuring up external walls, which are tough rendered or, indeed, indoor walls which have a rough surface (like bubbly ceiling paper), you will need to increase the amount of paint to allow for all the 'ups and downs' of the rough surface. This can double the quantities needed.

The painter's tool kit

There are two approaches to buying decorating tools: the first is to buy cheap tools and then throw them away after use; the second is to buy good-quality tools and look after them. The second is by far the better as your filling knives will not rust, bristles will not fall out of your brushes and your rollers will not go hard.

Abrasives

Paintwork, bare walls and bare wood need to be 'rubbed down' with abrasive paper before you apply new paint. This will ensure a smooth surface – and, for existing paint, a slightly roughened surface to which the new paint can adhere.

There is a wide range of sandpaper types available, with surface finishes from very fine to coarse; for best results always use the paper wrapped around a cork sanding block or on the rubber pad of a powered sanding machine (an orbital sander, for example).

Fillers

You will need two main kinds of filler when preparing surfaces for painting: **wall filler** for making good holes and cracks in plaster and **wood filler** for doing the same on

woodwork. Both come in interior and exterior grades; where you are filling a gap between two different materials (which will expand and contract at different rates) some kind of **flexible filler** or **mastic** is needed.

If you have very large holes to fill – such as the one left around a waste pipe going through the outside wall, you can buy expanding foam fillers, which can be cut back with a knife once set, and DIY plasters which can fill the hole in one go. DIY plaster can also be used for making good sections of damaged plaster, but if the whole wall needs plastering (or an external wall needs to be re-rendered), you should call in a professional.

Filling knife

You will need a flat-bladed filling knife for making good holes and cracks in walls and also in woodwork. You want a largish one for walls and a smaller one for woodwork – sometimes a putty knife can be used on woodwork instead.

Hot-air gun

This looks a little like a hair dryer, and it speeds up the process of stripping paint from woodwork by softening it before you take it off with a scraper. Using a hot-air gun is much

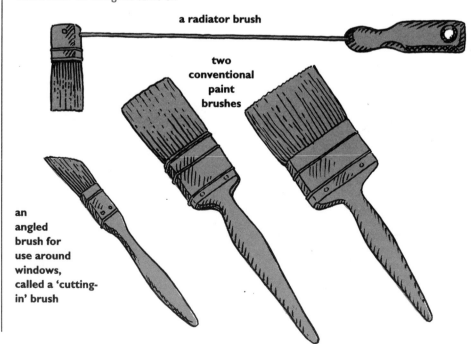

a radiator brush

two conventional paint brushes

an angled brush for use around windows, called a 'cutting-in' brush

safer than the more traditional blow lamp –
this can set fire to paint shavings, burn the
wood and crack glass if used carelessly – and
safer, cheaper and less messy than using
chemical paint strippers, though paste-type
chemical strippers are the answer for
removing several layers of paint in one go or
for use on complex mouldings where it is
difficult to get a scraper in.

Paint brushes

Paint brushes are generally used for applying
paint and varnish to wooden surfaces. The
best quality paint brushes are made from
pure boar's bristle, which comes only from
Chinese boars. Different qualities and lengths
of bristle are 'blended' together to give the
characteristic paint-brush shape with the 'split
ends' of the bristle spreading the paint.

You will generally find three price ranges of
paint brush available. The most expensive is
aimed more at the tradesman and
experienced DIYer: for most DIYers, it is best
to buy the middle range and look after the
brush by cleaning it thoroughly after use. If
you intend to throw the brush away, go for
the cheapest ones – but be prepared for the

**Although perfect for oil-based
paints (most varnishes and gloss
and eggshell paints), bristle
brushes are not ideal for use with
the increasing number of
environmentally friendly water-
based ('quick-drying') paints and
varnishes. The water causes the
bristles to swell and it is better to
use a brush with synthetic bristles.**

individual bristles to come out on the wet
paint, and so spoil your brushstrokes!

Special brushes, with synthetic bristles and
a non-rusting ferrule (the metal band which
holds the bristles in place), are sold for use
with emulsion paints.

Varnish brushes

The traditional paint brush is known as a
varnish brush and comes in sizes from 6 mm
($\frac{1}{4}$ in) up to 10 cm (4 in). For most purposes,
just two sizes are needed – 5 cm (2 in) for
painting large clear surfaces and 25 mm (1 in)
for narrow sections and fine work.

Crevice brush

This has small bristles mounted at right angles
on a long handle so that it can be used for
painting inaccessible places, such as the back
of a radiator.

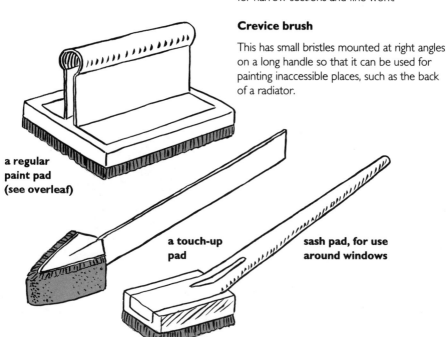

**a regular
paint pad
(see overleaf)**

**a touch-up
pad**

**sash pad, for use
around windows**

Cutting-in brush

This brush has its bristles cut at an angle and is specifically designed for painting along an edge, such as on a window next to glass.

> **When putting your brush down for a short break, wrap the bristles in cling film to prevent drying out.**

Paint kettle

It is generally much easier to decant a small amount of paint from the tin into a proper 'paint kettle' and then to carry this to the work. This keeps the paint tin relatively clean, allows you to use only a small amount at a time, and with older paint you can 'filter' the paint (through nylon stockings) to leave any solid bits behind.

Most paint kettles have hooks which can be used to attach them to a ladder or step-ladder.

Paint pads

These are an alternative to using a brush or a roller for applying paint. They have short mohair bristles attached to a foam backing pad fixed to a plastic holder. Many different shapes are available, including large pads for painting walls, smaller pads for painting woodwork, crevice pads, corner pads, pads with edging wheels for painting next to a corner above a moulding and exterior-grade pads for outside walls. Often a selection of pads will be sold as a 'kit' with the containing box doubling as a paint tray. Compared with a brush, a paint pad is much easier to use: it puts the paint on faster and gives a better finish. But it generally applies less paint, which can be a problem when painting over a strong existing colour, and can be difficult to clean. They are inexpensive, but have a limited life.

rollers for textured paint

standard paint rollers, in wool, mohair and foam, and roller tray

pipe roller

Paint rollers

Paint rollers are generally used for painting walls. The cheapest type use foam for the roller sleeve, but these are not generally recommended – they splash a lot in use, can leave bubbles on the surface (which explode leaving tiny 'craters'), and are difficult to clean. Much better is a roller sleeve which has a natural or synthetic pile sleeve – medium pile for most surfaces and most paints, but short pile for very smooth surfaces and for solid emulsion paint and long pile for more textured surfaces. There are small rollers on long handles for painting behind radiators.

Rollers usually come apart for cleaning; some have provision for an extension pole for use on high walls and ceilings. A roller cannot normally be used right up into a corner so when painting a wall, you will have to go round the edges painting these with a brush first.

A roller needs a proper roller tray in order to load it with paint; like the roller sleeve, this must be thoroughly cleaned after use.

Painting chemicals

All paint chemicals should be kept in the original containers and well out of the reach of children and pets. You will need:

- ☞ **paint stripper** for removing paint, especially from awkwardly shaped mouldings
- ☞ **paint-brush cleaner** for cleaning paint brushes and pads used with oil-based paint or varnish
- ☞ **sugar soap** for cleaning old paintwork
- ☞ **white spirit** (turpentine substitute) for thinning paints and varnishes and for cleaning previously painted surfaces
- ☞ **wallpaper stripper** for difficult-to-remove wallpaper.

You may also need a mould cleaner for removing algae and mould from walls and a stabilising solution for use on dusty walls. Two useful chemicals are liquid sander, which prepares the surface for painting, and knotting which is put over knots in bare wood to stop the resin 'bleeding' though the paint.

Shavehook

A shavehook is used with a hot-air gun or after applying a chemical paint stripper to remove paint from woodwork. The tool is used to pull the paint off the wood with a scraping action and there are different shapes of shavehook – flat (three scraping edges arranged in a triangle), curved (two convex curved shapes and one concave one) and combination (one flat, one convex and one concave scraping edge) – for different types of surface.

Window scraper

Where too much paint has got on to the glass of a window (it should only just cover the putty line) a window scraper can be used to remove it. This holds a trimming knife blade and is moved across the glass with a pushing motion.

Stripping knife

A flat-bladed stripping knife looks a little like a filling knife, but has a more rigid blade. Its main use is for stripping wallpaper off walls; a less wide version with a sharpened edge can also be used for stripping paint – it pushes the paint off the surface.

Types of paint

When you look along the shelves of the average DIY store, the apparent choice of paint is bewildering. But most of the paints available can be broken down into one of five types:

- ☞ emulsion paints for walls
- ☞ gloss paints for woodwork
- ☞ varnishes
- ☞ paint for outside woodwork
- ☞ masonry paints for external walls

There are also several speciality paints, usually described by their use rather than by their type.

Emulsion paints for walls

All emulsion paints are water-based and contain 'vinyl'. What can vary is the amount of solids put into the paint, which is usually reflected in the price. Cheap emulsion paints are fine for use on bedroom ceilings, where you are painting white over white, but several coats could be needed on walls where you are overpainting a stronger colour.

The other thing which varies is the surface finish the paint gives. Most emulsion paints give a matt surface finish, but more popular over the years are the 'silk' and 'satin' finishes which give a slight sheen. These are easier to keep clean than matt (all emulsion paints are washable once they have dried) and better at reflecting light into a room, but they will be more likely to show up any defects in the surface.

'Solid' emulsion paints can be applied directly from their container.

Gloss paints for woodwork

The traditional gloss paint, designed for use both inside and outside, is a three-coat system:

- ☞ primer
- ☞ undercoat
- ☞ gloss

For use inside, this has now largely been replaced by self-undercoating gloss paints (oil-based) and quick-drying gloss paints which are water-based, making them more user-friendly (the brushes wash out in water and the paints are easier to use) and environmentally friendly. Both still need a primer when used on bare wood (or a different primer if used to overpaint metal), but neither needs an undercoat unless a very strong colour is being overpainted.

Gloss paint for wood also comes in a non-drip (thixotropic) form. This is solid in the tin, but becomes liquid when you brush it out on the surface and does not fall off the brush between the two. This type of paint should not be stirred.

Varnish

Varnish is like paint without any solid pigment to give it colour or opacity (hiding power). It is applied in exactly the same way, but needs no primer or undercoat – and usually three or four coats of varnish is recommended. Most varnishes these days contain polyurethane, which is extremely hard and proves a surface which resists both heat and water – vital if used on occasional tables or shelves, for example.

As with gloss paint, varnishes come in both oil-based and water-based ('quick-drying') versions; as well as clear varnish, you can get coloured varnishes which change the appearance of the wood as well as protecting it.

> These paints form a skin when partially used. To avoid this forming on top of the paint, store the tin (well closed) upside down. Then when you open the tin, the skin will be on the bottom of the paint.

Paint for outside woodwork

Traditional three-coat gloss paint is still used for exterior woodwork, but there is now a range of specially formulated paints for use here.

The main characteristic of these paints is their flexibility (to cope with the movement of the wood) and their ability to 'breathe' – that is, to let moisture out of the wood, but to prevent water getting in. This property is often called 'microporosity' and the paints are sometimes known as 'microporous' paints. Different types are available, including both oil-based and water-based paints; some need an undercoat while others are self-undercoating and some self-priming, too.

A matching range of exterior stains is also available for painting hardwood or softwood doors and windows which you want to leave with the natural wood effect.

Masonry paints

These are specifically designed for external walls, mainly those which have already been rendered (covered with a sand/cement 'plaster').

Two main types are available: smooth and textured. Smooth masonry paint is for use on flat surfaces in good condition; textured masonry paint contains small particles which give a rougher finish, but one which will cover up hairline cracks and other surface defects.

Speciality paints

As well as these five main types of paint, you can get the following paints for more specialised uses:

- ☞ **radiator paint** (resists yellowing)
- ☞ **anti-condensation paint** (insulates the surface)
- ☞ **garage floor paint** (keeps the floor clean)
- ☞ **rust-inhibiting paint** (for metal gates and railings)
- ☞ **doorstep paint** (for a red welcome)
- ☞ **cork and floor varnish** (to seal and protect)
- ☞ **anti-damp paint** (to form a waterproof barrier)
- ☞ **anti-stain paint** (to cover up unsightly stains)

☞ **zinc-rich primers** (to combat rust on metal surfaces)

☞ **aluminium wood primer** (to provide a water-resistant layer).

Painting techniques

The method you use for painting depends very much on the type of paint you are applying, the tool you are using to apply it, and the surface to which you are applying it.

The one thing which is common to many painting tasks is the need to keep what professional decorators call a wet edge – that is, making sure the edge of the area you have just painted is still wet so that it can be used to start the next area of painting.

Before you start painting, all surfaces should be clean and dry and all holes and cracks filled with any rough bits smoothed over.

Using a brush for doors and woodwork

First load the paintbrush, by dipping just the first third of the bristles into your paint kettle (or paint tin) and wiping any surplus paint off on the top rim.

When painting a large surface like a door, start at one top corner. Hold the brush between your finger tips and apply

▲ **Top: apply paint in dabs approximately 5 cm (2 in) apart, joining them together with neat strokes.**

▶ **Right: follow the numbers to paint various parts of a panelled door.**

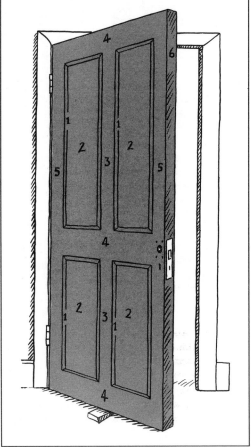

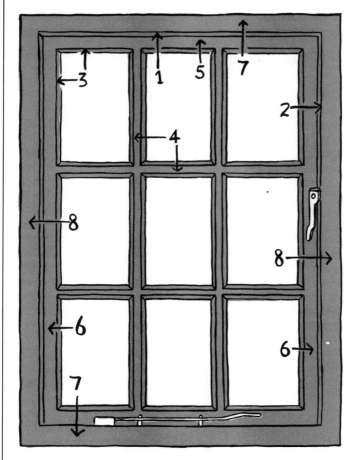

▲ **Follow the numbered sequence when painting a casement window, painting the window before the frame.**

the paint in vertical strips or dabs around 2.5 cm (1 in) apart. Then brush across these in both directions; at the side of the door, paint towards the edge, never away from it or you will get paint building up on the corner. Complete a block like this around 40 cm square (16 in – or roughly one-eighth of the door) and finish by using long vertical light strokes across the paint surface from the bottom of the block up to the top edge of the door, without re-loading the brush with paint. This is known as 'laying off'.

Repeat for the other top corner of the door and then work down the door in more blocks, each time finishing off with long light

strokes back into the areas which you have painted.

You need to adapt the technique slightly when painting doors with panels or when painting window frames. With windows and glazed door, use a 'cutting-in' brush (see page 76) to paint the wood next to the glass.

Using a paint pad for doors and woodwork

A pad can put on paint much faster and more evenly than a paint brush, so you adapt the technique by painting down the door or window in vertical strips, the width of the pad until it runs out of paint.

Make sure when loading the paint pad, that only the bristles are allowed to touch the paint – do not get paint into the foam backing – and wipe off excess paint on the side of the tray. Use a 'wand' paint pad to paint the mouldings of a panel door or the thinner parts of a window and a larger pad for the main body of a panel door or the whole of a flush door.

Using a paint roller for walls and ceilings

Load the roller by first tipping a small amount of paint into the tray and then moving the roller across it – experience will show the right amount of paint to use. The basic painting technique with a roller is to paint first of all a 'W' or 'X' shape on the wall and then to use the roller across this both horizontally and vertically so that the paint is spread around.

Walls should be painted in horizontal bands, starting from the top, and ceilings should be painted in bands working away from the main or only window.

Using brushes and pads on walls and ceilings

When using a emulsion paint brush on walls, the technique is very much the same as the using a roller – that is, to get the paint quickly on to the wall and then to work it around; grip the brush in the palm of your hand.

Special large paint pads are sold for use when painting walls and ceilings and the technique is similar to using a smaller paint pad for gloss paint – that is, to apply the paint in long smooth strokes until the pad is empty. Because the paint goes on more thinly than with a brush or a roller, you may need an extra coat, especially if you are covering a dark colour with a lighter one. On rough or textured surfaces, use a scrubbing action with the pad to work the paint into the hollows.

Some paint pads come with small wheels which allows them to be used right up to edges – whether it is the join between ceiling or wall or the join between wall and skirting board.

▼ **With your paint roller, paint a 'W' or 'X' shape first, and then roll across it vertically and horizontally.**

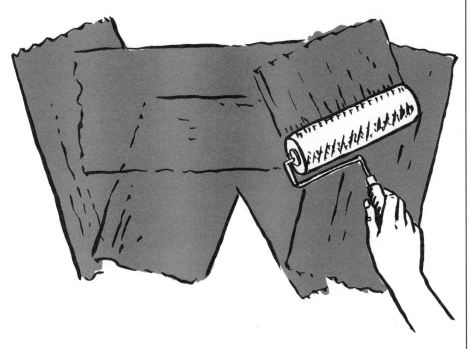

▲ **When painting masonry, protect your downpipes with newspaper.**

Painting outside

When painting outside woodwork, the technique is exactly the same as when painting woodwork inside – except that you are working from the top of a ladder or the platform of a scaffold tower, which makes being organised and being careful much more important.

When painting walls, however, you use quite a different technique. For a start, you need a stiff-bristled brush for applying masonry paint and if the surface is rough, a 'stippling' action (dabbing the tips of the bristles into the wall) is required. A long-pile roller can also be used. Divide the wall up into sections, preferably broken by natural features such as drainpipes and windows, and complete one section at a time. Wrap newspaper around downpipes to keep the paint off them.

> **When painting outside, the rule is to 'follow the sun' – that is to work round the house clockwise after the sun has had a chance to dry out the next part you are working on. This will now be in shadow which makes it easier to see where you have painted.**

Wallpapering

Wallpapering has the advantage of producing a coloured and patterned wall surface very quickly. The wallcovering will cover up many surface defects in the wall – and often covering the wall with lining paper is the prelude to painting.

As with painting, however, preparation is all-important: old paper should be stripped off unless it provides a uniform surface and all defects in the wall made good (and the wall cleaned) before you start.

Measuring up

The standard roll of wallpaper is 53 cm (21 in) wide and 10 m (33 ft) long – so you can use either metres or feet and inches to measure up your walls and ceilings before buying the paper. The chart below shows how many rolls you will need for walls – read off the appropriate perimeter (the distance right round the room in metres, ignoring doors and windows) against the height of the wall from skirting to ceiling (or lower height such as a picture rail if the wallcovering will stop there). When buying wallcoverings, make sure that all rolls come from the same batch – it is better to buy too many rolls rather than too few – any spare material can be used for patching in the future and most shops will take back unopened whole rolls.

The wallpaperer's tool kit

Although you can get away with using inferior tools and equipment, it will make wallpapering much easier if you buy decent equipment to start with – after all, it is going to last you years. This applies primarily to the most important piece of equipment – the pasting table. Making do on the kitchen table is a waste of time, but do not be tempted to buy one of the cheapest tables available in DIY stores: they are often flimsy rubbish and do not make the task of pasting wallpaper any pleasure. Far better to go for ready-pasted paper, which in theory needs no pasting table (though somewhere to lay the paper out while it is being cut is useful) or for a decent, sturdy, pasting table which will make life much easier.

Filling knife

Needed for making good holes in walls – see *The painter's tool kit*, pp. 76-9.

PERIMETER	HEIGHT (METRES)				
(m)	2.0 – 2.2	2.2 – 2.4	2.4 – 2.6	2.6 – 2.8	2.8 – 3.0
9	4	4	4	5	5
10	4	4	5	5	5
11	5	5	5	6	6
12	5	5	6	6	7
13	5	6	6	7	7
14	6	6	7	7	8
15	6	6	7	8	8
16	6	7	8	8	9
17	6	7	8	9	9
18	7	8	9	9	10
19	7	8	9	10	11
20	8	9	10	11	12

Chalk line

A piece of string covered with chalk, used for marking out a straight line along a ceiling.

Paperhanging brush

A soft-bristled brush which is used to smooth a piece of wallpaper out on to the wall (or ceiling) after you have placed it in position. An essential tool.

Pasting brush

A coarse-bristled brush which you use for applying paste to the back of a wall covering. You need a **bucket** in which to mix the paste – tie a piece of string across the top to give you somewhere to rest the brush after use.

Pasting table

A flat surface on which to lay wallcoverings while you cut them and subsequently paste them. The table needs to be wider than the width of the wall covering – so you can slide it first to one side for pasting and then to the other, which keeps paste off the table surface – and it is a good idea to make a note of the exact length of the table so that you can use this to help you measure. If you need 2.1 m (7 ft) , for example and the table is 1.8 m (6 ft), you need only mark the length of the table plus 30 cm (12 in).

Paperhanging scissors

Scissors for paperhanging are much longer than normal scissors, which helps when cutting straight lines. They should be kept clean and always washed and dried after use to prevent them rusting. Do not use them for anything else. Use both for cutting lengths on the pasting table and for trimming them on the wall (a pair of very small scissors is also useful for tricky corners).

Plumb line

Few houses have straight, flat or vertical walls. So you need a plumb line to hang the first piece of wallpaper accurately on each wall. A proper plumb line (a weighted bob on a piece of cord) is ideal; you could improvise with something like a paperclip or screw on a piece of black thread.

Seam roller

Helpful, but not essential, for pressing down the seams of wallpaper once hung. Should not be used on relief (textured) wallpapers.

Stripping knife

Needed for removing old wallpaper from walls – see *The painter's tool kit*, pp. 76-9.

Trimming knife

Useful, in addition to wallpapering scissors, for cutting wallpaper once it is hung. If you are using it on ordinary wallpaper which is still 'wet', the blade must be absolutely sharp or it will tear the wallpaper. Professional decorators use trimming knives with 'snap-off' blades, using a new blade for each piece of wallpaper.

Steam wallpaper stripper

An extremely useful tool which makes the task of removing old wallpaper very much easier. What it does is to drive steam into the wallpaper, softening the adhesive underneath, so that you can then use a stripping knife to scrape it off. You can buy your own steam stripper or can hire one: hired wallpaper strippers are more effective, but quite hard work to use.

For painted or impermeable wallpaper, you also need a **wallpaper serrator**, which will scratch holes in the surface to allow the steam through.

Wallpaper paste

Choose the type of paste to match the type – and weight – of the wallcovering. Some wallcoverings require a special adhesive (check the instructions); impervious wallcoverings (such as washable wallpaper and vinyl wallcoverings) require the use of a paste containing a fungicide to prevent mould growing under the wallpaper.

Types of wallcovering

There are five main types of wallcovering:
- ☞ 'whites'
- ☞ relief papers
- ☞ normal wallpaper
- ☞ washable wallpaper
- ☞ vinyl wallcoverings.

There are also some 'exotic' coverings, such as **seagrass**, **hessian** and **silk** which not only require special adhesives but also need some skill to hang correctly.

Whites

The two main members of this family are lining paper which you hang before another wallcovering (or before painting) to give a smooth flat surface – under another covering, lining paper is hung in horizontal strips so that the joins do not line up with the vertical strips of main wallcovering – and woodchip wallpaper, which is an excellent and cheap way of covering up a damaged wall surface prior to painting.

Relief papers

Also part of the 'whites' family, these papers (typically Crown Anaglypta and Supaglypta) give a sculptured surface to the wall which is then painted. Not the easiest of wallcovering to hang, but highly effective.

Normal wallpaper

Traditionally the most common type, but now largely being replaced by vinyls. Basically a plain paper overprinted with a pattern, it comes in a wide range of designs and is easy to hang.

Washable wallpaper

Now largely out of fashion, washable wallpaper is a normal wallpaper with a surface layer of plastic, making it easy to clean (and so ideal in children's rooms and bathrooms). It, too, has largely been replaced by vinyls as it is difficult to hang and even more difficult to strip.

Vinyl wallcoverings

Now the most popular type, vinyl wallcoverings have the advantage over normal wallcoverings that the pattern is infused into the vinyl surface, allowing much richer colours and more imaginative patterns. Most types are strippable – that is the covering can be pulled off, leaving its backing paper on the wall – making them easy to replace, and are also washable or scrubbable, making them easy to clean.

Foamed vinyls, the latest type, can have even more interesting patterns, including ceramic tile effects.

Exotic wallcoverings

These include:
- ☞ cork
- ☞ felt
- ☞ flock
- ☞ foil
- ☞ grasscloth
- ☞ hessian
- ☞ silk
- ☞ sisal
- ☞ suede effect
- ☞ woolstrand.

Some types require considerable skill in hanging and many of these types require you to paste the wall with a special paste rather than the wallcovering.

Wallpapering techniques

What is described here applies to all the main wallpapering types, but not to 'speciality' wall coverings. Where we talk about 'paper', this includes other wallcoverings, such as vinyl.

Surface preparation

You can paper over existing wallpaper if it is clean and in good condition – but avoid having the joins in the same place. Normally, though, it will be better to strip of the old wallpaper, make good the wall surface below with filler and start again. Stripping can be done with ordinary water (though washing-up liquid or a preparatory wallpaper stripper makes it easier), but a steam wallpaper stripper speeds the job up considerably.

◀ **Begin at the top wall, with about 5 cm (2 in) extra at the top, bringing it down beside your plumb line.**

On freshly plastered or very absorbent walls, the surface should be sized before putting up the wall covering – usually with diluted wallpaper paste, but sometimes with special size (available at DIY shops).

Cutting the wallcovering

Measure up the length of each 'drop' of wallpaper and then cut the paper at least 10 cm (4 in) longer than this – more on papers with a spaced pattern (with these, don't cut the second piece until the first piece is up).

Transfer the measurement to the back of the paper, using a try square and straight-edge to draw a square line across the paper, and cut the paper (or marking the measurement on both sides if you are sure the other end is square) with wallpapering scissors.

Pasting the paper

Lay the paper face down on the pasting table with one end just overlapping one end of the table. Start by pasting a central strip the whole length of the table and then slide the paper away from you until the edge just overlaps the far side of the table and paste the strip on that side. Then slide the paper to overlap the table edge nearest you and paste this strip. Fold this end of the length of paper over on itself and repeat for the other end and fold this over, too. With some papers (check instructions) you need to leave the paper to soak for a few minutes before applying it to the wall.

Putting up the first piece

Mark a true vertical line, using your plumb line, next to the largest window in the room.

Carry the paper to the wall and unfold the top half. Apply this to the wall down your marked line, with 5 cm (2 in) projecting at the top, and smooth it down with your wallpapering brush. Smooth away from the centre so that all air bubbles and globules of paste are carried to the outside. Wipe down with a sponge to remove excess paste.

Use the back of the wallpapering scissors to mark a line where the paper joins the ceiling or picture rail, peel the paper back and cut carefully along the line. Brush paper back

► **Allow about 12 mm ($^1/_2$ in) on each side to go around external corners. Make sure the wall-paper is still vertical.**

up on to the wall. Repeat at the skirting board.

Hanging subsequent pieces

Use the edge of your first piece as a guide for hanging the second piece. With a large 'drop' pattern, check before cutting that the second piece will line up with the first (it is sometimes better to cut alternate pieces from different rolls). When you get to a corner, cut the strip before hanging so that it goes about 12 mm ($^1/_2$ in) around the corner. Then mark a new vertical line (this is important) to hang the rest of the piece into the corner overlapping the first piece. The joint won't be noticed, tucked in the corner.

Awkward points

Papering straight stretches of wall is relatively easy – though you should allow around twenty minutes for each piece to be realistic. Problems happen when you come to external corners, chimney breasts, door frames, windows and light switches, electric socket outlets, and radiators.

External corners As with internal corners, the trick here is to cut the piece which meets the corner so that it goes round the corner by at least 12mm ($^1/_2$ in)- too much and the paper will wrinkle. Fit the next piece (against a vertical line) so that it covers the first piece, preferably on the side away from the light and preferably in as vertical a line as possible.

Chimney breasts You will want to centre a strip of wallcovering on a chimney breast. So do these first (or last), finishing off at the two internal corners where the breast juts out from the wall.

Door frames It helps if you can work out how much space there is between the last strip and the door frame – you do not want much less than around 2.5 cm (1in), but ideally there will be more than this. Mark out the shape of the door frame on the paper, allowing 2.5 cm (1 in) for trimming, and carry the paper very carefully to the bit of wall immediately before the door frame. Brush the paper down and then cut along the edge of

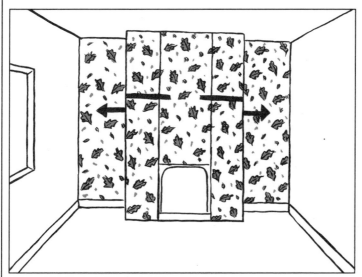

◀ Work from the centre outwards on a chimney breast.

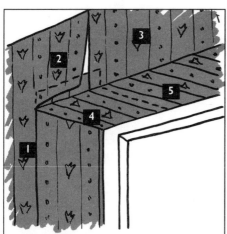

◀ Follow the numbered sequence, using patches of wallpaper to match the patterns. Each patch should be cut slightly larger than the area it is covering, and then area 2 + 3 brushed down over it.

◀ Cut the wallpaper into the corner of the architrave and crease it into the space between this and the wall, using the flat edge of the scissors. Trim off any excess.

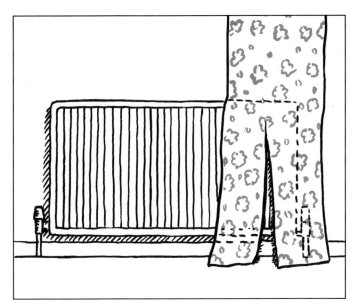

the architrave (the decorative wood around the door frame) – a trimming knife will be easier than scissors here, but take care not to rip the paper. You will need to cut another piece to fit the other side of the door frame and to meet up with the first piece over the top.

Windows The problem here is that most windows are positioned in the outer edge of the wall, leaving a window 'reveal' which needs to be papered. Provided the piece which would overlap the window does so by at least the depth of the reveal, there is no problem wrapping this piece round and trimming it to size. Nor is there a problem wrapping the top piece into the top of the reveal, but you will be left with two awkward squares to fill with an offcut of paper. The best way to do this is to fit the offcut first and then shape the covering piece to sit squarely along the edge of the reveal.

Switches and sockets When you approach a light switch or a socket outlet, you should turn off the electricity – water and electricity do not mix. Some professional decorators will actually remove both sockets and light switches, paper over them, cut out a recess and then put the sockets or switches back. If you do not feel confident about doing this, you can simply loosen the securing screws of the switch or socket, cut a cross in the paper over the switch or socket position and then cut the paper to fit just under the edges of the socket or switch.

Radiators Unless you are confident enough to remove a radiator, you have to cut a slit in the paper to fit round the radiator bracket and then push the paper down behind the radiator – a long-handled roller is a good tool for doing this.

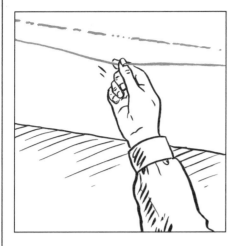

▲ **Use a chalked line to guide the placement of the first piece of wallpaper on the ceiling, and after that, every subsequent piece.**

Wallpapering ceilings

When wallpapering ceilings, you need to paste much longer lengths as you do not want joins in the middle of the ceiling. The paper is pasted in the same way, but folded up concertina fashion so that you can support it on a broom or with a spare roll of wallpaper while pasting it to the ceiling. Start by 'snapping' a chalk line all along the ceiling 10 mm ($\frac{1}{2}$ in) less than the width of the wallpaper from one edge. This is done by taping a string to the ceiling, running from one side to the other. The string is rubbed with chalk, then pulled back slightly so it 'snaps' against the ceiling, leaving a chalk line. Then paste the first piece, using the line as a guide for one edge and trimming at the wall. Repeat across the ceiling until you get to the far edge, where you may have to cut a piece to fit.

▼ **Fold paper concertina style and hold it up with a spare roll of paper.**

▲ **Construct a platform tower with step ladders and planks to make hall papering much easier.**

Wallpapering stairwells

The biggest problems with wallpapering a stairwell is providing a suitable platform for standing on while you apply the paper. Most platform towers can be re-constructed inside a stairwell, but a good compromise is a three-way combination ladder which you can set up to give you suitable points at which to stand.

The golden rule when you are papering stairwells is to hang the longest piece first.
Once you have done this, the procedure is identical with wallpapering walls, except that many of the pieces will need to be cut at an angle rather than straight across.

▲ **Use a tile-cutting jig for accurate and easy cutting.**

Tiling

Ceramic tiles are in many ways the perfect wallcovering for kitchens and bathrooms. They are easy to clean, they do not stain, they are heat-resistant and they provide a decorative backdrop.

They are not, however, cheap – something you particularly need to consider when creating a shower enclosure, for example – so you should think carefully about exactly how much of the wall you want to tile. In kitchens, this will usual be the space between the worktop and the wall cupboards; in bathrooms, you could consider having just a 'splashback' around a basin or bath, rather than tiling the whole wall.

Measuring up

The easiest way of counting the number of tiles you need is to make yourself a **gauging stick** from a square wooden batten around 1.2 m (4 ft) long. On each side of this, you can mark lines which represent the two main sizes of tile:

☞ 10 cm (4 ¼ in)
☞ 15 cm (6 in)

Then you can use this across your proposed tiling area, not just to count the number of tiles, but also to work you where they should be positioned to the best effect – for example, centred over a basin.

▶ **Use a notched spreader to cover the tiling space with adhesive. Press the first tiles into place against the batters and use it as a guide for the others.**

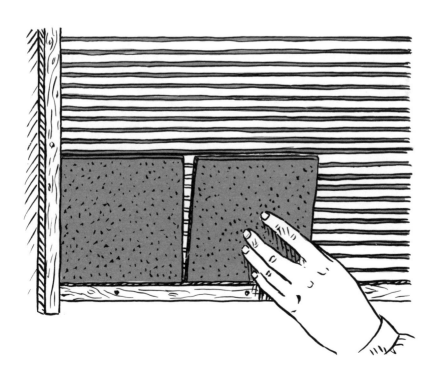

Tiling tool kit

The main tools you need are for cutting and shaping tiles. You also need devices for spreading tile adhesive and grout, plus a sprit level and straight-edge for getting the run of tiles horizontal and flat to the surface.

Tile cutters

Tiles are hard-baked ceramic biscuits, so are cut like glass – a firm score across the surface followed by 'snapping' the tile over an edge such as a match or a nail. You can score the tile with a variety of cutters; special **cutting jigs** and **snappers** are available to make the job easier. A **pair of pincers** is invaluable for 'nibbling' a thin edge of a tile. It is quite simple, especially on thinner tiles, but it is best to tackle the snapping with confidence.

Tile shapers

You will need to cut tiles into 'L' shapes to fit around socket outlets and the corners of windows. The best tool is a **tile saw**. Cut down one leg of the 'L' with the saw and then score and snap for the other leg. A **tile file** is also useful for smoothing off snapped and sawn edges.

Spreaders

A spreader for the adhesive is usually supplied in the tub, but you will need a **squeegee** for spreading grout across the tiles surface (this fills the gaps between tiles) plus a **shaping tool** for making the grout lines concave.

Tiling techniques

As with other decoration, the surface must be thoroughly prepared – which for tiling means having a moderately **flat** surface as well as a clean and undamaged one.

Having worked out the area you are going to tile and centred the position of the tiles correctly, the starting point is to attach two wooden battens to the wall – one at the base height of the second row of tiles (use a spirit level to ensure it is horizontal); the other vertically at one edge. These can be secured to the wall with masonry nails.

Using an adhesive spreader, put the tiling adhesive on the wall in ridges, working horizontally right across the area – in areas subjected to water (such as around a shower) use a waterproof adhesive. Then, put the tiles on the wall, simply pressing them into place, starting at the corner between the horizontal and vertical battens, allowing excess adhesive to squeeze out around the edges. Continue like this until the whole area is covered, cutting tiles to fit around socket outlets, internal window sills and the edges of windows, as appropriate. Some tiles are square-edged and need spacers to be fitted between them; others have spacing lugs; universal tiles have an angled edge requiring no spacer.

At the outer edges of the tiles, you have three choices. With some types of tile, there are tiles with one or two rounded edges (one for a top or side edge, two for corner); with others the square or angled edge of the tiles simply have extra glazing; the third choice is to use a preparatory edge strip which fits under the last tile and has a rounded edge.

Once the main body of tiles is in place, you can remove the battens and add the bottom row. If the worktop, skirting board or vanity basin top below is not exactly level, you will have to cut the bottom row of tiles to suit.

Once the tile adhesive has had time to set (at least twenty-four hours), you can apply the white or coloured grouting. Normally, this is a separate powder which you mix up with water, but if you use a combined adhesive and grout, it is the same as the adhesive.

Start by spreading the grout all across the tiles, making sure that it goes into the gaps between them. Then use a lolly stick or a specially shaped plastic tool to shape the grout into a slightly concave shape and finally wipe across the whole surface with a sponge to remove any traces of grout – if you leave it to dry, it will be very hard to remove.

CHAPTER THREE **Homecare**

Judy Williams

Previously Food Editor at the Sun, Judy now writes for Essentials, Family Circle and Take A Break. She has written five books altogether on crafts, food and children's parties.

As Mrs Beeton once said, 'The young housekeeper should never deem any of her duties ignoble ones', and of course nowadays this applies to young men, too. There are many jobs involved in the smooth running of a household, some of which we learn from our parents and others that seem to be a complete mystery. Lots of them are boring and repetitive, but essential to a clean, tidy and peaceful domestic situation. Once the skills, methods and short cuts are mastered, the time spent doing these tasks should be minimal, especially with our busy lives today. People who are working and trying set up a home together don't want to spend too much time on mundane household chores.

This section of the book aims to set out basic information to make jobs as quick and simple as possible, while including the skills needed to make setting up home fun.

Laundry and dry cleaning

Washing

Most households have a washing machine and if you are considering appliances for a new home, it's one of the most convenient time-saving purchases you can make. There are dozens of brands on the market, each of which offers different combinations of features. To simplify matters, remember the following:

- Automatics are the most efficient and straightforward.
- Don't be carried away by multi-programme washers; most people use only three: 90°C with a long spin, 60°C with a long spin, and 40°C with a short spin.
- There is energy-saving value in being able to wash at lower temperatures, but it can take quite a while to recoup the extra cost of these machines.
- Do look at spin speeds; the faster the spin, the drier the clothes. Bear in mind, however, the fact that anything above 1000 rpm is hardly worth the extra expense.
- Check the door opens in the direction which suits you and the room.
- Make sure the soap powder drawer is easily accessible (many are too short to go under protruding work-surfaces.

Getting things dry

Our unpredictable weather makes this the most difficult part of laundering. The machine will spin things practically dry and if the weather is fine there's nothing like the smell of clothes that have been hung outside on a line.

Clothes will also dry well round the hot-water tank, and an airing cupboard can be hung with removable lines to dry clothing away from household activity.

An airing rack can be stood in a warm place and the washing draped over it but

**Dyeing fabric –
colour mathematics**

If you can't purchase the right
colour, mix and match to create
what you need, making sure to test
it on a corner of fabric first.

• **Red and yellow = orange/red**
• **Blue and yellow = green**
• **Yellow and pink = coral**
• **Green and yellow = lime**
• **Light brown and red = rust**
• **Red and blue = purple**
• **Pale blue and pink = lilac**
• **Yellow and brown = golden
  brown**

• **Dark brown and light red =
  reddish brown**

Dyeing know-how:

• **Always wear rubber gloves**
• **Weigh the article carefully and
follow the instructions for that
weight**
• **Always dye wet items or the dye
may take unevenly**
• **Remove all stains beforehand**
• **Wash the garment first**
• **Don't use your washing machine
for dyeing – it can leave traces that
will colour other clothes.**

these can be inconvenient in a small house.
Smaller racks that fit over a radiator are
available but you'll end up with washing
hanging around for a while. The
condensation created by laundry over
radiators can create damp problems (see *A
new home*, page 49).

An expensive, but effective, option is a
tumble dryer. This process is not suitable for
all clothes and can shrink some items – check
your care label before use. Don't forget it
also runs on electricity and too much use will
bump up your bills.

Washing and cleaning symbols

The HLCC (Home Laundering Consultative
Council) is a voluntary organisation
concerned with the laundering and dry
cleaning of clothes and textiles. They teamed
up with various industries, including domestic
appliance and washing powder manufacturers,
to work out a universal labelling scheme to
help us take better care of our fabrics. All
participating groups ensure a label is sewn
somewhere on the garment that gives advice
about the washing or dry cleaning of that
item. So make sure that care label is seen
before you clean!

These symbols help you get the best wear
out of your clothes and keep them looking
good for longer.

General guidelines

● Some items can be mixed but only at the
lowest temperature and with a reduced
wash action.
● Always follow any special instruction such
as 'hand wash only' or 'wash separately'.
● Dark colours should never be mixed with
the white wash.
● Really dirty clothes should be washed
separately.
● Don't overload the machine as the
clothes cannot be washed properly and
the spinning action will be overloaded.
● Act on stains quickly to make removal as
successful as possible.
● Rinse thoroughly to remove all particles
of dirt and soap powder.

• **Items without the bar can
generally be washed together at
the lowest temperature.**
• **Items with the same bar
symbol can also generally be
washed together at the lowest
temperature.**

• White cotton and linen articles without special finishes. A vigorous wash that maximises whiteness and removes staining.

 • Cotton, linen or viscose articles without special finishes where colours are fast at 60°C. Still a vigorous wash but slightly cooler to stop colours fading.

 • (Not used in the UK) White nylon and white polyester/cotton mixtures are included in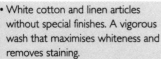
The temperature is high enough to maximise whiteness but the cold rinse and short spin reduce creasing.

 • Nylon; polyester/cotton mixtures; polyester cotton and viscose articles with special finishes; cotton/acrylic mixtures. The slightly cooler water in this wash preserves colour and finish.

 • Cotton, linen or viscose articles, where colours are fast at 40°C but not at 60°C. A fairly vigorous wash but the lower temperature safeguards colour.

 • Acrylics, acetate and triacetate, including mixtures with wool, polyester/wool blends. A much more gentle wash to help more delicate garments keep their shape and colour.

 • Wool, wool mixed with other fibres, silk. The low temperature and minimum agitation help garments keep their shape, and to preserve colour and finish.

 • Not used in UK) see items included in and
Minimum agitation and cool water make this a much more gentle wash.

 • (Not applicable in UK) A high temperature wash for cottons with a special finish. It helps keep whiteness but garments need drip drying to prevent creasing.

 • Handwash only (Do not machine wash)

 • Do not wash

Other international care labelling symbols

BLEACHING • Chlorine bleach may be used

TUMBLE DRYING • May be tumble dried • where dots appear means high heat setting means low heat setting

IRONING • Hot iron – Cotton, Linen, Viscose • Warm iron – Polyester, Mixtures, wool • Cool iron – Acrylic, Nylon, Polyester

DRY CLEANING • May be dry cleaned. • Other letters and/or a bar beneath the circle will indicate the required process to the dry cleaner.

A cross through any symbol means 'do not' ✕

Ironing

Although most of us use an automatic washing machine and some of us have a tumble dryer, most clothes will need ironing to make them look neat and crisp. Of course, if you can avoid ironing ...

Carefully smoothing things before pegging them out, or hanging them out on a coat hanger or drying them flat means less creasing and therefore less ironing. Keep it to a minimum. It's not necessary to iron towels, flannels, tea towels, bedding and underwear, so if it doesn't need it, leave it.

Irons

A **dry iron** is the most simple and cheapest type of iron available. They are light to use, have a temperature control with various settings and a basic flat plate that heats up when switched on. They should be used with a separate water spray.

Steam irons have their own water container that needs to be filled with either distilled or tap water. The water drips down on to the hot plate and turns to steam on contact. This means clothes don't need dampening first.

Steam/spray irons are the most expensive choice. Press a button and a fine spray of water comes out of the front of the iron and dampens the material as it is ironed. Some also emit a blast of steam. This makes ironing much easier, although these irons are bigger and heavier than the basic dry iron.

It's tempting to go for a very light iron, but the extra weight of a heavier-duty model can help you press out the creases.

Water spray

Ideal for dampening clothes that are too dry to get all the creases out. Use a plant spray,

available from a garden centre or hardware shop. Fill with water, spray clothes, roll up and allow dampness to penetrate fabric. Don't use on fabrics that are easily watermarked.

Ironing board

There is a huge selection of ironing boards available and the choice is really up to you and how much money you want to spend. It is important to have the board at the correct height – place an iron on the board and check the handle is the same height as your elbow, even if you prefer to iron sitting down!

Choose one with an asbestos impregnated rest for the iron as they are much safer than wire rests, especially with children around.

Covers will need changing when they become scorched and the material splits and frays.

A table covered with a blanket and then a sheet can also be used, especially for larger items like sheets or dresses, but smaller things are much more fiddly and the curved end of the iron is very useful.

NEVER LEAVE AN IRON UNATTENDED
Children or pets are naturally inquisitive and accidents can happen. Always turn it off even if you are leaving for a moment.

Sleeve board

A smaller board that sits on the large one that a sleeve or trouser leg can be slid over to make pressing easier.

Ironing guide

Getting the temperature right is crucial. Lighter, flimsier fabrics will melt and shrivel if the iron is too hot. Follow the care label in the garment. The iron should also have settings and a temperature guide on it .

$***$ HOT IRON
$**$ WARM IRON
$*$ COOL IRON

Avoid ironing woollies!
Woollens, acrylics and jumpers can be spread out carefully over a damp towel and patted into shape. Leave overnight, take the towel away without disturbing the jumper too much and leave the jumper to dry.

> **Add a few drops of perfume or toilet water to the water in the steam iron to add a fresh scent to your ironing.**

Pressing

COTTON	Press on the right side with a hot iron while the fabric is still damp.
CORDUROY EMBROIDERY	Press on the wrong side with a hot iron. Place a thick towel between the item and the board. Iron carefully to preserve the pattern or pile.
LINEN	Press on the wrong side with a hot iron while still damp.
VISCOSE AND RAYON	Press on the wrong side with a hot iron. Roll garment in a damp towel before ironing rather than spraying or steaming.
POLYESTER AND COTTON	Press on the right side with a warm iron while still damp.
SILK AND SATIN	Press on the wrong side with a warm iron. Roll in a damp towel rather than spraying or steaming.
WOOL	Press very lightly with a warm iron if necessary. Do not stretch.
TRIACETATE AND ACETATE	Press on the wrong side with a cool iron while damp. Only iron if necessary.
ACRYLIC	Press on the wrong side with a cool iron while still damp.
NYLON AND POLYESTER	Iron on the right side with a cool iron while still damp.
VELVET	Don't iron. Hang in a steamy bathroom and allow creases to fall out.

> **There are various iron cleaners on the market if you do scorch or burn the iron. Look out for them in hardware departments and shops.**

Ironing know-how

- Ironing on the wrong side of some fabrics will not flatten the pile and prevents others becoming shiny.

- Test the heat of the iron before touching the fabric, then try on a part of the garment that doesn't show. This is more important on finer and synthetic fabrics as they can melt, mark or shrivel.

- Place the item over the ironing board carefully, keeping the grain as straight as possible and avoiding any unnecessary creases.

- Work on the wrong side and press all the small parts first – cuffs, collars, seams, button bands and round the neck. If the main body of the shirt is ironed first it will get crushed when doing these smaller areas. But because these parts are usually double-thickness they won't crease again so easily.

- Some people like to have a sharp crease down the top of the sleeve, in which case iron one side of the sleeve flat, pressing carefully along the top edge before turning over and pressing the second side. If you prefer no crease, then the sleeve must be ironed on a smaller sleeve board, or iron smaller areas while constantly turning the sleeve to avoid any crease being ironed in.

- Sweat shirts and T-shirts should not be ironed 'double' as the imprint of any motif or seam will show through on the reverse side. Take care with any raised plastic patterns or lettering as they will melt and smudge over the fabric as well as marking the iron.

- Iron the bodice of a dress first, and then the skirt.

- Lay the waist end of a pair of trousers over the ironing board first. Press the waistband and inside the pockets and fly. Then iron outer zip and fly, the seat and the pockets area in a single layer, rotating the trousers as necessary. Then lie one of the legs, with the seams at the sides, on the board and press each one flat, in a double layer, taking care not to iron in a crease down the side of the seam.

Hold the trousers upside down by both legs and allow all four seams to come together. Lay the trousers back on the board and press the creases down the front and back of each leg, keeping the seams matching all the time. Use a damp cloth on dark-coloured trousers to prevent material going shiny.

 Larger items like long dresses, dressing-gowns and large shirts may touch the floor, so cover the floor round the ironing board to protect the clothes from dirt.

 Pleats need ironing a few at a time and, especially on a dark-coloured skirt, with a damp cloth as the fabric may go 'shiny'.

Iron care

Marks made by melting manmade fibres can be removed from the face of the iron by bringing it up to temperature and scraping off as much as possible with a wooden spatula. Let the iron cool down and scrub any remaining marks with a kitchen scouring pad.

If your steam iron gets 'furred up', half-fill with vinegar. Allow to reach temperature and spray vinegar until the container is empty. Fill with distilled water and repeat the process to rinse through. This should clean the iron ready for use.

Try putting a double layer of kitchen foil under the ironing board cover. As you iron the foil will heat up and warm the clothes from the other side, too.

For best results clothes should be ironed when still damp. If they have dried too much dampen the items and roll together or put in a plastic carrier bag so they stay damp until needed. Don't leave them longer than twelve hours; they will start to smell and mildew will form.

Household cleaning

Although cleaning the house isn't a favourite job, it has to be done, so it's best to find a way to make it as quick, easy and as painless as possible.

Set aside a certain time in which to get the job done. The time allotted will vary enormously, depending on where you live. A small one-bedroomed flat won't take long to clean and as there will be fewer people in the place it shouldn't get so untidy or dirty. Tidy as you go – deal with clothes as soon as you take them off, rinse the shower tray properly and wash up regularly to keep jobs short and simple.

A larger house will often mean more people and maybe a family. This will automatically mean more housework, and not all the mess is your own! Encourage children to be responsible for their own rooms and to help out with other jobs. Just rinsing the bath round, making and changing their beds, and washing up occasionally can make a huge difference. Here are some ideas for jobs that children can do:

- Dusting dado rails.
- Hang up their coats.
- Sort laundry into colour loads.
- Sweeping the garden path or front walk.
- Tidying away toys at the end of the day.

For younger children a 'star' chart makes their responsibilities seem fun.

Vacuum cleaner

Choose one that suits your house and lifestyle. A small flat may only need a small vacuum cleaner unless you are planning to move in the near future. A bigger house will need a more substantial vacuum cleaner, as it will have to work harder – or even two, one upstairs and another down.

An upright vacuum cleaner is ideal if you have large rooms with lots of fitted carpets as it cleans more quickly. They come with all sorts of various gimmicks from illuminated fronts, and air fresheners to variable suction actions and extra cleaning attachments. However, they can be tricky to fit under furniture and into corners. Choose a lightweight one if you have lots of stairs.

A cylinder is much more versatile. They come fitted with a long, flexible tube and several assorted attachments for curtains and upholstery. They can reach into corners and under furniture and are excellent for cleaning stairs as it can be easily transported. But they are less efficient than an upright and are being superseded by a more up-to-date equivalent.

The wet/dry multipurpose cleaners are becoming more and more popular. Again they have a flexible hose, move around on wheels and come with various attachments for different jobs. They can pick up wet and dry waste but they seem to be noisier. Some have a carpet shampoo facility which can be very useful, especially with lots of children or pets.

> **Keep recyclable rubbish separate; recycling centres have sprung up in even the smallest villages, so put aside your drink cans, newspapers, bottles, etc., and make a trip to the centre a weekly occurrence. Buy a few plastic boxes to keep outside a back door, or in the cellar to keep your recyclable rubbish out of sight and separate from your main collection.**

Other equipment

You'll also need:
- ☞ Long-handled broom
- ☞ Dustpan and brush
- ☞ Feather duster – for picture rails, pictures and curtain rails
- ☞ Sponge pan cleaners – coarse on one side with sponge on the other for bathrooms and kitchens
- ☞ Large sponge – for washing tiles and painted surfaces
- ☞ Disposable cloths for general use
- ☞ Yellow dusters for woodwork
- ☞ Appropriate cleaning agents

Making a clean start

- Close all doors and windows to contain the room. Start at the top of the room and work down.
- Dust surfaces including picture rails, pictures, lampshades and radiators, before wiping up any sticky marks and dealing with any stains (see A–Z of Stains).
- Wash paintwork if necessary, again starting at the top and working down, taking care not to make the carpet wet.
- Rinse with clean water and rub a dry cloth over.
- Beware of getting walls wet – paper can stain and emulsion paint can show the tide mark horribly.
- Lastly vacuum the floor or carpet working towards the door so you don't have to walk over the clean surfaces.
- Have one last look round to make sure you haven't missed anything.
- Rinse out any cloths or dusters and the brushes, too, if necessary.

Cleaning guide

Supermarket shelves are packed with cleaners for everything you'll ever want to sparkle. It's almost mind boggling looking at them all. Take time to read labels carefully as the wrong product on the wrong surface can ruin it forever. Some are more dangerous than others and all should be treated with caution. Try to wear rubber gloves and work in an airy room as some fumes can be harmful.

> **• Be methodical – start in one room and finish it before moving on. Work at a steady pace and check the room afterwards.**
> **• Put all the smaller cleaning equipment in a container that can be carried from room to room.**
> **• Take a rubbish sack with you and empty bins as you go.**

A – Z of general cleaning

Baking tins

Put stained and very greasy baking tins (not non-stick) and sheets in a strong solution of washing soda and water. Rinse and dry well, preferably in a warm oven to prevent rusting.

Baths and basins

There are lots of bathroom cleaners on sale, the most popular being the liquid type, since they aren't as abrasive as powders.

- Tidemarks and scratches on plastic baths can be removed by rubbing with metal polish or toothpaste on a soft cloth, but not every day, as the polish is also abrasive.
- Porcelain baths can be cleaned with white spirit before rinsing thoroughly.
- Rust marks can be removed with lighter fuel.
- Clean gold-plated taps with a baby shampoo as it won't scratch the metal at all.
- Scrub round the taps with a toothbrush kept specially for the purpose.

Bedding

Bed linen should be changed regularly, especially if you use any bath preparations or body lotions as they will eventually stain the sheets.

Some smaller duvets and pillows are machine-washable, but the weight of wet bedding can put a huge strain on the machine. It's best to take them all to the dry cleaners (check first whether they'll have to send them away as you might have to make other arrangements for a few days).

Shake duvets well and remember to turn the mattress occasionally to make it wear evenly.

Small blankets can be washed in the machine but benefit from added conditioner in the rinse cycle. Larger blankets might be too heavy for the machine, try taking them to the dry cleaners. Launderettes generally have larger machines than domestic washers and some offer a service wash for washable duvets and pillows.

Blinds

Roller blinds need sponging clean without getting too wet, but check instructions.

Festoon, Roman and Austrian blinds should be vacuumed regularly and either washed or dry-cleaned according to fabric.

There are several gadgets on the market for cleaning Venetian blinds – fingers of sponge that wipe between each slat – but take care as the slats are often sharp. Try wearing a thick cotton glove to remove dust. If you are planning to wash the blind, check manufacturer's instructions first. If the blind is washable, line the bath with a thick towel and place the blind in warm soapy water – but don't let the operating mechanism get wet. Rinse and stand up to drip dry before re-hanging.

Cane

Wash cane seats with warm soapy water and rinse well. This can sometimes tighten up sagging seats, too!

Carpets

Vacuum carpet regularly as dirt and grit will wear it out more quickly. Remember to go round the edges as most dust collects there.

Carpets should also be shampooed occasionally, especially after a party or several spillages. Some vacuum cleaners have shampoo facility but it's possible to hire a machine to do the job. Special shampoos are available from the hire shop or a hardware store and instructions on the bottle should be followed carefully. It's advisable to carry out a colour-fast test first.

Older, more precious carpets and rugs should be shampooed professionally.

Long-haired rugs need handwashing in warm soapy water but they should all have a label with washing instructions stitched on them.

Ceramic cooker tops

Marks on these hobs should be dabbed with hot white vinegar and left for five to ten minutes, depending on severity of mark, then wiped off and rinsed clean. Get a paint-scraper from the DIY store – they are ideal for scraping off burnt residue from ceramic hobs and glass oven doors.

China

Washing regularly should keep china clean but badly stained crockery should be left soaking in a bleach solution.

Stained china mugs can also be scrubbed clean with washing machine powder and water, or try a dab of toothpaste – a gentle abrasive with bleaching action.

Rub decorative plates over with methylated spirits for a really shiny finish.

Don't put china with gold or silver decoration in the dishwasher as the metal will be worn away. Rub persistent marks with salt and a cloth rather than scouring powder. Porcelain china should always be washed by hand. Check with manufacturer, if in doubt.

Clothes

(See *Laundry and dry cleaning*, page 97.)

Cork

Rub cork mats with sandpaper rather than wash them clean.

Floor tiles should be swept or vacuumed and mopped with warm water and Flash, not anything abrasive or the shiny finish will be scrubbed off. If they have a polished surface already then buff with polish, but don't otherwise.

Cookers

Electric cookers should be switched off and all shelves, shelf rests and the grill pan removed. Leave them all to soak in very hot soapy water.

Wipe the top and clean with a liquid cleaner. Don't use an abrasive powder as this will scratch the enamel. There are also plenty of spray and pad cleaners that can be left on overnight, some on a warm oven and others on a cold one, so read the instructions carefully. Always wear rubber gloves.

Gas ovens can be cleaned in much the same way; take care not to accidentally turn on the gas.

> **Line the grill pan with kitchen foil to catch as many spills as possible. Throw away and re-line. To protect against grease, sprinkling the inside of the oven and grill with bicarbonate of soda will help keep them much cleaner as it soaks up the grease. Once it gets discoloured, wipe off, clean and sprinkle again.**

Cupboards and drawers

Shelves, drawers and doors of all bedroom cupboards should be wiped with a damp cloth and warm soapy water. Line shelves and drawers with paper to keep them, and the clothes, cleaner and tuck tablets of soap or lavender bags among the clothes to keep fresh smelling.

Kitchen cupboards and shelves get much dirtier and greasier and consequently need much tougher and more regular cleaning. Choose one of the many kitchen surface cleaners that are available. Use an abrasive pan cleaner for really tough marks, wipe, rinse and wipe dry. Finger marks can also be wiped off this way.

Line shelves and drawers with paper and change regularly.

> **To remove dust without having to take the whole drawer out, roll some sticky tape round your fingers and dab on the fluff.**

Curtains

Curtain rails should be dusted and wiped with a damp cloth.

When your curtains are down take the opportunity to give them a proper clean or wash, depending on what they are made of.

Rub or spray the sliding track with polish to make the gliding movement more fluid.

Curtains should really be dry-cleaned. Some are washable fabrics but they often shrink.

Vacuum curtains when you clean the house to keep as free from dirt as possible and hang them out for a blow if the sun is shining.

Net curtains should be washed regularly as they discolour quickly. They can usually be washed in the machine (short spin or none at all) and hung back straight away so they dry in position. There are also powders and liquids for sale that brighten nets if they look rather dull.

Dishwasher

Clean with hot water and dishwasher powder.

Don't put any gold china, cutlery, pewter or bone-handled knives in the machine. Check instruction booklet.

Don't let silver or silver plate touch stainless steel items or the silver will discolour.

Drains

It's a good idea to clean out drains from time to time.

Put a few lumps of washing soda over the drain and pour boiling water over the top.

Use a strainer that fits over the plughole in the sink and throw away any bits that collect in it. Never throw coffee grounds or rice down the sink as they can lead to blockages.

Leave fat to set and throw away rather than pour down the sink. If this is unavoidable then squeeze plenty of washing up liquid and very hot water down with it. If the drain does become blocked with fat pour a cupful of salt and another of bicarbonate of soda down the drain and pour over a kettleful of boiling water.

Dustbins

Keep bins lined with bin liners and scrub out regularly with hot soapy water and some disinfectant or bleach. Turn upside down to dry. Use plastic bin liners in the kitchen as well to keep mess and smells to a minimum.

> **GREEN TIP Save plastic carrier bags from your shopping trips to line small wastepaper bins.**

Fridge

Keep food wrapped to prevent the smells contaminating other foods and the fridge itself.

Turn the fridge off to clean it. Take out the shelves and ice trays. Wash everything with warm water and bicarbonate of soda. Rinse well and return.

The freezer should also be defrosted regularly. Leave until the ice has melted after putting a thick towel or newspapers on the floor by the door to catch any drips. Wash as for the fridge, wipe clean and dry before turning on again.

> **If you leave the fridge switched off when you go on holiday, make sure you prop the door open to stop mildew growing.**

Glasses

Wash drinking glasses in warm soapy water and rinse well under hot water. Leave to drip dry or use a clean cloth. Don't wash very fine glasses in a dishwasher.

Kettles

To descale your kettle, put 1 tablespoon of borax in the kettle, bring it to the boil and leave to cool before rinsing, ready for use.

There are also plenty of de-scaling gizmos for sale in supermarkets and hardware shops that work well.

Wash the outside with cleaning fluid, taking care not to get the electrical parts wet.

Kitchen surfaces

Most surfaces can be cleaned with proprietary kitchen surface cleaners.

Brown rings from tea or coffee spills may need light bleaching to disappear completely, or try rubbing gently with toothpaste.

Lavatory

Lift the seat and pour a lavatory cleaner or bleach around the bowl. Scrub with a long-handled brush. Use a cloth and disinfectant cleaner to clean the round the top of the bowl, both surfaces of the seat and the lid. Don't forget the handle.

Don't put anything other than human waste down the toilet – have a separate bin for other rubbish, including sanitary towels and dental floss.

Check the floor round the base of the loo for spillages and splashes, especially with small children or men in the house.

Linoleum

Some marks can be removed with a pencil rubber, or silver polish may also work. After vacuuming or sweeping, wash with warm soapy water with a shop-bought cleaner or add a few drops of paraffin.

Marble

Benzine or copper polish will clean marble. Some marks can be removed with lighter fuel, but test a small area first.

Not-too-serious drink stains can be shifted by rubbing powdered chalk or pumice into the mark and rinsing. Dry well.

Microwaves

Unplug the oven, lift out the turntable and sprinkle bicarbonate of soda over a damp cloth. Rub over all surfaces.

Wash glass turntable in warm soapy water, rinse and reassemble.

Mirrors

Make up a solution of equal parts methylated spirits and water and wipe over the mirror. Rub dry with chamois leather or crumpled newspaper.

There are also lots of sprays that are available, or use warm soapy water to wash and a rubber scraper to remove the water.

Paintwork

Wash walls with warm soapy water, always starting at the top in order to wipe up drips and smears as you work downwards.

Complete one wall before starting another to avoid leaving any discoloured lines.

> **It can often be much easier to re-emulsion paint a blotchy wall than to wash it.**

Woodwork can also be washed in the same way as painted surfaces, but you might need a cleaner that is slightly abrasive for really grubby marks.

Pans

Non-stick pans should never be scoured with abrasive sponges or powders. Check manufacturer's instructions as new finishes are always coming on the market.

Aluminium and stainless steel pans shouldn't be scoured either; the fine scratches will make grime stick more easily.

Put water in a burnt pan and bring gently to the boil, leave the pan to soak overnight.

Woks should be 'sealed' following instructions and after cleaning an iron one, drizzle a little oil in the pan and rub round with some kitchen towel to prevent rusting.

Piano

Ivory notes should be cleaned with methylated spirits or lemon juice; avoid water altogether.

Keep the keyboard lid open as the dark encourages the keys to yellow.

Shower curtains

Many shower curtains are machine-washable so launder regularly.

If they start to go black and speckled with mildew soak the curtain in a very mild bleach solution overnight.

Silver

Silver dips, cleaners and cloths are easily available in supermarkets or hardware stores.

Try putting 2 tablespoons bicarbonate of soda in an aluminium saucepan with 2 litres (4 pints) water. Put the silver in and heat to almost boiling point. Remove from heat and leave for ten to fifteen minutes and the tarnish should have lifted off. Rinse and dry thoroughly.

Methylated spirits and toothpaste will also clean silver. Rinse well afterwards.

Avoid putting silver cutlery in a dishwasher, always wash by hand.

Sinks

Put a little warm water in a china sink and add 3 to 4 tablespoons of bleach. Leave until stains start to lift. Rub a cloth round the sink using the water. There are also many cleaners available in the shops that will do the job.

Plastic sinks can also be cleaned in much the same way.

Black marks on white sinks can be scrubbed off with some slightly abrasive cleaning fluid, or a little bleach.

Don't leave bleach on the sink overnight as can ruin the surface.

Stainless steel sinks should also be cleaned with hot soapy water and might need a cleaning liquid to remove tougher staining. Don't use an abrasive sponge as this will mark the surface. A little vinegar rubbed over the surface will also bring back the shine.

Spectacles

Wash with warm soapy water, rinse and polish dry. Some people find nail varnish remover also keeps the lenses clean.

Stainless steel

Use bicarbonate of soda on a damp cloth to clean stainless steel.

Methylated spirit will remove water marks.

Teapot

An aluminium teapot can be cleaned by putting 2 to 3 tablespoons of borax in the pot and filling with water. Place on a cooker and bring the water to the boil. Pour the water away and rinse before use.

Bicarbonate of soda or salt can be rubbed into badly stained china teapots. Denture cleaning powder is also good for shifting stains. Wash the teapot well after use and don't allow the staining to build up too much.

Telephone

Methylated or white spirit will clean the telephone. There are also special cleaning fluids and cloths for the receiver available from supermarkets and hardware stores.

Thermos flask

Fill the flask with boiling water and add 2 tablespoons of bicarbonate of soda. Put the lid on and shake well. Leave for fifteen to thirty minutes. Rinse well and leave to dry.

Tiles

Treat decorated tiles and ones with special finishes with care as rough abrasives and fluids will spoil the shiny surface. Check with the manufacturer or shop. Most will look fine after washing with hot soapy water and buffing dry. Rinse and dry after use to keep them looking their best.

Shampoo and soap splashes can be removed with a solution of one part white vinegar and four parts water.

Discoloured grouting should be scrubbed with a toothbrush and a solution of one part bleach to five or six parts water. Again, don't allow the grouting to get too discoloured before treating.

Upholstery

(See A–Z of stain removal, page 114.)
Keep clean and vacuumed to stop the build-up of dust.

Loose covers can be removed and should be dry cleaned to prevent shrinkage.

If you can wash your own put them back on while they are still damp so they can stretch back into place more easily.

Suites without loose covers will need shampooing for best results. Protect them with a spray like Scotchguard once dry.

Vinyl tiles

Warm soapy water should get vinyl tiles clean but if they get badly marked you may need a more abrasive cleaner.

Place aluminium foil over a cracked or badly stained vinyl tile and press with a hot iron. The tile will soften and the heat melt the glue underneath. A hot air gun (used for paint stripping) will also do this. Make a hole through the middle of the tile and lift off, taking care not to damage adjoining tiles.

Wallpaper

Washable wallpapers should be wiped over with a damp cloth, after checking with manufacturer's instructions.

Thinner wallpapers need more careful treatment because too much water will leave a stain.

Some dirty marks can be removed with an eraser.

A traditional idea is to make a dough from 8 tablespoons plain flour, 4 tablespoons white spirit and a little water. Knead well and use to rub over the marks. The dirt should be lifted off, but do test a small area first. Sometimes bread will work as well.

Talcum powder can similarly lift greasy marks.

To remove sticky tape stuck to the wall, place a piece of newspaper over it and press with a hot iron. The heat will melt the adhesive and the sticky tape can be peeled off.

Windows

Wash windows on a grey day, as smears will be left in bright sunlight.

Use a solution of methylated spirit with water and apply with newspaper. Polish with a chamois leather or soft cloth.

Clean bird droppings off with vinegar.

Wood

Wood should never be allowed to get really wet as it warps and cracks as it dries. This especially applies to wooden chopping boards and bowls. Wipe boards and bowls clean but if they have to be washed use minimal water and dry well. Lightly oil to prevent shrinking.

There are plenty of polishes and preparations to keep sealed wood bright and shining. Oiled wood will need re-oiling occasionally.

A guide to cleaning agents

Most cleaning agents are readily available, but they must all be used carefully. Follow instructions and remember to test the fabric on a corner, or out-of-sight fold. There are also many ready-to-use stain removers that can be found on shop shelves. The following is a list of the products you'll find most useful in your house.

Acetic acid

This is available from chemists in its pure form, but remember that vinegar is also an acetic acid and can be substituted for it. Dilute 2 teaspoons of the acid with 1 litre (about 2 pints) water and use to brighten coloured fabrics and silks by rinsing away hard water residues. It also counteracts any alkaline spills on fabric.

Acetone

Available from chemists; use it as a solvent for nail varnish, paint and oils. Not suitable for all fabrics (it will actually dissolve some synthetics) and it's very flammable.

Ammonia

Used with water, this colourless gas helps dissolve grease. Do not use on delicate fabrics, follow instructions carefully and wear rubber gloves. Available from chemists.

Bicarbonate of soda

A powder that is used mostly as a raising agent in cooking so it's easily available in shops and is not poisonous. It removes stains from glass, china, tiles, work-surfaces, refrigerators and cookers.

Borax

Available from chemists, borax is usually sold in crystal form. Mixed with water it can be used to remove stains; never soak for too long as the colour will fade.

Bleach

Easily available from supermarkets. Use neat to clean sinks, baths, tiles, toilets and work-surfaces, and a very dilute solution to bleach linens and cottons, including stained tablecloths and napkins. Test before use and never leave fabric in the solution too long or it will rot.

Bran

Good absorbent for carpets and soft furniture. Available from supermarkets and healthfood shops, it can be sprinkled on spills to absorb the liquid. Hoover or brush off when most of the stain is removed.

Citric acid

Use like acetic acid. Squeeze some juice in your rinsing water to brighten fabrics, or use as a descaler in your kettle.

Detergent

Dissolve biological detergent powder in warm water and soak gravy, blood and egg stains overnight. Washing-up liquid is a milder detergent and good for greasy stains on washable fabrics.

Disinfectants

Dilute in water and use to eliminate urine and vomit smells. Available from shops and chemists. A teaspoon in your wash will remove odours and leave your wash fresh-smelling and free of bacteria that might normally survive a cold or warm wash.

Dry cleaning solvents

These are used by dry cleaners and each has its own symbol to indicate the fabrics for which they are suitable.

Glycerine

Available from chemists and useful for softening substances like paint, chewing gum or glue, to 'ease' them out of fabrics or hair.

Scouring powders or creams

Many products are now available to gently scrub away stubborn stains and build-up of grease or food without scratching the surface. Available at supermarkets and most convenience shops, scouring creams and powders can be used on most kitchen surfaces, including the floor, hob and the outside of your oven, all bathroom surfaces, and on most washable painted surfaces, like window sills or children's furniture. An easy scouring cream which you are likely to have to hand is toothpaste – but beware, it can bleach surfaces and fabrics.

Methylated spirits

Dissolves oils, ballpoint pen ink, grass stains, some oils and some medicines. Also used for cleaning glass and mirrors. These spirits are available from the chemist or supermarket and are highly flammable.

White spirit

Available from DIY stores, but handle with care as it is poisonous and flammable. Traditionally a thinner and remover for paint, it is also good for removing oil-based stains.

Pest problems

Most houses are infested with some bugs at some time or another. If in doubt call in the experts. Your local authority or the telephone directory will be able to put you in touch with the right people. But you could try the old-fashioned remedies first.

 Ants

 **A dish containing a handful of lavender soaking in white vinegar will attract and then drown the ants; a saucer upside down with a spoonful of honey on top, will attract and trap them.**

A bunch of fresh chervil, or a saucer of cloves and paraffin will repel ants, hopefully sending them off the property for good.

Sprinkle bicarbonate of soda, powdered borax or cloves on shelves and drawers to deter ants.

Boiling water poured on to ant nests will destroy the ants but not their nest, so it's not an effective long-term solution to an ant problem.

There are also plenty of branded ant powders available from garden centres and hardware stores. Puff round the nest or along floor to deter ants from coming in. They are very harmful to animals and children so take care when sprinkling.

Draw a chalk line across the floor or step where ants enter the house and they won't cross it any longer.

 Bats

Bats are a protected species under the Wildlife and Countryside Act 1981 and must not be exterminated. Contact your local authority or The Nature Conservancy Council for advice.

 Bed bugs

These round, mahogany-coloured beetles lurk in your bedroom and wander about at night. They are very hard to eliminate and if insecticidal aerosols don't shift them you may need to call in the Environmental Health Department.

Bees

Place honeyed or sugared water outside your house to deter the bees from entering.

Don't be tempted to tackle a bee's nest on your own. Call in professional help.

Carpet bugs

These small grubs of the fur beetle attack carpets, fur, wool, etc. Look out for discarded furry skins.

Keep fluff in drawers, wardrobes and cupboards to a minimum.

Spray with carpet beetle killer or call in professional help.

Cockroaches

These resilient pests are very hard to exterminate. They range in size, the larger ones being around 5 cm (2 in) long.

If there aren't too many try an insecticide otherwise contact your local authority.

To deter cockroaches, sprinkle washing soda in the cracks where they appear.

Flies

Balls of cotton wool sprinkled with a few drops of lavender oil placed on saucers can an effective way of deterring flies. Fresh lavender has the same effect.

 To keep flies away, grow mint or basil in pots on your windowsill inside the kitchen, or outside in a windowbox.

To deter flies, mix a teaspoon of black pepper, 2 teaspoons of brown sugar and 2 tablespoons of milk in a saucer. Flies won't come anywhere near.

Spray fly killer is also available from your local supermarket, chemist or hardware store. Don't spray near food. Cover all food or put it away and keep all rubbish well covered and away from the house to deter them as much as possible.

Fleas

These insects are carried on cats and dogs so make sure these animals are regularly treated with spray or powder available from your vet, or kit out with a flea collar.

Vacuum and shampoo carpets and remember to treat or destroy the pet's bedding as well.

> **Green Tip** **To destroy fleas and lice, burn the leaves of the common fleabane or wormwood (herbs available at your local healthfood shop, or grow them in your garden). Allow the fumes to fill the room, but avoid breathing them yourself.**

Lice

Head lice are very common and often brought home from school by children. The symptoms are an itchy head and small oval eggs cases attached firmly to the hair about 1 in (2 cm) from the scalp. There are often small red bites around the ears and neck, and eggs deposited around the backs of the ears.

A special shampoo available from the chemist or clinic will successfully get rid of them. The whole family needs to wash their hair at the same time for it to be effective, and bedding and clothing must also be washed at a high temperature.

Add a few drops of lavender oil to your shampoo to prevent reinfestation.

> **Green Tip** **An infusion of thyme (thyme leaves soaked in boiling water) can be used to rinse hair and act as a parasiticide.**

Mice

Block up any holes and make sure all food is stored in jars or the fridge to discourage mice.

There are commercial traps and baits available from the hardware store but if the problem is greater than that or persists contact the local authority for advice.

> **Green Tip** **Hang bunches of watercress (fresh or dried) in your cupboards to prevent mice. If you can find the mouseholes, paint their exterior with oil of peppermint, which will deter them indefinitely. Mint and tansy will prevent mice from appearing.**

Mites

These pests are very small and look rather like dust. They live on particles of shed human skin that are found in soft furnishings. It's these mites that have been known to exacerbate asthma and sufferers will need to have special bedding.

Regular cleaning and vacuuming will help keep numbers down, and they hate a dry atmosphere, but they are impossible to get rid of completely.

Try a few drops of tea tree oil (available from an aromatherapist or healthfood shop) in your rinse water when doing laundry – it will kill the eggs that might survive even high-temperature washes.

Similarly, a few drops in boiling water can be spritzed on to your carpet and furnishings, or when dusting washable surfaces, to help prevent infestation.

Mosquitoes

Mosquitoes are found around still or stagnant water so keep damp areas as dry as possible and water butts and ponds well away from the house and eating areas.

Spray exposed skin with a mosquito repellent before sitting outside in the evening and burn mosquito coils indoors.

Mesh bags, made for oranges, potatoes and onions, can be filled with cotton wool balls and sprayed with insecticide. Hang them in open doors and windows to deter mosquitoes.

> **Dab a few drops of lavender oil, mixed in something like apricot kernel or grapeseed oil, on your face and body (keeping the oil away from eyes) to deter mosquitoes from biting you.**

Candles placed on outdoor tables during a meal will help discourage mosquitoes from joining you.

To stop a mosquito bite itching, dab it with lemon or ammonia.

Moths

The pale-coloured moths aren't responsible for destroying clothes, it's the grubs that do the damage.

Launder clothes and bed linen if they aren't going to be used for some time, and store in sealed plastic bags.

> **Small muslin bags, filled with plants such as mint, rosemary and thyme, placed among your clothes in your wardrobe and drawers will deter moths.**

Spray curtains and carpets with moth proofer that should be available from your hardware store.

There are also anti-moth bags, that contain tansy, lavender, orris root and cloves, which can be hung in the wardrobe.

Rats

These are reputedly on the increase at the moment and need to be discouraged.

Get rid of all rubbish promptly and don't allow newspapers and outdoor rubbish to collect and rot in piles, especially near the house.

There are proprietary rat poisons available or contact your local authority.

Many of the mice deterrents are useful for preventing rat infestation.

Silverfish

These small slim silvery-grey insects are most often found in the kitchen and bathroom as they are attracted by damp. They aren't seen often as they feed at night, but you might find them trapped in the sink or bath in the morning.

Keep these rooms as dry as possible and treat the silverfish with an insecticide spray for crawling insects.

There are a number of herbs that will deter silverfish, including garlic and basil.

Wipe washable surfaces in any room prone to silverfish with methylated spirits to deter them.

Wasps

Fill jam jars with water sweetened with honey or jam. This will attract wasps and they will drown in the water.

Although there are insecticides available to spray on wasp's nests it is advisable to contact the Environmental Health Department or other professional to dispose of it safely.

> **Burn dried leaf of *Eupatoria cannabinum* (Sweet Joe Pye) will deter wasps.**

Weevils

A real problem in the larder, especially if your dry stores sit for any period of time between use.

 A few bay leaves in flour, rice and dried pulses will prevent weevils, but may flavour the food.

Woodworm

Woodworm are actually wood-boring beetles and although small areas can be treated yourself, professional help will be needed for larger problems. You can buy woodworm treatment products at your DIY store.

Traditional remedies include injecting paraffin into woodworm holes. Then fill them with household ammonia, and repeat the operation. Leave at least for twenty-four hours and then wipe away any excess.

To seal old holes paint the woodworm holes with paraffin so it enters the wood, and spread melted beeswax over the entire surface. Polish and the holes will be sealed. If any new holes appear, treat promptly.

Stain removal

Most of us have some item of clothing or furniture that has been stained by spilling something over it. Although there are lots of chemical cleaners on the market at the moment, as well as lots of cheaper homemade alternatives, there are no guarantees that all stains can be removed. But there are steps you can take to limit the damage as much as possible.

If you know what has made the stain the chances of removing it are much higher, as it can be treated correctly. If you are unsure then follow the step-by-step identification.

Colour check

As a general rule, the darker the stain, the older it is. Pale sugary marks dry to a darker caramel colour and so do things like tomatoes, sauces and wine. Paint, nail polish and some glues hardly change at all.

Touch check

Older stains may feel more crusty or hard and the texture is another clue. Sugary things tend to be more crispy and don't seem to soak in so much. Dried sugar stains turn white when scratched. Oily things like pickles, mayonnaise, butter, mustard and motor oil will stay softer. If the stain is dark and soaked into the fabric it will probably be oil or grease. Perfume, beer, alcohol and some food stains can be identified by their smell, so try scratching and sniffing.

Room check

Look round the house and see if there are any clues as to what the stain might be. See where the item was last worn or used and what the wearer was doing.

STEPS TO SUCCESS
always:
• **Act quickly. Scrape, spoon or blot off as much spillage as possible and keep the area marked to a minimum. This will help prevent a small spot becoming a permanent stain.**
• **Identify the stain first before deciding what treatment to follow.**
• **Try to remove as much of the stain as possible as any residue will turn into a darker stain**
• **Make sure the mark is removed before applying any heat to the area, as this will fix the stain. Rinse with cold water unless care instructions say otherwise.**
• **Make certain that no scrubbing or rubbing is done until the stain has been identified. Keep rubbing to a minimum as the colours will fade and the texture of the fabric can change.**

STEPS TO SUCCESS
always:
• **Pre-test an area before embarking on treatment. Try out the solution on an area of the fabric that will not show – the underside of a cushion, the hem or inside of a pocket. Place a tissue or paper towel on either side of the fabric and press together. If no colour shows on the paper then proceed. If colour comes off ask your dry cleaner for professional help.**
• **If you are ever in doubt, ask your dry cleaner for expert advice.**

Shop-bought cleaners

In-Wash is a stain remover that is added to your washing powder. It acts on stubborn stains like tea, coffee, red wine, grass and cocoa. There is also a stain remover for items that need handwashing.

Stain Devils do a huge range of stain removers that are individually designed to deal with different types of marks, so you can choose which one will suit you best. There is a list on the back of the packaging that tells you which type to use for what.

Needlework shampoos are also on sale to clean your works of art. Items need handwashing, rinsing and drying flat. Larger items might need pinning in shape while they dry to prevent any distortion.

• **Always wear rubber gloves when dealing with chemicals and cleaning agents.**
• **Work in a ventilated room and wash hands and eyes if they come into contact with any chemicals.**
• **Don't smoke while you work and keep children and animals out of the way.**

Stain remover sticks can be used on smaller marks. Rub in and leave for three minutes before brushing off. Repeat again if necessary.

More serious marks like tar, grease and oil can also be shifted with Stain Slayer.

A – Z of stain removal

Alcohol (including beer, white wine, mixed drinks)

Blot up as much of the spill as possible with a sponge and cool water.

Rub neat washing-up liquid mixed with a few drops of vinegar into fresh stains. Rinse with cold water. Launder any washable items or take to the dry cleaners. Don't use any soap if the drink contained fruit.

Garments with older stains will need soaking overnight in cold water. Then use the washing-up liquid and vinegar as above. Articles that need dry cleaning should have warm glycerine rubbed into stain and be allowed to sit for thirty minutes before treating as above.

As a last resort soak washables in an enzyme detergent. Mix powder to a thick paste and put on the stain on items that need dry cleaning. Rinse with warm water.

Sponge wool carpets with warm water and for synthetic carpets mix 1 tablespoon methylated or surgical spirit with 2 tablespoons of water and rub well.

Remove a fresh stain from wood by rubbing with a cloth dampened with methylated spirits. For an old stain mix cigarette ash with linseed oil to make a paste and rub gently until the mark disappears. You could also try metal polish rubbed over the stain, working with the grain of the wood.

Sweet or sticky marks can be removed from varnished wood by gently rubbing with used coffee grounds. Wipe over and polish.

Adhesive

For all fabrics, washable and non-washable, place a piece of absorbent cloth on the right side of the stain and dab the wrong side with cotton wool dampened with non-oily nail polish remover.

To remove the adhesive from a wool carpet dab with non-oily nail polish remover, but if the carpet is synthetic, or if you aren't sure, use amyl acetate.

Test for colour fastness first.

Epoxy resin (Araldite): act immediately as only fresh marks can be removed. Place a piece of cotton wool on the right side of the stain and dab the wrong side with thinners or methylated spirits. For manmade fibres use lighter fuel, a wool carpet will need non-oily nail polish remover and a synthetic one will need amyl acetate.

Animal stains (including urine, excreta and vomit)

Scrape any surface deposit off washable fabrics and sponge with a biological washing powder, or a solution of 1 tablespoon borax crystals dissolved in 600 ml (1 pint) warm water for more delicate fabrics.

Non-washable fabrics should be scraped clean of any deposit and as much liquid as possible blotted up with absorbent paper or a cloth. Sponge with the borax solution, sponge with clear water and blot dry. Clear any remaining traces with a cloth dampened with methylated spirits.

Carpets should be scraped and blotted dry before being rubbed with warm soapy water with 2 tablespoons vinegar in it. Blot again and rinse again.

If your animal urinates in the same place all the time scrubbing with a disinfectant will leave another smell that will encourage them to urinate again. Look out for the special solutions from pet stores that will deodorise the area and eliminate all smells.

Anti-perspirants and deodorants

Mix equal amounts of vinegar and water and rub over the stain. Or use warm water and detergent. Rinse well with cold water.

More persistent stains can be shifted with methylated spirits.

More delicate fabrics can be treated with a 50/50 solution of water and ammonia.

Treat carpets the same way, but check for colour fastness.

Beer

Rinse washable fabrics and table linen in cold water before laundering in the usual way.

More stubborn stains can be removed by soaking the linen in a weak solution of bleach and cold water before laundering in the usual way.

Blot excess beer from the carpet before rinsing in warm soapy water. Older stains can be removed by rubbing with methylated spirits.

Bird droppings

Scrape off excess before soaking washable fabrics in a biological detergent overnight then washing as usual.

Stubborn stains will need dabbing with a solution of 1 tablespoon hydrogen peroxide diluted with 4 tablespoons water. White cotton can be soaked in a solution of 2 tablespoons bleach and 2 litres (1 gallon) warm water.

Scrape any deposit off any non-washable fabrics and sponge with 1 tablespoon ammonia diluted in a 300 ml (½ pint) water. Blot and sponge again with white wine vinegar, rinse and leave to dry. Treat carpets the same way.

Garden furniture can be cleaned by scrubbing with a solution of 1 tablespoon washing soda and 1 tablespoon detergent dissolved in half a bucket of warm water. Canvas furniture should be cleaned of any deposit, rubbed over with a bar of soap and sprinkled with washing soda. Leave for thirty minutes and rinse well. Stubborn stains may need treating more than once,

Blood

Fresh blood stains should always be rinsed and then soaked in cold water immediately, never hot, as this will help fix the stain. Rinse in warm soapy water.

Stubborn stains will need soaking in a solution of 2 tablespoons bleach and 2 litres (1 gallon) water for about five minutes before rinsing well.

Non-washable fabrics will need sponging with a mixture of 1 teaspoon ammonia diluted in 300 ml (½ pint) water.

Dried stains are much more difficult to remove. Try placing a pad of cotton wool or soft cloth on the right side of the stain and sponge the back with a very dilute solution of ammonia and water. Or try spraying on some starch, leave for a few hours and brush off. Wash in soapy water and rinse well. You may then dab with the weak ammonia solution before rinsing again.

Candlewax

Scrape off as much wax as possible with a blunt knife, or put the garment or linen in the freezer and break off excess wax. Then place the item between sheets of newspaper and press with a hot iron, This will melt the wax and the paper will absorb it. Change the paper as soon as it is saturated. Sponge off any remaining marks with dry cleaning fluid. or methylated or white spirit.

Scrape off excess wax from carpets and cover the stain with blotting or absorbent paper. Use a warm iron to melt the wax. Again use methylated or white spirit to remove any remaining greasy stains.

Polished wood is best treated by putting ice cubes in a plastic bag and holding it on the wax to set it hard. Scrape off as much as you can with fingernails or card. Wash off remaining marks with a little warm soapy water and finally use a little lighter fuel to clean up completely.

Chewing gum

Put the garment in the freezer and chip off the gum when it is frozen.

For larger items put ice cubes in a plastic bag and hold over the gum to freeze it. Again

chip or break off as it freezes. Use dry cleaning fluid, methylated or white spirit remove final traces.

Soak the stain with liquid stain remover and rinse with cold water.

The method using ice cubes in a bag can also be used on carpets and hair.

Chocolate

Work liquid detergent into the stain and rinse with cold water. Any stubborn stains can then be removed with liquid stain remover.

Non-washable fabrics will need sponging with warm water and blotting dry before sponging with a solution of 1 teaspoon borax dissolved in 150 ml (¼ pint) warm water. Rinse and blot dry. Use cotton wool dampened with surgical spirit to remove final traces.

Blot as much chocolate off the carpet as possible. Use liquid stain remover or methylated spirit to finish off.

Coffee

Follow instructions for chocolate, and act as quickly as possible.

Cosmetics

All washable fabrics should have liquid detergent worked into the stain and the item rinsed.

Dried stains should be dabbed with an equal mixture of glycerine and water and left for an hour before washing in warm soapy water.

Non-washable fabric should be sponged with methylated spirits before being rinsed and blotted dry. Carpets should be treated the same way.

Crayon

For fabrics follow directions for cosmetics.

Wallpaper should be tested before larger areas are cleaned. Rub carefully with bicarbonate of soda on a damp cloth and leave to dry.

Vinyl wallpapers, floors and lino can be cleaned with silver polish.

Curry

Curry and any of the spices used, like turmeric, stain very badly. Scrape off as much food as possible, keeping the marked area to a minimum. Soak washable fabrics in warm water before rubbing in a solution of equal quantities of glycerine and water. Leave for at least an hour. Rinse well and reapply if necessary. Wash with biological washing powder.

Non-washables should be scraped carefully and sponged with a solution of 1 tablespoon borax to 600 ml (1 pint) warm water. Blot carefully, rinse and blot again.

Carpets should be treated as above but check carefully for colour fastness.

Egg

Egg, cooked or raw, will usually wash out of clothes if laundered as soon as possible. Soak in salty water for a while before washing.

Scrape off any excess egg and sponge area with warm salty water. Rinse with clear water and blot dry. Stubborn marks can sometimes be shifted with upholstery shampoo or stain remover.

Carpets should be cleaned with stain remover after scraping off any excess material. It might need shampooing to get rid of the mark and smell entirely.

> **Using a specialist shampoo on a small area of carpet will probably change the colour slightly and a lighter area may be the result. You might find it best to do the whole lot at the same time.**

Felt-tip pen

Buy water-soluble, not permanent, markers. Soak the item straight away in warm water. Wash as normal.

Non-washable fabric and carpets should be blotted carefully and washed in warm soapy water, rinse and blot dry.

Food colourings

Sponge fresh stains immediately with cold water. Work undiluted liquid detergent into the stain and rinse. Sponge gently with methylated spirits before rinsing again.

Manmade fibres and carpets should be treated with a solution of one part methylated spirits and two parts water. Dab any remaining traces with hydrogen peroxide and rinse again.

Fruit, fruit juices, berries

Don't use soap on washable fabrics as this will fix the dye. Rinse items with cold water before working some liquid detergent into the stain and leaving to soak for a few hours. Wash as normal.

Delicate fabrics should have glycerine rubbed into the stain and be left for an hour. Wash out with warm soapy water.

Sponge non-washable items with cold water, work liquid detergent into the stain and rinse. Any remaining traces can be dabbed with ammonia. Rinse and blot dry. Or try glycerine left on the stain for a few hours and sponged off with warm soapy water. Rinse and blot dry.

Carpets should be blotted and then shampooed. Any remaining traces can be dabbed with methylated spirits.

Grass

Dab washable fabrics with methylated spirits and wash in the usual way.

Non-washable fabrics should be treated with a one part methylated spirit to two parts water solution. Rinse and blot dry.

Carpets can be treated as above or dabbed with non-oily nail polish remover.

Gravy

Soak washable fabrics in cold water for about an hour before washing in the usual way. Any remaining traces should be treated with a stain remover.

Table linen should be soaked in a biological detergent solution and then washed.

Grease, oil and fat

Dab stains with eucalyptus oil before sponging lightly with water.

Washable fabrics should have the grease spots dabbed with dry-cleaning fluid or methylated spirit before being washed in the normal way.

Fresh stains on non-washable fabrics should be sprinkled with talcum powder. Press into the fabric and when it has caked together and dried, brush off. Repeat if necessary or use a spray dry-cleaning fluid and leave overnight.

Ice cream

Remove all excess ice cream and soak in warm soapy water. Use a liquid stain remover on any stubborn marks.

Non-washable fabrics need light sponging with warm soapy water and then treat as above.

Ink

To remove ballpoint pen marks, dip a cotton bud in methylated spirit and rub gently. Rinse and wash as normal. Some fountain pen cartridges contain ink that washes out but more obstinate marks should be rubbed with lemon juice and sprinkled with salt. Leave for an hour and wash as usual.

Use the methylated spirit technique for ballpoint pen marks on carpet. Then rinse and blot dry. Fountain-pen ink on the carpet should be lightly dusted with talcum powder. As soon as the talc is stained it should be Hoovered up and fresh applied until it is not coloured at all. Make up a paste by mixing a little white spirit with talc, spread over the stain and leave until dry. Hoover up the talc. The process may need repeating several times.

Jam

If clothes are washed immediately the jam will wash out. Stubborn or older, dry stains will need soaking in a solution of 25 g (1 oz) borax dissolved in 600 ml (1 pint) water.

Non-washable fabrics should be sponged with warm soapy water, rinsed and blotted dry. Older stains should be rubbed with borax, left for a few minutes before rinsing and blotting dry.

Carpets should be wiped as clean as possible but will need shampooing to get really clean.

Make-up

(See *Cosmetics*)

Mildew

Brush off as much as possible before sponging with a weak hydrogen peroxide solution – one part to twenty parts water – and rinsing washable fabrics as normal.

Non-washable fabrics will need specialist treatment so check with the dry cleaners.

Carpets will need sponging with carpet shampoo. Rinse before rubbing with a weak bleach solution – don't forget to test a small area first. Rinse again and blot dry.

Walls, tiled floors and surfaces should be washed with a solution of 300 ml ($\frac{1}{2}$ pint) bleach mixed with 1 litre (2 pints) water. Rinse with clean water and rub dry.

Some shower curtains are machine washable and this should remove most of the marks. But stubborn stains can be shifted by sponging them down with 2 tablespoons bleach mixed with 600 ml (1 pint) water. Rinse well and dry.

Milk

Washable fabrics should be washed in the normal way and this should remove stains.

Non-washable fabrics need rubbing with dry-cleaning fluid and sponging with warm soapy water. Rinse with clear water and blot dry.

Carpets should be rubbed with warm soapy water and shampooed to remove all traces and smell.

WARNING Before using bleach, amyl acetate, borax or any other products, test a small area of the fabric or carpet first. If there is any discoloration or alteration in the texture or substance, discontinue use.

Nail varnish

All fabrics should be blotted with paper towel or tissues to soak up as much of the excess as possible. Try not to spread the polish too much. For natural fibres put a pad of cotton wool or newspaper under the fabric and dampen some cotton wool. Dab on non-oily nail varnish. Any remaining traces can be dabbed with methylated spirit.

Manmade fibres should be dabbed with amyl acetate that is available from chemists. Do not use nail varnish remover.

Carpets should be blotted with amyl acetate. Some will work with the polish remover but test a small area first. The carpet might need shampooing to restore completely to its former glory.

Oil

(see *Grease*)

Paint (water-based)

Washable items should be washed as soon as possible, preferably before the paint hardens for best results. Dried stains will need a bit of help. Dilute methylated spirit with an equal amount of cold water, rub into the paint and give the paint a chance to soften before washing as usual.

Non-washable fabrics should also be wiped as quickly as possible.

Carpets should also be treated the same way.

Better to cover and protect furniture and carpets with cloths and avoid the problem altogether.

Paint (oil-based)

Blot washable fabrics with cotton wool or paper towel dipped in white spirit or paintbrush cleaner. Then wash as normal.

Non-washable fabrics should be treated much the same way – dab carefully with white spirit, rinse with cold water and blot dry. Dry stains are harder but placing a wad of cotton wool soaked with white spirit over the mark and leaving for at least an hour can help loosen up the paint. Rinse with cold water. Rub in a little diluted washing-up liquid and rinse again. Repeat the procedure if necessary.

Buy a bottle of white spirit when you buy gloss paint so it's ready to wash brushes and mop up any spills.

Carpets should be lightly sponged with white spirit or brush cleaner before rinsing with cold water.

Perfume

Rub the mark on washable items with a little white spirit before washing in warm soapy water. If the stain has dried rub with a mixture of equal parts of water and glycerine before rinsing well.

Non-washable fabrics should also be lightly sponged with a white spirit solution before rinsing carefully and blotting dry.

Carpets should be blotted with paper towels or tissue to soak up as much as possible, dab with white spirit, rinse and blot again.

Perspiration

Dampen the fabric and dab with 1 teaspoon ammonia mixed with 600 ml (1 pint) water solution. Or leave suitable fabrics to soak in a biological detergent. Wash items as usual. If the colour has been changed white wine vinegar can sometimes shift it, but test the fabric properly first.

Non-washable fabrics should be sponged with a solution of equal quantities of water and ammonia.

Plasticine

Scrape excess material off washable items and place a wad of paper towel or tissues underneath the mark. Dab with liquid stain remover or lighter fuel. Wash as usual.

Non-washable fabrics should be treated as above but sponge the fabric.

Carpets should also be treated as above.

Rust

Cover the stain with salt and squeeze lemon juice over the top. Leave for an hour or so before rinsing well with cold water. You may have to repeat this procedure several times. Check for colour fastness first.

Non-washables should be treated in the same way but check for colour fastness first as the lemon juice might bleach it.

Salad dressing

(See *Grease*)

Salty water

Sponge all fabrics with a solution of one part vinegar and two parts water before washing as usual.

Leather shoes can get marked from holiday and walking in the snow. Dissolve a little washing soda in about 150 ml (¼ pint) hot milk. While it is still warm use a soft cloth to rub over the marks. Leave until the shoes are dry before polishing as usual.

Scent

(See *Perfume*)

Scorch marks

Very bad scorch marks cannot be removed.

For light scorches, use fingertips to lightly rub the scorched area with a solution of one part glycerine and two parts water. Then soak the item in a solution 1 tablespoon borax and 600 ml (1 pint) warm water. Rinse well and wash as usual. Lighter marks can sometimes

be shifted by rubbing with granulated sugar dampened with water.

Non-washable fabrics will probably need expert attention as it's doubtful anything can be done.

Small marks on a carpet can be rubbed out carefully with hydrogen peroxide, but colour test first because it can bleach.

Try trimming the scorched ends of a carpet with nail scissors.

Shoe polish

Scrape off any excess polish from washable fabrics and dab with a liquid stain remover. Any remaining stains should be dabbed with slightly diluted methylated or white spirit. Rinse with cold water and wash as usual.

Non-washable fabrics should be treated the same way. Older stains can be loosened by rubbing with a solution of equal parts glycerine and warm water. Rub into the stain before dabbing with liquid stain remover. Rinse and blot dry.

Carpets should be treated the same way.

Suntan lotion

(See *Grease*)

Sweat

(See *Perspiration*)

Tar

Marks on washable fabrics can be dabbed with non-oily nail polish remover, but not manmade fabrics. Larger stains should be rubbed with butter, margarine or glycerine and worked in with fingers. Leave for at least an hour, sponge with a liquid stain remover and wash as normal.

Non-washable fabrics can be rubbed with a solution of half glycerine and half warm water. Leave for at least an hour before sponging with clean water. Blot and dab with liquid stain remover.

Carpets should be treated in much the same way.

Pet's paws should be rubbed with eucalyptus oil to loosen the tar.

Tea

(See *Chocolate*)

Tomatoes, juice or purée

(See *Fruit*)

Urine

(See *Animal stains*)

Vegetable stains

(See *Grass*)

Vomit

Scrape any excess off washable fabrics and rinse thoroughly in cold water. Leave to soak in a biological washing powder and then wash as usual.

Non-washable fabrics should also be scraped as clean as possible. Sponge with a solution a warm water with a few drops of ammonia added.

Carpets should scraped and blotted with paper towels. Mix 3 tablespoons borax with 600 ml (1 pint) of warm water and rub well. Rinse and shampoo well. Rinse again with warm water with a few drops of disinfectant added to help get rid of the smell.

Wine (red)

As soon as the wine is spilt sprinkle with a thick layer of salt and leave overnight. White wine poured over the same mark can remove the redness. Washable fabrics should then be soaked in a biological detergent before washing as usual.

Non-washable fabrics should be blotted to remove as much of the mark and liquid as possible. Sponge with warm water and blot again. Sprinkle the damp area with talcum powder, wait fifteen minutes and sweep or Hoover up. Repeat process until the fabric is clear.

Spills on the carpet should be sprinkled with salt and left overnight. Hoover or sweep up the salt in the morning. Lightly sponge any remaining marks and blot again.

Yoghurt

Scrape off as much yoghurt as possible and treat as *Milk*.

Zinc and castor oil cream

Make stained area damp and rub with a little white spirit. Leave for five to ten minutes and rinse with warm water. Wash as normal.

Non-washable fabrics should be dampened and rubbed with white spirit. Blot dry and rinse before blotting dry. Remember to test fabric first.

Treat carpets as above.

Waste disposal

According to Friends of the Earth we throw away twenty million tons of household rubbish and another 460 million ton are disposed of from shops, offices and other commercial properties every year.

Our comparatively affluent society spends more money and as most things we buy come in packaging we also throw away a lot more rubbish. Newspapers have got much bigger, there are more magazines and we consume tons of drinks and ices every year – all this contributes to the huge amount of waste.

Household waste

Most households use plastic liners in the kitchen bin as it saves so much mess and contains smells. Once full, these bags should be tied or taped up and transferred to the dustbin. If you have a plastic bin supplied by the council then they may not need plastic lining, but often you have to put out black sacks.

In Britain, our household rubbish is collected by the local council once a week and all we have to do is bag it up and put it out. The local council is legally obliged to collect rubbish on a regular basis but there are rules and regulations attached to this.

☞ You must use the type of container that is specified by your council, whether it's plastic bins or black rubbish sacks.

☞ The rubbish, and this is only household rubbish, must be left at a particular point every week and the earliest it can be put out is the night before collection.

☞ If you have a lot of extra rubbish, or gardening waste, you will have to contact the local authority about removal or take it to the local dump yourself.

Take care to wrap any broken china or glass to prevent any accidents. It helps the rubbish collectors if you mark it as broken glass or china.

If you have very large items to get rid of, like furniture, old bikes or kitchen equipment, check that no local charity can use it, and then contact your local authority who can advise you or arrange disposal. The council will also need contacting if you need to get rid of an old car. After filling in a form and handing over the log book they will take the vehicle away. Ask if they will charge you for this service.

Council dumps are also open for the public to dispose of rubbish themselves. They are usually tucked away somewhere and contain several huge skips. Rubbish may need to be sorted into types before dumping as they like to keep different materials separate ready for recycling or disposal.

Between 80 and 90 per cent of this rubbish is buried in landfill tips and the other 10 per cent is burnt. Only a very small amount is recycled and we should be doing more to protect the earth's dwindling resources.

What can you do?

Take your sorted rubbish to the appropriate recycling centres.

Glass bottles should be returned to shops where possible or re-used at home. Take jars and bottles to the bottle bank where they are sorted by colour. The glass will then be taken away and melted for re-use.

Paper of most types, including newspapers, can be pulped ready for more paper products. There are often recycling bins near the bottle banks.

Cans and foil come in two types – aluminium and steel. It's easy to differentiate as steel is magnetic and aluminium isn't. Cooking foil is also aluminium and both these

products are recyclable, so return your empties. Schools and other associations often collect these items so look out for further information.

Plastics can be recycled but there isn't such heavy investment in it. So save your carrier bags and use them to line small rubbish bins rather than buy more. Refill bottles wherever possible and use again.

Textiles including clothes, linen and wools can be donated to charity shops or jumble sales for re-use by other people. Some charities ship them abroad to developing countries and others who are in need. Otherwise fabrics can get shredded and used to make upholstery stuffing, roofing felt and wiping cloths. Unfortunately, there aren't many textile banks in this country at the moment.

White kitchen equipment like fridges, cookers and washing machines are often reconditioned and sold secondhand. Fridges need treating carefully as they contain CFCs that could damage the ozone layer if they are allowed to escape.

Before dumping larger pieces of furniture, ask your local authority in case they know people in need.

Batteries also need disposing of carefully as they contain heavy metals that are very poisonous. When collected they are often recycled. Wherever possible, buy rechargeable batteries – it's also more economical.

It is illegal to pour car oil down any drain or to dump it in the soil; although that's what happens to much of it. It can be recycled but it's quite hard to find a recycling plant.

Wood is often burnt or buried in landfill sites to rot with other organic waste. Timber from demolished buildings can be used to make garden sheds, pallets and cases. Small pieces should be shredded for use in chipboard or a mulch for garden parks.

Some tyres can be retreaded and re-sold but they are also used in boatyards, weights for silage clamps or for crash barriers in children's playgrounds.

Sewing repairs

Clothes naturally get damaged, worn out and eventually thrown away but sometimes a simple repair is all they need to extend their life. Day-to-day running repairs can often rescue a favourite shirt, coat or pair of trousers.

BASIC SEWING KIT
- **Needles, large and small**
- **Tin of pins**
- **Small scissors**
- **Thimble**
- **Tape measure**
- **Reels of cotton in black, white, brown, beige, and colourless**
- **Black button thread**
- **Thin elastic**
- **Trouser band hooks**
- **Hooks and eyes**
- **Seam ripper**

Buttons

Sewing on a button is one of the more simple repairs that you can do quickly and without any previous sewing experience.

Buttons must be sewn on to double fabric to prevent tearing. If the fabric is single then it will need to be reinforced with a 'stay'. This can be made of more of the fabric, ribbon or a piece of binding. This should be stitched, self-adhesive, or ironed on the back of the buttonhole area.

If you are making your own clothes, buttons should be positioned and sewn on after button holes are made, but before button loops are stitched.

Trim and pull out any remaining threads from a lost button. Quite often the holes will still be visible for you to use as a guide. (Many garments come with a spare button sewn inside in case of loss.)

If there is no replacement try taking a button from somewhere that doesn't show on the garment.

Thread a needle with matching cotton, using it double for extra strength. Fasten on the wrong side with a small double stitch.

Two-holed buttons will need six or eight stitches passed through the holes, trying to sew through the same holes all the time to form a neat bar of stitches on the wrong side of the fabric.

Don't sew the button tightly to the fabric. It will need a shank or stem to allow the buttonhole side to fit under it. Leave 5 mm ($\frac{1}{4}$ in) between the fabric and the button, more if the fabric is particularly thick.

Hold the button at this distance while you stitch it in position. Having made several stitches you will now have made a shank.

Wind the cotton round this shank several times, thread back into the fabric, make a few small stitches over the bar to secure the end and cut the excess thread off.

Stitches for four-holed buttons either form a two-bar pattern or make a cross. In either case the stitches should be sewn alternately.

Buttons with a moulded shank should be sewn on with six or eight stitches forming a bar on the wrong side.

Sometimes a small flat button is stitched on the reverse side of a larger button, on coats for example, to give extra strength.

Button covers can give you a new look without any sewing at all.

Button loops

Loops should be sewn after all buttons are in position.

Use strong matching thread for the job.

Make a tack mark or stitch on the buttonhole side of the fabric to mark the centre of each button. These will also mark the centre of each loop.

Put a pin either side of this central stitch to mark the size of the button, which will also decide the size of the loop.

The size of the loop away from the edge of the fabric should be half the width of the button.

Bring the needle up through the fabric by the left-hand pin. It is often easier to work

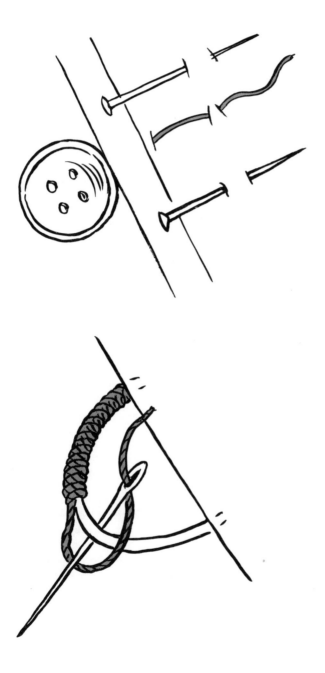

▲ Top: Measuring and marking
where to place your button.
Bottom: To make button loops,
loop stitch over threads.

with the edge of the opening facing you. Make one or two small stitches to fasten the thread and then go back through the fabric at the right-hand pin and under the fold to come up again at the left-hand pin, leaving enough thread in a loop to fit comfortably over the button. Repeat this stitch several times – more for thicker fabrics and less for finer ones.

Brush a little clear nail polish on to the threads of plastic buttons on clothes to make them last longer.

Use the same thread to make looped stitches over the four or five strands of thread to hold them together. The first and last stitches should be made through the fabric as well, and finish off with a couple of back stitches before cutting off excess.

Press studs

Don't use this method of fastening clothes where there is going to be any strain on them – they have a tendency to pop undone! They are most often used on children's clothes, as secondary fastenings or on lingerie.

The press stud (also called a popper) is made up of two parts that are sewn on opposite sides of the fabric and lock when pressed together.

The knobbed part should always be sewn on the overlapping or outer part of a garment.

Sew press studs fairly close together, about 2.5 cm (1 in) apart, to give them more strength.

Sew on all the knobbed parts first. Make a couple of small back stitches (see page 130) first that will be hidden by the press stud.

Sew in position by making three or four small stitches through each hole. Rub the knobs with chalk and press the other side of the fabric on to them. These chalk marks will tell you exactly where to place the dipped side of the press stud before sewing it on in the same way. Use pins to mark positions if you have no chalk or the fabric is too pale. Take care: it's very easy to sew this part of

the press stud upside-down – both sides look rather similar.

Look out for fashion poppers that come in packs with their own gadget for fixing them in place. They are brightly coloured and can be used to decorate or renovate clothes.

Hooks and eyes

Fasten thread with a double backstitch on the back of the fabric and where it will be hidden by the hook.

The hooked part should be approximately 3 mm ($\frac{1}{8}$ in) from the edge of the fabric so it will not show from the outside. Sew in position with four or five small stitches over each metal loop, making sure they don't show through on the right side of the fabric.

Finish off with a double backstitch and cut off excess thread.

The eye should be sewn exactly opposite the hook, but on the front of the fabric with the actual loop projecting over the edge of the fabric by about 3 mm ($\frac{1}{8}$ in).

Again, fix the thread with a double backstitch and make small stitches over the eyelets. Finish in the same way, not allowing any stitches to show on the right side.

Zips

There are three basic types of zips – conventional, open-ended and invisible.

The **conventional** type is closed at one end and sewn into a seam in most garments.

The **open-ended** zip is used in coats, jackets etc., and opens at both ends.

The **invisible** type is also closed at one end but blends into the garment much better.

Most have a chain of metal or plastic teeth that link together as the zipper 'tab' is pulled up. Metal and nylon zips are of a similar strength so the choice of which type to use is entirely up to you. Metal ones are usually heavier, seem slightly chunkier and come in heavy-duty types as well for use in jeans, jackets, etc.

Always do up zips before washing clothes as it helps them keep their shape better.

New zips

The degree of difficulty of putting in a new zip depends on how the zip is set into the garment. Some are part of the design and show clearly, others, like skirts and dresses are centred and semi-concealed. You may prefer to get professional help to replace zips in smart skirts and trousers, which are concealed with a fly front.

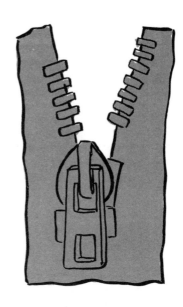

> **In an emergency, stitch yourself into the clothes and fix it later.**

To replace a semi-concealed, central zip – unpick the stitches round the old zip and remove it. Pull out any remaining threads. Tack the seam together so it looks as if there is no longer a zip. Press carefully. Pin the new zip in position on the inside and tack in place. With a zip foot in place (it lets you machine right up to the teeth of the zip), machine round the edge, taking care on the corners. Remove tacking stitches.

> **Buying a zip of a set length: the measurement of a zip is from the top of the slide to the end of the teeth.**

Repairing a zip.

Sometimes the energetic pulling means the zipper foot comes off one side of the zip. One way to make a quick repair is to cut two or three teeth out of the very bottom of the zip, on the opposite side to the zipper foot.

This will allow you to slip the cut end into the zipper foot – and the teeth will close up as the zipper moves up again. Sew a few stitches above the cut to stop it opening again.

The only disadvantage is that the zip is a bit shorter than before (if the garment is very tight you may have a bit of trouble putting it on again!)

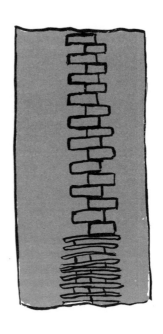

Darning

Darning is a sewing technique that weaves small stitches together to fill in a worn-out area or hole. The darning thread should be the same texture and thickness as the fabric of the garment as well as being as close to the colour as possible.

If the area is quite thin but not yet a hole, weave threads through horizontally to reinforce the fabric. If it's really thin then you will have to dam vertically as well.

Work tiny running stitches in close rows on the wrong side of the fabric, blending in with the texture as much as possible.

For a really perfect match pull out threads from somewhere that doesn't show, like the hem, and use them for the darning.

▼ **Below: Web darning.**
Run stitches around the outside of the hole and then work vertical and horizontal stitches across it.

Web darning

This type of mending is ideal for woollen garments and woven fabrics but you may need a darning mushroom to carry it out successfully. Not many people bother darning socks and things today as they just replace them instead. But when a favourite item needs renovating, this technique might just come in handy.

Tack a row of small running stitches round the outside of the hole. Trim any tatty bits if absolutely necessary but take care knitting doesn't unravel.

Work on the vertical stitches first. Start at one side just inside your tacking line. Use an extra long needle and make a few small stitches up to the hole, lay the wool in a straight line across the hole and sew a few more stitches on the other side. (The first few rows will not go across the hole but they will be inside the tacking line.)

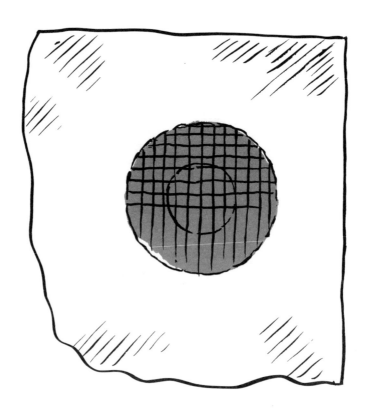

Then work another row next to the first one, always going as far as the tacking line. Once you have filled the area with vertical rows, start weaving the darning thread horizontally under and over the vertical stitches, until the hole is filled.

> **When darning jumpers or woolly items make sure you pick up any dropped stitches and include them in the weaving or the jumper will continue to unravel.**

Invisible mending

A very useful technique for mending holes such as cigarette burns in favourite clothes. Darning is excellent for woolly garments, but it won't be very successful on finer or patterned textiles.

To mend something invisibly means using a piece of the same fabric and weaving it in place so that the hole vanishes.

Study the weave of the fabric carefully so you can see what the pattern and weave is like. Look out for any colours that only figure in one direction or if there is any particular pattern.

You will have to pull threads from the hem of the garment. They should be of the right colour, texture and longer than the area to be darned.

For best results, stretch the area over an embroidery hoop with the wrong side uppermost. If the threads you have collected are short then weave the needle through the fabric leaving the eye exposed, then thread the needle and pull through until the thread is in the right place. If the threads are long enough then thread the needle before starting as usual.

If the hole is too large to darn you'll have to repair it by weaving in a piece of the same fabric.

Cut a patch from the hem that is one and a half times the size of the hole, matches the missing pattern or colour, and is as near to the same shape as possible.

Fray the edges slightly until the solid central part is practically the same size as, but still a little bigger than, the hole. Fray the edges of the hole area, too, until the solid fabric shape fits into the hole.

Using the technique opposite, use a needle to weave the frayed edges of the patch into the garment, matching the texture of the fabric. Weave the frayed edges of the hole into the patch as well to blend the patch into the article of clothing.

An iron-on patch on the reverse of the fabric can help to secure the new fabric.

It does take time and care to invisibly mend. If you can't face doing it yourself, a good dry cleaners will do it for you.

Machine darning

Lots of sewing machines darn. There is usually a special foot to fit on the machine and you'll need to check the manual for details.

After sewing a few tacking stitches round the edge of the area to be darned it should be stretched over an embroidery hoop, right side up, to keep fabric tight.

Turn the frame over so the fabric is resting flat on the surface and machine the area as suggested in your manual.

Repairs to elastic

It's very easy to replace snapped elastic inside a waistband or sleeve or to let out a garment that is now too tight.

Unpick a few stitches along the lower inside edge of the waistband near a seam and pull the elastic out. If the elastic hasn't broken it will obviously need snipping first.

Take a new piece of elastic of the same type and measure the exact length required. Add on 2.5 cm (1 in) and cut.

Attach a closed safety pin to one end and push it through the waistband casing until it comes out the other end. (Hang on to the other end though, don't let it disappear into the waistband!)

Check the elastic is flat before overlapping the ends by that extra 2.5 cm (1 in) and stitching the elastic together.

Tuck back into the waistband and stitch opening closed.

Elbow patches

Leather or suede patches can either be cut yourself or you can buy them ready-made, and often punched with holes.

Ideally sew them on while the fabric or wool is still intact.

Use a matching thread or wool to stitch in place.

Sewing elbow patches on to blazers before school starts will add life. Similarly, the trousers of crawling babies will benefit from the same attention being given to the knees.

Iron-on mending

Department stores or haberdashery shops usually stock a large range of quick repairs for clothes, and a lot of them can be ironed in place, rather than sewn.

Iron-on patches are placed over the hole or tear on either the right or wrong side of the fabric, according to which type you buy.

A hot iron is placed over the patch, the heat melts the adhesive and sticks the repair in place.

Pockets

There are various types of 'pockets' that can be bought and sewn into trousers or jeans to replace a torn one.

Cut the old one out and simply stitch the new pocket in its place.

Elasticised cuffs and waistbands

Repair tracksuits, long-sleeved T-shirts and children's clothing with elasticised cuffs and waistbands, which can be bought in packs in various colours with complete instructions for fitting.

Simple stitches

Backstitch

Use this for embroidery purposes: it forms a strong, solid line. Bring the needle up to the right side of the fabric and make a running stitch backwards. Bring the needle back up one full stitch length in front of it. Take one running stitch backwards to fill the gap and continue. Use a stitch length of approximately 2–3 mm ($\frac{1}{16} - \frac{1}{8}$ in).

Blanket stitch

As the name suggests, an edging stitch which can be used in buttonholes or on any fabric which will required a finished edge. Using a small needle, secure the thread to the fabric edge. Push the needle from the right side to wrong side, about 6 mm ($\frac{1}{4}$ in) from the edge with the needle pointing towards you. Ensure the thread is under the needle before pulling the needle completely through. Repeat the process, making the stitches fairly close together. Continue in this way.

Blind stitch

This stitch is hidden from view when worked between two layers, such as hems and facings. Turn down the upper fabric approximately 6 mm ($\frac{1}{4}$ in) and make a small diagonal stitch, catching one thread of the lower fabric. Now make a small diagonal stitch back to the upper fabric. Continue in this way.

Gathering stitch

All gathering can be worked by machine, which is always easier because you have two threads to gather with, instead of the single, hand-worked thread. If you do damage this stitch by hand, run the needle in and out of the fabric, in a basting style stitch (see tacking), securing it at one end. Run a second row beside this in exactly the same way and pull the unsecured ends of the thread together.

Slipstitch

This stitch will give an almost invisible finish. It is perfect for attaching linings or for handworked buttonholes. Make a running stitch through the folded fabric, emerge directly below this point and make a tiny stitch to the lower fabric. Take the needle immediately back up into the folded fabric and repeat. The only visible stitch will be the tiny v-stitch which joins the two edges together.

Tacking or basting

This is a temporary stitch, used to keep more than one layer in place until it is permanently stitched. Use it also for gathering. Work it as a continuous, even, running stitch, with a 13 mm ($\frac{1}{2}$ in) space between each stitch of about the same length.

Zigzag stitch

Most sewing machines will do this stitch, and it can be done in various widths or lengths. See your sewing machine manual.

Knitting

The beginner will only need the wool and some suitable needles, but as you become more experienced and tackle larger projects you'll need a few extras to do the job properly.

Needles

Knitting needles come in variety of lengths, diameters and materials and you need to match the size with the thickness of chosen wool.

Finer wools will need finer needles, there will be more stitches and the item will take longer to knit. Therefore it follows that thicker needles should be used with thicker wools, there will be fewer stitches and the garment knits up more quickly. Using large needles with a fine wool will make a very 'holey' garment indeed.

Knitting needles, or knitting pins, are sold in pairs for flat knitting but there are double-pointed needles for round knitting.

There are at least seventeen different sizes of diameter ranging from 2 mm for very fine work to 10 mm for chunky knits.

Knitting needle size equivalents		
mm	**GB old**	**US**
2	14	0
2$\frac{1}{4}$	13	1
2$\frac{1}{2}$	—	—
2$\frac{3}{4}$	12	2
3	11	—
3$\frac{1}{4}$	10	3
3$\frac{1}{2}$	—	4
3$\frac{3}{4}$	9	5
4	8	—
4$\frac{1}{4}$	—	6
4$\frac{1}{2}$	7	7
5	6	8
5$\frac{1}{2}$	5	9
6	4	10
6$\frac{1}{2}$	3	10$\frac{1}{2}$
7	2	—
7$\frac{1}{2}$	1	—
8	0	11
9	00	13
10	000	15
		16

Knitting needles come in lengths of 25, 30 and 35 cm – the choice is up to you. Some people prefer to knit with more manageable short needles but others knit with long ones that tuck under the arms, so it depends on your technique. Of course if you're knitting doll's clothes short needles will be fine, but the number of stitches cast on for a larger item may require longer ones.

Cable needles

These are short double-pointed needles that are used to hold some stitches out of the way while you knit with others.

Stitches are slipped on to them and the needle is held either at the back or in front of the knitting while other stitches are knitted.

Those held on the cable needle are then knitted back into the garment.

They are used mainly in making cable patterns.

They come in varying sizes but it's not essential to have them the same size as your knitting needles (although it's better if they are thinner as they won't stretch the wool, because the stitches are only held on them for a very short time).

Cable needles are also useful when picking up dropped stitches.

Mittens, socks and sleeves may be knitted completely on cable needles – usually four at a time, creating an enclosed circle without seams.

Knitting bag

It's handy to have a bag to keep all your knitting, extra wool and other equipment together. There are bags made specially for this but a carrier bag will do to start with, although they will eventually get punctured by the needles. Keep a tape measure, pins, stitch holder, small scissors, cable needles, wool needle and a row counter to hand.

A **stitch holder** is rather like a large safety pin and will hold stitches on finished item, like the top of a sleeve, in readiness for the making up.

A **wool needle** is shorter and slightly thicker than a normal sewing needle with a very large eye to make threading the wool for sewing up much easier.

A **row counter** is a small gadget that slips on to the end of one of the needles. It has numbers that can be moved so you can keep track of how many rows you've knitted. This is vital when counting rows between patterns or increasing or decreasing on sleeves and fronts. It needs moving on one number after each row and it helps to get into a routine of doing this at the same point so you know you haven't forgotten, even if you have put the knitting down for a few days.

Yarn

This is the name given to any fibre suitable for knitting and they are either natural or manmade.

Natural yarns divide into two groups – yarn made from plants which include cotton and linen, and yarn made from hair, wool or the fur of animals. Although they are very popular they are also very expensive and need special care when laundering and drying.

Manmade yarns are manufactured from chemicals. They are hard-wearing and often machine-washable. There are also yarns made from a mixture of both.

Buying yarn

The pattern you follow will specify what type of yarn you need to use. Most wool shops will let you reserve wool and collect and pay for it as you go and others will take back unused balls of wool. Check at the time of purchase.

Make sure each ball has the same dye lot number or the colour may vary and make the knitting look uneven.

Read the washing instructions and make sure you can comply with them.

> **Sometimes patterns call for yarn in Imperial measurements, but the balls of wool are in metric. As a rough guide: 100 g = 3 ½ ounces**

Getting started

Flat knitting is working on two needles. As you knit you are actually making rows of loops that interlock and make the knitting grow longer. Sections of the garment are worked separately and then they are 'made up' or knitted together to make the complete garment.

Round knitting means what it says; there is either one long, flexible, double pointed needle or you work on four needles. The knitting grows longer and you just keep knitting, there's no swapping needles from hand to hand.

Casting on

A beginner should start with a piece of flat knitting as it's easier to deal with and you can see the progress you are making.

- ☞ Casting on is the name given to making the first row of loops on the needle that will eventually be the 'hem' of the garment.
- ☞ Knitting patterns will tell you how many stitches to cast on for each section of the garment.
- ☞ There are several ways to cast on and the one you use depends on the amount of elasticity or firmness required.

▲ **A slip knot. Make a loop 15 cm (6 in) from the end of the yarn and insert the needle as shown. Draw up the loop on to the needle and tighten the knot.**

Here are two simple methods of casting on, although there are several more. Once you've got the knitting bug you'll need to refer to specialist books for in-depth information.

The thumb method

You'll need a ball of yarn and one knitting needle.

1. Make a slip knot about 15 cm (6 in) from the end of the yarn and put over the needle. Hold the needle in the right hand. Wrap the yarn around the left thumb and grasp between the palm and last three fingers.

2. Turn thumb away from you so the wool makes a loop. Slip this loop on to the needle and pull thumb out.

3. Pull the long end of the yarn to tighten the stitch round the needle. Repeat this

procedure to make as many stitches as you need.

The knitting-on method

You'll need a ball of yarn and two needles. Each new stitch is formed as knitting and is made on one needle before being slipped on to the other.

1. Make a slip knot on the needle held in the left hand. Push the right-hand needle through the slip knot and wind the yarn round it, in front of the slip knot. This will make the new stitch.

2. Carefully withdraw the right-hand needle, bringing the new loop with it. When you have pulled it through the slip knot, put this loop on to the needle in front of the slip knot to make the new stitch.

3. You should now have two stitches on your needle. The following stitches are made by always putting the right-hand needle through the last stitch slipped on to the left-hand needle, as explained above.

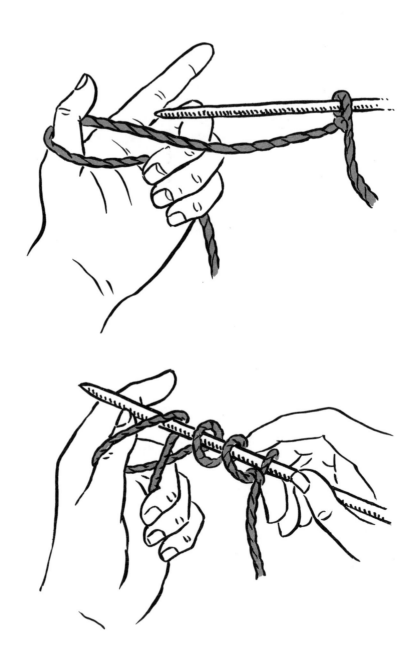

▲ **Thumb method of casting on.**

▲ Casting on by knitting.

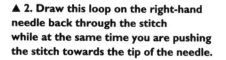

▲ **The knit stitch.**

1. Insert the right-hand needle into the back of the first stitch, from left to right. Take the yarn round the tip of the right-hand needle that is poking through the stitch, going beneath and then over the same needle. Pull the thread towards you.

▲ **2. Draw this loop on the right-hand needle back through the stitch while at the same time you are pushing the stitch towards the tip of the needle.**

Stitches

There are two basic stitches – knit and purl.
- ☞ The knit stitch forms a flat vertical loop that becomes the face, or right side, of the garment.
- ☞ Purl stitch makes the reverse side of the garment and it's actually a horizontal semi-circle of a loop.
- ☞ One row of each stitch is usually knitted alternately to become the finished garment.

Purl stitch

This is actually the reverse of the knit stitch.

Follow the drawings opposite for steps 1, 2 and 3.

Repeat these steps with the rest of the stitches on the left-hand needle until the new stitches are on the right-hand one.

Swap this needle to the other hand to knit the next row.

▲ **3. Let the stitch slip off the end of the left-hand needle, but the loop you've just made remains on the right-hand needle and becomes the new stitch.**

▲ **The purl stitch.**
1. **Hold the needle with the stitches in your left hand with the first stitch approximately 2.5 cm (1 in) from the tip of the needle.**

Knit stitch

The needle holding the cast-on stitches should be held in the left hand, with the first stitch about 2.5 cm (1 in) from the point of the needle.

Follow the drawings opposite for steps 1, 2 and 3.

Repeat these steps with the rest of the stitches on the left-hand needle until all the new stitches are on the right-hand needle.

The right-hand needle will now have to swap to the left hand so you can knit the second row.

> **You'll know when to do a knit row because the flatter, smoother side of the garment will be facing you. When the bumpier side is facing you, it's time for a purl row.**

▲ **2. Insert the right-hand needle into the front of the first stitch, so it goes over the top of the left hand needle, going from right to left. Take the yarn backwards, over the right hand needle and the stitch and beneath and over the tip of the same needle. Draw this loop on the right-hand needle back through the stitch while at the same time pushing the stitch towards the tip of the needle.**

▲ **3. Let the stitch slip off the left-hand needle but the loop you have just made remains on the right-hand needle to become the new stitch.**

Get knitting

All patterns suggest you knit a small square to start with, to check the tension of your work. Some people knit very tightly so it's hard to get the needle through the loops, and others knit too loosely. This could mean the garment will end up smaller than the pattern or much too big.

The pattern will say the tension should be a certain number of stitches to the centimetre (or inch). When you have knitted your tension square, which should be around 7.5 x 7.5 cm (3 x 3 in), count the number of stitches you have knitted to the cm/inch.

If there too many stitches, try knitting another square using needles that are one size larger, but if there are too few stitches use needles one size smaller.

If you have the tension right, start knitting, if not you may have to try another pattern.

Starter square

Try casting on about 30 stitches if this is your first attempt, using either method mentioned before.

Start with a knit row.

Take your time, it's quite tricky to get the hang of picking up new loops and dropping old stitches, so it's worth practising before embarking on a huge jumper.

Sometimes it's worth doing every row as a knit row to start with, just to master the technique. The resulting pattern – with an horizontal ribbed effect – is called a **garter stitch**.

Try alternating knit and purl rows until both stitches are mastered and the knitting looks neat. This is called **stocking stitch**.

> • **Knitting into the front of the stitch makes a looser stitch than knitting into the back of it.**
> • **Keep cast-on stitches as neat as possible as any unevenness will show, and try to knit them fairly loosely to make them easier to work.**

Casting off

Once the garment or your starter square is the right size you'll have to cast off the stitches. This is a way of finishing off or knotting the last row of stitches so the knitting doesn't unravel and it looks neat.

There are several ways to cast off but the basic method is the plain, or knit, cast-off.

Knit the first two stitches of the row in the normal way. You should now have two stitches on your right-hand needle.

Using the tip of your left-hand needle, slip the first stitch over the second stitch and off the needle, so you have only one stitch left.

Now knit another stitch from the left-hand needle, so there are two on the right-hand needle again and slip the first one over the second and off the needle.

Keep repeating these instructions until there is only one stitch left and that is on the right-hand needle. Cut the yarn until only three or four inches remain hanging, and then thread the end of the yarn through the stitch and pull tight to knot the end. Cut off excess yarn.

This casting-off method, or one like it, will also be used to start the decreasing – for example – at armholes when several stitches need to be cast off in one go.

Decreasing

Decreasing is used to shape the garment by making it narrower, but it can also be used in the making of various patterns. There are two main methods of decreasing and they vary slightly depending on whether it's a knit or purl row.

Slip stitch decrease

☞ KNIT (sl 1, K1, psso) Instead of knitting a stitch it is slipped straight on to the right-hand needle. The next stitch is knitted and then the slipped stitch is passed over that knitted stitch and dropped.

☞ PURL (sl1, P1, psso) A stitch is slipped straight on to the right-hand needle and the next stitch is purled as usual. The slipped stitch is then passed over it and dropped off the needle.

Knit together decrease

- ☞ KNIT (K2 tog) Knit two stitches together through the front of the loops. This will make one stitch instead of two.
- ☞ PURL (P2 tog) Purl two together through the front of the loops.

If the pattern says (tb l) it means put the needle through the back of the loops.

How to read a pattern

K	knit
P	purl
K2 tog	knit two stitches together
P2 tog	Purl two stitches together
tbl	through back of loop
alt	alternate
beg	beginning
dec	decrease
inc	increase
patt	pattern
rep	repeat
rnd	round
foll	following
rem	remaining
cont	continue
sl	slip a stitch
st	stitch
psso	pass slip stitch over
ybk	take yarn to back of work
yfwd	take yarn to front of work
yon	yarn over needle
yrn	yarn round needle
DK	double knitting yarn
st st	stocking stitch
g st	garter stitch
M	make a stitch

Your pattern will give you figures for a number of different sizes, within brackets (). Where only one figures appears, this applies to all sizes. For example, the sizes for the sweater or jumper you are knitting might be 10, 12, 14 and 16. They will appear as 10 (12, 14, 16), and the instructions for knitting will follow that pattern throughout. You might be asked to cast on 50 (62, 74, 86), which would reflect the stitches required for the respective sizes.

- ☞ Work figures given in square brackets [ ], the number of times stated afterwards.
- ☞ Where 0 appears, no stitches or rows are worked for this size.

Yarns

All amounts are based on average requirements and should be regarded as approximate figures. If you cannot find the exact yarn called for in the pattern, you can substitute one of a similar weight. But make sure that the substituted yarn knits up to the tension specified in the instructions.

Making up

When the garment is finished you will have all the component parts to stitch together. The best way to do this is to use mattress stitch, as it avoids making a chunky seam and keeps them looking smooth.

Use the same yarn as the item you are knitting and thread up the wool needle. Start by sewing up the shoulder seams and press using a damp cloth. If the sleeve needs sewing in it should be stitched in next.

Mark the centre of the top of the sleeve with a pin, as well as marking the halfway point between the top and the armhole shaping on either side of the sleeve. Do the same thing on the jumper.

Pin the matching pins together and sew in place, easing the knitting if necessary.

Then sew up the side and sleeve seams and press using a damp cloth.

Washing for wearing

This helps complete the finished look.

Machine-washable yarns will have instructions printed on the label and these should be followed carefully.

Natural fibres will need handwashing and it is best to wash them before they get too dirty so the laundering can be less vigorous.

Wash in lukewarm water using a very mild detergent or even washing-up liquid. Wash gently, trying not to rub or wring out too hard.

Rinse several times in clear water. Lift out of the final rinse with both hands and squeeze gently to remove as much water as possible. Leave to drain for few moments before wrapping in a towel and squeezing again.

Don't hang up a wet woollen garment or it will stretch it out of shape. Dry woollens on a flat surface or a rack if possible.

Curtains

Curtains are one of the easier soft furnishings to make yourself at home, as long as you have a sewing machine and a bit of patience, especially when it comes to measuring up. This is the crucial part as any error here will spoil the whole effect, so it's worth checking and double checking before you cut any fabric.

Furnishing fabrics are wider than dress fabrics and most of them will be suitable for dry cleaning only. As machine washing will shrink some materials, check before you buy.

Before you get started you'll have to decide what sort of track the curtains will run on and what will suit the window you want to dress. For instance, it won't be sensible to have brass rods in a small bay, you'll need a flexible track to fit the shape. Smaller windows let in more light if the track is a bit longer to allow the curtains to sit either side of the window rather than covering it up.

Install your choice of track before measuring for curtains.

Measuring up

Nets

Material for nets or smaller curtains to fit inside the window recess should be worked out by measuring the width and the length of the window.

The width measurement should be multiplied one and half or two times (even three), depending on how full you want the curtains.

Use half this measurement for each curtain if you are making a pair rather than just one.

The length should be from the track to the windowsill with approximately 20 cm (8 in) extra added for hems.

Curtains

Curtains which are to hang outside a window recess should be measured in much the same way, but taking the measurement from the length of track.

Double or triple that figure to allow for fullness. If you have two curtains, divide the overall figure by two; if you have three, your figure should be divided by three, and so on.

The length of your curtain will depend on your taste. If you want them to touch the window sill, measure from the top of the curtain track to just below the sill, adding at least 20 cm (8 in) for hems and seams.

Curtains will 'fall' slightly once they are hung, adding extra length, so don't worry if they are just slightly too short. Remember this when making floor-length curtains; however, the weight of the curtains will make them fall more, and they may end up dragging along the floor.

You will need extra fabric to match a pattern, and that will depend very much on the length of the pattern (the repeat – see below). Ask your fabric supplier or haberdashery assistant for help in adding the difference.

Allowing for pattern repeat in curtains

As a rule of thumb, you can usually add the length of one pattern for every width of fabric you'll need. In other words, if you have a window that is 150 cm (5 ft) high, and 120 cm (4 ft) wide, and fabric which is 60 cm (2 ft) wide, you would need 4 lengths to go across the window, allowing for double fullness, each length being about 170 cm. If your pattern is 40 cm (16 in) long, you'll need four times that, or 160 cm (64 in) of extra fabric, to allow for matching those patterns. Therefore, altogether, you'll need 6 m (20 ft), plus 160 cm (64 in) for the pattern, for a total of about 7.5 m.

Basic curtains

Measure window carefully.

Cut fabric to size. Turn a 1 cm ($\frac{1}{2}$ in) double hem down each side of the length of the curtain and tack in place.

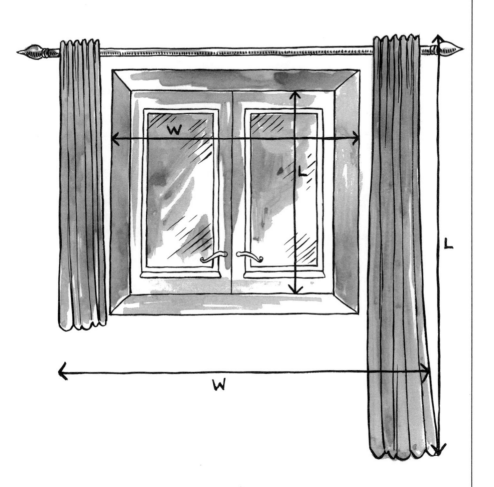

▲ **Measuring up for curtains (see opposite)**

Some fabrics can be machined but hand sewing leaves a much neater and looser hem.

Selvage edges (the finished edges of the fabric) are often snipped before hemming to allow the fabric to give slightly.

Making a gathered heading

To make a simple gathered heading for the curtain you'll need to buy a standard curtain gathering tape. Cut tape 8 cm (3 in) longer than the width of the curtain. Pull about 4 cm (1½ in) of the drawstring out of one end of the tape and knot ends together.

Pin the tape along the top of the curtain, folding knotted end under at the end which will be in the middle of the window (for two curtains).

Pull the drawstrings out of the tape at the other end (the outside edge of the curtain).

Fold excess tape under and pin to leave cords free.

Machine or hand stitch along the top edge of the tape, then the bottom edge. Take care not to machine over the end of the tape with the free strings hanging on it.

Pull the two strings, gradually easing the fabric as you go, to gather the top of the

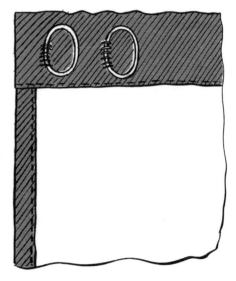

▲ **The wrong side of curtains with a gathered heading. Pull your drawstring out of the holes at each end.**

▼ **Sew your curtain tape to the curtain at the top and bottom. Tack the threads at one end and draw them tight. Put the hooks into the appropriate places along the curtain and hem.**

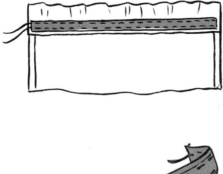

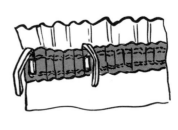

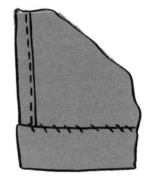

Gathered

Pencil pleat

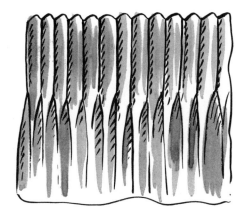

Pinch pleat

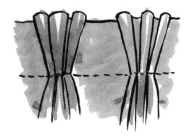

Scalloped

curtain to the correct fullness for the window. Tie the drawstring ends together and wind on a card keeper. Do not cut in case you want to open curtain out again for cleaning or laundering.

Insert curtain hooks through the special loops made by the gathered tape at 8 cm (3 in) intervals

Hang curtain in position and pin hem to correct length. Remove from track, fold over hem and hand stitch the hem closed.

Others headings

Heading tape helps you create the effect you want; e.g., pencil pleats, loose gathers, or pinch pleats.

▲ **Types of curtains.**

> Patterned fabrics look much more professional if the patterns run across the window as well as up it. You will have to allow extra fabric for this (see page 140) so take it into account when purchasing.

The strings are arranged to make this easy for you and the tape provides the correct stiffening.

In general, thicker tape should be used for heavier fabrics and a thinner tape for lighter ones.

Simple gathered heading is used on unlined curtains and is ideal to use when a pelmet is going to cover the top. You'll need one and a half to two times the length of the rail.

Pencil pleats need to be more tightly gathered so you'll need to allow for this when measuring the curtains. The tape will need to be about 10 cm (4 in) more than the width of the window multiplied by the fullness figure. In other words, using the example on page 140, if your window is 120 cm (4 ft) wide, and you will have curtains of double fullness, the width of the fabric required will be 240 cm (8 ft). Add 10 cm (4 in) to this figure for the length of your heading tape, and you'll need 250 cm (a little over 8 ft).

Pinched pleats are more decorative and especially suited to long curtains. They are ideal for thicker fabrics as there is less gathering than pencil pleats.

Scalloped tops are most often used on curtains that are hung on a pole. They hang flat as there is no gathering and it uses less fabric. It's popular also on café curtains (these hang on a pole halfway up the window).

Blinds

Blinds are becoming increasingly popular, especially used in conjunction with fabric curtains. They are easy to make and usually cheaper as they use less material and are most widely used in bathrooms and kitchens.

There are lots of kits available from DIY stores now that contain instructions and everything you need to finish the job, except the fabric, of course. Look out for ready-made ones, too.

Venetian blinds are made from slats of plastic or metal and work on a two-pulley system. One pull the slats up and down and the other tilts them open or closed. They come in a fantastic range of colours and can be wiped clean fairly easily. They are bought ready-made.

Vertical blinds are made up from vertical strips of stiffened fabric that twist open or closed. They don't collect as much dust as Venetian blinds but still restrict the view a lot,

even when fully open. Most often used on large picture windows.

Bamboo blinds are very cheap and have to be rolled up manually. The thin bamboo sticks are closely stitched together in horizontal strips and are rolled up and down with thin string on a pulley. They look very natural but don't give much privacy, especially at night when the lights indoors can be seen from outside.

Plisse blinds are made from thick pleated paper or stiffened fabric that give complete privacy when closed. The working cords run up either side through punched holes.

> **To clean Venetian blinds, wear an old sock on each hand, then wash with one hand and dry with the other.**

Making blinds at home

It's actually quite easy to make simple blinds at home. There are lots of kits around that can be made up quickly, but you'll need to take care when measuring up. One of the advantages to having blinds is the fact they can be made to fit just about any window.

Roller blinds

There are all sizes of roller mechanisms and therefore blinds can be individually made to fit any window.

They usually come in a kit that will also include the batten to stiffen the bottom, a cord and cord holder.

The roller will need cutting to size and should be 1 cm ($\frac{1}{2}$ in) narrower than the window.

When cutting the length of fabric allow an extra 30 cm (12 in) for hems and turnings. Stiffened fabric will not need side seams so it can be cut to the same width as the roller. If the sides need hemming, allow an extra 2.5 cm (1 in) for each side.

The kit will come with precise instructions but basically a tunnel is sewn across the bottom to slide the batten through and to attach the pull cord. The fabric at the other end is wrapped round the roller mechanism and stitched in place. The extra fabric at the sides is folded over and hemmed.

Roman, Austrian or festoon blinds

For Roman blinds measure the actual window size and then add an extra 45 cm (18 in) to the length of the fabric (blinds are usually longer than the actual window to allow some fullness).

Allow an extra 2.5 cm (1 in) to the width for each side seam.

Start by turning and sewing side seams.

Fold over 5 cm (2 in) at the top and bottom and stitch hems.

Stitch vertical rows of ring tape about 30 cm (12 in) apart across the back of the fabric (this tape is available from department stores and haberdashery shops).

Start by sewing the central row, then one down each edge of the curtain and the rest at regular intervals in between (approximately 30 cm (12 in), depending on the width of the blind).

A cord is tied to each bottom ring and threaded up through the rings above it. These are then threaded across the top row and gathered together at one of the top corners of the blind.

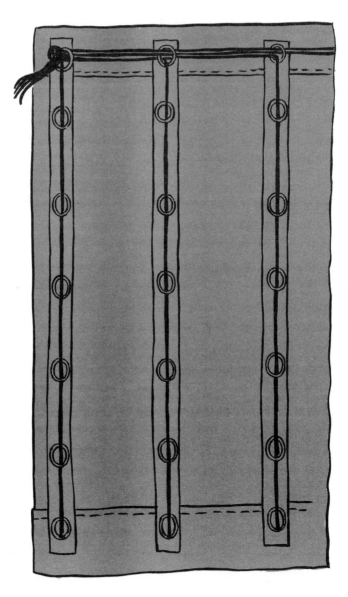

▲ **For Austrian and Roman blinds, sew ring tape in evenly spaced vertical rows, running the cords from the bottom and up through the rings to the top, where they'll come together as one cord.**

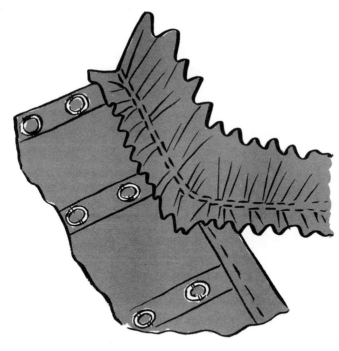

1. Cut fabric twice the width of the desired frill plus 1 cm ($\frac{1}{2}$ in) for seams.

2. Fold in half lengthways, right sides together.

3. Stitch 1 cm ($\frac{1}{2}$ in) from raw edge, using loose tacking stitches. Turn right side out and pull up threats to gather fabric.

4. Top stitch the frill to the edge of the blind.

Hanging blinds

Lightweight blinds may be fixed using Velcro.

1. Staple Velcro to a 2.5 cm (1 in) square wooden batten nailed to the window frame.

2. Stitch the other side of the Velcro to the top of your blind.

3. Screw an eyelet into the end of the batten and pass the cords through it.

Window dressing

Of course you don't have to sew curtains, there are other ways to decorate windows.

Drapes

Fix a brass rod or wooden pole to the wall above the window.

Twist and drape muslins, silks, satins, old sheets or other fabric loosely round the horizontal pole and allow it to hang down either side in an informal way.

These curtains can't be closed of course!

▲ **Add a frill or a row of lace to the bottom of your blind, sewing to the wrong side.**

With the blind laid out flat, tie all the cords together, allowing enough cord to hang down one side to where you can reach them when the blind is put in place. Or tie them all together and tie a simple cord to the knot if you think this is neater.

Festoon or Austrian blinds are made in much the same way. Before sewing the vertical rows of ring tape, baste the outside seams and each vertical line where you expect to sew on ring tape. Pull the threads so that the seams are lightly gathered and have a ruched effect. Carry on as for Roman blinds, sewing on ring tape and finishing accordingly.

Frills

You may want to have a frill running round the bottom or all sides of the curtains.

The amount of fabric will need to be at least twice as long as the length of the edge to be decorated.

**Curtains difficult to pull?
Spray furniture polish along the
curtain rail and they'll glide
beautifully.**

Pin ups

Use a favourite piece of fabric, damask bedspread, patterned tablecloth or antique net that is practically the same size as the window and pin along the top edge over the window.

With a tasselled rope tie back, or another piece of the fabric, tie the fabric in the centre, pulling it up and out above the knot to create a ruched effect.

This improvisational curtain cannot be opened further, but can be closed by removing the tie.

Alternatively, sew a length of attractive fabric to a pole, letting it fall to the windowsill or floor. To open, pull to one side, where it can be held back by a curtain tie or hook.

Table linen

It's very easy to make your own table linen. As well as brightening up the room, tablecloths can be used to cover up scratched tabletops, make a meal more festive or a dinner party more formal. And smaller side tables can also be covered to add extra colour.

Fabrics

Choose washable fabrics like cotton or a poly-cotton mix . Always check washing instructions before you buy.

There are also printed fabrics to suit special occasions; for example, around Christmas, which can really set the scene.

Plain colours can be decorated with ribbons, tapes, fabric dyes and sprays, but check the fastness of colour and washing instructions before use.

Although fabrics for this use are often wider than dress fabrics, round and very wide tables may still need two widths stitched together.

Buy extra fabric or a complementing colour so you can make napkins and table mats to match.

There is also PVC fabric that can be bought by the metre and thrown over the table, without the need for hemming, to give a completely waterproof surface that's ideal for the kitchen or anywhere that there are lots of kids around. It comes in many colours and patterns which can be co-ordinated with your decor.

Measuring up

Measure the area of the table top and decide on the amount of overhang you want on each side.

A shorter overhang is better for everyday use, especially if you have children, but a longer drop looks extra special for a more formal occasion.

Add twice the overhang to the length and width of the tabletop, then add an extra 2.5 cm (1 in) on each edge for 147 hems.

Try to find a fabric that is as near to the right width as possible, but if you have to sew two pieces together, buy twice the·length you have measured, plus enough for the pattern repeats (see *Curtains*, page 140).

Round cloth

Measure the top of the table (from side to side) and allow extra for the overhang (twice the length you'd like the cloth to hang down from the top) and the hem – about 5 cm (2 in).

Buy a square piece of fabric that is practically the right size. Fold into four.

Hold a piece of string in the middle of the table and cut it off an inch below where the

▼ **Making a round tablecloth**

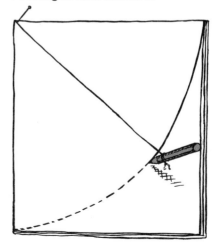

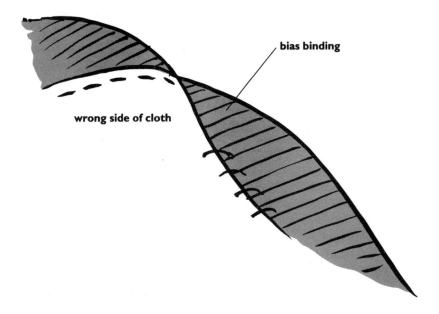

bias binding

wrong side of cloth

▲ **Stitch bias binding tape around the cloth to prevent edges from fraying. A bias tape in a complementary colour looks nice.**

overhang would finish. Now pin one end to the corner which is the central point of the folded fabric.

Holding a pencil or chalk at the other end of the string, draw a quarter of the circular shape on to the fabric.

Take care not to wrinkle the fabric. Cut out carefully and open out to reveal a circular shape.

Sew a length of bias binding to the raw edge of the fabric, turn up and stitch in place to make the hem. Or run some gathering stitches round the raw edges. Turn up a hem, gathering up and easing the fabric to fit as you go.

Square or rectangular cloth

If the fabric is wide enough it will only need hemming and pressing before use.

To make a cloth for a table wider than the fabric, buy twice the measured length and cut in half across the width. One of the halves will now be the part that covers the table top. Cut the remaining piece in half lengthways and sew one piece on each side of the larger piece, matching up any patterns if necessary. This means the larger piece of fabric will be central and the seams will not show as much, as they should be around or just below the table edge.

Napkins

Adjust the size of the napkins so they will fit evenly into the width of fabric to waste as little as possible.

Fold a double hem round the edge of each one and press the fold lines.

Unfold and cut a small triangle off each corner to the first fold line to make the corners less bulky. Fold up again and machine round the edges.

Slip stitch the corner seams closed and press.

Table mats

Make matching or complementary table mats with fabric that is slightly thicker than the cloth itself to give more protection to the table.

> **You can buy many fabrics already quilted, which are perfect for table mats, and can be made the same way as the napkin.**

If you want your mats to match the cloth, double the tablecloth fabric, slip a layer of quilting wadding between, sewing around the outside to fix the wadding carefully between the two layers of fabric, and finish with bias binding tape around the outside.

Each mat should be large enough to take a plate, a side plate, cutlery and a napkin.

Bed linen

With duvets the ability to create your own bed linen becomes more attractive. Not only can you make curtains and duvet covers to match but any other soft furnishings can also be co-ordinated with the room. Pillowcases, plain and fitted sheets and cushions can all be made at home.

There are lots of fabrics and different types of sheeting available now and it comes in much wider sizes, usually 228 cm (90 in), although it can be more difficult to find the king-size width. Easy-care polyester cotton mixtures are the most suitable as they wash easily and dry more quickly than thicker cotton fabrics. They are excellent for fitted sheets as the fabric is often non-iron and the colours don't wash out.

▼ **Making bed linen. Measure carefully as described overleaf.**

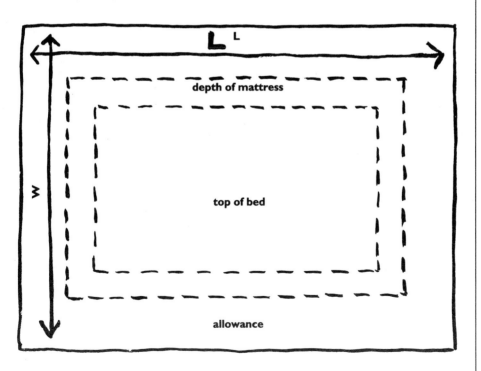

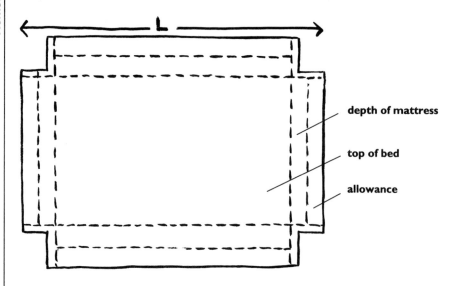

depth of mattress

top of bed

allowance

▲ For a fitted sheet, you'll need the same basic measurements, but the corners will be cut out.

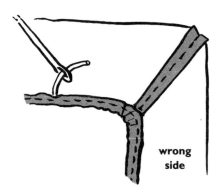

wrong side

▲ Cut pieces of elastic and pull them through the hem at the corners.

Measuring up

A rough guide to the amount of fabric you'll need is as follows:

A single bed is usually 90 cm (3 ft); a double bed is 135 cm (4 ft 6 in); a king-size, 150 cm (5 ft).

		Width	Fabric
Flat sheet	single	176 cm	2.8 m
	double	226 cm	2.8 m
Fitted sheet	single	90 cm	2.5 m
	double	135 cm	2.5 m
	king	150 cm	2.8 m
Duvet	single	140 cm	2.9 m
	double	200 cm	4.1 m
	king	230 cm	4.8 m

Flat sheets

You'll need to measure the length, width and depth of the mattress.

Don't forget to take all four sides of the mattress into account. Add another 60 cm (2 ft) to the width to allow room to tuck in.

Allow an extra 25 cm (10 in) for top and bottom hems.

With fabric the right width, a plain sheet will just need hemming round the edge. The

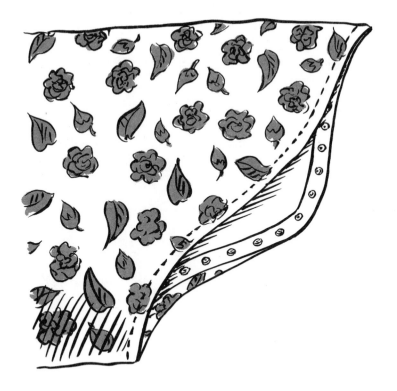

▲ Your duvet cover can be closed with poppers, zips or fastening tape.

top edge usually has a larger 4 cm (1½ in) double hem.

Fitted sheets

A fitted sheet is slightly more complicated. The basic measurements are the same but the corners will need cutting out, as shown.

With the right sides together, as shown, machine stitch the corners closed with an open seam.

Machine stitch the hem all the way round the sheet as above.

To elasticate the corners you'll need to unpick a 2.5 cm (1 in) section of the hem 25 cm (10 in) away from each corner seam, as shown.

Cut four 20 cm (8 in) pieces of strong elastic fine enough to fit through the hem,

and thread on to a bodkin or needle with a very large eye.

Pin one end at one of the entry holes and thread needle along the hem to come up at the hole on the other side of the corner.

Pin to hold in place. Stitch both ends firmly in place before removing pins. Sew the small openings in the hem closed.

Duvet covers

Use the same type of sheeting fabric as for other bedding so it's washable and matches the rest of your bedroom.

Measure the duvet's length and width and add 2.5 cm (1 in) to both measurements to allow for seams. If the fabric isn't wide enough and you have to make joins, try to put one centrally or two equally spaced on each side of a central panel.

With the right sides together pin one of the shorter sides together. This edge will have the opening in it so leave the central part open and machine about 45 cm (18 in) in from each outside edge, leaving the opening in the middle.

With the right sides together machine stitch all round the rest of the outside.

Fastenings

Turn the duvet cover right side out and press the seam allowance to make a sharp fold.

Cut a piece of fastener tape to the same length as the opening and pin in place so that one edge aligns with the pressed fold and machine stitch in place.

Sew press studs at regular intervals, about 15 cm (6 in) apart along the tape.

You can buy fastener tape that has the press studs already in position and just needs machining into the opening. This should be available in large department stores or haberdashery shops.

Alternatively make the fastenings. Machine stitch 15 cm (6 in) tape or ribbon every 15 cm along the opening on one side. Stitch more on the opposite side of the opening to match the first so they can be tied together once the duvet is inside the cover.

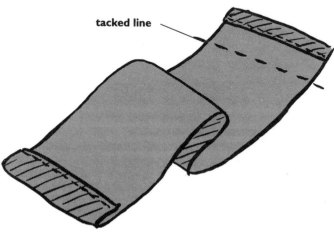

tacked line

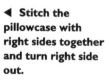

right side

▲ **Top: To make pillowcases, fold over at the tacked line to allow the pocket for the end of the pillow to sit in.**

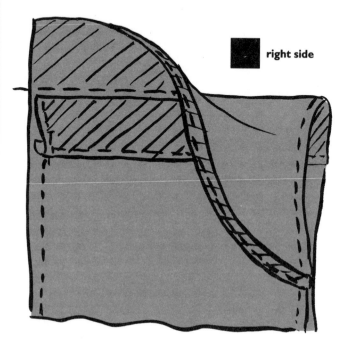

◄ **Stitch the pillowcase with right sides together and turn right side out.**

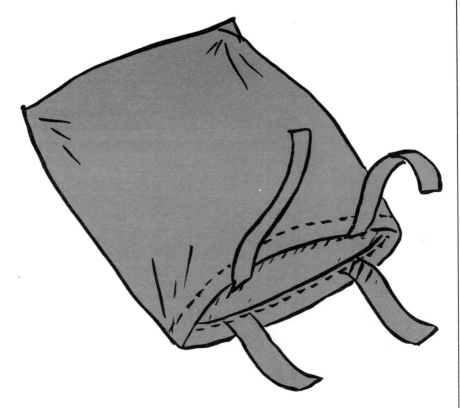

Pillows

Measure the length of a pillow and double it. Add 20 cm (8 in) for the tuck-in part and another 8 cm (3 in) for the top hem, plus another 2.5 cm (1 in) on both ends for seam allowance.

Measure the width of the pillow and add on another 2.5 cm (1 in) for a seam allowance. Cut fabric to size.

Baste a line of stitches straight across the fabric 20 cm (8 in) from one end. Turn fabric over and stitch a narrow hem across this same end, folding the hem to the wrong side of the fabric.

Turn 1 cm ($\frac{1}{2}$ in) over at the other end and press.

Turn over another 6 cm ($2\frac{1}{2}$ in) and neatly machine stitch across. This will be the top end.

Put right sides together and fold the top end up to the line of basting stitches across

▲ A quick pillowcase can be tied shut at one end instead of having a pocket to keep the pillow self-contained.

the pillow case at the other end. Baste fabric together down both sides.

Fold the other end of the fabric wrong sides together along the line of basting and baste in place down both sides.

Machine stitch down both sides through all layers, leaving a 2.5 cm (1 in) seam allowance.

Turn right side out and press well.

Quick pillowcases

Measure the length of the pillowcase, double it and add 15 cm (6 in).

Measure width and add 5 cm (2 in) seam allowance for both sides. Cut fabric to size.

Turn a 1 cm (½ in) hem on both short edges of the fabric. Press to make a sharp fold.

Cut four 20 cm (8 in) lengths of tape or ribbon and position two on each of the short edges of the pillowcases, approximately 10 cm (4 in) from each edge. Sew tapes to the turnings.

Machine stitch the side seams together. Turn edges of the opening over another 6 cm (2½ in) and press. Fold tapes back on themselves and machine stitch round the opening through the tapes. Press well.

> **Buy inexpensive pillow covers and decorate them to match your room. Fabric paints can be stencilled on to match your walls, or try sewing on various shapes (perhaps reflecting your wallpaper, border or curtains), ironing the edges under and sewing it with a blanket stitch (see page 130).**

Cushions

Either buy the cushion pads already stuffed and cover them yourself, or make the cushion cover first and then stuff it. Obviously it's easier to cover a ready-made shape but you will be restricted by the sizes available.

Measure the length of the shape and double it, allowing 2.5 cm (1 in) extra on each side for seams.

Unlike pillowcases, cushions look most professional with a seam on all four sides. Cut two pieces of fabric to the required size and pin right sides together. Machine down three of the sides and snip the excess fabric at the corners to stop them being so bulky. Put the cushion inside.

Hand stitch the last seam closed. You may prefer to use press studs or tie-up ribbons for this seam so the cover can be removed for washing. Otherwise this seam can be slit open, the cover washed and stitched closed again when dry.

> **Place a cushion in the centre of a large piece of fabric and gather up the excess material together. Tie in a knot, or wind ribbon round the gathering to make a quick cushion.**

Once you have mastered this simple cushion cover you can move on to 'dressier' seams. One of the neatest is a piped look in the same or a contrasting fabric. Simply measure the four sides of the cushion and add 2.5 cm (1 in) to each measurement. Cut four lengths of fabric, 2.5 cm (1 in) wide, to the same length. Fold and press in two, lengthways. Placing the raw edges along the raw edges of the cushion cover fabric, trap the strips between the two pieces of fabric. Pin in place before sewing round the three sides as before.

> **To create plump cushions, make your cushion cover a little smaller than the pad.**

Choosing fabrics for soft furnishings

Buying fabric for the home can be a tricky business. The sheer choice is overwhelming and mistakes could be expensive. The following guidelines might serve to make the decision-making process a little easier.

• If you are buying a large amount of fabric for, say, a pair of curtains, take sample colours of other upholstery or fabric in the room. Carry with you, for example, an offcut of the carpet or a dab onto a postcard a little of the paint you are trying to match.

• Always buy fabric in natural light. If necessary, carry the roll of fabric over to a window to view the texture and colour.

• If you can, take a large swatch of fabric home with you. Some shops will agree to refund you should you decide to return it.

• To check a fabric for creasing, scrunch a corner in your hand. If the fabric remains creased after a few minutes you can select another more suitable for your purposes.

FABRIC WIDTH CONVERSION CHART

35" – 36" 90 cm	44" – 45" 115 cm	52" – 54" 140 cm	58" – 60" 150 cm
1 ¾ (1,60 m)	1 ⅜ (1,30 m)	1 ⅛ (1,10 m)	1 (1 m)
2 (1,90 m)	1 ⅝ (1,50 m)	1 ⅜ (1,30 m)	1 ¼ (1,20 m)
2 ¼ (2,10 m)	1 ¾ (1,60 m)	1 ½ (1,40 m)	1 ⅜ (1,30 m)
2 ½ (2,30 m)	2 ⅛ (2 m)	1 ¾ (1,60 m)	1 ⅜ (1,50 m)
2 ⅞ (2,70 m)	2 ¼ (2,10 m)	1 ⅞ (1,80 m)	1 ¾ (1,60 m)
3 ⅛ (2,90 m)	2 ½ (2,30 m)	2 (1,90 m)	1 ⅞ (1,80 m)
3 ⅜ (3,10 m)	2 ¾ (2,60 m)	2 ¼ (2,10 m)	2 (1,90 m)
3 ¾ (3,50 m)	2 ⅞ (2,70 m)	2 ⅜ (2,20 m)	2 ¼ (2,10 m)
4 ¼ (3,90 m)	3 ⅛ (2,90 m)	2 ⅝ (2,40 m)	2 ⅜ (2,20 m)
4 ½ (4,20 m)	3 ⅜ (2,90 m)	2 ¾ (2,60 m)	2 ⅝ (2,40 m)

Decorative fabric finishes

There are several easy ways in which you can add a decorative finish to cushions and bed linen. **Ribbons** come in an array of colours and textures – from polyester satin and jacquard to velvet and taffeta. Attach narrow ribbons to fabric by stitching them down the centre. Wider ribbons are best machine-stitched down both sides. Remember to stitch in the same direction to prevent puckering.

Ribbon bows in a contrasting colour might look pretty on a child's duvet. To attach the bows, thread narrow ribbon through a needle and push it through all the layers of fabric from front to back then to the front again. Cut the ribbon and tie securely using a double knot followed by a bow.

You can create **tassels** for cushions by winding embroidery or crochet thread a dozen times around a piece of card. Remove from the card and wind thread around one end to secure and snip the other end to form the tassel.

Lace looks pretty used as an edging for pillows. Cotton eyelet, for example, is available flat and pre-gathered. Lace is available in an assortment of colours but it is also easy to dye if you cannot find it in a colour to suit your fabric. See the chart on page 98 for reference.

NEEDLE CHART

Fabric type	Hand	Machine
Very light fabric chiffon, silk, lace	9, 10, 11 12	9, 11 (70, 80)
Light fabric silks, lawn, taffeta, voile	8	11 (80)
Medium light fabric gingham, cotton, satin, wool crêpe	7,8	11, 14 (80, 90)
Medium fabric flannel, velvet, pique, corduroy, linen	6,7	14 (90)
Medium, heavy fabric towelling, denim, tweed, felt, fleece, chintz, fake fur	6	14, 16 (90, 100)
Heavy fabric wax-covered ticking, corduroy, canvas, upholstery, fabrics, leather, suede	1, 2, 3	16, 18 (100, 110)

Flowers around the home

Fresh flowers lend life to a home, adding colour, texture and scent. They bring tremendous pleasure for relatively little cost.

The following tips will bring out the best in cut flowers and help keep them fresher longer:

• Strip off the leaves that will be submerged by water. They rot quickly under water and over time give off a foul smell.

• Add a pinch of plant food such as Phostrogen to the water. If you do not have any, try crushing an aspirin, adding a pinch of sugar, or using carbonated water, tonic or lemonade diluted with normal water (about $\frac{1}{2}$).

• Cut off about 2 cm ($\frac{1}{2}$ in) from each stem. Liquid trapped in the stem might have caused it to seal.

• For wooded-stem flowers (e.g. chysanthemums) use a rolling pin to open up the base of the stem.

• For roses split the bottom of the stem and stand in a tall jug of boiling water for 20 seconds. Remove and place in a deep vase of cold water. (Boiling water opens up the stem and enables water to reach the head.)

• Plants like ivy, hydrangea and heather like to be totally immersed in cool water before arranging.

Essential check list for flower arrangers

☞ Floral foam: Handy for fresh and dried flowers. There are two types: the green kind, commonly known as Oasis, which has to be soaked in water before use; the other variety is brown and is useful for dried flowers. The foam is easy to cut to the shape you require.

☞ Wire mesh: Use plastic coated rather than ordinary chicken wire. Mesh can be crumpled and squeezed into any shaped container to hold flowers in position.

☞ Scissors and secateurs: Buy the best you can afford.

☞ Knives: A good sharp knife is useful for slicing woody stems. A dinner knife is suitable for cutting foam.

☞ Tape: You can buy a rubber-based tape called gutta percha which is used for binding stems together or covering ones already bound with fine wire. It comes in shades of green as well as brown and white.

The cut flowers that last longest are carnations, tulips and gladioli.

Tips for flower arranging

• Remember to keep the background wider and taller than the rest.

• Use Oasis or wire to keep flowers in place.

• If using Oasis with softer stemmed flowers you might need to insert a cocktail stick in the stem for extra support.

• You can create a triangular-shaped flower arrangement by inserting the tallest flowers first in the centre, then filling in.

Reconditioning your flower arrangements

To revive drooping flowers, trim about 2.5 cm (1 in) off their stem ends and place them in hot water for at least ten minutes.

When tulips start to droop, push a pin beneath the head of the flower. This will disperse trapped air bubbles. Or try using carbonated water to perk up tired blooms.

Floral touches make great accompaniments for dinner parties, buffets or garden parties. Try trailing ivy or Russian vine around candlesticks and night lights. Float chrysanthemum heads in shallow glass dishes or decorate a plate of rich red summer fruits with dazzling scarlet geranium heads.

A – Z cut flowers

Alstroemeria *(Alstroemeria sp.)*
A good cut flower. Trim ends of stems and stand in shallow water.

Anemone *(Anemone sp.)*
Good range of colours available. Trim ends of stems then dip into about 1 in/2.5cm of boiling water for a few seconds before transferring to cold water.

Carnation *(Dianthus sp.)*
Lasts well as a cut flower. Stems should be trimmed between joints before standing in shallow warm water.

Chrysanethemum *(Chrysanthemum sp.)*
Lasts fairly well. Stem ends should be crushed before soaking in cool water.

Cornflower *(Centaurea dealbata)*
Deep blue colour. Trim stems and arrange in water.

Daffodil *(Narcissus sp.)*
Lasts fairly well. Inexpensive. Trim stems and arrange in cool, shallow water.

Dahlia *(Dahlia sp.)*
Brightly coloured. Trim stems and arrange in water.

Delphinium *(Delphinium sp.)*
Tall, blue and purple. Turn them upside down, fill stems with water and plug with cotton wool.

Forget-me-not *(Myosotis sylvatica)*
Lasts fairly well.

Freesia *(Freesia sp.)*
Good scent. Trim stems and arrange in cool, shallow water.

Gerbera *(Gerbera sp.)*
Good range of bright colours. Trim stems diagonally and dip into boiling water for a few seconds before arranging in cool water.

Gladiola *(Gladiola sp.)*
Tall, red, yellow, orange or white flowers. Trim stems and arrange in cool, shallow water.

Gypsophila *(Gypsophila paniculata)*
Tiny white flowers. Look good arranged with roses.

Iris *(Iris sp.)*
Blue, purple and yellow flowers. Does not last very long. Trim stems diagonally before soaking.

Lily *(Lilium sp.)*
White, pink and orange with different patterns and markings. Split stems vertically and arrange in cold water.

Peony *(Paeonia sp.)*
Pink and red. Trim stems and place in warm water.

Poppy *(Papaver sp.)*
Red flowers. Burn stems with a flame until the tip goes black.

Rose *(Rosa sp.)*
Long-lasting cut flowers. Crush stem ends and dip in boiling water for up to 20 seconds before arranging.

Scabious *(Scabiosa sp.)*
Blue or white flowers. Arrange in tall vase of cool water.

Stock *(Matthiola sp.)*
Good scent; pink, white and mauve. Do not last very well. Crush stem ends and strip lower leaves.

Sunflower *(Helianthus annuus)*
Cut ends and place in deep container of water. If they start to droop, immerse the whole plant in warm water.

Sweet pea *(Lathyrus odoratus)*
Good scent and range of colours; lasts fairly well. Trim stems and place in cool, deep water.

Tulip *(Tulipa sp.)*
Last well as cut flowers; good range of colours. Trim stems diagonally and arrange in cool, shallow water. Stop the heads drooping by pricking the stem with a pin just under the head.

How to dry flowers

The three chief methods of preserving flowers and foliage are

- by air
- using drying agents (dessicants)
- with glycerine

Most garden flowers can be dried. The secret of drying plants successfully is to pick them at their best. Gather them on a dry day, ideally around noon when the plant is well nourished. Choose blooms that are just about to peak – they will open up when you dry them.

Colours alter as the flowers dry – all will fade to some degree. Some shades hold their colour better than others – for example, red and mustard yellow dry successfully, while pink and yellow can look dirty and blue does not hold well.

Drying by air

The simplest and most common form of drying flowers. Hang them upside down in bunches in an airy place out of direct sunlight. Turn them around occasionally if necessary. Some flowers – for instance, teasels or pompon chrysanthemums – dry better if placed upright in a container or piece of foam.

Others – like hydrangea or gypsophila – benefit from being dried in a little water. Don't top it up once it has evaporated.

Using drying agents

This is the best way as flowers retain their colour and form. The most common drying agent is silica gel, which is available from chemists. It comes in blue or white crystals – the blue turns pink as they absorb the moisture.

Cover the bottom of an airtight container and lay the flowers on the top. Gently spoon more crystals over the flowers. Attach the lid and leave until dry – the petals should feel like tissue. This might take anything from one to four days.

You can also use borax for drying flowers. This is cheaper than silica gel but is slower, taking up to two weeks. Mix the borax with dry silver sand (3:2).

Using a microwave oven can help speed up the drying process. Pack the flowers and silica gel as described above and place them in the oven, uncovered, together with a glass of water. Set the oven to high power and microwave for one to four minutes.

Preserving with glycerine

This is only suitable for foliage and enables you to dry it with a supple and glossy finish. Some plants ideal for drying by this method are bracken, hawthorn, eucalyptus and beech.

Mix one part glycerine to two parts hot water. Pour a little into a tall container. Bash the ends of the stems with a rolling pin and stand them in the solution. Gradually the plants will drink the mixture, turning a rich bronze shade in the process. This will take about four weeks.

Arranging dried flowers

Attaching wires to flowers makes them much easier to handle and arrange. Wires can be purchased from florist shops. To attach the wire, take a flower in one hand and carefully bind the wire three times around the stem.

You can cover the wired flower stems with tape, also available from florist's. Hold the wired flower in one hand and, starting at the top of the wire, twist and pull the stem tape round it tightly till the wire is covered.

Finally, you will find brown florist's foam best for dried flower arrangements.

**Herbs to discourage insects:
Bay, basil, mint, pennyroyal,
rosemary, elder, rue**

A – Z of dried flowers

Carnation
Preserve with dessicants

Chrysanthemum
Some can be preserved with dessicants

Dahlia
Some can be preserved with dessicants

Delphinium
Air dry or preserve with dessicants

Freesia
Preserve with dessicants

Gypsophila
Air dry

Love-in-the-mist
Seed heads can be air dried

Peony
Air dry or preserve with dessicants

Poppy
Seed heads can be air dried

Rose
Air dry or preserve with dessicants; can also be dried in a microwave

Scabious
Preserve with dessicants

Sea lavender
Air dry

Statice
Air dry

Strawflower
Dry by hanging upside down

Sunflower
Dry by hanging upside down

Pot pourri around the home

Capture the fragrance of dried flowers, herbs, aromatic seeds and foliage by making your own pot pourri. Adding essentials oils will give depth and intensity to your pot pourri mixture and will impart a delicious perfume around the house. You can use lavender for perfuming bed linen; rose petals and clover for a sleep pillow; wild flowers for scenting wedding gifts; roses and bay leaves for fragrant drawer liners and writing paper; pine shavings and bay leaves to perfume a coat hanger or a pillow.

> **Remember that you can use spices from the store cupboard for 'fixing' the fragrance in your pot pourri. Cinnamon, mixed spice, cloves, nutmeg and sea salt are all suitable.**

With pot pourri there are few rules: you can use virtually any flower, herb, grass, seed or foliage. Gather them on a dry day and discard any bruised or damaged materials. You can create your own recipes, adding different herbs and flowers, or mixing oils and spices to produce an original fragrance. Bear in mind colour and texture as well as perfume. It is a good idea to keep a few whole flowers in reserve for sprinkling on top of your pot pourri.

How to make pot pourri

Spread the flower heads on sheets of newspaper and leave in a warm, airy place to dry. Check on progress every few days. Store dried materials in airtight containers until you are ready. Keep flowers groups separate.

The dried material will have a subtle fragrance but this will begin to fade if you do not use a fixative. Orris root is perfect for this, although you can also use other products from the pantry such as cinnamon, mixed spice, cloves, nutmeg, sea salt, lemon and orange peel.

Mix together all the ingredients in a big wooden or glass bowl. Next introduce the fixative and lastly add a drop or two of essential oil. Combine well and store in an airtight container for about four to six weeks. This is to ensure that the mixture has matured and that the perfume is held.

Essential oils

Made by distilling different kinds of plant material, essential oils are an important fixative for pot pourri mixtures.

All essential oils should be used with caution: they are not to be taken internally and should not be used on the skin or used instead of aromatherapy oils.

To keep them at their best, store oils in plastic bottles, in a cool place. Do not let them come into contact with varnished wood or a naked flame and keep them out of the way of children.

The best way to add essential oils is a with a dropper – and one single drop will greatly enhance a pot pourri fragrance.

Flowers suitable for pot pourri:

- **Geranium**
- **heather**
- **lavender**
- **chamomile**
- **lemon balm**
- **marigold**
- **rose**
- **pansy**
- **yarrow**

CHAPTER FOUR
Food and drink

Gilly Cubitt

Editor of Essentials; previously deputy editor of Family Circle and cookery editor of Woman.

There are thousands of cookbooks from which to choose recipes representing countries around the world. This is not another cookbook, but a comprehensive guide to all you need to know about setting up, running and enjoying your own kitchen. You'll find advice on planning and equipping your kitchen so you can decide exactly what you will need, and go shopping for equipment fully armed with information and the right questions. If you've ever wondered who you could possibly ask about the best way to get enough Vitamin D, how to fillet a trout, which knife and fork you should lay where, what on earth a *bain marie* is, and what Chablis actually tastes like, the answer is to look no further. You'll find all this information and more in this chapter.

Your kind of kitchen

A well-designed kitchen saves time and effort on the part of the cook. The basic principle of good kitchen design is to create an efficient work 'triangle'. This allows that food and equipment generally moves from storage to the cooker via the sink, with all these areas being linked by work-surfaces. For example, you take meat and vegetables from the fridge or freezer and vegetable rack, wash them at the sink, chop and mix them on the work surface and then cook them. The process also works in reverse. Some of the food may need to be drained at the sink before dishing-up, leftovers are returned to the fridge, washing-up follows.

Where do I start?

Whether you're starting from scratch or just updating your kitchen, remember that the ideal plan keeps the work triangle – the distance between sink-cooker-fridge – as short as possible. It is possible to create this work triangle in any shape of kitchen and any style, from English country kitchen to Mediterranean-style to the highest high-tech – and any in between!

Small kitchens

Corridor kitchen

You've not much choice but to position all units and the sink-cooker-fridge in the same run of units. Make maximum use of wall-mounted cupboards to keep the minimal work-surface clear.

Galley kitchen

Fit units along both sides – try to allow 145 cm (4 ft) between facing units to allow for bending and opening doors – with one of the work-triangle elements on the opposite side to the others two.

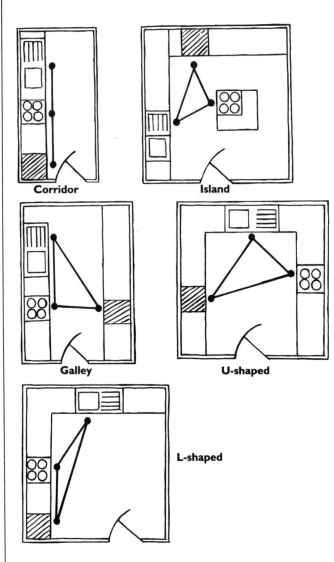

Corridor   **Island**

Galley   **U-shaped**

L-shaped

▲ **Design your kitchen around your work triangle.**

Average kitchens

L-Shape

Arrange runs of units at a right angle around two sides of the kitchen, with one of the work-triangle elements on one side, two on the other. This is especially useful in a kitchen with more than one door or where you want space for a table and chairs.

U-Shape

Arrange units around three sides of the kitchen, with one work-triangle element in each side. Remember to keep the triangle as short as possible, or you'll be walking around more than necessary.

Large kitchens

Island

A central island unit containing one of the work-triangle elements – a hob or fridge – will reduce the distance from one side of the kitchen to the other, and can provide informal eating space.

Planning on paper

Draw a floor plan of your kitchen to scale on graph paper, putting in doors, windows, water, gas and electric service points. Cut to scale paper shapes to represent any units, equipment, and furniture you want or need to incorporate, and move them around on the floor plan to determine the best arrangement. If you are going for a fitted kitchen, check manufacturer's brochures for dimensions – although most are standardised, many manufacturers offer slimline and larger appliances as well. Most kitchen unit manufacturers offer a free planning service – many can provide computerised three-dimensional drawings so you can get a clearer impression of the end result. Shop around for the best service and prices.

Pre-planning pointers

Start your plan by deciding what you would like for the three key areas – sink-cooker-fridge/freezer.

Sink

Decide whether you need one or two sinks and on which side you prefer a draining board.

If you opt for one sink, a small **half-sink** is helpful for rinsing, washing vegetables or hands, or disposing of slops, while the sink is full of washing-up water.

A **waste disposal** in the half-sink is a useful extra especially if you don't have a compost heap.

Sinks are made from stainless steel, fibreglass, plastic or ceramic.

Light-coloured sinks can stain in time, dark sinks can show up limescale, and stainless steel can scratch.

Draining racks, cutlery baskets and draining board extenders are accessories you may like to consider.

Cooker

You may have a choice of fuels – gas, electric or solid fuel – and most people have a preference. The technology is constantly updated so it is worth shopping around to decide which features are best for you. See *Choosing large equipment*, pp. 165-8.

☞ Don't site a cooker in a corner where it's difficult to get to, or under a window where people might need to stretch across it. Plan in a work-surface on each side.

☞ A built-in oven at eye level occupies valuable work-surface space in a small kitchen.

Fridge and freezer

Again, there are many options available, see *Choosing large equipment*, pp. 168-72.

What else do I need?

Work-surface

Make all worktops at the same height, for most people waist-height is about right. Many cabinets are standard height, but you can adjust the plinth according to the height you need. Some companies are now offering work-surfaces that go up and down to suit whomever is using them at any particular time!

As far as possible, have a seamless surface to avoid food getting caught in cracks. Go for a smooth, tough, easy-clean surface like laminated plastic. Tile surfaces look good but can be cracked by heavy pans and the grouting will eventually discolour. Solid wood needs regular oiling.

Create a splashback around messy areas like hobs and sinks. Washable paint or tiles are suitable for this.

Power supply

Decide as you go, where you will need to position electric-plug sockets to make them accessible but not in the way, and how many you will need for both large and small cooking equipment, laundry and ironing, lighting and vacuuming.

Water supply

This may be established and immovable, in which case you will have to work around it. As a rule, try to keep all equipment needing plumbing – sink, dishwasher, washing machine – as close together as possible.

Storage

Aim to keep equipment near to where it is likely to be used; i.e., saucepans near the cooker, cleaning materials near the sink, etc.

Use wall-mounted cupboards and shelves for storage to keep work-surfaces clear, especially in a small kitchen.

Many kitchen unit ranges offer shelves, baskets and other accessories that are specially designed to take advantage of the space under the wall units and above the work-surface.

Consider a carousel fitting inside deep corner cupboards, it cuts down on the available space but does make items more easily accessible.

Use the more awkward storage spaces – the corners or highest points – for items that are used less frequently.

Keep electrical aids like mixers or food processors out on a surface – if you have to dig it out of the cupboard, it probably won't get used.

Flooring

Your choice of flooring will partly be dependent on the floor beneath – whether it is solid or wooden boards. Wooden floors often have too much movement for ceramic tiles. Vinyl flooring or carpet tiles need a smooth, level surface so it may be necessary to hardboard over the floor first.

Kitchen floors need to be hard-wearing – there's a lot of traffic – and also easy to clean.

Check the surface won't be slippery when wet.

Soft flooring, like cork tiles, cushioned vinyl or rubber are easier on your legs when you stand for long periods.

Ceramic or quarry tiles look great but are harder and colder than other floors – and anything breakable can shatter quite spectacularly if dropped on these tiles. Perhaps not the most practical for children.

Lighting

This is important for safety's sake and to create the right atmosphere. A single central light is of no use – you'll always be working with your back to it, in your own shadow.

Consider where the natural light falls. Some people like the sink under a window so they can enjoy the view. If you eat in the kitchen you may prefer your table by the window.

Fluorescent lights fitted under wall-mounted cupboards throw light directly on to the work-surface.

Spotlights on tracks can be useful, to light an island unit or display shelves.

If you have a dining area in the kitchen, plan more subtle lighting, perhaps with a dimmer switch to adjust the mood in that part of the room.

Ventilation

Kitchens can be hot steamy places, and without good ventilation condensation will form. Obviously you can open windows and/or doors, but this may not be suitable in winter, or if you have small children around. Some extra help may be required.

Cooking smells are a delicious appetite stimulant, but you don't want them to linger for hours! A cooker hood fitted over the hob will extract smells and smoke (see *Choosing large equipment*, page 167).

An extractor fan fitted into a window or a wall can be used as extra ventilation for busy cooking sessions. An efficient one should change the air in the room at least ten times an hour.

Eating area

Even if you have a separate dining room, you may want space in the kitchen for breakfast or informal eating.

In a small kitchen, a breakfast bar, with chairs or high stools, or an island unit, can make a casual eating area. Or a half-table, fastened to the wall and able to fold down, may be the answer.

In a larger kitchen, units arranged so they jut out into an open area as a 'peninsula' can form a room divider between the kitchen and a table and chairs.

Display

A kitchen gets its character from its finishing touches. A stream-lined, high-tech kitchen may look best minus cooking paraphernalia, while country-style kitchens cry out for a dresser laden with pretty china and clutter. Allow for this individual style when you are planning your ideal kitchen, because it may affect your storage and lighting plans.

Choosing large equipment

Cookers

Your own cooker is perhaps the most potent symbol of independent life. Here are some guidelines for choosing the one that's right for you.

What fuel?

You may not have total freedom of choice – check what services are, or can be, laid on to your home. The traditional differences between cooking with gas and cooking with electricity have been reduced by improved technology but, generally speaking:

A **gas hob** offers instant reaction. **Electric plates** or **radiant rings** adjust more slowly. Electric plates keep things warmer for longer after the heat has been turned off.

Electricity is cleaner and the oven temperature is considered to be more even.

Solid-fuel cookers are harder work – they need fuelling (and space to store the fuel), as well as regular emptying and cleaning. Different cooking techniques are also required, but solid fuel cookers do provide constant oven and hob heat.

 Green Tip   Friends of the Earth research shows that running appliances like fridges, washing machines, cookers and televisions accounts for about one-fifth of all the electricity produced in the UK. If we were to choose and use the most energy-efficient appliances available, a UK Government report suggests a 45 per cent savings on this figure. And that could mean £65 pounds a year less on your electricity bill, too.

Green Tip   Friends of the Earth suggest that swapping from an electric cooker to gas, would save on average per year
* **360 kg of carbon dioxide**
* **4.8 per cent of your household emissions**
* **£25**

What's on offer?

Unlike many other appliances there is relatively little difference in the size and shape of today's cookers, whatever fuel they use.

• **Free-Standing Models** with one or two ovens, four burners or plates, a grill and possibly a plate-warming/storage drawer. Offers flexibility of siting, subject to position of gas or main cooker point, and you can take it with you when you move.

• **Slip-In Models** are free-standing models designed to fit into a run of units to give a built-in look. They tend not to have splashbacks, or eye-level grills, but they may have a lid which provides extra work surface when the hob is not in use. Free-standing and slip-in models still account for 80 per cent of cooker sales in the UK.

• **Built-In Models** come in two parts. The oven is usually sited between the wall-mounted and floor-standing kitchen units in a fitted kitchen, so there is no bending to the oven. A separate hob is set into an adjacent work-surface. More suitable for large kitchens where work-surface space is not at a premium and for households with small children as oven is out of reach.

• **Built-Under Models** are fitted in a housing in the run of floor-standing kitchen units, underneath the work-surface with the hob set into the work-surface. If the grill is situated in the oven you won't be able to use them simultaneously.

Once you've decide which type of cooker model you prefer, you have still more choices to make – **traditional** or **fan-assisted**? Traditional ovens have temperature zones. In a **gas oven** the temperature set by the thermostat is for the middle shelf. Shelves above will be at a slightly hotter temperature,

---

SAFETY NOTE Check your cooker has been tested and approved as having the highest safety standards. For gas cookers – British-made models should have the BSI (British Standards Institution) mark. European-made models should have an EN30 mark. For electric cookers – British models should have a BEAB (British Electrotechnical Approvals Board) mark. European models should have an EN60 mark.

---

shelves below slightly cooler. This can be useful when you are cooking more than one dish at a time.

In an **electric oven** the top and bottom thirds are the hottest zones, the centre is cooler. **Fan-assisted ovens** have a fan situated in the back wall of the oven which circulates the air and so evens out the temperature throughout the whole oven. They often have an extra shelf as they are ideal for batch cooking. If you do a lot of baking this could be the best oven for you. **Solid-fuel cookers** usually have two ovens, one hot and one cooler. The temperature is trickier to adjust.

Hobs

There are a number of types of cooker hobs available, and again, each has its particular uses.

Gas hobs

- ☞ Check for sealed hotplates with rounded corners for easy cleaning.
- ☞ Some have gas cut-off if a burner should go out.
- ☞ Check fold-down lids have a safety cut-off device which automatically shuts off gas if lid is closed while one of the burners is alight.
- ☞ Check for easy to reach, grip and use controls and clear markings as to which of the burners they operate.

- ☞ Look for automatic ignition or push-button spark ignition to save using matches.
- ☞ The pan racks may not be as stable as electric rings, especially for small pans.

Electric hobs

There is a considerable choice of electrically heated hobs.

- **Radiant Rings** are effective but can be difficult to clean. They may be dual-circuit; i.e., you can heat just the inner part of the ring for small pans or for simmering.
- **Solid Plates** take longer to heat up and cool down, but are easier to clean. There may be simmer control in one or more plates.
- **Ceramic Hobs** have a completely smooth surface of heat-resistant glass, so are easy to clean. Reaction to adjustment of temperature is fast. The position of the cooking 'rings' is marked and they glow when on. You need to use saucepans with machine-ground bases for good contact with the hot surface.
- **Halogen Hobs** are like ceramic hobs but with tungsten halogen lamps as the heat source. Temperature control is pretty much instant and cleaning is easy.
- **Magnetic Induction** is another ceramic hob, but heat is only produced when a ferrous (iron/steel) metal pan is placed on one of the marked rings. The molecules in the metal and magnets in the surface react to produce heat for cooking.

Solid fuel hobs

These consist of two huge, solid hot-plates, capable of taking more than one pan each. They are kept covered by a lid when not in use. Temperatures can also be controlled by moving pans so they are only partly on the hot plate.

Built-in hobs

Appart from solid fuel all the above can be built into a work-surface. You can also mix them. A mixed-fuel hob with two gas burners and two electric plates – solid, radiant, ceramic or halogen – is ideal. Use the gas for frying where you want good adjustability from the initial high temperature to the lower 'cooking through' heat. The electric plates are reliable for simmering and longer cooking. Some hobs come with extras like a griddle plate or deep-fryer.

Grills

Whatever fuel you are using, always check the following points:

- ☞ The position of the grill – do you prefer it at waist-height or eye-level?
- ☞ Can you use oven and grill simultaneously?
- ☞ Is there a dual-heat facility; i.e., can you use only half the grill for smaller quantities?
- ☞ Is the grill-pan handle well-balanced and easy to grip?
- ☞ Is the grill pan fully supported when pulled out so you can use both hands to turn the food?

Other extras

Think carefully before you spend about whether these extra functions are worthwhile for the kind of cooking you expect to do, because they all add to the price.

A second oven Many electric and solid fuel, and some gas cookers have a second small oven, also thermostatically controlled. This may double as a grill. Use this when you're just cooking one dish, and for plate-warming.

Stay-cool oven doors Essential for households with children, these special doors stay cool to the touch even when the oven is on.

See-through oven door and light Allow you to keep an eye on what's cooking without constantly opening the door and so reducing the temperature.

Self-cleaning linings Catalytic oven linings convert food splashes to carbon so they burn away. This makes one of the most tedious of kitchen cleaning jobs so much easier.

> **SAFETY NOTE** **Turn pan handles to the back or side of the hob; don't leave them sticking out where they can be knocked by passers-by or grabbed by a child.**

Automatic timer Allows you to set the start and finish times and temperature so that food can cook in your absence.

A spit/rotisserie Some grills are fitted with a rotating spit for roasting joints and poultry.

A griddle plate A solid plate that can be used for cooking steaks, burgers, drop scones, etc., or for keeping food hot.

Touch controls Technology is constantly updating and improving control panels. Expect more developments in this area.

> **Green Tip** **Don't heat more water than you need in pans and kettles.**

Do I need a cooker hood?

A cooker hood, sited above the hob, helps to remove steam – which causes condensation – cooking smells and greasy vapours, by sucking in air and filtering it. Some types are simply extractors and others recirculate the air. Most hoods also have built-in lighting which can be used separately.

Do I need a microwave oven?

These small free-standing or built-in ovens operate by stimulating the water molecules that all foods contain, with electro-magnetic waves. This causes rapid movement which creates enough heat to cook the food. These ovens are a very useful adjunct to a conventional cooker.

What microwave ovens do best

☞ Thawing frozen food, fast.

☞ Reheating food, fast.

☞ Cooking fish and vegetables to preserve their flavour, colour and texture.

☞ Melting chocolate, butter or gelatine.

☞ Speeding up cooking processes, e.g., cooking jacket potatoes.

Green 🌍 Tip **There are dozens of energy-saving tips that can be incorporated easily into your day-to-day life:**

• **Put lids on pans and reduce heat once the contents have boiled.**

• **Don't let gas flames lick up the sides of a pan, adjust the flame.**

• **Don't heat the main oven for just one item if you can help it. Use the smaller oven or cook the side-dishes, pudding or an extra lasagne/pie/cake for the freezer.**

• **Cook two vegetables on one burner; e.g., steam green vegetables in a metal colander on top of the potatoes.**

Friends of the Earth suggests that developing these energy efficient habits when using an electric cooker could save on average per year:

• **150 kg (325 lb) of carbon dioxide**

• **2 per cent of your household emissions**

• **£12**

What microwave ovens can't do

☞ Brown food (although some models do have a browning element).

☞ Cook large quantities.

☞ Make tough foods, like cheaper cuts of meat, tender.

Combined Microwave/ Conventional cookers offer flexibility, with faster cooking times and more traditional results.

Getting the best from your microwave oven

☞ Know the wattage of your oven. These vary and you should check that the model you select has the power to cook the kind of food you usually prepare.

☞ Check the wattage and the timing specified in a recipe. If your oven wattage is different the cooking time will need to be altered. Check your instruction manual for how to do this.

☞ Don't skip 'standing time' at the end of the cooking time. Food continues to cook after it has been removed from the oven.

☞ Don't cook in metal dishes or use foil (although prudent use, to shield corners of a cake to prevent overcooking, for instance, may be acceptable. Check your manufacturer's guidebook). Don't put your best china in if it has a metallic trim!

☞ Don't switch on an empty microwave oven.

☞ Follow recipe instructions about pricking, stirring and covering food during cooking.

☞ Follow cooking instructions on ready-made foods and always make sure food is piping hot when you eat it.

☞ Keep the interior of the oven, and especially the door seal, clean.

Choosing and using your fridge

What size?

Chances are, whatever size you buy you'll always fill it. As a rule of thumb allow one cubic foot (25 cm) of space per member of the household, plus one (25 cm) extra.

Free-standing or built-in?

This will depend on your kitchen plan (see *Your kind of kitchen*, pp. 161-4). Most are standard sizes to fit in with kitchen units. You may have a choice as to whether the door opens to left or right – again consult your kitchen plan for what will work best in your work triangle.

Star rating

Ice-making compartments in fridges have an efficiency-rating in the form of stars. Check it to make sure the fridge you choose will do what you need it to do. (see *safety note*, page 171).
* One star. Safe for storage of ready-frozen food for up to one week.
** Two stars. Safe for storage of ready-frozen food for up to one month.
*** Three stars. Safe storage for ready-frozen food for up to three months.
**** Four stars. Safe for freezing and storing fresh food – you'll see this mark on freezers, too.

SAFETY NOTE **You should not put in fresh, unfrozen meat, fish, vegetables or ready-meals and expect them to freeze safely in fridge ice-compartments that carry a star rating of less than two stars **.**

Painless defrosting

Look for models with **automatic defrost**. This happens continuously with the water dripping into a channel at the back of the fridge. This must be kept clean and clear. The water then evaporates on the compressor.

With **semi-automatic defrosting** you press a button to initiate defrosting, then empty the drip tray.

What's on offer?

Standard fridge

The body of this and other fridges is maintained at between 2 and 8°C (35 and 45°F), controlled by a thermostat. There is an automatic light that comes on as the door is opened. Features may include:
❉ an ice-making compartment (see *Star rating*)
❉ salad crisper drawer
❉ door storage for eggs, dairy products and bottles
❉ top shelf with hinged section for taller bottles.

Standard fridges may be built-in under a work surface or higher as long as you can reach the ice-making compartment.

Larder fridge

As above, but without an ice-making compartment. This model is perfectly acceptable when you have a separate freezer in which you can make ice and store frozen foods. Can also be built in under units or at eye level.

American-style fridges

Usually the size of a wardrobe, with double doors and fitted with all sorts of gadgetry, such as drink-dispensers fitted in the outside of the door, ice-cube makers and dispensers. You need plenty of space and money.

Use a fridge thermometer to ensure the upper shelves don't get too warm without ice compartment to cool them.

Fridge/Freezer

Can be free-standing or built-in. The two compartments – fridge and freezer – share the same compressor. The size of the two compartments varies so you should be able to find the combination that works for you. The fridge section is a larder fridge (see above), and the freezer will normally be fitted with shelves or drawers and possibly a fast-freeze section. Generally it's more convenient to have the fridge on top.

Green Tip New energy-efficient fridges are available and may even be cheaper than conventional ones. According to Friends of the Earth, if you buy a new fridge, which runs on less than 150 units of electricity a year, you would save on average each year:
- 160 kg (360 lb) of carbon dioxide
- 2.1 per cent of your household emissions
- average cost: nothing to £40 above the cost of a typical model
- £14

If you need to buy a new fridge/freezer, buying one which runs on less than 350 units of electricity a year would save, on average, per year:
- 320 kg (720 lb) of carbon dioxide
- 4.2 per cent of your household emissions
- average cost: nothing to £50 above the cost of a typical model.
- £25

❄ Look for ozone-and-climate-friendly fridges containing propane and butane, instead of CFCs. Many fridges are reducing CFCs to use 50 per cent less, but the substitutes – HCFCs and HFCs – are still greenhouse gases.

❄ Don't dump your old fridge and risk CFCs escaping to damage the ozone layer. Check with your local authority and press for your fridge to be collected as part of a CFC reclamation scheme.

How to use your fridge

Set thermostat between 0°C (32°F) and 5°C (41°F) Check with a fridge thermometer. You may need to alter the thermostat in very hot weather or when the fridge is very full.

The atmosphere inside a fridge has a very drying effect. Wrap foods to prevent drying and smells transferring – milk and eggs easily pick up strong odours. But leave a bit of space inside wrappings for air to circulate

COOK'S TIP Store eggs pointed-end down in the rack. For some recipes, they need to be allowed to come to room temperature before use. Also, remove meat for roasting from the fridge at least an hour before cooking, so cooking starts from room temperature, not fridge temperature, which could alter the cooking time.

Don't mix raw and cooked food, as cross-contamination can occur. Keep cooked foods and food, like cheese, which may be eaten uncooked, near the top of the fridge. Keep raw meat and fish in the centre on a large dish and covered so juices can't drip on to vegetables and fruit on the bottom shelf. Keep salad stuff in the crisper drawer.

Green Tip Don't leave the fridge door open for longer than absolutely necessary. Don't put hot food in the fridge or it will raise the internal temperature.

Choosing and using your freezer

What size?

Like fridges, this depends on how many of you there are in the household. But it depends more on what sort of cooking you do, how you like to shop, and whether you grow your own fruit or vegetables and want to freeze them. A small freezer – probably a fridge/freezer model – will suffice if you tend to buy ready-meals and just want room for a spare loaf of bread and some ice-cubes.

Free-standing or built-in?

Consult your kitchen plan. You'll also have to decide which way you want the door to open, if you're buying an upright. Chest freezers tend to be big and bulky and many people prefer to put them in a utility room or secure garage.

What's on offer?

All freezers work by maintaining an internal temperature of 0°C (-18°F). At this low temperature the action of bacteria and enzymes which cause food to spoil, are arrested. Many freezers have a fast-freeze area and a control which reduces the temperature further to speed up initial freezing. This causes smaller ice-crystals to form so the structure of the food is not damaged as it would be by large jagged crystals formed by slow freezing. After a few hours – depending on how much food is being frozen at once – the fast-freeze action can be switched off and the freezer returned to its usual temperature.

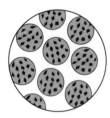 

▲ **Small ice-crystals formed by fast freezing**

▲ **Large, jagged ice-crystals caused by slow freezing**

Upright freezers

Available in many sizes as free-standing models or built-in. They have shelves or drawers to make storage more convenient and orderly; for example, you might keep all meat in one drawer, and baked goods in another. Many have their own in-built labelling system.

> **SAFETY NOTE** Check the star rating system (see page 169). If the freezer doesn't have a four-star rating it is only suitable for storing ready-frozen food.

Chest freezers

Although bulky, these are cheaper to run as less cold air is lost when the lid is opened. Choose one if you plan to freeze bulky items, your own homegrown produce or you cater for a crowd on a regular basis. Disadvantages include having to rummage through it to find anything (although hanging baskets in the top help organise the contents), awkwardness of cleaning and the need to keep the top clear if it's in pretty regular use.

> **Green Tip** **Empty freezer space wastes energy. Try and keep it as full as possible, and keep the door or lid open for the minimum amount of time.**

How to use your freezer

❄ Tape over the plug and socket switch so the freezer doesn't get turned off by mistake!

❄ Check your freezer is on and working properly regularly, especially if it's out of sight in a garage or utility room.

❄ Freezing arrests breakdown and spoilage, it doesn't reverse it. So freeze fresh, good-quality foods only.

❄ Freezers have a very drying action. Wrap food very well in heavy-duty foil or polyethylene bags. Overwrap supermarket packs or contents will suffer freezer-burn. This makes the surface look very dry, pale and fibrous and spoils the texture.

❄ Label all freezer packages. Frozen, cleaned squid can look remarkably similar to stewed apples six months later and doesn't make nearly such a good Sunday pudding.

❄ Don't keep food too long. Generally fatty foods keep least well.

❄ Here's a rough guide to how long food can be safely kept in the freezer:

Meat and poultry – joints
and made-up dishes ....6 months
Pork and pork products ..3 months
Fish and fish products......3 months
Seafood, shellfish ....I month
Cakes and biscuits,
baked goods ....6 months
Made-up puddings
and desserts......................6 months
Fruit and vegetables ......I2 months
Ice cream..........................3 months

POWER CUT! Don't open the freezer and let precious cold air escape. Food will stay frozen up to twelve hours, longer if your freezer is packed full. After a lengthy power cut, switch on fast-freeze for a few hours to reduce temperature quickly.

❄ Spread open-freeze squashable foods like meatballs, piped cream rosettes or raspberries out on a baking tray. Pack in rigid containers once frozen. Treat vegetables the same way, then bag, to make free-flow packs where you can shake out just the amount you need.

❄ Most vegetables need to be blanched before freezing. Check your freezer instruction manual.

❄ Leave headspace – room for expansion – in the top of polyethylene boxes.

❄ Don't put all your tins and dishes in the freezer. Use a large piece of foil to line the dish, add the food and freeze until solid. Remove block of food, wrap in the foil and put in a polyethylene bag in the freezer. Unwrap and return to the original dish to thaw and reheat.

❄ Pastries and other crisp items need to be 'refreshed' – re-crisped – after thawing. Put in a hot oven for just a few minutes.

❄ Not all food is suitable for freezing. Consult your freezer manual.

❄ Defrosting – you'll need to do this once or twice a year, preferably when the freezer is at its emptiest.

❄ Don't re-freeze thawed frozen foods, especially ice-cream, dairy products, seafood and meat.

❄ Some foods must be thawed thoroughly before cooking – especially poultry and pork. Many foods can be safely cooked from frozen, but make sure they are properly heated through. Food must be piping hot all the way through to the centre to be safe to eat.

A cook's tools

'Bad workmen blame their tools,' goes the old saying, and in the kitchen it is certainly true that the right tools make the job much easier.

Knives

Essentials

☞ A small (7.5 cm/3 in blade) paring knife for peeling and trimming vegetables and fruit

☞ A utility knife (15 cm/6 in blade) for general slicing and dicing

☞ A chopping knife (20 cm/8 in blade) for chopping and slicing

☞ A bread knife with a (25 cm/10 in) serrated blade

☞ Palette knife – with a long, extra-flexible, round-ended blade for lifting and spreading

Useful extras

☞ Carving knife – with a long (30 cm/11 in) slim, flexible blade

☞ Grapefruit knife – with a short serrated blade, curved to cut under the segments

Best buys

● Look for a knife where the blade metal continues in one piece inside the handle – this is called the **tang**. In the strongest knives, the tang runs all the way through the handle, held in place by rivets.

● Stainless steel knives blunt more quickly than carbon steel, but carbon steel blades discolour when in contact with acid foods.

Care

- Store knives in a block or rack, not in a drawer where they can get damaged or cut someone.
- Don't use knives for cutting paper or string or levering off lids.
- Don't leave knives in washing-up water, it loosens handles and can cause cuts to unwary washers-up.
- Use knives on a wooden or polypropylene board, not on a hard surface, which can damage the blade.
- Sharpen knives on a steel. Hold the steel point-down in a dishcloth. Press the handle-end of the knife blade at a 45-degree angle to it and slide it down and towards you in one smooth movement (so the whole length of the blade is wiped against the whole length of the steel). Repeat several times. Repeat the process on the other side of the knife blade.
- Knife-sharpening gadgets are available and some are very effective – but they will wear away the blade more quickly than using a steel.

Chopping boards

Essentials

- ☞ A wooden or polypropylene board for chopping and slicing fruit and vegetables
- ☞ A separate board reserved for raw meat, poultry or fish

Useful extras

- ☞ Bread board
- ☞ Cheese board

Best buys

- A large board, so you've plenty of space, but not too thick and heavy. Price is a good guide when choosing a wooden board.
- Polypropylene boards are available with colour-coded handles so you can confine use to one type of food; e.g., raw meat.

Care

- Don't leave boards soaking in water, the surface will soften and boards may split.
- Scrub with a stiff brush, wipe with kitchen paper then leave to dry at room temperature. High heat may warp the board.

Graters and slicers

Essentials

- ☞ A multi-purpose grater

Useful extras

- ☞ Parmesan grater – a container put on the table so each diner can grate cheese over their pasta, without actually handling the cheese
- ☞ Nutmeg grater – some conical ones can store nutmegs inside
- ☞ Hand-held bean-slicer – a tiny gadget with a series of blades through which you push runner beans to make fine, even slices

Best buys

- A pyramid-shaped stainless-steel grater with several different grating surfaces. Some surfaces consist of small curved raised blades. Use the coarsest ones for cheese and vegetables, the finest ones for citrus rind. Other surfaces are made of jagged punched holes. Use the coarsest for breadcrumbs, the very finest for nutmeg. The pyramid shape stands steadily on a board and allows plenty of food inside without clogging.

Care

- Wash in soapy water, using a stiff brush if necessary to unclog holes.

Measuring equipment

Essentials

- ☞ Weighing scales – either spring-balance or traditional balance scales with weights, and Imperial and Metric options
- ☞ A heatproof measuring jug with Imperial and Metric calibrations. Heatproof glass jugs make it easy to check the level of liquid inside. A large jug (1 litre/1 ¾ pt) is the most versatile but make sure there are a lot of calibrations and they are easy to read
- ☞ A set of standard measuring spoons

Useful extras

- ☞ American cups for following American recipes
- ☞ Smaller measuring jug – more accurate for small quantities

Best buys

- ● Choose scales with a large scale pan. If choosing the type where you weigh your own bowl first, check a large bowl won't obscure the dial.
- ● When measuring liquid, put jug on a level surface and bend so you read the calibration at eye level.
- ● Check that calibrations are easy to read.
- ● Wall-mounted spring-balance scales save space on the work-surface.
- ● Traditional balance scales look attractive and are useful for large quantities.

Care

- ● Check scales are on zero before starting to weigh. Most are adjusted by a simple screw.
- ● Keep loose weights in a safe place.

Bowls

Essentials

- ☞ Large mixing bowl
- ☞ Pudding basins in different sizes

Best buys

- ☞ Toughened, heatproof glass. Plastic bowls are light but can't be used over hot water like glass. Stoneware bowls can be heavy.

Care

- ● Don't drop them!

Tools and utensils

Essentials

- ☞ Slotted spoon – for lifting and draining
- ☞ Fish/egg slice
- ☞ Hand whisk – choose a spiral or balloon whisk
- ☞ Sieve
- ☞ Ladle
- ☞ Kitchen fork
- ☞ Tongs
- ☞ Potato masher
- ☞ Wooden spoons
- ☞ Kitchen scissors
- ☞ Corkscrew
- ☞ Potato peeler
- ☞ Rolling pin
- ☞ Pastry brush
- ☞ Rubber spatula

Useful extras

- ☞ Skewers
- ☞ Poultry shears
- ☞ Cooking thermometer
- ☞ Garlic press
- ☞ Melon baller
- ☞ Piping bag and nozzles
- ☞ Pastry cutters

Best buys

- ● Look for stainless steel tools with well-fixed handles.
- ● Check tools are well-balanced and comfortable to hold.
- ● Use special plastic tools in non-stick pans.

Care

- ● Hang the tools you use most on a rack or stand them in a jug so they are always at hand.

- Don't leave wooden handles soaking in washing-up water, or they will loosen.

Saucepans

Essentials

- ☞ Small milkpan with pouring lip
- ☞ 4 saucepans in varying sizes, with lids
- ☞ Steel colander, to double as a steamer
- ☞ Non-stick frying pan (cuts down on fat needed for frying)

Useful extras

- ☞ Omelette pan – don't use it for other frying
- ☞ Egg poaching pan – you may be able to get a poaching set that will fit in your ordinary frying pan
- ☞ Deep-fat frying pan
- ☞ Double saucepan – for sauces or porridge
- ☞ Preserving pan – for jams and pickles, bulk cooking
- ☞ Fish kettle – for poaching whole fish

Pans are available in many different materials. Choose from:

Aluminium – easy to clean but can be marked by acid food or boiling water.

Stainless steel – thin bases can cause burning in 'hot spots'. Ideally choose ones with copper bases, but they are expensive.

Enamel-coated steel – often decorative exteriors; cheap, but food has a tendency to stick and burn.

Non-stick – many different non-stick surfaces are available, some much better than others. Price is generally a good guide.

Cast iron – attractive pans which give even cooking; but very heavy, especially the larger sizes.

Best buys

- Saucepans and frying pans with fairly heavy, even bases.
- Ground-base pans for cooking on electric hobs. Thin pans burn in 'hot spots' and can become misshapen and wobbly with use.

- Handles and lid knobs should be heatproof and well-secured.
- The handle should balance the pan – feel strong and well-supported even when the pan is full and heavy.
- Lids should fit tightly.

Care

- Use plastic tools in non-stick pans, and don't stack them or they'll scratch. Hang them up.
- Try and avoid burning food so you don't need to scour aluminium or steel pans. Boil water in them to loosen burned-on food and scrape gently with a wooden spatula.
- Keep pans in a dry place.

Baking tins

Essentials

- ☞ Roasting tin (may come with your cooker)
- ☞ 2 baking trays
- ☞ Wire cooling rack

Useful extras

- ☞ Bun tray
- ☞ Flan tin
- ☞ 2 sandwich tins
- ☞ Round or square cake tins – 19 or 20 cm (7 or 8 in) are probably the most useful sizes
- ☞ Spring-form tin

Best buys

- Sturdy tins that don't bend and flex and won't rust. Some have non-stick linings, but cost more.

Care

- Treat them gently so they don't get dented or scratched, or they may rust.
- After washing return them to a still-warm oven to dry completely.

Electric labour savers

There is a huge selection of electrical gadgetry to help today's cook. What you need depends on the type of cooking you do. Try to assess how often you will use the device, before you buy, and if it is worth:

- ☞ the money
- ☞ the space it will take in the kitchen
- ☞ the effort of assembling it to use it
- ☞ the effort of dismantling and cleaning.

Then shop around to check out the latest developments and the keenest prices.

Blenders and liquidisers. A tall jug with rotating cutting blades at the bottom. *Best for:* puréeing fruits, soup, making small quantities of breadcrumbs. Mainly good with wet mixtures.

Grinders. Smaller versions of blenders but with tougher blades for hard foods. *Best for:* dry food – coffee beans, nuts, whole spices Keep your spice grinder for spices alone, the flavours will transfer otherwise.

Food processors. Giant blender/mixers with a large bowl and a range of functions. *Best for:* The metal chopping blade prefers drier mixtures – lots of liquid will swish around, so you may need to purée the lumps of a soup in just a little of the liquid, then mix it. A plastic blade is provided for mixing cakes, batters etc. Most machines have grater and slicer plates, some offer whisks (food processors won't whisk egg whites unless without this attachment) – and dough hooks for kneading bread. Check the booklet for details.

Food mixers. May be hand-held or come with a bowl and a stand to leave your hands free. *Best for:* aerating mixtures, making sponges, meringues. Creaming cake mixtures, whipping cream.

Kettle. For your cooker (get one that whistles) or an electric kettle, with automatic cut-out when boiling.

Toaster. Uses less fuel than switching on the grill. Choose one that takes items of different thickness; e.g., muffins or crumpets as well as thin-sliced toast, and 'pops up' toast once it's done.

Deep-fat fryer. A large pan with a frying basket and a special lid that filters grease and cooking smells. It's thermostatically controlled so food cooks at the correct temperature. *Best for:* a family who eat a lot of fried food! They are bulky, take a lot of oil (although it can be strained and used again) and are difficult to clean.

Microwave oven (See *Choosing large equipment*, pp.167-8)

Crockery

You need two main types of crockery – the plates and bowls, cups and saucers you'll eat off, and the dishes that you'll cook, and possibly serve in.

- ☞ You may want a dinner service in fine china for entertaining, and cheap and cheerful stoneware for everyday eating.
- ☞ Check it's dishwasher-proof, if you have one.
- ☞ Serving dishes can be oven-to-table glass, classic French white porcelain, terracotta dishes brought back from your holiday, or a junk-shop find. The choice depends on your taste and your budget – most homes end up with a mixture of the lot!

Glass

The same rules apply to glasses. Is it worth having glasses you're frightened to use? Serious wine drinkers like thin glass with a tulip-shaped bowl to trap the bouquet, but there are no firm rules about wine or any other glasses. If you do decide to collect a matching set, check replacements will remain available. Bric-a-brac buy glasses can also be delightful.

SHOPPING TIP **If you are going to collect a formal dinner service, choose one that won't date, and check that pieces will be available for the foreseeable future. You might be able to register with the company who makes them, and they'll advise you when they plan to discontinue a range so that you can buy some pieces in advance.**

A to Z of cooking terms and techniques

All you need to know to understand any recipe!

Acidulate

To make water acidic, by the addition of lemon juice. Used to prevent fruit or vegetables browning after peeling and slicing; e.g., apples for a pie left in acidulated water will not discolour, as they would if left exposed to air.

> **COOK'S TIP Float a plate on the surface of the acidulated water to hold the fruit in.**

Activate yeast

Yeast needs moisture (and warmth and food in the form of sugar or flour) in order to start creating the carbon dioxide gas that gives it its rising qualities. Fresh yeast is creamed with water then added to the dry ingredients. Dried yeast granules are sprinkled over warm water and left in a warm place for about 15 minutes until frothy before being mixed in.

Aerate

To incorporate air into a mixture. There are two main ways to do this:

- mechanical
- chemical

Either way, it means that air is trapped in a mixture to make it light in texture (in the case of a mousse, for example) – or so that, during cooking, the air will expand and force the mixture to rise (for example, a cake), giving it a light, open texture.

Mechanical means physically adding air. When rubbing fat into flour for pastry you can let the mixture fall from a height into the bowl in order to trap air. In puff pastry, air is trapped between the layers of dough during the rolling and folding process. Whipping

cream or whisking egg whites causes air to be trapped inside in tiny bubbles.

Chemical methods rely on yeast or baking powder which, in contact with moisture and warmth, creates carbon dioxide gas. The gas expands during cooking and the oven heat sets the mixture in a framework around the bubbles, forming an open lacy texture (e.g., sponge cake).

The exceptions to the rules are batter pudding and choux pastry, where the raising agent is steam, produced by the combination of a large proportion of water in the recipe and a high cooking temperature. As the steam forms it forces up the mixture, which then sets in its risen shape.

Bain marie

A bain marie is a water bath in which you sit a cooking dish or dishes. It is easily improvised by using a roasting tin filled one-third full with water. The object is to create a steamy atmosphere in the oven and to temper the heat so that delicate mixtures like egg custard cook slowly and evenly. A double saucepan (also called a double boiler) also acts as a bain marie. With the liquid in the bottom pan kept at below boiling point, sauces and soups thickened with eggs and cream can be safely kept hot without the mixture overheating and 'scrambling' or curdling.

Bake

To cook in the oven, in dry heat. The temperature of the air inside the oven is controlled by a thermostat, but ovens can vary and most cooks get to know how their ovens perform through trial and error. For most recipes it is important to preheat the oven so food goes into the oven at the correct temperature. This is usually indicated when the thermostat light on the oven-control panel goes out.

Bake blind

To cook a pastry flan or tart case without a filling in order to achieve a crisp result. Line the tin with pastry in the usual way and prick the base all over with a fork. Put a piece of greaseproof paper slightly larger than the tin inside the pastry case and weight it down with dried beans or special ceramic baking beans. This helps to support the sides of the case and stop the base from lifting. Cook as directed in the recipe. Remove paper and beans and cook for a further 5 to 10 minutes to dry the base of the case. You can use the beans over and over again.

> **COOK'S TIP** **To avoid a soggy bottom when using a ceramic flan dish, put a baking tray in the oven during preheating. Stand the dish on the tray to bake blind.**

Barbecue

A method of grilling over glowing charcoal which gives a characteristic smoky flavour to the food.

Bard

To cover the breast of poultry or game birds with bacon fat or rashers to prevent the meat drying out during roasting.

Baste

To spoon fat and cooking juices over meat or poultry during roasting to keep it moist and plump and to improve the colour and flavour.

Bat out

To flatten meat to an even thinness, to speed up cooking and/or tenderise it. Beef steak is batted out to make it easier to roll up into beef olives. Veal is batted out thinly to make quick-frying escalopes. Chicken breasts are sometimes batted out for layering in terrines or for stuffing. Delicate meat like chicken should be placed between sheets of dampened greaseproof paper and beaten with a rolling pin, starting at the centre and working outwards. Steaks can be batted out with a steak hammer designed to tenderise them. A proper steak hammer also gives them a characteristic 'dimpled' appearance.

Bind

To add liquid – often egg, water or milk – to dry ingredients to make them stick together.

Blanch

To pre-cook – usually in boiling water – either to preserve natural colour, or to loosen skins. For example, potatoes are brought to the boil before roasting and tomatoes are plunged into boiling water for 20 seconds to make skins easy to remove. Almonds can be slipped out of their papery brown skins after blanching in boiling water for a few seconds. Also used to reduce excess saltiness; for instance, from gammon or a bacon joint. The meat is covered with plenty of cold water and brought slowly to the boil. The water is discarded and the meat cooked in fresh water.

Blister

A technique to remove skins, usually from tomatoes and peppers. Tomatoes can be speared on a fork and held in a gas flame until the skins blister and char. The skin is then easily stripped away. Peppers are more usually grilled, turning frequently until the skin – but not the flesh – is blackened. Put in a polyethylene bag and leave for 10 minutes for the steam to loosen the skins further, then peel them. This technique makes peppers more digestible and also gives an appealing roasted flavour.

Blend

To mix ingredients evenly – usually a solid, such as cornflour, with a liquid. To avoid lumps, the liquid is added gradually and stirred in thoroughly between each addition. Alternatively, the instruction may mean to mix ingredients in an electric blender or liquidiser, where the fast action of sharp whirring blades purées and combines solids and liquids, for example, to make a smooth soup from vegetables simmered in stock.

COOK'S TIP It is dangerous to fill a blender more than half-full, especially with hot liquid. Hold the lid on firmly with a folded tea towel to ensure the initial whoosh of action doesn't force off the lid.

Boil

To cook in liquid at 100°C (212°F). Many foods we describe as boiled are actually added to boiling water but then cooked at a simmer. But for some foods it's essential that the water remains at a rolling boil – which is easy to recognise as it looks exactly as it sounds, with the water rolling and heaving with large bubbles.

Dried red kidney beans, for instance, need 10 minutes of this vigorous boiling to destroy toxins. And **pasta** is prevented from sticking together. But it's too fierce an action for vegetables which would disintegrate. Puddings in a basin need a slow but steady boil, characterised by a stream of bubbles breaking the surface gently. Flour-thickened sauces must be brought to the boil and boiled for 2 min to cook away the flouriness. It's important to be vigilant and stir well at this stage to avoid burning the bottom. Egg-and-cream-thickened sauce must not be allowed to boil or they will curdle.

Bone

To remove bones from meat or poultry before cooking.

Feel the meat first so you understand where the bones are. Then, using a sharp knife, start cutting and scraping the meat away from the visible end of the bone. Work along the bone, and keep the knife scraping against it. You probably won't have to cut through bone anywhere if you sever tendons at joints and continue working along the following bones, feeling your way and turning the meat inside out as you go.

Bottle

To preserve fruit or vegetables by bottling in syrup or brine and sterilising by raising to a high enough temperature. It's not as popular now that most households have freezers. You need special jars, lids and seals. Follow recipe instructions regarding sterilising time carefully and check jars really are sealed before storing.

Braise

To cook using a method that combines roasting and stewing. The food – meat or vegetables – is gently sautéed first until browned all over, then cooked in the oven in a covered dish with a little liquid. This moist cooking method, like stewing, helps to tenderise tougher meats and game. The liquid is usually thickened and served as a gravy or sauce with the meat.

Brand

To scorch decorative markings on to food with a hot skewer. Heat a skewer or skewers until very hot under a grill (hold the skewer with an oven glove as all the metal will get extremely hot). Press on to the surface of a grilled steak or fish to create criss-cross lines These branded markings echo the natural marks you would get from cooking on a charcoal grill and rotating the steak during cooking. Puff pastry, heavily dredged with icing sugar can be branded in the same way to give a professional-looking finish and pleasant caramel flavour to pastry gateaux.

Brick cooking

Baking in a special terracotta 'brick' – a special pot and lid – is said to preserve all the natural flavours of chicken or fish as it cooks very simply in its own juices combined with steam from the brick. Follow brick manufacturer's

---

COOK'S TIP Rub your hands with a handful of salt after chopping onions or garlic to help remove the odour from your skin. Then wash.

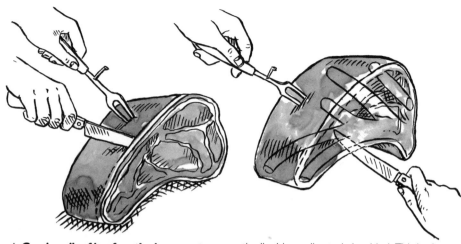

▲ **Carving rib of beef on the bone: cut with a gentle sawing movement so that the knife pastes cleanly through the meat. Carve it downwards, cutting across the grain on to and between bones.**

instructions, but usually both halves of the brick are soaked in cold water for about 30 minutes and the brick is put into an unpreheated oven to prevent it cracking. Add extra flavour by tucking onions, lemon or herbs inside the bird or fish.

Brown

An early stage in many recipes including casseroling which helps to give an appealing colour and savoury flavour to the end result (think of the taste difference between boiled onions and fried onions). Meat and vegetables are sautéed (see entry) over a moderate heat, and turned frequently until evenly coloured. The brownness and meat juices adhering to the pan or casserole dish dissolve in the cooking liquid, helping to darken and colour the gravy. French onion soup depends on the long, gentle but thorough browning of the onions for its colour and delicious caramel flavour. If the onion burns the flavour will be bitter.

A **brown sauce** is made like a white sauce but the roux – the fat and flour mixture – is allowed to brown gently, before

the liquid, usually stock, is added. This basic sauce is varied in many ways to create classic French sauces.

Carve

To cut cooked meat or poultry or game into neat slices for serving. This is a simple process with boned and rolled joints, slightly trickier with meat on the bone. It's a good idea to have a good look and feel of meat on the bone, before you cook it, so you get some understanding of the number, shape and direction of the bones. Most butchers will bone meat for you to make carving easier.

Carving beef: (topside, sirloin, riib [boned and rolled]). Remove strings, cut downwards in thin slices. Ribs on the bone look like a giant chop or chops. Ask the butcher to chine it for you – this means he saws through the thick bone where the ribs join the spine. Carve meat down through the fat covering to the rib bone then cut horizontally along the rib bone to release the slices.

Carving lamb leg. Cut a V-shaped wedge about 2.5 cm (1 in) deep out of the centre of the top of the leg of lamb (the side with the thicker fat layer). Cut thickish slices from each side of the wedge following the contours of the original wedge shape. When you have carved all the meat from the top, cut long slices from the sides parallel to the leg bone.

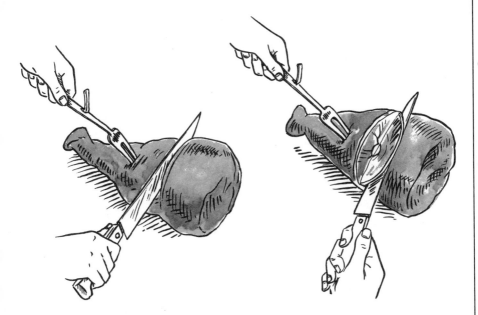

▲ Carving leg of lamb: carve slices from either side of the first cut, slanting knife to obtain longer slices.

Carving shoulder of lamb. This is more difficult to carve because it has three bones. Before you roast, feel for the triangular blade bone and cut round it using a sharp knife. The shoulder will start turning inside out as you work towards the point of the triangle inside the shoulder. Cut through the tendons to detach the blade at the ball and socket joint. This creates a space for stuffing if you like. Tie or skewer the shoulder back into shape and roast as usual. You can then slice downwards through about half the shoulder. Cut the rest

of the meat away from the bone as neatly as you can.

Carving lamb loin, best end. These are respectively the loin chops and the cutlets left in a strip. Ask the butcher to chine the joints for you. (See *Carving beef*, left.) Then you can cut between the rib bones to divide the meat into chops to serve. If you prefer to slice it thinly, ask the butcher to bone and roll the joint for you.

▼ Prepare a shoulder of lamb before roasting by removing the blade bone.

Carving pork (belly, loin, neck end, sparerib). Ask your butcher to bone, roll and tie these awkward-shaped joints. Or treat loin as for lamb and divide into chops. Before cooking, score the crackling at frequent intervals. The scoring allows you to cut through the crackling when the pork is cooked, so be sure to score at intervals at which you'd like to eventually slice. Carve through the crackling and meat.

Carving pork leg. The fillet end of leg is a very lean joint with a neat central bone, so it's easy to carve. Carve from the top down to the bone, turn the joint upside down and carve the other side. The shank (narrow end) has a larger central bone but is carved in the same way.

Carving poultry (chicken and turkey). Cut through the skin between the legs and breasts and press the legs outwards, away from the breast. Cut through at joint to separate them from the carcass. Carve the breast downwards in long thin slices. Cut through the joint between the drumstick and thigh and serve either on the bone or carve the meat from them.

Carving game birds and duck. Larger game birds like pheasant are carved in the same way as poultry. Smaller birds and duck are usually cut in half or jointed. To halve the bird, turn it upside-down on a board. Use poultry shears or strong kitchen scissors to cut out the spine, starting from one side of the tail and cutting forwards. Cut through the carcass on the other side of the tail and spine to remove it complete. Serve half the bird per person or cut in half diagonally between the wing and leg.

Casserole

A deep French cooking pot with a lid which has also given its name to the contents. Like braising, casseroling combines two cooking methods – in this case frying (or sautéing), to brown and flavour meat and vegetables, and slow stewing in liquid to tenderise the meat and make a tasty gravy.

Clarify

To clear and clean fats – most often butter – of milk solids and salt. These are the elements that burn first, so reducing butter's ability to survive high frying temperatures. Melt the butter (or margarine) gently. It will separate into yellow oil and white sediment. Pour off the oily part which is the clarified butter and store in the fridge. Discard the sediment. Use the clarified fat for shallow-frying.

Coat

To cover food with a protective layer, generally prior to a harsh cooking method. Coatings like egg and crumbs or batter protect soft and tender foods from the intense heat of deep or shallow-frying. The coating also traps juices in the food, preventing them from leaking into the oil.

Core

To remove the central pith and seeds from fruit. This is easiest when the fruit is quartered. You can use a coring gadget which is pushed into the centre of an apple to remove a thick plug of core and seeds. The easiest way to core pears is to hollow them out from the base with a small teaspoon.

Cream

Used as a verb, this means to beat together fat and sugar until pale and fluffy and aerated – usually the first stage of mixing sponge cakes and puddings, and biscuits. All-in-one cakes use soft margarines so the initial creaming stage is omitted, but an extra raising agent is added to compensate for lack of air incorporated mechanically (see *Aerate*).

Crimp

To pinch the edges of a raw pastry pie crust to create a decorative scalloped edge. This helps to seal the lid to the pastry or dish rim below and prevent the contents boiling out. Either pinch the edge with thumb and first finger all the way round, or press the flat of your thumb into the pastry and indent on each side with the back of a knife, without cutting the pastry. Repeat all the way round the rim. This looks especially attractive on puff pastry pies (see also *Knocking up*) .

Crystallise

To coat fruit or flowers with egg white and sugar to make stiffened and sparkling decorations for cakes and desserts. Paint dry, perfect blooms – violets, rose petals or primroses, or tiny seedless grapes or strings of red currants – with egg white using a fine paintbrush. Sprinkle with caster or fruit sugar until lightly coated and shake off excess. Leave to dry. Use crystallised fruits within 12 hours – flowers will last longer. Blanched shreds of orange or lemon rind can be treated in the same way and used to decorate syllabub, cheesecake, mousse or iced sponge cakes. Preserved crystallised fruits are more complicated – involving long soaking in sugar-rich syrup to prevent decay.

Deep-fry

The term given to cooking in enough hot oil for the food to be completely submerged. This means cooking is fast and more even than shallow-frying. Because it's fast it's not suitable for tough foods, only for tender delicate chicken, fish, shellfish and vegetables.

> **COOK'S TIPS**
> • **Never fill a frying pan more than one-third full with oil. It could overflow when you add the food.**
> • **Cut food into small, even-sized pieces for fast, even cooking.**
> • **Don't overcrowd the pan or the temperature will drop.**
> • **Drain fried food thoroughly on kitchen paper towels.**
> • **Never, under any circumstances, leave a fat pan on the heat unattended – it is a major fire hazard as it automatically ignites above a certain temperature. Should a pan catch fire, switch off the heat and place a fire blanket or bread board over the pan to smother the flames.**

Getting the oil to the correct temperature is the key to success. Too cool and the food will absorb oil and end up greasy, too hot and the outside will burn while the inside is undercoated. Check the recipe and use a special deep-fat frying thermometer, or add a small piece of the food to be fried. At the correct heat it should rise to the surface surrounded by bubbles within 10 seconds. Not all fats and oils are suitable for frying – check the label. Frying oil can be re-used. Cool then strain back into the bottle. Discard once the oil darkens in colour.

Deglaze

To dissolve the cooking juices and brown sediment left in the pan after roasting meat or shallow-frying meat or fish. Wine or stock is added after the food has been removed, and stirred over a gentle heat to incorporate the pan juices or drippings in an intensely tasty, but small quantity of sauce. Or these juices can be added to a larger quantity of gravy or a brown sauce.

Degrease

To remove or skim fat from the surface of a sauce or casserole. The easiest way to do this is to let the food cool completely so the fat solidifies. It is then easy to lift it off. If there isn't time to wait, skim off the excess with a spoon and soak up the rest with kitchen paper towels.

Derind

To remove the rind from bacon rashers. This is easiest with sharp kitchen scissors. Some recipes call for bacon rashers to be derinded and stretched. Stretch them by running the flat of a knife blade along the length of the rasher.

Devil

To coat food for frying or grilling with hot, spicy and sharp seasonings.

Dice

To cut food into neat cubes of even size. First cut thick slices then cut through the stacked-up slices at intervals equal to the thickness, to make sticks. Turn the stack and cut across the last cuts at the same intervals, to make cubes.

Dredge

To dust evenly with flour or sugar. A dredger is a canister with holes in the lid, usually used to flour the work-surface before rolling out pastry (see also *Dust*).

Dripping(s)

The fat that drips out of meat as it is roasting. Use it to baste the meat during cooking (see *Baste*). Pour off the dripping leaving just a tablespoonful in the tin to make the roux or the gravy. Reserve the dripping in the fridge and use for roasting potatoes.

Dropping consistency

This describes the correct texture for some cake mixtures. Lift a heaped spoonful above the bowl, tip it and watch that the mixture falls from the spoon without a sharp shake. If it flops off the spoon and flattens out in the bowl it is 'soft dropping consistency'.

Dust

To sprinkle food lightly with flour (for example, a loaf of bread before baking, to give a soft crust) or with icing sugar (for example, cakes or pies).

Egg and crumb

To cover food, such as fish, chicken or croquettes with a protective coating of egg and fine breadcrumbs, usually prior to shallow or deep-frying. Dry the food thoroughly and

> **COOK'S TIP** Sift icing sugar through a fine-meshed sieve, held several inches above the cake or pastries to be dusted, so the sugar drifts down to cover with a light dust. Add a half teaspoon of caster sugar to icing sugar for extra sparkle. Place a lacy paper doily on a cake before you dust with icing sugar to create a pretty pattern.

dust with flour, to help the coating stick. Beat the egg on a plate, spread the crumbs on another plate. Dip food into egg until coated, lift, allowing excess egg to drain off, then press into crumbs. Shake off surplus (see also *Coat* and *Deep-fry*).

En croûte

Wrapped in pastry (or literally, 'in a crust'). The most famous is *Bœuf en croûte*, where rare-roasted beef fillet is wrapped in pastry. Everything from a middle cut of salmon to lamb chops to pears can be cooked en croute. Wrap large pieces in pastry as you would a parcel. Chops and apples or pears can be 'bandaged' with a long strip of pastry.

En papillote

Wrapped in paper or foil. Delicate foods like fish steaks can be folded in a greaseproof-paper parcel so they steam gently in their own juices. They are generally served in the parcel so the juices can be enjoyed, too. To make a parcel, cut a wide, shallow heart-shape from greaseproof paper or baking parchment – the size depends on the item to be wrapped. Fold the heart in half. Open out and butter to prevent sticking. Put the food and any flavourings on one half of the heart and fold over the other half. Fold in the open edges of the paper, about 1 cm ($\frac{1}{2}$ in) all the way round. As you fold around the curve the edge will start to overlap the previous folds and this secures the parcel.

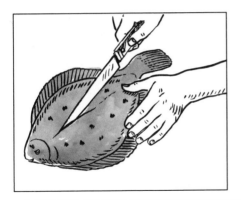

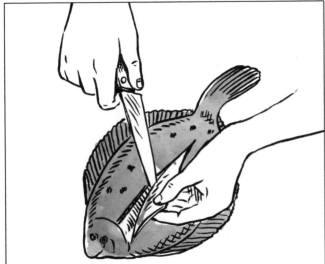

How to fillet a flat fish in three stages:

1. Cut along the centre to the central bone.

2. Slide tip of knife under flesh and cut away in short strokes.

3. Keep blade flat against the bone and detach the fillet.

Enrich

Egg yolks and cream are the most commonly used enriching agents because of their high fat content. They may be used separately or beaten together, usually in soups or sauces. Egg yolk added to sweet shortcrust pastry makes rich shortcrust – more golden and shorter in texture than plain shortcrust. Some yeast doughs, especially sweet, fruited buns and loaves are enriched with eggs and melted butter.

Fillet

To remove the bones from uncooked fish. For flat fish like plaice, cut along the centre, just down to the central bone. Slide the tip of

a sharp knife under the flesh of the fish and gradually cut away from the rib bones in short strokes. Keep the underside of the blade flat against the bone and continue until you can detach the fillet. Repeat on the other side, then turn the fish over and repeat to give you four fillets (see also *Skin*).

With a round fish, like a trout, cut off the head. Put fish on a board with the sides of the opening where the fish was cleaned spread out on the board. Press with your thumbs along the length of the backbone to loosen it. Turn the fish over and lift the backbone, with all the fine bones attached, away from the flesh. Remove any stray bones. Cut along the centre to divide the fish into two fillets.

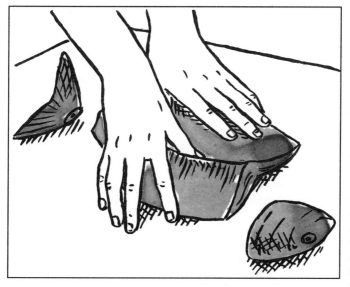

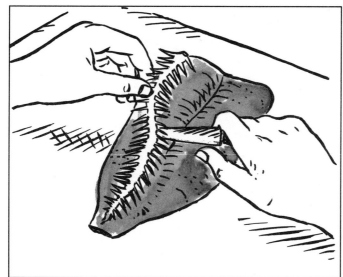

spirit most commonly used. Any spirit needs to be warmed in a small pan first, to release the alcoholic vapours. Pour warmed brandy into the pan with the fried steaks or crepes (thin sweet or savoury pancakes) and ignite, at arms length, with a match. Serve once the flames have died down. Burning off the alcohol intensifies the flavours and reduces any greasiness, although the main purpose of flambéing is to impress!

> **COOK'S TIP**
> **Never pour straight from the bottle as the flames could light the contents leaving you holding a highly deadly bomb.**

▲ **How to fillet a round fish (see page 185).**

Flake

To divide cooked, boned and skinned fish by separating the natural flakes from each other.

Flambé

To flame or set fire to alcohol to produce a dramatic flourish at serving. Brandy is the

Fold in

To add ingredients to a mixture in a gentle fashion so that air bubbles are preserved. Previously whisked egg whites are folded into sauces to make soufflés; sugar is folded into egg whites for meringues; flour is folded into whisked sponge mixtures. Use a large metal spoon or spatula to do this as a chunky wooden spoon will knock out air. Scrape the spoon around the back edge of the bowl, gradually turning it over as you reach the part of the bowl nearest you, to fold the mixture back on itself. Turn the bowl slightly as you repeat this motion and be sure to cut through and lift the mixture from the bottom of the bowl, too.

Flour

You may find this instruction in a cake recipe which calls for a greased and floured tin, especially a ring tin which is difficult to line with paper. Brush the tin with oil. Add a spoonful of flour and shake the tin until the base is evenly covered. Tip the tin, holding it over the sink, and turn it through a complete circle so the flour moves around the sides coating them. Hold upside-down and tap the tin to shake out excess flour.

Frothing

A little trick to give roast beef, poultry or game birds an attractive crispy surface. About 15 to 20 minutes before the end of cooking time, dust a little seasoned flour over the meat and baste with the hot dripping. The flour will froth initially as the starch grains burst, then cook to a thin crust.

Fry

To cook food in hot fat or oil, usually with the intention of creating a crisp and tasty outer surface (see also *Deep-fry, Sauté, Shallow-fry, Stir-fry*).

Garnish

To decorate foods or dishes with prettily cut vegetables or fruit, fresh herbs, spices, bread or pastry shapes.

Glaze

To create a shiny surface. Beaten egg is the usual glaze for pastry, but egg yolk alone makes a deep golden glaze that's very appealing on puff pastry. Milk or beaten egg white and a sprinkling of caster sugar gives a shiny, crispy surface to sweet pies. Sticky buns get their glossy finish from sugar dissolved in milk, brushed on while buns are still hot. Fruit tarts served cold often have an apricot glaze made by melting sieved apricot jam in a little water. This looks marvellous spooned thickly over fruit toppings and it helps stop the fruit drying out, too. Hot fruit tarts are often glazed by dredging with icing or caster sugar and returning them to a hot oven to melt the sugar.

Grate

To shred into fine strips, using a grater. Most graters have a choice of surfaces for different foods; e.g., coarse blades for cheese, vegetables, etc., finer blades for citrus rind and tiny punched holes for grating fresh nutmegs, etc. (see also *Graters and slicers*, page 173).

Grease

To prepare a tin or dish by applying a thin film of fat or oil to prevent food sticking to the surface. Use only clean oil – not oil that has been used for frying – and brush on as little as possible to avoid a greasy surface on the finished food. For speed, use a wrapper from a block of butter or margarine.

Griddling

A form of dry frying where food is cooked on a heavy metal plate on the hob. Burgers, steaks, drop scones all cook successfully on a lightly greased griddle.

Grill

A method of cooking using dry heat radiated directly on to the food – not indirectly through water or hot oil. It is a fast and fierce cooking method, best suited to tender foods of even thickness. Most recipes require that the grill is preheated. As well as using the thermostatic control you can regulate the temperature by moving the grill pan closer to, or further from, the heat. When grilling, try to turn the food once only, otherwise juices that form continually on the surface of the food will be lost into the bottom of the grill pan.

Grind

To chop dry foodstuff, like coffee or spices, into tiny fragments or crumbs in a machine with strong blades, so they release more flavour on cooking.

Hazing

This slight, shimmering movement in the air above the pan when heating fat or oil for shallow-frying indicates that the fat is hot enough to sear and seal the food. Once both surfaces are sealed, the temperature is normally reduced to allow the food to cook through to the centre.

Headspace

This refers to the space you need to leave when packing food for the freezer. Liquids expand on freezing and if a container is filled to the brim, the lid will be forced off. Leave 2.5 to 5 cm (1 to 2 in) headspace between top of food and the lid.

▼ **Interlard: you can use a special interlarding needle.**

Hull

To remove the stalk and ring of leaves from strawberries and soft fruits.

Infuse

To soak flavourings in liquid to extract the flavour. This can be by pouring boiling water over and leaving to soak as in making tea, or by bringing the flavouring almost to the boil in liquid, then leaving to soak. A vanilla pod may be infused in milk in this way to make custard. An onion spiked with cloves is infused in milk to make bread sauce.

Interlard

To thread strips of fat through very lean cuts of meat to baste it internally and keep it moist during roasting. A special needle with a hinged end that grips the fat is used traditionally, but it is possible to thread strips of bacon or salami in and out of slits cut in lean meat like chicken breasts, which also gives an attractive finish.

Jam setting point

Jam must have the right amount of pectin (see *Pectin*) and be boiled to the right temperature in order to set. To test if this point has been reached, stir the jam and check with a special cooking thermometer. The temperature should be 105°C (221°F). Don't let the thermometer touch the bottom of the pan or you will get a false reading. Without a thermometer, take jam pan off the heat (so it stops cooking) and spoon a small blob of jam on a chilled saucer. Leave

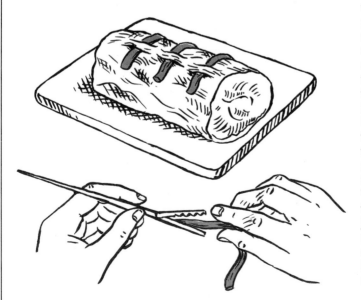

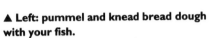

▲ **Left: pummel and knead bread dough with your fish.**
Right: pastry requires gentle kneading – use fingertips only.

for a minute or so to cool, then slide your finger into the jam or blow on it. If the surface wrinkles, the setting point has been reached and you can pot in the usual way. If not, return the pan to the heat, continue to boil, then retest.

> **COOK'S TIP Always remove the pan from the heat while testing so jam doesn't over-boil and chill several saucers in the fridge in case you need to test more than once.**

Joint

To divide poultry prepared for the oven into smaller pieces, usually on the bone. Pull the legs away from the body to reveal the joint where thigh joins carcass. Cut through this joint. Cut through joint between drumstick and thigh to give two pieces (you can leave as one large leg portion). Repeat on other side. Remove wings in the same way, cutting through where they join the breast, or leave them attached to the breast portions. Cut horizontally through the rib bones underneath the breasts to separate them from bony base (use this piece for stock).

Place breast portion skin side up and cut downwards through central breast bone to divide into two.

Julienne

Fine matchsticks cut from vegetables – usually carrots, celery and leeks – used as a garnish for clear soups or fish. Occasionally julienned vegetables or even fruit (like lemon peel) are required within a recipe and not just as a garnish.

Knead

To use your hands to work dough until it is smooth. With yeast dough, kneading must be vigorous to stretch the dough and develop its elasticity. Bend your fingers and use the heel of one hand to push into the dough and away from you. Then, in a continuous movement, use the knuckles of the same hand to lift the back of the dough and fold it towards you. Repeat, using the other hand to rotate the dough slightly between each movement. Continue for 5 minutes until the dough is smooth and elastic. Pastry in contrast needs a delicate touch when kneading, because you don't want elasticity but a short, crumbly texture. Use the fingertips of one hand only to lift the underneath of the back of the ball of dough and fold it into the centre. Rotate the dough with the other hand. Continue for only a few seconds until the pastry is just smooth. Overhandling will make the end result tough.

▲ **Left: base-lining a shallow tin.
Right: lining the sides and base of a deep
cake tin.**

Knock back

This is a stage of bread-making. After the
dough has been left to rise for the first time it
will contain a lot of large, uneven air bubbles
which would give the finished loaf a holy,
uneven texture. So the dough is kneaded
again to 'knock back' these bubbles, before
shaping.

Knock up

This describes the technique of creating deep
flaky edges to a puff pastry pie top. Puff pastry
is rolled out thicker than short pastry – about
6 mm (¼ in). Once it is positioned on the pie
dish or baking sheet, take a sharp knife and
make light horizontal cuts into the sides (the
thickness) of the pastry to resemble flakes.
Repeat all the way round. This encourages
the flakes to separate and the edge of the pie
will have extra depth and lightness. Crimp the
edge after knocking up (see *Crimp*).

Lard

(See *Interlard*)

Line a tin

To put a paper lining inside a baking tin to
prevent food from sticking. To line the base,
stand tin on greaseproof paper and mark
round it with a pencil or knife tip. Cut out,
just inside the line. To line sides of a deep tin,
cut a strip of paper a little longer than the
circumference of the tin and 4 cm (1½ in)
deeper. Fold one long edge in 2.5 cm (1 in).
Snip at intervals up to the fold. Put in the
greased tin so fold is in bottom corner and
snipped sections overlap slightly. Put base
lining paper on top and grease.

> **Cook's tip To measure
> circumference, simply wrap a
> piece of string or cotton round
> the outside of the tin to get the
> right length of paper.**

Macerate

To soften food by soaking it in liquid; e.g., you
may soak dried fruit in sherry, tea or fruit
juice before adding it to a rich fruit cake.

Mandolin

A very useful flat tool with a fitted blade, for
fast and even slicing. The food, say a potato, is
passed quickly up and down over the blade,
which may be crinkled or plain. The thickness
of the slice may be adjustable.

Marinade

The flavoured liquid – wine, vinegar, lemon juice, often with herbs, oils and spices added – used to tenderise and flavour meat, fish or poultry. Oil in the marinade helps keep food that is naturally low in fat moist during cooking.

Marinate

The act of soaking food in liquid to tenderise and flavour it. Acidic marinades (e.g., containing wine, vinegar or fruit juice) should not be used in metal bowls – use glass or china instead. Add the food and keep cool and covered. Turn the food occasionally so the marinating is even.

Mince

To cut food into small pieces using a mincer which forces the food – usually meat – through holes, then slices it off in short lengths.

Mirepoix

A mixture of chopped vegetables – usually onion, carrot and celery – which is fried gently without browning (see *Sweat*) then used as a base on which to sit meat for braising. It helps to flavour the gravy.

Mould

i) A decorative dish or tin in which food is shaped. The food isn't served in the mould, it is turned out to show off its shape. To turn cold food (e.g., mousse or jelly) out of a mould, first loosen the top edge by pressing gently with your fingertips. Dip the mould into a bowl of hot water almost to the brim for 10 seconds, then place the serving plate on top. Gripping plate and mould firmly, turn it upside-down and give a short sharp shake. The food should slip out on to the plate. If not, repeat the process.
ii) A tiny plant which grows on food in warm moist conditions. Some moulds are deliberately introduced, e.g., into blue-veined cheeses to give them their unique flavour, and

these are harmless. However, it is now considered safest to discard the entire piece of cheese or jar of jam (not just scrape off the mould) if mould has formed through poor storage conditions.

Open-freeze

To freeze food spread out on a tray so each piece freezes individually rather than in a block. Used for squashable foods like raspberries or meatballs, and for vegetables like runner beans to make 'free-flow' packs.

Pan juices

The juices that run out of food when it's fried, grilled or roasted and mingle in the cooking fat. These tasty juices are usually incorporated in the sauce or gravy.

Par-boil

To partially cook food in boiling water before the next stage of cooking, which may be by another method like frying or roasting.

Pare

To peel and trim fruit and vegetables with a small sharp knife.

Pectin

A natural substance found (in different amounts) in fruits and some vegetables. It forms a gel in water and is responsible for setting jam (see also *Test for setting*) Some fruits are naturally high in pectin and so set easily into jam (e.g., blackcurrants, gooseberries, Seville oranges). Others are low in pectin (e.g., strawberries or cherries) so commercial pectin (made from apples) or lemon juice is added to boost it.

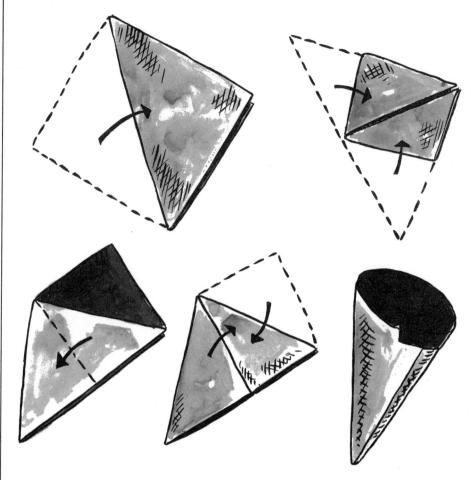

▲ **How to make a paper piping bag. Use greaseproof paper.**

Pipe

To force soft food through a piping tube or nozzle to shape it into fingers, rosettes or other shapes to create a decorative effect. You can buy piping tubes and piping bags (also called forcing bags) in different sizes – small ones for icing or chocolate, larger ones for piping cream, meringue, potato or biscuit doughs. To make a simple piping bag, cut a square of greaseproof paper. Fold it in half diagonally, then fold both corners of the folded edge up to the top of the triangle to make a square. Fold one of these corners out again, fold the other over towards it, twice.

> **Cook's tip** To fill a large fabric or plastic piping bag cleanly, stand it in a tall jug or glass and fold the top inside-out. Spoon in the mixture, fold the bag the right way out, grip it just above the mixture between finger and thumb and twist it round several times to force the mixture into the nozzle. To use, wind the twisted part around your thumb. Twist the bag into the palm of your hand until the mixture appears at the nozzle. As you pipe, keep twisting the bag into your hand to force the mixture out.

Squeeze the triangle open to make a cone. Fold over the top edge once or twice to keep the layers together. Snip off the tip of the cone to use with or without a piping tube. Fill the bag half full, fold the top down several times and hold the bag with your fingertips under the folded paper and your thumb on top. As you pipe, keep folding down the paper to force the icing out.

Poach

A gentle method of cooking – used especially for delicate foods such as a whole salmon, eggs or peach halves – in liquid that is kept at just below simmering point. The surface of the liquid shouldn't be broken by bubbles – it should just 'tremble'.

Pot roast

Similar to braising, but usually meat is cooked in a pan on top of the stove, in fat and a little liquid, instead of in the oven.

Prove

This is a term used in bread-making. When the dough has been kneaded, it is set aside in a warm place to prove – rise to double its size. Return the dough to the mixing bowl and cover loosely with oiled cling film to prevent a skin forming and put in a warm place like an airing cupboard or above the cooker. Don't put in direct heat or the yeast will be killed. Once dough has doubled in size it is knocked back, then shaped into a loaf or rolls (see *Knock back*). It is then proved again, until doubled in size, before cooking.

COOK'S TIPS
• **Knead pastry as little as possible, just until the underside is smooth. Turn it over so the smooth side is on top and tap the sides with your hands to make the pastry into the shape you require (e.g., a rough round or square).**
• **Use short, light strokes with the rolling pin, working from the centre and always rolling away from you. Rotate the dough a half-turn, clockwise, between each rolling.**
• **Don't turn the pastry over. Keep patting the edges to keep the round or square shape. If you lean too hard or over-stretch the pastry it will shrink back during cooking.**
• **The rolled side is the neatest side of the pastry so use it where it will show – upwards on the top of a pie, downwards (on the outside) of a flan case.**

Refresh

1. To reheat and re-crisp bread, pastry or biscuits after storing or freezing, by putting in a moderate oven for a few minutes.
2. To cool hot food quickly; i.e., if you want green beans in a salad, rinse them with cold water as soon as they are cooked to stop them cooking further and preserve their bright green colour.

Relax

Pastry is wrapped and chilled after handling and before cooking in order to relax it. There is a substance in flour called gluten, which when mixed with water and kneaded becomes stretchy, giving pastry or bread its flexibility. Allowing it to relax reduces the risk of the gluten contracting causing the pastry to shrink during cooking.

Render

To extract fat from food by gentle cooking. For example, the suet that naturally surrounds kidneys can be rendered by slow roasting, then used for basting roast meat or potatoes.

Roll out

To flatten pastry to an even thickness and the required shape before cooking.

Roux

Equal quantities of fat (e.g., butter) and plain flour, cooked together to make the thickening for white sauce. It must be cooked very gently, without browning, for 2 minutes to remove all flouriness before the liquid is added. For classic brown sauces, the roux is allowed to brown.

Rub in

To incorporate fat into flour when making pastry, crumble topping and some cakes. The aim is to coat each flour grain with fat to stop long chains of gluten forming, thereby giving the pastry a 'short' crumbly texture.

> **COOK'S TIPS**
> • **Keep everything cool to avoid melting the fat. Rinse your hands with cold water. Use cold but not rock-hard fat, cut it into cubes.**
> • **Lift the lumps of fat and flour, and rub backwards and forwards between your fingertips, letting the crumbs fall through your fingers back into the bowl.**
> • **Hold your fingers high over the bowl so the mixture is aerated as it falls into the bowl.**
> • **Shake the bowl from side to side so any large lumps remaining come to the surface.**
> • **Don't over-rub the mixture or it will be oily and difficult to handle. Stop when the mixture resembles fine breadcrumbs**

> **QUICK TIP   You can use a food processor to rub in. Process fat and flour for few seconds only. Trickle in the water with the machine running, again just for seconds. Knead lightly and continue with recipe**

Sauté

To fry quickly in shallow fat over a high heat. Shake the pan frequently to keep the food tossing and turning or 'jumping', for even cooking without sticking.

Salt

As well as being a flavour enhancer, salt helps to draw moisture from food. Sliced cucumber, lightly salted and left to drain, becomes firmer and crisper. Aubergine slices are salted to draw out the bitter juices. Rinse them and squeeze out the water before frying.

Scald

To heat a liquid – usually milk – until almost boiling.

Scale

To remove the scales from fish to be cooked whole. You can get a special gadget to do this, but it's just as easy to use a knife.

> **COOK'S TIPS   Grip the fish tail (salt your fingers to help you get a firm grip) and scrape with the back of a sharp knife blade against the scales – from tail to head. Rub skin with salt to detach remaining scales, rinse well before cooking.**

Score

To make a shallow cuts just through the skin (e.g., of pork to make crackling, or around the centre of an apple or a potato before baking, to prevent it bursting). Score also the skin of hard vegetables like squash to enable them to cook faster.

Sear (or seal)

To put food into hot fat or on to a hot griddle to brown rapidly and seal the surface.

Segment

To divide a citrus fruit into its natural sections. Using a serrated knife, slice off top and bottom. Stand the fruit on a board or plate and cut the peel and white pith away from the sides, following the contours of the fruit. Hold the fruit in one hand and cut very close to each side of the dividing membranes just to the centre, to release whole segments. Squeeze out juice from membranes.

Separate eggs

To separate the yolk from the white of an egg. Cradle the egg in one hand and tap sharply with a knife across the centre. Hold the egg over a bowl. Insert both thumbnails into the crack and pull the shells gently apart, turning them upright as you do so, so one half shell forms a cap. The white will flow over into the bowl, leaving the yolk in the shell. Tip the yolk from shell to shell to pour off all the white.

▼ **How to skin fish fillets.**
Make sure you use a sharp knife.

> **COOK'S TIPS** Egg whites won't whisk to a stiff foam if they contain egg yolk, so for meringues, etc., take special care. Separate whites individually into a small bowl or cup before mixing them, in case you ruin the lot with the last egg.

Shallow-fry

To cook in shallow hot fat (see also *Fry, Sauté, Stir-fry*).

Sieve

To press food through a sieve to purée it.

> **COOK'S TIPS** Use a wooden spoon to rub food through a sieve. If possible, use a nylon sieve for acid fruits or they may pick up a metallic flavour.

Sift

To shake dry foods through a sieve to remove lumps, to aerate the mixture or to mix baking powder, spices, etc., into flour evenly.

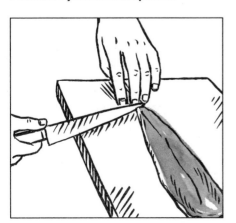
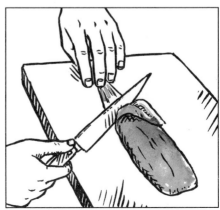

Skim

To spoon off surface scum from boiling or simmering food, like bacon joints, beans or jam.

Skin

To remove the skins from fruit or vegetables, poultry or fish (see also *Blanch*, *Blister*).

> **COOK'S TIPS   To skin fish fillets, place skin-side down on a board. Grip the tail (salt your fingers to improve your grip) and slide a sharp knife between the skin and the flesh. Hold the knife at an angle and, using a sawing movement from side to side, work forward to detach the fillet from the skin.**

Slice

To cut food into flat, even sections with a sharp knife.

> **COOK'S TIPS   To regulate the thickness of the slices, use the back of the fingers of the hand holding the carrot or whatever as a guide for the knife. Tuck your finger tips under so they are clear of the knife.**

Sponge

Not just a cake, a term used in dissolving gelatine. The gelatine granules are sprinkled over a little liquid in a bowl and left for few minutes to 'sponge' or soak up all the liquid. The bowl is then placed in a pan of simmering water and the mixture stirred until the gelatine dissolves.

Spatchcock

To flatten a chicken or other bird, usually for grilling or barbecuing. Put the bird breast down on a board. Using poultry shears cut along both sides of the tail and spine and remove it whole. Turn the bird over, open out the sides then press down firmly on the breastbone to break the ribs and flatten the bird. Tuck the legs and wings against the breast so that all the meat is of approximately the same thickness and fix in place with skewers.

Spit-roast

To cook on a huge, rotating skewer. As the meat rotates it is automatically basted by its own fat, and the whole surface is browned and crisped.

Spreading space

Some mixtures, especially biscuits, spread during cooking so you need to leave enough room between the uncooked portions on the baking tray to keep them separate.

Steam

An indirect method of cooking where food is cooked in the steam driven off boiling water or stock. This can be done in several ways. The food is put in a perforated container, which could be a trivet that goes inside a pan with a little water, or a steamer or metal colander which sits above a pan with a lot of boiling water. Puddings in basins, cooked in a covered pan with just enough water to come a third of the way up the basin, are described as steamed, but are in fact only partially steamed.

Stir-fry

A fast method of cooking over very high heat, in very little oil, which preserves natural colours and flavours. Food is cut into fine, even pieces and kept moving all the time it is over the heat, to prevent it burning. Traditionally done in a wok where the deep sloping sides allow you to 'dig and toss' – turn over the food with a wide flat tool – without tossing the food out of the pan!

Sweat

To fry vegetables very gently, without browning them, to 'sweat out' their natural flavours. This is the first stage of making vegetable soups and in braising (see *Mirepoix*).

Strain

To pour liquids through a sieve to separate from any solids.

Thicken

To change the consistency of thin liquid or cooking juices by the addition of a thickener, such as flour or cornflour. When starch grains are boiled in liquid they burst, absorbing some of the liquid and thereby thickening it. Dry flour cannot be added or lumps will form. You need to blend it with a little water, milk, stock or wine first to make a thin, smooth paste, then stir that into the sauce to be thickened. Bring to the boil, stirring constantly so the flour is evenly incorporated into the sauce. Boil for at least 2 minutes to remove any flouriness. Egg yolks, usually blended with cream, are also used as a thickener for delicate soups and sauces. In this case the liquid must be heated gently to a temperature at which the egg will thicken but never allowed to boil. The addition of starchy vegetables like potatoes, lentils or beans or rice or pasta to soups or casseroles also has a thickening effect.

▼ **Trussing a chicken or other poultry (see page 198). Dental floss makes a good tie which won't fray or disintegrate.**

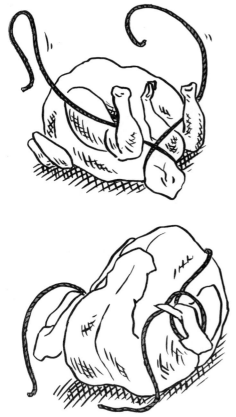

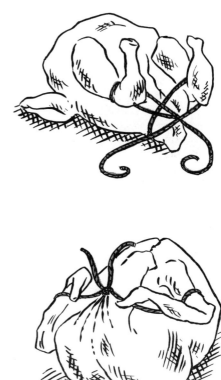

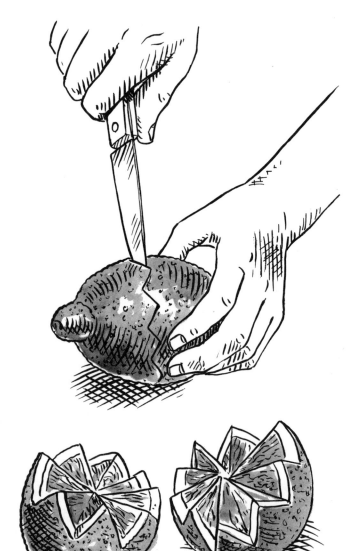

Top and tail

To snip off stalks and ends of gooseberries or podded vegetables.

Truss

To tie meat – especially poultry – into a compact shape for even roasting. Place chicken breast side up. Take a length of string, centre it under the tail. Cross the ends, taking them up over and around the legs. Cross them again over the tail then take them under the bird, loop them round the wings and tie them together in the centre.

Vandyke

To cut a decorative zig-zag edge when halving tomatoes or melons to create 'waterlilies'. Insert a small sharp knife at a forty-five degree angle, just to the centre of the fruit. Withdraw it then insert at the mirror image angle next to it. Repeat all the way round the fruit.

▲ **Vandyke a lemon as a garnish. Any round fruit can be vandyked.**

Waterbath

See *Bain Marie*.

Toast

To brown the surface of bread or nuts to add colour and a roasted, slightly caramelised flavour.

Whip

To beat rapidly in order to add air and thicken the consistency of cream.

Whisk

This term is usually reserved for egg whites or egg yolk and sugar mixes for soufflés or sponges, but generally means the same as 'Whip', which is to beat rapidly in order to add air and thicken the consistency (see also *Aerate*). Whisked egg whites go through several different stages and different recipes call for different consistencies. **Soft peaks** means whites stand up but tops flop over. They look glossy and wet. **Stiff peaks** means the tops don't flop over. Tradition has it that you should be able to hold the bowl upside-down above your head without the whites falling out. The next stage is stiff and dry-looking. Follow the recipe instructions.

Zest

To remove just the coloured part of citrus rind, which contains the flavoured oil. A fine grater will do this, or you can use a gadget called a zester. It has five tiny round blades and when you drag it across the rind it removes it in long, very fine shreds. You can remove the flavoured oil without the rind by rubbing a sugar lump over the outside of the fruit – this is sometimes required in cocktail recipes.

Weights and measures

While many types of cooking offer a level of freedom and preference when it comes to the proportions of different ingredients, some – such as cakes and pastry – need careful balancing in order to be successful. These proportions are expressed in weight for dry or solid foods, in volume for liquids. At present, two systems are in use in the UK:

☞ **Imperial**, our traditional system, using pounds (lb) and ounces (oz), pints (pt) and fluid ounces (fl oz).

☞ **Metric**, the system common in Europe, using kilograms (kg), grams (g), litres (l) and millilitres (ml).

Many recipes give quantities in Imperial and in Metric. Don't mix the two. Because the actual conversions are awkward fractions and

difficult to measure, metric recipes are adapted, not just translated, so the two are not interchangeable. For example, one ounce (1 oz) actually converts to 28.4 g; one pound (1 lb) converts to 454 g, one pint (1 pt) converts to 568 ml.

Remember also that the American pint is smaller than the British pint, which is 20 oz. American recipes do not always discern between the two.

Different sources of recipes sometimes use different conversions. You may see 1 lb expressed as 450 g or 500 g, or one ounce as 30 g or 25 g. This is another reason the two systems are not interchangeable.

WEIGHING TIPS
• **Do you need to weigh? All packs of food are marked with their weight. You may be using all of it, or in the case of block fats, you may be able to divide the block by eye.**
• **Check the scale is on nought before you weigh.**
• **Measure dry ingredients before sticky ones, fats, etc., to save washing the scale pan.**
• **To measure sticky ingredients like honey or syrup, put the can or jar on the scale and spoon out the contents until the weight is reduced by the quantity demanded in the recipe.**
• **Check the recipe source to see whether spoon measures should be level or not. A 'rounded' tablespoon has as much above as below. Any more than this and it's a 'heaped' spoonful.**

There are:
• 20 fluid ounces (fl oz) in 1 pint
• 100 millilitres (ml) in 1 litre (l)

Dry Measures	
Imperial	Metric
½ oz	10 g
1 oz	25 g
1½ oz	40 g
2 oz	50 g
3 oz	75 g
4 oz	125 g
5 oz	150 g
6 oz	175 g
7 oz	200 g
8 oz	225 g
9 oz	250 g
10 oz	275 g
11 oz	300 g
12 oz	350 g
13 oz	375 g
14 oz	400 g
15 oz	425 g
16 oz (1 lb)	450 g
24 oz (1½ lb)	700 g
32 oz (2 lb)	900 g (or 1 kg)

Fluid measures	
Imperial	Metric
½ fl oz	15 ml
1 fl oz	25 ml
2 fl oz	50 ml
3 fl oz	75 ml
4 fl oz	100 ml
5 fl oz (¼ pt)	150 ml
6 fl oz	175 ml
7 fl oz	200 ml
8 fl oz	225 ml
9 fl oz	250 ml
10 fl oz (½ pt)	300 ml
11 fl oz	325 ml
12 fl oz	350 ml
13 fl oz	375 ml
14 fl oz	400 ml
15 fl oz (¾ pt)	450 ml
16 fl oz	475 ml
17 fl oz	500 ml
18 fl oz	525 ml
19 fl oz	550 ml
20 fl oz (1 pt)	600 ml

Which way to weigh?

Most kitchen scales offer a choice of Imperial and metric measurements. If you use a traditional weighing scale it is possible to buy loose metric weights. It's helpful to use proper standardised measuring spoons – you can buy Imperial and metric sets.

American measures

The American system of weights and measures is based on measuring by volume, not weight, using special measuring cups and spoons. It is impossible to give weight equivalents, as every ingredient varies; e.g., a cupful of butter would weigh more than a cupful of cornflakes. You can buy American cup measures in good cookshops, otherwise use an ordinary coffee mug – something that holds about 225 ml (8 fl oz). It's keeping ingredients in the right proportions that counts.

☞ An American pint is 475 ml (16 fl oz)
☞ An American cup measure is 225 ml (8 fl oz).
☞ Don't pack food tightly into the cup unless instructed to do so in the recipe.
☞ Shake cup to level the surface and measure accurately.

Oven temperatures

The way in which the temperature of your oven is described depends on the fuel that powers it and the age of the model. Most recipes state all options; e.g., Gas Mark 4, 350°F, 180°C.

Gas cookers use a Regulo or Gas Mark which represents a known temperature. These numbers mark 25°F increases or decreases in temperature. The temperature may also be described in words; e.g., cook in a moderate oven, Gas Mark 4.

Electric cookers display the actual temperature, either in degrees Fahrenheit (F) or, in newer models, degrees Celsius (C).

Solid fuel cookers usually have one hot oven and one cooler one. Check your instruction manual for how to regulate the temperature.

°F Fahrenheit	°C Celsius	Gas Mark	Solid fuel
225°	110°	¼ (very cool)	very slow
250°	130°	½ (very cool)	slow
275°	140°	1 (cool)	
300°	150°	2 (cool)	warm
325°	170°	3 (moderate)	moderate
350°	180°	4 (moderate)	
375°	190°	5 (fairly hot)	fairly hot
400°	200°	6 (fairly hot)	hot
425°	220°	7 (hot)	
450°	250°	8 (very hot)	very hot
475°	275°	9 (very hot)	

Sizes

The other measurements you may need to know for a recipe are dimensions. Cake recipes are given for a specific size of tin. If you make it in a different size tin, the cooking time and finished depth will be different. Measurements are given in Imperial (inches/in) or metric (centimetres/cm).

There are:
• 1000 centimetres (cm) in a metre (m)
• 10 millimetres (mm) in a centimetre

Imperial	Metric
¼ in	6 mm
½ in	12 mm (1.2 cm)
1 in	2.5 cm
2 in	5 cm
3 in	7.5 cm
4 in	10 cm
5 in	12.5 cm
6 in	15 cm
7 in	18 cm
8 in	20 cm
9 in	23 cm
10 in	25 cm
11 in	28 cm
12 in	30 cm

Healthy eating

A healthy, balanced diet is one in which you eat anything you like, but in moderation. This means a diet of only grapefruits or Southern-fried chicken isn't healthy, no matter how much weight you may gain or lose. We need to eat a wide mixture of foods so that nutritional pluses outweigh the minuses and because it increases our chances of getting all the nutrients we need – not just to live, but to live in the best of health. The following guidelines explain how to balance our daily meals. Don't be alarmed: humans are flexible and a poor day in nutritional terms – where you don't eat much or it's mostly junk or empty calories (i.e., food that supplies energy in the form of calories but few other nutrients) – is easily compensated for in an all-round healthy diet.

As a guideline for planning a healthy menu, choose what you eat, and what proportions, from the following food categories. The food we eat every day should include:

Protein

Essential for: Growth, repair and maintenance of the cells that make up our body. Also as a source of energy, although this is an 'expensive' way to get calories. We should try and meet our energy needs from carbohydrates.

Source: Meat, fish, eggs, cheese, milk, soya products like tofu, Quorn (protein from vegetable sources), nuts, beans, pulses (peas and lentils) and grains. Note: the body also needs complex carbohydrates (see below) in order to utilise fully vegetable protein.

Daily requirements: Eat two portions of food from this category.

Deficiency: Very unlikely in the Western world. In deprived countries, protein deficiency causes poor growth and development.

Excess intake: Not harmful, just wasteful as excess protein is converted to energy or excreted.

Vitamins

Vitamin A (retinol)

Source: Milk, butter, margarine, cheese, egg yolk, liver, green vegetables, especially cabbage, watercress. Yellow vegetables like carrots and tomatoes.
Function: Healthy eyes, skin, teeth and gums and hair.
Deficiency: Temporary or permanent eye damage, dry and infected skin, poor resistance to disease.

Vitamin B-complex

(There are at least 13 substances in this group, hence the name complex. The three main B vitamins are niacin, riboflavin and thiamine.)
Source: Cereals, especially whole-grain cereals like brown rice. Food made from cereals like flour, bread, pasta; yeast, yeast extract (e.g., Marmite); pork, bacon, ham; liver, kidney, fish roe, milk and eggs.
• B1 (thiamine)
Function: Metabolic process; i.e., the conversion of carbohydrate to energy; for normal growth, maintaining good health, and healthy nerve function.
Deficiency: Anxiety, loss of concentration, possibly depression. Inflamed nerves, weakened muscles and reduced reflexes.
• B2 (riboflavin)
Function: Normal growth, and for bodily processes that release energy from protein and fat.
Deficiency: Skin and eye disorders, mouth problems including a sore, swollen tongue.
• B3 (niacin)
Source: To aid release of energy from food.
Deficiency: Skin problems, loss of appetite, diarrhoea, depression.

Vitamin C (ascorbic acid)

Source: Citrus fruits, blackcurrants, strawberries, potatoes. Green vegetables like cabbage, peppers, peas, broccoli.
Health note: Vitamin C is fragile – it's lost in cooking water, destroyed by heating and by exposure to air. We need to eat Vitamin C-rich foods every day.
Function: Construction of body tissue. Aids absorption of iron. Helps build strong bones and teeth. Maintains healthy blood circulatory system and lining of the digestive system.
Deficiency: General weakness and irritability. Pain in muscles and joints. Bleeding gums. Anaemia.

Vitamin D (calciferol)

Source: Egg yolks, margarine (added by law), oily fish, liver, sprouted seeds, milk and dairy products, especially in summer. Vitamin D is one of the only vitamins that is synthesised by our bodies, and they need sunlight for this process to occur. This also happens in cows, so summer milk contains the most Vitamin D.
Function: Aids the supply of calcium to make strong bones and teeth. Helps absorption of calcium and phosphorus.
Deficiency: Weak teeth and bones.

Vitamin E (tocopherol)

Source: Most foods. It's fat soluble, so its found in most fats, including egg yolk, milk and milk products, grains, peanuts and seeds.
Function: Normal functioning of red blood cells and muscles. Resistance to infection.
Deficiency: Unknown, since it is so widely available.

Vitamin K (menadione)

Source: leafy green vegetables, especially spinach. Also produced by the healthy bacteria (flora) present in our intestines.
Function: For normal clotting of the blood, especially after injury.
Deficiency: Very rare.

Minerals

Calcium

Source: Dairy products, milk, cheese, white flour and bread (added by law), edible bones in canned fish, broccoli, nuts and seeds.
Function: Combines with phosphorus to build and maintain strong and healthy bones and teeth. Helps blood to clot. Needed for normal functioning of nerves and muscles.
Deficiency: Weak bones and teeth. Poor function of nerves and muscles.

Phosphorus

Source: Occurs naturally in all organic foods, but best sources are fish, poultry, whole grains, eggs, nuts and seeds.
Function: Works with calcium to allow normal bone and tooth structure, to assimilate niacin, to regulate heart and kidney functioning, and for production of energy in the body.
Deficiency: Can lead to rickets and pyorrhoea; in excess phosphorus can cause calcium deficiency.

Iron

Source: Organ meats, including kidney and liver, cocoa, red meats, white bread (added by law), dried fruit, eggs, nuts, fortified breakfast cereals, oatmeal and oysters. Leafy green vegetables are also a good source.
Function: Necessary for building red blood cells which supply oxygen to every cell in the body to maintain cell functions.
Deficiency: Occurs most often in babies three months after birth. (They are born with three months' supply, but afterwards breast milk is not a good source of iron.) Also menstruating and pregnant women may need extra iron. Deficiency causes weakness, fatigue, low resistance to infection and possibly anaemia.

Magnesium

Source: Figs, lemons, citrus fruits, yellow corn, apples, milk, meat, eggs, pulses, nuts and grains.
Function: Essential for nerve and muscle functioning, helps to convert blood sugar into energy, helps prevent depression and heart attacks.
Deficiency: Unlikely.

Potassium

Source: Citrus fruits, watercress, mint, sunflower seeds and oil, bananas, potatoes.
Function: Works with sodium (see below) to regulate water balance, heart, nerve and muscle function, blood pressure and immune system.
Deficiency: Can cause hypoglycaemia, weakness, poor reflexes and high blood pressure.

Selenium

Source: Wheatgerm, bran, tuna, tomatoes, broccoli, onions and shellfish.
Function: Antioxidant (slows down the ageing process and the hardening of tissues caused by oxidation; so may provides protection against some cancers and heart disease)
Deficiency: Premature ageing, heart disease.

Sodium Chloride

Source: Salt, shellfish, carrots, artichokes, bacon, beets.
Function: Ensures the normal functioning of muscles and nerves; essential for normal growth.
Deficiency: Very rare, except in extreme heat; can cause impaired digestion and nerve damage.

Zinc

Source: Lamb, pork, wheatgerm, yeast extract, eggs, ground mustard, seafood.
Function: Accelerates healing, treats infertility, promotes mental agility, controls cholesterol, helps in the formation of insulin, controls the efficiency of body processes.
Deficiency: heart disease, infertility and fatigue.

Carbohydrates

Essential for: Supplying energy. Many carbohydrates deliver fibre, vitamins and minerals, too.

Source: Complex carbohydrates are starches like flour, bread, cereals, pasta, rice, potatoes, grains. Simple carbohydrate sources are sugars like cane sugar, honey, jam, fruit and some vegetables.

Daily requirements: Eat four portions from this list, concentrating on getting your carbohydrates from starches and not from sugars.

Deficiency: Highly unlikely in the West unless on a very strict diet, or suffering from an eating disorder such as anorexia nervosa or bulimia, where reduced energy is the result.

Excess intake: Excess carbohydrate is converted to fat and stored under the skin as an emergency energy reserve. Can lead to overweight and obesity. Excess sugars can cause tooth decay and gum disease.

Fat

Essential for: Providing a concentrated source of energy, surrounding and protecting internal organs like the kidneys, and providing a layer of insulation under our skin. Also a source of fat-soluble Vitamins A, D, E and K.

Source: Dairy products, especially butter, cheese, milk, yoghurt; margarine, lard, dripping, meat, oily fish, egg yolk, vegetable oils.

Daily requirements: Eat two portions of dairy food, but keep fat consumption low, especially saturated fats which tend to be the hard fats, from animal sources. Fish oils – from sardines, herrings and mackerel – are beneficial. Pure vegetable oils, like sunflower or olive oil are unsaturated and less inclined to cause circulatory and heart disease. Use all fats sparingly. Use pure vegetable oils for cooking where possible; use skimmed milk and grill; steam or bake food instead of frying it. Trim visible fat from meat and skin from poultry. Be aware of hidden fats – in pastry, patés, sausages, salami, pork pies, cakes, crisps and chocolate.

Deficiency: Unlikely, but can lead to lack of energy and low body weight.

Excess intake: We become overweight, possibly obese and arteries and heart can become blocked with fatty deposits, which may result in a heart attack.

Vitamins and minerals

Essential for: Vitamins are chemical substances required to maintain and regulate growth and to control most body functions (see chart, pp. 202-3). They are only required in tiny quantities, but most cannot be manufactured in the body so we have to have regular supplies from our diet. Minerals control body processes and bodily fluids and help to maintain good health. We need at least twenty mineral elements over and above the carbon, hydrogen and oxygen we get when protein, fat and carbohydrate are broken down.

Source: All foods, especially fresh foods and particularly fruit and vegetables (see chart).

Daily requirements: Eat four portions of fresh or lightly cooked fruit and vegetables, more if you like.

Deficiency: Lack of vitality (see chart for specific symptoms of deficiency).

Excess intake: (see chart).

MEAL PLANNING TIP When planning your menus, check the chart to ensure a good nutritional mix. Once you've grasped the basic idea, you can see why it is a good idea to have one green, one yellow or red vegetable at a meal, to have spaghetti with meat sauce or chips with fish. As long as you eat a variety of foods, at each meal of the day – even if it's only a tuna and salad sandwich lunch – you are almost certain to fulfil your nutritional needs.

Fibre

Not strictly speaking a nutrient, fibre is nonetheless an essential part of a healthy diet. Fibre is the cellulose or indigestible element of plant food that our guts cannot break down.

Essential for: Causing the swift evacuation of waste products from the body. The toxic remains of the food we have digested pass through the large intestine by the action of it expanding and contracting alternately to propel the faeces along. A high proportion of fibre in the faeces absorbs water, bulking out the stools and keeping them soft and easy to pass.

Source: Whole grains, cereals and bread, beans, pulses, fruit and vegetables, dried fruit, nuts and seeds.

Daily requirements: About 25 g (1 oz) a day. A mixed diet, as described above, with four portions of starchy carbohydrate and four portions of fruit and/or vegetables should easily supply this. Drink plenty of fluids, too, or you may find it difficult to pass. If you are eating enough fibre your stools should float.

Deficiency: Irregular bowel movements, leading to constipation and more serious bowel problems.

Excess intake: Bloated feeling and wind, poor absorption of iron and other minerals, bowel disorders.

Water

Water is essential to life. Seventy per cent of the human body is water, and while we can live for several days without food, we cannot go for long without water.

Source: Water and other liquids taken as drinks, also from fruit and vegetables. Water is also a by-product of some processes within the body.

Function: All bodily fluids – like saliva and other digestive juices, blood, sweat and urine – are dependent. Also keeps linings of mucous membranes, the digestive tract and the lungs moist. Lubricates joints. Essential for many metabolic reactions – the conversion of food to energy – and absorption of nutrients from food.

Daily requirements: 2 to 3 litres (3 to 5 pints) a day. Water is continuously lost through our breath, urine and perspiration. More may be needed in very hot weather, after sickness or diarrhoea leading to

dehydration, and by women who are breastfeeding.

Deficiency: Thirst, dehydration and in extreme cases, death.

Excess intake: Loss of appetite and dilution of other nutrients.

Cooking for special diets

The amount and type of food we need to eat to stay in good health, and particularly to maintain a sensible body weight, varies according to the following factors:

- ☞ Age – whether we are going through a period of growth or slowing down due to ageing.
- ☞ Sex – men tend to be physically larger than women and so generally need more energy (calories).
- ☞ Physical activity – a child or anyone with a strenuous job or someone taking a lot of exercise will need more calories in relation to their body size.
- ☞ Body state – pregnant or breastfeeding women have special dietary needs. And sick people and people with severe food allergies may also require a different diet.

Feeding babies

The ideal food is human breast milk, which is the best combination of nutrients, easily digested, sterile and containing antibodies which will build up immunity to illness. Powdered baby milk is cow's milk modified to resemble human milk more closely.

From around three or four months old, or when the baby reaches a certain weight, a breastfed baby may need extra iron or Vitamin C. Since this is often the stage at which weaning begins, you can usually

---

> **SAFETY NOTE** Always make up a baby's formula according to manufacturer's instructions – too much powder to water can cause strain on the baby's kidneys and unnecessary weight gain.

supplement the baby's diet with suitably fortified foods. Consult your GP or health visitor.

Weaning babies

At some point between four and six months your baby may want to start on solids – he'll let you know by not seeming satisfied at the end of a feed or by starting to wake up in the night, having previously slept through.

Start your baby on soft, sloppy puréed food. Baby rice or specially modified cereals are a common first choice. It's important not to introduce anything potentially allergenic in those first months of solid foods. Try to avoid wheat and anything with cow's milk, in particular. Carrots, potatoes, apple or pear, home-cooked without salt or sugar are ideal first foods. Avoid eggs, peanuts, honey and any foods that are high in fat, salt or spices, before the age of one year.

Don't rush your baby, introduce a teaspoonful before his regular milk feed while he is hungry. Add new foods gradually – introducing too many too soon can cause allergies. Introduce them one at a time so you can spot any reaction.

Later on – about eight months – you can introduce slightly lumpier foods and teach your baby to take liquids from a cup with a drinking spout.

SAFETY NOTE
• **Consult your GP or health visitor about any changes to your baby's diet.**
• **Never leave your baby alone with food – he could choke.**
• **Avoid all nuts, especially peanuts, until pre-school age – they are a common allergen and can cause choking.**

Feeding children

Because children are going through a rapid growth period and because they lead such active lives and need a lot of energy, they need a healthy mixed diet, high in the following nutrients:

MENU-PLANNING TIPS
• **Make food look interesting and colourful.**
• **Encourage your child to taste a little of everything but don't make mealtimes stressful.**
• **Remember too, that this is an important time for children to learn good eating habits (and table manners).**

☞ Protein – for growth and repair
☞ Calcium and Vitamin D – especially from full-fat milk, for strong bones and teeth
☞ Starchy carbohydrates – for energy and fibre. Sugary and fatty processed foods provide a lot of calories but don't have much other nutritional value; keep them to a minimum
☞ Vitamins and minerals – from fresh fruit and vegetables (see *Healthy eating*, pp. 201-5)

Feeding vegetarians

There are two types of vegetarians:
☞ **Lacto-vegetarians**, who don't eat, meat, poultry or fish, but do eat eggs (free-range), cheese (vegetarian cheese set without animal rennet) and other dairy products. Menu-planning is not usually a problem because of the variety of foods from which to choose.
☞ **Vegans**, who don't eat meat, poultry, fish or dairy products – in fact anything from animal sources at all. They get their protein from soya products, beans and pulses, grains, nuts and seeds. Because of the lack of animal fats vegans may suffer from a lack of calcium, B-complex vitamins and Vitamin D and so require supplements.

MENU-PLANNING TIPS
• **Check labels on products carefully; those suitable for vegetarians carry a special symbol.**

Feeding slimmers

There are two main ways to slim:

☞ Eat fewer calories (cutting down on fat is the most important way).

☞ Burn up more calories by taking more exercise.

The best bet is a combination of both.

Feeding diabetics

Diabetics suffer from raised levels of sugar in their blood. They do not produce enough insulin to convert the sugar to energy, so eventually there is a build-up of harmful ketones (toxins caused by the unconverted sugars) in the blood which can cause the diabetic to go into a coma. Some diabetics can control their sugar levels by adjusting their diet; some need drugs, too. Detailed information is available from your GP.

Allergies

Some people have to modify their diet
because of food allergies – often intolerance
to milk and milk products or to wheat flour
and gluten. Others find dietary changes offer
some relief from eczema, asthma, irritable
bowel syndrome, migraine, etc. It is beyond
the scope of this book to discuss the various
diets available for allergy sufferers, but your
GP can give you advice, and there are dozens
of books available on the subject. Many
organisations offer self-help groups which can
offer help and advice in meal planning.

Religious objections

Some religions forbid the consumption of
various foods. Many Jews won't eat pork or
bacon products, shellfish or eels, or serve milk
and meat together (or within several hours of
one another). Meat must be slaughtered in a
special way and is never served at the same
meal as milk.

Muslims won't eat pork and other meat
must be halal – slaughtered according to their
holy ritual. Hindus regard the cow as sacred
and won't eat products which involve cows
being killed.

Keep it clean

Hygiene is of special importance in the
kitchen in order to avoid contamination and
its possible consequence – food poisoning.

Hygiene in the shops

Be vigilant when you're shopping for the
following signs of poor hygiene:
- ☞ dirty floors with rubbish and spills on the
  floors
- ☞ old dusty and dented tins and food
  packets that indicate a slow turnover
- ☞ staff with dirty hair or hair not tied back,
  grubby hands and nails, soiled overalls or
  aprons
- ☞ animals wandering in the shop

Hygiene at home

- ☞ Keep work surfaces, cooker and sink
  clean – wipe up spills as you go.
- ☞ Bleach or renew your dishcloth frequently
  and relace soiled tea towels often.
- ☞ Wrap waste in newspaper before putting
  in the bin, preferably in a bin-liner. Keep
  the bin in a cool place, and tightly
  covered against pets and insects. Empty
  and bleach (or disinfect) regularly.
- ☞ Keep all food clean, cool and covered.
  Store food promptly, keeping raw and
  cooked foods separate – in the fridge and
  during preparation (e.g., use different
  chopping boards for meat or fish and
  bread or salad).
- ☞ Wash up in the hottest water you can
  stand – wear rubber gloves so you can
  increase the heat.
- ☞ If possible, use another room for doing
  your laundry.

☞ Don't allow pets on kitchen surfaces.

☞ Keep pet food and dishes separate from yours, keep a special washing-up brush or cloth just for them.

☞ Make sure food is thoroughly thawed before cooking, especially large or rolled joints and poultry.

☞ When reheating ready-meals follow the pack instructions carefully. Make sure all hot food is piping hot right through to the centre before you eat it.

Personal hygiene

☞ Wash your hands frequently, and ALWAYS after using the loo, blowing your nose, touching your face or hair, stroking pets and handling raw meat or fish.

☞ Tie your hair back or otherwise keep it out of your eyes and out of your cooking.

☞ Cover up cuts and grazes.

☞ Don't lick spoons or your fingers and then handle food with them.

Shopping for food

Even with the biggest fridge, freezer and storecupboard, shopping for food is a pretty regular activity. It's a matter of personal preference – transport, budget and storage facilities permitting – whether we do it daily, weekly or monthly. Shopping in dribs and drabs in small local shops can prove time consuming and possibly costly, but bulk buying can lead to bulk consumption. Most people find a mixture is the most realistic option.

What do I need?

Obviously this depends on what you want to cook, but a good basic storecupboard of items you could use in many different recipes, is a good idea. And with the following items in stock you'll never be stuck for a meal.

Staples

✔ Baking powder
✔ Bicarbonate of soda
✔ Breakfast cereal
✔ Cocoa, for drinking or cooking
✔ Coffee
✔ Dried beans or pulses
✔ Dried fruit
✔ Flour, plain, for pastry, sauces, coating, etc.
✔ Flour, self-raising, for cakes and puddings
✔ Nuts (store in the freezer to stop them going stale)
✔ Oil – sunflower or similar for cooking and salad dressing
✔ Pasta, any shape you like!
✔ Rice, long grain or basmati for side dish
✔ Sugar, caster, for desserts, pastry
✔ Sugar, granulated, for tea and coffee, stewed fruit, etc.
✔ Tea

Seasonings and flavourings

✔ Chutney
✔ Herbs
✔ Honey
✔ Jam
✔ Ketchup
✔ Mayonnaise
✔ Mustard
✔ Pepper/peppercorns
✔ Pickles
✔ Salt
✔ Savoury or sweet spreads
✔ Soy sauce
✔ Spices
✔ Stock cubes
✔ Tomato purée
✔ Vinegar

Canned goods

✔ Beans
✔ Fruit
✔ Sardines
✔ Tomatoes
✔ Tuna

Refrigerated foods

✔ Bacon
✔ Butter
✔ Cheese, for cooking or snacks
✔ Eggs
✔ Lard, for roasting or pastry
✔ Margarine, block or soft, for cooking or
   spreading
✔ Milk
✔ Yoghurt

Frozen foods

✔ Ice cream
✔ Bread
✔ Vegetables
✔ Puff pastry

Vegetable rack

✔ Cabbage
✔ Carrots
✔ Garlic
✔ Onions
✔ Potatoes

SHOPPING SAVVY

✎ **Make a list. Use the categories on the left to write your own shopping list. Add: 'meat', 'fish', 'dairy', 'fruit and vegetables', 'drinks' and 'bread' categories, once you've planned your menus. If you just can't face planning meals for a whole week, stock up with basics like minced beef, chicken or fish in the freezer and 'create' a dish using storecupboard items as the fancy takes you.**
✎ **TAKE THE LIST WITH YOU!**
✎ **Try not to shop when you are hungry, otherwise you'll find a trolley full of snacks and goodies.**
✎ **Look for good practice in handling food. Raw meats and food that will be eaten uncooked, like cold cooked meats and cheese, should not be displayed together or handled consecutively. Check assistants look clean and tidy and that they use tongs or gloves where appropriate.**
✎ **Check that food is not piled above the load line in freezer cabinets, as it won't be at the correct temperature. Beware of bags of 'free-flow' vegetables that have solidified, they may have partially thawed.**
✎ **Check 'best before' dates, particularly on dairy or ready-made meals.**
✎ **Loose fruit and vegetables are usually cheaper than pre-packed equivalents.**
✎ **Don't leave shopping hanging around. Get it home and unpacked into the fridge and freezer as soon as possible.**

Understanding the label

All packaged foods carry a label stating the contents and country of origin. What else can you discover from it?

The ingredients list shows contents in order of weight; i.e., there is most of the first ingredient on the list and least of the last ingredient on the list. Dairy products and alcoholic drinks are exceptions to the rule.

Many products also carry nutrition information labels showing typical values per 100 g of the contents. The energy (calorie), protein, carbohydrate, fat, sodium and fibre values are given, as well as other nutritional messages such as suitable (or not suitable) for certain dietary needs, e.g., vegetarian, cow's milk-free, gluten-free.

The description of the product is revealing, too. The inclusion of the word 'flavour' may mean that there is no genuine banana in a 'banana flavour drink', for instance. There must, by law, be some banana in a 'banana drink'. Check the ingredients list.

Colourings and preservatives used in the product must be listed on the label by name and what purpose they serve or by E number. If you suspect you have an intolerance to any additive invest in a directory of E numbers to find out more (see page 430 for a list of good and bad E numbers).

The black striped bar code is of use purely to the retailer, for whom it provides price and stock control information.

How much to buy?

When you can help yourself, for instance from supermarket displays of meat or vegetables, it easy to assess by eye the quantity you'll need. Try imagining the meal on the plate – how many chops, how many potatoes, how many green beans?

As a rule of thumb, you'll need 125 to 175g (4 to 6 oz) boneless meat or fish per person, but twice as much if on the bone.

Allow about 75 g (3 oz) cheese per person for a meatless main dish and two or three eggs for an egg-based meal (e.g., an omelette). Allow about 225 g (8 oz) of potato per person, about 125 g (4 oz) of each other vegetable. Allow about 50 g (2 oz) uncooked weight of pasta or rice per person as an accompaniment, more if it's the main component of the meal.

How long will it keep?

All packaged food carries a 'best before' date. This is the period in which the food will remain in prime condition and be safe to eat. While many foods are still all right to eat beyond this date because manufacturers err on the side of safety, it is not recommended.

☞ Keep all food clean, cool and covered.

☞ Use the 'best before' date to rotate storecupboard supplies and food in your fridge.

☞ Use fresh meat and fish within a couple of days. Use minced meat, sausages and other partly prepared meat as soon as possible, preferably the same day.

☞ Store fresh fruit and vegetables in a cool, dark place. Remove from polyethylene bags as they may sweat and go mouldy. Allow air to circulate around them. Use vegetables as soon as possible to get maximum nutritional value from them.

☞ Keep dry stores, like flour, beans and pulses in insect-proof jars or containers. Brown flours don't keep as well as white, because of the fat content. Use within six months.

☞ Store tea and coffee in airtight containers after opening and use within one month.

☞ Keep jams, pickles and chutneys in the fridge once opened. Use within three months.

☞ Keep biscuits in an airtight tin once opened. Don't store with cakes, which will make them go soggy.

☞ Most canned foods will keep for one to two years, although acidic foods like tomatoes keep less well. Don't buy rusty or dented cans.

☞ Check can tops for puffiness. These cans are described as 'blown' and it's a sign that the food inside is spoilt. Throw them away.

Entertaining

Cooking for friends is an enjoyable business.
There's nothing like gathering people around
a table over food and wine to get
conversation flowing.

Menu planning

The two main principles of menu planning are
to provide a nutritious and enjoyable meal.
The nutritional balance is obviously most
important in everyday menu planning (see
Healthy eating, pp. 201-5) for more details.
When you're entertaining, the emphasis is on
relaxation and enjoyment (though everyday
eating should be a pleasant affair, too). The
occasional meal that is not particularly
balanced never hurt anybody!

How many people?

Don't over-stretch yourself. Consider the
following before you plan your event:

- ☞ The number of people you can seat
  comfortably whether it's a sit-down meal
  or buffet supper.
- ☞ How much crockery, cutlery and glass
  you own or can borrow.
- ☞ How much oven or fridge space you
  have.
- ☞ How much money you can afford to
  spend.
- ☞ How much time you can spend.

What shall we eat?

The main aim is for variety and interest:

Variety of flavours. Don't follow pork
and apple sauce with apple pie. But don't feel
you have to batter their tastebuds with every
spice and herb under the sun. Balance strong-
flavoured foods with the natural flavours of
simple ingredients; e.g., lamb spiked with garlic
served with the first new potatoes of the
season.

Variety of colours. Think about the
different courses and ensure they're not all
red or brown. Introduce colourful vegetables
and garnishes, or fruit. Great big tossed salads,
brimming with red, yellow and green peppers
and colourful lettuces are nutritious and

attractive – top them with stilton, pine nuts
or crumbled bacon for something more filling.

Variety of textures. If you're serving a
soft and saucy main course, like fish in white
wine and cream sauce, consider a crisp salad
to start and perhaps a pastry-based dessert.

Variety of richness. Avoid heavy,
creamy sauces or other rich mixtures in every
course. Contrast rich puddings with simple
main dishes. (Most people seem to manage
an obscenely rich pudding.)

Make it easy on yourself

It's your evening too!

 Plan to prepare as much as possible in
advance. A cold starter or dessert can be
prepared on the morning, or even the
day before.

 Make a rough time-plan of what to do
when, bearing in mind that you won't
serve dinner as soon as the guests arrive.
Decide a time to start eating and then,
with a list to remind yourself, what time
you need to put on the oven/vegetables,
etc.

 Don't add unnecessary stress. Good
ingredients, simply prepared and well
cooked are always appreciated.

 Don't cook too many dishes you've
never done before. Don't leave yourself
too much between-course/last-minute
work – stick to checking seasoning,
dishing up and garnishing rather than stir-
frying, tricky sauce-making or sugar-
spinning!

How to get ahead

- ☞ Shop well in advance so you can adjust
  the menu if a vital ingredient is
  unavailable. Don't forget wine, water and
  aperitifs (see *Choosing and serving wine*,
  page 219).
- ☞ Plan and lay the table as early as possible,
  gathering up china, cutlery, glasses and
  linen. Plan how to warm the plates. Sort
  out after-dinner coffee-making equipment
  and cups, liqueurs and glasses and leave
  ready on a tray.
- ☞ Do as much advance preparation as
  possible, including freezing food.

Otherwise, the day before, make pastry and cook cases if appropriate. Make and chill frozen or set desserts. Make paté, soup, croutons, sauces and salad dressings and store in fridge.

☞ Early in the day, trim, bone, fillet, stuff meat or fish. Prepare vegetables. Keep potatoes in cold water; plastic bag other vegetables or washed salad and keep chilled.

☞ Do any smelly work – like frying – as early as possible, rather than in your party clothes.

☞ Don't forget your microwave oven for last-minute cooking of vegetables, melting butter or reheating.

SAFETY NOTE **If you are preparing or part-preparing food in advance, make sure you cool it quickly and keep it clean, cool and covered. Make sure any reheating is thorough – hot food should be served piping hot.**

Setting the style

When you've spent time and trouble planning a menu and cooking for a dinner party, it's a pleasure and pride to present it in style. It's also a compliment to your guests. Laying the table in the classic way is not just a fussy formality – it helps avoid confusion and allows your guests to relax and enjoy themselves.

Covering the table

Whether you cover the table with a cloth or use place mats is a matter of personal preference (and the state of table surface).
If you do use a cloth:

☞ Put a thick blanket or special plastic table protector underneath to preserve a precious polished surface.

☞ Don't put mats under a cloth as the uneven surface could result in spills.

☞ Don't let the cloth trail on the floor where it may get tangled in guests' feet and cause an accident.

Lighting

Keep lighting low enough to encourage relaxation and intimacy, but not so low that guests can't see what they are eating or each other.

If using candles, keep them low so your guests can see over them. (The same goes for flowers and other table decorations.)

Place settings

Lay the cutlery at each place setting in the order in which it is used. The golden rule for the diner is to start with the cutlery on the outside and work inwards through the courses. Lay knives on the right-hand side (even if your guest if left-handed) and always face the blades in, towards the plate. Make sure you leave enough space for your dinner plates to fit between the cutlery.

Starter

The knife and fork, or spoon and fork for a starter go on the outside – the knife or spoon on the right of the plate, the fork on the left of the plate.

Main course/fish course

Put the knife and fork for the main course inside the starter cutlery – knife on the right, fork on the left of the plate. If serving a fish course between the two, lay cutlery for it before the main course cutlery and after the starter cutlery. As a guest, you can look at the cutlery when you sit down and work out how many courses to expect. Generally the largest knife and fork are for the main course.

Bread and butter

Put a small knife on the side plate.

Dessert

Place a dessert spoon and fork above the space where the plate will go, with spoon on top with the handle to the right and the fork beneath it with the handle to the left.

Cheese/fruit

Lay a small knife with the dessert spoon and fork.

Side plates

A side plate for bread is positioned to the left of the plate, on the outside of the cutlery.

Napkins

Fold neatly and arrange in the space in the centre of the cutlery, in the wine glass, or on the side plate.

Glasses

Group in the top right-hand corner of each place setting. In a restaurant, plates are cleared from your left-hand side to avoid a clash between a plate and a raised glass. Lay one glass for red wine, one for white and one for water (provided you are serving all three, of course). A large glass, preferably a tulip-shaped glass on a stem is generally used for red wine, and sometimes for water. White wine is usually served in a smaller glass. Don't fill wine glasses more than half-full, so you have space to enjoy the bouquet of the wine.

Entertaining etiquette

A hostess/host

- ☞ Gives guests advance warning of what sort of evening to expect – a casual supper in the kitchen or dressy dinner party.
- ☞ Checks in advance if guests have any dietary no-nos – eating meat, allergies, religious objections.
- ☞ Welcomes guests appearing relaxed and in control (even if he or she really isn't ...)
- ☞ Introduces guests to each other and seats them at table in such a way as to maximise conversation.
- ☞ Serves the main course on to the plates, allowing guests to help themselves to side-dishes.
- ☞ Notices if someone needs a dish passed to them, whose glass needs re-filling, who needs bringing into the conversation.

- ☞ Doesn't notice if someone is politely leaving something they don't wish to eat.
- ☞ Doesn't clear plates away until everyone has finished eating that course.

A guest

- ☞ Arrives on time.
- ☞ Doesn't start eating until everyone is served.
- ☞ Doesn't help themselves to more than their fair share.
- ☞ Doesn't use their own cutlery in serving dishes or handle food other than their own.
- ☞ Eats bread or a roll by breaking off bite-size pieces and spreading with butter from a dab on the side of their plate, one bit at a time as they eat it.
- ☞ Is aware of others, notices when to pass things, when to engage someone in conversation.
- ☞ Paces their speed of eating so they don't finish long before, or after, everyone else.
- ☞ Rests cutlery on the plate while chewing, rather than waving it in the air.
- ☞ Makes a polite and reasonably convincing excuse for leaving or refusing food/second helpings.
- ☞ Doesn't start clearing away or stacking plates unless requested to by the hostess.
- ☞ Offers to help with clearing or washing up, but doesn't insist if hostess firmly refuses.
- ☞ Phones or writes to thank the hostess.
- ☞ Doesn't insult other guests.

Catering for a crowd

Feeding larger numbers than those for which you usually cater is not necessarily difficult – especially if you plan the menu so you can get a lot of work done in advance. (See *Menu planning*, page 212.)

The amount of food and drink you will need to buy and prepare depends on the type of party, the time of day and, obviously, the appetite of your guests.

Whatever kind of party you have, the food is almost certain to be served as a buffet. There are two main types of buffet.

☞ At a formal buffet, guests may all eat at the same time, coming to the table and helping themselves, or being served with food, then eating it at other tables. They may return to the table to collect a dessert.

☞ At an informal buffet food may be laid out constantly and guests can just help themselves when they choose and eat standing or temporarily seated.

Drinks parties

The implication of this kind of party is that food is secondary to drink. Guests will probably expect nibbles or simple food like cheese and bread, but not a main meal.

Formal cocktail party

Serve a limited range of drinks (unless you can afford to hire a barman for the evening). Cocktails take a while to prepare so you could end up working all evening with your guests queuing for a drink and a chat with the host or hostess!

Best drinks

☞ One kind of cocktail or mixed drink, made up in large quantities – say, Margueritas, Pimms or Kir – in a jug for instant re-filling
☞ Sherry – have a variety of dry (Fino), medium to dry (Amontillado) and sweet
☞ Wine or champagne
☞ Water, soft drinks for drivers

Best food

Keep the food small enough to eat in two bites at the most and don't choose crumbly, gooey or staining food that's difficult to eat with fingers.

☞ Nuts and crisps
☞ Olives
☞ Tiny savoury pastries, bite-size pizza and cheese straws
☞ Crudités (raw vegetable sticks) and dips
☞ Sausages, mini frankfurters with spicy dips
☞ Satays on sticks
☞ Grilled prawns with a honey sauce for dipping.

Informal drinks party

A good way to enjoy company without having to seat everyone. Most guests would expect to bring a bottle – suggest it on the invitation, if you like, otherwise it can prove expensive.

Best drinks

☞ Wine – doesn't have to be top-quality, some of the country wines are very appealing with food or on their own. Go for lighter. easy-drinking reds, plus white wines – some dry and some medium. (See *Choosing and serving wine*, page 219.)
☞ Serve well chilled – put them in a clean dustbin or the bath with cold water and plenty of ice.

> **SHOPPING TIP   Unless you know the majority of your friends like red wine, buy a ratio of about one-third red wine and two-thirds white wine.**

☞ Beer – bitter and lager in bottles or cans. If you want bulk beer speak to your wine merchant well in advance of the party. A barrel of real ale will need time to settle in its party place before serving.

Best food

'**Finger food**' is the most appropriate:
☞ sausage rolls, chicken drumsticks, French bread, pizza etc., that doesn't require cutlery
☞ Bread and cheese or paté, with celery, radishes and pickles

Food that needs **cutlery**, but is quite easy to prepare and serve includes:
☞ Selection of cold meat and fish, quiches, various salads, new potatoes

Hot food can be suitable, and there are lots of easy menus that can be prepared with minimum fuss and expense. Some traditional favourites include:

☞ Sausages and mash with onion gravy
☞ Shepherd's pie and beans
☞ Lasagne and green salad
☞ Curries and rice
☞ Pizza and salad
☞ Chilli and bread

Puddings and **desserts** are always successful; you might even consider serving these alone – with steaming Irish coffee or mulled wine over the winter months, or some inexpensive fizzy wine or Sangria in summer.

☞ Strawberries and cream
☞ Pastries or gateaux (profiteroles or rich chocolate cupcakes are easy to eat and prepare)
☞ Cheesecakes
☞ Fresh fruit salad
☞ Trifle
☞ Chocolate mousse (try white chocolate with a swirl of summer fruit sauce)

BUFFET TIPS
• **Position the table and arrange the food to allow maximum access to the table, otherwise there may be queuing.**
• **Divide each dish between several plates along the length of the table, again for maximum access.**
• **Put plates and cutlery at various points, or place them (and the drink) away from the main table to keep people circulating.**
• **Expect people to try a 'little of everything' and cater accordingly.**

• **Choose food that is easily portioned if people are helping themselves; i.e., if you have individual pieces of fish or chicken in a sauce, use a garnish on each to denote one serving.**
• **Cut quiches, gateaux, etc., into slices rather than letting guests cut their own. It's neater and faster.**
• **Choose food that's easy to eat on a balanced plate with just a fork.**
• **Choose food that can be prepared (and preferably frozen) in advance.**
• **Make soft desserts like mousse or trifle in individual glasses (like borrowed wine glasses) if possible as they look messy once they've been scooped into. It also helps control portion size as well!**

Barbecues

Barbecues are a popular way of feeding a crowd when the weather is good, probably because the garden takes the strain rather than your carpets, and it's good family entertainment that children can enjoy, too.

Best drinks

Stick to the standard favourites (see *Drinks parties*, page 215), with the possible additions of:

☞ Extra beer or a fruity punch
☞ Pimms or something like freshly squeezed lemonade with gin or vodka is nice served out of doors
☞ Drinks for the children

Best food

Nibbles and **starters**

☞ Cold soups (serve in borrowed bowls or paper cups)
☞ Melon
☞ Mexican tortilla chips and dips
☞ Taramasalata, humous and pitta bread

Main courses

☞ Good sausages (try some flavoured with stilton or leeks, for example) and burgers, buns and relishes

☞ Small chicken joints, Chicken tikka, spare ribs

☞ Steaks or kebabs, barbecue or satay sauce

☞ Small whole fish – sardines, red mullet, skewered, prawns or fish kebabs

☞ Salmon or tuna steaks – look out for special offers throughout the summer months; they aren't as expensive as you might think

☞ Garlic bread, hot or cold new potatoes, jacket potatoes rice salad, tabbouleh (cracked bulgar wheat salad), pasta salad

☞ Vegetable kebabs or ratatouille, assorted salads, corn on the cob, barbecued peppers, aubergine and courgette

Puds *and* Desserts

☞ Barbecued bananas (slit the skin, add a little dark rum, a dot of butter and sprinkling of sugar, and seal again to cook)

☞ Fruit kebabs, marshmallows

☞ Fresh fruit – watermelon, peaches, strawberries dipped in chocolate

☞ Summer pudding

☞ Ice cream cones or sundaes with hot fudge sauce

SAFETY NOTES
• **Don't brush marinade from raw meat or fish over food unless it's got at least five more minutes to cook.**
• **Never ever pour petrol on a lit barbecue – it could light back into the can or set fire to splashes on your clothes.**

BARBECUE TIPS
• **Fresh air seems to stimulate appetites so cater accordingly.**
• **Don't forget vegetarians. Falafel (spicy chickpea balls), onion bahjias, tofu kebabs, veggie burgers cook well on the barbecue. Keep them well away from the meat, or even borrow a barbecue to keep them separate.**
• **Have plenty of charcoal and allow it to burn for at least one hour or until the coals are grey before starting cooking.**
• **Try to turn food once only or you'll lose all the juices from the surface.**
• **Use the heat zones, moving food to outer parts or raising or lowering the barbecue grid to cook food through without the outside burning.**
• **Marinate foods to tenderise and flavour them. Brush with marinade during cooking to keep them moist.**

Children's parties

Parents may dread them but children love them – and they usually only come round once a year. Like any other occasion when you're feeding a crowd, planning ahead takes away the headaches.

Best drinks

Depends on the age of the children, but generally they get very thirsty and drink a lot.

☞ Soft drinks bought in bulk bottles work out cheaper but may be more easily spilt than cans or cartons with straws (spilt milk or blackcurrant makes the worst stains on carpets and furniture)

☞ Older children may like a fruit punch or mixed drink (non-alcoholic) 'cocktail'

Best food

Familiar foods tend to be the most popular, especially with younger children:

- Mini sausages, chicken 'nuggets', cubed cheese
- Small sandwiches, pizza fingers, cheesy biscuits, crisps
- Sausage rolls, rolled-up ham, cucumber rounds dotted with cream cheese

Hot food

- Hotdogs in buns
- Burgers in buns with relish and oven chips, pizza.
- Jacket potato wedges or 'skins' with cheese and bacon

SAFETY NOTE Don't give peanuts to children under five years old.

Puddings and cakes

- Ice cream with fruit/sauces and 'sprinkles'
- Chocolate 'crispy' cakes, biscuits, mini Swiss rolls
- Birthday cake
- Jelly with fruit, topped with cream
- Animal-shaped biscuits or tiny fruit muffins

CHILDREN'S PARTY TIPS

• Send written invitations stating the exact time the party begins and ends. Make it clear whether parents are welcome or not.

• **KEEP IT SHORT.** Two hours of non-stop fun is better than three hours of 'What shall we do now, Mum?'

• Don't invite more children than you can cope with. Remember to count in the party child's brothers and sisters, too, including perhaps a friend of their own.

• Ask for help. Get another parent to help with supervising or to help lay out the tea while you organise games.

• Fill the time – plan and prepare some party games with small prizes. Get a book from the library for ideas. Even games you may think are old-fashioned or out-dated can go down really well. Get a short video for the quieter end of the party, or if parents are late collecting their children.

• Allow for a hectic teatime – children don't necessarily eat food in the same order at a party as at home. Try a couple of quieter games before tea so they calm down a bit if they've been dashing about.

• Relax and enjoy it!

Choosing and serving wine

It's impossible in a general reference book like this to describe all the wines available, with virtually every country in the world now producing and exporting their own. But the following guidelines will help you make your initial buying decisions. Once you've tasted some of the different options it's up to you to decide which you like best.

Wine myths

- There are no hard and fast rules about serving wine. The object of drinking wine is enjoyment – you don't have to drink what you don't like!
- You don't have to serve white wine with fish and red wine with red meat.
- It's not illegal or immoral to serve red wine lightly chilled.
- You don't have to lay down wine for years before it's ready to drink.

Why is there so much choice?

The difference in colour, flavour, dryness or sweetness of wine depends on:
The variety of grape
- the country of origin
- the soil of the vineyard
- the climate
- weather conditions (which vary from year to year)
- different methods of growing wine
- different methods of production

How can I tell the difference?

The only way to decide which types of wines you like is by tasting them. This is different from sipping them absent-mindedly at a party (which is fine, but this is the way to get to know them first):
- Fill the glass only about one-third full. Hold it by the stem so your hands don't change the temperature.
- Look at the colour – tilt the glass holding it above a white background. Generally, the paler the wine is, the lighter-bodied it will be. A deeper colour. whether red or white, indicates a fuller-bodied wine.
- Swirl the wine around the glass to release the aroma or 'bouquet', then sniff it. Repeat after a few more seconds. What does it smell of? Fruit? Flower? Is it smoky because it's been matured in oak barrels?
- Now taste. Different areas of our tongue register different tastes – acidity, sweetness and bitterness – so you need to roll the wine around your mouth so it comes in contact with your whole tongue. This is easier if you imagine you are chewing the wine.
- Try and breathe in small gulps of air at the same time through your slightly parted lips (this takes practice!) This allows the vapours to waft to the back of your throat where they can be identified and appreciated by your sense of smell.
- Think about the flavours. Can you taste fruit? Is the acidity right – enough to be fresh-tasting without being too sharp? Or is it sweet, possibly floral? Is it well-rounded? What other flavours does it remind you of? Most important, do you like it? Now swallow ...

What style of wine might I like?

The type of wine you want to serve will depend on your personal taste preferences but also possibly on the occasion for serving it. You may want a lighter wine if you're not eating, or fancy a robust wine to complement a meaty main course. The following general descriptions suggest some different styles of wine, but remember that the origin, age and price of the wine mean that there will always be variations, even in the same grape types.

White wines

Dry delicate wines with no really distinctive fruit

From **France**:
- Muscadet
- Bordeaux sec
- Mâcon blanc
- Pinot blanc

From **Italy**:
- Soave
- Frascati
- Verdicchio

Others:
- Cheaper Californian and Spanish table wines
- Laski Rizling from Yugoslavia

Dry crisp whites, reminiscent of sharp apples or gooseberries

From **France**:
- White burgundy
- Bordeaux Sauvignon
- Touraine Sauvignon
- Sancerre
- Pouilly-Fumé

From **Australia**:
- Sauvignon Blanc
- Semillon

Others:
- New Zealand Marlborough Sauvignon Blanc

- New Zealand Chardonnay
- Californian Sauvignon Blanc
- Orvieto from Italy

Light aromatic whites, ripely fruity but not over-sweet

From **Germany**:
- Riesling
- Mosel
- Liebfraumilch
- Kabinett
- Spatlese
- Hock

From **France**:
- Vouvray
- Graves
- Chablis
- Gewurztraminer from Alsace

Others:
- Californian or Australian Gewurztraminer
- Californian Zinfandel
- Italian Pinot Grigio
- Sicilian white
- White Dao or Vinho Verde (slightly sparkling) from Portugal
- Greek Retsina (flavoured with pine resin)

Rich and buttery full-bodied whites

From **France**:
- Chardonnay, matured in oak barrels for a slightly smoky flavour
- Pouilly-Fuissé

Others:
- Californian or Australian Chardonnay
- White Rioja from Spain

Rich white wines with honey and ripe fruit tones

From **France**:
- Sauternes
- Barsac
- Monbazillac
- Beaumes de Venise

Others:
- Some Rieslings and Gewurztraminers, especially from Alsace
- Hungarian Tokay
- Moscatel from Spain

Red wines

Youg, easy-drinking reds (often served lightly chilled)

From **France**:
- Beaujolais
- Mâcon Rouge
- Vins du Pays (country wines)
- Côtes du Luberon
- Côtes du Ventoux
- Bergerac
- Red Anjoux
- Pinot Noir from Alsace

From **Italy**:
- Valpolicella
- Bardolino (sold as 'Novello' or young)
- Lambrusco (sparkling)

Others:
- Spanish Navarra
- Greek Demestica

Medium-fruit, medium-reds

From **France**:
- Côte du Rhone
- Corbières
- Bordeaux Rouge
- Saint Emilion
- Beaujolais Villages
- Minervois
- Côtes du Rousillon

From **Italy**:
- Valpolicella
- Bardolino

Others:
- Spanish Valdepenas
- Dao
- Bairrada
- Alentejo from Portugal
- Merlot from Chile

Strong, plummy, blackcurranty, fleshy reds

From **France**:
- Bordeaux Supérieurs
- Claret
- Graves
- Red Burgundy
- Rhône Crozes-Hermitage
- Châteauneuf du Pape

From **Italy**:
- Barolo
- Barbaresco
- Chianti Classico
- Montepulciano d'Abruzzo

Others:
- Australian Shiraz
- Cabernet Sauvignon/Shiraz

Dark reds

From **Spain**:
- Rioja, especially 'Reserva' or 'Gran reserva', which are aged longer in oak

Others:
- Argentine Cabernet Sauvignon, oak-aged

Rosé wines

From **France**:
- Tavel
- Anjou Rosé
- Côte de Provence

Others:
- Mateus Rosé (slightly sparkling) from Portugal

Sparkling wines

Only wine produced in the Champagne region of France is allowed to call itself champagne, though there are many sparkling wines available. Their dryness or sweetness is described on the label in the following terms:

> **Brut** = extra dry
> **Sec** = dry, but with slight sweetness
> **Demi-sec** = medium sweet

Champagne

Usually a blend of three wines from vineyards in the Champagne region, so as to maintain a standard quality each year. It is made by the 'méthode champenoise', which allows a secondary fermentation in the bottle. If you see this description on a bottle, it means the contents were made in this same way, but not within the Champagne region.

Vintage Champagne

Made from grapes of one vintage (one year's harvest alone). Consequently it will vary from year to year.

Others sparklers:

- Crémant de Bourgogne
- Crémant d'Alsace
- Crémant de Loire from France
- Freixenet or Cordiony from Spain
- Californian and Australian bubbly
- Lambrusco (red)
- Asti Spumante (demi-sec) from Italy
- Sekt from Germany
- Angus Brut from Australia is particularly nice

Shopping for wine

Many of us buy wine at a supermarket along with our weekly or monthly food shopping, but if you're shopping for a party, a wine-merchant or wine warehouse may be a better bet, as they may buy back what you don't drink and may also lend or hire you glasses. Note: most warehouses only sell wine by the case (twelve bottles), although most will mix a case.

How much to buy?

There are about six glasses in a standard (75 cl) bottle. It's better to be safe than sorry and over-buy if you don't know much your guests may drink. You will probably need to allow about one bottle per person for a dinner party, unless you plan to serve pre-dinner drinks and port, brandy or liqueurs. Most people like to drink mineral water, too, so this makes the wine go further.

Storing wine

If you're keeping wine for a few weeks, or longer, try to keep bottles on their sides so the cork stays moist. If they dry out and shrink air can get in and spoil wine. Keep out of direct sunlight or the wine may discolour.

Serving wine

Generally white wines are served chilled. but not so cold that you can's taste them. A couple of hours in the fridge is about right. Red wine is usually served at room temperature, although young wines can be improved by a brief chilling. Err on the cool side of room temperature rather than central heating on full blast.

> **PARTY TIP** **Open and recork six to twelve bottles before your guests arrive for a big party. Then you won't spend the first hour fiddling with a corkscrew.**

> **PARTY TIP** **Use a clean dustbin, baby bath or the kitchen sink filled with water and ice cubes or frozen cool-box ice blocks to chill lots of bottles for a party. Remember, however, that you won't be able to return unopened bottle if the labels have floated off...**

Opening the bottle

- Choose a corkscrew with a long screw as it's less likely to leave half the cork behind, and preferably one with a cage that fits on to the neck of the bottle to keep the screw central and to lever out the cork.
- Cut around the capsule that covers the cork; it may be made of lead or plastic. Trim it away from the top so it won't come into contact with the wine.
- Wipe the rim and top of the cork.
- Insert the screw into the centre of the cork and screw well into, but preferably not through, the bottom of the cork. Going right through could leave bits of cork in the wine.
- Continue twisting or lever up the cork (depending on the design of the corkscrew).
- Wipe inside the neck of the bottle again.

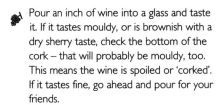

Pour an inch of wine into a glass and taste it. If it tastes mouldy, or is brownish with a dry sherry taste, check the bottom of the cork – that will probably be mouldy, too. This means the wine is spoiled or 'corked'. If it tastes fine, go ahead and pour for your friends.

If the cork breaks off...

Try and insert the corkscrew into the remaining piece of cork. at an angle, so it's pressed against the side of the bottle, rather than pointing down, which may just force the cork into the bottle. If it won't come out this way you may have to push the cork in anyway and then strain the wine before you drink it.

To open champagne

Have a bottle chilled and unshaken, and glasses ready. Remove the foil and carefully untwist the wire until you can remove it. If the bottle has been shaken, the cork might fly out at this point, so aim the bottle out of harm's way and hold the top on with a cloth. Grip the cork firmly through the cloth and twist the bottle until the cork comes out. Pour slowly into glasses, pouring just an inch at first, then topping up the glasses as the bubbles subside.

Fortified wines

These are table wines which have had additional alcohol added to them.

Sherry

There are six main kinds of sherry of varying degrees of sweatness. Dry sherries are often served chilled as an aperitif, sweet sherry may be served before, or after a meal as a dessert wine.

- Fino, very pale gold in colour, very dry
- Manzanilla, another dry fino, said to have a slight saltiness
- Amontillado, a fino, aged so it has a deeper colour and a nutty flavour. Sold as medium sherry

- Oloroso, full-bodied and generally sweeter and more alcoholic than a fino
- Cream, oloroso sherry with extra, added sweetness
- Pale cream, fino sherry with extra sweetness added

Port

Port can only come from Portugal, where brandy is added to wine. Like champagne the name is protected by law. There are four types available, all sweet.

- Ruby port, deep plum-red in colour, thick and sweet-tasting. In Britain, traditionally served with cheese, especially Stilton, at the end of a meal
- Tawny port, blended port from several years, matured in a cask so it takes on a golden colour
- White port, made from white grapes, so pale-golden. Slightly dryer and pleasant served chilled as an aperitif
- Vintage port, wine from one year only, that is allowed to mature in the bottle for at least ten, often more, years. It needs to be carefully decanted before serving to leave behind the deposit or 'crust' that will have formed.

Vermouth

Wine is fortified with brandy and flavoured with herbs to make Cinzano, Martini or Gancia in Italy, Chambery or Noilly Prat in France. There are three main types and they can be drunk neat with ice and lemon or mixed to make long drinks or cocktails.

- Secco, pale yellowish-green colour, dry with a mildly herbal flavour
- Bianco, light in colour, medium-sweet in flavour
- Rosso, reddish-brown and sweet-tasting, faintly spicy-medicinal

Picnics

What better way to spend a sunny day than with a bottle of wine, some good food and company (or a great book). Picnic basics are easy to remember:

☞ never take anything that might go rancid, like butter or homemade mayonnaise

☞ Keep a checklist of essentials (see below)

taped to the lid of your picnic basket. Think how many picnics have been compromised because something was forgotten (like the corkscrew, or something to wipe your hands)

☞ Take drinks that don't need chilling; i.e., red wine instead of white. Freeze still drinks like Ribena and lemonade the night before; they'll be a nice temperature by the time you need them.

PICNIC ESSENTIALS:
• **paper cups and plates (china or acrylic are fine, of course, but they do require washing-up!)**
• **cutlery – there are lots of firm ones made of plastic, or bring some from home**
• **kitchen roll or towelling to mop up the inevitable spills**
• **a tub of water for wiping fingers**
• **salt, corkscrew and a bottle/tin opener**
• **plastic bags for litter**
• **rugs and umbrellas (in the UK, certainly)**
• **a sharp knife for cutting**

SIMPLE MEALS:
• **cold pizza, sausages, chicken drumsticks and cold meats**
• **pasta, potato and green salads**
• **fresh bread spread with cream cheese (butter will go rancid). Cut it before you go – or bring a knife!**
• **hard-boiled eggs, olives, crudités and crisps**
• **mini sandwiches, cold satay sticks**
• **water melon, melon, fruits in season. Try sprinkling a carton of washed strawberries with some balsamic vinegar and a couple of teaspoons of caster sugar**
• **cheeses**
• **sweet biscuits (not chocolate, which melts)**

Most important, don't make preparations that can't be changed in the event of rain!

CHAPTER FIVE **Health care**

Dr Susan Barton

A clinical assistant in Accident and Emergency and mother of three, Dr Barton also writes for Home Health Fact File and My Child.

Our health is something we tend to take for granted. Most people suffer no significant health problems until well into middle-age, or even later. That doesn't mean we don't all experience the odd ache and pain, cold or even broken bone, but none of these are serious threats to our life, or ability to carry on normally. Clean water supplies, childhood vaccinations and free access to health care, including maternity care and contraception, are factors that have contributed to our overall good health.
Health care normally passes through different stages as we age.
In the early years, the emphasis is on prevention. Vaccinations as children and a healthy lifestyle keep most serious illness at bay. During the middle years, we become more aware of the spectrum of ill-health, often through the responsibility of caring for sick children or elderly relatives. Towards old age, illness becomes much more common, and we have to learn how to live with it, and what treatment is available.

The human body is incredibly complex, yet it is the most common things that account for the majority of illness. Professional medical care is available to us twenty-four hours a day, 365 days a year when illness strikes. Against that background, an understanding of some of the basics is necessary to ensure that we get the kind of health care we need, whether that is knowing that it is safe to take a couple of aspirins, or getting emergency admission to hospital.

The home first aid and medicine cabinet

There are three reasons for having a proper place in the home containing some basic medical supplies:
- ☞ To provide a safe, childproof storage space for all medicines in the home, whether this is aspirin from the supermarket or drugs from the doctor.
- ☞ If they are always kept in the same place, you can lay your hands on them in a emergency.
- ☞ To have available a range of treatments to deal with the day-to-day illnesses and injuries that crop up in the home.

It is worth thinking about what sort of cupboard/container to use, so that it fulfils the necessary requirements. Children have died from eating such seemingly harmless tablets as paracetamol and iron, so one of the most important features should be that it is childproof: **out of reach and lockable**.
It should be in a **visible** place, otherwise it is easy to forget to take regular medicine. Over the sink in the bathroom (where the door serves as a mirror) is a popular place for this reason. It should be **large enough** to contain everything. Safety is compromised if bottles and packets of medicine end up sitting on top. Finally, it should provide the right conditions for **storage** of medicine which, in most cases, is out of direct sunlight and in a cool place.

What's inside?

The contents of the medicine cabinet should include things required to treat the minor illnesses and accidents that can be dealt with at home. These include:

- ☞ colds and flu
- ☞ muscle sprains
- ☞ rashes and insect bites
- ☞ small cuts
- ☞ burns
- ☞ digestive upsets.

Colds and flu

For relieving fever and aches in adults: **aspirin** and **paracetamol** tablets. For children: paracetamol syrup (Calpol, Disprol). **Cough medicine** can be soothing, but should not be used for prolonged periods. Your pharmacist will be happy to advise the best type for a particular cough, but if the cough persists, you should see your doctor. Cold and flu remedies are no more effective than aspirin or paracetamol, and can be expensive. **Anaesthetic throat lozenges** (Tyrozets, Dequacaine) are useful for sore throats.

Muscle sprains

The **non-steroidal anti-inflammatory drugs** (NSAIDs) are a group of drugs that are particularly effective at reducing the inflammation, and hence the pain and swelling, associated with sprained muscles and ligaments. They are also useful general analgesics (pain killers) for a range of other things, such as arthritis and period pain. They are available from the pharmacist without a prescription, but should not be taken by people with peptic ulcers.

Sprays that cool the skin are available for the treatment of sprains, but they are no more effective than putting ice on the injury.

Rashes, insect bites

Itchy rashes (heat rash, nettle stings), sunburn and insect bites can be treated with **Caladryl lotion** or **ointment**, which contains an anti-histamine in addition to soothing calamine.

Burns

Small burns should immediately be placed under cold water. A **local anaesthetic gel** (Xylocaine) will relieve the pain. Large burns should be taken immediately to casualty.

Digestive upsets, gastro-enteritis

Heartburn can be relieved by an **antacid**. Magnesium Trisilicate Mixture is effective, or there are many proprietary brands such as Rennies, Asilone or Maalox. Your pharmacist will help you choose.

Laxatives for the treatment of constipation should be used with caution: fibre in the diet is better, but lactose or Sennacot are effective short-term.

Diarrhoea and vomiting of short duration is best left untreated, as the body is trying to eliminate the cause. Medicines to prevent diarrhoea such as **kaolin** should not be used in acute gastro-enteritis. Sachets of **electrolyte replacements** (Dioralyte, Rehydrat) prevent dehydration in children or the elderly. A teaspoon of sugar and a teaspoon of salt in a pint of water is an effective alternative. If symptoms persist, or occur in a baby, see the doctor.

Infant colic responds to **gripe water**, and failing that Infacol, available over the counter at your local chemist.

Teething

Paracetamol suspension (Calpol, Disprol) and an **anaesthetic cream** for the gums (Dentinox, Calgel) will relieve the pain of teething. Homoeopathic **teething granules** may also soothe the pain and agitation caused by teething.

Miscellaneous

The following are all worth having in the home:

- ☞ skin disinfectant for small wounds (Dettol, TCP, Betadine)
- ☞ cream for dry, chapped skin (Cream E45)
- ☞ antihistamine for hay fever (Triludan)
- ☞ cream for inflammation of the skin (only to be used sparingly and upon advice from your doctor)

In addition to medicines, the cabinet should contain a basic range of equipment and dressings:

☞ tweezers for removing stings or splinters
☞ scissors
☞ crepe bandage for supporting a sprain
☞ soft dressings (gauze, cotton wool or sanitary towels) for covering and applying pressure to a bleeding wound
☞ range of sticking plasters

It is possible to buy a ready-made first-aid kit from the pharmacist, but there is no reason not to develop your own 'customised' version. Smaller, ready-made kits are useful to keep in the car, or take with you if you are travelling abroad.

Having some basics in the home can avoid unnecessary visits to the doctor, but are no replacement for professional treatment.

Consult your doctor if:
• **you are uncertain about the diagnosis**
• **symptoms persist**
• **a baby or small child is ill**
• **you are already receiving treatment**

Basic first aid

Many accidents happen in the home, and some are potentially fatal. There are times when a knowledge of basic first aid can actually save a life. The aims of first aid are to preserve life, prevent the condition from worsening and promote recovery, during the interval it takes for expert medical assistance to arrive.

Accident prevention

As with all medical conditions, prevention is better than cure. Many accidents in the home can be prevented with a little thought and planning, particularly where children are involved.

Supervision

There is no substitute for the careful supervision of small children. From the age of about eighteen months, when children become mobile and curious, until about five, when they have developed a greater awareness and understanding of danger, small children need almost constant supervision. They should remain where you can see or at least hear them all the time. All mothers develop the instinct that tells you that if a child has gone quiet, you need to drop whatever you are doing and go and check on them.

Removing potential hazards

All potential poisons should be kept out of reach. This includes **cleaning materials**, **toiletries** and **garden chemicals** as well as the more obvious **medicines**. **Matches** and **lighters**, **polyethylene bags** and **tiny objects** on which a child might choke are other hazards to think about. **Electrical appliances** should be properly wired and kept out of reach, including table lamps.

Safety precautions

● Stair gates should be installed, and large plate glass windows should be of reinforced glass. Covering internal glass doors with a film of adhesive plastic reduces the risk of damage if they are broken.

- Upstairs windows should have catches to prevent an inquisitive child from being able to open them and fall out. Open the top windows, not the bottom, in any room where children might be playing. In blocks of flats, safety bars may be necessary.
- The balustrade of landings or balconies should be high enough to prevent a child from being able to fall over them. Never leave a chair or table where a child can climb on to it and gain access to an open window.
- Outside, the play area should be clearly visible from the house, and access to the road should be blocked. Ponds should be avoided, filled in, or fenced off, irrespective of their depth. A small child can drown in a very small amount of water.
- Children should not be allowed near live flames unsupervised, as they hold a fascination for them. This includes gas cookers, open fires and garden bonfires.
- Smoke detectors are relatively inexpensive, and should always be installed, as they really do save lives should a fire break out.

The list of potential hazards to a child in the home is almost endless, and also depends on the type and location of your home. It is not always possible to see them before they actually happen. A sensible measure is, when your first child begins to walk, to go round the house carefully, trying to identify problems. An environment cannot be made totally accident-proof, but an awareness of where danger lies is an important aspect of prevention.

Emergency first aid

When a major, life-threatening accident occurs to an adult or child, prompt action can save a life, yet the natural response is one of total fear and panic. No untrained person can expect to know about first aid in any depth, but everyone should know the basics of

resuscitation. The St John Ambulance and the Red Cross run first aid courses throughout the country, and you might like to consider going on one.

When presented with a situation where someone has sustained a life-threatening injury, and is lying unconscious, there are three observations to make:

Does the casualty have an open AIRWAY?
Is the casualty BREATHING?
Have they got a CIRCULATION?
This is the ABC of emergency first aid.

The body is dependant on the delivery of oxygen to the tissues for survival. Without this, death from lack of oxygen to the brain will occur in about five minutes. Air, containing oxygen, enters the body through the airway, which is made up of the nose and mouth, trachea (windpipe), bronchus and lungs. The airway is normally wide open, allowing air to pass in and out of the lungs as we breathe.

Breathing is necessary to get the air in and out of the body. Even if the airway is patent, without breathing, air (and therefore oxygen) is not going to reach the tissues.

The oxygen is transported to the tissues by the blood, which circulates around every part of the body. This circulation depends on the heart functioning as a pump. If the heart stops, the oxygen does not reach the tissues.

These three factors, airway, breathing and circulation, must be present for survival. If any one of them fails, death will occur.

Maintaining an airway

In an unconscious person, the airway can be blocked simply because the tongue has fallen to the back of the throat, or dentures have fallen backwards, or the person has vomited. *Action:*

- Lift the chin forwards and upwards. This may immediately restore breathing. If not:

▲ Tilt back the head to maintain an airway.
Possible obstructrions can include: tongue dropped back, narrowed air passage, vomit at back of the throat.

- Sweep round the back of the mouth with the fingers to remove any loose object.
- Turn the head to the side, keeping the chin supported.

Breathing

If clearing the airway does not restore breathing, you may have to assist the casualty's breathing by mouth-to-mouth ventilation. This involves blowing the air from your lungs (which still contain a lot of oxygen) into theirs.

Action:

- Take a deep breath, and squeeze the patient's nose shut with your fingers.
- Place your mouth over their mouth.
- Blow gently into their mouth, watching to see if the chest rises. Remove your mouth, and the chest should fall as the breath is exhaled.

▼ **You may have to assist breathing by mouth to mouth ventilation. See above.**

Circulation

If the unconscious person has a clear airway and has started breathing, then you must check their pulse to see if they have an adequate circulation. If you cannot feel a pulse, the heart may have stopped beating, and you are going to have to start **external cardiac massage**. The heart is situated between the sternum (breast bone) in front and the spine behind. By pressing on the sternum, the heart can be squeezed, and empties blood in the way it normally does when it contracts. The circulation is a closed system, so that when the pressure on the sternum is released, the heart fills with blood again. Rhythmic pressure on the sternum will sustain circulation of the blood, even if the heart has stopped.

Action:

- Make sure the patient is lying on their back on a firm surface. Move them if necessary (e.g., pull them off a soft bed).
- Place the heels of both hands over the sternum, about two-thirds of the way down its length.

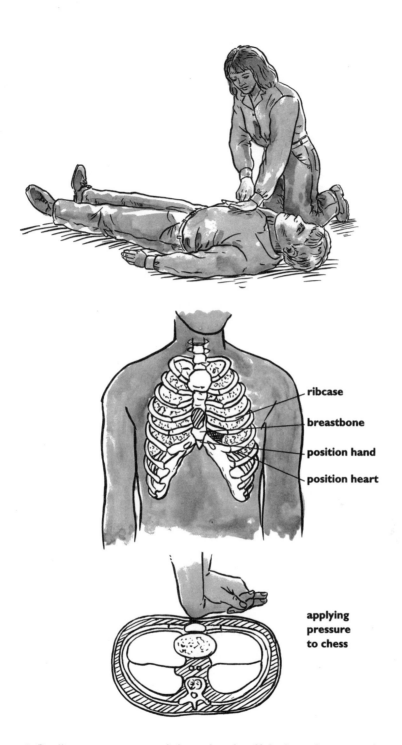

ribcase

breastbone

position hand

position heart

applying
pressure
to chess

▲ Cardiac massage must only be undertaken if the heart has stopped.
If there is no pulse, find the correct position and press down firmly,
to stimulate contraction of the heart.

- Keeping your arms straight, lean forward and press down on the sternum. Remove your hands and allow the chest wall to spring back.
- Repeat this at a smooth regular rate (eighty compressions per minute) for fifteen compressions. Then stop and give two breaths of mouth-to-mouth ventilation.

This ABC of resuscitation applies to any unconscious person, whatever the nature of their injury. Unless the circulation is maintained until help arrives, they will die. Fortunately, situations requiring this level of first aid are unusual, but if it does happen you should be prepared.

Minor first aid

Controlling bleeding

The extent of bleeding from a wound will depend on the nature of the injury. A graze, even if it quite large, is shallow and the bleeding is only from tiny blood vessels called capillaries. These can contract and reduce blood loss, and clotting should occur fairly quickly. A deeper wound may cut a vein, in which case there is a more significant, but steady flow of blood. If a wound cuts an artery, then blood will spurt out under pressure every time the heart beats. Blood loss is large and rapid and potentially life-threatening.
Action:
All types of bleeding are treated in the same way.
- Cover the wound – ideally with a sterile dressing, but any absorbent, soft pad will do.
- Apply firm pressure over the dressing, either by holding it, or applying a bandage.
- Lift the wounded part. This reduces the blood pressure to the area, and slows the bleeding. Call for help, and do not remove the dressing until expert assistance is available. If the person becomes shocked (pale, faint and sweaty), get them to lie down and raise their legs above the level of the heart.

Unconsciousness

Being faced with an unconscious person can be alarming. There are several reasons that people become unconscious, some of which are relatively harmless and some very serious.
- A blow to the head may cause loss of consciousness, which may be momentary or prolonged.
- Disturbance in the blood supply to the brain causes unconsciousness. This can arise from the slowing of the blood flow, as may happen in a simple faint, or more seriously, from a heart attack or stroke.
- Lack of oxygen, from strangulation, drowning or asphyxia produces loss of consciousness, as does lack of adequate blood sugar, which sometimes occurs in people with diabetes.
- An overdose of drugs or alcohol can cause unconsciousness.
- Convulsions or fits are followed by a period of unconsciousness. Fits may occur for the first time in people who have previously been well, due to some underlying disease such as a brain tumour. They can also occur in small children due to a high temperature (febrile convulsions), or they may occur on a regular basis in people who suffer from epilepsy.

Whatever the cause of unconsciousness, it is important at first to respond in the same way with some basic first aid. It may not be possible to identify the cause, but the initial management of the unconscious person is nevertheless the same.

Action:
- Open the air passages by lifting the jaw and tilting the head back.
- Check for breathing and circulation. If necessary, start artificial ventilation and external cardiac compression.
- If the person is breathing and has a pulse, quickly check for tight clothing or bleeding.
- Place the person in the recovery position. This involves gently turning them on their side, then bending the upper arm at the elbow to support the upper body, and the upper leg at the knee to support the

lower half of the body. The head should be gently adjusted to rest with the chin tilted slightly upwards. Once an unconscious, but still breathing person with a pulse has been placed in this position, it is safe to leave them momentarily to call for help.

The position of the chin means that the tongue cannot fall to the back of the throat and obstruct breathing. The position of the head means that the air passages are open to their fullest extent. If the person vomits, it will drain freely away, rather than choking them.

Fractures

Fractures, or broken bones, are a relatively common occurrence. They are usually caused by a direct injury of some force, although in the elderly and small children the bones are more fragile and a relatively small injury may be sufficient to produce a fracture.

Fractures can be divided into **closed fractures**, in which the skin over the broken bone remains intact, or **open fractures**, where the skin and overlying tissues are also damaged, and the broken ends of the bone may protrude from the wound. In this case, the fact that the bone is broken is fairly obvious. In a closed fracture, the clues that suggest a fracture include:

☞ An audible crack or snap at the moment of injury, followed by pain.
☞ Difficulty in moving the affected part.
☞ Pain and swelling over the injury.
☞ Obvious deformity. For example, a leg may be bent or twisted at an unnatural angle, or appear unnaturally short in comparison to the other.
☞ **Multiple fractures**, or fractures of large bones such as the thighs or pelvis may also be accompanied by shock (pallor, sweating, faintness) due to loss of blood from the fracture site.

The aim with a fracture is to immobilise the affected bone while waiting for, and during, transport to hospital. **Immobilisation** reduces pain, and reduces the risk of damage to any nerves or blood vessels that may lie near the broken bone ends.

The key to immobilisation is **splinting**.

The form this will take depends on the site of the fracture, but basically, the broken part should be firmly strapped to an adjacent healthy part. So, for example, a broken leg should be strapped to the other leg. A broken arm should be strapped to the chest. Broken fingers or toes should be strapped to the next ones.

Bandages, hankies, ties, and **scarves** are all suitable for strapping and splinting a fracture. They should be tied firmly enough to limit movement, but not so tightly that they interfere with the circulation. Before and again after strapping, you should feel for the pulse beyond the fracture (i.e., at the wrist for arm or finger fractures, the neck for collarbone or rib fractures, the ankle for leg or foot fractures).

An A to Z of common ailments

Abdominal pain

Most people experience pain in their abdomen (the region between the bottom of the ribs and the base of the trunk) at some time in their lives. In the majority of cases, the cause is a minor, self-limiting problem such as indigestion, mild gastro-enteritis or period pain. Abdominal pain may be serious if:

☞ It is a new, unfamiliar pain.
☞ It does not wear off after a relatively short period of time, i.e., an hour or two.
☞ It is accompanied by other symptoms.
☞ It is so severe that it produces faintness or shock.

On the whole, most people find it easy to distinguish between something minor and something more serious, but pain in the abdomen can be alarming, and may be associated with the fear that there may be something serious underlying the pain.

Pain in the abdomen can arise from any of the organs within it.

The stomach, duodenum and large and small bowel form the gastrointestinal tract. This is the site of digestion of food. Colicky (comes and goes in waves) pain is characteristic of pain arising from the gastrointestinal tract. If accompanied by no other symptoms, this is usually 'indigestion'. It may also be a symptom of constipation.

The sudden onset of colicky pain accompanied by vomiting and diarrhoea is usually due to gastro-enteritis, but if the onset has been insidious, especially in the elderly, then medical advice should be sought as it may indicate an obstruction.

The pain due to a peptic ulcer is often sharp, and may be constant, or brought on by food or drink.

Any bleeding from the gastrointestinal tract should be considered serious until proved otherwise (haemorrhoids, or piles, are actually the most common cause). Bleeding into the bowel may turn the stools black.

The pancreas is an organ that secretes enzymes into the bowel. Inflammation of the pancreas (pancreatitis) produces severe constant pain that goes through to the back. It is an illness that is more likely to affect heavy drinkers.

The spleen and liver are organs tucked under the diaphragm. They are not a common site for abdominal pain, although they may be ruptured by abdominal trauma.

The gall bladder may become inflamed or form gallstones, which produce pain, typically brought on by eating a fatty meal.

The kidneys are located towards the sides and back of the abdomen. A severe urine infection may give rise to painful kidneys. Stones may also develop in the kidneys which cause very severe pain, often accompanied by blood in the urine.

The female reproductive organs (uterus, ovaries and fallopian tubes) are located at the base of the abdomen. Pain arising from these organs often gives rise to a change in the menstrual cycle. The pain may occur at a fixed point in the cycle.

AIDS (Acquired Immune Deficiency Syndrome)

The Human Immunodeficiency Virus (HIV) that may eventually cause AIDS is caught from the body fluids of a person already infected with the virus. This may be through sexual intercourse, the sharing of needles, or a blood transfusion with blood containing the virus.

The length of time between becoming infected with the virus, and developing AIDS is variable. In some people, it may take less than a year. There are now people who have been HIV positive (infected with the virus) for fifteen years who have not yet developed AIDS.

To avoid HIV infection:
☞ Practise safe sex and always use a condom.

If you are going abroad:
☞ If you are going to remote, undeveloped areas, take a simple sterile suture kit, and needles for any injections you might require.
☞ If a blood transfusion becomes necessary, try and have blood donated by a travelling companion. A sterile blood giving set can also be obtained here for emergency use abroad.

Angina

Angina is chest pain arising from lack of oxygen to the muscles of the heart. Blood vessels called the coronary arteries provide the constantly contracting muscles of the heart with oxygen. If they are unable to provide sufficient oxygen, then the muscles develop 'cramp'. This pain is typically described as a crushing pain, that feels like a tight band around the chest. It may spread down the left arm, or to the left jaw. It usually only lasts for a few minutes before wearing off.

Angina occurs in people whose coronary vessels have narrowed. The blood supply to the heart is maintained at rest, but if the heart requires more blood, as it does during exercise, the arteries can no longer provide it and angina develops. Men are more likely to have narrowed arteries than women, although it can develop in women, particularly after the menopause. Other factors that speed up narrowing of the arteries with age are cigarette smoking, diabetes, high blood pressure and high cholesterol levels.

Angina can be well controlled with medicines, but eliminating the risk factors such as smoking is also important. Severe narrowing of the arteries may result in a heart attack. The arteries can be surgically stretched, or in very bad cases, they can be replaced with a coronary by-pass operation. Many people can live with angina for years, modifying their activities to avoid bringing on an attack.

Alzheimer's disease

Alzheimer's disease is the name given to a condition characterised by gradual loss of intellectual function ending in dementia. It is rare under the age of fifty. Some deterioration in brain function, such as increasing forgetfulness or confusion, is common with increasing age. In Alzheimer's, this deterioration is progressive and remorseless, until the victim is eventually left with virtually no intellectual function. They become incontinent, and are incapable of feeding or dressing themselves, or of comprehensive speech. It is a very distressing condition for relatives to cope with, as the victim becomes unable to recognise even familiar faces, and may become irrational, angry and abusive with the very people who are trying to care for them.

The cause of the condition is a shrinkage and destruction of the actual substance of the brain. In the later stages of the disease, the diagnosis can be confirmed with a brain scan that shows the damaged parts of the brain.

Unfortunately, there is no treatment. There are no preventative measures either. Although the condition is thought to have a genetic basis, it is not possible to predict who, or when, any individual may develop it.

Back pain

Back pain is very common, but rarely has a serious cause. The spine is made up of a string of small bones (vertebra) separated by disks of cartilage, and joined together by a series of small muscles. The back has to support the weight of the upper body, and is put under strain by any movement of the upper body such as bending or twisting.

Back pain is usually brought about by a sprain of the muscles of the spine. It may be

▼ **The spinal column is made up of thirty-five vertebrae with dishes between them, allowing a range of movements.**

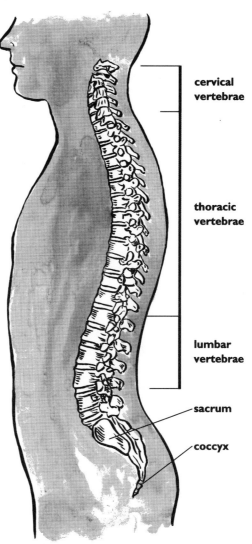

cervical vertebrae

thoracic vertebrae

lumbar vertebrae

sacrum

coccyx

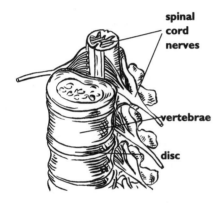

spinal
cord
nerves

vertebrae

disc

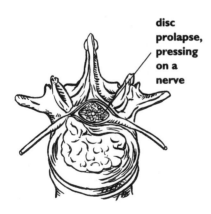

disc
prolapse,
pressing
on a
nerve

Top: vertebrae of the spine, with intervertebral discs pressed between. Centre: a cross section of the spine. Bottom: prolapse of the disc, pressing on the nerves

acutely painful at the time, but usually clears up spontaneously if the back is allowed to rest. A severe strain on the back may cause one of the cartilaginous disks to pop out from between the bones. This is known as a slipped disc. Surgical repair of a slipped disc is usually considered only if there is evidence that the nerve supply to the lower body has been affected. This is not the case in the vast majority of cases, no matter how severe the pain.

Treatment of acute back pain is by:
☞ Resting flat on a firm surface (a soft mattress puts greater strain on the spine; a too-hard surface however prevents the normal curves of the spine from being properly supported).
☞ Pain-relieving drugs.
☞ Physiotherapy.

Chronic, dull back pain is best dealt with by preve-ntative measures. These include:
☞ Using a firm mattress.
☞ Exercising to strengthen the back.
☞ Avoiding undue strain by bending the knees to lift.

Bronchitis

Bronchitis is a common infection, particularly during the winter months. The bronchi are the tubes that connect the lungs to the mouth and throat. They are lined by a membrane that warms and moistens the air that we breathe before it reaches the lungs. Bronchitis is caused by an infection that inflames this membrane.

Most cases of bronchitis start with a simple viral illness of the nose and throat (a cold). If the body does not manage to shake this off, then a second bacterial invasion can spread further down the airway to the bronchi. The risks of this happening are increased in smokers, because the lining membrane is already irritated and inflamed by cigarette smoke.

The symptoms of bronchitis are a cough and a temperature. The cough is usually productive, with yellow or green phlegm. This in turn may cause nausea, or even vomiting after a prolonged bout of coughing.

Severe bronchitis is an unpleasant illness,

but in an otherwise fit person, it is rarely serious and responds rapidly to antibiotics. In the elderly or chronically ill, however, it can actually be fatal.

Cleaner air, and a reduction in the number of people who smoke, has led to a reduction in bronchitis.

Chronic bronchitis is the regular development of a productive cough during the winter months, which often lasts for a long time. It may lead to permanent lung damage.

Cancer

Cancer is a disease that can arise in any part of the body, at virtually any age. It is this, and the fact that curative treatment is available for only a few types of cancer, that makes it such a feared illness.

Nevertheless, although some types of cancer are relatively common, most are rare, and it remains a disease much more likely to develops in the elderly than in the young. The reasons why a particular cancer starts to grow are still poorly understood. There are known risk factors, such as smoking and radiation, but this does not explain why it only occurs in certain individuals, not others.

Cancer develops in normal tissue that loses its ability to control growth. The abnormal cancer cells begin to grow and divide rapidly, forming a tumour. Not all tumours are malignant, but cancer is usually taken to mean those that are. Malignancy means that as the tumour grows, it sends off cancer cells into the bloodstream. These cells can lodge in a different part of the body and start to grow into another tumour. Eventually the body becomes riddled with cancer, the vital organs can no longer function, and death ensues.

The chances of treating cancer are much better if it is detected at an early stage, particularly before it has had a chance to spread. Cervical smear tests are aimed at identifying cervical cancer before it can spread. Mammography is aimed at the early detection of breast cancer.

Unfortunately there are not many other ways of effectively screening a healthy person for cancer, and early detection therefore relies on reporting any suspicious symptoms

to your doctor. Again, there is a problem, in that the majority of early symptoms of cancer can also be symptoms of mild, insignificant illnesses.

The following are some symptoms that may be serious, although to have them does not necessarily mean that you have developed cancer:

- ☞ Coughing up blood (haemoptysis)
- ☞ Unexplained weight loss
- ☞ Change of bowel habit
- ☞ Difficulty swallowing (dysphagia)
- ☞ Blood in the stool, vomit or urine
- ☞ Bleeding or discharge from the nipple
- ☞ Chronic fatigue
- ☞ Abnormal vaginal bleeding
- ☞ Any lump or ulcer that persists or grows
- ☞ Persistent worsening headache
- ☞ Loss of sensation in any part of the body
- ☞ Fits
- ☞ Lump or changed shape in the testicles or breasts
- ☞ A mole which changes shape or bleeds

Diabetes

Diabetes mellitus, or sugar diabetes, is a common condition affecting two to three per cent of the population. It is caused by a complete or partial inability of the pancreas (a gland situated in the abdomen) to secrete a hormone called insulin.

Normally, as the food we have eaten is digested, it produces a rise in the level of sugar in the blood. This in turn causes the secretion of insulin, which enables the sugar to be taken up from the blood into the tissues, where it supplies energy to the cells. In diabetes, not enough insulin is produced, so the levels of sugar in the blood remain high. Sugar starts to be excreted in the urine, something that never usually happens. Testing the urine for sugar is therefore a simple way of diagnosing diabetes.

Too much sugar in the blood produces a range of symptoms. In the undiagnosed diabetic, the commonest symptoms are:

- ☞ Excessive thirst.
- ☞ Large quantities of urine.
- ☞ Weight loss.

Other problems that may be due to diabetes are:

- ☞ Disturbances of vision.
- ☞ Recurrent infections of the skin or mouth.

Once diabetes is diagnosed, there is no cure, but the condition can be managed with medical treatment, and most diabetics lead a perfectly normal life. There are two broad categories of diabetics:

- ☞ Insulin-dependent diabetics are those who produce no insulin whatsoever, and need to inject themselves with insulin on a regular basis. These tend to be people who develop diabetes at an early age.
- ☞ Non-insulin-dependent diabetics produce some insulin, but not enough to completely prevent the condition. This can be controlled with a modified diet and tablets. This form of diabetes may develop in later life.

Diabetes itself is no longer a fatal condition, but it can cause other health problems eventually. The high blood sugar can damage small blood vessels and nerves, which may result in kidney disease, loss of sensation, and damage to the eye. These problems can be minimised by careful medical treatment that keeps the blood sugar levels as close to normal as possible.

Depression

Emotional, as opposed to purely physical, disorders occur in as many as fifteen per cent of the population. These can range from the natural grief of bereavement through to serious mental illness. One of the most common forms of emotional disorder is depression. Many people experience a mild form of depression at some point in their adult lives, a general sense of being fed up with everything and not having any energy or enthusiasm. At its most severe, depression can be a very disabling illness, preventing people from leading a normal life and ultimately, make them contemplate, or even commit suicide.

There is some evidence to suggest that depression is at least partly due to a physical (biological) cause. That is, the level of some of the transmitter substances in the brain fall

to low levels. Anti-depressant drugs work by increasing the levels of these substances in the brain, and the fact that they are, on the whole, effective, gives support to this.

Depression tends to occur in adults between the ages of thirty and fifty. The characteristic features are:

- ☞ General depression of mood.
- ☞ Tearfulness.
- ☞ Sleep disturbance.
- ☞ Loss of appetite and energy.
- ☞ General change in personality, which may take the form of anxiety or irritability.

Sometimes people who are physically fit but depressed may develop all manner of physical symptoms including headaches and chest pain.

Some people experience recurrent bouts of depression, but return to normal in between. Once recognised for what it is, all but the most severe depression responds well to anti-depressant treatment and counselling.

Endocrine disease

The endocrine glands are a group of glands situated in different parts of the body. Their function is to secrete hormones, which they do in response to signals from other parts of the body, including the brain. The purpose of the endocrine system is to control the general internal environment of the body, enabling it to grow and develop in a normal way. Endocrine disease is, broadly speaking, caused by the production of too much or too little of these respective hormones.

- ☞ The pituitary gland is situated in the centre of the head, just beneath the brain. One of the hormones it produces is growth hormone, responsible for the normal acceleration of growth in adolescence. Deficiency leads to stunted growth, excess to gigantism. The pituitary gland also produces hormones responsible for stimulating the normal production of sperm by the testes and eggs from the ovaries. Pituitary dysfunction can be a cause of infertility.
- ☞ The thyroid gland is situated in the neck. It produces a hormone called thyroxine,

responsible for general metabolism. Too much, thyrotoxicosis, causes an increase in metabolic rate, with weight loss, sweating, hyperactivity, palpitations and insomnia. Too little, hypothyroidism, has the opposite effect: weight gain, drowsiness, constipation.

☞ The parathyroid glands are situated beside the thyroid in the neck. They are tiny glands which control the levels of calcium in the body, including the amount taken up by bone. Deficiency can cause osteoporosis.

☞ The adrenal glands are situated just above the kidneys in the abdomen. They are responsible for controlling the levels of minerals and salts in the body. The hormones they produce are known as steroids. People who take extra steroids can suppress the normal steroid production of their own glands which can cause problems.

☞ Insulin production by the pancreas is part of the endocrine system. Diabetes is one of the most common endocrine disorders.

☞ The testes and ovaries also act as endocrine glands in their own right, producing hormones. In the male, testosterone is produced which is responsible for male sexual characteristics, such as facial hair and libido. In the female, the hormones produced by the ovary control the menstrual cycle.

Certain disorders of the endocrine system are not uncommon, such as diabetes and thyroid disease. Others, such as growth-hormone excess are extremely rare. Some people develop a condition known as an auto-immune disease, in which their own body treats some of its own tissue as 'foreign'. This often affects the endocrine system, affecting more than one type of gland.

The symptoms of endocrine disease are typically a group of apparently unrelated conditions, such as:

☞ A change in weight.
☞ Pain or swelling in the head, neck or eyes.
☞ Loss of libido or impotence.
☞ A change in the texture of the skin.

Most forms of endocrine disease are treatable, and this is increasingly so with the production of artificial hormones.

Epilepsy

People who suffer from epilepsy have fits, or convulsions. There are two common forms of 'idiopathic' epilepsy (epilepsy that occurs spontaneously, rather than having an identifiable cause):

☞ Petit mal, in which the 'fit' is no more than a brief period of 'absence'
☞ Grand mal, where a convulsion of the whole body occurs.

Epilepsy is diagnosed from a recording of the electrical activity of the brain, an electroencephalogram (EEG). In people with epilepsy this shows a characteristic alteration in the electrical activity of the brain.

Sometimes epilepsy can follow damage to the brain, such as a head injury or brain tumour. Often, especially in children, there is no apparent cause. Many children grow out of it, especially if they have only had petit mal.

Although a grand mal convulsion may be alarming to witness, the fit itself rarely causes harm; the danger lies in accidental injury during a fit, such as falling from a height or into a fire. Most people with epilepsy find that it can be well controlled by anti-convulsant drugs. Most lead perfectly normal lives once the epilepsy is controlled on treatment.

Fibroids

Fibroids are benign (non-cancerous) growths, mainly consisting of muscle fibres, that develop in the womb. They are very common, and twenty per cent of women over the age of thirty-five will have fibroids. The majority cause no symptoms, and are harmless. They range in size from less than one centimetre, to the size of a football, and it is the fibroids that grow to such a large size that usually cause symptoms.

They tend to occupy four sites:

☞ The external surface of the uterus (subserous).
☞ The internal surface (submucous).
☞ Inside the uterine wall (intramural).

☞ Within the neck of the uterus (cervical). Cervical fibroids may protrude from the cervix. Fibroids are usually multiple.

The symptoms caused by fibroids may include:

☞ Heavy periods (menorrhagia)
☞ Bleeding between periods
☞ Pressure on the bladder causing urinary frequency or retention
☞ Pressure on the veins causing varicose veins
☞ Abdominal swelling
☞ Abdominal pain
☞ Reduced fertility

Fibroids may be diagnosed incidentally during an internal examination, such as for a coil-fitting or a cervical smear. The uterus is enlarged and lumpy, and cervical fibroids may be visible. They may also be found on an ultrasound scan (sound waves are directed at the abdomen, producing an image of the internal organs, including the pregnant uterus, on a screen), or during a Caesarean section. In women who have passed the menopause, fibroids often become calcified (where the calcium salts that form bone are deposited in the tissues). This does not produce any symptoms, but the fibroids may then show up on an ordinary abdominal X-ray.

If they are not causing any symptoms (the majority), they are small, and the diagnosis is certain, fibroids are not treated.

Larger fibroids may cause symptoms, in which case they can be removed. For women who wish to become pregnant, an operation called a myomectomy, where the fibroid alone is removed, can be performed, although the fibroids have a tendency to recur. Once a woman has completed her family, a hysterectomy is the preferred operation.

The majority of fibroids are totally harmless. Many women who have them are never aware of their existence. The few that produce symptoms can be removed. Fibroids may cause problems during pregnancy. Malignant change (where the fibroid becomes cancerous) occurs in less than one in two hundred cases.

Flu

Flu (or more correctly influenza) is a common illness caused by a virus. The symptoms of flu often start as those of a simple cold:

☞ Sore throat
☞ Runny nose
☞ Headache

This is followed by:

☞ Fever
☞ Muscle aches
☞ Dizziness and light-headedness

And sometimes:

☞ nausea
☞ vomiting
☞ abdominal pain
☞ diarrhoea

Whereas a simple cold may last up to ten days, but is often much better within a week, flu may last a week to ten days, followed by several weeks of general fatigue and loss of energy and appetite.

As with all illnesses caused by a virus, antibiotics are ineffective. Treatment is aimed at relief of pain and fever, by taking aspirin or paracetamol, bed rest and drinking adequate fluids. These simple supportive measures control the symptoms and allow the body's own defence mechanisms to shake off the illness. Once you have had flu, you are then immune to that particular strain. Unfortunately, viruses have the ability to change into a different strain, to which you will not be immune.

Flu can be debilitating, but not serious in a normal healthy person. To the elderly, or chronically ill, it can be potentially fatal. Flu vaccination is aimed at these groups, but needs to be done annually.

Gall bladder disease

The gall bladder is a small sac that sits beneath the liver. It is connected to the bowel by a narrow tube. Bile is a substance produced by the liver that has an important role in the digestion of fatty food. Bile collects in the gall bladder, and after a meal, the gall bladder contracts squeezing the bile into the bowel where it mixes with, and helps to digest, food.

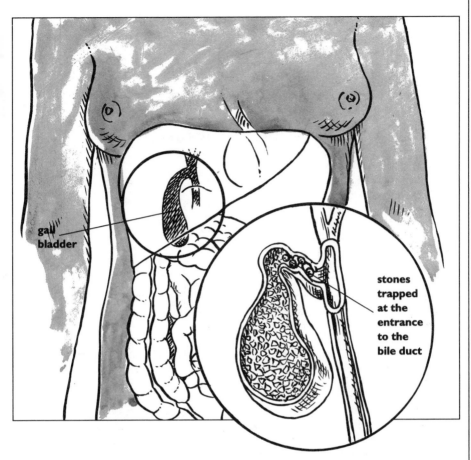

gall
bladder

stones
trapped
at the
entrance
to the
bile duct

▲ **Common site of gallstones.**

It is quite common for small stones to develop in the gall bladder. The reason why some people are particularly prone to developing gallstones is not known. They tend to be more common in fat middle-aged women, but they also occur in young adults and males. Many people with gallstones never know of their existence. Unfortunately, sometimes a stone may pass into the tube leading to the bowel. This produces an acute pain across the top of the abdomen, particularly on the right side (biliary colic). If the stone passes right into the bowel, the pain eases after a few hours. If the stone gets stuck in the tube, the gall bladder becomes swollen and inflamed (acute cholecystitis). Pain and fever are accompanied by jaundice, pale stools and dark urine.

Once someone has suffered one or more episodes of biliary colic or cholecystitis, then if stones are still present, the recommended treatment is surgical removal of the gall bladder (cholecystectomy). Like the appendix, the gall bladder is an organ we are unaware of until it becomes inflamed and causes illness, whereupon its removal is indicated, and we can manage perfectly well without it.

Gout

Gout is one of those illnesses that we have all heard of, and associate with fat elderly gentlemen who are fond of the port. In fact, gout can occur in women and men any time after puberty, although it is rare in women until after the menopause. Gout is caused by crystals forming in a joint and it is incredibly painful. Usually, only one joint is affected at a time. The big toe is most commonly affected, but the crystals can form in any joint, or in the tendons of joints. People who suffer from gout may also develop crystal deposits in the lobes of the ears.

Gout is due to a genetic disorder in the metabolism of uric acid, one of the body's waste products. Normally uric acid dissolves, and is excreted by the kidneys. In people with gout the levels of uric acid in the blood are far higher than normal, and eventually the crystals appear, giving rise to the symptoms.

Gout is not a life-threatening illness, and can be treated with anti-inflammatory drugs in the first place, followed by a drug called allopurinol, that reduces the levels of uric acid in the blood.

Heart disease

Heart disease is the major killer in the Western world, and Britain has the highest incidence in Europe. In 1990, 448 per 100,000 men and 167 per 100,000 women died from heart disease. Heart disease is the term used to describe illness arising from gradual blocking of the arteries that supply the heart (the coronary arteries) and covers a spectrum of illness that includes sudden death from a major heart attack at one end, to mild angina on exertion at the other.

Although there are recognised risk factors for developing heart disease:

- ☞ Diabetes
- ☞ High blood pressure
- ☞ A history of heart disease in the immediate family
- ☞ Smoking
- ☞ High cholesterol levels

the reason why some populations, such as Britain, have a higher incidence than a similar population such as France, remains one of medicine's unanswered questions.

Hepatitis

Hepatitis is inflammation of the liver. There are two main types of hepatitis. The most common is Hepatitis A. This is caused by a virus, and is transmitted by eating contaminated food, such as shellfish, or drinking water that has been contaminated, often in areas of poor sanitation.

The incubation period between infection and the onset of the illness is two to three weeks. The illness itself starts with a period of about two weeks, during which symptoms include:

- ☞ A general feeling of being unwell
- ☞ Loss of appetite and energy
- ☞ Vomiting
- ☞ Diarrhoea
- ☞ Fever

After two weeks, jaundice and itching of the skin develop and the liver becomes enlarged and tender. The illness persists for another week or two, most people recovering within six weeks from the beginning of the symptoms. Maximum infectivity is during the first three weeks of the illness, just before the onset of jaundice. Most people make a full recovery.

Hepatitis B, and the rare C,D,E are also caused by a virus that acts in a very different way. A person may become an asymptomatic carrier of Hepatitis B, and they then infect other people by sexual or blood transmission. The illness is common amongst homosexuals and intravenous drug users. The symptoms of Hepatitis B are similar to those of A, but the incubation period is much longer, from one to five months. The illness itself may be more severe, and the patient may become a carrier of the virus. Although recovery is normal, there is a risk of permanent liver damage.

Vaccination against both types of hepatitis is available, and should be taken when travelling abroad or by anyone at risk.

Hysterectomy

A hysterectomy is the surgical removal of the womb. There are different types:

- ☞ A radical, or Wertheim hysterectomy involves complete removal of all the reproductive organs: womb, cervix, Fallopian tubes ovaries plus associated blood vessels and lymph nodes.
- ☞ A total abdominal hysterectomy is the removal of womb and cervix, but leaves the ovaries behind.
- ☞ A partial, or sub-total hysterectomy is the removal of the womb but not the cervix.
- ☞ A vaginal hysterectomy is the same as a total hysterectomy in that both womb

and cervix are removed leaving the ovaries, but the operation is performed through the vagina, leaving no abdominal scar.

The reasons for performing a hysterectomy are:

☞ Cancer of the cervix, uterus or ovaries.
☞ Uncontrollable bleeding after childbirth.
☞ Fibroids.
☞ Endometriosis (small deposits of cells from the lining of the womb in the wrong place giving rise to abdominal pain).
☞ Prolapse of the womb.
☞ Chronic pelvic infection.
☞ Cervical abnormalities.

For women who have completed their families, a hysterectomy removes forever: periods, which may be heavy and painful, the need for contraception, the need for regular cervical smears, and the opportunity for cancer to develop in the womb or cervix. Many women, relieved of these anxieties, say that a hysterectomy has given them a whole new lease of life.

A hysterectomy is a major operation lasting at least an hour and requiring a full general anaesthetic. It usually means a hospital stay of up to ten days and a convalescence of between six weeks and three months. Like all major operations, it is not without risk, and a tiny proportion of women do die following hysterectomy, although they are usually already desperately ill.

Other complications which can follow include wound infections, venous thrombosis (a clot in the vein, usually of the leg) and damage to the bladder. Some women experience psychological problems arising from the inability to bear children, and fear of sex after the operation. If the ovaries are removed, then women experience menopausal symptoms, although these can be alleviated with hormone replacement.

Endometrial ablation is a new technique where the lining of the womb is destroyed by a laser beam, preventing bleeding but leaving everything else intact. It can be done as a day-case procedure, causes very little postoperative pain or bleeding, and women are back to normal within days, rather than weeks. It may be that before long,

hysterectomy will be used as a last, rather than first line of treatment.

Infertility

Infertility affects between one in ten and one in twelve couples. It is not diagnosed until a couple have been having effective unprotected intercourse for at least a year. There are a variety of causes:

☞ Defects of sperm or ejaculation in the male.
☞ Failure of ovulation.
☞ Fallopian tube damage or blockage.
☞ Endometriosis.
☞ Failure of intercourse.
☞ Cervical problems, including mucus hostile to sperm.
☞ Complete absence of sperm in the semen.

In at least a quarter of cases, no cause is ever found.

The treatment of infertility is aimed at identifying a cause, then if no cause is found, offering explanation and counselling.

Modern techniques have offered new hope to infertile couples.

IVF (In Vitro Fertilisation) consists of removing an egg from the woman, artificially fertilising it in the laboratory with the husband's sperm, and then returning it to the womb. A normal pregnancy results from 15 to 20 per cent of cycles. It is particularly suitable for women with blocked or damaged Fallopian tubes.

GIFT (Gamete Intra-Fallopian Transfer) is similar to IVF in that the egg and sperm are mixed in the laboratory, but then they are returned to the Fallopian tube to allow fertilisation to take place naturally. The success rate is slightly higher than IVF. This is particularly suitable for a couple where the husband has a low sperm count, or where there is no apparent cause of the infertility, but it is not suitable for women with blocked tubes.

Other ways of treating infertility include drugs that stimulate ovulation, and surgical treatment of damaged Fallopian tubes.

Irritable Bowel Syndrome (IBS)

The bowel normally contracts in a regular pulsatile way, pushing partly digested food, and then waste along its length until it reaches the rectum. We have all experienced the sensation of excess wind in the bowel, or indigestion brought on by particular food, or the watery feeling in the bowel produced at times of extreme anxiety. The Irritable Bowel Syndrome is a condition that is an extension of these normal variations, into a form of illness that cause significant distress.

The characteristic symptoms of the irritable bowel are diarrhoea interspersed with episodes of constipation, accompanied by abdominal pain. The pain usually occurs low on the left side of the abdomen, but can occur in any part of the abdomen. It may be relieved by defecation or the passing of wind. Appetite is usually normal, and weight stable. The symptoms are made worse by stress or depression.

It is thought that the symptoms of the irritable bowel are due to the contractions of the bowel becoming irregular and erratic, and out of sequence.

Treatment is aimed at restoring the movements of the bowel to normal, and this includes a high-fibre diet and drugs that relieve spasm of the bowel muscle. In some cases, particularly the elderly who suddenly develop symptoms, or if there is blood in the stool, then hospital investigation may be required to rule out a more serious cause, such as cancer or ulceration of the bowel.

Joint pain

The skeleton is made up of numerous bones which are connected at the joints. Movement can take place at the joints, giving the skeleton considerable flexibility. Most joints consist of a small cavity between the bones. The ends of the bones are covered in a rubbery substance, like a shock absorber, called cartilage (gristle). The rest of the joint capsule is lined with synovial membrane, which lubricates the surfaces and allows free movement of the joint. The whole joint is surrounded by muscles, tendons and ligaments which hold it in place. Joint pain can

be caused by any disease within a joint (usually called arthritis). It can also be mimicked by pain in the surrounding soft tissues.

Joint pain is a very common symptom. In most joint complaints, like a sprained ankle or frozen shoulder, the pain arises from the muscles and ligaments surrounding the joint, rather than within the joint itself. Joint disease can be serious and disabling, but with modern drug therapy and advances in surgical joint replacement, treatment is often highly successful.

Some common causes of joint pain include the following.

- ☞ Joint degeneration
- ☞ Joint inflammation
- ☞ Connective tissue disease
- ☞ Foreign material in the joint
- ☞ Reactive arthritis; following Gastro-enteritis
- ☞ Urethritis (Reiter's disease)
- ☞ Joint infection (septic arthritis):
- ☞ Trauma

Rest and analgesia will bring about recovery in most cases of isolated joint pain. You should see your doctor if:

- ☞ A painful joint persists or becomes worse.
- ☞ A painful joint is swollen, hot, red or associated with a generalised illness.

Knee injury

The knee joint is susceptible to injury because it bears the whole weight of the body. It is designed to bend (flex) and straighten (extend) in one plane only. The knee is not designed to rotate, so accidental rotation of the knee is one of the most common ways that the knee is damaged.

Joint problems tend to be more common in the elderly, but the knee is often damaged in young people during sporting activities, particularly football.

The knee joins the bottom of the thigh bone (femur) with the top of the two bones in the lower leg (tibia and fibula). Between the end of the bones are two cushions of cartilage (the menisci). On either side of the joint are two ligaments connected to the bones above and below the joint. To the front of the joint is a broad ligament connecting the powerful thigh muscles to the lower leg. Situated in this ligament is a small bone called the patella.

The knee is most prone to damage when it is partially bent, and then subjected to a blow from the side, as often happens during a football tackle. This can tear the cartilage or the ligament, on either side according to the direction of the blow.

When the knee is bent, and the front ligament is under strain, a blow to the front of the knee can fracture the patella.

Whatever the nature of the injury, a characteristic feature is swelling of the knee. This can be quite dramatic, and happen very quickly following a knee injury. Because the joint is a confined space, any bleeding, or inflammation producing excess fluid in the knee cannot escape, and the knee rapidly swells and becomes hot, stiff and very painful.

The initial treatment of a knee injury includes an X-ray of the joint to exclude a fracture. If the patella is broken, then an operation may be required to wire it together.

If there is no fracture, the excess fluid may be aspirated from the knee, which produces instant relief from most of the pain. Examination will reveal whether or not the side ligaments have been torn. If so, the knee will be immobilised to give them a chance to heal. Tears of the cartilage may give rise to 'locking' of the knee. These may require an operation called arthroscopy.

The inside of the knee joint is examined using a flexible telescope. Any torn or loose pieces of cartilage can be removed.

Many knee injuries will recover completely within a few weeks. However, because of the continued burden placed on the joint during normal activity, some will continue to be stiff, painful, or swell up intermittently. Physiotherapy to strengthen the muscles is useful in these cases.

Serious knee injuries can bring a professional sporting career to an end, but in most people, they recover adequately for normal life to be resumed.

Laryngitis

Laryngitis is inflammation of the larynx. The larynx (voice box, Adam's apple) is situated in the throat. It contains the vocal cords, which produce the sounds of speech as air from the lungs pass over them.

Laryngitis is most frequently caused by a viral infection, often in conjunction with inflammation of the nasal passages and the pharynx (upper throat), as in the common cold. Inflammation of the larynx produces a sore throat and hoarse voice.

Viral laryngitis is a self-limiting condition which recovers spontaneously within a few days. Treatment is aimed at relief of symptoms:

☞ Plenty of cold fluids
☞ Aspirin and paracetamol
☞ Throat lozenges
☞ Gargles

Laryngitis can sometimes be caused by a bacterial infection. If it does not improve within a week it may need a course of antibiotics. Chronic laryngitis tends to occur in people who put their vocal cords under a lot of strain. Smokers are prone to laryngitis because of the irritant effect of smoke on the lining of the air passages. People who use their voice a lot, such as singers and actors, may develop chronic laryngitis, and need to rest their voice to allow it to recover completely.

Harmless nodules can sometimes develop on the vocal cords, producing a hoarse voice. These can be removed surgically.

The onset of a constantly hoarse voice, particularly in the elderly and smokers, may indicate a tumour of the vocal cords, and needs medical investigation. This involves examining the vocal cords using a laryngoscope (an instrument designed to pass over the tongue to reveal the larynx).

Lung disease

Disease of the tissues of the lung fall into three main groups:

☞ Infections, such as pneumonia
☞ Damage to the lung tissue
☞ Tumours

The predominant symptoms of lung disease are coughing, shortness of breath and chest pain associated with breathing.

Pneumonia remains a relatively common lung disease. It is usually caused by a bacterial infection, but can also be caused by a virus, as a side-effect of radiotherapy, from inhaling vomit and as an allergic reaction of the lung tissue. Bacterial pneumonia remains a significant cause of death. It was expected that the incidence of death due to pneumonia would decrease dramatically following the widespread availability of antibiotics. This has been the case in children, but it is offset by an increase in death from pneumonia in the very old.

The onset of pneumonia can be rapid, with a temperature and a dry cough that is painful. Breathing becomes shallow and rapid. After a couple of days, the cough becomes productive, with rust-coloured sputum. The diagnosis can be confirmed by chest X-ray. Treatment is with antibiotics and physiotherapy to encourage coughing to clear the lungs.

In a fit person, recovery from pneumonia can be swift and uncomplicated, but in someone who is chronically ill, or has existing lung disease, admission to hospital is required.

There are a range of viruses that cause pneumonia. One of these is legionella, responsible for outbreaks of Legionnaire's disease.

Tuberculosis (TB) is caused by a bacteria that can affect all parts of the body, the lung being the most common site. It does respond to antibiotics, but needs prolonged treatment and can permanently scar the lung. Vaccination programmes have reduced the incidence of TB in this country, but it is still a significant cause of lung disease worldwide.

Damage to the lung tissue can occur for a variety of reasons. The surface area of the lungs is actually quite vast, so they can be exposed to significant concentrations of inhaled substances. The commonest is tobacco smoke. Smokers damage their lungs by the combined effect of the inhalation of smoke, and repeated chest infections. This can cause scarring of the lung tissue, which then loses its elasticity and becomes less efficient at absorbing oxygen. This condition is known as emphysema. People suffering from emphysema may need oxygen supplies in the home to help them breathe.

An emphysema-like condition can be caused by the long-term inhalation of chemical substances, such as coal dust.

Tumours of the lung that are malignant (cancerous) fall into two categories:

☞ Primary tumours, arising from the lung itself.
☞ Secondary tumours, arising from a primary tumour elsewhere in the body, which has spread to the lung.

Primary lung cancer is responsible for more deaths than any other form of cancer. There has been a rise in the number of people who develop lung cancer over many years. Although this now appears to have levelled off in men, it is still rising in women. The main risk of developing lung cancer is in smokers. Lung cancer is extremely rare in young people. The main symptoms of lung cancer are cough and chest pain, followed by rapid loss of weight. It is very difficult to treat.

The lung is a common site for the secondary spread of cancer from other parts of the body. This is due to the high blood flow through the lungs. Secondary cancer differs from primary in that there is not usually a single isolated tumour in the lung, but a wide scattering of small tumours throughout the lung fields.

Migraine

Approximately one in ten people suffer from migraine. It is characterised by episodes of particularly severe headache and ranges from a severe and disabling condition through to headaches that, although recurrent, are otherwise very like the normal 'tension' headaches that most people experience from time to time.

Classical migraine begins with a prodromal phase that may include disturbances of vision, such as flashing lights or the appearance of jagged lines. It may also be accompanied by numbness or tingling in the face, or down one arm, and rarely, difficulty in talking. Nausea is a common feature. This phase may last for up to an hour, and then the headache occurs.

This typically starts in one place and spreads, but is often confined to one side of the head only, although this is not invariably so.

The headache may last for several hours, together with nausea, vomiting and intolerance of bright lights. Once it wears off, sleepiness and an increased passage of urine may occur.

The cause of migraine is unknown, but it is thought to arise from swelling of some of the blood vessels in the brain, which stimulates the nerve endings lying adjacent to them, giving rise to the symptoms.

Some people who suffer from migraine find that they are able to identify things that trigger an attack, such as certain food or drink. Chocolate, cheese and red wine are often implicated. Women may find that they are more likely to have an attack of migraine around the time of a period. They are also more common during puberty and at the menopause. In some women, the oral contraceptive pill may trigger migraine for the first time, or make the existing condition worse.

Migraine is very rarely associated with any kind of brain disease, but because it is common, it may occur in people who go on to have strokes or develop a brain tumour in later life. The sudden onset of migraine in people who have never had it before requires medical advice.

The treatment of migraine is based on three things:

☞ The avoidance of risk factors, such as foods that trigger an attack.

☞ The relief of symptoms, drugs for the pain of the headache and to settle nausea and vomiting.

☞ Prevention of attacks. There are some prescription drugs that are effective at preventing migraine in some, but not all, people who suffer from frequent attacks.

Nerve disorders

The nervous system includes the brain, the spinal cord, and an enormous network of nerves that supply every single part of the body. The function of nerves is to transmit information from one part of the body to another. This information can arise from outside the body, where it is detected by our senses:

☞ Sight
☞ Touch (including pain)
☞ Taste
☞ Smell
☞ Sound

Other information arises from inside the body: feelings of hunger and thirst, the need to empty the bladder.

In addition, we have nerves detecting the position of our body and limbs, balance and temperature.

There is a great deal of nerve activity that we are unaware of, unless it goes wrong. Things like the movements of our bowels, the movements of our chest as we breathe, and the beating of our heart are under a degree of autonomic (or automatic) nerve control.

Because the nervous system is so complicated and is involved in every part of the body, diseases affecting the nervous system cover a host of conditions. Some are specific to a single nerve, some to the nervous tissue of the brain and spinal cord, some affect certain groups of nerves, and some affect nerves in general, in which case the symptoms may arise in any part of the body.

A feature of nerve tissue that makes diseases of the nervous system potentially serious, is that, unlike tissue in other parts of the body, it does not heal well, or even at all. Once nerve tissue is damaged, it may never recover.

Like other tissues of the body, nervous tissue is susceptible to infection, inflammation, damage from trauma, and tumours.

Symptoms suggestive of nerve (neurological) disease include:

☞ A change in the level of consciousness
☞ Mental state
☞ Awareness of who, what and where you are
☞ Changes in intellect and memory
☞ Speech difficulties
☞ Problems with balance, posture and walking
☞ Loss of co-ordination
☞ Muscle weakness, twitching and wasting
☞ Loss of skin sensation

☞ Pain along the path of a nerve
☞ Headaches, dizziness

Some of the most common disorders of the nervous system are:

Herpes zoster (shingles)

In some people the virus responsible for chicken pox can lie dormant in some of the nerves for a long time. What causes the infection to re-emerge and attack the nerve is unknown, but it may be due to a decrease in immunity. It tends to occur in the middle-aged and elderly. The first symptoms are of pain and tingling along the length of the nerve, often those supplying the upper body or face. This is followed by the eruption of blisters on the skin along the nerve track. Shingles can be very painful, and lasts for three to six weeks. Treatment is with the anti-viral agent acyclovir, or steroids.

Sciatica

The sciatic nerve is a large nerve that emerges from the spinal cord and passes through the buttock to supply the leg. Conditions affecting the lower spine, including slipped disc or arthritis, can inflame the sciatic nerve. This causes pain that spreads down the side of the thigh towards the knee. In severe cases it can cause weakness in the leg. Treatment is by non-steroidal anti-inflammatory drugs (NSAIDs), and physiotherapy to improve posture.

Bell's Palsy

This is a common nerve disorder, thought to be caused by a virus that attacks one of the nerves supplying the face. It produces a one-sided paralysis of the muscles of the face. It usually recovers spontaneously within a couple of weeks, but in some people it may take up to a year to recover.

Parkinson's disease

One in two hundred people over the age of seventy develop Parkinson's disease, making it very common in elderly people. It is caused by a chemical imbalance in the brain. The characteristic symptoms are slowness and development of a tremor in the hands and arms. Loss of facial expression, stiffness and changes in posture and walking may follow. In the later stages of the illness, speech becomes slurred and eventually dementia may develop. Parkinson's disease is slowly progressive over a period of fifteen to twenty years. Treatment is aimed at correcting the chemical imbalance using drugs. On the whole these are effective, but side-effects or resistance to the drugs after a period of time are problems.

Trigeminal neuralgia

The trigeminal nerve receives sensation from the side of the face: the eye, cheek and jaw. Trigeminal neuralgia is a type of hypersensitivity of this nerve, in which chewing, washing or a cold wind may bring on acute knife-like pain in the side of the face. The pain only lasts a few seconds, but may occur several times a day. The cause is unknown, but it is more common in the elderly. Drugs that are used in the treatment of epilepsy have been found to be useful in controlling this condition.

Multiple sclerosis

Multiple sclerosis is one of the better known neurological diseases – partly because it is quite common, and partly because it affects young people and is responsible for a significant degree of disability in the population as a whole. Like many neurological diseases, the cause is unknown. The mechanism of the disease is progressive damage to the sheath which surrounds the nerves. This damage 'de-myelination' can occur in nerves in any part of the body.

The diagnosis is based on a series of nerve disorders occurring in different parts of the body. Disturbances of vision and intermittent weakness and paralysis are some of the commoner symptoms in the early stages. In some people with MS, the disease follows a 'relapsing and remitting' course. Periods of disease are followed by periods of apparent recovery, often lasting quite a long time. In such cases, MS sufferers can lead reasonably normal lives. In some people, the disease is more aggressive and advances rapidly, causing serious disability.

All manner of treatments have been attempted, and research goes on into the cause and treatment of MS all the time.

Osteoporosis

The bones consist of soft tissues made rigid by the deposition of salts within their structure. Calcium is one of the main components of these salts. Osteoporosis is a decrease in the density of bone. The bones become softer and more brittle, and are more likely to break after even a relatively small injury. Bone density in men is greater than that of women, and men are less likely to develop osteoporosis, although the overall density of the bone decreases in everyone with increasing age. The hormone oestrogen protects against osteoporosis, making it unusual in young women.

It is women after the menopause who are at greatest risk. Once a fracture occurs, it takes longer to heal. The most common sites for fractures in people with osteoporosis are the wrist, hip and top of the thigh bone (neck of femur). Fracture of the wrist often occurs after a fall on the outstretched hand. The top of the thigh bone can be broken by a simple fall, often just getting out of bed. The bones of the spine (vertebra) can collapse. This may go unnoticed or give rise to back pain. Gradual collapse of the spine is the reason some elderly women have a shrunken, hunched back appearance.

Prolonged bed rest also increases the development of osteoporosis. In young people, exercise and plenty of dietary calcium build up the density of the bone, which can then last into old age. Increased calcium supplements in people with established osteoporosis may not reverse the condition, but can prevent it worsening.

The replacement of oestrogen, in the form of hormone replacement therapy, has been shown to be very effective in preventing osteoporosis from developing in post-menopausal women.

Osteoarthritis

Arthritis, the painful swelling and stiffening of joints, has many different causes, the most common being osteoarthritis. Joints are the junction between two or more bones, and their main function is to act as a 'hinge' allowing movement, so providing flexibility in the skeleton, which is made up of otherwise rigid bones. Some joints allow relatively little movement, such as the junctions between the ribs and the sternum (breast bone). Others such as the hip joint, allow a wide range of movement in several directions.

Joints consist of cartilage over the ends of the bones, which provide a smooth surface across which movement can occur, and also act as shock absorbers. Many of the larger joints also contain fluid. This fluid is called synovial fluid, and is produced by the synovial membrane which lines the joint. It acts as a lubricant.

Osteoarthritis is the result of wear and tear on the joints. It is common in the joints that are exposed to the greatest strain: the weight-bearing joints such as knee hip and lower spine. It is relatively uncommon in the joints of the upper limbs, although it does occur in the neck. The small joints of the feet and hands are rarely affected.

The changes include thickening of the joint, sometimes accompanied by bony swelling around the joint. The joint becomes painful and stiff, with limited movement. The stiffness is worse in the morning and tends to wear off during the day. The condition is isolated to the joints, and is not usually accompanied by any symptoms of general ill-health. Joints that have been previously damaged are more likely to develop osteoarthritis.

The initial treatment of osteoarthritis is with drugs called 'Non-steroidal anti-inflammatory drugs', or NSAIDs. As their name suggests, these drugs reduce inflammation in the joint, which relieves the pain. Steroids are very effective at reducing inflammation, but are used sparingly in the treatment of osteoarthritis because of their side-effects. There are many different NSAIDs on the market. They resemble aspirin in the way they work. They are now available from the pharmacist without a prescription. They are very effective. Their main drawback is that they may irritate the lining of the stomach in some people.

For very severe osteoarthritis, where the joint has been almost completely destroyed, surgical joint replacement is performed. Hip replacements are now a fairly common procedure. Replacement of the knee joint is becoming more widespread. These operations can be spectacularly successful.

Panic attacks

Panic attacks are a condition brought about by anxiety. It is one condition in a group that come under the general heading of 'anxiety-related disorders'. Others include generalised anxiety, agoraphobia, social phobia, post-traumatic stress disorder and some obsessive disorders. Anxiety-related disorders affect up to 15 per cent of the population and are aggravated by stress. They can be difficult to identify, in particular they can easily be confused with depression, which if mild, may have many similar symptoms.

Panic attacks are a specific condition, occurring in people with a level of underlying anxiety. The factors that trigger a panic attack differ from person to person, but are usually a stress-inducing situation. This may be having to attend a social event, or meet someone, or entering the workplace, or even leaving the house.

The symptoms are a feeling of panic, which is followed by:

- ☞ Palpitations (an awareness of the heart beating)
- ☞ Shortness of breath
- ☞ Chest pain
- ☞ Pain in the limbs
- ☞ A choking sensation
- ☞ Eventually loss of consciousness.

What happens during a panic attack is this: The underlying anxiety produces an increase in the rate of breathing (hyperventilation). This reduces the levels of carbon dioxide in the blood, which in turn have an effect on the blood chemistry causing spasm of the muscles and pounding of the heart. The levels of anxiety, and the degree of overbreathing increase, until they eventually lose consciousness. Once they have lost consciousness, breathing returns to normal and they promptly wake up again. This may

happen several times, and sufferers may even be rushed into hospital with a suspected heart attack before the diagnosis becomes clear.

The treatment of panic attacks is usually successful. In some cases, simple explanation of what is happening will suffice. When the early symptoms develop, the person can make themselves take slow breaths until the symptoms subside. Demonstrating that it is overbreathing and nothing worse that produces the symptoms can be useful. Anyone who forces themselves to breathe very fast will develop dizziness and tingling in the feet and hands.

If a panic attack is developing, re-breathing into a paper bag is effective. By inhaling some of the exhaled carbon dioxide, the symptoms do not develop. Relaxation techniques are useful in controlling the underlying anxiety. If the basic level of anxiety is high, then drugs may be necessary. These drugs, tranquillisers, may be effective used alone or in conjunction with psychological counselling.

Panic attacks are a condition that can usually be managed by the GP. Only in the most severe cases, where there is often more serious underlying mental illness, including severe depression, will referral to a psychiatrist become necessary. Since panic attacks are generally related to factors in a person's life, such as relationship problems, or a stressful job or situation, such as moving house, they may cease once the underlying cause has been changed.

Rheumatic fever

Rheumatic fever is still a common disease affecting children and young adults in some parts of the world, although in Britain the number of cases has fallen dramatically over the last seventy years. In the 1920s, it affected one in ten people; now it affects only one in ten thousand. This is due to improved sanitation and the availability of antibiotics.

Rheumatic fever starts as a fever with pain in the joints. It may be accompanied by loss of appetite, fidgety movements (Sydenham's chorea) and skin rashes. The heart may be affected, giving rise to a fast pulse and a heart murmur.

Rheumatic fever is due to an infection with the streptococcus bacteria, which commonly causes throat infections. Treatment is with antibiotics (usually penicillin), aspirin and in severe cases, steroids.

Recovery is normally rapid and uneventful. The danger of rheumatic fever lies in the involvement of the heart. Although this may settle with treatment, the valves of the heart may be permanently damaged. This may not cause problems until later in life, although a heart murmur might be permanently present. As the heart ages, this underlying damage can result in the development of heart failure. Ultimately this may mean that the damaged valves have to be surgically replaced with artificial heart valves. Although now rarely fatal, rheumatic fever is still a serious infection that requires prompt treatment.

Sinusitis

The sinuses are air pockets situated in the bones of the skull and face. They are lined by a membrane that produces mucus, and their function is to warm and moisten inhaled air, and to add resonance to the voice.

The frontal sinuses are situated in the forehead, between the eyebrows. The maxillary sinuses are situated in the cheek, just beside the nose. These are the largest and most important sinuses. If you develop a cold, the lining of the sinuses becomes inflamed. This causes the runny nose, blocked sensation, and pain in the face and head. Normally, this will clear up by itself within a short space of time. Because the entrances to the sinuses are fairly small, inflammation can block them off, preventing the normal drainage of mucus. This may then become infected with bacteria, producing greenish mucus from the nose, and increased pain over the cheek or forehead.

☞ Antibiotics are not always very effective at treating this, since they cannot penetrate into the sinuses very easily if they are blocked. Treatment is therefore aimed at improving drainage of the sinuses.

☞ Inhalation of steam makes the mucus more runny, and so able to drain. This is also the effect of drugs called mucolytics.

☞ Decongestant sprays are used to settle the swelling of the membranes. Decongestant tablets work in the same way. The problem with these is that although effective in the short term, once they have worn off, the membrane may swell more than before. They should therefore be used with caution, and under medical advice.

Some people are particularly prone to developing sinusitis after a cold. Often this is simply due to the particular shape of their sinuses, which happen to become easily blocked. It is also more common in smokers.

Allergic sinusitis is swelling of the membranes in response to an allergen such as pollen, and is one of the features of hay fever.

☞ Anti-histamine drugs are effective in the treatment of allergic, but not infective, sinusitis.

Chronic sinusitis can develop in some people, where the sinuses become blocked and the condition does not improve after prolonged treatment with antibiotics. This can be helped by a washout of the sinuses by an ENT (Ear, Nose and Throat) surgeon.

Sexually Transmitted Diseases (STDs)

STDs are infections that are transmitted primarily by sexual intercourse. Until the last two decades, STDs were primarily considered to be one of the following, also known as Venereal Disease:

☞ Gonorrhoea
☞ Syphilis
☞ Chancroid
☞ Lymphogranuloma

Today, however, this list has grown to include:

☞ Chlamydial infections
☞ Trichomonas
☞ Genital herpes
☞ Scabies
☞ Pubic lice
☞ Genital warts
☞ HIV infections
☞ AIDS

Diagnosis and treatment are usually offered at specialist clinics, often by specialists in genito-urinary medicine. Treatment is always confidential and often consists of antibiotics, and then assessment to see if the patient is still infectious. Safer sexual practice has meant that STDs are on the decrease, and treatment of previous partners (traced through a confidential contact tracing procedure) has meant that major outbreaks are less likely. With the advent of AIDS, STDs took on a whole new meaning, becoming a threat to life, not just sexual activity, and that has also served to decrease the prevalence.

cervical erosion

This is a harmless change that can take place on the surface of the cervix (neck of the womb). The linings of the womb and vagina are made up of different types of cells. The junction between the two, known as the transition zone, is usually situated inside the cervical canal. Under certain circumstances this junction moves on to the surface of the cervix, giving it a red, roughened appearance. This is visible during an internal examination and is described as an 'erosion'.

Most erosions do not cause any symptoms and are an incidental finding during an internal examination. Symptoms arise when an erosion becomes infected. This can produce an offensive discharge or bleeding after intercourse. An erosion that is not causing any symptoms requires no treatment.

Sometimes an erosion causes an 'inflammatory' appearance on a cervical smear. If inflammatory changes persist on repeated smears, or the erosion is producing symptoms, then treatment is aimed at clearing up infection, with an antiseptic vaginal cream, or a course of oral antibiotics.

If an erosion on an otherwise healthy cervix continues to produce symptoms, then the usual treatment is cryo-cautery (freezing) or diathermy (burning) of the affected area.

Vaginal discharge is rarely due to a serious condition, but you should consult your doctor if you experience any of the following:

- ☞ Bleeding between periods
- ☞ Bleeding after the menopause
- ☞ Bleeding during pregnancy
- ☞ Change in cycle associated with weight loss
- ☞ Pain inside during intercourse (Dyspareunia)

thrush

Candida albicans is an organism commonly found on the skin. It is also found in the vagina of many women with no symptoms. An attack of vaginal thrush produces white discharge and itching, then soreness around the vagina.

Why it should flare up and cause symptoms requiring treatment in some women more than others is not fully understood, although there are some common factors.

- ☞ The use of vaginal deodorants and washes alters the normal bacterial content of the vagina, and may allow thrush to flourish.
- ☞ Diabetics and pregnant women are more prone to thrush.

The treatment of thrush is with drugs such as Canesten, which can be used in cream, pessary or oral tablet form. Some women find that natural live yoghurt, applied internally, is effective. Live yoghurt contains bacteria called lactobacilli, which form a large part of the normal, healthy, bacterial content of the vagina.

trichomonas

Trichomonas is a sexually transmitted disease. The condition is caused by infection with a protozoa (a single-celled organism larger than a bacteria) called Trichomonas Vaginalis. The organism is introduced into the vagina during sexual intercourse. Once established, it multiplies rapidly, killing off the protective bacteria that normally inhabit the vagina. The vaginal acidity is neutralised, allowing harmful bacteria to invade and exacerbate the infection. This produces inflammation of the vaginal walls and copious vaginal discharge.

Trichomonas is common, and together with thrush, accounts for 90 per cent of cases of abnormal vaginal discharge.

The diagnosis of trichomonas is confirmed by looking at a sample of the discharge under the microscope, where the organism can be seen swimming about.

Treatment is with an antibiotic, usually metronidazole, which can be given as a large single dose or smaller doses over several days, and clears the infection very quickly. Occasionally, the organism can lodge in the vaginal or urethral glands and act as a reservoir, causing re-infection, which again must be treated with metronidazole. It is important that the sexual partner is also treated with a course of metronidazole, whether or not he has symptoms, otherwise, re-infection will occur with every act of intercourse.

Trichomonas infection may accompany (and mask) the symptoms of a more serious infection, such as chlamydia or gonorrhoea. Swabs of the discharge, and from the cervix and urethra, are taken at examination, and sent to the laboratory to check whether other organisms are present. If so, then both partners are treated with high doses of antibiotics such as amoxycillin or oxytetracycline.

Tinnitus

Tinnitus is the sensation of ringing in the ears when there is, in fact, no such noise. It is suggestive of a problem with the ear, or the nerve along which sound passes to the brain. There are several things which can affect the ear, or its nerve, giving rise to tinnitus. Dizziness, deafness and occasionally pain in the ear are the symptoms which usually accompany tinnitus.

The most common cause of tinnitus is a condition called Meniere's disease. This is a disease of unknown cause. Sufferers experience sudden attacks of dizziness, deafness and tinnitus, which may last from a few minutes to several hours. The attacks may continue with variable frequency for several years. Eventually permanent deafness occurs in the affected ear and the dizziness disappears.

The symptoms of the acute attack can be lessened by the use of drugs, but there is no cure for the underlying condition.

Ulcers

An ulcer is generally round in shape, with a raised edge surrounding a central hollow of damaged tissue. Ulcers occur in different sites, but the most common are mouth ulcers, skin ulcers and ulcers inside the stomach or small bowel. They have different causes.

Mouth ulcers are common and often accompany a viral illness. They are known as apthous ulcers. They tend to occur during adolescence and clear up spontaneously with age. They are very shallow and painful, but heal up without treatment within a matter of days.

Occasionally recurrent mouth ulcers are associated with diseases of the gastrointestinal tract such as Crohn's disease and ulcerative colitis.

Tiny ulcers can form in the stomach and duodenum (the first part of the small bowel). These are known as peptic ulcers. They arise from a combination of excess stomach acid, together with underlying infection that damages the gut lining, allowing the acid to burn an ulcer through the protective coating. Peptic ulceration is very common. It causes pain related to eating, and the diagnosis is confirmed by examining the lining of the stomach and duodenum using a gastroscope (a flexible telescope) where the ulcer can be seen.

Symptoms are relieved by antacids, but the ulcer may come back. Drugs that reduce the acid produced in the stomach are effective. There is an increasing tendency to give these together with an antibiotic to clear up the underlying infection. This is caused by an organism called helicobacter pylorii, and its role in the development of peptic ulcers has only recently been identified.

Skin ulcers on the lower part of the legs are common, particularly in the elderly. The shin does not have a very good blood supply, as there is very little tissue between the skin and the bone. As the blood supply generally becomes less efficient in the elderly, the shin is at particular risk. A relatively small injury, possible just nicking the skin, takes ages to heal. Sometimes it does not heal, but becomes infected and develops into an ulcer.

☞ Some skin ulcers, particularly those occurring in sites other than the leg, such as on the face, can be more serious. They may actually be a cancerous ulcer. Removal of a small piece of tissue for examination under the microscope (a biopsy) may be needed to confirm the diagnosis.

☞ Basal-cell carcinoma, known as a Rodent ulcer, is an ulcer that typically occurs on the face in fair-skinned people who have had long exposure to the sun. Although cancerous, it grows very slowly and is usually completely healed by surgical removal.

☞ Malignant melanoma is a more serious form of skin cancer that is also more common in those exposed to prolonged sun. It develops from an existing mole, which may grow, bleed, or ulcerate, suggesting that it has become malignant. Early surgical removal is successful, but once it has spread it can prove fatal.

Vaginal discharge

Many women find it difficult to know what constitutes a normal vaginal discharge. The amount of normal vaginal discharge increases during pregnancy and mid-cycle at the time of ovulation, is inoffensive, and does not necessitate wearing any form of sanitary protection.

Vaginal discharge is abnormal if it is:
☞ Offensive
☞ Bloodstained
☞ Green or yellow
☞ Causes soreness or itching
☞ Requires sanitary protection

The three most common causes of excessive vaginal discharge are:
☞ Infection with candida albicans (thrush)
☞ Infection with *trichomonas vaginalis*
☞ A cervical erosion

Warts

Warts are a common condition initially caused by a virus which disrupts the normal skin. There are several different types.

Common warts occur mainly on the hands and knees in children. They sometimes spread by contact with damaged skin. For example, nail-biters with warts on their fingers may develop warts around the mouth.

☞ Plantar warts (verrucas) occur on the soles of the feet, and often resemble a pit in the skin, rather than a lump. They can be very painful when squeezed or pressed.

☞ Plane warts are smaller, flat lumps that occur on the skin of the face, and may be pigmented.

☞ Genital warts form pale clusters around the vulva and vagina in women, and on the glans of the penis in men. There is some evidence to suggest that they may be sexually transmitted. Genital warts in women are associated with a higher incidence of cancer of the cervix.

Warts tend to disappear spontaneously, sometimes within a matter of days, sometimes after a few weeks or months. This makes it difficult to be absolutely certain whether treatment has been effective or not.

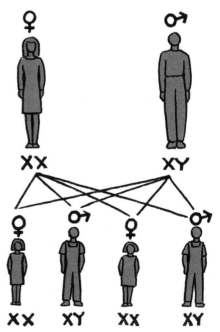

There are two main forms of treatment:
- The application of paints that contain an acid that dissolves the wart.
- Surgical destruction of the wart. The wart may be cut out (curettage), frozen (cryotherapy) or burned (diathermy).

Generally, warts are entirely harmless.

X-linked conditions

Each cell in the body contains 46 chromosomes. Chromosomes carry the genes which form the genetic 'blueprint' of the body, and are what makes each individual unique. Of the 46 chromosomes, there are 22 identical pairs plus the pair responsible for determining what sex we are. In a female this pair consists of two X chromosomes. In a male, one X and one Y.

There are certain genetic abnormalities that exist on the X chromosome only. Genes can be dominant, i.e., they have an effect if they occur on just one of the pair of chromosomes, or they can be recessive i.e., both chromosomes need to carry the gene

for it to become apparent.

The main example of an X-linked condition is haemophilia. This is a recessive gene. A female with one gene for haemophilia and one normal gene will not have the condition, but will be a carrier and she may pass it in to her offspring. Males, on the other hand, will have the condition if they inherit the gene, because there cannot be a second, normal X chromosome to oppose the abnormal gene. X-linked haemophilia is therefore a genetic condition which occurs in men but is carried by females. If a female is a carrier, the chances are that half her female children will be carriers, half not, and half her male children will have the disease, half not.

There are other X-linked genetic disorders. Most are extremely rare, but they include colour blindness, albinism and Duchenne muscular dystrophy.

▼ **X-linked conditions – how they are passed on.**

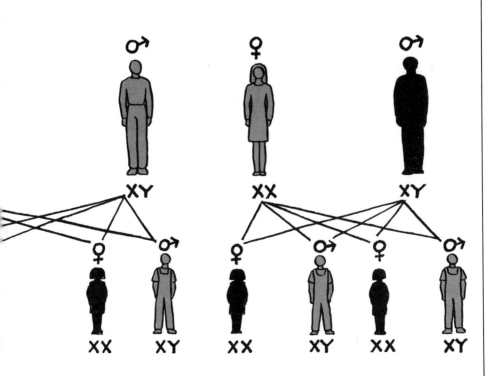

255

Contraception

The purpose of contraception is to prevent an unwanted pregnancy. Modern methods are freely available and on the whole, safe and reliable. They are not all completely devoid of a degree of minor inconvenience, but this must be measured against the major problem of an unwanted pregnancy. There is, as yet, no such thing as the 'perfect' contraceptive: one that is reversible, 100 per cent effective, has no side effects and does not require you to remember to use it. However, some come fairly close. The best method of contraception is the one that suits you.

Contraceptive advice and supplies can be obtained from several sources:

☞ Family planning clinics deal specifically with women seeking contraception.

☞ Health Authority clinics are run by doctors and nurses who specialise in family planning. They deal only with contraception; for other problems, such as vaginal discharge, you would be referred back to your doctor.

☞ Most doctors offer family planning to their patients. This may be done during normal surgery times, run as a separate clinic, or combined with a 'Well woman' clinic. Any female problems, including hormone replacement therapy, can be dealt with. If you feel uncomfortable about seeing your own doctor, or he does not provide the service, then it is possible to go to another doctor for family planning only.

☞ Charities such as the Marie Stopes clinics or the Brook Advisory Centre also offer family planning, and there are private clinics that specialise in vasectomy and female sterilisation operations.

☞ Pharmacies sell caps, condoms, spermicides and fertility charts and thermometers. Supermarkets sell condoms.

Your Local Family Health Service Authority will be able to tell you which Health Authority clinics are available. They are also listed in the phone book and Yellow Pages The advantages of these are:

☞ Anonymity.

☞ They are usually staffed by female doctors.

☞ They are often held outside normal working hours.

Brook Advisory Centres and Marie Stopes clinics are listed in the Yellow Pages under 'clinics' or 'family planning'. You do not need a referral from your doctor, but you do need to make an appointment before you attend.

When you go for professional contraceptive services for the first time, you will see a doctor, who will ask about your contraceptive requirements. You may already know what method of family planning you would prefer. The doctor will then ask for all details about your medical history, with particular reference to your menstrual cycle and any pregnancies. You will not be asked embarrassing questions about your sex life, but you should always offer any information that might be relevant (such as a previous abortion) as this will help the doctor find the best method for you.

You will have your blood pressure checked, urine tested, and may undergo an internal examination and cervical smear.

The methods of contraception available are:

☞ Hormonal methods, which include the normal combined pill, the progesterone-only mini pill, and the progesterone injection.

☞ The intra-uterine contraceptive device (IUCD, known as the coil).

☞ Barrier methods: the diaphragm or sheaths, used with a spermicidal cream.

☞ 'Natural' methods: predicting ovulation and timing intercourse.

☞ Permanent sterilisation.

The Pill

Oral contraception is a method of birth control in which taking a regular small dose of hormone in tablet form (known as **the Pill**), prevents pregnancy. Such tablets are only available for use by women at present.

The Pill works by preventing ovulation. For conception to occur, an egg must be released from the ovary (ovulation), and fertilised by a sperm. The high levels of the hormones oestrogen and progesterone, naturally circulating during pregnancy and in the second half of the menstrual cycle, inhibit further release of eggs from the ovary. Oestrogen and progesterone cannot be taken by mouth, being inactivated by the digestive system, so it was not until synthetic versions of these hormones were developed, that the Pill became available, in the early 1960s.

In addition to preventing ovulation, the pill acts on the uterus, preventing implantation of a fertilised egg, and making the cervical mucus hostile to sperm.

The **combined** oral contraceptive pill contains both oestrogen and progesterone. The oestrogen component of the combined pill may produce nausea, fluid retention, breast tenderness and increased vaginal secretions, whereas progesterone causes acne, hirsutism and vaginal dryness. These effects are dose-related, so are less of a problem with low-dose pills, and often improve after a few months of pill-taking. They can also be minimised by tailoring the relative doses of oestrogen and progesterone to the symptoms. In some cases, the side-effects are beneficial; e.g., acne may be improved by an oestrogen-dominant pill, breast-tenderness by increasing the progesterone.

The other beneficial side-effects of the Pill include:

- ☞ shorter, lighter, less painful, regular periods.
- ☞ a reduction in pre-menstrual symptoms.
- ☞ A reduction in the risk of pelvic inflammatory disease, ectopic pregnancies, ovarian cysts and painful, lumpy breasts.

In spite of the fact that the Pill has been in widespread use for so long, there is still no convincing evidence that it causes any type of cancer. What has been shown is that it reduces the risk of cancer of the ovary and body of the uterus.

Dangerous side-effects of the pill are due to its effect on the blood and circulation in a small group of 'At risk' women.

Contra-indications to the pill

Absolute (The Pill should not be taken.)

- ☞ Circulatory disease: Venous thrombosis, angina, heart-valve defects, crescendo angina.
- ☞ High levels of lipids in the blood and a family history of strokes and heart attacks.
- ☞ Diabetes with complications (eye or kidney damage).
- ☞ High blood pressure.
- ☞ Heavy cigarette smoking (more than 50 per day).
- ☞ Increasing age (smokers only).
- ☞ Severe obesity (more than 50 per cent above ideal body weight)
- ☞ Liver disease
- ☞ Focal migraine
- ☞ Undiagnosed vaginal bleeding
- ☞ Steroid-dependent breast cancer

Relative (The pill can be taken provided only one of these risk factors is present.)

- ☞ Family history of arterial disease, but normal blood lipids.
- ☞ Uncomplicated mild diabetes.
- ☞ Slightly elevated blood pressure.
- ☞ Smoking more than 50 per day.
- ☞ Age over 35.
- ☞ Moderate obesity (less than 50 per cent above ideal weight)
- ☞ Long-term immobilisation.
- ☞ Crohn's disease.

If you wish to start taking the Pill as a method of contraception, you should see your doctor before you have intercourse. Once you are on the Pill, you will be asked to return for a check-up every six to twelve months. You should also see your doctor if you have an attack of gastro-enteritis, as this might interfere with the absorption of the pill.

You should also see your doctor if you develop any of the following symptoms, after taking the Pill:

- ☞ Pain in the calf.
- ☞ Chest pain.
- ☞ Breathlessness.
- ☞ Abdominal pain.
- ☞ Migraine.
- ☞ Fainting.
- ☞ Weakness or numbness.
- ☞ Disturbance of speech or vision.
- ☞ A severe rash.

If you forget to take a pill, but it is less than twelve hours since you should have taken it, take it immediately and carry on as normal. If it is over twelve hours, or more than one pill has been missed, take two pills, then carry on with the pack, but use other methods as well (e.g., condoms) for the next seven days. If the pack you are taking finishes during these seven days, continue with the next pack without a break.

The 'morning after' pill (post-coital contraception)

If unprotected intercourse has taken place, a special, relatively high dose of the Pill can be used to prevent pregnancy, provided it is taken within seventy-two hours of intercourse. Two 'morning after' tablets are taken immediately, and a further two after twelve hours. Depending on the stage of the menstrual cycle, this will prevent ovulation or implantation.

The 'mini-pill'

This only contains progesterone, no oestrogen. It acts by preventing implantation rather than ovulation. It is a little less reliable, so every pill has to be taken regularly, at more or less the same time each day. It is suitable for women who may have some medical reason for not taking the combined pill. The mini-pill is taken constantly, with no monthly break. Bleeding is less regular, and may stop altogether.

The progesterone injection

This is an injection that lasts for six months at a time. It works in exactly the same way as the progesterone-only pill. The main advantage is that you don't have to remember to take a pill every day. The main drawback is that it is not instantly reversible, but has to wear off.

Intra-Uterine Contraceptive Device (IUCD, Coil)

An IUCD is an object that is inserted into the uterus (womb) to prevent pregnancy. The IUCDs currently used in the UK are made of plastic with a thin coating of copper wire, and come in several shapes.

For fertilisation to proceed to pregnancy, the egg must become embedded in the lining of the womb (implantation). The IUCD prevents this from happening.

Larger IUCDs are better at preventing pregnancy than small ones, but they also cause more side-effects. The addition of copper wire to the device improves its contraceptive effect, allowing smaller devices to be used. IUCDs that slowly release the hormone progesterone are currently being tested, as they are likely to be even more reliable.

Inserting an IUCD:

☞ Proper insertion of an IUCD has been shown to reduce many of the potential problems associated with its use, so insertion is always carried out by an experienced family planning doctor. This may be your own family doctor, or a doctor at the family planning clinic.

☞ The actual insertion can be performed at any point of the menstrual cycle, but is usually done towards the end of a period as this excludes pregnancy, and the cervix is soft and slightly dilated at this time, making insertion easier and more comfortable.

☞ Some doctors prescribe a dose of oral painkiller about an hour beforehand.

☞ The procedure starts with a bi-manual (two-handed) examination, where the doctor places one hand on the abdomen, and the other inside the vagina, to feel the size and position of the uterus

☞ A speculum is inserted into the vagina, giving the doctor a clear view of the cervix. The cervix and vagina are then swabbed with antiseptic, to prevent vaginal bacteria being introduced into the uterus. The cervix is held steady with forceps, while a special instrument is

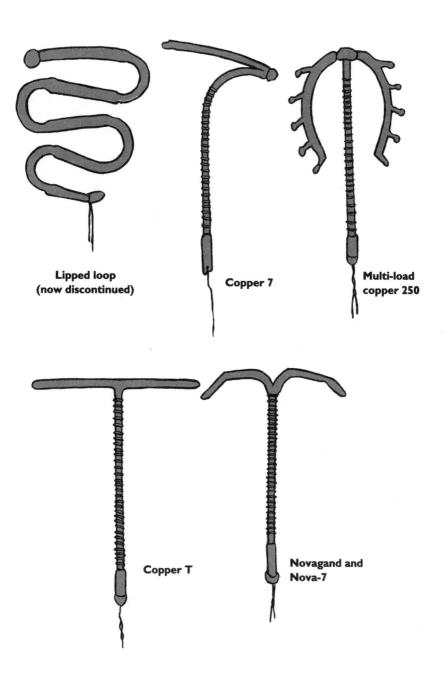

**Lipped loop
(now discontinued)**

Copper 7

**Multi-load
copper 250**

Copper T

**Novagand and
Nova-7**

▲ The IUCD (Intra-Uterine Contraceptive Device)
is placed inside the womb to prevent implantation
and thereby pregnancy.

carefully inserted to measure the dimensions of the uterus, and detect any anatomical abnormalities that would prevent the fitting of the IUCD.

☞ The sterile IUCD is fitted into its applicator, which is passed into the uterus. On withdrawal of the applicator, the IUCD assumes its normal shape.

☞ The threads of the IUCD are cut to leave just a couple of inches in the vagina.

☞ There may be some slight spotting of blood, but provided you do not feel faint, you will be able to go straight home. Mild cramplike pains may occur for a few hours afterwards. The contraceptive effect is immediate, and you can have intercourse as soon as you feel comfortable.

Following a pregnancy, an IUCD can be inserted six weeks after delivery, or two weeks after termination. It is not done sooner, because pregnancy makes the uterus soft, and more easily perforated.

An IUCD inserted within five days of unprotected intercourse will act as a 'post-coital' contraceptive.

As a method of contraception the IUCD is:

☞ Reliable. If a hundred women used it for a year, the number of pregnancies would be between one and six.

☞ Reversible. Fertility returns on its removal.

☞ Not related to intercourse.

☞ Without effects on the rest of the body, so suitable for women who cannot take the Pill.

The disadvantages of the IUCD are:

☞ Insertion may be uncomfortable.

☞ It may cause heavy, painful periods.

☞ It may be expelled, resulting in pregnancy.

☞ It may cause infection, leading to infertility.

☞ It does not protect against sexually transmitted diseases (STDs).

☞ Most types need changing at intervals of five years to remain fully effective.

☞ It carries a slight increased risk of ectopic pregnancy.

The IUCD is a good method of contraception for women who cannot take the Pill. It is not the best choice for women who have never had children, because of the slight increased risk of developing **pelvic infection**, and because insertion may be more difficult. It should also be avoided by women who have had a previous **ectopic pregnancy**, have **active pelvic infection**, an **anatomical abnormality** of the uterus or **allergy to copper**.

They are very suitable for the woman who has completed her family, but is not happy about having an irreversible sterilisation.

Once the IUCD has been inserted, you will be asked to check to see if you can feel its threads in the vagina. This indicates that it is in place. You will be checked by the doctor after your next period (this is the most likely time for an IUCD to be expelled from the uterus). If all is well, you will be instructed to check for the threads after each period, and you will return annually. Depending on the exact type of IUCD, you will return to have it removed and replaced with a new one after five to seven years.

A woman having a copper-containing IUCD inserted over the age of forty-five need not have it removed until the menopause, no matter how many years later that is.

You should see your doctor if you develop any of the following with an IUCD in situ:

☞ Heavy, prolonged bleeding.

☞ Bleeding between periods.

☞ Absent periods.

☞ Abdominal pain.

☞ Persistent low backache.

☞ Vaginal discharge.

☞ Missing threads.

☞ Pain on intercourse.

Barrier contraception

The term 'Barrier' is rather unfortunate in the context of contraception, dealing as it does with the intimacy of sexual intercourse. However, it covers those methods of contraception which involve placing a physical barrier between the male sperm and the female cervix. There are two main types: the **condom**, or sheath, used by the male, and the **diaphragm**, or cap, used by the female.

Condoms

A condom is a sheath of fine latex which is designed to fit over the erect penis. It simply catches the sperm during ejaculation, thereby preventing it from entering the female. All makes are basically the same, but some have ridges, or are of different colours and thickness.

Condoms are readily available. They can be obtained free from any Family Planning clinic, or purchased from the chemist or numerous other outlets, including supermarkets. They are easy to use and inexpensive. They require no medical supervision, and have no associated health risks. If used properly, they can be very effective (about five in every 100 users may fall pregnant).

Important advantages include the facts that:

☞ They offer considerable protection against **sexually transmitted diseases** (STDs), including the HIV virus that causes **AIDS**.

☞ There is also some evidence that they may protect women from **cervical carcinoma**.

☞ Condoms are a visible method of contraception, which may be reassuring to both partners. They also involve the male in sharing the responsibility for contraception.

☞ They may help men who suffer from **premature ejaculation**, and they reduce the odour of intercourse in women.

There are several disadvantages:

☞ A new condom must be used for each act of intercourse. This may reduce spontaneity, and means a supply must be at hand.

☞ They decrease male sensitivity.

☞ They may rupture during intercourse, or semen can leak before or after ejaculation.

☞ They can be messy to handle.

Within a stable relationship, condoms are a useful method where a small risk of pregnancy is acceptable, such as spacing a family.

They should always be used whenever unpredictable intercourse occurs. In terms of contraception, they are considerably better than nothing at all, and even if another method is being used, they guard against sexually transmitted disease.

The diaphragm

The diaphragm is a thin dome of latex with a circular spring around the edge. This is the most commonly used design, although there are some that fit over the cervix alone.

The diaphragm is placed at the top of the vagina, covering the cervix, where it is held in place by the spring. It is used in conjunction with spermicidal cream. It acts by holding the spermicidal cream against the cervix (where it must be in order to be effective), and holding sperm away from the cervix for long enough for them to die in the vagina. Unlike the condom, it does not form a complete physical barrier to the sperm, and must be left in place for at least six hours after intercourse in order to work.

If used properly, diaphragms are even more effective than condoms (there is a 2 per cent chance of pregnancy occurring), and there are numerous other advantages:

☞ They are more independent of intercourse than the condom. If correctly fitted, they cannot be felt by the woman once in place, and cannot be felt by the man during intercourse, so there is no loss of sensation.

☞ It is a method over which the woman has total control, and it only needs to be used when required.

☞ They can be useful when intercourse occurs during menstrual bleeding.

☞ Like the condom, they also offer some protection against sexually transmitted disease.

☞ They do not cause widespread side-effects, or alter the nature or duration of menstrual bleeding.

The disadvantages are:

☞ They require a certain amount of forethought: the woman must have her diaphragm and a supply of spermicide available, and use it before intercourse.

☞ If intercourse occurs more than once, more spermicide must be used. Some women find the insertion messy and distasteful.

☞ Initially, a diaphragm needs fitting by a suitably qualified family-planning doctor, with proper instruction in its use.

☞ Some women experience discomfort on passing urine after using the diaphragm. This is because the spring may press against the bladder or urethra. This can often be overcome by using a different size, or type.

☞ Some women are, or become, allergic to the spermicide or rubber, which causes soreness of the vagina.

With few exceptions (such as virgins or women with an anatomical abnormality), most women can use the diaphragm effectively. It is an alternative to the IUCD for women who cannot use hormonal methods of contraception. For many women, it is simply a matter of personal choice, especially when intercourse is not particularly frequent.

Natural contraception, rhythm method (natural family planning, fertility awareness)

The human ova survives for a maximum of twenty-four hours after ovulation. Sperm can survive for a maximum of seven days in the Fallopian tubes. Conception can therefore only occur up to seven days before ovulation, or a day after. This is the 'fertile' phase of the menstrual cycle. In theory, if no intercourse takes place during the fertile phase, pregnancy cannot occur. The **rhythm method** is basically an attempt to establish the fertile phase for an individual woman, so that intercourse takes place during the 'infertile' phases of the menstrual cycle only, and pregnancy is avoided.

In a woman with a perfectly regular menstrual cycle of twenty-eight days, with ovulation always occurring on day fourteen, then the fertile phase would be between days seven and fourteen. The problem is that women have very different menstrual cycles, and even in an individual woman, the cycles can vary from month to month. Ovulation may occur on day fourteen, but it can also occur as early as day twelve or as late as day sixteen. In practical terms, the modern rhythm method aims to identify the time of ovulation as accurately as possible, rather then relying on a calendar alone.

Ovulation can be detected after it has occurred, which means that the infertile phase in the second half of the menstrual cycle can be determined with some accuracy. Prediction of the exact time of ovulation before it occurs is virtually impossible, which means that the infertile phase in the first half of the menstrual cycle carries a greater risk of pregnancy.

Detecting ovulation

☞ The hormones produced after ovulation produce a small but constant rise in the basal body temperature. This rise is only about 0.5°C, so a special thermometer is used to detect it.

☞ The temperature must be taken first thing in the morning, before eating, drinking or smoking.

☞ It is plotted on a chart, and the rise which occurs at ovulation can be seen.

☞ The infertile or 'safe' phase begins on the morning of the third consecutive higher temperature.

☞ The cervix undergoes changes during the menstrual cycle. It becomes soft and rises in the vagina towards ovulation, then becomes firm and descends again towards the end of the cycle.

☞ The cervical mucus is clear and elastic (like egg white) before ovulation, but becomes opaque, thick and inelastic in the second half of the cycle. These changes can be detected, and used in conjunction with the temperature to identify when ovulation has occurred.

☞ In some women, there are other changes that occur at the time of ovulation that can help them pinpoint it with accuracy. One of these is 'Mittelschmertz', or ovulation pain, that occurs twenty-four to forty-eight hours before ovulation. Some women have a show of blood at ovulation. Pre-menstrual symptoms such as acne, breast tenderness and mood changes occur only after ovulation.

Provided intercourse takes place only during the second infertile phase (after ovulation), the rhythm method can be as effective as most other methods, and sometimes more effective (with a possible three in every 100 cases becoming pregnant). Intercourse in the unpredictable first half of the menstrual cycle (before ovulation) is associated with a higher failure rate.

Advantages of the rhythm method include:

☞ It is entirely 'natural' and free from all side-effects.

☞ It is acceptable to many cultural and religious groups.

☞ The method is under the personal control of the couple, who can start or stop using it without any medical intervention.

☞ Once established, it is free and requires no further expense or follow-up.

☞ It can be used in conjunction with barrier methods to provide even greater reliability.

☞ When a pregnancy is wanted it can be 'reversed' to assist early conception.

Disadvantages:

☞ The major disadvantage is that some women find it impossible to detect ovulation with any accuracy. This may be because they have erratic cycles, which is common around the time of the menopause, or no easily discernible change in body temperature.

☞ Some find the daily taking of temperature inconvenient, or examining the cervix and cervical mucous distasteful.

☞ The use of lubricants or intercourse itself can interfere with cervical mucus assessment.

☞ An infection that produces a rise in temperature can interfere with the chart.

☞ The method requires abstinence during the fertile phase.

There are already electronic thermometers that can record the basal body temperature, and indicate that the 'safe' phase has been reached. There are also kits available that detect the hormone changes at ovulation. These are currently aimed at couples hoping to become pregnant, but they may become cheap enough to be used on a regular basis

as part of the rhythm method. A device that aspirates fluid from the vagina is undergoing assessment, as the volume may correlate with the other changes at ovulation. It is possible that eventually the price and design of ultrasound machines may enable a woman to use one in the home to actually visualise ovulation as it occurs.

Female sterilisation

Female sterilisation is an operation to block the Fallopian tubes. This prevents the egg released from the ovary from being fertilised, so pregnancy cannot occur. It is an irreversible method of contraception.

The uterus and ovaries are left intact so periods continue as before, and hormone replacement is not necessary.

There are two methods:

☞ One involves a small incision in the abdomen (a mini-laparotomy), and the cutting and tying of the Fallopian tubes (tubal ligation).

☞ The other method is laparoscopic sterilisation. This is performed with a laparoscope (a telescopic instrument that enables the surgeon to look directly into the abdomen) and an applicator that places rings or, more commonly, clips on to the Fallopian tubes. The laparoscope and applicator are inserted into the abdomen and manoeuvred into position. The open clips are placed over the Fallopian tubes with the applicator, then pressed tightly shut, which occludes the lumen of the tube.

Diathermy, or surgical 'burning', of the Fallopian tubes has largely been abandoned now because it posed a risk to adjacent organs, like the bowel.

New methods are constantly under review, including means of performing sterilisation through the vagina and uterus, but these are currently experimental.

Female sterilisation is the contraceptive method of choice for the woman who never wants to become pregnant, and wishes to be relieved of any further contraceptive responsibility. It is therefore suitable for a woman who has completed her family and is

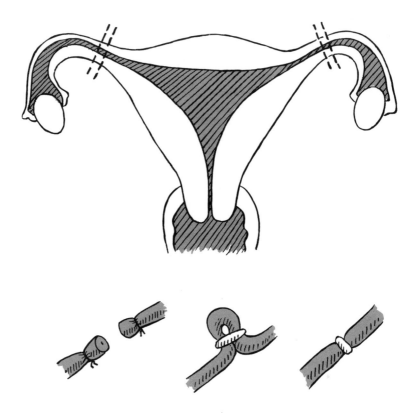

▲ **Female sterilisation by tubal ligation –
the Fallopian tubes are cut, tied or have
rings or clips placed over them.**

a long way from the menopause. Some
women, who never want children, or who
should not have children for medical reasons
may also choose sterilisation.

If you are considering sterilisation, then you
should see your doctor to discuss it. It is
irreversible, so you should not be in any
doubt about it. If you suffer from any other
gynaecological problem such as menorrhagia,
prolapse, abnormal smears or endometriosis,
then it might be advisable to consider
hysterectomy, rather than undergo two
operations. However, hysterectomy is a
major operation, with significantly greater risks
than sterilisation, and should never be
performed solely as an alternative to female
sterilisation.

· If you are getting close to the menopause
your doctor might advise an interim method
like an IUD, rather than an operation.

Over the age of forty-seven, fertility is low,
and the menopause imminent, making
sterilisation less suitable.

If you decide to go ahead, your doctor will
refer you to a gynaecologist, who will
perform the operation. If you have been
taking the Pill, you may be told to stop before
your operation. You should use an alternative
method in the meantime.

If there is a chance you could be pregnant,
then you should have a pregnancy test before
the operation. A laparoscopic sterilisation
may be performed on an out-patient basis,
and you will be able to go home the same
day. You may be given a choice of general or
local anaesthetic.

Tubal ligation is done under general
anaesthetic, and since it involves an incision
into the abdomen, you may be in hospital for

a day or two. Sterilisation can be done at the same time as a Caesarean section, or soon after childbirth. If you are pregnant, and do not want any more children, it is worth discussing this with your doctor early in your pregnancy.

☞ Both types of sterilisation are short, safe procedures and you should be back to normal within a week or so. You are immediately sterile after the operation and do not need to take any further precautions.

☞ Complications are rare, but there is always a small potential risk from any surgery and anaesthesia. Sterilisation has been shown to be a low-risk procedure, otherwise it would not be acceptable as a contraceptive method for otherwise healthy women.

☞ Post-operatively, there may be some pain arising from the damaged tubes. This is variable, but up to 50 per cent of women have no post-operative pain.

☞ Wound infection is less likely with a laparoscopic sterilisation, where there are just two small puncture marks in the abdomen.

☞ Later on, some women experience abnormal menstrual bleeding. This is rarely related to the sterilisation itself, but due to some other cause.

☞ Method failure can occur, resulting in an unwanted pregnancy. The risk of this is low. It is lower with tubal ligation, than clips or rings.

☞ The risk of an ectopic pregnancy is slightly increased after sterilisation.

☞ Some women have difficulties coming to terms with their infertility.

☞ Successful reversal of a female sterilisation is almost impossible. In Vitro Fertilisation makes pregnancy after sterilisation theoretically possible, but this still has a low success rate so should not be viewed as a viable option.

☞ Research continues into reversible methods, such as removable plugs in the Fallopian tubes, but they are not very effective at blocking the tubes in the first place.

Advantages of sterilisation include:
☞ Permanent.
☞ No further contraceptive precautions necessary.
☞ No side-effects once completed.
☞ Not dependent on partner.
☞ Independent of intercourse.
☞ Safe.
☞ Effective.

Disadvantages include:
☞ Irreversible.
☞ Operation involved, with potential risks.

Vasectomy

A vasectomy is a simple surgical procedure to cut the vas deferens (the two tubes connecting the testes to the penis along which sperm travel during ejaculation). It is done as an outpatient procedure under local anaesthetic.

The purpose of a vasectomy is to render a man sterile without interfering with sexual performance in any way. It is to all intents and purposes irreversible. As a method of family planning it is ideal for couples who do not wish to have any more children. It is more effective than reversible methods, which all have a small failure rate, and it carries none of the risks of the Pill or the coil.

Once a couple have decided that a vasectomy is the right method of contraception for them, they need to see their doctor and be referred to the surgeon who will perform the operation.

☞ During a vasectomy, the scrotum is cleaned and shaved, and then local anaesthetic is injected into the skin. This makes the whole area go numb. The rest of the procedure is completely painless.

☞ The surgeon removes a small portion of each vas deferens, and these are sent to the laboratory to ensure correct identification.

☞ The tiny incision on each side of the scrotum is then closed with a few stitches. These will absorb as the wound heals, so do not have to be removed. The area is covered with a dressing.

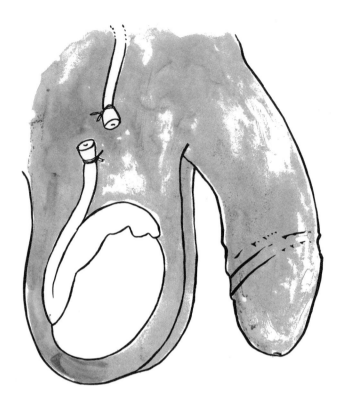

▲ In a vascectomy the vas deferens is cut and sealed so no sperm can pass.

☞ The local anaesthetic wears off after a couple of hours. Any pain or discomfort after this is easily relieved by aspirin or paracetamol, and will go within twenty-four hours.

☞ The wounds take seven to ten days to heal completely, but most men can return to work after a day or two.

☞ The vas deferens are full of sperm along their length, and it takes over ten ejaculations to clear them. The vasectomy is effective only after two consecutive specimens of ejaculate are examined by the laboratory and pronounced completely free of sperm. These tests are usually carried out about fourteen to sixteen weeks after the vasectomy. During this interval it is still necessary to continue using contraception.

Of the thousands of men who have vasectomies each year, the vast majority suffer no complications whatsoever. Occasionally the wound may become infected or develop some bruising. This usually clears up quickly with a course of antibiotics. For some men the volume of ejaculate decreases noticeably, but this does not interfere with sexual pleasure. A few men suffer a temporary psychological impotence but this quickly disappears when they realise that everything is still in good working order.

In a very small percentage, a vas deferens manages to re-connect, resulting in a partner's pregnancy at a later date. Modern surgical procedures make this less likely.

A vasectomy should be considered irreversible, so if you have any doubts it is better to use a reversible method. However, an operation to reverse a vasectomy is possible, and does have a success rate of about 50 per cent. Research continues into methods of reversible vasectomy.

User-failure rates for different methods of contraception:

(A measure of the number of pregnancies likely to occur among a hundred women using a method for one year)

Male sterilisation	0.02	Spermicides alone	11-9
Female sterilisation	0.13	Fertility awareness	15.5
		(Rhythm method)	(3 if done properly)
Low-dose combined pill	0.27		
		Contraceptive sponge	25.0
Progestogen-only pill	1.2		
		No method, young women	80-90
IUCD	1.5		
		No method, age 40	40-50
Diaphragm	1.9		
		No method, age 45	10-20
Condom	3.6		
		No method, age 50	0-5
Coitus Interruptus (withdrawal)	6.7		

REMEMBER:
- **Unprotected intercourse results in pregnancy.**
- **Withdrawal is unreliable.**
- **Contraception is necessary while breastfeeding (unless you are feeding on demand, with no supplementary feeds of milk or water, and before solids are introduced).**
- **After childbirth you can get pregnant before your first period; an alarming proportion of women are pregnant at their six-week post-natal check.**

Nursing sick children

Caring for a sick child

Most illness in childhood is caused by infection, which produces symptoms such as **vomiting**, **temperature** or **rash**, together with changes in behaviour, such as **tiredness**, **loss of appetite** or **irritability**. The majority of infections are caused by viruses, and the child will shake it off in a few days with nothing more than paracetamol syrup to alleviate the symptoms, and a lot of comforting from parents.

Of course babies can't talk, some children learn to feign illness, and some illnesses have a slow and gradual onset. No one wants to call the doctor out for a fever that may respond to Calpol and be better in the morning, but at the same time, no one wants to miss something serious like meningitis.

Identifying illness

Symptoms of illness in babies include:
- ☞ Fever
- ☞ Refusal to feed
- ☞ Persistent crying
- ☞ Diarrhoea and vomiting
- ☞ Noisy, laboured breathing
- ☞ Pallor, jaundice or cyanosis (a blue tinge to the skin)
- ☞ Failure to gain weight

Young children quickly learn that illness has its rewards. In the absence of any actual symptoms, like temperature, rash or vomiting, a 'wait and see' attitude is worth adopting.

See if the complaints are consistent by asking 'show me where it hurts' at intervals, and seeing if the pain moves around.

Watch them, unobserved, to see if they recover when you are out of sight.

Note whether the complaints are associated with a particular time, or activity. The tummy ache that always develops on a Monday morning during term-time is not likely to have a medical cause.

When a child develops an illness that begins slowly, it can be hard to spot. Be on the look out for:

- ☞ Failure to grow at the expected rate
- ☞ Unusual fatigue
- ☞ Permanent pallor, even in the summer
- ☞ Frequent, recurrent coughs and colds that take a long time to clear
- ☞ Unusual persistent bruising

With experience, most mothers learn to tell when a child has a mild viral infection that will respond to paracetamol and rest within a day or two. Otherwise, most mothers prefer to have the doctor see their child, for fear that they might be missing something serious. A child who wakes in the night with the first symptoms of an illness does not need an urgent visit from the doctor. You should take the child to the surgery the following day.

Call the doctor urgently if your child:
- **Has a fit**
- **Has difficulty breathing**
- **Is in severe pain**
- **Is unrousable**

Most children who become ill can be cared for at home. The basic requirements are a thermometer, paracetamol syrup and common sense.

Keep the child in a warm, well-ventilated room. If they have a temperature, then try and cool them down by removing clothes and bedding, and occasionally sponging with tepid water.

Make sure the child takes any prescribed medicine at the right times. Babies can suck medicine from the bottle. It can be diluted with water, but try and ensure that they drink it all. If older children are reluctant, you can disguise it in cold drinks.

The sick child often want nothing more than to be cuddled by his mother. Try and do this, even if it means time off work, or abandoning housework for a couple of days. Otherwise, make sure the child is left in the care of someone they know and trust, who can contact you in an emergency.

Make sure they have plenty to drink. If they are not vomiting, try and encourage them to eat, by temptation, not force.

Allow them to sleep as much as possible avoiding distraction (other children, the television).

Treat uncomfortable, itchy rashes with a soothing lotion, like calamine. A warm bath and clean pyjamas can help.

For an infectious disease, keep the child away from unvaccinated children and babies, and pregnant women. Keep soiled linen separate (including flannels and towels) and wash it as soon as possible. Looking after a sick child can be exhausting, so you must try to ensure you that you eat properly, and rest when you can.

More serious, or prolonged illness may require admission to hospital. All children should have some understanding of hospitals, in case they ever need admitting in an emergency. Reading them stories about children going to hospital, or pretend play with teddies and dolls is a good away to teach them.

If hospital admission is required, they won't be so frightened if they know what to expect:

☞ Explain it as fully as possible.
☞ Don't show them that you are worried, even if you are.
☞ Make sure they take any favourite toys or comforters with them.
☞ Talk to the staff, so that you understand what is going on, and they know of any special requirements for your child.
☞ Try and stay, if there are facilities for parents.

Tell brothers and sisters about it (they can find it a distressing experience to visit a child in hospital, especially if mother has gone, too).

Large numbers of children suffer from chronic conditions such as **asthma**, **diabetes** or **epilepsy**. These can usually be controlled with drugs, allowing the child to lead a virtually normal life. The importance here is to not 'medicalise' the child's entire existence, but to adhere to treatment, and know how to cope in an emergency. The child should understand as much as possible about their own illness, and be taught to manage their own inhaler, or injections, as early as possible.

Sadly, some children develop illnesses like **leukemia**, which require repeated hospitalisation for treatment, and long periods of quite severe illness. Professional help with the nursing, and counselling for the family is available under these circumstances.

Medicines for children

The only medicines you really need for children are paracetamol syryp (**Calpol**, **Disprin**, etc) and a soothing skin lotion for rashes and stings (**Caladryl**).

Paracetamol is fatal in overdose, so you must never exceed the stated dose, and always keep the bottle out of reach.

If your child has been prescribed medicine, make sure you know how much to give, and when to give it, and ensure that the course is completed.

Never give your child a medicine formulated for adults, or left-over prescription drugs. Children under the age of ten should never be given aspirin.

If your child needs injections or inhalers, you and your child should be given proper instruction in their use. If you are worried or unsure, don't be afraid to ask your doctor questions.

ABC of common childhood illnesses

Asthma

Asthma is a very common respiratory disease affecting about one in ten children. The disease is not curable but is treatable and tends to get less severe as children get into their late teens or early twenties.

The symptoms are:
- ☞ Recurrent cough
- ☞ Wheeze
- ☞ Chest tightness
- ☞ Shortness of breath.

Not all the symptoms are present in each child, and often a child's only symptom is a recurrent cough which does not respond to courses of antibiotics.

Asthma is usually worse in the night and **night waking** with **chest symptoms** is a good indicator of under-treatment.

Asthma is often triggered by:
- ☞ Exercise
- ☞ Change in air temperature
- ☞ Fumes, including perfume
- ☞ Animals
- ☞ House dust.

Nearly always a runny nose or sore throat will trigger the cough and parents frequently believe that every time their child gets a cold it goes straight on to the chest. In fact, the cold stays where it is but it triggers off the asthmatic cough.

Asthma, eczema and hay fever often run in families. The incidence of asthma is rising but the reasons for this are unclear; it's likely to be related to increased environmental pollution, among other things.

Treatment is with two types of drug:
relieving drugs and **preventing drugs**.
- ☞ The relieving drugs such as salbutamol (Ventolin) and terbutaline (Bricanyl) act within minutes to open the airways and bring relief from symptoms, but wear off within a few hours and fail to deal with the underlying inflammation of the airways.
- ☞ Preventing drugs such as beclomethasone (Becotide), budesonide (Pulmicort), or sodium chromoglycate (Intal) do deal

with the inflammation in the airways which is the root of the problem. They act slowly over several hours and their full effect may not be apparent for several days. These drugs should be used regularly, whether the child is well or ill in order to keep the inflammation at bay and prevent long-term permanent damage to the airways.

Balanitis

Balanitis is inflammation and soreness of the foreskin of the penis. It is common in boys with a very small hole in the end of the foreskin, making it difficult for the urine to flow out easily. The foreskin often balloons when the child passes urine. Treatment is usually **circumcision**.

In boys in early puberty balanitis is often due to vigorous masturbation, and the complaint rarely recurs, even without the intervention of an adult, because the child usually works out why his foreskin is sore.

Chickenpox

See under *Rashes*.

Cough

Coughing is the most common symptom presented to doctors. It may be due to a respiratory infection, usually viral, to asthma or to a post-nasal drip. If the child has not lost his appetite and has no difficulty breathing through his mouth then the cough will usually settle within a week or two without any treatment. Recurrent or prolonged coughs may be due to asthma.

A cough associated with a runny nose is often worse at night because the mucus runs backwards when the child is lying down and trickles down the throat. This triggers a reflex cough which protects the lungs by throwing the mucus forward to be swallowed. In babies the mucus may be so indigestible that they vomit to get rid of it from the stomach. In this case the child may vomit only once in twenty-four to forty-eight hours, the mucus is clearly visible in the vomit and the baby is otherwise well and happy with a good appetite and no temperature.

Diarrhoea

Diarrhoea is common, especially in warm weather. It may be associated with vomiting and abdominal pain and is usually due to an infection or toxin in the bowel, when it is known as gastro-enteritis. Avoiding solid foods and taking plenty of fluids for twenty-four to forty-eight hours will usually settle it down, but close attention should be paid to hand-washing, food hygiene and refrigeration of food so the problem does not spread to other members of the household.

In prolonged diarrhoea or diarrhoea following foreign travel, medical advice should be sought so that a sample can be sent for analysis. Very occasionally the analysis will indicate that an antibiotic is needed.

Toddler diarrhoea is a profuse diarrhoea in an otherwise well toddler who continues to have a good appetite and to gain weight. It often contains undressed food particles giving rise to the name 'peas and carrot' diarrhoea. No treatment is needed and the problem resolves when the child is potty-trained.

Ear infections

Infections of the ear are common in children; the child will appear:
- ☞ unwell
- ☞ feverish
- ☞ off their food
- ☞ crying
- ☞ in pain
- ☞ tired.

Older children can say clearly that the pain is in the ear, but younger children may not give a clear indication what is wrong. The child pulling the ear is a good clue.

Infections of the outer ear, right down the hole to the eardrum, are outer ear infections, and commonly present a milder illness with a discharge from the ear. Beyond the eardrum, where even the doctor cannot see with his auroscope, is the middle ear. It is here that most ear infections occur, with the eardrum becoming bright red.

Treatment with antibiotics and paracetamol is usually effective, but some deafness may persist for a week or two until all the pus has drained away via a narrow tube to the throat.

Eczema

Eczema is a skin condition which is often found with asthma and hay fever running through the family (atopic eczema). This form is treatable but not curable, and frequently goes through good and bad spells. Other forms of eczema are due to sensitivity to certain chemicals in contact with the skin (contact dermatitis) or to certain foodstuffs.

- ☞ Contact dermatitis is present on or near the skin exposed to the allergen; e.g., nickel dermatitis is found where cheap jewellery is in contact with the skin under necklaces, bracelets or pierced ears. Biological soap powders produce dermatitis under clothes but spare hands and face.
- ☞ Eczema, often severe and widespread, can be due to a protein in cow's milk. The common infant formula milks are based on cow's milk so it is worth trying a soya-based or goat's milk infant formula to see if the eczema settles.
- ☞ In atopic eczema, and in other eczemas where the cause cannot be eliminated, treatment needs to be continuous.

Glandular fever

Glandular fever is a mildly infectious disease which typically affects teenagers and young adults. Symptoms include a sore throat which does not improve with time nor with antibiotics; tiredness and fatigue, often profound; mild depression and irritability and swelling of the lymph nodes ('glands') under the jaws, in the neck, in the armpits and in the groin. It may last from a week or two up to several months but a full recovery always occurs eventually. Treatment includes rest and sympathy, tolerance of the irritability and a balanced diet.

German measles

See under *Rashes*.

Headache

Headache in children is a common symptom with most feverish illnesses. Most childhood fevers with headache are due to an infectious illness such as a cold, ear infection, gastro-enteritis or tonsillitis. However, headache and fever are also the signs and symptoms of the much rarer meningitis which can cause brain damage, fits or even death if untreated.

In meningitis typically there is headache, fever, vomiting, neck stiffness and photophobia (dislike of bright light). In the dangerous form, meningococcal meningitis, there may also be a faint rash but this is an unreliable sign. Not all the signs and symptoms are present in every case. If meningitis is suspected then medical help must be sought at once because a child with meningitis can get worse rapidly.

Headache without fever may be due to:

☞ Stress (tension headache).
☞ Problems at school, at home (including rows involving other family members), or worries about feeling unattractive or socially inept.
☞ Migraine.

Migraine is usually one sided, often severe and may involve nausea, vomiting, photophobia and eye symptoms such as flashing lights or zig-zag lines. It occasionally causes symptoms in an arm or leg too, and may last for a day or two before settling. It does not produce a raised temperature and thus can be distinguished from meningitis.

Migraine tends to be recurrent and is triggered off by certain things – different for each individual. If the trigger factors can be identified and avoided then the number of attacks can be reduced without long-term drug treatment. Common trigger factors are stress, periods, food and drink (e.g., some food colourings/flavourings, chocolate or even strawberries) or a flickering television or computer. Migraine often runs in families. In small children the discomfort is often felt in the abdomen, causing sharp pains or nausea and vomiting, and may later develop into classic migraine. Other symptoms can include:

☞ Eyesight problems
☞ Heat stroke

There are many other types of headache, some serious and others harmless; any persistent or chronic (long-term) headaches must be seen by a medical practitioner.

Impetigo

Impetigo is an infection of the skin which causes weeping and scabbing sores to develop and spread rapidly to adjacent areas of skin. It is highly contagious and the child should be excluded from school or playgroup until the lesions are dry. It commonly starts on the face, the sores growing and spreading over a few days. The child remains otherwise well and happy with a good appetite. Treatment is usually very effective and involves antibiotics, either by mouth or in an ointment. Some doctors also prescribe a type of liquid soap to sterilise the rest of the skin and scalp, too, where the bacterium may be lurking without causing any signs.

Jaundice

Jaundice is yellowing of the skin and whites of the eyes caused by an underlying illness. Jaundice develops because the liver is not disposing of waste products fast enough or the waste products are being produced in very large quantities, so the liver can not cope. The commonest causes in children are jaundice of the newborn and hepatitis.

☞ Newborn babies developing deep jaundice are monitored with blood tests for bilirubin. If the bilirubin is rising too fast then the baby is put under lights (phototherapy). If the bilirubin level is allowed to rise too high then brain damage may ensue.
☞ Hepatitis is an infection of the liver, commonly caused by viruses such as glandular fever, hepatitis A and hepatitis B. Hepatitis A is endemic in Britain, often appearing as a 'flu-like' illness with diarrhoea and vomiting from which children usually make an uneventful recovery.

Kidney disease

Urine infections, common in adult females (cystitis), need investigating carefully in children. Passing urine frequently, burning or stinging when passing urine, blood in the urine, abdominal pain, wetting the pants and bedwetting are the signs and symptoms of a urine infection, although they may not all be present. In some children the only signs are loss of appetite, being 'off colour' or failure to thrive.

Left untreated the infection may rise further to the kidneys causing abdominal pain and often fever and malaise. Kidney damage may ensue and, if recurrent or untreated, may eventually lead to kidney failure, dialysis or kidney transplant.

Investigations are aimed at seeking a cause for the infection because in some children a congenital abnormality makes them prone to urine infections. Surgical correction can prevent recurrent infection and thus prevent lifelong kidney problems.

Nephrotic syndrome is an uncommon disease of the kidneys in which the child looks very puffy, particularly in the face. An abnormality develops which causes the kidneys to leak protein into the urine. The mainstays of treatment are a high protein diet and steroids, which usually lead to a cure.

Leukaemia

Leukaemia is an excessive quantity of white cells in the blood.

Untreated it may progress to cause anaemia (insufficient red blood cells), bleeding, or allow infection to develop without the normal defence reaction from the body. Symptoms include:

- ☞ Fever
- ☞ Malaise
- ☞ Nose bleeds
- ☞ Mouth ulcers
- ☞ Muscle aches and pains

There are a variety of types of leukaemia, and a range of different treatments, all carrying varying prognoses. With some forms of leukaemia it is possible to be optimistic about the outcome but others are frequently fatal.

Mumps

Mumps is a viral infection of the salivary glands which run from the ear down to the angle of the jaw and then wrap around the angle of the jaw on each side (the parotid glands). These glands become swollen and tender making the child look like a hamster.

Usually the child also feels unwell, runs a fever and loses his or her appetite. In adolescent or adult males the virus may also affect the testes causing aching and sometimes subsequent sterility.

Treatment is with fluids, paracetamol for the pain and fever, and rest. Complete resolution is usual in a week or two. All children in Britain are now offered a vaccine to protect against Measles, Mumps and Rubella (MMR vaccine) between the ages of twelve and twenty-four months. It is so effective that mumps is rarely seen here any more.

Nappy rash

Urine and faeces, especially diarrhoea, cause a chemical burn if kept in contact with the skin for long. Nappies tend to do exactly this and so nappy rash is very common. It is particularly common at teething time.

Prevention is better than cure. Changing the nappy frequently, washing away the urine and faeces thoroughly and applying a liberal layer of barrier cream (e.g., zinc and castor oil, or Vaseline) are helpful. The barrier cream acts as a waterproof layer between the soiled nappy and the delicate skin.

Treatment is in the same vein, but dunking the whole bottom in clean water at each change and leaving the nappy off altogether for several hours each day promotes healing. Occasionally the fungus candida albicans (thrush) may grow in the raw areas and this needs specific treatment with an anti-fungal cream.

Nits or lice

This is an infestation of tiny insects which bite the skin to feed from the blood. These parasites lay their eggs, which are visible as tiny grey dots, on the hair shafts. Head and body lice are itchy and are highly contagious. They are a common problem among schoolchildren and seem especially to like clean hair. A shampoo, purchased from your pharmacist, will deal with the problem, but wash all towels, clothing and bedding in boiling hot water, and disinfect combs and hair brushes after treatment.

Poisoning (accidental)

Each year hundreds of children attend accident and emergency departments having swallowed a drug or chemical which may cause poisoning. Most of these poisonings are preventable.

☞ All medicines should be kept out of reach of children, preferably in a locked cupboard.

☞ Ask your pharmacist to dispense medicines in containers with childproof lids.

☞ Household detergents and bleach should also be stored out of reach and not in the cupboard under the sink. Many of these now also come in childproof containers. Where you have a choice, select one that does.

☞ The garage or shed provides endless fun as a place to explore or build a den, so the same precautions should apply here, too, with creosote, white spirit, petrol, weedkillers and similar noxious substances.

Because something tastes awful, it does not mean the child will not drink it. It is remarkable how much bleach a child will drink, when an adult would have choked on the first drop.

Rashes

In a small baby, a rash on the body is often heat rash, as they have ill-formed sweat glands. The rash disappears on cooling down. Rashes in children are very common, most of them being caused by acute viral illnesses. Most of the viral rashes are accompanied by a fever, loss of appetite and malaise, although some (e.g., rubella) are not.

Many of the rashes have a typical appearance such as the sparse itchy blisters in a spot of red skin that characterise chickenpox. Others produce a generalised non-specific rash, frequently mimicking rubella (German Measles), to which it may be impossible to attach an accurate label without unnecessary blood tests. What they all have

in common, however, is that they settle in a week or two and do not respond to antibiotics. Calamine lotion may soothe the itchy ones, while paracetamol is useful if they come with a fever.

Squint

When a child has a squint the eyes do not look at exactly the same spot at the same time, so the brain receives two different images. When the brain can not make the two images match, it ignores one of them so it can make sense of the remaining image. If treated by the age of six this complication can be avoided. If untreated by the age of ten, the eye is likely to be useless for life.

Squints are looked for at the routine child development examinations, but it may be intermittent, so it is important to voice your concerns if you suspect your child may have a squint.

Stomach-ache

There are many causes of stomach-ache in small children and babies. In infants, it may be a sign of colic, or simply wind. In older children, a bowel movement may relieve any abdominal pain or discomfort. Over-eating, tension, gastro-enteritis and abdominal migraine are other causes. If vomiting or diarrhoea is present, contact your doctor. A warm drink, a hot water bottle on the tummy, and avoiding solid food should ease the pain. If stomach-ache is recurrent and eased by a bowel movement, constipation may be the problem. In those circumstances, increase fluid intake and fibre-rich foods, and cut down on refined and processed foods.

Temperature

The child with a raised temperature will feel hot or cold, may perspire or shiver, will feel hot to touch and usually look flushed. He will lack energy, wanting to flop around or sleep rather than run everywhere as usual, be miserable and off his food. Babies may cry despite being cuddled, and be difficult to settle. If untreated a high temperature will commonly cause a child to vomit, and rarely the child may have a fit (febrile convulsion).

The fever can be confirmed by measuring the temperature with a thermometer. If you are using a mercury thermometer, it should first be shaken down so that the mercury is all below the beginning of the scale.

☞ In a baby or young child the bulb should be put in the armpit and the arm held to the child's side to keep it in place for at least a minute, preferably two, before reading it.

☞ In an older child the bulb should be placed under the tongue with instructions to close the mouth without biting it. After removing it, rotate the thermometer between your fingers until the mercury can be seen clearly against the scale.

☞ The temperature is raised if it is higher than 37°C. (98.4°F.)

Treatment is simple:

☞ The child should be cooled down by removing clothes and excessive blankets, and if necessary sponging with tepid (not cold) water, which is then allowed to evaporate.

☞ Paracetamol should be given regularly, four times per day.

☞ Cool drinks should be offered frequently.

In most childhood illnesses the temperature will subside in about forty-eight hours (two disturbed nights). If it persists much longer, medical help should be sought.

Urticaria

Urticaria is an itchy blotchy rash commonly called hives. It is a curious form of allergic reaction which is harmless, does not make the sufferer feel unwell, but can be very irritating.

The causes of urticaria are many and vary from person to person. In some a particular food or drink may provoke it, in others simply getting hot or too cold may bring it on. In these cases the rash recurs whenever the stimulus is present, but sometimes the rash occurs only once. In this case the cause is often a sore throat to which the body has mounted an excessive defence response.

Vomiting

Children vomit for many reasons including having a raised temperature and food poisoning. Whatever the cause the treatment is initially the same – starvation and fluid replacement.

☞ Starvation should be for twenty-four hours at first with no solid food at all.

☞ The best fluid replacement is a mixture of clean water (one pint), sugar (one tablespoonful) and salt (one or two pinches). Flavouring such as squash may be added if the child refuses to drink without it. When the first pint has been drunk, another should be prepared. If even this gets vomited, then sips of it should be offered rather than a cupful. In this way the stomach can usually be persuaded to keep some down.

☞ Babies may be offered full-strength or half-strength milk.

If the vomiting has not stopped after twenty-four hours then the starvation needs to be continued for a further twenty-four hours. When feeding is restarted it is wise to begin with a quarter slice of dry toast (no butter), then wait for an hour. If it stays down, more can be offered. Then a small quantity of another food can be offered, followed by a further hour's wait. If other food causes vomiting, then revert to the foods which were safe. If they cause vomiting, return to starvation and fluids.

If you are concerned about your child's vomiting, or it has no recognisable cause (an accompanying fever, excess mucus, perhaps), contact your doctor immediately.

Whooping cough

Whooping cough (pertussis) causes bouts of coughing and frequently vomiting, especially in younger children. It gets its name from the characteristic whoop when the child draws in his breath for the next bout of coughing but the whoop may be absent in older children.

It starts with a runny or snuffly nose for about a week together with the cough, which is always worse at night. There may be as many as fifty paroxysms of coughing which can be so severe that the face goes red or blue and the eyes bulge. The cough improves slowly over many weeks, often taking months to settle completely.

Pneumonia and convulsions may ensue, the mortality being highest in children under the age of one. It is highly infectious. Children should be excluded from school for twenty-one days from the onset of the cough.

There is no treatment to shorten the illness; only time will cure it. However a very effective vaccine to prevent the illness is available and offered to all babies. Vaccination rates of over 90 per cent of children are now being achieved in many parts of Britain, saving lives and reducing anxiety about this awful illness.

Zzz sleep disorders

Children who will not sleep can pose tremendous problems for the parents. It often starts after an episode of illness in which the parents have to attend to the child through the night for very good reasons. When the illness is over the normal sleeping pattern does not resume and the parents continue to attend to the child despite the fact that they are now well.

Disturbed sleep can be seen as a behaviour disorder. If a child does something good, parents praise the child, giving attention, smiles, cuddles and perhaps even a sweet or a drink. These things are rewards which the child likes. The child may repeat the good behaviour in order to get more rewards, and so good behaviour patterns are founded.

Unfortunately these are exactly the same rewards parents tend to give to a child who wakes. By rewarding the behaviour, the child is likely to wake again for more rewards and so a sleep disorder is founded.

The cure is to withdraw the rewards.
- ☞ If the child needs lifting, it should be done without cuddling.

- ☞ If the child craves a drink, water only should be offered, and preferably the child should take it from a bedside table without the help of an adult.
- ☞ Requests for anything else should be firmly but pleasantly refused with an explanation that it is time for sleep.
- ☞ If the child cries the moment the parent leaves the room, then the parent should stay, all night if need be, but refuse to give in to any other demands. Alternatively, controlled crying (waiting for five minutes and then re-entering the room, then ten, or fifteen with each subsequent cry) is also a successful technique, and teaches the child that it's not acceptable to waken his parents, but leaves him secure in the knowledge that they are still there.
- ☞ Getting into bed with a child is also a reward (cuddling). Save the rewards, which may be fulsome, for the morning after a full night's sleep.
- ☞ Only a few nights of this firmness will usually cure the problem. But weaken and all the child has learned is to cry and make a fuss for longer!

Child development birth to five

During the first five years, a baby develops from total dependence into an independent person capable of movement, speech and appropriate social behaviour. In the majority of children, most skills develop at a similar age. These are known as 'milestones of development'.

How is development tested?

Formal testing by healthcare professionals (doctors, midwives, health visitors) takes place at intervals throughout the first five years. This can vary slightly from region to region.

☞ The first assessment is made at birth when the baby is checked for any obvious abnormality.

☞ On leaving hospital, the baby is usually checked by a paediatrician, who listens to the heart and lungs, and tests the reflexes.

☞ At six to eight weeks the baby is again checked by the clinic or family doctor, and the mother asked about any difficulties.

☞ At about eight months, most infants have their first proper developmental check, when their behaviour and movements are observed, and their hearing is tested.

☞ This may be done again at eighteen months and certainly before the age of two and a half.

☞ At three, or just slightly older, there is another test, including an eye-sight test.

☞ After the age of five, testing becomes the responsibility of the school medical service. Most children are seen by the school doctor in their first year at school.

Factors affecting normal development

There are situations or influences which can produce less-than-perfect test results without there being anything serious to worry about.

☞ Illness, particularly chronic or severe illness requiring a long stay in hospital, can temporarily delay normal development.

☞ Due allowance must also be made for prematurity. Children born prematurely will achieve the milestones closer to the age they should have been, rather than their actual age. They usually catch up by the age of three.

☞ Environmental factors, such as poor diet and lack of sensory stimulation can inhibit normal development. This is reversible in most children, who will quickly catch up when provided with the right conditions.

☞ Often, perfectly normal children will not co-operate when being tested. The people performing the tests recognise this, and always listen to the parents. Most developmental problems are recognisable without the child being willing.

While the milestones of development are relatively constant, there is an enormous variation in the way in which different children develop. As a predictor of eventual potential, development testing is of very limited value. It is simply a method of spotting any potential problems as early as possible.

The chart on page 278 is a guide to development; please remember that it is very common for children to be ahead in some areas and behind in others. Failure to attain a single milestone on time does not mean a child is backward.

Child development six to twelve years

In terms of child development, the period between the ages of six and twelve may not appear as dramatic as the preceding five years, or the subsequent major changes of puberty.

Physical growth continues, but not as rapidly as in infancy. Development builds upon the skills learnt in the first five years, but the biggest advances are made in the spheres of academic and social competence. Children in this age group are in full-time education, and able to gain a great deal from it. They have overcome the traumas of starting school, and have none of the rebelliousness of adolescence.

Child development birth to five

Gross Motor development

At about

6 to 8 months	Sits unsupported
12 to 18 months	Walks
18 to 24 months	Runs, can throw without falling over
2 years	Climbs stairs unaided
2 ½ years	Jumps with both feet
3 years	Stands on one foot, pedals tricycle
4 years	Hops, skips
5 years	Jumps over a low obstacle

Visual Motor

At about

2 months	Follows an object with the eyes
4 months	Grasps with both hands in a co-ordinated way
6 months	Transfers an object from hand to hand
9 months	Probes with forefinger
12 months	Develops pincer grasp. Lets go of an object
15 months	Builds a tower with two bricks. Scribbles
18 months	Fills and feeds with a spoon
2 years	Builds a tower with five bricks. Removes clothes
2 to 3 years	Unbuttons clothes. Holds pencil properly
3 years	Dresses and undresses with little assistance
4 years	Catches a ball
5 years	Ties shoelaces. Spreads with a knife

The timing of teeth arriving varies enormously, but most babies will have at least one tooth by twelve months. Regular visits to the dentist should start at about the age of three, or when the child has eight or more teeth.

Language

At about

1 month	Alert to sounds.
2 months	Smiles.
10 to 12 months	Uses two words appropriately.
15 months	Runs two or more words together. Follows simple commands.
18 months	Uses 7 to 20 words. Names some parts of body.
2 years	Uses 50 words. Names objects.
2 ½ years	Uses plurals, past tense and 'I' correctly.
3 years	Relates experiences. Knows own sex.
4 years	Recites from memory.
5 years	Prints own name.

Social

Interaction with other people is an essential part of normal development.

At about

1 month	Looks at faces.
3 months	Anticipates feeding.
9 months	Explores surroundings.
12 months	Imitates actions. Responds to own name.
18 months	Plays with other children.
2 years	Asks for food, drink and the toilet. Tells own name. Performs simple tasks unaided.
3 years	Shares things with others.
4 years	Shows imagination in play.
5 years	Can play competitively and follow rules.

Child development six to twelve years

Gross motor development

There is no great difference in the physical achievements between the sexes at this stage.

Newly acquired skills include complex co-ordinated activities such as learning to skip, ride a bike or horse, swim, do athletics or ballet, and participate in team games.

There is evidence to suggest that plenty of physical activity now is good for future health.

Physical development

Between six and eleven, the baby teeth are replaced by secondary teeth.

Between the age of ten and eleven the breast buds start to appear in girls. By twelve, overall growth accelerates and pubic hair appears.

Early pubertal changes begin a year later in boys; there may be some increase in testicular size between eleven and twelve.

Visual motor development

The acquisition of literacy and numeracy is one of the most important achievements for the young child. Failure to learn to read and write at this stage holds back learning in other fields, and needs special help.

Language

By school age, the normal child should be able to talk clearly. There is an inherent desire to increase the vocabulary, and parental encouragement is important.

The child should be shown how to use the library and how to look up words they don't understand in the dictionary.

Social

Children at this age are sociable. They enjoy participating in organised group activities like Cubs and Brownies.

They should be able to relate to their peers, and be encouraged to become less dependent on their parents.

Sex education should be provided for all children before puberty.

Vaccination timetable

When to protect your child

At 2 months	Diphtheria Whooping cough Tetanus *	DPT one injection
	Polio	by mouth
At 3 months	Diphtheria Whooping cough Tetanus *	DPT one injection
	Polio	by mouth
At 4 months	Diphtheria Whooping cough Tetanus *	DPT one injection
	Polio	by mouth
At 12-18 months (usually before 15 months)		
	Measies Mumps Rubella *	MMR one injection

3-5 years (around school entry)		
	Diphtheria Tetanus	booster injection
	Polio	booster by mouth
Girls 10-14 years		
	Rubella	one injection
Girls/Boys 13 years		
	Tuberculosis	one injection BCG
School leavers		
	Tetanus	one injection
15-19 years		
	Polio	booster by mouth

If your child has missed any of these immunisations, or started them late, don't worry. Your doctor will tell you how to fit them in so that your child is fully protected.

* Haemophilus b vaccines are aimed at thwarting the deadly haemophilus influenza b (Hib) bacteria that can cause a wide range of very serious infections in young children, including meningitis and septicaemia.

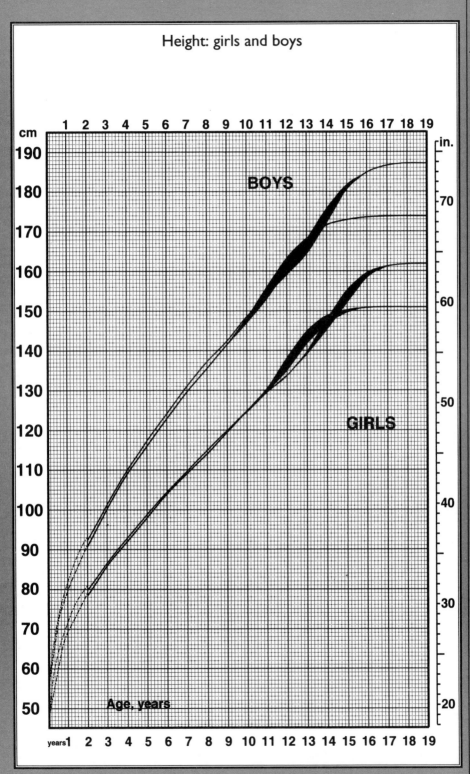

Height: girls and boys

Compared to other animals, humans have an extremely long period of childhood. This is partly due to the complexities of our society. A child needs to learn how to operate within it. A lot of the social and academic skills learned during this period form the basis of later adult behaviour.

Formal developmental testing ceases after the first school medical. The subsequent progress of the normal child is the responsibility of the parents, with the professional backup of the teacher and doctor.

• **Bedwetting still occurs in up to 5 per cent of children by the age of ten, and is not a serious problem; most will grow out of it.**
• **Treatment is purely behavioural retraining, and either the use of an enuresis alarm (to alert the child when he or she wets) or a star chart of dry nights usually works.**
• **Faecal soiling (encopresis) in older children is a serious problem, and in the absence of a physical cause may need referral to a child psychiatrist.**

Physical health

The largest cause of death in this age group is accidental, mainly on the roads, but also in the home including fires and poisoning.

☞ The commonest causes of illness are infections of the respiratory tract. The other infectious diseases, like whooping cough and measles are common, but provided the child has been immunised, rarely present a serious health threat.

☞ Chronic illness, such as asthma, diabetes and epilepsy can be well controlled with proper medical care. Children with these disorders should be encouraged to lead a normal life, and not be treated differently.

☞ Between the ages of six and twelve, children should receive at least one health check from the school medical service.

☞ Abnormal development should have been picked up by now, but minor deficits in hearing or sight may have gone unnoticed. Correction should start as soon as possible, as it can interfere with the child's ability to learn.

☞ Good nutrition is vital for maintaining growth and preventing future illness. A low-fat, high-fibre diet varied enough to provide all necessary vitamins and minerals is essential.

☞ Between the ages of six and eleven the baby teeth are replaced by the second, permanent dentition. Regular use of fluoride toothpaste has dramatically reduced the incidence of dental disease. Its use from an early age helps build stronger teeth.

☞ Between the ages of ten and fifteen children are tested for their immunity to TB, and vaccinated if not immune.

☞ Between eleven and thirteen all girls are vaccinated against Rubella (German measles), although this is due to change now that vaccination against measles, mumps and rubella takes place by the age of two.

Emotional wellbeing

Healthy emotional development is dependent on a degree of constancy in the early years of a child's life. Some of the main causes of stress (and this can lead to physical as well as emotional problems) that commonly affect children are:

☞ Separation from parents or siblings by death or divorce.

☞ Parental discord.

☞ Erratic handling: something is forbidden one minute, allowed the next.

☞ Lack of stimulation can lead to developmental delay or delinquent behaviour.

☞ Sibling rivalry.

☞ Unreasonable parental expectations.

☞ Acute emotional shock, e.g., witnessing a nasty accident.

☞ Bullying.

Parents should not delay in seeking professional help if their child suffers an emotionally damaging experience and/or exhibits abnormal behaviour compared to their peers.

Travel vaccination

Travel vaccination is necessary because you may encounter diseases abroad for which you have no natural or acquired immunity.

Travel vaccination is an injection of an attenuated or 'safe' form of the organisms that cause a particular disease. It stimulates the body's immune system to produces antibodies against the organism. If you then become infected, you will only experience a very mild form of the disease.

All children are routinely vaccinated against the serious diseases that are, or were, 'endemic' (regularly found in the population) here in Britain. You should ensure that your Tetanus vaccination is up to date, and be vaccinated against diseases that are endemic in the area you are to visit. This will depend upon your destination (see pp. 284-5).

Those commonly required are:

Polio

Polio is a painful, potentially fatal virus infection. It is transmitted by the 'faeco-oral route', a common mode of transmission, where the organism is present in the faeces of an infected individual and is inadvertently eaten by another, often as the result of unhygienic food handling.

An oral (taken by mouth) booster dose is required if it is more than ten years since you had your polio vaccination or last booster.

Typhoid

Transmission of infection is by contaminated food and water. The vaccine is effective for about a year. Pain at the injection site and fever are common reactions to the vaccine. A new oral form of the vaccine has recently been developed and is effective for three years.

Cholera

Cholera is transmitted by the faeco-oral route, and causes profound diarrhoea. With proper hygiene, the risk of catching it is small, and provided water and electrolytes lost in the diarrhoea are replaced, the mortality is very low. As the vaccine is only 50 per cent effective, the World Health Organisation no longer recommends it.

Hepatitis A

A true hepatitis A vaccine has only recently become available, and its use is recommended for frequent travellers to areas where hepatitis A is endemic, or those planning to stay for long periods. Otherwise, immunoglobulin that already contains hepatitis antibodies is used. This is known as 'passive' immunisation, i.e., the antibodies are given to you rather than being produced by your own body. It is possible to have a blood test to check whether you are already immune before having the vaccine.

Yellow fever

Yellow fever is a potentially fatal disease transmitted by mosquitoes. One dose of vaccine gives ten years protection after ten days.

Meningitis

There are several forms of bacterial meningitis (inflammation of the membranes surrounding the brain). The vaccine is effective against those caused by types A and C, but not B. Unfortunately, meningitis B is the form that occurs in Britain, which is why vaccination is not routine. A single dose of the vaccine will protect against types A and C for three years.

Generally speaking, vaccines are not advisable when suffering from an acute illness with fever or diarrhoea and vomiting, in children under one year of age, or pregnant women. In someone who is 'immuno-compromised' (their immune system is impaired because they are taking certain drugs, or have an illness such as AIDS), live vaccines should also be avoided.

Up-to-date information about which vaccinations you will need, if any, can be obtained from the travel agent, the relevant embassy or your doctor's surgery.

Group 1

Polio booster only:

All of Europe, including Eastern Europe and the former USSR, USA, Australia, Azores, Bermuda, Canada, Canary Islands, Cyprus, Greenland, Iceland, Japan, New Zealand

Group 2

Polio, Typhoid and Hepatitis A:

Most African, South American and Middle-Eastern countries, including Egypt, Israel, Turkey, Hong Kong, the Seychelles and South Africa.

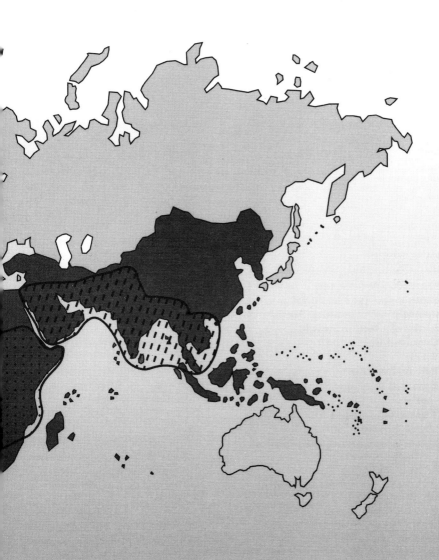

Group 3

Polio, Typhoid, Hepatitis A, plus Yellow Fever.

Mainly South America, including Brazil, Colombia, Peru and Venezuela.

Group 4

Polio, Typhoid, Hepatitis A, plus Meningitis:

The Indian sub-continent, including Nepal, Saudi Arabia and Senegal.

Group 5

All vaccines required:

Certain African countries including Ethiopia, Uganda, Kenya and Nigeria.

If you need vaccines, are planning to travel for any length of time, or have a condition such as pregnancy, diabetes or heart problems, you should see your GP in plenty of time. He will be able to advise you about travel medicine generally, and administer most of the vaccinations.

Yellow fever vaccination can only be obtained from a designated Yellow Fever Vaccination Centre. This may also be your local surgery, but if not, your doctor or travel agent will be able to tell you the whereabouts of your nearest one. Some countries require evidence of vaccination before allowing travellers to enter. An International Certificate of Vaccination can be issued when you receive them.

Vaccines are available for other conditions where the traveller may be at particular risk, e.g., rabies for animal handlers. Your GP will be able to advise you.

WARNINGS Avoidance of contaminated food and drink is as important as vaccination. Possible sources of infection include:
- **Unpeeled fruit**
- **Salads**
- **Raw fish/shellfish**
- **Reheated food/food from street vendors**
- **Tap water, including ice in drinks**
- **Unpasteurised milk**

A healthy lifestyle

☞ Take regular exercise. Vigorous exercise for twenty minutes, three times a week is all that is required to reduce your risk of heart problems, keep your weight down and prevent osteoporosis.

☞ Eat sensibly. A healthy diet does not mean a strict regime of 'health foods', but one that is balanced and contains more carbohydrate and protein than fat. Fresh fruit and vegetables supply necessary fibre, vitamins and minerals. If you are on an appropriate diet for your height and age, you should neither lose nor gain weight. If your weight starts to creep up, reduce your calorie intake a little before your weight gets out of control and dieting becomes a constant misery (see page 288 to check the ideal weight for your height). Adequate fibre in the diet means that a normal person should never have to use laxatives.

☞ Patterns in eating may well be established early in life and it is probable that fat mothers unconsciously encourage excessive intake in their children. Overweight people suffer from:
- high blood pressure;
- diabetes of the maturity-onset variety;
- an increased incidence in women of cancers of the breast, womb, ovaries and gall bladder;
- an increased incidence in men in cancer of the colon, rectum and prostate gland;
- orthopaedic problems, such as osteoarthritis and foot trouble;
- depression

☞ Drink sensibly. The recommended maximum for men is 21 units per week, for women, 14. Moderate regular drinking is not harmful. Binge drinking, and regular heavy drinking are.

Blood alcohol concentrations, in milligrams per 100 millilitres

AVERAGE-SIZED MAN				AVERAGE-SIZED WOMAN			
Units	At 1 hour	At 2 hours	At 3 hours	Units	At 1 hour	At 2 hours	At 3 hours
1	20	0	0	1	30	10	0
2	40	10	0	2	60	20	10
3	60	30	20	3	80	40	30
4	80	60	40	4	100	80	60
5	100	80	60	5	140	110	80
6	120	100	90	6	170	140	120
7	140	120	100	7	200	170	140
8	160	150	110	8	220	200	170
9	180	170	150	9	250	220	200
10	210	190	170	10	300	250	220

Note that the blood concentrations will vary with the weight. The lighter the person, the higher the concentration for a given input.

Effects of various blood alcohol concentrations on a person of average tolerance (moderate drinker)

BLOOD ALCOHOL (mg/100 ml)	EFFECTS
20	Performance is generally unaffected.
40	Less inhibited in social situations.
60	Judgement is probably impaired. Slowing of speech.
80	Definite loss of coordination. This is the current legal limit for driving in Britain.
100	Staggering.
160	Some people become argumentative and pugilistic.
300	Likely to lapse into a coma.
500	Dead.

TEN TIPS FOR GOOD HEALTH

1. Don't smoke.
2. Drink alcohol in moderation only.
3. Eat less fat, sugar and salt.
4. Eat more fibre, fruit and vegetables.
5. Do stretching exercises every morning.
6. Do twenty minutes of aerobic exercise three times a week.
7. Have regular medical, dental and optical check-ups.
8. Have a bath or a shower every day.
9. Drink plenty of water.
10. Try to keep cheerful!

☞ Avoid smoking. If you do smoke, try to give up, or at least cut down. Try smoking one less a day for a week, then one less for the next week and so on.

☞ Smoking is the commonest cause of cancer death in men and the second cause of cause of cancer death in women, after cancer of the breast. Statistics clearly show that smoking dramatically shortens life expectancy and the longer you continue to smoke the shorter your life will be.

☞ Attend for health screening tests when invited. Early detection of problems means that treatment is more likely to be successful.

☞ Keep up to date with vaccinations.

☞ Try and avoid or control stress in your life. If you can learn to adopt a healthy lifestyle in terms of exercise, diet, sensible drinking and giving up smoking, then you will undoubtedly feel better. This in turn will help you control stress.

☞ Try to be happy. More than 100 studies have established, statistically, that there is a positive correlation between a satisfactory and happy state of mind and good physical health.

Are you a healthy weight?

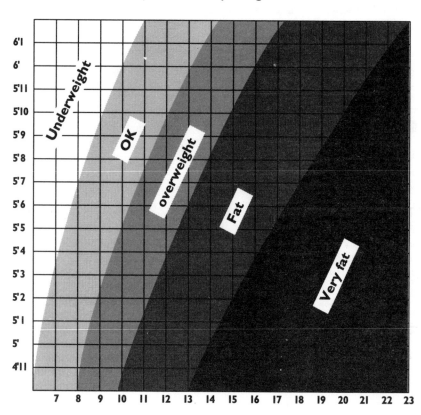

Height in feet and inches (1 ft = approximately 0.3 m)

Weight in stones (1 pound = approximately 0.45 kg)

CHAPTER SIX

Personal finance and legal matters

Kathy Gunn

Currently edits the financial pages of the People; previously city editor at Today and has written for Financial Weekly, The Times and Investors' Chronicle. Kathy has written three books: Nightmare on Lime Street: Whatever Happened to Lloyd's of London, High Street Robbery: How the banks hold up their customers and Fraud; The Growth Industry of the Eighties.

A basic knowledge of financial and legal matters can save a lot of time and money. This chapter advises on the most efficient ways to borrow money (pp. 292-7), savings and investment (pp.298-303), mortgages (pp. 306-9), insurance and pensions (pp. 310-19). There is also advice on the legal aspects of tenancy (pp. 323-8), consumer rights (pp. 333-6) and a range of other situations in which it is wise to be as well informed as possible.

Budgeting

Before you can budget you need a clear picture of where your money currently goes. So first jot down all your weekly or monthly income. Then list what you spend it on, starting with rent or mortgage payments, fuel and food bills, daily travel expenses, clothing, and including things like newspapers, TV and video rental, alcohol and cigarettes, eating out, cinema trips – everything that you do on a regular or semi-regular basis and consider a necessary part of your lifestyle.

Can you spread the cost of bulky bills?

Spread the cost of large bills by setting aside something each month towards gas, electricity, and phone costs (and half-yearly water bills). Put the money in an interest-earning, instant access account at the bank or building society and only use that account to pay the bills. It is also possible to take up one of the budget, stamps, or payment book schemes set up by the gas, electricity, telephone and water companies.

Most of these utility companies have a system to help you pay quarterly bills in monthly stages. For example, British Gas's payment plan allows you to pay a regular sum each month direct from your current account. Payments are revised if your consumption changes dramatically. Or ask about paying weekly instalments as you go along. Gas stamps are also available, which you should be able to buy at any gas showroom – it's a useful way to start saving towards your next bill if money is tight.

Electricity companies offer budget plans for monthly payments, which are taken direct from your account. Some also offer plastic budget cards to use in the showrooms to pay regular instalments. Payments are based upon your previous twelve months' electricity consumption – and if you've just moved into a new address, that of the previous occupants. Water companies usually send out bills twice a year but also offer instalment plans either by direct debit, or with a payment book to use either weekly or monthly at Post Offices and bank counters.

British Telecom also offers discounts on residential call bills. If your quarterly bill is regularly over £40 it's worth going on to Option 15 which costs £4 a quarter. It will provide you with a ten per cent discount if your bill tops the £40 mark. Light phone users whose bills are under £10 a quarter can have a rebate of 12.3 pence for every 10 pence below £10 that their bill adds up to. You can check the latest information on these BT schemes on Freephone 0800 800 862. BT competitors have similar schemes to help you spread the cost of telephoning.

Can you cut the weekly shopping bill?

It may be cheaper to buy supermarket own-brands instead of more expensive labels. They are often made for supermarket groups by the same food or household goods manufacturer as the more recognisable brands anyhow. Fresh fruit and vegetables in season are cheaper and healthier than canned ones. Local greengrocers may also sell off produce more cheaply when it looks 'tired'. Supermarkets mark down food that is on or near its sell-by date; if cooked and consumed within a day or so, they are fine. Sell-by dates are guidelines for the vendor, not the consumer, so you can quite safely add a few days to any date, and still have perfectly edible produce.

Try to buy things on special – in particular, the multi-buy purchases. Spending a few more pounds one week could save at least that amount over the next three or four, if you buy in bulk. If you have the freezer space, buy meat and baked goods that have been marked down.

Look for larger items you need at markets and car boot sales – but be careful: things like electrical goods may be faulty or even dangerous. Take advantage of discount sales in shops to get things the family really needs, but try to avoid impulse buys.

Can you increase your income?

Before you start cutting down on loads of things, pause to consider whether you can increase your income instead (or as well). For instance, you're allowed to earn more than £3000 a year tax-free and after expenses,

> **If you have taxable savings and a non-taxpaying spouse why not give your nest-egg to him or her so they can register to receive the income tax-free? The gift has to be genuine, so beware – if your spouse runs off, you could lose out.**

from letting a furnished room in your home. Ask the local tax office for its leaflet explaining how this scheme works (see also pp. 323-8).

Can you cut your tax bill?

A little planning could cut your tax bill enough to make a handy difference to your disposable income.

Husbands and wives can each earn several thousand pounds – at the time of writing this is £3,445 each – before tax is levied. This is your personal tax allowance. So, if one of you runs a business and the other isn't working, why not pay yourself less and give your spouse a salary matching the personal tax allowance to do some part-time work? They will get the money tax-free when you'd pay income tax on it. But your spouse really does have to do some work for this – the taxman won't be fooled if you pay them for doing nothing.

Couples can also choose whether to split the married person's tax allowance fifty-fifty, or allocate it to just one partner. If one of you is earning just enough to be in the lowest, twenty per cent tax rate band, allocating the married person's allowance to the lower earner might take that person out of tax altogether.

Suggest to your employers that they move to a profit-related pay scheme whereby staff can have up to twenty per cent or £4,000 of their salary (whichever is less) tax-free if it is linked to the company's performance. It means trading in part of your guaranteed but taxable salary for a tax-free share of the annual profits – so don't suggest it to a struggling business – and the end result can boost your monthly after-tax income quite sharply.

Check if your company car is worth having, now that they are so highly taxed. It may actually work out cheaper to trade in the kudos of the car for a bit more taxable salary. Other tax wheezes include having a company van instead of a car, or a 'classic' car instead of a modern one.

Make sure your savings are in tax-free form

Why pay tax if you don't have to? Put your major savings into tax-free form – for example National Savings Certificates, Tessas, PEPs, and pension plans. See pp. 299-302 and 316-19.

> If you do have more than one home in the UK, you can decide each year to elect (for tax reasons) which one to describe as your main home. So if you are selling one and keeping the other you might be able to avoid capital gains tax on the one being sold if you elect it as your main home for that tax year – and spend some time in it. Your local tax office has leaflets about CGT and how it works.

Can you raise extra cash?

The proceeds of selling off your 'chattels' attract no tax and every adult has an annual exemption from capital gains tax (CGT) on the first (at the time of writing) £5,800 of gains from selling their assets (including shares). Your main home never attracts this tax, though 'second' or holiday homes do.

Can you persuade the family to help?

Anyone can choose to give unlimited lots of £250 to different people each tax year, and one lot of £3000 to just one person.

If you are getting married, your parents can each give you £5000 and grandparents £2500. Anyone else can give you up to £1000, tax-free, to celebrate the day (see also page 343).

Can you claim any state benefits?

If your circumstances have changed, it is worth checking whether you have become eligible for any state benefits. For example, if the family income falls because a breadwinner has been put on short-time working, you may be eligible for help from the Department of Social Security (DSS) even if you have several thousand pounds worth of savings. So ask about the various benefits available to people working less than sixteen hours a week (family credit), and to those working more than that a week but still on a low wage (income support).

Once on income support or unemployment benefit, you may also qualify for Housing Benefit. Apply for this to the local council. Recipients can still have substantial savings. New mums who are on income support, family credit or other allowances can get a Maternity Payment from the social fund for essentials such as a cot or pram. The fund also makes crisis loans to replace things like the cooker or a bed, which can be repaid in very small weekly amounts.

All parents get child benefit so don't forget to collect that. New widows get a lump sum to tide them through the bereavement.

Have you got the best kind of bank account?

If you manage to stay in the black most of the time, you should have a bank or building society chequebook account that pays

> If you are about to lose your job tell the DSS at once. Unemployment Benefit is paid whatever savings or redundancy money you have, to people who have paid National Insurance contributions for the previous two tax years. You need a letter from your ex-employer stating you are being or have been made redundant, however, so beware of redundancy schemes that try to describe what's happened as a career opportunity or some other euphemism.

interest on credit balances. Some require a minimum opening deposit or only start paying interest above a minimum balance.

Can you reduce your debts and cut interest bills?

Paying interest can be an expensive business. First, list everything you owe. Now put your debts in order of priority, starting with the essential ones that you need to meet to keep your home comforts such as rent, community charge and fuel bills. It's important to keep paying these if you can (see page 296 for advice on how to negotiate with your lenders if you are in a tight spot). Assuming you're coping but would like to cut down your debts, start with your credit cards. If you have a large amount outstanding on a credit card that you feel you'll never whittle down, it may be cheaper to take out a bank loan that is repayable in manageable monthly amounts at a lower interest rate. Use it to clear the credit card debt. If you then continue using your credit card, try to clear the balance every month (see pp. 303-6).

Alternatively, use a debit card or a charge card instead. Debit cards are like cheques without the hassle; the money comes out of your bank account about three days later. Charge cards have to be paid off in full every time you get a statement, which puts an automatic brake on your spending urges!

If you regularly dip into the red before your salary goes into your account, negotiate an agreed overdraft limit with your bank before you next overdraw. Agreed overdrafts cost far less in annual interest charges at than unauthorised ones.

Borrowing

Only organisations or individuals with a credit licence can legally offer you credit. You can be confident that well-known high street banks, hire-purchase organisations, and building societies are licensed to offer credit. Do check that any smaller lender is licensed before you take out a loan.

The main providers of most loans to consumers are the banks and building societies.

If you need a large overdraft for a few months for a specific purpose – for example, to borrow £1000 for five months to pay for repairs to your home – it's a good idea to arrange a separate overdraft account. This way you can keep your normal current account in credit, avoiding bank charges on all your regular transactions. You make one transfer each month from your normal account into the overdraft account to reduce the borrowing – perhaps £200 a month for the five months. This means only one set of bank charges on the overdraft account each month. A final payment in month six clears the interest owed.

Banks operating in the UK are regulated by the banking laws, and are overseen by the Bank of England; building societies have their own Acts of Parliament and are overseen by the Building Societies Commission. Both, however, follow a voluntary Code of Banking Practice, laying out your (and their) rights and responsibilities, and free copies of this are available from their branches.

Signatories to this Code, are also members of the Banking or the Building Societies Ombudsman schemes. These Ombudsmen can intervene on your behalf in disputes with these organisations.

Personal borrowing from a bank or building society

Overdrafts

There are several different ways to borrow money from a bank or building society. You may have an overdraft, for instance, linked to your bank or building society cheque (current) account. Overdrafts are a form of unsecured lending – which means they are not guaranteed against any of your assets. Overdrafts come in two forms – agreed overdrafts, and unauthorised overdrafts.

An agreed or authorised overdraft is when your bank agrees that you can overdraw by up to a certain figure and what the interest rate for such borrowing will be. They'll also tell you what other bank administration charges may be involved. Your overdraft limit should not be regarded as a borrowing target, but the top limit of your facility to overdraw. Try not to run it up to the limit and leave it there, but just use it from time to time to absorb lumpy bills and costs, and clear it as often as possible.

Overdrafts have to be repaid on demand and the lender has the right to ask for repayment in full at any time if they consider you to be in breach of your agreement. Most overdrafts are set up on a yearly basis and renegotiated, or confirmed, once a year. So if your bank sees you are constantly up to your overdraft limit, they may grow concerned and reduce your limit next time round. Never go over your limit without permission – it will cost you more in interest and the bank may start returning your cheques unpaid.

Unauthorised overdrafts are when you overdraw your current account without the bank's agreement, or go over your agreed overdraft limit. They are far more expensive than agreed overdrafts as the banks levy a punitive interest rate for unauthorised borrowing, in an attempt to stop you from doing it. Your bank may still honour your cheques, up to a point, but you will pay dearly in interest rate and bank charges for this. Again, unauthorised borrowing has to be repaid upon demand.

Always complain to your branch at manager level first, regional office next (if there is one) and then the head office. Then, if the dispute is still in deadlock, you can take it on to the Ombudsman. Try to get a letter from the bank or building society concerned confirming that deadlock has been reached; if this is not forthcoming after several weeks (or a deadline set by you for its arrival) you can still go to the appropriate Ombudsman.

If you think you are going to overdraw and have no overdraft agreement, or realise that you may go over your limit (perhaps because someone else is late in paying you), alert the bank and explain the circumstances. They may agree to grant you an agreed overdraft, or extend your existing limit (perhaps temporarily) or at least to allow the extra borrowing on this occasion without sending back your cheques unpaid. This is particularly important for small businesses, as your credibility with suppliers could be at stake.

Set-offs

If you want to borrow money for something rather than use up your savings, your bank may suggest that you keep the savings but use them (perhaps transferred into one of the bank's savings products!) as security for an overdraft account. This makes it a 'secured' overdraft, which you repay in monthly instalments. In return for the increase in money on deposit with them, the bank will charge you less interest on your overdraft than it would normally do. So set-offs can be a cheaper way of borrowing. However, if you default on the loan, your savings can be used to repay it and meet the interest due.

Unsecured personal loans

Personal loans are loans of a set amount of money, arranged for a fixed period of time; for example, £5,000 for three years. Throughout the fixed term, the loan is repaid in set, regular instalments which include the interest owed. Both banks and building societies offer personal loans that are not tied to any particular purchase or use of the money, and are not usually 'secured' against any of your assets.

You can either have a personal loan with a variable interest rate – one that fluctuates in line with UK interest rates generally – or a loan at a fixed rate of interest which means the amount of your monthly repayments doesn't vary.

Fixed-interest personal loans

These are (usually) for a specific purpose; for example, to buy a car, or a boat, or even to pay for an exotic holiday. You agree with the lender at the outset exactly how much you are borrowing, at what interest rate and for how long. Provided you keep up the regular payments and any other conditions attached to the loan, the lender can't alter those terms. Fixed-interest loans are for at least one year, and a maximum of five years – and (at the time of writing) the most you can normally arrange to borrow this way from a bank is usually £10,000. Building societies are allowed to lend you up to £25,000 as a personal unsecured loan but loans of over £10,000 are usually in connection with helping people to overcome "negative equity" problems (when your home has fallen to a value that is less than you owe on the mortgage) and not for new spending. Most building societies prefer to make 'secured' personal loans (see below).

Mortgages

Banks and building societies lend larger sums of money for longer periods of time to buy your home. A mortgage is a long-term loan of money, secured against the asset – the home – bought with that cash (see pp. 306-9)

Secured loans

These are smaller than mortgages and are also loans secured against one of your assets, which will usually be your home. If you default on the loan, the lender can repossess the asset concerned to get its money back. A secured personal loan would normally be for a specific major project – like a home extension, when your home is worth more than any mortgage on it and you want to borrow some more cash to add an extra room or a conservatory. Sadly, you can't get tax relief on the interest on money borrowed for home improvements.

Both banks and building societies make secured loans.

Budget accounts

These are low-interest bank accounts intended to let you borrow up to a set limit in any month in order to help you budget. There is a low rate of interest and it is suitable for spreading bills evenly across all twelve months of the year. However, they are not currently offered as frequently as they

used to be, as too many canny people used to take out cash up to the borrowing limit and invest it at a higher rate at the building society, making their monthly repayments from the building society account! The banks saw this as an abuse of their budget account system. Nowadays if you ask for a budget account you are more likely to be offered a credit card to pay your larger bills.

Mastercard and VISA credit cards

These are issued to many customers of banks and building societies. See pp. 303-6 for more details about borrowing this way.

Borrowing from retailers

Some retailers offer budget and option accounts, or credit sales.

A budget account with a shop means you have an account there, usually based on a plastic card, with a credit limit and a system of regular monthly payments. The credit limit is set at a multiple of your monthly repayment; for example, 20 times £20 a month = a limit of £400. You can buy items from the shop up to the level of your credit limit, and you get monthly statements showing what you currently owe, the repayments due, plus the monthly interest on the account, and what spending is still available on your credit limit.

Option accounts are more like credit cards – the retailer sets your credit limit and you can spend up to the total of that amount with your card at its stores. Each month when you get your statement you can either pay off part of the money owed, plus interest on the balance, or you can clear the lot at no-interest cost.

Credit sales are usually offered on expensive items such as electrical goods, fridges and washing machines. The credit may be supplied by a finance house rather than by the store group itself. You buy the goods on credit, paying for them in monthly stages over an agreed period of time. There may be interest to pay, or the deal offered may be a special zero-per cent credit sales promotion. Either way, you own the goods outright from day one – unlike a hire-purchase agreement.

Mail order shopping is another form of retail credit as you can pay in instalments for

WARNING Loan sharks do not always turn out to be legitimate – and licensed or not, they often charge exorbitant interest rates. Never deal with anyone that asks you for your benefit book – it's illegal for anyone to do so. If you are on income support and in dire straits, try asking for a Social Security Loan.

the goods you order. Some mail-order shopping is even interest-free. Not all mail-order items are cheaper than in the high street shops, however, especially well-known brands of goods, so it's worth checking around before you purchase. You are entitled to return mail order goods that you decide aren't suitable, and most mail-order companies have standard arrangements for this.

Hire purchase (HP)

HP is still a popular way to buy very expensive items such as a new or secondhand car. With a hire purchase deal, you are actually agreeing to hire the car (or item concerned) for a set period of time, paying a monthly sum including interest on the financing deal. At the end of the time agreed, you either become the owner of the car automatically, or may have the option to do so by paying a very small extra sum.

HP agreements usually have a brief cancellation period in which you can change your mind and opt out of the deal to buy the goods. Check for this, and the terms of cancellation, before you sign the agreement.

If you change your mind after this period is up, you will have to return the goods and pay at least half the cost, if your repayments have not already reached that amount. And if the item(s) have become rather battered, you may have to pay extra on top.

If you don't keep up your monthly HP payments, the shop or showroom that sold you the goods is entitled to repossess them. But if you have already paid more than one-third of the total cost involved by the time you run into difficulties, the seller must go to

court for a court order before they can demand the goods back. And even if you have paid off less than one-third of the total involved, the seller can't just walk into your home and take the goods back. They need your permission to do so, and without that permission, they will need a court order to enter your home.

Bailiffs are not allowed to break into your home to gain entry, but once you have opened the door to them, or if you have (for instance) left a window open through which they can enter without doing any damage, they are legally permitted to seize the goods concerned.

Credit unions

Credit unions are formed by a group of people who have agreed to put money regularly into a common fund from which each member of the union can borrow when necessary. There is usually an initial period of membership, with regular savings, before you will be able to borrow. Interest rates tend to be low, so they are a cheap way to borrow, and the income from the loans can be divided up as a dividend between members. Credit unions have to register with the Registry of Friendly Societies, and since they are very much a business proposition, should be run by members with a fair amount of financial know-how.

What can I do if I'm refused credit?

Lenders use credit reference agencies to check how good or risky a customer you may be. All sorts of factors come into play, including your age, and address, as well as any information available about your financial management, such as what credit cards you hold and whether your card issuers have found you to be a habitual slow payer of those bills, for instance.

If you are ever turned down for credit, the retailer who has refused you must tell you –

upon request – which credit reference agency they used. You can write to the agency and pay a small fee (e.g., £2) to get a copy of your own credit reference. If there is something on this that is wrong – perhaps you have been mixed up with someone of a similar name who used to live at what's now your address – you can ask them to add a correction to your record so that future lenders will see the right information.

> **If you have had a county court judgment (CCJ) against you in a financial matter, this will stay on your credit record for six years. But if you have now cleared that debt, tell the credit reference agency this and ask them to enter the information on your record – it may help with future requests for credit.**

What happens if I just can't cope with my debts?

Never ignore debt problems and hope they'll just go away – like naughty children seeking attention, they tend to get worse if ignored. If it's one particular debt that is the headache, talk to that lender about ways of re-organising it.

For example, you may be able to convert an overdraft into a 'term' loan and pay it off over two or three years. You could ask to have the variable interest on a major debt frozen, so that it stops mounting up, giving you a chance at least to repay the capital and any interest accrued so far.

With a long-term loan, such as a mortgage, you may be able to agree to reduce the monthly payments and increase the term of the loan, paying it off more slowly. This costs more in the long run but may be more manageable month by month. Or you may be able to agree to reduce your monthly payments while you get back on your feet and then pay a larger monthly sum later on, to catch up. It is always worth asking. Never just hand in the keys and walk away – if the subsequent sale of the house doesn't raise

enough money to clear the loan, you are still liable for the balance.

If you are in a mess with debt, don't panic.

First, 'prioritise' your debts: decide which ones are the most important to meet. These are the debts that could cost you your home or your liberty if you don't come to an agreement. Examples of these are the mortgage – non-payment of it could lead to your home being repossessed (and again, if it doesn't fetch enough money on being sold to clear the loan you are still liable for the balance) – and your council tax bill or any legal fines whose non-payment could ultimately land you in jail. Then tot up your other debts.

Now you can work out a strategy with which to approach each of your lenders, explaining the overall situation and offering to pay each one a different, but affordable, amount each month. Write to your creditors with a schedule of your income, outgoings and debts so they can see the full picture, and tell each one what you reckon you can afford to pay per week towards meeting the particular debt that you owe.

Suggest realistic amounts that you can afford to pay week after week over a long period of time. It can be helpful to bring in a third party such as the local Citizens Advice Bureau (CAB), or your local authority debt advice centre, to help you draw up this schedule and to negotiate with your lenders on your behalf.

> **Using a third party takes some of the worry out of the situation and stops individual lenders from bullying you into an agreement that would only solve part of the problem. Most lenders will pay more attention to a well thought-out proposal brought to them on your behalf by a mediator. And they would always rather get back at least some of their money, than none at all. So if you are in trouble, don't soldier on alone. With the right approach, there is nearly always room for a deal.**

Data Protection Act

Have you a sneaking suspicion that someone has got your details wrong on their computer records? You can check. The Data Protection Act, 1984, gives you the right to see personal data about yourself which is held on any organisation's computer system, and to get it corrected if it's wrong. You can also complain to the Data Protection Registrar if you are unhappy about the way information about you held on computer is being collected or used – and you can even take the organisation concerned to court to get things sorted out.

You may be able to get compensation if damage (other than just distress) has been done to you by the unauthorised disclosure, or the loss, or even the unauthorised destruction of your personal details held on a computer. Manually processed paper records are not covered by the Act.

What information can be held on computer?

The Act says holders of 'automatically processed' – i.e. computer – data about living people must:

☞ obtain and process the information they hold fairly and lawfully;

☞ register the purposes for which they hold the information;

☞ not use or disclose it in a way contrary to those purposes;

☞ only hold information that is accurate and (where necessary) kept up to date.

It must also not be held for any longer than necessary; and when requested, individuals must be given copies of information held about themselves and the holder must, where appropriate, correct or erase that information. Finally, the holder must take appropriate steps to keep the information safe.

Can I always see my records?

Almost always. Even if a firm just keeps names and addresses on computer file it's supposed to register under the Data Protection Act.

The only times when you can't gain access to your records are if they are held:

☞ for the purpose of preventing or detecting crime;

☞ for catching or prosecuting offenders;

☞ to assess or collect tax or duty.

But even then, holders of this type of information are only allowed to refuse you access to it if letting you see it would hinder these purposes. Sometimes your access to health or social work details are also restricted. So if you are ever refused the right to see your computer records, check with the Date Protection Registar whether the refusal is correct or not.

If you just keep your own personal, family and household affairs on computer you don't have to register under the Act. You are also exempt if you just keep information for preparing the text of documents, calculating wages or pensions, keeping your accounts and records for accounting purposes, or mailing lists to send out articles and information to the people on your records. Sports and recreational clubs that are not limited companies are also exempt. But if you do keep a mailing list, or run a club that keeps information on computer, you must get the permission of the people concerned (the data subjects) to use their details. So, if in doubt about your position, ask the Registrar's Office for guidance (see page 298).

> **WARNING Breaches of the Act by data-holders can result in criminal prosecution initiated by the Registrar if an information-holder fails to put matters right when instructed to do so!**

How do I get a copy of my computer record?

To get the details of your own file you need to write to the organisation direct (the data user), asking for a subject access report; and the Registrar's Office can tell you where and to whom to send your letter (see page 298). The data user must reply to your letter with a copy of the information held about you, within forty days (and is allowed to charge a small fee, at the time of writing of up to £10 per entry, though some may let you have the copy for free).

If you don't get a reply within forty days you can complain to the Registrar, or ask for a court order for access to the data user's files on you. If the data held is inaccurate you can complain to the Registrar, or apply to the courts to get it corrected or deleted; and even ask for compensation if you've been damaged by the errors or ommissions.

Consulting the Data Protection Registrar

The Registrar is an independent official whose office can tell you if an organisation is registered under the Act; the sort of information that organisation holds; the type of people about whom it holds it; what in general terms the information is used for, where obtained, and to whom disclosed. It can help you get errors corrected.

Registrar is based at
Springfield House,
Water Lane,
Wilmslow,
Cheshire SK9 5AX

The Registrar's Office produces leaflets for people wanting to check their computer files, and for data users to help them check that their record-keeping is on the right side of the law.

Savings & investment

There's an important difference, which is often overlooked, between 'saving' and 'investment'.

Savings are – as much as anything can be – risk-free. You are tucking money away safely for a rainy day or a specific project, and earning some interest on it.

But investment involves a bit of risk – you are putting money into something that should grow and increase your capital by more than your savings are likely to grow, but which could run into squally financial weather.

In return for the risk you take, you are paid an income on the money – but the higher

this income or 'return' on your capital, the greater is the potential risk! So don't be greedy, always remember that the return you are offered is itself a measure of the risk involved (or, that 'risk equals return'); and that risks sometimes do turn into real losses!

So select your mixture of savings and investments according to how 'risk averse' you are, and your own plans for the future.

Savings are the right home for money you cannot afford to risk in any way. Investments are for money that you are not likely to need in a hurry, so that if things don't go well you can either bear the loss, or wait patiently until things improve. Some types of investment are much less risky than others.

Saving

The type of account you decide to put your savings into depends on how quickly you want to be able to get your hands on the money. Banks and building societies all offer a wide range of different savings accounts. Some will be designed for regular, monthly saving, and others for lump sums as and when you have some cash to spare.

It's important that you select the type of savings vehicle that best fits your plans at a particular stage in your life, including your tax position.

Always check first what the minimum investment is, whether you can increase your payments to the account later, how easily you can withdraw the money if you need it early, and what the interest payment arrangements are.

Basically, the more money you tuck away and the longer you agree to tie it up, before dipping into it, the higher the interest rate you will receive.

If you withdraw high-rate savings early, you may face a penalty – so you should always have some of your savings in a lower-paying, 'instant access' account for emergencies, treats, or holidays.

Instant access accounts are offered by banks and building societies, or you might prefer one of the National Savings products at the Post Office. Leaflets there will tell you about all the different National Savings schemes.

Always check how many days' notice are required for you to withdraw your savings even on these accounts – it may be a week, for instance. Sometimes higher rates are available on large sums in some quick-access accounts.

Most higher-interest paying accounts offered by banks and building societies require anything from ninety days' to a whole year's notice of withdrawal so use these as homes for longer-term savings. Early withdrawal from these accounts can result in an 'interest penalty' – you are docked a month or three months (for example) of the high interest already earned on the cash.

Some accounts will pay variable interest which changes in line with UK interest rates generally; others will offer a fixed rate of interest for a set period of time.

Different types of savings plans are also designed to appeal to different kinds of savers – for instance, there are accounts for children, and higher-interest bearing accounts for the over-65s, who may need to supplement their income. There are also National Savings 'Granny Bonds' (five-year savings schemes for the over-65s), on which the interest is paid gross but is taxable, and one-year First Option Bonds on which the interest is paid net of basic rate tax.

There are postal accounts which also pay slightly better rates of interest for those who don't require instant cash transactions; and 'escalator' bonds offered by building societies which pay a rising annual rate of interest on the capital put in, over a set number of years.

Tax & savings

Most types of savings are taxable but some are tax-free. Interest on bank and building society savings and some National Savings products is usually paid after they've taken off (net of) basic rate tax. So higher-rate taxpayers will have to stump up the difference. But non-taxpayers can fill in a form to register to have their interest paid gross – that is, without tax being docked. This saves you the bother of having to reclaim the tax.

Children also have a personal tax allowance, but rarely have the taxable income to offset it against! If your child has a bank or building society savings or deposit account, remember to fill in one of these forms so he or she can receive their interest without tax (up to the level of the personal allowance).

Tax-free savings

Some savings schemes are entirely tax-free, provided you leave your cash in them for five years. So once you have started your rainy-day savings fund, these are a good haven for longer-term savings.

National Savings

These are a very safe way to save money as you are lending your cash to the government in return for interest on the money. Some types of National Savings schemes are tax-free including National Savings Certificates, and Index-Linked Certificates which protect your savings and the interest earned on them from inflation. But if you cash them in during the first year you get no interest, and less than the offered rate if you withdraw the cash in under four years.

National Savings Yearly Plans are also tax-free. You put in a regular sum each month for a whole year during which you get no interest at all if you withdraw the money. But if you get to the end of the year you do get an annual interest payment, and if you leave it in for four more years, it earns a better rate of interest for the whole period.

National Savings Children's Bonds are a long-term tax-free way for a child under sixteen to build up a modest lump sum. These bonds can be held until the 'child' is twenty-one.

Save as You Earn schemes

These are regular savings schemes with some building societies. Each saver can only have one of these plans, which let you put aside £20 a month for five years. The interest you receive is in the form of a tax-free bonus payment of fourteen months' worth of savings on top of what you have tucked away by the end of the five years. Leaving the money in the scheme for a further two years, earns you a second lot of fourteen months' worth of extra money. You have access to your money throughout but get no interest at all if you withdraw it during the first year, and a lower rate of interest if you take it out between years two and five than if you stay the full course. You can also miss some monthly payments and still get the top rate of interest provided you catch up again by the end of the five years.

Friendly Societies

These offer a tax-free savings scheme which lets savers, including children, put up to £18 a month (or £200 in lump sums per year) aside for ten years. All the accumulated interest is tax-free at the end of the ten years. You can only have one plan per person at a time, but children can renew their plan to take them up to age twenty-one.

TESSAS

These are Tax Exempt Special Savings Accounts, and are probably the best-known tax-free bank and building society accounts for personal savers over eighteen. But to get the tax break you must leave your money in for five years. You can get at the money earlier if you suddenly need it, but you will lose the tax breaks on any sums withdrawn early (and some TESSA providers also levy an early withdrawal penalty so check that before you choose one). At the time of writing, you can save up to £9000 in a TESSA over five years, starting with up to £3000 in year one and no more than £1800 per year after that until you hit the £9000 ceiling.

TESSA plans vary but most are structured to let you make both regular deposits and lump sum payments, whichever suits you best. Some TESSA providers pay extra bonus interest on the first year of your investment.

You can withdraw TESSA interest any time net of tax, and will get the tax credited to your balance after the five years are up (except on any capital that you withdrew early). Or you can leave the interest in to roll up and earn even more interest on the balance.

> There is more than one kind of share. The ones described below are 'ordinary' shares. You may also come across various 'preference shares' which come higher up the pecking order for repayment, and pay a fixed rate of interest rather than a dividend. It is also possible to trade in 'options' on shares but these are more suitable for very experienced stock market investors.

Annuities

When you retire your pension fund buys an annuity. If you have another lump sum later in life, you can do this for yourself, too. An annuity puts the money into interest-bearing investments from which it pays you an agreed monthly income for the rest of your life (however long you live for). You or your heirs do not get back the lump sum, however. The cost of an annuity – i.e., the amount you pay upfront for the amount of guaranteed monthly income you will get – varies in line with events in the gilt-edged market (see Investment, below).

Investment

There are many forms of investment – the best known are probably buying shares and government bonds, known as 'gilt-edged stock' on the stockmarket.

Shares

When you buy shares in a company, you are literally buying a share in the ownership of that company. You hope it will do well and that its shares will rise in value. Meanwhile the company distributes part of its after-tax profits to its shareholders each year in the form of dividends (paid either half-yearly or in some cases, quarterly). Dividends are paid net of basic rate tax and there is also capital gains tax (CGT) to pay on the profits when you sell up. But you can reduce that tax bill by the amount available on your annual capital gains tax allowance.

There are no guarantees – if the company does badly the value of its shares will fall. If it goes bust, the shareholders are last in the pecking order to be repaid out of the assets left, and usually get nothing or just a few pence per share back often after a wait of several years. So shares, also known as 'equities', can be risky, depending on the strength of the company you invest in. However, generally speaking, investing in a careful selection of shares can be very profitable if you are prepared to tuck your money away for several years and wait for the companies concerned to grow. Shares of very strong, successful British companies are known as 'blue chip' shares after the highest value gambling chips!

Shares can be bought new from a company when it issues new sharepaper, or be bought and sold secondhand on the stockmarket through a stockbroker or sharedealing service. Most people buy and sell them this way. Share price movements reflect levels of demand for a particular company's shares, and the general economic outlook and 'mood' of the stock market. A stockbroker can advise you on what to choose, the timing of sales and purchases, and will charge you a commission based on the value of your transaction; an 'execution-only' telephone-based sharedealing service won't give advice but will just carry out your orders and therefore charges a lower commission or fee.

Gilts and bonds

When you buy a bond, you are lending your money to the business or government that has issued the bond, in return for which you are paid an annual interest rate. Your money is pretty safe as the issuer also guarantees to repay the bond at its full face value at a set date. Companies can issue bonds; and if the company runs into trouble the bondholders get repaid out of what is left before the shareholders do (but if there is not enough in the kitty to go round all the creditors, even the bondholders can get back less than they invested).

British government-issued bonds are generally regarded as the safest of all – hence the nickname 'gilt-edged stock', often shortened

> The interest you earn from investing in British government stocks is paid net of basic rate tax but there is no capital gains tax to pay on any profits you make when you sell your gilts.

to 'gilts'. Gilts and other bonds (also called loanstocks) are also traded secondhand in the stockmarket.

Collective investments

There are ways to invest in the stockmarket without committing large sums of money. You can buy units in a **unit trust** group. These are investment funds that pool lots of small investors' money to buy a wide range of different stocks and shares. Some specialise in shares of certain types of company and/or the stockmarkets of certain geographical regions. Units are bought and sold directly from and to the fund, which levies an annual management fee on the general pot and may also charge an initial, entry fee deducted from your own opening investment.

Or there are **investment trusts**, which invest broadly in the same way as unit trusts. The difference is that instead of you buying units in the fund in which the trust is investing, you buy shares in the trust itself – these shares are traded on the stockmarket so to get them you need to go through a stockbroker.

Tax-free Personal Equity Plans (PEPS)

With these you can invest tax-free in shares, or in investment trusts, or in unit trusts.

PEPs allow you to invest in equities (but not gilts), take any eventual gains tax-free, and meanwhile get the dividend income tax-free as well. Each person over eighteen can put up to £6000 a year into a 'general PEP' (i.e., holding shares in more than one company, or in one or more unit or investment trusts), and another £3000 a year each into a PEP holding the shares of just one UK Stock Exchange traded company.

But you must do this through an approved PEP provider; you can't just buy shares and claim the PEP tax breaks. To qualify for

'PEPping' the money involved must also be predominantly invested in shares of UK or European companies. Many PEP plans are offered by unit and investment trusts, and by the fund management arms of insurance companies as well, and are often advertised in the press. Some building societies have also arranged PEP schemes. Management charges and dealing costs are levied within your PEP and should be shown in its literature.

Life policies

You probably haven't thought of a life policy as a form of stockmarket investment, but it is! The premiums you pay to secure your life cover and with-profits element, are mainly invested in stocks and shares. The payouts on life policies when there is a claim, or upon their maturity, are tax-free.

Guaranteed Income Bonds

These invest a lump sum for a set number of years, during which you receive a regular (guaranteed) monthly, quarterly or annual income. The fund pays tax but you don't. At the end of the day you get your capital back and, depending on the terms of your bond, possibly a share of any additional investment gain. But, be careful – if things don't go well your capital may have to be tapped into to make some of the guaranteed income payments so you may get less capital back at the end of the day than you put in at the start. Check the terms of your bond carefully before investing. The bad news for non-taxpayers thinking of investing in these is that they cannot reclaim tax paid by the fund!

Growth Bonds

Your lump sum is committed for a set number of years and the income earned on it is reinvested, in a variety of ways, to grow your capital faster. At the end of the day you should therefore receive a larger lump sum. Again the fund pays tax, but you don't.

Stock market or equity-linked growth bonds

A variety of investment bonds are offered, often by building societies, which promise to pay out at the end of a set period whatever percentage growth the stock market has seen over that time (as measured by one of the Stock Exchange indices). Usually there is an undertaking to pay a minimum return; e.g., your capital back plus another twenty-five per cent – and a method for 'smoothing' out any dramatic falls in stock market values during the final year. The money is not usually directly invested in the stock market but in a mixture of 'derivatives' that reflect market movements. Normally the fund is run for the building society by an international investment bank which gives the building society a guarantee that the fund will pay investors at least the promised minimum return at the end of the period.

Investor protection

Always check anyone giving you advice on investment or taking your money is legally authorised to do so by the appropriate regulator. If they are not, they are operating illegally – and you are not protected by the Investors Compensation Scheme (ICS) if there is a disaster caused by their inefficiency, failure, or fraudulence. The ICS repays up to ninety per cent (the maximum ceiling) of your money.

You can check their authorisation by ringing the central register run by the top financial watchdog, the Securities and Investments Board, on 0171 929 3652 or by dialling *SIB# on a Prestel terminal – or your local library or Citizens Advice Bureau may have one.

Insurance salesmen and tied agents are authorised by the firm they work for, and will only tell you about the products of that insurer or pensions firm – but must not sell you an unsuitable product (if they do you can unravel the deal). Independent financial advisers (IFAs) are not tied to any one product provider and must select the best example of the best kind of investment, to their knowledge, for you. From January 1995 all financial advisers, whether independent, tied, or in-house, must tell you what commission they are set to make from selling you the product concerned! And from mid-1995 all providers of financial products are supposed to tell you about how all their charges work.

If you have any complaints about a provider of personal financial advice or investment products, you should contact the Ombudsman of the Personal Investment Authority in London, which in July 1994 became the regulator that polices this area for the SIB. But if your complaint is about a stockbroker, you should contact the complaints bureau of their regulator, the Securities and Futures Authority.

Banks are governed by the Bank of England and the banking laws. Building societies are governed by the Building Societies Acts and overseen by the Building Societies Commission. There is a Banking Ombudsman scheme and a Building Societies Ombudsman, to whom you can turn if you have complaints. Banks and building societies all provide leaflets with details of how to do this, so ask for a copy at your branch. There is a compensation scheme for bank customers who suffer if a bank defaults.

Credit cards and other payment cards

Payment by plastic card has soared in popularity over the last decade. The best-known form of plastic card is the credit card which, like all the other types of card, is a convenient way to pay for goods, avoiding the need to carry lots of cash or to spend time writing out cheques. But unlike other payment cards, credit cards let you spread the cost of purchases over several weeks, months, or even years. In return, you pay interest on the amount borrowed.

Some card issuers also charge an annual fee for having the card, and a lower rate of interest; others charge no annual fee but tend to levy a higher rate of interest on credit balances. Some credit card issuers will waive their annual fee if you are a very big spender with their card (and keep to the rules of card use).

Credit cards are mostly provided by banks and building societies, who issue cards connected to either the VISA or Mastercard credit card operators.

A credit card allows the holder to buy goods and services on credit, up to a personal credit limit granted to you by the bank or building society that issued the card to you.

Each month you receive a statement showing your transactions and the total owing. You must pay off at least a minimum amount, shown on the statement (usually five per cent of the total borrowed at that point) but otherwise you can clear the balance as and when you like.

It's unwise to exceed your credit limit; your card issuer may decide to withdraw your right to use the card and demand repayment of the total amount owed.

Under the Consumer Credit Act, using a credit card also gives you certain additional consumer rights, explained on page 305.

Other types of plastic payment card include:

Storecards

These give you credit at a particular store or chain of stores.

Charge cards

These have a much higher spending limit than do credit cards, but the money spent using the card must be paid off in full every month. There is no interest cost (unless you fail to pay your bill on time) but there is a substantial annual fee for having the use of the card.

Examples include the green, gold and platinum series of American Express cards, and Diners Club cards. Some charge cards are issued by banks in the form of gold Mastercharge cards, which again should not be confused with credit cards. Charge cards are not covered by the Consumer Credit Act (see below), though some issuers (i.e., American Express) do in practice extend the same rights to users as if they were covered by the Act.

Debit cards

These are payment cards that behave like cheques; the money comes out of your account within a couple of days of the purchase made with the card. Debit cards either (so far) belong to the Switch system or the VISA Delta system (i.e., Barclays Connect card). Don't confuse a VISA Delta debit card with a credit card; debit cards are not covered by the Consumer Credit Act unless you were overdrawn (and in practice, this would normally be within an agreed overdraft) when you made a purchase. Under these circumstances, the Consumer Credit Act may apply!

Many cheque guarantee cards are three-in-one cards – functioning as either a Switch or a VISA Delta debit card in stores set up to take payment this way; as a cash card for withdrawing money from 'hole-in-the-wall' (automated teller) machines; and as a traditional cheque guarantee card.

How do credit card interest rates work?

You will be charged monthly interest on the amount you borrow on your credit card. Different card providers start the interest clock ticking at different stages. Some only charge interest on new borrowing from the monthly statement date, for instance, while others start racking up interest from the date of each purchase. Other card issuers wait until the date your next payment was due and only levy interest on the outstanding balance. But if you use your credit card for a cash withdrawal from a hole-in-the-wall machine, interest is usually always charged on the cash from the day it was withdrawn.

How do I compare credit cards for the best deal?

The various different combinations of annual fee, monthly charges and interest dates can be rather confusing for card users, and the only way to compare the true interest costs of different cards is to look at what each one's system of levying interest plus any annual fee works out at per year.

This is known as the annual percentage rate, or APR, and credit card users must tell you what their card's APR is as well as the monthly rate and the level of any annual fee. In late 1992 the major credit card issuers in the UK agreed to calculate their APRs in the same way, based on a £1000 credit limit, so that consumers really can compare cards.

The cheapest credit card on 1 June 1994 was a card with a £12 annual fee and an 0.95 per cent monthly interest rate, which worked out at an APR of 13.9 per cent on purchases – and at 15.4 per cent on cash withdrawals. This was cheaper than an overdraft at most banks at the time. But a more expensive card with £12 annual fee and a 1.6 per cent monthly charge, had an APR of 22.4 per cent on purchases and on cash withdrawals. Another card with no annual fee and a 1.6 per cent monthly interest rate levied from different start dates for purchases and cash, worked out at an APR of 20.9 per cent on purchases and at 22.9 per cent on cash withdrawals.

Borrowing for a whole year on these two cards was therefore more expensive at the time than having an overdraft for a year at some banks (depending on the individual bank's overdraft charges).

The exact cost of borrowing money on a credit card, however, depends on how long you take to pay off the balance.

If you use your card to buy Christmas presents, or a major holiday, clearing the balance within three or four months usually works out cheaper than using a bank overdraft for a few months. But if you expect to need longer to clear the balance, using a pre-arranged bank overdraft or even a one-year term loan (see *Borrowing*, page 292) to finance your purchases will probably cost you less interest in the end.

But if you usually owe money on your credit card for several months at a time, then you should choose one with a low monthly interest rate, to keep your interest bill as low

> **If you always clear the full amount shown on your statement every month, you should probably apply for a card that offers good perks. Many credit cards now offer 'points', awarded according to how much you use your card and how much you borrow on it; the points can be exchanged for a range of items from bottles of wine to discounts on buying certain cars.**

as possible. Many credit card issuers and some chargecard issuers, will provide free insurance against loss or damage to goods within the first 100 days of being bought with their card. This is a useful extra service. Many card issuers also offer other services to their customers, such as a travel agency.

What are my rights if I use a credit card?

Credit card agreements are regulated under the Consumer Credit Act 1974. You can end your credit card agreement any time you want by settling the amount owed and writing to cancel the agreement. If you change your mind soon after applying for the card, you have five days after signing the card agreement to cancel it in writing without incurring any costs, and if you repay any amounts already borrowed on the card before your first statement is due, or in instalments within a month of signing the agreement, you should not have to pay any interest.

Under Section 75 of the Act, if you paid for something worth at least £100 and up to £30,000 by credit card and the goods don't arrive or if the goods are defective, or not as the supplier claimed them to be, you can pursue either the supplier or the credit card issuer to get your money back. This is particularly useful if the supplier has gone bust. This applies even if you only paid part of the total by credit card. For example, if a tour operator goes under after you have paid by credit card for all or part of a holiday costing over £100, you can get your money back from your card issuer.

This is called 'connected' lending. The card issuers don't like this clause, but it is the law. In the past they have tried to wriggle out of it by refusing to meet claims from cardholders who've suffered misrepresentation or breach of contract by overseas suppliers of goods. However, in spring 1994, they had their knuckles rapped for this by the Director General of Fair Trading and were told that such refusals on their part were illegal. Never leave your card slips lying around for others to see your number. Keep them as your own record of the transaction. If you do use a credit card to order goods by phone,

> **When paying for expensive goods and services such as a holiday, Section 75 means you have more protection if you pay with your credit card than by cheque, cash, or charge card. So it's important to be sure the card you use really is your credit card rather than a bank-issued chargecard which may show a Mastercard symbol but does not come under the Consumer Credit Act. If using a different charge card, such as American Express, check first with that issuer whether it still follows a policy of extending this protection voluntarily to all its customers.**

make sure you're buying from a well-known, reputable supplier.

If your number is misused by someone else (or a fraudulent supplier) to buy other goods dishonestly, you could have difficulty proving to your card issuer that you had nothing to do with the transaction.

If you do have a dispute with your credit card provider, check your rights through your local trading standards officer or a Citizen's Advice Bureau, and enlist their help on your behalf. If you run into financial problems, don't put your credit card debts top of the list, and don't tackle your debts one by one. Credit card issuers can be very persistent but in fact these are not your most important debts – you can't lose your home over a credit card debt, for instance, as these are not 'secured' against it or any of your other vital assets. It's better to look at your whole debt problem and work out an overall strategy to tackle it. Do ask the Citizens Advice Bureau (CAB) for its free help in negotiating with all your lenders – they can often persuade lenders to agree terms to freeze the interest that would otherwise mount up, and let you repay the debts in regular small amounts for a long period of time.

Once you have struck a deal with a lender it's important to stick to it; if circumstances change, go back and renegotiate with all of them, again through a third party like the local

CAB, if you find that less stressful. (For more information, see page 296).

What happens if I lose my credit card?

Tell your card issuer at once if you lose your card; as soon as you have alerted them, you are only liable for the first £50 that is stolen with your credit card. Now the banks also extend this protection to three-in-one cheque guarantee, debit and cash cards that are genuinely stolen or misused.

It is a good idea to join one of the card protection services that card issuers will suggest to you – it only costs a few pounds a year to list all your credit card, storecard, debit and chargecard numbers with the one organisation. Then if any cards go missing, just one phone call to this service is all you need to make. It will advise the card issuers of each card's loss for you.

Mortgages

A mortgage is a loan secured against the property that you intend to buy with that loan. You pay regular interest, set at an annual rate, on the loan during its life, as well as eventually repaying the loan itself (the "capital").

Mortgages are normally lent for twenty or twenty-five years, but you don't have to stay in the same house for the whole time. When you sell up and move, the sale price of the home should repay the remaining loan (any profit left over is yours).

There are several types of mortgage to choose from, but all are based on one of two main varieties: repayment mortgages and interest-only mortgages.

Repayment mortgage

With a repayment mortgage, you pay off a combination of interest and capital each month, reducing the debt gradually until it is completely repaid.

Early on in a repayment mortgage's life, your monthly payment is mostly the interest on the debt, and very little goes towards repaying the capital. But as the interest

element is paid off, you gradually repay more and more of the capital. By the end of the term of the loan, every penny of capital has been cleared and all the interest has been paid, too.

Interest-only mortgages

With interest-only mortgages you only pay the lender's interest each month. Meanwhile, you put money into an investment plan that is intended to grow to repay the capital at the end of the period of the loan. The most popular version of an interest-only mortgage is an endowment mortgage.

Endowment mortgage

This is an interest-only loan linked to a special type of life assurance policy. As well as your monthly interest payment to your lender, you pay a smaller sum of money each month to the life assurer. This is the 'premium' which goes into an investment fund that grows. Your policy is designed to mature and pay out a lump sum at the same time as your loan falls due for repayment. Meanwhile, if disaster strikes and you die during the term of the mortgage, the life assurance company will pay off the loan completely so your family can afford to stay in the house.

You can choose either a unit-linked endowment policy or a with-profits endowment policy. With a unit-linked policy, if the investment fund grows faster than expected, you can use it to repay your mortgage early.

With a with-profits policy, the idea is that the fund should grow big enough to clear the loan at the end of the day and provide extra money (tax-free) as well. But there is an element of risk with both schemes, as you are relying on the expertise of others to make profits which they can share with you. Not

---

With a with-profits endowment, if money is tight later, you can borrow from the insurer against the surrender value of the policy. Or you may be able to sell the policy through a trader for more than its surrender value.

> **Consider taking out a cheap life policy as well as your PEP, to give your family a lump sum in the event that you die early.**

every company is successful in this and you should check how things are going as the mortgage nears the end of its life, just in case any top-up premiums are needed.

If you move and/or repay your loan, try to keep the endowment policy going as an investment – you will then collect the whole of its maturity value in due course. You get less value from an endowment cashed in early.

PEP mortgage

Interest-only mortgages can also be linked to a tax-free savings vehicle called a Personal Equity Plan, or PEP for short. This is known as a PEP mortgage. You pay interest each month to your mortgage provider and also put a monthly sum into a PEP looked after by an investment house. Here again the idea is that the plan should grow to repay the loan, and with luck, leave some money over for you, tax-free.

Pension mortgage

If you are in a pension plan you can use it to clear your mortgage. Pension plans guarantee you an income on retirement plus a tax-free lump sum. With a pension mortgage, you earmark the lump sum to repay the home loan.

You will not be able to touch the money in your pension fund until the plan matures, so if you are only twenty-five now, you would be paying the mortgage interest until sixty or sixty-five – that's for thirty-five or forty years! So pension mortgages are better suited to people over the age of forty who are sure they won't need the lump sum to supplement their pension.

Discount mortgage

Sometimes lenders will offer you a discount on the normal interest rate for the first year or more – for example, two per cent off.

During that time, whatever normal mortgage rates do, you will always be charged two per cent less. So if rates are eight per cent your loan will start at six. If rates rise to ten, yours will only go up to eight. When the time limit is up, your loan interest rises to the normal daily rate.

Capped mortgage

These loans have a ceiling limiting how much the interest rate on the loan can rise during an agreed period of time, for example five years.

Collared mortgage

These are home loans with a floor beneath which the interest rate charged will not fall during the agreed period. Often loans are Cap and Collar mortgages which have both a floor and a ceiling between which the loan rate can fluctuate but can't breach during the agreed period.

Currency mortgage

These are very risky because you are borrowing the money in one or more foreign currencies – which is fine if their interest rates are lower than ours. Currency mortgages are not a good idea if sterling suddenly falls in value against these currencies – you'll have to make up the shortfall or add it to your debt. The latter also means you have to pay more interest each month, and hope things will balance out later.

> **A currency mortgage may suit you if your earnings are also paid in the same foreign currency. But otherwise, steer clear.**

What about the interest rate?

Two main types of interest rates are offered, whatever kind of mortgage you choose. They are variable interest rates, and fixed interest rates.

Variable interest rates rise and fall in line with UK bank base rates – in other words, they vary. But in order to help homeowners keep track of what their payments will be, the

> **WARNING** Lenders offering special low-cost deals are allowed to tie you to their choice of insurer for the building and even your house contents.

rate on many variable rate loans only alters once a year. So with one of these annual or 'budget' mortgages, if UK interest rates fall, you must wait for a particular date to come round before your payments are reduced. But when rates rise, you also get the benefit of a delay before you have to pay more, giving you time to adjust your budget accordingly. **Fixed** interest rates are set at an unchanging rate for an agreed period of time, after which your mortgage moves on to a variable rate. Rates can be fixed for as little as a few months or as long as ten or even twenty years. The shorter the period the rate is fixed for, the lower the rate will usually be for that time.

The appeal of a fixed rate is that you know exactly what your monthly payments will be during the agreed period. But if you agree to a very long 'fix' and later change your mind, you can be charged a penalty for repaying the loan early, usually a set number of months in interest – so check the rules first!

A mortgage whose interest is fixed at a very low rate for one year gives first-time buyers a chance to recover from all the other expenses of moving before moving onto the higher, normal variable rate. These are known as low-cost, deferred or even starter mortgages. But make sure you will be able to afford the higher mortgage bill when the low-cost period is up.

Some mortgages are also 'portable' – meaning you can take that lender's loan with you to the new house, topping it up if need be, rather than clearing one loan and starting a new one. This can be very useful and save you quite a lot of expense.

Mortgage question and answers

Is there any tax relief?

You get tax relief on the interest on the first £30,000 of your mortgage. This is knocked

straight off your monthly payments by your lender, and is known as Mortgage Interest Relief At Source – or MIRAS for short. In 1994-95 MIRAS is granted at a twenty per cent tax rate but in 1995-96 it is scheduled to fall to just a fifteen per cent rate. This adds roughly £9.50 a month to your mortgage bills from Spring 1995.

How much can I borrow?

Your borrowing is based upon two things – the value of the house or flat for sale; and how much you earn.

The value of the home you want may turn out to be a bit different from the price the seller wants for it – which is why your lender insists that a surveyor checks the home out before it will make you a firm offer of a mortgage on that property.

If the asking price is more than the valuer says the home is worth, you may be refused a mortgage on that particular place. Or you may be offered a lower mortgage, in which case it's wise to ask if the seller will also accept less for it. Otherwise, house-hunt again for a better deal.

Few mortgage providers will lend you the full value of the home you buy (a hundred per cent loan). Most will lend a maximum of ninety or ninety-five per cent of its value, so you will need some savings for the balance, and also for the other costs involved in buying a home.

Your mortgage provider will lend you two-and-a-half and sometimes up to three times your annual earnings. This is the multiple. For a couple, this sum can be based on your joint annual income. So if one of you earns £20,000 a year and the other £10,000, you should be able to borrow at least £75,000 and possibly as much as £90,000, depending on which 'multiple' your lender uses.

A single person earning £20,000 a year could borrow at least £50,000 and possibly up to £60,000.

> **Most lenders will charge a lower interest rate on a loan which is a smaller percentage of the property's value.**

Lenders may ask to see payslips as proof of income. Only your guaranteed earnings may count, as bonuses tend to come and go. If you are self-employed, show them your accounts.

How do I know how much I can afford to borrow?

Before you even begin househunting, work out what you can afford to pay for a mortgage each month. Write down your monthly income. Then work out what you need to live on. To do this, write down your monthly spending on food, fares to work or any car costs – and include a monthly contribution towards each quarter's heating and phone bills, your water rates and council tax, TV rental (and licence). Do the same for newspapers, clothes, and nights out – but leave out any rent you currently pay as that will be replaced by your monthly mortgage payment. Add up all these and any other outgoings and subtract the result from your monthly income. The balance is what you can afford to spend on monthly mortgage payments. If it looks small, you can boost it by deciding to cut back a bit on luxuries. Try not to budget all the fun out of your life or you won't enjoy your new home.

Where do I go for my mortgage?

You can get a mortgage from a building society, or from a bank's mortgage division. Some friendly societies are also moving into home loans. You don't already have to be a saver or account holder with any of these to ask a lender about a mortgage, but it may help, as they will know how well you handle your money. Ask a mortgage broker or even a solicitor to help you find you a good deal with a suitable lender.

What other costs are involved?

Quite early on, you will have to pay the valuer's fee on the home you hope to buy, plus the fee for any more detailed, structural survey that you may decide to have undertaken. It's usually more economical to pay the valuer for the more detailed survey, but do check by shopping around beforehand.

As you get closer to finalising the purchase, you will be asked to pay a deposit – usually around five per cent but possibly up to ten per cent of the purchase price – on the house. This is due once your offer to buy has been formally accepted, legal checks have been carried out, and contracts are on the point of being exchanged.

> **If the home you want costs £50,000, you will need at least £2,500 handy to pay the deposit, and about the same again for all your survey, legal and moving-in bills. That means you need at least £5,000 in savings or other financial help, plus the difference between the mortgage and the property's price.**

Exchange of contracts and the payment of a deposit mean you and the seller are committed to going ahead with the deal. It may take another four weeks for the deal to be completed (although technically it can be done in days), and then you can move in.

If you are borrowing more than seventy-five per cent of the value of the home, be prepared for the lender to ask you to pay a mortgage indemnity premium (see page 311) upon 'completion' of the purchase.

Once the deal is done, you will get your lawyer's bill, which will include the fees for the searches he has to do, to check that nothing drastic is planned for the building or the area, and for registering the change of ownership.

As soon as you own the property, it's up to you insure the fabric of the building – which your lender will also insist upon. It's wise also to insure the contents of your home (see page 311). Some lenders will give you 'cash back' out of your loan towards your legal fees, moving-in costs, and even new furnishings, but that also means you pay interest on this money, so it's cheaper to use your own cash if you can. Find out if any of your family are flush enough to lend – or give! – you a helping hand. Gifts of up to £3000 can be tax-free, and more if they are wedding presents (see page 343).

Insurance

Insurance is designed to protect the insured against the unexpected. You cannot insure against the inevitable. Even certain life policies have a maturity date on which you collect the accrued money – and you don't have to die to benefit from the premiums paid (see Savings, page 300).

You can however insure against the unexpected occurrence, in your life, of most things.

Insurance policies may provide long-term cover, or be brief one-off things like insuring the village fête against being rained off on that day (called pluvius insurance, after the Latin for rain). Specialist cover is also available against the wrong kind of weather wrecking sporting events; and parents and schools can buy insurance protection for children against sporting or other accidents, for instance.

If you want to find out if cover is available for something, however unusual, ask an insurance broker for help. They can arrange most sorts of specialist cover. If you are a budding pianist, you can insure your hands against injury, for example. An insurance broker will happily shop around for your more normal insurance requirements, too.

But for home, contents and motor policies, you may find that you can also get cheap cover through some of the 'direct' (telephone-based) insurance companies that have developed recently. The advantage of these is that one phone call can be all it takes to arrange insurance cover without delay, and claims are handled quickly by phone as well.

If you approach a big general insurer for a quote, rather than going through a broker, it is worth asking them to register you as a 'direct customer' – which means you should get the percentage of your premium that's normally allocated to the insurance broker's commission knocked off the cost.

Insuring your home

Though we all know storms happen, we don't, for example, go round expecting a tree to fall through the attic. So if you own your home, insure the 'fabric' of the building against natural and other disasters.

> **WARNING Never make a false or exaggerated insurance claim. If you are caught out, this will invalidate the genuine part of your claim and your insurer will be entitled to refuse to pay out a penny for any of it. Insurers watch like hawks for any sign of 'dodgy' claims.**

Then, if trouble strikes, you can claim on the insurance for the funds to put it right. If you are a tenant, the building should be insured by your landlord, but you will need to buy cover for your own possessions.

If you have a mortgage on your home, your lender will insist that the fabric of the building is insured, from the date of completion of your purchase. Some low-cost starter mortgages may be conditional upon you taking out a buildings policy with the lender's choice of insurer (and on which the lender receives a commission). So check the premiums before you accept the mortgage.

Once the low-cost period of the loan is over you should be free to switch to another insurer, so shop around nearer that time for cheaper comparable cover. But the new policy you pick must still be acceptable to your lender. And check if your lender charges a one-off administration fee – for example, £20 or £30 – for the 'inconvenience' and loss of commission it suffers when you switch insurers. Standard loans leave the choice of insurer up to you.

Buildings cover is renewed annually. To buy cover, you pay a premium each year. This can be a once-a-year bill at the start of each insured period; or you may be able to opt to pay by monthly instalments (which may cost a little bit of interest in return for the extra time to pay). The amount of your premiums will reflect rebuilding costs, and how prone your area is to flooding, or subsidence, for example. Some insurers have started to offer policies that exclude cover for things that never happen in a particular area, which can make the policy cheaper. But be careful – the unexpected may still happen! Many insurance companies provide helplines for customers to call for advice in an emergency and which can put you instantly in touch with approved local builders, glazers, plumbers or electricians. Some also provide legal advice helplines.

From time to time, check that your level of buildings cover is still keeping pace with the market value of your home, and rebuilding costs. Your insurer should advise you on this.

> **If your house ever has to be underpinned for subsidence caused by dry weather, or mining, you may find that while your current insurer will still cover it, anyone to whom you try to sell the home may have trouble getting insurance for it. This will make your home almost impossible to sell to anyone needing a mortgage. But specialist cover may be available through the Subsidence Advisory Bureau in Bexhill-on-Sea.**

Mortgage indemnity cover

If you are buying a house, you may be asked to pay for a Mortgage Indemnity Policy or MIP for short. This is an insurance policy that your lender is legally required to arrange on loans exceeding seventy-five per cent of the value of the property. It protects the lender's deposit-account customers if the lender has to repossess your home and cannot sell it for as much as is still owed on it. But you, the borrower, have to pay for it.

However, there is just one single premium, paid right at the start of your mortgage. It's levied as a percentage of the difference in money terms between seventy-five per cent of the value of the home and the actual percentage that you borrow.

For example, on a £50,000 house a seventy-five per cent loan would be £37,500 and a ninety-five per cent loan would be £47,500. The MIP premium for the ninety-five per cent loan is levied at seven per cent of the £10,000 difference – and costs you £700. Your lender may let you add this to your total loan, but if you do that you'll also be paying interest on it for the life of the mortgage. So it's cheaper to use cash or savings if you can.

Contents insurance

Whether you own or rent your home, it is always wise to insure the possessions you keep there, as replacements can be expensive. This is generally referred to as contents cover. (Some low-cost mortgages may also specify a contents insurer for the low-cost period, in which case remember to budget for that cost as well when comparing loans.)

Contents cover is renewed annually. The annual insurance premium – which can be paid monthly – reflects the area you live in and how common crimes like burglary are in that area, as well as your own past claims record. Often premium bands are set according to your post code.

The cost will also reflect whether you are buying cover to replace items 'as new' or at their estimated value at the time of the loss or damage to them. Replacement as new is usually a good idea or you could find yourself out of pocket when trying to replace expensive burgled electrical items, for instance.

Contents cover is available either on your own room-by-room estimate of what your possessions are worth, or as 'bedroom-based' cover. The latter usually provides £30,000-£35,000 worth of cover for a home with up to four bedrooms and can work out cheaper even if your home has only two bedrooms, than the room-by-room method of insuring.

But if you have very few possessions, or lots of very valuable items, then room-by-room cover may be better value for you. If you can choose your own cover, ask insurers for quotes on both types of cover before you decide.

Your insurer will usually ask you to specify individual items worth over a particular value – jewellery, for example. If you do not list these individually, you could find that you cannot claim for their full value if they are stolen or damaged.

The other thing to watch out for is whether or not your policy covers accidental damage to your possessions in your home – this means things like the toddler smashing the TV screen, or you dropping a hammer in the sink while doing a spot of DIY. Not all of them do.

Your insurer is entitled to insist that your doors and windows have proper locks of a particular type. After paying a claim, they may require you to increase your security before they will continue your cover.

Always read your policy documents and if you are not clear exactly what is or isn't covered, ask your insurer to clarify any of those areas to you. House and contents insurance policies do not normally include the cost of replacing damaged or stolen garden plants and trees, though sheds, fences, garden equipment and some patio plants in pots may be covered. Check with your insurer just what is and isn't covered by your policy before you need to make any storm damage or theft claims. One way to discourage light-fingered garden and household thieves is to surround your home with hedges of very prickly plants – this can be quite a deterrent – and always keep garages and sheds locked up. Otherwise, not only may expensive garden equipment go missing but your ladder may be used by a burglar to gain access to an open upstairs window.

Can I get a discount?

Yes. Discounts may be available if you do additional things to protect your home. For instance, some insurers will give you a discount of around five per cent if you join the local neighbourhood watch. Others will reduce your premiums if you have fitted a smoke alarm – apparently statistics show that people who fit these tend to be good at locking up their homes properly and not leaving clues that the place is empty when they're away!

Fitting a burglar alarm of a make approved by your insurer can sometimes knock up to fifteen per cent off your premiums. There are also discounts for older residents – passing your fiftieth birthday for instance. Some insurers offer graded discounts from age thirty-five! So ask your insurer if they do this. The idea is that the older you are the more care you tend to take to protect your home and its contents.

Another way to keep the cost down is to agree to an 'excess'. This means you agree to meet the first part of any claim yourself, which earns you a discount on your

> **If one of you stops work and is likely to be at home a lot in the day, ask your insurer if that also qualifies you for a discount. You may find it does. Keeping a dog does not usually qualify for a discount, but it's always worth enquiring.**

premiums. A £100 excess means you'll pay the first £100 of any claim – which can earn you as much as fifteen per cent off some contents policies. The higher the excess, the cheaper the premium for your cover should get.

Working from home & insurance

If you work from home, do tell your insurer or your normal household insurance may be completely void – even if you have a normal burglary and only lose household or personal items.

This is because running a business from home can mean a higher risk of theft or accident – if lots of people you don't know well are coming in and out, for instance, and seeing what's in your home.

For an extra premium you can add your work equipment to your household cover, but it may be cheaper to take out a special policy for those items. If you have any staff working for you the law requires you to have public liability cover to protect them, or any customers coming to the house, should something happen to them while on the premises.

An insurance broker will help you find inexpensive, specialist cover for small businesses that includes all the insurances that you must legally have.

Motor insurance

If you own or drive a car you must by law be insured to do so. It is an offence to drive without having this cover and a valid driving licence. You can have your own policy, or you may be a 'named' driver on someone else's policy, which means you are insured to drive that particular car.

Motor cover is either third party, fire and theft, or comprehensive cover. Third party, fire and theft meets the minimum legal requirement to protect other people, other vehicles and any property damaged as a result of your car being involved in an accident. You are not covered for repairs to, or the replacement of, your own car if it is damaged or wrecked beyond repair in an accident.

But your own car is covered for damage resulting from theft, or fire other than a fire caused by the road accident you are in. If your car just catches fire of its own accord, or is burnt in, say, a forecourt fire, it's insured (but not if you deliberately torch it yourself!). Replacement of a shattered windscreen is not usually covered but can often be added to a third party, fire and theft policy if you ask.

Comprehensive cover does protect your own vehicle as well as other parties, and it costs more. As well as all the events described above, comprehensive cover insures your personal belongings that are in the car – but only up to a limited, specified value – and some personal accident, injury and death cover for you and your spouse, plus limited medical expenses. Damaged windscreens are included, and if your car is less than a year old and repairs will be very expensive, the insurer will replace the car with a new one.

The younger a driver is, and the sportier the car, the more their motor insurance will cost. This is because older drivers and more sedate cars tend to be involved in fewer accidents. Once a driver is over twenty-five, their insurance premiums should become lower.

What about learner drivers?

Learners using a driving school car will come under the school's insurance but if they are learning or practising on someone else's car, they come under that car owner's policy. So if your policy only covers named drivers, you need to add the learner on to it or they will not be insured if something goes wrong.

If your policy covers any driver, the learner is covered – but it is wise to tell your insurer all the same. Some insurers may refuse to pay up if an accident is caused by a learner, rather than by someone else driving in to them.

For a learner driver, and often also for anyone up to age thirty, insurers will usually specify an excess (for example, £250) which the policy holder must pay in the event of any claim before the insurer picks up the rest of the bill.

Once your learner has passed their driving test, it may be cheaper to buy a young driver in your family an old banger and help him or her with the cost of insuring it in their own name, than it costs to add them to the insurance policy on the family car. This way the young driver also starts to build up their own no-claims record with an insurer, cutting their future premiums down dramatically once they get to twenty-five.

What's a no-claims bonus?

Drivers who have not had to claim against their insurance build up a 'no-claims bonus', which provides a rising, and ultimately substantial, discount on their car insurance premiums. If you make a claim, you lose your no-claims bonus.

For a small extra premium, it is often possible to take out additional cover with your motor insurer that protects your no-claims bonus! Then if you do make a claim, you don't lose the valuable discount that you've built up over the years.

If you have had a lot of claims, endorsements or even had your licence taken away for a time for an offence (and now have it back), or drive a very sporty car, the new 'direct' motor insurers may be able to help you return to the road.

> **Statistics show that women are more cautious, and less accident-prone, drivers than men so women tend to be charged lower motor premiums. But recent studies suggest that, after age thirty-five, women's claims record rises – not because the women start to have more accidents, but because their teenage kids borrow mum's car rather than dad's and are more likely to become involved in an accident!**

Some now offer special cover for 'hard to insure' drivers who would not be able to get insurance from a standard provider of motor cover, or could only get cover at a very high price. Even so, it still costs more than normal cover – but then you are also a higher risk for the insurance company. Without at least third party, fire and theft insurance you cannot legally drive on public roads.

Motoring abroad

If you are taking your car abroad you must get insurance to drive in that country. If you are hiring a vehicle abroad this should be available through the hire company. You need a valid driving licence – this usually means taking your national licence to somewhere like an AA shop to get an international licence as well. If you are going to take your own car to Europe, ask your own motor insurer for a 'green card'. If you drive a company car, ask your company for the green card supplied by its insurer. The green card extends your UK cover to the European Union country in which you plan to drive, protecting any third parties or vehicles involved in an accident with you. Take your vehicle registration document with you, too.

In Spain, you will need a 'bail bond' – again ask your insurer about this.

You should also take out additional insurance to give you breakdown, personal accident and medical cover, and general cover for your possessions during your travels abroad.

Travel insurance

When you go away it is wise to take out travel cover for the area to which you're going, and the duration of the trip. Typical travel insurance packages include medical expenses cover – medical costs can be very high overseas especially in the USA – accident cover, payments if you lose a limb or an eye, or are killed, repatriation costs, third-party cover if something you do injures someone else or damages property, and basic insurance for your possessions and money.

These policies usually also insure against expensive delays in your journey, and cancellation for a range of reasons listed in the policy (other than you just changing your mind). They will exclude certain activities – dangerous sports, for example – so if you are going skiing, or bungee jumping, make sure you take out special ski or otherwise appropriate cover.

Some policies also cover a certain amount of legal costs and assistance – if you become involved in a court case overseas as the result of an accident, for example.

If you are going to Europe, fill in form E111 (ask for it at the Post Office) which extends your British NHS cover to the country you're in, and get it stamped at the Post Office. In some countries, treatment will be free on production of the form. Others will still charge you but you can claim the cost back from the DHS when you get home. Always keep receipts for any medication or medical charges. Even with Form E111, it's still wise to have travel cover as well.

Health cover

There are various kinds of insurance available to protect you against the costs of falling ill. They should really be regarded as part of your long-term financial planning, when you are considering your savings and investment plans.

They vary from inexpensive Hospital Cash Plans, which pay you a set amount of money per night in any hospital, to full Private Medical Insurance (PMI) which pays for private hospital treatment including surgeons' fees, medication and dressings, and so on.

PMI is different from Permanent Health Insurance (PHI) which is designed to pay you an income for the amount of time you are off sick or are incapacitated. This protects you and your family from having nothing with which to pay the mortgage, for example.

In fact, your mortgage lender may ask you to take out a very basic Mortgage Protection Policy that will pay your mortgage in case of sickness, or of redundancy. These policies are very cheap, at a few pounds a month, and sensible to have – especially if you are an employee. But read the small print to find out what they exclude and when as they are not always as good as they sound.

Paying for redundancy cover is pointless for a self-employed person – these policies exclude the self-employed! But you could still use cover which guarantees to meet your mortgage payments, or a PHI policy to provide you with an income, if you become too ill to work. Always check the small print to make sure you know exactly which circumstances and illnesses are not covered as well as which are.

You can top up your insurances with Critical Illness Cover. These policies insure you if you go down with one of a list of incapacitating illnesses or heart conditions, for example. Some pay an income, others a lump sum that you can take when the illness is diagnosed, to use as best suits your situation. It is even possible to get cover against developing AIDS in certain circumstances.

Life cover

Life assurance is also really part of your long-term financial planning. There are two main types – life policies that are also investment vehicles, building up a lump sum by a set maturity date. These are 'with profits' or 'unit linked' endowments, often linked to mortgage deals, which will pay up if you die during the term of the policy – clearing the loan or (if not attached to the mortgage) providing your bereft family with capital. If you live, they run to maturity and will pay out the proceeds upon the date fixed at the outset.

If all you want is cheap cover to give your family a lump sum if you die early, but are not interested in the savings element, you want 'whole life' cover. The premiums on this are much lower than for endowment policies.

If you have a family and your mortgage is not an endowment-linked one, it is a good idea for both parents to have some 'whole life' cover to give the family a capital sum if one of you dies leaving the other to cope with raising the children alone.

Whole life cover can also be a way of leaving your family money without incurring inheritance tax problems, as there is not normally any tax to pay on the proceeds of an insurance policy (though higher-rate taxpayers may in certain circumstances find they do have to make up the difference between basic rate tax and their own tax rate).

But if you have no family likely to be in need of cash upon your sudden demise, you're better off saving money towards your own future.

There are also 'term' policies, which just provide life cover for a fixed period; i.e., ten years. If you die in that time, the policy pays up. But if you outlast the policy, it expires and there is no payment to you. Term policies are sometimes used to provide cover for a fixed-term bank loan, so that if you drop dead the loan is cleared. They can also be used as ways to leave money tax-free – but only if you actually die within the term of the policy! So if you live longer than you expected, you may end up taking out a series of these policies.

> **If you have a complaint about an insurance company and are getting nowhere, you can contact the Insurance Ombudsman's offices in London. Your insurer should provide details of the scheme if asked, or call directory inquiries.**

Pensions

A pension plan is a savings scheme that will provide you with a regular income to live on after you retire from full-time work. There are different types of pension schemes, and the law concerning how pension funds are administered is being revised in the wake of scandals in the recent past. This section outlines the pension system but, as with any investment, pension planning is a very personal matter and it's always wise to consult a properly authorised financial advisor about what's best for you. Retirement may be a lifetime away, but it is important to feel comfortable that you will have anough to live on when you are less able to look after yourselves. It's also nice to think you'll have enough money to have a bit of fun when you are older. These days, pensioners are doing everything from walking in the Himalayas to taking up sailing and martial arts.

The state pension

Everybody who works and pays either Class 1 National Insurance (NI) contributions or Class 2 contributions (paid by the self-employed), is building up a basic state pension that will be paid to you weekly from the state retirement age.

Not all your NI contributions are pension contributions; some of the money goes towards your entitlement for other benefits – which is also why the self-employed, who don't qualify for unemployment benefit for example, pay less NI.

The state retirement age is changing – from being sixty for women and sixty-five for men, women's retirement age is to be brought up to sixty-five, to make it the same for both men and women. The change is being phased in steadily from the year 2010, when women

born between 6 April 1950 and 5 May 1951 will find they have to work an extra month, to age sixty years and one month, before collecting their pensions. The phasing-in continues like this in stages until, by March 2020, women born after 5 March 1955 must wait to reach 65 before they can collect their state pensions. (See how this might affect you from the table on page 317.)

People earning less than what's known as the 'lower earnings limit' don't pay any NI and are not building up a state pension. There are situations in which NI contributions are automatically credited to your pension record – for example, for people on some state benefits, and those born after 5 April 1957 who were still at school between sixteen and nineteen years old or while they were at training college.

To get the full basic state pension at sixty-five you will need to have built up an NI contributions record for ninety per cent of your working life. That's set at forty-four 'qualifying' years, or thirty-nine years if you are a woman still able to retire at sixty (i.e., retiring before 2010). Otherwise you will end up with a reduced basic state pension calculated on the percentage of your potential working life in which you actually paid NI contributions. But you are allowed to plug gaps in your NI record with voluntary Class 3 contributions to beef up your basic state pension entitlement.

The basic state pension is not very big. It aims at paying about a quarter of a single person's national average earnings, but in future may not work out at even that much. So if you can put more aside, it's wise to do so. If you decide to go on working after retirement age, you can opt to defer drawing your state pension for up to five years after that. Additional pension benefits may accrue during that time, without you having to make any extra NI contributions.

What are the arrangements for married women?

Married women can either qualify for a state pension through their own NI contributions record if they worked, or may draw a pension based on their husband's contributions.

> **To check how your NI record stands and what level of pension you'll get, go to your local Social Security or Benefits Office for Form BR19. Filling in and returning this will get you a state pension forecast.**

> **Although your outgoings fall once you retire, to maintain your quality of life you'll probably need a pension income that's a good two-thirds of your old salary.**

The latter means that once he has retired and the wife is already over (or once she reaches) what would have been her own retirement age, she can receive a state pension worth approximately sixty per cent of the value of his basic pension.

By the time you read this, changes in legislation may have made pensions part of the marital assets in a divorce. If this has not yet happened, you should still ask for the value today of any pensions belonging to your estranged spouse (to which you might lose your share of any entitlement after the divorce) to be taken into account in reaching your financial settlement. Either way, if you are divorcing, make sure your lawyer looks into this area for you.

New state retirement age for women

Use these examples, compiled from lists published by the Department of Social Security, to work out how the change may affect you.

Date of birth:	New pension age:	Pension starts:
6.4.50	60 yrs 1 ms	6.5.2010
6.5.50	60 yrs 2 ms	6.7.2010
6.6.50	60 yrs 3 ms	6.9.2010
6.12.50	60 yrs 9 ms	6.9.2011
6.3.51	61 yrs	6.3.2012
6.12.51	61 yrs 9ms	6.9.2013
6.6.52	62 yrs 3ms	6.9.2014
6.1.53	62 yrs 10 ms	6.11.2015
6.3.53	63 yrs	6.3.2016
6.12.53	63 yrs 9 ms	6.9.2017
6.1.54	63 yrs 10 ms	6.11.2017
6.3.54	64 yrs	6.3.2018
6.12.54	64 yrs 9 ms	6.9.2019
6.2.54	64 yrs 11 ms	6.1.2020
6.3.55	65 yrs	6.3.2020

The state earnings-related pension scheme

This is known as SERPS, for short, and is an extra state pension that can be built up by employees through their Class 1 National Insurance. SERPS is designed to bring your pension income a bit closer to the level of your earnings in the final stages of your working life.

Companies must also pay NI contributions on behalf of their staff, but not all companies choose to contract into the additional SERPS system. If your company is in the SERPS system, you will pay a higher level of Class 1 National Insurance than if you were only contributing to the basic state pension.

> **At present men within five years of retirement age who have already stopped working, for whatever reason, are automatically credited with NI payments which protect their pension entitlement at sixty-five. The plan is to extend the same arrangement to women aged between sixty and sixty-five in due course.**

It's important to realise that Class 3 NI payments only top up your basic state pension and don't count towards SERPS.

If your company is not in SERPS, the rules that let it contract out of the state system ensure that it must provide a company pension at least as good as its staff would have received from SERPS. Many companies do opt out of SERPS. You have the right to opt out of their company plan and take out your own personal pension plan instead, in hope of increasing your income after retirement that way. But this is not always advisable as the company scheme does have to beat SERPS, whereas there is no guarantee that the personal plan you pick will do so.

If your firm remains in SERPS, you also have the right to contract out of that part of the state scheme yourself, in preference to a personal pension plan. All personal pension plans are automatically outside SERPS but if you ever look likely to be worse off this way, you do have the right to contract back into SERPS.

Any pension adviser who suggests you switch to a personal plan must now show you written comparisons of what you stand to gain or lose by leaving either a SERPS or a non-SERPS company scheme. If you go ahead, your new pension provider should also alert you if they ever think changing circumstances mean you might be better off contracting back into SERPS. If in doubt at any stage, ask for the SERPS position to be checked again.

Company pensions versus personal pension schemes

Many companies do provide a pension scheme for their employees.

This may be a contributory scheme – into which you make some payments (this is as well as your Class I NI contributions to your basic state pension) – or a non-contributory one, in which case only the company puts money into the pension scheme.

You get tax relief on any payments you make to a company pension scheme, or to a personal pension plan. But the tax does not come back into your paypacket – it is rebated to your pension and adds to the growing retirement fund you are building up. You get tax relief at your top tax rate; so pension contributions are a very tax-effective way to save.

Company schemes can be 'final pay' schemes or 'money purchase' schemes. Final pay schemes provide a pension that takes into account both the length of time you've been in the plan, and what your salary has risen to by the time you retire. For instance, a good scheme might pay you a pension of one-sixtieth of your final year's salary multiplied by the number of years you've worked for the firm. (Forty years service at one-sixtieth, would give you an annual pension worth two-thirds of your final year's salary.)

'Salary' can include overtime, bonuses, commissions. It all depends on the terms of the particular scheme. With a final pay scheme, you will be able to work out how much pension you can expect to get.

You may come across an 'average pay' scheme. This is just like a final pay scheme except that the calculation is based on a proportion of what your pay averaged during your time at the firm rather than on what it reached by the end of it.

> **Final pay schemes work out better for people who stay with the same employer a long time, than for those who move around a lot.**

With a money purchase scheme, the pension fund that has accrued in your name is used to buy an annuity that then pays you an income for life. So how much you get, depends on how much you and your employer have paid into the scheme, how well the fund has been invested, and how good an annuity the proceeds can buy. This means you don't really know for sure, in advance, what your pension income will be. But on the other hand, changing your job has less impact on a money purchase scheme than on a final salary one.

Some employers offer a mixture of a final pay scheme and a money purchase one.

How much can I put into a pension scheme?

There are strict rules about how much of your earnings you can put aside into your company or personal pension fund each year. For a start, all pension contributions have to be made out of earned, taxable income. So if you are not working, you cannot make pension contributions.

However, there are rules that do allow you to bring recent years' contributions up to the permitted limit for each of those years, so when you have any spare cash you may find you can improve your pension prospects that way. A pensions expert can advise you on the latest rules.

Employees can put in a slightly smaller percentage of their income into a company fund than people with a personal plan. In both cases, the amounts you can put in rise in stages with your age. In 1994-95 for instance, employees under thirty-five could put fifteen per cent of their taxable earnings into their company pension plan, whereas someone under the age of thirty-five with a personal plan – for instance a self-employed person – could put in 17.5 per cent.

Since your earnings may also rise as you get older and climb the business ladder, this should mean the value of your fund grows faster as you grow older.

Most company schemes do not take the full allowance out of your earnings to put into the pension plan, particularly as the company is also contributing something to the plan. So employees are free to make 'additional voluntary contributions' to take their pension provisions up to the limit if they wish. These are known as AVC in pension jargon.

There are two types:

- AVCs that go into an AVC scheme provided by the company.
- Freestanding AVCS.

If the company has an AVC scheme, that's where any AVCs you pay must go.

But if it hasn't, then you are free to pay Freestanding AVCS (or FAVCs) into a personal pension plan of your own choosing. You'll probably need a pensions expert to help you pick the best one out of all the available plans.

> **You cannot be in a company pension scheme and start a personal pension as well, unless you have extra earnings from some other activity, or are paying into an FAVC scheme.**

So what about a personal pension plan?

If your company does not provide a company scheme, or you want to opt out of the one it does offer (perhaps because you are in the kind of work that involves frequent job moves), or if you are self-employed, you can start your own pension plan. You can transfer money built up in company schemes that you have belonged to in the past, to a personal pension plan (or to your current company's scheme if it accepts transfers).

Be very careful to get a proper written comparison of what pension is forecast by the old fund and what the new fund says it can provide, before you decide whether to make a transfer. You may be better off leaving the money where it is, especially if it's in a fund to which your old company contributed a lot. There are strict formulae for these forecasts, and no financial adviser or salesman should try to persuade you to do this without providing written comparisons for you to study.

All personal pension plans are money purchase schemes (explained above) and, if you wish, you can take twenty-five per cent of the fund as a tax-free lump sum when the maturity date is reached. Personal pensions can be more flexible than company schemes in that you can tailor your retirement date to suit yourself – if you want to retire at fifty, for instance. If you then decide to go on working, you can extend your pension planning.

Personal pension plans can also be timed to mature when, for example, an interest-only mortgage is due for repayment, as you could use the lump sum element towards clearing the loan. If you are using your pension for this sort of additional financial planning, however, it is wise to take advice about financing your general plans for the future as well.

There are hundreds of personal pension plans to choose from, provided by insurance companies, investment groups and fund management houses, and your bank or building society almost certainly offers a pension plan, too.

To cope with the maze of choice, it may be better to take advice from an authorised independent financial adviser – rather than a tied agent or salesman from just one provider – who specialises in pensions and who can suggest which of the many plans available looks right for you.

Making a will

There's no point in being superstitious about making a will – it won't send you on your way any faster and if you don't make one, the result could be that your money speeds its way to someone you never meant to get it –

or worse, to the Treasury when it could at least have gone to a worthy charity!

What happens if I don't make a will?

If you die without making a will – called dying 'intestate' – your money and assets (your 'estate') are divided up according to a set of rules spelt out in the Administration of Estates Act.

For example, here's what happens to the estates of people who normally lived in England or Wales, wherever they died (though if they also owned property abroad, foreign law comes into play with regard to those assets).

For married couples, when one dies intestate, and everything (home, money and possessions) totals under £125,000, the whole lot goes to the surviving spouse. (This ceiling may change in future Budgets.) If there are children, they don't get a penny unless the estate is worth (at the time of writing) more than £125,000, in which case they do get something.

First that £125,000 is still due to the surviving spouse, along with the house's contents and the deceased's personal effects. (If the house alone is worth more than £125,000 the spouse is not always entitled to keep the house itself.)

The rest is divided into two equal parts of which one is divided equally between the children. If they are under eighteen, the assets concerned or proceeds of them, are held in trust for them until their respective eighteenth birthdays.

The other half of what's left over is held in trust for the surviving spouse during the rest of his or her lifetime – but he or she can only receive the income from it. The money or

assets themselves – the capital – will finally go to the children when the second parent dies.

If there are no children, and the estate is worth more than £125,000, things are a bit different. Then, the first £200,000 is earmarked for the widow or widower plus the house's contents and the deceased's personal effects. Then half of the rest of the estate also goes to the widow or widower, and the remainder is split between either the deceased's surviving parents or, if they too are no longer alive, any brothers and sisters of the deceased who are still living. If there are none, then the widow or widower gets the lot.

If you were not married when you died intestate but did have children, all your property will go equally to your children (including stepchildren or adopted children) or on down to their respective children. If you die single and without children, it is split evenly between your parents if they are still living. If they are no longer around, the estate is split between your brothers and sisters. If you were an only child or your siblings are also dead, then the estate reverts to the other branches of the family tree. First, any surviving grandparents you have will share the loot. But if they are dead, the next in line are your aunts and uncles or, failing them, their children or, on down the line, their children's children.

But if none of your grandparents' direct descendants are left, then more distant cousins don't get a look-in. The estate goes to the Crown.

So, if you are living with someone but are not married to them, they get nothing at all if you die without having made a will.

If you are divorced and have not made a new will since your change of status, your estate is also treated as if you had died intestate. In a family tragedy, if a couple both die, say in an accident, without having made a will, all the money is held in trust for their children until they are eighteen and there are very strict rules about how it can be invested meanwhile.

If you have not said who is to be guardian of the children in such an event, there can be bitter family arguments about who brings them up. Worse, the children could end up in care even if there are relatives who would

> **The sequence of delegating an estate means a favourite item among your personal effects that you might have liked to hand on to a particular child of yours, will first go direct to your spouse – who may not be aware of your wishes and who may in turn decide to leave it to someone else altogether.**

like to give them a home. So it's very important that you do specify a guardian for them when you make your will – 'a testamentary guardian' – to avoid further upset if the worst does happen. The guardian does not need to be the same person as the executor of your will.

Can I draw up my own will?

Yes, if your estate and bequests are very simple and don't involve things like foreign property, family trusts, a family business, and if you have not made any large gifts in your lifetime to family or friends. Will forms are available from legal stationers.

But do make sure you pay attention to detail when you fill one in, and word your bequests very precisely – for example, not just saying 'I leave all my money to....' if by that you also mean your house, and some stocks and shares, for example. Specify each type of asset, saving or investment even if they are all going to the same person. Otherwise, things could unravel badly after your demise.

Another important thing to know is that whomever you name as an executor of the will can also be a beneficiary, but the witnesses cannot be.

You need two witnesses, both of whom must witness your signature to the will in each other's presence – not on separate occasions, or even in different rooms. If this is not adhered to the will is void, and your estate is treated as if you had died intestate.

If you make any inserts, crossings-out or alterations to the document, make sure you and both witnesses also initial each change; and all three of you should also initial every page in each other's presence. Failing to do this could invalidate the entire will.

Professional executors will charge for the job and their bill comes out of your estate! Some banks' charges for this work are pretty high. So if your estate is not large, appoint a sensible, competent friend or relation as your executor(s).

Make sure your completed and properly witnessed will is kept in a safe place and that you leave a note amongst your general papers about where it is or who has it. You can lodge it at your bank, for example.

It's a good idea to name two executors – but you can't have more than four – to share the work of administering your estate. It's best (but not necessary) to ask them first if they are happy to named as executors, and it's a nice gesture to leave them a little something as a thank-you for doing the job, if they are not already on your list of beneficiaries. They can be family members or friends, or you might prefer to name your solicitor or accountant or even your bank.

Is it wiser to use a solicitor to make my will?

Frankly, yes. And if you are leaving money in trust to children aged under eighteen, it is essential that you get a lawyer to draw up the details. Then if there is a cock-up, your heirs can at least sue the solicitor (or try to). If your estate is complicated by ownership of shares in a family business, property abroad, if you want to set up trusts for any of the beneficiaries – or if you want to do any tax planning today that can reduce the risk of inheritance tax being levied on your estate later – then it is essential that your will is drawn up by an expert.

On the whole it is not expensive to go to a solicitor or a professional will writer to have a will properly drawn up – the cost can be as little as £30 or £40 for a very simple will, more for a more complicated one. Couples can have 'mirror' wills drawn up, with exactly the same terms for whoever predeceases the other, at little more than the cost of just one person's will.

The outlay of £50, or even a few hundred pounds on expert advice now, may mean thousands of pounds more from your estate go to your chosen beneficiaries rather than to the wrong people or, worse, to the taxman.

Is there legal aid for getting wills made by a solicitor?

You may be eligible to fill in a 'green form' to get this service free if your income is under £61 a week (at the time of writing) or your capital (savings) are fairly modest. You will also qualify for this help if you are over seventy; seriously handicapped, blind, deaf or dumb; the parent of a child with a serious handicap; or a single parent who wants to appoint a guardian for your child.

What does an executor do?

The executor's job is to wind up your estate after your demise and deal with the practical arrangements. He (or she) should notify the doctor of your demise, and the coroner if the circumstances are unusual, register your death (within five days), and see that you are buried or cremated according to wishes expressed in your will.

The executor is empowered from the moment of your death, though he usually also has to have his authority to act confirmed by the High Court (see Probate). He gets your assets valued, collects any debts owed to you, and pays any outstanding bills out of your estate – including the funeral costs if not already pre-paid by you under a funeral plan – and your final gas, electricity and phone bills, and of course the taxman.

Then he (or she) distributes the balance to the beneficiaries as specified in your will, and submits a final statement of account to them – which they may need for their own tax purposes.

What is probate?

If you have made a will, your executor has to 'prove' the will before your assets can be distributed to the heirs. This means getting a Grant of Probate from the High Court that confirms the executor(s) legal authority to handle your estate.

If you die intestate, i.e., without a will, the Court appoints administrators to handle your affairs and divide your assets in the order described earlier – in which case the person(s) appointed gets Letters of Administration giving them this authority.

> **Executors can always check what should be done by asking the local Probate Office (look in the phone book) for advice and help.**

If your estate is very small, a grant of probate or letter of administration may not be necessary. If what you leave behind is just cash and personal effects, probate is not needed. Or if your assets were not more than £5000 in National Savings or Premium Bonds, or money held in pension funds and friendly societies, probate may also be unnecessary. But there are various forms that will have to be filled in to inform the savings organisation of the death and to arrange transfers of the money to the heirs. (Premium Bond numbers can't be inherited; they are encashed and their face value is handed on.)

What about inheritance tax?

You can't escape death in the end – but you can help your heirs escape inheritance tax. It is normally levied at forty per cent on the value of your estate exceeding £150,000, and only on the balance above that amount. But it has to be paid before any bequests are handed out. By planning ahead to reduce the estate's exposure to tax, you can end up giving your heirs more. There are several ways you can do this:

Gifts

One is to reduce the size of your estate by making gifts of money or assets in your lifetime to your intended heirs. You can give a certain amount away free of all tax.

For a start, any gifts between spouses are tax-free anyway, however large. That includes inheritances. You can make as many small gifts a year in your lifetime as you like, worth up to £250. If your child is getting married, each parent can give him or her a tax-free £5000 as a wedding present that year.

If your grandchild is getting married, each grandparent can give him or her £2500 tax-free as a wedding present. (These exemptions apply to every child or grandchild.) If you are not a parent or grandparent but want to give money to someone else who is getting married, you can give that person £1000 tax-free. And you can also make a separate, single gift of £3000 to somebody every year without any tax liability to your estate or the lucky recipient. You can give the money to a different person each year if you want, or to the same person. If you give a larger sum of money to someone other than your spouse in any tax year, provided you live for another seven years, there will also be no inheritance tax to pay on that gift's value.

But if you die within the seven years, the taxman claws inheritance back from the recipient, using a sliding scale. If you die within three years of making the gift, the tax is clawed back at the full forty per cent of its value at the time the gift was made. After that the liability gets less. The table below shows how to work out the tax due.

Years between gift and donor's death:	What % of the normal rate must be paid:
3 years	100% (of 40% rate)
3-4 years	80% (of 40% rate)
4-5 years	60% (of 40% rate)
6-7 years	20% (of 40% tax)
7 years+	0%

EXAMPLE If the gift was worth £10,000 and the donor dies after a couple of years, the full £4000 tax is still due. If the giver lasts three and a half years, the recipient will get a tax bill for eighty per cent of £4000, which equals £3200. If the donor dies after four and a half years, the tax liability is down to sixty per cent of £4000, making £2400. If the donor dies after six years, the tax due is twenty per cent of £4000, making just £800. If the donor is still alive seven years on, there will never be any inheritance tax to pay on that gift.

If you are reducing your estate's liability to tax by making regular gifts in this way, don't give away so much that you'll end up destitute if you live far longer than you anticipate! Assume a long life, just to be on the safe side. It's better for your estate to pay a bit more tax at the end of the day, than for you to end up on the streets. Your relatives and friends may already have spent all you gave them – or could just pocket it and decide not to care for you after all!

Tax planning

Another way to plan to reduce inheritance tax is for a couple not to leave everything to each other. If you each leave up to £150,000 to your children, for example, then on the death of the first spouse, that £150,000 will be passed down tax-free to the children as it does not exceed the inheritance tax threshold. Meanwhile, whatever the surviving spouse inherits on top will be tax-free anyway. Then he or she can still leave the first £150,000 of their own estate to their heirs without tax on that either.

That way your heirs can get up to £300,000 tax-free, whereas if it all goes to the surviving spouse and then is handed on to the heirs, only £150,000 of it will be tax-exempt. This assumes your combined estates are likely to be worth more than £150,000 between them, of course. There is no point in leaving your widow or widower destitute just to protect your children from inheritance tax!

Trusts

You can save inheritance tax by leaving your capital in trust to your heirs, while keeping a lifetime interest in the income from it for yourself. If you do this by giving some of your capital to the trust and lending it the rest, you can even top up your annual income by taking back some of the capital each year as a loan repayment. But trust law is complex and you will definitely need a lawyer to sort the details out for you. There is no inheritance tax at all on farms, and tax is levied at half-rate on family businesses being handed on to the next generation to run. But once again, it's important to clarify these bequests and you should definitely consult a solicitor in drawing up a will involving these assets.

Renting and letting

Tenancy agreements

The law surrounding residential tenancy agreements is complicated, not least because there are several different Housing Acts in force – at least three in England and Wales since 1977; and one in Scotland. Which one governs your lease depends on which Act of Parliament was in effect at the time in the region where that particular tenancy started. Where a lease is unclear, or does not mention a particular situation, normally the appropriate Housing Act will govern the tenants' rights, no matter what else it says in that lease.

Even if you have inherited an old tenancy because you shared the accommodation with a deceased relative, the lease is still covered by the Act of Parliament under which it was granted.

So don't just believe what a lease says or your landlord tells you – this area is so complex that he or she could be mistaken or have drawn the lease up wrongly in the first place.

This section will give you a guide to the overall picture, although it would be impossible within the scope of this book to cover every point of all the different housing laws. If you are ever worried about your legal rights as a tenant, or as a landlord, it is very important that you check all the facts covering your particular situation with a solicitor specialising in housing law – preferably before you sign any lease or agreement. And, since housing law can and does change, remember that any new Act that comes in is likely to be the one that governs any tenancy that you subsequently start from scratch.

If you are subletting from someone, or taking on their tenancy, it's equally important to check the details. For instance, if you are renting from someone who has a mortgage on that property and has not told their lender about the tenancy, if the house is ever repossessed the lender is entitled to chuck you out. The borrower's failure to get its lender's permission will leave you with no right of tenure in a repossession case. This is a very common cause of people finding themselves forced to leave a rented property. And landlords should note that letting your home without your mortgage provider's permission is a breach of the terms of the mortgage – and therefore would entitle the lender to start repossession proceedings over your home. Though in practice this would be unusual, it is still a danger!

Your local Citizens Advice Bureau gives free legal advice about renting and letting; and the Consumers Association also offers guidance.

What does leasehold mean?

Don't confuse renting a home with owning a leasehold. With a leasehold, the holder buys the right to live in the property for the duration of a very long lease, usually at least ninety-nine years. But the leaseholder does not own the land on which the property stands, for which he also pays a very low, annual 'ground' rent. Leaseholds can be sold on.

Leaseholds come in two sorts:

A long lease on a house, for ninety-nine years or considerably longer. The Leasehold Reform Act 1967 granted holders of these leases, the right to buy the 'freehold', the land under the house, in certain circumstances.

A long lease on a flat, again usually for at least ninety-nine years. Ground rent is payable. Landlords are meant to keep the building and common parts in good repair but the leaseholders must contribute to these maintenance costs. The Leasehold Reform, Housing and Urban Development Act of 1993 extended to leasehold flat-owners the right to club together to buy the freehold of the building in certain circumstances. It can be simpler, however, for each leaseholder to exercise a different right to a whole new lease instead. If you want to do any of these things, you will need the help of a solicitor.

What's the difference between a tenancy and a licence?

A tenancy or lease buys you the right to occupy the property concerned, exclusively, for an agreed period – even if the property changes hands in that time.

For the agreement to count as a lease, the dwelling concerned must also be self-contained, with its own kitchen and bathroom rather than facilities shared, say, with the landlord.

Depending on the type of lease, you may have security of tenure beyond the originally agreed period. Leases can also be assigned by the tenant to someone else, or sublet (subject to any prohibitions in the terms of that particular lease). And they can be transferred to a spouse or relative after the original tenant's death.

A licence cannot be passed on to anyone else. You do have some protection from summary eviction and harassment during its life, but you do not have the right to stay on after the licence period expires.

If you are sharing rented self-contained accommodation with friends, and came looking for the place together, you are probably joint tenants, even if you each signed a separate agreements with the landlord. But if from time-to-time different flatmates move in and out of the place, and no one has been designated exclusive occupation of any particular room, then you may find you only count as licencees, with no security of tenure. If in doubt, check with a legal expert.

What types of tenancy are there?

Leases can be 'fixed term' (e.g., set for six months) or 'periodic' (e.g., monthly) and each kind is governed by different rules.

There are three main areas of tenancy in England and Wales, each with different kinds of protection for tenants and landlords:
- ☞ Private sector tenancies.
- ☞ Public sector tenancies (e.g., being a council tenant).
- ☞ Leases from a housing association or housing co-operative.

Private sector tenancies

That is, renting from a private landlord – those granted before 15 January 1989 come under the Rent Act 1977, while those granted after that date are covered by the Housing Act 1988.

1977 Rent Act tenancies. These are either 'protected' or 'secured' tenancies. They also have controls on the amount of rent that can be charged. You can ask to have its fairness assessed by the local rent officer.

A 'protected' tenancy grants you this right to rent control, and also gives a spouse, or partner of the opposite sex who lived as your husband or wife, the right to take on ('succeed to') the tenancy after the main tenant's death. The successor then becomes a 'statutory' tenant (see below). Or family members living there for at least two years before the original tenant's death (after 15 January 1989) can succeed to the tenancy,

but they only become an 'assured' tenant (explained later).

A tenancy is a 'protected' one if the home is let as a separate (self-contained) dwelling to an individual and is generally used as their main home. Holiday lets are not protected tenancies! Nor are lets where part of your rent is for board, or service; e.g., if the landlord provides meals, or cleaning services.

Under the old 1980 Housing Act, there are a few **protected shorthold' tenancies** left but these are mainly petering out. These are lets for fixed periods, after which the landlord has a mandatory right to have the property back but under a rather complicated procedure that, to be successful, he must abide by.

When a protected tenancy under the 1977 Rent Act is ending, in most cases if you stay put you will automatically become a **'statutory' tenant** – providing you are a person not a company and provided that you go on living there.

Becoming a statutory tenant gives you security of tenure. Provided you stick to the terms of the lease, you can't be evicted unless the landlord can prove one of the grounds for repossession given in the Rent Act.

Some of these are discretionary, which means the landlord has to convince the court that his reasons for wanting to repossess the place are reasonable. Others are mandatory – which means the court has to grant him a possession order.

Mandatory grounds include an absent owner-occupier now wanting his home back, an out-of-season holiday let coming to an end, retirement homes now being needed by the owner for that very purpose, and returning servicemen wanting to live in their UK home – though in all these cases the tenant must have been given a warning notice in writing right at the start of the tenancy that this might happen.

Discretionary grounds for seeking to evict you, include your non-payment of (reasonable) rent, annoying the neighbours, using the place for immoral or illegal purposes, neglect of the property, ill-treatment of the furniture, subletting or assigning the lease without the landlord's permission or at an exorbitant rent. Others include the dwelling being required for an employee of the landlord, or if you are now an ex-employee of the landlord, and if the landlord (reasonably) needs the place for himself or certain members of his family.

1988 Act tenancies. There are two types of these – 'assured shorthold' tenancies, and 'assured' tenancies. They are available to people, either as joint or individual tenants, but not to companies, and only on rented accommodation that is to be the tenant's main home (holiday trips won't affect that).

'**Assured shorthand**' **tenancies** are for a fixed term only, of at least six months. After the time is up, the landlord is entitled to repossess the dwelling providing he follows the procedure laid down in the 1988 Act. Shorthold leases cannot be terminated by the landlord within the first six months, though the terms of the lease may permit the tenant to end them sooner.

The tenant does not have security of tenure once a shorthold lease expires, but he is entitled at the start of the tenancy to have the amount of rent checked by a rent assessment committee. It can only be reduced, however, if it is significantly higher than other rents in the area on similar properties.

'**Assured**' **tenancies** do give you the right to stay put at the end of the lease, unless the landlord can show a good reason for getting repossession. Again, some grounds for repossession are mandatory, while others are at the court's discretion. Mandatory ones include the original owner-occupier needing the house back as his or his spouse's principal home; substantial rent arrears exceeding thirteen weeks of weekly rent, or three months of quarterly rent.

Discretionary grounds include any rent arrears, or persistent delay in paying the rent – so be careful! As with other types of lease, neglecting or damaging the property or furniture is another potential ground for eviction. Always check with a solicitor what could lead to repossession of your rented dwelling before you sign a lease.

Rent

With an assured tenancy, the landlord can charge what rent he can get, though to raise the rent once you are in, he has to follow a set procedure correctly.

If the assured tenancy is a 'periodic' one (e.g., month by month) and there is nothing in the lease about rent rises, he must suggest a new rent to you which you can ask to have assessed to check that it is reasonable for the area. If it is, then that's what the new rent can be.

If it is a fixed-term assured lease, the rent can't go up without the tenant's agreement unless the terms of a rent rise are already specified in the lease. Once the fixed term ends, you can stay put as a periodic, statutory tenant – and the landlord can seek to raise the rent provided he sticks to the rules of the Act.

Transferring the lease

You can assign or even sublet a fixed-term assured tenancy whenever you like, unless the lease specifically forbids this – so check it. Sublets must be shorter than the original lease.

But with a periodic assured lease, you cannot normally assign or sublet without first getting the landlord's consent, though you can take in a lodger to share the place with you. If in doubt about what you can or can't do, do consult a legal expert (try the Citizens Advice Bureau for free guidance).

Genuine sub-tenants get the same protection from their immediate landlord (the assured tenant) as he had from his landlord – but they should still double-check with a lawyer to see whether there are circumstances in which the ultimate head-landlord could turf them out.

Can I inherit an assured tenancy?

When an assured tenant dies, the tenancy passes to any surviving joint tenant or to the person nominated to receive it in a sole tenant's will. If there is no will, it goes to the next of kin according to the law of intestacy (see Wills, page 319). This can only happen once however – these leases can't be passed on from generation to generation.

What about resident landlords?

If you are sharing the house, as a lodger, with your landlord, you almost certainly only have a licence to be there, not a lease – especially if the landlord has access to your room to clean it, provides linen, or other services such as meals. If the owner sells up, or dies, you have no statutory right to stay on in the house.

If you live in the same property as the landlord and it has been divided into flats, any leases on those flats may not be assured tenancies and therefore would also be without security of tenure. It all depends on the landlord(s) living there (other than on holiday or for brief absences) throughout the entire tenancy, from start to finish. If he does not do so, the lease is an assured tenancy. (The death of a resident landlord does not, however, create an assured tenancy!)

If you were already a tenant in a property before the landlord moved in, any new lease he subsequently grants you will retain your former lease's status of an assured tenancy. Flats in a purpose-built block of flats in which the landlord occupies one flat, can also count as assured tenancies.

What about becoming a landlord?

If you are considering becoming a landlord by letting part of your home or a property you own, don't just buy an off-the-shelf lease form at a stationer's.

It really is essential that you get proper legal advice first, and have a rental agreement drawn up that fits in with what you want to achieve. The law can be so precise that even a simple mistake or omission in the wording of a lease can change the intended nature of the tenancy. This can leave a landlord, who wanted a brief let, with a tenant able to stay put for the rest of their life – and possibly even their next-of-kin's life, too! For any would-be landlord, it is always worth spending a bit of money now on expert legal advice to save a lot of potential grief, argument and expense later.

Public sector tenancies

These come under the Housing Act of 1985 and include being a tenant of a local authority, development corporation – or of a housing association whose leases do not come under the 1988 Housing Act. The 1985 Act gives you 'secured tenancy'. This grants you

considerable rights to stay put – provided you don't mistreat the place or abuse the neighbours – but there you have no control over the amount of rent you can be charged. The place being rented must be your only or main home.

If the tenancy is for a fixed term, at the end of that time you can stay put as a periodic tenant, on a month-by-month basis.

You must stick to the terms of your tenancy agreement but if you do breach them, the landlord can't turf you out without a court order against you. A notice to quit on its own is not enough.

To get the court order, the landlord must follow the procedures laid down in the Housing Act 1985. There are sixteen grounds under which the landlord can seek a court order, but he has to prove that the grounds he is claiming are justified.

The sixteen, however, include you not paying the rent that is lawfully due, or failing to meet some other legal obligation laid down in the tenancy agreement. Causing nuisance or annoyance to the neighbours is another ground. So are being convicted of using the house for illegal or immoral purposes; neglecting or damaging the place, or mistreating the landlord's furniture; gaining the tenancy by lying to the landlord; or overcrowding the home.

Other grounds reflect the kind of house it is – for instance, if it's been adapted for a disabled person, you aren't disabled and now the landlord needs it for someone who is. Government-approved plans to redevelop the area can also be grounds for wanting the house empty.

If your landlord is seeking a court order to evict you, ask a legal advice centre or Citizens Advice Bureau for (free) guidance.

Can I inherit a secured tenancy?

Sometimes. When a tenant dies their spouse or the person living with them as their husband or wife, 'succeeds to' this tenancy and can go on living there. Where there is no spouse but a relative has been living with the tenant for at least twelve months before the death, the relative can succeed to the tenancy. But this can only happen once in a tenancy.

In other cases, you can't get permission to assign a secured tenancy to someone else except where a property adjustment order is made in connection with divorce or a separation, or if it's a straight swap with another secure tenant.

> **WARNING Assigning without permission will lose the tenancy its secured status.**

Council house tenants have the right to buy their homes at a discount after a certain period of time. Ask your local council for details. Remember that once you own the property, all repairs and maintenance become your responsibility.

Housing associations and housing co-operatives

If you are the tenant of a housing association, and with a tenancy granted before 15 January 1989, it will usually be regarded as a public sector tenancy under the 1985 Housing Act. Tenancies started after that date usually count as private sector ones under the 1988 Act.

Members of housing co-operatives are in effect both the tenants and the landlords. With co-op tenancies begun before 15 January 1989, tenants have no statutory security of tenure but you should be OK provided you stick to the rules (the constitution) of the co-op – and you are still entitled to seek checks that the rent is fair. Co-op tenancies begun after that date are exempt from the 1988 Housing Act so your rights are only what are spelt out in the tenancy agreement, though the co-op does have to guarantee to manage the property well.

Inside, the landlord has to keep water, gas, electricity, heating, hot water, and sanitation systems in good order. Generally speaking, tenants are expected to look after minor maintenance matters within the dwelling. Repairs are not the same as making improvements, however, which may require negotiation between landlord and tenant; and the landlord does not have to repair any fixtures that are yours and which you would take away with you. He has rights of access to carry out repairs, even if this is not specified in the lease, though he may have to give you twenty-four hours' notice in writing.

If your landlord does not keep things in good repair, you can seek a court order to carry them out; or do the repairs and make a claim for damages to get back the cost. Or you can give him notice that the repairs need doing and set him a time limit in which to meet his obligations.

If the property you rent is in really bad condition you may be able to call in the help of the local authority under the Environmental Protection Act 1990 – which extends to premises whose state could be damaging to health. It may be simpler to persuade the local authority to serve an abatement notice on your landlord to 'abate the nuisance' from a state of poor repair, than to sue him yourself under the Landlord and Tenant Act.

You and your home: rights & responsibilities

When you own your own home, you take on a lot of new responsibilities. Security, maintaining, repairing and decorating the place are up to you; there's no landlord to badger to get things fixed. So if your overflow is dripping down the wall, it's you who has to get it fixed. Don't just ignore it or you could end up with a nasty damp problem and, if it's affecting the flat downstairs for example, possibly a bill for putting right the damage there as well. You have a legal responsibility not to cause a 'nuisance' to your neighbours – and you in turn can take action if their behaviour is unreasonable.

> **Always keep a note of how and where to turn off the electricity, gas and water in your home, in case of an emergency; and put a list by the phone of emergency numbers to call, such as the local electricity company or a good 24-hour plumber.**

Maintenance

If you're a tenant, the landlord has to keep the fabric of the building in good repair (see Renting, page 323). If you've bought a leasehold flat, the managing agents of the building will be responsible for arranging the upkeep of the fabric of the building and the common parts, such as stairs and hallways, at regular intervals. But you'll have to pay your share of the cost – and looking after the interior of the home and your own fixtures and fittings is down to you.

If you've bought a house, looking after the outside of the building and the roof, is all yours, as well as caring for the interior (see Insurance, page 310).

Newly built homes

If you buy a house built in the last ten years it should have either a 'Buildmark' guarantee from the National House-Building Council (NHBC) or, possibly, a similar guarantee from the insurance group Zurich Municipal.

The most common one in the UK is the Buildmark. It protects the first buyer of the house against the loss of his or her deposit should the housebuilder go bust before he finishes the work, and covers defects that occur because of bad workmanship within the first two years – in which case the builder has to return to fix the problem. It also covers against financial loss whomever owns the house in the subsequent eight years if major structural defects emerge.

But the guarantee doesn't cover basic wear and tear, nor does it cover problems caused by land subsidence, nor any damage that's caused by the homeowner's own activities. Installations put into the building, like central heating, may not be covered either – so when you get your guarantee, make sure you read the small print and look after your property.

Improvements

If you're having work done to your home by someone else, ask any contractors you approach to give you estimates (the final price may vary from this) or quotations (a fixed price for the job which should not alter)

> **If you are buying a newly built home, check that the builder is NHBC-registered and that the house is covered by a Buildmark guarantee. Ask around about the builder's reputation, if that's possible. See if he keeps the site tidy – a messy site may bode ill. Look out for any defects such as chips in a basin, for example, before you buy the property and write to tell the builder you want them put right first. And keep a copy of the letter. See addresses, page 437, for details of the NHBC's address.**

for the work before you commit yourself to one of them. Ask friends or neighbours if they can recommend anyone.

If a contractor offers you a guarantee for the job, this will be in addition to your legal rights (see Consumer Rights, page 333). But don't let an amazing guarantee from a tinpot outfit be the factor that wins you round; if the firm goes bust the guarantee is worthless!

Make sure you get a written agreement or contract for the work to be done, and try to avoid paying for work in advance, because again if the firm goes bust, you may not get the money back or the work done. Offer to pay in stages, if you like, or when the job is done. Always keep a quarter of the bill back to be paid when the work is finished. If you aren't satisfied you can withhold payment until things are completed to your satisfaction. But be reasonable – don't refuse to pay just for the sake of it.

Pests and other hazards

No home is guaranteed to last forever, and there are all kinds of unpleasant things that can attack the fabric of a building. Regular checks, and regular maintenance, will help to keep these at bay. The Royal Institution of Chartered Surveyors (see page 437 for details) produces a booklet that lists the problems that can happen, by symptom, and tells you the solution.

Keeping your home free from pests, such as vermin or a nasty outbreak of fleas brought home by the cat, is also your headache as a homeowner. If you have a problem, your first port of call should be the local council to see if they have a pest-control unit that will come round for free; failing that, look in the telephone book or Yellow Pages for a private firm.

Rats must always be reported to the local environmental health officer – whether they are invading your land or just in the area. But if you think a neighbour has a rat problem, talk to them about it first. If they don't act, then call in the environmental health officer yourself. He can serve a notice on them to clear the pests. If you think an empty property is infested, contact the local council, which should be able to trace the owner.

Be nice to the neighbours

There are other responsibilities shared by all householders, not just home owners. Causing 'nuisance' to the neighbours is an offence that can in extreme cases get tenants evicted, for example. Anyone upsetting the neighbourhood enough, can be taken to court and ordered to stop – either by being sued by the sufferer, or the local authority, or even the Department of the Environment.

All kinds of things can count as 'nuisance', but noise is usually the main bone of contention – whether it's caused by a constantly barking dog, frequent loud music, or inadequate sound insulation between flats or terraced houses.

Sound is caused by fluctuations in air pressure, which change in frequencies rather like ripples on a pond, widening out as they move further away from where a stone has been dropped in. High-pitched shrieks are high-frequency, low rumbles are low-frequency sounds.

What can I do if I have noisy neighbours?

If you have noisy neighbours, or live near a noisy business, the best first step is to approach them informally, explain what the problem is, and ask them to stop, reduce the problem, or change the time of day they do

Noise is measured in decibels, often using what's called the 'A' frequency weighting which closely mimics how the ear responds to different frequencies. Decibels measured as 'An increase of 10 decibels (dB) on the A weighting', say from 70 dBA to 80 dBA, actually measures a doubling of the loudness of that sound to the human ear. A reduction of 10 dBA is a halving of the loudness. A fridge humming emits a sound of about 40 dBA, according to the Department of the Environment, while a pneumatic drill five metres away from you is a much louder, 90 dBA sound. A discotheque loudspeaker belts out 120 dBA to anyone just a metre away from it.

whatever it is they do. If that gets nowhere, you can complain to the local authority. It has powers, under section 80 of the Environmental Protection Act (in England and Wales) or section 58 of the Control of Pollution Act 1974 in Scotland, to deal with noise that constitutes what is known as a statutory nuisance. This could be anything from loud music constantly playing, to excessive noise from construction if they are having building work done – including vibration. Action can also be taken to prevent anticipated noise, or anticipated repetitions, as well as to deal with an existing problem.

Talk to the local authority's environmental health department, which will send someone to check out the problem. If they decide the noise really is a statutory nuisance they will probably contact the culprit to try and get them to agree to solve the problem. But if that does not work, the authority can serve the culprit, or the owner or occupier of the premises concerned, with a notice to abate the nuisance. It may also say what they should do to achieve this.

If the person getting the notice ignores it, they can be taken to the magistrates court or, in Scotland, the Sheriff Court. Or, if the local authority thinks more drastic action is required, it can seek an injunction in the High Court (or an interdict in the Court of Session or in the Sheriff Court in Scotland).

You can do the same to curb noise from industrial, trade or business premises. Conviction can result in substantial fines for the main offence, plus a daily fine for every day that the offence continues after conviction.

If the local authority decides not to start proceedings against the noisy person or premises, or if you don't want to involve them, you can still complain directly to the magistrates court yourself under section 82 of the Environmental Protection Act 1990.

But the magistrate will need to be convinced that the noise really is as bad as you claim – so keep a written record of when it happens and how much of a nuisance it is, and take that to court with you.

It is still a good idea to write to the culprit first, explaining that the noise bothers you so much that you believe it amounts to a nuisance and that unless they can stop or reduce it, you will have no choice but to complain to the magistrates court.

If you decide to go ahead, you need to give the noisemaker at least three days notice in writing, with details. Date the letter, and keep a copy. You can deliver the letter by hand, or post it. If still nothing improves, contact the clerk of the court and say you want to make a complaint under section 82 of the Environmental Protection Act 1990. You'll be asked to go and explain the problem and what your evidence is – and you will be expected to say whether or not you have already involved the local environmental protection officer.

If you appear to have an arguable case, a summons will be issued against the alleged culprits with a date and time for a court hearing, to which you should also go, to make your case. In England and Wales you do not have to have a solicitor (and you won't normally get Legal Aid for this, but you may eligible for a little bit of free legal advice under something called the 'green form' scheme, see page 338). The clerk of the court will advise you on how to conduct your own case.

If you win the case, the magistrates will make an order requiring the culprit to 'abate'

the noise, and saying how this should be done. He can also be fined at that point. (If you have incurred costs in bringing the case, the magistrates may also decide to make the noisemaker pay them.)

The order may also forbid any repetitions of the noise nuisance (if there are any, the culprit can also be fined for that) so if it does recur, keep a diary of what happens.

If you are bringing the case in Scotland you have to apply to the Sheriff Court and your application must be drawn up by a solicitor. Then the Sheriff clerk will give you a warrant, which must then be legally served, plus the application, to the noisemaker either by a solicitor or a Sheriff officer.

A third option is to take civil action yourself. You can either seek an injunction to restrain the noisemaker from making it; or you could seek damages for loss if you have suffered financially as a result of the problem. Again, it's up to the court to decide whether your claims are reasonable. Civil actions can be costly, so there's no point in pressing ahead if the noise merely irritates you but does not upset anyone else in the area. Being hypersensitive is not a good enough argument.

Alarms

If you have a burglar alarm on your home or car, remember that if these keep going off it is you who could end up in court for creating a nuisance!

Burglar alarms should have an automatic cut-out after they have rung for a while, and car alarms should stop quickly and only go off again if the car is interfered with. It's an offence to sound your horn in a stationary car, unless you're in danger from another, moving vehicle, and it's an offence to sound the horn between eleven-thirty p.m. and seven a.m. if you are in a restricted road – that's a road lit with lamps not more than 200 metres apart.

Loudspeakers can't be used in the street between nine p.m. and eight a.m., though car radios are OK – unless you turn the volume up hugely and regularly waken the neighbourhood. If they are being used to advertise things, loudspeakers aren't allowed in the street in the day-time either, with certain exceptions. Ice cream vans are allowed to play their jingles between noon and seven p.m., for instance, but even they must not annoy the locals too much.

Traffic trouble

If constant, loud traffic or aircraft overhead are driving you crazy, complain to the Department of Transport. You may be able to get traffic re-routed, or your home insulated against the sound. If the problem comes from a construction site, go to the local authority for action. And if noise at your place of work is upsetting you, there are Noise at Work Regulations that may help with finding a solution.

Parking

You have no territorial rights over the piece of road directly outside your front door as it's not part of your property. So anyone can park there. But you do have a right of access to your own driveway or garage, so if someone frequently blocks that, their parking habits are illegal and you can report them to the local police station, or ask the highways department of your local council to intervene.

Boundaries

If you think your neighbour is spreading on to your land, check the lie of the boundary shown at the Land Registry (or the Registers of Scotland and Northern Ireland), and with the solicitor who did the conveyancing when you bought your place. If the boundary is still unclear, consult a surveyor. If it looks as if your neighbour has indeed expanded into your land, you can seek an injunction, in the same way as you do to get him to curb noise, from the local county court (or an interdict from the Sheriff Court). If he ignores an injunction he runs the risk of a fine – or even being jailed for being in contempt of court.

> **Owners of land who don't claim it back from uninvited users within twelve years (ten in Scotland) may find they have lost the right to it!**

If you are ever on the receiving end of an injunction, make sure you obey it in good time.

Trees

If your neighbour's tree or garden bush is overhanging your land, you are entitled to prune it, but only to the boundary line. And check first with your local council that the tree isn't covered by a preservation order – if it is, you could be fined for pruning it back. The other thing to watch for is whether your home is in a conservation area. If it is, you need to give the council a six-week period in which to decide whether there should be a preservation order on the offending tree.

Walls and fences

If you and your neighbour's home share a wall – a party wall – you both share responsibility for its upkeep, but you can't force your neighbour to do repairs to his side.

When it comes to fences, you can put one up on your side of the boundary line and as long as it's no more than two metres high where it borders your neighbour's land, or one metre where it runs along public land, you shouldn't need to seek planning permission. But there may be restrictions in your title deeds, or locally, on the building of fences or walls, so do check both the deeds and with the local authority before you start the work. It is the job of the owner of a fence to repair it. Again, check the title documents to be absolutely certain but you can usually work out ownership of the fence based on which side the support pillars are on – if they're on your side, it's your fence. In England, Wales and Northern Ireland, you have the right to gain access to your neighbour's land to carry out repairs to your own fence.

Extensions

If your neighbour is planning an extension to his or her home – and that includes conservatories – they need planning permission. Your views have to be taken into account before final permission is (or isn't) granted for the original proposal, or for a modified version. So if the extension will block light from part of your home, for instance, you may be able to get it altered, or even forbidden altogether.

* Either the planning department (in England and Wales) or the developer (Scotland) has to notify the neighbourhood via a site notice, or individually, of the plan, after which you have up to three weeks in which to voice any objections.

You can arrange to meet the planning officer to discuss what worries you have about the project, but you should send any objections to him or her in writing. If the planning officer says he intends to recommend the project for planning permission, you can still send copies of your objections to local councillors and members of the planning committee – and you can include your own suggestions for amending the proposed extension (i.e., making it lower).

Your neighbour can appeal if he is refused planning permission; but if he is granted it, you can't appeal against that decision. So it is vital to make any protests in time for them to be considered by the planning officer and committee. And if, at the outcome, you think the case has been mishandled in any way, you could finally try complaining about what's happened to the local government ombudsman.

Your consumer rights

Consumers have legal protection against poor conduct by shops, traders and providers of services, but not many of us realise what our rights are.

Shopping

The Sale of Goods Act 1979 gives consumers statutory rights. It says that goods must be of merchantable quality. This means they must not have major faults, except any defects that the shop points out to you – such as being shop-soiled, or 'seconds'.

Goods must also be fit for the purpose for which they are being sold. This not only means that the item must do what it says it can do or be used for, but also that if you tell the sales assistant that it has to work with a

particular item (i.e. a new camera lens for your old camera body), they mustn't sell you one that is not suitable.

Thirdly, goods must be as described on the packaging or in the display sign. If the sign says a dress is 100 per cent silk, it must not be made of anything else.

These rights apply to food as well as to other items. They must be honoured by sellers of items like bricks or window frames, bought in by a builder who is providing a service by working on your home, exactly as if you had bought the items directly.

Your rights are the same whether the goods come from a shop, are in a sale, were bought in a street market, from a mail-order catalogue or even from a door-to-door salesman. Only auctioneers are exempt. If the goods you buy are delivered to your door, and you're asked to sign a delivery note, write on it that you have not yet inspected the goods, in case they turn out to be faulty when you do open the package.

The law also applies to cars, and secondhand cars bought from dealers, but doesn't include those purchased at auction (see Buying a Car, page 369). Private sales give you fewer rights than buying from a dealer. If you are not convinced a seller really owns the goods, don't buy them. If they have been stolen, and are traced, they belong to the original owner (or his insurer if they have paid out for the item), even if you have paid someone else for them.

What happens if I find something wrong with what I've bought?

As soon as you realise there is a fault in the goods you've bought – other than anything pointed out to you when you bought them – you should contact the seller.

Go back to, or contact, the shop and take your receipt with you if possible. Explain the problem, and be ready to say what you would like done about it – i.e. you'd like a refund, or a replacement. It's a good idea to set a deadline by which you'd like your refund, if, for instance, you have bought by mail order. Many shops will be helpful to the point of replacing or refunding items whose only 'fault' is being a size too large, even though they don't have to do this.

If you take the goods back straightaway, or alert the shop to the fault, it means you haven't accepted the goods and can get your money back. If you can't get back to the shop within a few days, phone to tell them about the fault and keep a note of the conversation and with whom it took place, so that when you do go in, there should not be a problem. (If the defective goods are bulky you can ask the seller to collect them – you don't have to pay for their return yourself.)

What happens if the seller refuses to co-operate?

The law makes it clear that it is the seller – except for auctioneers – who is responsible for selling merchantable goods, and must therefore respond to complaints about faulty items or mis-sold or misdescribed goods. Shops and traders cannot refer you directly to the manufacturer. So, unless you want to exercise your rights under the manufacturers' guarantee, remind the seller of the law. He or she can't argue that the goods were sale goods and therefore no refunds are available – that's against the law too, and you can report them to the local trading standards office for trying that line of argument (and for displaying 'no refund' signs on sale goods).

Even if you have lost the receipt, your rights are still intact, though keeping it does help you to prove when and where the goods were purchased. If an item was a gift, and proved faulty, however, the person who bought it should either take up the problem with the place from where it was purchased, or write you a letter authorising you to complain on their behalf. The statutory rights laid down in the Sale of Goods Act only apply to the actual buyer of the goods.

If the seller offers you a replacement, a free repair, or a credit note, you don't have to accept that – the law says you are entitled to a full refund of your money. If you do agree to a repair, it means you are also accepting the goods, so it may be difficult to get the money back afterwards if the repair does not work out. Fortunately, however, if the repair is a disaster, you are still entitled to a replacement, or compensation if no replacement is available.

If you accept a credit note, remember that it will probably only be valid for a limited time, and if the shop never has anything else you want, you'll lose out. It's far better to stick to your rights and insist on a full cash refund.

If the fault in the goods caused damage to something else you own, you can seek compensation for that.

If a visit in person has got you nowhere, put your complaint in writing to the manager or, if the shop is part of a chain, write to customer services at the head office, or even to the company chairman, about your complaint.

If the company's response is unsatisfactory, talk to the trading standards office, a Citizens Advice Bureau, or the seller's trade association, which may be able to mediate. However if arbitration is offered, this may mean you cannot subsequently take your case to court if you are still unhappy – so check that first.

If you do decide to take the matter to court, the best thing is to go via the small claims procedure (for claims of under £1000 in England and Wales, or £750 in Scotland). It's not expensive, and Citizens Advice Bureaux, consumer bodies, and the local County or (in Scotland) Sheriff Court will be able to tell you how to do this.

Door-to-door sales

Doorstep sellers may try to persuade you to sign a deal on the spot, often in return for a discount or free gift. Pay no attention and make sure you read any documents carefully. If need be, say you want to have it checked by an expert or a consumer adviser before you are ready to sign.

If you do buy or agree to anything worth more than £35 (at the time of writing) from an uninvited doorstep seller, the law gives you seven days grace in which to change your mind – except in the case of perishable items, and home extensions! Always check before signing that you do have cancellation rights, which should be given to you in writing.

If you pay by credit, and the items cost £50 or more, your right to cancel is valid whether the seller was invited to call on you or not, as long as you discussed the deal face to face (not just on the phone beforehand) and you don't sign it on their business premises. (For more about your other rights when buying by credit, see page 305.)

What is the point of a manufacturer's guarantee?

Guarantees give you additional rights on top of your statutory rights as a consumer. If the goods come with a registration card, make sure the seller fills in details of the purchase (or the guarantee may not be validated). You also need to fill in your details, and return it to the address shown on the card. Keep the documents that tell you how to claim. Repairs must be done within a reasonable period of time.

What about extended warranties?

Extended warranties are offered by some shops, especially on electrical items, adding one or more years to the guarantee period. They usually cost extra and retailers make a fortune from them, as only a fraction of these warranties are ever actually claimed under. Check what the warranty offered to you covers, before you agree to this extra expense.

What happens if I buy at an auction or secondhand sale?

Auctioneers are the only traders allowed to refuse to accept responsibility for the quality of the goods for sale. Once your bid has been accepted, you have to pay up. So examine items carefully during the viewing time.

But when buying secondhand goods from any other trader, you do still have your statutory rights – except that you know the goods are secondhand, so you can't expect them to be in mint condition. But if items turn out to have faults that weren't obvious, or weren't pointed out to you at the time, you can claim your money back, or the cost of any repairs.

Buying goods privately is another matter. They don't have to be fault-free but even they must be as described, in the ad in the local paper for instance, or from the door-to-door salesman. Check the goods carefully before parting with your cash. If the seller does mislead you, you are entitled to seek your money back. It may be hard to prove, so take along someone who can act as a witness when you buy privately.

Be extra vigilant at car boot sales – not only may you never be able to find the seller again, but he or she may be a trader masquerading as a private seller. This can happen in newspaper small ads, too. If they are a trader and not a private person, your full statutory rights apply – if you can prove what they're up to! Look out for lots of small ads giving the same telephone number, for example, and alert the local trading standards office.

Services

When you go to a restaurant, or to the hairdresser, have your car repaired, or buy a holiday from a travel agent, you are buying a service.

Legally, the service you get should be carried out with reasonable care and skill. That means it has to be done to a proper standard. It should also be done within a reasonable amount of time – it shouldn't take weeks and weeks to get your car back, for instance. And, if no fixed price was agreed at the outset, the charge for the work should also be reasonable. If you did agree to a fixed price, or some method of calculating the charge, you can't easily complain afterwards that you don't like the bill.

With travel agents, it's a good idea to use ones that belong either to the Association of British Travel Agents (ABTA) or the Association of Independent Tour Operators (AITO) because they have bonds that will cover the cost of continuing your holiday and getting you home, or compensating you, if your tour operator goes bust.

> **Ask if the provider of the service you are buying is a member of a trade organisation. Often these bodies have codes of practice by which their members are expected to abide; if something goes wrong, you can ask the trade association to intervene.**

Complaining about poor services

If a service is shoddy, complain to the provider or supplier of that service first. If that doesn't solve the matter, complain in writing to the manager, head office, customer services or chairman, say what you'd like done about it, and set a deadline.

Keep copies of all correspondence on this, and notes of any telephone conversations. You could ask an expert to give you an opinion on the problem. For example, if your complaint is about overcharging, check what other providers charge for similar services in the area. If all this still fails to produce a satisfactory response, contact the local trading standards office. Or, if your complaint is about unfit food, dirty restaurants or shops, contact the local environmental health officer.

The supplier's trade association is also a good port of call, and may offer to arbitrate (but again, check whether this will affect your ability to go to court later).

If your complaint is about your local electricity, gas, water, or telephone service, contact the customer service or the users' association whose numbers should be shown somewhere on your bill. (Check the print on the back.)

If your complaint is about a provider of financial services, start by complaining to the organisation itself and if that gets nowhere, seek a letter confirming the deadlock and then you can approach the appropriate ombudsman (if this letter is not forthcoming after several weeks you can go straight on to the ombudsman).

Going to the ombudsman does not affect your right to go to court if you wish, but if you have already started court action the ombudsman cannot also take up your case.

Alternatively, you can complain to the regulator of that part of the financial industry. If you decide to go to court, the size of your claim will affect whether you go the small claims route, described above, in which case you don't have to use a solicitor – or whether you want more substantial compensation. Under these circumstances, you should take legal advice first. You can get free legal advice on whether your case stands a good chance of success from the Citizens Advice Bureau or local legal advice centre.

Divorce

The grounds for getting a divorce are broadly similar in England, Wales, Northern Ireland and Scotland, though the legal proceedings themselves vary in the three different regions.

Before you decide that divorce is definitely what you want, cool down, and weigh up all the financial and personal implications. If you think it's worth trying to rescue the marriage and sort out your differences, you can improve your chances with the help of a reconciliation or marriage guidance counselling agency.

It's also a sobering process to list the marital assets, and consider how you will manage when they have to support two households, as opposed to one. Check with the Citizens Advice Bureau or local benefits office about other financial help for which you might become eligible after a divorce or judicial separation. Then you'll have a clearer idea of what life after divorce may hold.

Judicial separation can be sought when the marriage has broken down and you wish to separate but, perhaps for religious or other reasons, not to divorce. You can still seek a full divorce later (but remember that means a second set of legal costs).

Even before a divorce or separation, you can apply for maintenance from your spouse for yourself. Make your application to a local magistrates' court or to your county court. In most cases the Child Support Agency will deal with maintenance for children. Only very rarely will the courts retain jurisdiction over

> **When you divorce or agree to a judicial separation, the cause of the marriage's breakdown does not usually affect how the marital assets are divided between you – or how any children are catered for (unless your other half's behaviour has been particularly bizarre). So don't assume that being the wronged party will entitle you to all the money. All parties have to be reasonably provided for out of the available pot.**

the arrangements for them, but they might, for example, if one parent is abroad.

What are the grounds for divorce?

If you live in England or Wales, or in Northern Ireland, there is only one main ground for divorce – the irretrievable breakdown of the marriage – but there are several different ways to prove it. These are:

- ☞ Adultery and the intolerability of continuing to live with the unfaithful spouse.
- ☞ Your spouse's unreasonable behaviour.
- ☞ Desertion for at least two years.
- ☞ Separation for two years with your spouse's agreement (sometimes called a 'no-fault' divorce).
- ☞ Separation for five years whether or not the other party wanted the separation.

Northern Irish divorce proceedings are largely similar to the law in England and Wales, but Scottish divorce proceedings are different. Even in Scotland, however, the actual grounds for getting divorced work out much the same as further south. These grounds are:

- ☞ Adultery – except that here you don't also have to prove that living with your other half has also become intolerable as a result.
- ☞ Unreasonable behaviour.
- ☞ Desertion.
- ☞ Not living together (cohabiting, in the legal jargon) for two or more years and your husband or wife agreeing to the divorce.
- ☞ Non-cohabitation for five or more years, after which you don't need their agreement to seek a divorce.

Only one of you can actually apply, or 'petition' for the divorce. He or she is then known as the petitioner (or in Scotland as the pursuer) and the other spouse is the 'respondent' (or in Scotland, the defender) and is the one whose conduct may be given as one of the reasons for the breakdown of the marriage. If adultery is given as the reason for marital breakdown, the third party need not be named but if they are, they are known as the 'co-respondent'.

You or your spouse may not wish to admit to adultery or unreasonable behaviour. A 'defended' divorce can drag on and cost more in legal fees. So if you can agree, for example, to split up now and let one of you petition for a divorce with the other's agreement in two years' time, you may avoid lot of bitter argument and legal expense. Interestingly, the legal expenses – normally have to be paid for out of the joint assets, so it's in both your interests to keep the costs down.

What about the children?

Provision has to be made in your divorce for the maintenance of the children and where they will live. Despite the divorce, both parents nowadays retain parental responsibility for their children. Don't expect to be able to cut your partner off from them completely. It's also usually best for the children to be able to go on seeing both parents afterwards – just because you've split up doesn't mean they want to be divorced from either of you.

Early discussions between spouses about what to do with the children and the marital assets can be helped by going to a voluntary conciliation or mediation agency. Conciliation is not the same as reconciliation.

Reconciliation agencies will help you try and sort out your differences and keep the marriage on the road. Conciliation agencies will help you reach amicable agreement over how to manage the split. Doing this before you get too embroiled in legal proceedings will help to keep tempers cool and your legal bills down.

Does it matter how long we've been married?

It can do. Whatever the reason for the breakdown of the marriage, in England and Wales or Northern Ireland, you can't present a petition for divorce until at least a year after the wedding took place. But in Scotland, you don't have to wait for a minimum period of time after the wedding before formally seeking a divorce. The completion of a Scottish divorce also only involves one decree, after which you are legally divorced.

In the rest of the UK you are first granted a decree nisi, which allows you to apply to the court for the divorce to be made absolute six weeks and one day later. Until the decree absolute, you are still married to each other.

Does it matter where I got married?

No. Even if you got married abroad, if you decide your marriage has broken down irretrievably and you definitely want a divorce, you can do so in the area of the United Kingdom where you live now.

So if you or your spouse live in England or Wales, or have lived there for at least a year (short trips away during that time don't affect this time period), this is where you should seek your divorce.

If you normally live in Scotland, or in Northern Ireland, or have been living in that country for at least a year, apply for your divorce in that region.

Can I have a DIY divorce?

Sometimes. There is no DIY divorce in Northern Ireland; even uncontested or undefended divorces have to go to the court so you will need a solicitor.

However, in England and Wales, if you and your spouse agree about the divorce, how to sort out your assets, and what happens to the children, divorce need not be complicated and you can do all the paperwork yourself. Your petition and plans still need to be approved by the court, but an undefended divorce saves you the bother of actually going there yourself – it can usually all be done by post.

In Scotland, if your grounds for divorce are non-cohabitation for two or five years, and provided there are no children under sixteen, no disputes leading to financial claims by either spouse, and no other legal proceedings linked to the marriage waiting to be heard, you can organise your own divorce without the services of a lawyer.

Scottish DIY divorce forms are available from the courts or Citizens Advice Bureaux.

If there are any complications over money or plans for the children, then you really should take legal advice. As one solicitor cannot act for both sides, you and your

spouse will need different solicitors to handle the divorce proceedings.

How do I find a solicitor?

There are many branches of law, and many solicitors are specialists in some aspects and less knowledgeable in others. So it is important in a divorce to appoint a lawyer who is already thoroughly experienced in matrimonial law. Even if you have already used a solicitor, for example when buying your home, don't just assume that firm can also handle your divorce. In any case, if you have already been their clients as a couple, for whatever purpose, they may prefer not to act for one of you separately now in a contested divorce.

In England and Wales, the Solicitors Family Law Association (see useful addresses, page 437) can send you a list of suitable law firms. And the local Citizens Advice Bureau or library should also have lists of local solicitors who do divorce work.

North of the border, ask the Law Society of Scotland for a list of matrimonial lawyers.

In Northern Ireland, ask the Law Society of Northern Ireland for a list of local Family Law practitioners.

Can I get legal aid?

Possibly. There are two types of financial help with legal bills that may be available, but only to people with fairly low incomes and modest or no savings. Ask your solicitor about these, and what the income and capital limits for applicants currently are, the first time you meet. Or contact the Legal Aid Board for a leaflet explaining the scheme.

One is the legal advice and assistance scheme, often known in England as the 'green form' scheme (or in Scotland, 'pink form'). It doesn't apply in Northern Ireland.

The green form scheme gives you up to three hours of a divorce lawyer's time at a low price. Depending on your income and capital you may have to contribute to this or the state may pay it all for you. The scheme suits uncontested, straightforward divorces.

If you are not well off and your case is likely to be contested or complicated, ask if you are eligible for Legal Aid. This is available in all parts of the UK but again is strictly limited to people of modest means. Depending on your income and savings, you may still have to pay something towards your legal costs, even if you get legal aid. And if the divorce ends with you being awarded substantial sums from the marital assets, you may have to repay some of the legal aid you've received.

> It may be possible to have more of the legal costs awarded by the court against your spouse than yourself, if the conduct of their case has made the proceedings more complicated than they need have been. But don't count on it! And remember that if you are unreasonable in your demands during the case, it could be you that ends up with a larger share of the total law bills.

If you think your own lawyer's bill is too high at the end of the day, you can ask the court for it to be 'taxed'. This means that the judge looks at the bill and decides if it is fair or should be reduced.

What court will hear my divorce petition?

South of the border, normally your petition will be heard in a county court that has been classed as a Family Hearing Centre. You can go to any Family Hearing Centre in England or Wales if you prefer to avoid local publicity. Complicated or contested divorces may be transferred to the High Court. In Central London, the Divorce Registry is the home of both the county court and High Court divorce proceedings.

In Scotland, you would normally go to one of the local sheriff courts. You can bring proceedings in any sheriff court in whose area you or your spouse have lived for the past forty days. If you don't want to go to a sheriff court, you can go to the Court of Session in Edinburgh.

> Legal Aid is not available for divorce hearings at Scotland's Court of Session, except for unusually complicated or difficult divorce cases.

How do I prove to the court my grounds for seeking divorce?

Adultery

If adultery is given as the reason anywhere but Scotland, the petitioner must also state that living with their spouse has become intolerable as a result.

The petitioner will be asked to say when and where the adultery happened, if they know. You can ask your spouse for a 'confession statement' admitting to the adultery at a particular time and place, but they can refuse to disclose the other person's identity. This statement can then be incorporated into your divorce petition as evidence. If the third party, the co-respondent is named, you will need to provide an extra set of the divorce papers to the court to send on to him or her.

In England and Wales, you can have tried to save the marriage for up to six months since deciding on a divorce, without that affecting the reason given for going ahead with the divorce petition. If you go on living together for more than six months after confronting your spouse about the specific incident of adultery given in your divorce petition, you won't get a divorce on that ground. But the six-month time limit only starts ticking from the date you knew for sure about the adultery, and not from when you just suspected it might be going on. And, if the adultery is still happening, you can give the date of the most recent incident that you know about as the example for your petition, and start the time clock running from then.

In Scotland, if you forgave your spouse and continued normal married life with them for more than three months after discovering the adultery, this counts as 'condoning' it and you won't get a divorce on those grounds. You also won't get the divorce if you 'connived' at the adultery – which means actively encouraged it, such as agreeing to wife-swapping or a sex party.

Unreasonable behaviour

There is no clear legal definition of what counts as unreasonable behaviour. It could be anything like: violence to the petitioner or the children, excessive gambling and financial recklessness, constant nagging, refusal to have children knowing that the other spouse does want kids, or less dramatic but persistently strange or distressing habits, such as constant rudeness and derogatory remarks.

You will have to give examples, dates if possible, and details of particular incidents and, if you are still living under the same roof, make sure you include details of examples that occurred within the past six months.

If you go on living with your spouse for more than six months after the date of the unreasonable behaviour cited in your divorce petition, it may affect the court's decision. So you will need to give a detailed account of why you are still there despite your spouse's alleged unreasonableness.

Desertion

This means that your spouse left against your wishes and has now been gone for at least two years. You'll need to say in your divorce petition what happened, when; and that they left without your consent.

Separation with consent

Separation with consent means that you must show that you have been living apart for at least two years and that your spouse agrees to a divorce. If you tried living together again for up to six months (or periods of time that together add up to no more than six months) it won't affect your grounds for divorce but it will be added to your two-year timetable. So if you tried again for four months, for example, you'll have to wait two years and four months to get your divorce.

Separation without consent

If your spouse will not agree to seek a divorce, you will have to live separately for five years and then the petitioner can seek

the divorce on the grounds of separation without consent. If in the meantime your spouse agrees to a divorce after all, you can go ahead and seek it on grounds of separation with consent. Again, any periods of trying to live together that tot up to six months or less won't affect the divorce but will be added to the five-year wait.

If your circumstances meant that you have had to go on living under the same roof since splitting up as a couple, the court will want evidence that you really have separated. That means having different sleeping arrangements, not eating meals together or cooking and cleaning for each other, throughout the period of separation. In Scotland, 'non-cohabitation' for two or five years also means that if you have had to go on living in the same house while seeking the divorce, you'll need to show that you have been leading very separate lives there.

What will my divorce case cost me?

Lawyers charge at an hourly rate, usually divided into five-minute units, according to time spent on your case, including phone calls, paperwork, interviews with you, and court attendances.

You can expect an uncontested divorce to cost perhaps a few hundred pounds, but a contested one could run into thousands – all of which comes out of the marital assets you are fighting over. So be reasonable in your demands and you won't deplete the pot of money by generating too much extra legal work.

> **The more basic homework that you can do, such as drafting lists of assets, and the less time you spend just crying on your solicitor's shoulder or down the phone, the lower the bills will be.**

Do I need to make a new will?

Yes. After a divorce any wills the spouses had made previously become void and you will each need to make a new one. If you die without making a new will, your estate – including any life assurance policies – is treated as if you had died leaving no will at all. It's also wise to agree on who should be the children's guardian, and state this in your will, if anything should happen to the parents (whether divorced or still married). This can avoid extra distress and wider family arguments later.

What happens if I remarry?

Remarriage may affect payments to the ex-spouse receiving maintenance for themselves or the children. Your new partner's finances are not themselves tapped into, but if, for example, the new relationship means you are no longer having to pay as much for your own living costs, then the courts may decide that more of your money is now available to support your previous spouse. The Child Support Agency may decide that more should now go towards supporting the children. And, because your circumstances have changed again, you need to make yet another will.

Marriage, birth and death

Marriages, births, and deaths all have to be registered.

Marriage

There are two ways to get married in England and Wales. One is to have the marriage solemnised in a church belonging to the Church of England (or Church of Wales). The other is to have what is called a 'civil' service. Both legalise the marriage.

A civil service can be followed by a religious service, and the legal part of the ceremony does not have to be in a registry office – many religious buildings belonging to non-Church of England churches and chapels and to non-Christian religions are registered, by the Registrar General, as places where civil marriage proceedings can be held. So you can combine the two occasions into one event.

Alternatively, if you don't want any religious ceremony, you can go to your local register office for a short civil ceremony.

How do I arrange a church wedding?

You are entitled to be married in your own parish church, and other churches may also be prepared to marry you if you have been a regular attendee of that particular church for at least the previous six months.

With a Church of England (or Wales) wedding, there are several things you have to do before the big day. You must either have 'banns' published in both your respective parishes, announcing the intended marriage, on three successive Sundays before the wedding day. Or you must get a 'common licence' to marry, from the diocesan registrar or his 'surrogate' – in which case you don't need to have the banns read. Once you have this licence, you can get married straightaway.

Alternatively, in emergencies or unusual circumstances, you can seek a special licence granted by, or on behalf of, the Archbishop of Canterbury.

The priest-in-charge of the church where you plan to marry will tell you how to seek these licences.

You can also seek a licence from the superintendent registrar's office instead of having banns read, but then you must still wait at least twenty-one days after giving notice of the marriage to him before you can go ahead with the service.

If you are not a parishioner of the church in which you hope to marry, you may need a special licence to be married there. Discuss which route is right for your circumstances with the priest-in-charge at the church in which you hope to be married.

During the wedding service, as soon as the marriage vows have been exchanged, you will go into a room set aside to sign the register. You need two witnesses who will also sign the register, as will the priest officiating at the ceremony.

> **Don't forget that there are fees to be paid for the registration of your marriage, and a church fee! Usually it is the best man's job to settle the bill on the day, on the couple's behalf.**

What if I have been divorced?

If one or both of you have been divorced, you may find it hard to gain permission for a full church wedding. Some parish priests have 'discretion' from their bishops to remarry divorced people in church but they will want to discuss all the circumstances with you first. If you are not a member of that parish, the priest in charge may be unable to help you. However, many churches may be willing to conduct a service to bless your new marriage, in which case you need to go the registry office for the civil proceedings first, and have your religious service of blessing afterwards. Again, this will probably be in your parish church or another church with which you already have connections or have attended regularly.

Civil weddings

For a civil wedding, whether in a registry office or some other registered building, you must give notice of the marriage to the superintendent registrar. You can marry with a licence issued by him, or by certificate and licence.

For marriage by certificate you must each give notice at your local register office, which means two fees to pay! If you both live in the same area, you only need to notify the one registrar, and pay the one fee. You'll find the address and phone number of your registry office in the local phone book. You need to have lived in the area for at least seven full days before you can apply to be married by certificate at its register office.

At least one of you must go into your local register office(s) to give notice. If either of you was born overseas, you should take that person's passport or birth certificate in with you; and if either of you is divorced, take the decree absolute with you to prove that you are now free to remarry. And you will need to pay the district's fee to give notice at this point, too, so take cash or a cheque book. At the time of writing, it is £18 per district.

Do all this within three months of the wedding date, and at least twenty-two days before it, so that the notice can be displayed at the register office for a full twenty-one days before the wedding date (so anyone

who knows of an impediment can tell the Registrar). After the twenty-one days, all being well, the Registrar issues his certificate for the marriage to proceed (and on the wedding date, you pay the marriage fee, which at the time of writing is £21.50 – that's £2.50 for the certificate and £19 to register the marriage).

For marriage by certificate and licence, you only need to give notice at one register office. The person giving notice must have lived in the district for at least fifteen days beforehand. No notice has to be displayed, so if the registrar is satisfied that there is no impediment to your marriage he will issue the certificate and licence for you to go ahead and marry after one clear day (Good Friday, Christmas Day or Sundays do not count as a clear day so if one of them intervenes, wait two full days). The licence and certificate are valid for three months, so if the wedding is delayed that long, you will need to get new ones first.

Marriage ceremonies at a register office only take five or ten minutes. You need at least two witnesses to come with you, though there will be room for more people to attend if you like. The registrar will want to have a brief private chat with the bride and groom together, just before the ceremony. You will be asked to declare in front of your witnesses that you are free to marry, and then you make a contract to join each other as man and wife.

You can exchange wedding rings at a civil service if you want, but you don't have to. As soon as the ceremony is over, the marriage is registered – in special permanent ink!

What does signing the register involve?

The register records your names, ages, marital condition (for example, if you have been previously divorced), occupation, residence at the time of marriage, and the name of each partner's father and his occupation. The bride and groom, their two witnesses, and the person officiating at your ceremony, all sign the register. If you are marrying in church or a registered building, you sign the duplicate register kept there. At the register office, you sign the official register kept there.

What about the cost?

If you are having a big wedding bash, remember that it can costs thousands of pounds by the time you've bought wedding clothes, bridesmaids' dresses, paid all the marriage fees, and for wedding flowers, the cake, the reception and the honeymoon! Traditionally the bride's family foot the bill but these days many couples pay for their own weddings. You can buy insurance to cover damage to clothing and presents, delay or cancellation (but the insurer won't pay up if the wedding is cancelled just because one of you chickens out), and any accidents that happen to your guests or the venue during the wedding celebrations.

> Remember that the taxman lets each parent give their own child up to £5000 tax-free as a wedding gift, while grandparents can each give £2500 tax-free to their own grandchild. Others can each give £1000 tax-free as wedding gift.

Are there any tax implications?

As soon as you are married, you qualify as a couple for the married person's tax allowance from that date, in addition to the normal personal tax allowance which you will still each get in your own right.

But you need to tell the taxman about the wedding, for he won't automatically know. To avoid delays in getting the allowance through, it's a good idea to tell your tax office in advance what your wedding date will be.

For the tax year 1994-95 the allowance lets you keep an extra £1720 of your income as a couple tax-free. Nowadays, the tax break can only be offset against the lowest tax band. So with a 20 per cent minimum tax band, the allowance is worth an extra £340 a year in your pocket. The allowance will be allocated to the husband unless you ask for it to be allocated to the wife, or to have it split equally between you. You need Inland Revenue form 18 to alter the allocation and, apart from the year in which you marry, you will need to complete the form again before the start of each new tax year.

If only one of you is earning, make sure the married person's allowance is allocated to that person, to minimise tax.

As well as having your own personal tax allowance, you each still have an annual capital gains tax allowance, and can take out your own tax-free savings plans (see *Savings*, page 298). But if you are buying a home together, remember that you will only get one set of tax relief on the interest, which is knocked off the monthly payments.

> It's a good idea to read through the Inland Revenue's leaflets IR 80 'Income Tax and Married Couples' and CGT 'Capital Gains Tax, A Guide for Married Couples.' You can get copies at the nearest tax office.

So how should we plan our joint finances?

It's useful to decide before you get married if you will want to have a joint bank or building society account, at least for the household bills. If one of you already has a large overdraft, it may be a good idea to have the joint account at a different bank – otherwise you can both become liable for the existing debt!

You should also run through each other's savings and investments, and do tell each other about any debts you have, preferably before you tie the knot. Then you can plan for the future as a couple, especially if you are buying a home together. Take financial advice from an independent financial adviser, if you want to know about more than just the financial products of your own bank or building society. And if you are planning a family, start saving as soon as possible! Children can be expensive. But pick a flexible savings plan so that if a baby doesn't come along for ages, you can decide to use the money easily for something else.

If you're taking out a non-endowment mortgage together, you should still consider taking out ordinary life cover so that if one dies, there is another lump sum that could be used to clear the loan and stay in the home; and you may want to do some fresh pension planning too. You should also make a will. If you haven't had time to do all this before the wedding, try to sit down and sort it out soon afterwards, when life is a bit less hectic!

Births

All births, including still-births, must be registered within forty-two days. Doctors and midwives periodically pass lists of births to the local authority so sooner or later it will know if one has not been registered, and you will get a requisition form. Parents can be fined for failing to register a child's birth!

The birth must be registered by a 'qualified informant'. This can be either the mother, or the father if he was married to the mother when the birth took place, the occupier of the house in which the child was born, anybody present at the birth itself, and anyone with charge of the child. If a baby is found abandoned, either the person who found it or who is looking after it should register the birth. (If an abandoned still-born child is found, the finder should register it.)

The registrar will ask for your baby's date and place of birth, its name, surname and sex (the forenames can be added later if you haven't yet decided, but once registered they can't be changed). He also needs to know the full names of the parents and where they were born, the father's occupation, and the mother's maiden name as well as her married name.

If the father was not married to the mother when the baby was born, his details can only go on the birth certificate if he goes with the mother to register the birth and signs the register, if he makes a statutory declaration of paternity, or if the mother produces an 'affiliate order' naming him as the father.

For a still-born child, the registrar also needs to be given evidence from a doctor or midwife of the cause of death. He may also issue the certificate needed to authorise burial or cremation. Painful though all this is, you must register a still birth within three months of the event.

Usually the person registering a birth has to go in person to the local registrar of the district in which the birth occurred. But if this was not where you normally live, you can sign a declaration with all the details and post it to the correct register office. Many registrars visit maternity hospitals so the birth can be registered while mother and baby are still there.

Is there any financial help available to new parents?

Yes. Expectant mums get free NHS dental treatment and NHS medical prescriptions during the pregnancy and for a year after the birth. Fill in the forms in leaflets D 11 and P11, from your local benefits office. Or your local hospital may give you a card to send off.

Working mothers can get statutory maternity pay (SMP), via their employer, provided your earnings were at or above the UK's lower earnings limit (for National Insurance contributions) and if you have been with the same firm for the twenty-six weeks up to the fifteenth week ('the qualifying week') before the baby is due.

SMP is paid weekly for eighteen weeks and starts before the birth. See leaflet NI 17A for details. Employers are not allowed to escape SMP by firing you because you're pregnant. The first six weeks of SMP are paid at ninety per cent of your average weekly earnings (based on the eight weeks up to the qualifying week). Then it drops to a lower, standard rate. Tax and NI still have to be paid on SMP. If you can't get SMP – for instance if you have given up your job, or changed jobs recently, or become self-employed – you may be able to get maternity benefit instead, provided you had paid NI contributions in twenty-six weeks of the fifty-two weeks up to the fifteenth week before the baby is due. It can start to be paid from eleven weeks before the baby is due to be born. To claim, you need form MA1 from your local social security office. Send it in within fourteen weeks (not earlier) of the week the baby is due, along with maternity certificate MAT B1 which your doctor or midwife can give you.

If you can't get either of these benefits, inquire about sickness benefit, as you may qualify for that for six weeks before the baby is due until two weeks after the birth.

Once the baby is born you can claim child benefit, paid weekly. All mothers are entitled to this. Single parents may be eligible for One

Parent Benefit as well (leaflet CHI I). If you are hard up, you may qualify for other benefits such as income support, and housing benefit. Ask your local Social Security Office or Benefits Agency (look in the phone book) about these.

Death

Before a death can be registered, a doctor who attended the deceased during the final illness has, by law, to issue a certificate showing the cause of death. This certificate must be given by the doctor to the registrar of births and deaths – and this can be done by giving the certificate to a relative of the deceased who intends to inform the registrar of what has happened.

'Qualified informants' who can notify the registrar of the death can be, in order of priority, either a relative of the deceased, someone who was there when they died, the occupant of the house the death occurred in, or the person in charge of the arrangements for disposing of the body.

If a dead body is discovered, either the person who found it or the person subsequently in charge of it, can notify the registrar of the death.

You should either tell the registrar of the death within the first five days or notify him that a medical certificate of the cause of death has been signed by the doctor, in which case you have up to fourteen days in which to take it to the register office to record the death. The registrar needs to know:

- ☞ The date and place of death.
- ☞ The names and gender of the deceased – if a woman, that includes her maiden and married names.
- ☞ The deceased's date and place of birth.
- ☞ Their occupation and normal address.
- ☞ The cause of death.

He (or she) will also ask you to say which of the qualifications above as the notifier of the death, apply to you.

When there has been an unexpected, violent or unnatural death, or the victim died of an industrial disease, the register has to refer the death to the coroner. The police are also called. If the coroner decides there

need not be an investigation, he'll tell the registrar to register the death when notified of the details by a qualified informant in the normal way.

If he orders a post-mortem, the results may still lead him to decide there is no need for an inquest, and again he will tell the registrar that he can go ahead and register the death, with the cause of death recorded as given in the pathologist's findings.

If the coroner decides there should be an inquest into the death, it is the coroner who has to give the deceased's details to the registrar, and the findings of the inquest provide the details of the cause of death. In this case, there is no need for any other qualified informant to notify the registrar of the death.

> **If you are the executor of the deceased's will, you may find the item on probate, in *Making a will*, helpful (see page 322). You can ask the local probate office for guidance.**

When registering a death you may be asked for the deceased's medical card. This is so that he can be taken off the doctor's list of patients. If the person who has died was receiving any state allowances or a pension, the registrar will tell the authorities, and any professional bodies to which he or she belonged.

The deceased can't be buried or cremated until a registrar or a coroner has issued a certificate authorising this. A registrar can issue one of three certificates: one certifying that he has been notified of the death, one certifying that he has registered the death, or – if the person died abroad and the body was brought to England or Wales for burial – that no registration of the death is needed. If a certificate comes from the coroner, it is in the form of an order for burial or cremation.

All these come in three sections – one to be kept by the issuer of the certificate, one which counts as the actual certificate, and a detachable section to be filled in by the place carrying out the burial or cremation and returned to the registrar as confirmation of when and where it was done. If a cremation is to be arranged, the medical referee of the crematorium gives the final authority for it to go ahead. You will find that the staff of funeral directors are well-versed in what has to be done to register the death.

Owning a pet

Before you get a pet, stop and think about your lifestyle. It's important to house and train your pet properly so that you can keep it under reasonable control. Have your garden properly fenced, too, to stop it from straying. You could be fined or pursued for compensation if it causes an accident, damages land or property, or attacks someone. The only pet that can wander freely without running the risk of getting its owner into legal hot water, is a cat!

When training an animal, be sensible. Remember that if you mistreat your pet, including the cat, or any other animal, you can be reported to the police, or the RSPCA (Royal Society for the Prevention of Cruelty to Animals, see page 440) for instance, and may face prosecution and hefty fines.

What sort of pet can I have?

A constantly barking dog could get you into trouble with your neighbours, and local authority, which can order you to stop the problem, and fine you.

If you want an unusual pet, make sure you stay within the Dangerous Wild Animals Act (see page 347).

There are four types of very powerful dog that you can no longer acquire as a pet. These are:

- 🖙 pit bull terriers
- 🖙 the Japanese Tosa
- 🖙 the Dogo Argentino
- 🖙 the Fila Brazliero

All four are banned under the Dangerous Dogs Act. If you had one before the Act came into force, you are supposed to have registered it and had it tattooed. If this was not done, your ownership of the dog is illegal and it can be destroyed. You must also put a muzzle on it when you take it out.

Safety

Under the Dangerous Dogs Act, any dog must be kept under control in a public place – so if your dog attacks someone, you could be prosecuted and the dog could be destroyed. Train your dog properly and if in doubt about its temperament, muzzle it when you take it out. All dogs must also wear a collar with the owner's name and address on it.

Dog mess can be dangerous – it can carry a parasite called Toxocara Canis. Some cats also carry it. The parasite gets into the earth, and can cause serious illnesses, including asthma, epilepsy and blindness to anyone who becomes infected with it. It is a condition particularly dangerous to children. So if your pet constantly messes in someone else's garden, or a play area, you could find yourself being prosecuted under the Environmental Health Act! Complainants can call in the local authority's environmental health officer to investigate the problem; if he or she thinks it's serious, the local authority can fine you. Your local environmental health officer can advise you about dog-free zones in the area and any by-laws that the local authority has introduced to deal with this subject.

Roving pets

Be careful where you let a dog run free. A dog that kills or injures livestock (for example, farm animals) can provide its keeper – and that can be whoever is in charge of it at the time – with a hefty fine. And if a farmer catches a dog 'worrying' his sheep or other livestock, he is also legally entitled to shoot it on the spot.

If you find a stray dog, you can contact the local environmental health office and tell the dog warden. Or contact your local police station. If yours goes missing, try those two ports of call, and any animal homes in the area.

If your animal wanders off and is the cause of an accident, or damages someone else's property, you could end up being chased for compensation. Unless it's a cat! So keep your dog on a lead near roads, for instance, and play areas in case it gets over-excited and hurts a child. Don't let children tease your pet – it may snap.

Cat owners are not held responsible for what their felines do (provided it's a domestic moggy). A horse that strays is a different matter; its owner or keeper is responsible for what happens. And if livestock damages someone's land – a herd of cows invading the garden, for example – the victim may be able to claim compensation if the keeper of the animals can be shown to have been negligent.

If you run over a dog, horse, sheep, cattle, pig, ass, mule or a goat (but not a cat) you have to stop, and must report the accident to the local police station.

Don't forget that if you have a guard dog – on your business premises, for instance – you must display a clear warning notice on the property, and keep the dog properly secured. It can only roam about if it's under the supervision of its handler. You can be fined heavily for breaching these rules.

What happens if I have a complaint about someone's pet?

The first step is to try and sort something out with the pet owner. If this leads nowhere, try the local authority.

If you have been injured, consult a solicitor, or your local Citizens Advice Bureau, about whether you can claim compensation from the owner or keeper of the animal.

It's a good idea to get someone to take photos of the injury, or any other damage; and get the names and addresses of any witnesses. Your doctor can also supply medical evidence about your injuries.

If you have to sue to get satisfaction, it's simplest to go through the small claims court – where you don't need a solicitor, you can present your own case – but if the injury or damage is very serious and you want substantial compensation, that means going to a higher court and you should consult a solicitor.

If your animal starts to behave oddly, or obsessively, consult your vet. Better training or even a visit to an animal behaviourist may solve the problem.

If any animal ever attacks you, you can defend yourself within reason but, unless you think it's going to kill you, try not to kill it. Get out of the situation as best you can; the authorities will decide later if the animal concerned should be put down.

Unusual pets

If you want a pet that's out of the ordinary, consult your vet first. He or she should have lots of information about which animals come under the Dangerous Wild Animals Act and how they should be housed, fed and looked after. Wolves, 'big cats', bears, monkeys, some large birds, reptiles, lizards or snakes, and some spiders, are included in this category.

If the pet you want is classified as a dangerous wild animal, you must have a licence to keep it (this also involves a fee). That means the local authority will want to send a vet with specialist knowledge of that species to inspect your arrangements for housing and looking after it.

The local authority will also want to check your fire and emergency precautions, heating arrangements if it's an animal that needs to be kept warm (reptiles, for instance), and be satisfied that precautions are taken to prevent the spread of diseases between the animal and humans.

You can't normally get a licence to own a wild animal, but have it looked after by someone else, unless you are running a private zoo.

If you have an unusual or expensive pet it's a good idea to find out if you can insure against it doing anything odd, or accidents befalling it. Pet insurance is covered in *Insurance*, page 310 – but ask your house or contents insurer if your policy with them could be extended to cover pet-related incidents. This may not be cheap!

Changing your name

You can call yourself anything you like in Great Britain, just by choosing a new name and using it whenever you are asked for it. Providing you are not using the new name to defraud or deceive anyone, this is perfectly legal. It's known as changing your name informally 'by use and reputation'.

Deed poll

Though you can change, or add to, your name just by using a different one, it's actually better (and not expensive) to do so by deed poll. A deed poll is a legal document stating your old name, and the new one you are adopting. You should consult a solicitor about this. If you want the new name to be permanent, it's a good idea to 'enrol' it with the Central Office of the High Court, which means the change of name must be advertised in the UK's official newspaper, the *London Gazette*. A solicitor will tell you how to go about this.

Once your name is enrolled you can obtain official copies of your enrolment to show with your birth certificate if proof of your new identity is ever required.

Marriage

Married women don't have to switch to using their husband's surname – they can stick to their maiden name if they prefer. A married woman can decide to use her husband's name at any time, and can also switch back to her maiden name whenever she likes. If she becomes divorced, she can still use her ex-husband's name if she wants to, or revert to her maiden name if she prefers. It's up to her to use whichever name she wants.

What happens to my child's name if I remarry?

If a woman with a child or children of a previous marriage or relationship remarries, she may want the children to take the name of her new husband. However, this can only be arranged with the written consent of both of the child's natural parents, or by a Court order if the Court decides it is in the child's best interests to be known by their stepfather's name. Discuss this with a solicitor before taking any action.

What about adopted children?

When a child is adopted, the record of its birth kept at St Katherine's House in London is altered to show its new name, and a birth certificate is issued in the child's new name.

Passports

If you have started using a different name, and want a passport, you will need to provide some evidence that the name you are using is now your assumed name. A statutory declaration or affidavit sworn in front of a solicitor should be sufficient.

If you already have a passport and want to change your name in that – for instance a newly married woman wanting to use her husband's surname – you need to call in at the Post Office and ask for the UK Passport Agency's Form C. Fill this in and send or take it to your passport office. If you want to change your passport name in time to travel straight after the wedding (you can still travel under your maiden name if you wish) you need Form PD2. Remember to leave enough time for changes to be made and your passport to be returned to you before your departure date.

If you still have an old blue UK passport, you'll get it back with the new details added, so you don't have to send in a new photo unless your appearance has changed a lot. If yours is one of the new EC passports, you'll get back a replacement passport with the new details, valid until the expiry date of the old one. You'll need to send in two passport photos in this instance.

Children can also be added to passports with Form C but most parents prefer to get the child his or her own passport nowadays.

Who else needs to know?

For practical reasons, don't forget to tell your bank, building society, insurer, and any other organisation you save or invest through, that you want to be known by your new name. They may ask you to complete a form for their records and provide a specimen of your new signature.

Employment

Getting a job

Job hunting can be a full-time business. To avoid wasted effort, check the fields in which your qualifications will help you to get work. School and college leavers should make full use of any careers help offered by their place of education. Look in local and national newspapers for advertisements (and ideas), visit local job agencies to see if they've got anything suitable – and don't forget the government's free employment service. If you are unemployed, or looking for your first job, go to the nearest Job Centre (see below).

Draw up a neat, preferably one-page, curriculum vitae with your name and address, education, qualifications, experience and interests. You can send this to potential employers with a short covering letter when applying for a post, or use it as a prompt when filling in a company's application form. When going for a job interview, dress in a way that you think will make you look suitable for that job. First impressions in your favour are always worth having. Try to prepare yourself for the sort of questions a job interviewer may ask you about yourself, your qualifications, your ambitions and interests – and don't be afraid to ask a few questions of your own about the organisation, as this will help you decide if you'd like to work there. It also gives the interviewer the feeling you're genuinely interested in joining. Practise on a friend!

Job Centres

Not only will your local Job Centre help you to claim any state benefits to which you are entitled while out of work, but it will help you plan a strategy for getting a new job. It can help in several ways:

☞ Job Centres have display boards showing current job vacancies.
☞ They can advise you on how to go about looking for work.
☞ They'll help you prepare for job interviews and get work experience.
☞ They can even provide you with information on how to set up your own business (see page 433).

If you are out of work for over three months, the Job Centre can:

☞ Help you to revise your strategy.
☞ Send you on a seminar to get practical advice about job-hunting.
☞ Organise a job review workshop to see what kinds of work might be open to you.

At the time of writing, if after six months you've still had no luck, the Job Centre has a further series of programmes including training to acquire a new skill, to help you tackle the problem. (People with disabilities don't have to wait for three or six months to move on to the job-hunting seminar and other programmes.)

> TECs and LECs also participate in an 'open learning' system which allows you to study in your own time or at work, and at any age, to gain any extra skills you need, using any combination of books, videos, tapes, and computer disks. Back-up comes from a tutor and group meetings.

Can I get financial help to retrain?

Yes. There are career development loans of between £200 and £5000 available through the Employment Department to help unemployed people gain new skills, or update existing ones. The loans cover eighty per cent of one year's course fees and are available, via the Employment Department, from a choice of three banks. Find out about these loans at the nearest Job Centre or through your local Training and Enterprise Council (TEC) in England and Wales or local enterprise councils (LECs) in Scotland.

Your legal rights at work

Being an 'employee' means you have entered into or are working under a contract of employment with the business concerned. This will be a contract of 'service' or of apprenticeship, and gives you various legal rights.

Some of these are 'time-acquired' rights, which means they only apply after you have been working for the same employer for a certain period of time; and some are 'non time-acquired' which means they are your rights however short or long you have been in any job.

Time-acquired rights include entitlements to redundancy money and compensation for unfair dismissal.

Non time-acquired rights include the right of a pregnant woman to return to her old job after having her baby, the right to be protected against race or sex discrimination at work, the right not to be sacked for any action you take on lawful health and safety grounds (for example, you shouldn't be sacked for reasonably refusing to tackle a dangerous task unless issued with a safety helmet), and the right not to be fired for belonging – or even for not belonging – to a trade union at your place of work.

You also have the right not to be refused a job by a company or an employment agency on unlawful grounds such as race or sex discrimination.

This section runs through some of the areas that are most likely to crop up, and your local Job Centre and the Employment Department provide frequently updated booklets and leaflets clearly explaining your current legal rights, as an employee, in each of these circumstances.

What do I do if I think I've been unfairly treated?

If you think your rights as an employee have been breached you can refer your case to an industrial tribunal which will decide each case upon its merits and rule whether you should be compensated, or reinstated. Your local Job Centre or Unemployment Benefit Office will have the form you need to refer your case to a tribunal, and an explanatory leaflet.

A 1994 House of Lords ruling resulted in a review of certain rights which may by now have resulted in some changes – so if you have a particular problem, make sure you drop in to your nearest Job Centre for the latest information.

Depending on the cause of your case, there are various time limits within which you need to refer it to a tribunal or you could miss the opportunity (see below). Once you have sent in the form, you may be asked to go through an arbitration and conciliation process. If this is not possible, or does not

work, the tribunal will hear your case. Both sides need to attend the hearings. You can present your own case – you don't need a lawyer, but you may prefer to have one – or it can be presented for you by someone else, from your trade union, for example.

Unfair dismissal

Unfair dismissal can include your job being axed without warning; you resigning because the employer has breached its contract of employment with you in ways that show it did not intend to be bound by that contract; a fixed-term contract that you have with a firm expiring without renewal; and being refused the right to return to work after a baby when you have a legal right to do so.

If you are over eighteen and have been in your job for two continuous years of working more than sixteen hours a week, you are entitled to claim compensation if you are unfairly dismissed.

In the past, part-timers employed by the same firm for at least eight hours a week have had to wait five years before qualifying for compensation for unfair dismissal, and those working under eight hours a week didn't qualify at all. But in 1994 all this was put under review after a House of Lords ruling that time limits on employment rights should be the same for everyone, so check at your local Job Centre for the latest rules.

Non-employees: freelancers, independent contractors – people working abroad (except for most merchant seamen on British-registered ships and employees working offshore on oil and gas rigs in the British sectors of the Continental Shelf) – members of the police, armed forces and intelligence services, are not covered by the rules on unfair dismissal or unlawful refusal of employment.

New or recent mothers refused their old jobs back, people who believe their dismissal is linked to race discrimination, or trade union membership issues, or to their objection to something on health and safety grounds, can refer their claim of unfair dismissal to an industrial tribunal, whether they have been in the job for two years or not.

To prove your claim of unfair dismissal, or unlawful refusal of a job or of the services of an employment agency, you need to refer it to an industrial tribunal. You can also go to a tribunal if you think you have been unlawfully refused a job by a company or an employment agency on discriminatory grounds.

Redundancy

If you are over eighteen, have been in your job for two continuous years working more than sixteen hours a week, you are entitled to a tax-free payment if you are made redundant.

As with unfair dismissal rights, part-timers employed by a business for at least eight hours a week have had to wait five years before qualifying (and those working under eight hours a week didn't qualify at all), but this also went under review in 1994 after the House of Lords ruling so check at your local Job Centre for any new rules.

Redundancy payments do not affect your entitlement to unemployment or other benefits.

Self-employed people, fee-earning non-executive directors, and partners in firms, are not eligible for statutory redundancy payments. Nor are apprentices, people reaching normal retirement age, and civil servants (for whom there are other arrangements).

If you work abroad for a British company you are only entitled to redundancy payments if you are recalled to the UK before your contract ends. But someone on a fixed-term contract that is not renewed when it expires, may be entitled to a redundancy payment – provided that the contract was for less than two years and there was no clause in it waiving redundancy rights. So check the rules before you sign a fixed-period contract!

> **If your employer asks for volunteers for redundancy, and you successfully apply, make sure the company still formally dismisses you – or the tax man may argue that it wasn't a proper redundancy and that your pay-off shouldn't have been tax-free.**

What counts as redundancy?

There are strict rules about what constitutes redundancy. It usually involves being dismissed because the employer needs to reduce the work force, or because the business or a workplace is being closed down. Normally people who resign of their own accord from a job don't qualify for redundancy money – but an employer who behaves so badly that you become entitled to leave the firm without notice, may have to pay you.

Equally, employers who suddenly lay off workers without wages – or put them on short-time working at less than half a week's pay for four consecutive weeks, or for six weeks within a thirteen-week period – can also face valid claims for redundancy payments. If that happens to you, you don't have to wait to be made redundant to get a payment. Put in your own claim in writing to the employer.

What happens if my employer refuses to pay?

If there is a dispute about whether you are entitled to redundancy money, or if your employer has failed to pay up, write to them promptly to state your case. You can also refer the issue to an industrial tribunal, and again the form you need is available at the local Job Centre, so call in there.

There is a time limit for taking action, so make sure you start the ball rolling within six months of the date that your employment ended or you could lose out. If six months have already elapsed, it's still worth applying to a tribunal. It is possible that they'll decide you have a case, but do it quickly.

Once you have either written to the firm asking for your money or referred your claim to the tribunal, your right to a payment if you win is not affected by how long the case itself takes to hear.

What happens if I'm offered another job with the same firm?

If you take an alternative job with the same employer before the old job runs out, and start it within four weeks of the old job ending, you may find you are no longer entitled to a redundancy payment on the old job. But you can keep your options open for a bit. If you start the new job on a four-week trial basis – or for longer (by written agreement) if it involves re-training – without agreeing at the outset that you will accept it, you reserve your right to your redundancy money if the alternative job turns out not to be suitable (or if you have very good personal reasons for not wanting it). But you must reject the alternative job before the end of the trial period. Then you are entitled to be treated as if you had been made redundant from the day your old job ended.

Be careful – if at the end of the trial period you are still doing the new job, you will be regarded as having accepted it! So make sure you decide in good time.

How much redundancy money do I get?

Redundancy payments reflect how long you have worked for the employer, your age, and your weekly pay. At the time of writing, if you are aged between twenty-two and forty-one, you will get one week's pay for every complete year of employment with the company who are making you redundant.

If you are aged between forty-one and sixty-four you get one-and-a-half week's pay for each full year with that employer. If made redundant between sixty-four and sixty-five the same calculation is used but is tapered off to retirement age, by being reduced by one-twelfth for each full month over sixty-four you are when you leave.

People aged between eighteen and twenty-two get half a week's money per full year's employment with the firm concerned.

Pregnancy

Working mothers-to-be must not be unreasonably refused paid time off for antenatal appointments, though they can be asked to provide proof of the appointments. If your firm is unreasonable about this, complain to an industrial tribunal within three months of the date of the antenatal appointment concerned.

Women must not be dismissed because they are pregnant, or for reasons linked to the pregnancy.

You are entitled to return to your job within twenty-nine weeks of stopping work to have the baby. This can be extended, once, by four weeks, provided you give the firm four weeks' notice – that is, by twenty-five weeks into the break – that you want to take an extra month off. In order to be eligible, you must continue to be employed by the firm (even if you are physically off work!) up to the eleventh week before the baby is due. If you leave your job before then you lose your right to getting it back again afterwards. (Freelancers don't have the same rights.)

You must give your employer all the information they need, and (if practicable) three weeks – twenty-one days – notice of the date you plan to stop work. The length of maternity leave you get, and the level of maternity pay you get over and above any Statutory Maternity Pay (SMP), are up to the company and you to agree together.

If a redundancy programme undertaken while you are away means your old job no longer exists, the employer must offer you a suitable alternative to which you can return. If they can't, you are entitled to redundancy money. But if you unreasonably refuse a suitable alternative job, you could find you lose the right to any redundancy pay.

If the firm simply fails to let you come back to work after your time away, you can claim for unfair dismissal.

An employee who is sacked because of her pregnancy (or a related reason) or refused her job back, should complain of unfair dismissal to an industrial tribunal within three months of being dismissed.

If you win, the tribunal can either order your reinstatement or appointment to a similar job, or a cash compensation payment instead. But if the pregnancy makes it impossible – or unlawful – for you to do your job properly it may be possible for the employer legally to end your contract. First they must offer you a suitable alternative job if they have one. If you turn that down, you could lose your right to compensation for unfair dismissal. But if there is a suitable alternative post that you could take up or return to, and the employer does not offer it to you, then your dismissal from the old job does count as unfair.

CHAPTER SEVEN

Basic car maintenance

Maria Young

Associate Editor of AA Magazine.

Running a car can add freedom and flexibility to your life, enabling you to see more places, reach more people and get about more often. It can also be a big drain on your expenses. Yet with careful thought before you buy your car, and a smattering of regular attention afterwards, running a car can be cheap and fun. This chapter gives you the information you need to buy a car (see pp. 353-6), service and maintain it (see pp. 357-60) and deal with the other basic car ownership entails, like changing a wheel (see pp. 361-3). There is also advice on keeping your car safe from theft (see pp. 364-7) and getting it through the MoT test (see p. 360).

Buying a car

Next to buying a house, buying a car is probably the biggest purchase you'll ever make. It's a daunting prospect with plenty of scare stories to intimidate you further. While it is true that Trading Standards officers receive hundreds of complaints every week from dissatisfied customers, with a few common sense measures, buying a car should be no more risky than buying a table.

Before you even begin to look, think objectively about what you need from a car. Do you have passengers to ferry; a great deal of luggage to carry; a caravan or trailer to tow? Is speed important, or economy? What about safety features, air conditioning and colour? Once you know the kind of car you want, then you can start to shop around.

If you can afford to buy new, you will avoid having to take some of the precautions involved in buying secondhand, and of course you won't have to worry about the car's history. New-car dealers and manufacturers are keen to protect their reputations, so any problems you may experience when buying new car are likely to be dealt with sympathetically and efficiently.

In addition, most new cars carry a warranty for between one and three years, so you are covered should your car suffer a parts failure. However, the level of cover varies from manufacturer to manufacturer so, as always, check the small print. The current trend is for warranties to be more comprehensive, rather than less – many include breakdown assistance through the AA or RAC. The major manufacturers such as Rover, Ford and Vauxhall also offer the chance for an exchange or refund within the first month if customers are in any way dissatisfied with their purchase.

Before you sign on the dotted line, make sure you know what's included in the price. Delivery charges, number plates and tax can all come as extras.

Buying new has recently become more affordable with many manufacturers introducing flexible finance schemes, and there are few things more seductive than a gleaming new car. It's worth remembering that hundreds, if not thousands of pounds can be wiped off the value of a new car the second you drive it off the dealer's forecourt.

That's one reason why nearly 75 per cent of all car sales are used-car deals. By opting to buy secondhand, suddenly your budget can stretch to a bigger/faster/higher-specification model. But it is here that first-time buyers, in particular, are advised to temper enthusiasm for that irresistible bargain with some caution.

In general, there are three routes to buying a used car: a dealer's forecourt, the private seller through classified ads, or the auction house.

Dealers

The first is the least tricky, as dealers have to abide by consumer protection legislation.

☞ The dealer must have a legal right to sell the car.

☞ The car supplied must be the same as described by the dealer.

☞ The car must be of proper quality, save any defects brought to your attention prior to the sale.

☞ The car must be fit for the intended purpose.

☞ No misrepresentation of the vehicle's condition or history may be made.

Choose an established dealer, preferably through a personal recommendation. A local dealer with a new-car franchise that includes the model you're interested in would be a good bet, as there will be stocks of part-exchanged vehicles. Avoid back-street dealers whose trading names change regularly.

As with new cars, used vehicles purchased through dealers are likely to come with a warranty, but you may have to pay extra for this and they vary tremendously in value and level of cover. Read them carefully, they may not be worth the money. You can always opt to find your own warranty. Many used-car dealers sell warranties – which are really a special sort of insurance.

Private sales

If you shop for your car through the small ads, there is little consumer legislation to

---

> **SMALL-AD JARGON**
> **Fsh, pas, ice ... What does it all mean? Car ads are full of these strange abbreviations, but how can you understand this other language? Here's a brief guide:**
> **fsh** — full service history
> **pas** — power assisted steering
> **rww** — rear wash and wiper
> **ice** — in car entertainment
> **abs** — advanced braking system
> **e/s/r** — electric sunroof
> **c/l** — central locking
> **e/w** — electric windows

protect you – the often-quoted phrase 'caveat emptor' (let the buyer beware) sums it up. However, there are some tempting bargains to be had in this market, and once again if you're careful, you need not come unstuck.

There are many genuine ads from people wishing to sell their car in magazines such as *Auto Trader* and *Exchange and Mart* and in local newspapers. It may be your chosen medium when you come to sell your car. But the largest pitfall for buyers shopping through the classifieds is to end up dealing with a trader masquerading as a private seller.

If you see a car you like in the classified section of a newspaper or magazine, take the following steps to be sure you're not really negotiating with a trader.

☞ Avoid ads that specify a time to phone. Sometimes these numbers turn out to be for a public call box, or a third party not involved in the sale.

☞ When you call, don't specify the car in which you're interested. If the seller has to ask 'Which car?' he's probably a trader. Hang up.

☞ Never allow the seller to bring the vehicle to you, always insist on going to where the vehicle is on sale. Anyone who is less than honest will be put off by this approach.

☞ Look out for signs of casual car dealing, such as several other cars in the drive or parked nearby, or an unusual amount of spare parts stored in the garage.

☞ Ask to see the registration document, to check how long the seller has owned the vehicle. If it is only a short time, ask why it is being sold now. If the seller does not have the registration document, find out why not.

☞ Once you have established the seller is genuine, you need to take an objective look at the car. This also applies if you are buying from a used-car dealer.

☞ Bring along a friend who is mechanically minded and knows something about cars. If you can afford it, pay for a professional engineer to survey the car. The AA and RAC have vehicle-inspection services, which often prove to be well worth the money (from £100 upwards, depending on the model).

☞ Look out for rust, especially along door sills, wheel arches and the tailgate of hatchback models.

☞ Mis-matched paintwork may mean the car has been in a crash.

☞ Check the tyres for wear and damage and ensure the car sits evenly on its suspension.

☞ Check for leaks – excessive oil seeps are a warning something more serious may be wrong.

☞ Turn over the engine and leave it running, it should idle smoothly. If there are any rattles or misfires there may be a problem.

☞ Check the exhaust by looking for smoke as the engine is revved. Some black smoke is nothing to worry about, but blue smoke indicates worn engine components – an expensive repair, no doubt. Check the exhaust isn't 'blowing', as this means a new part.

☞ Test-drive the car, paying particular attention to the brakes, steering and gearbox. Make sure the gears can be selected easily and that the steering doesn't pull to one side when driving and braking. Listen out for any knocking noises and see that all the warning lights and indicators are working properly.

☞ Look into the car's authenticity, too, or you could end up buying a vehicle that is an insurance write-off, stolen, or belongs to a finance company. An HPI check can help here, at a price (around £25), but it is particularly valuable when buying privately. HPI hold computer registers for millions of cars using information supplied by the DVLA, police, insurers, rental companies and local government.

☞ Check the history of the car by looking at the service book and registration documents, as well as asking questions. How many previous owners have there been? Has the car any accident damage? What's the mileage? Are there any outstanding finance agreements? Be wary of cars with no service history, it may prove troublesome in the future and it prevents you from checking out the mileage.

☞ Check the chassis and engine numbers and ensure they tally with the registration document.

☞ Check the registration document for watermarks, spelling mistakes, typeface and over-typing – irregularities could indicate a forgery.

Auctions

Buying at auction used to be 'strictly trade only', but many auction houses are now positively encouraging private individuals to their sales. Even so, this is not good territory for the novice.

If you are determined to bid at auction, read the terms and conditions of the sale beforehand. These are normally displayed fairly prominently. More often than not 'caveat emptor' applies, but some auction houses are now introducing special warranties for private buyers. Whatever the terms, never

Green Tip Cars are a major contributor to air pollution, but catalytic converters significantly reduce many of the toxic gases usually associated with exhaust fumes. Most petrol-powered cars sold after January 1993 are fitted with catalytic converters. So for a greener car pick one registered after that date.

forget that at auction, a sow's ear can be made to resemble a silk purse.

Pay several visits to your chosen auction prior to bidding, so you know the format and feel at ease. On the day you go to bid, decide on your budget and stick to it – it's all too easy to get carried away in the heat of the moment.

Wherever you buy your car, don't let your heart rule your head. Remember there really are plenty more cars to see, and unless you're shopping for a rare classic, there will be dozens more much like the one with which you just fell in love.

> **Green** 🌍 **Tip** **If the car you are interested in is registered prior to October 1990, it may not necessarily run on unleaded petrol – ask the seller which petrol it takes. Check if it can be easily converted to unleaded.**

Selling a car

Eventually you will no doubt want to sell your car, either because your circumstances have changed, or you need a different sort of vehicle, or because you would like to trade up to a better model. Whatever the reason, you have a choice of how to dispose of it. You can trade it in with a dealer as a part-exchange for another car, sell it to a garage, put it to auction, or sell it privately.

Firstly, you need to get a good idea of what the car is worth by scanning dealer's forecourts and advertisements for similar models. Many motoring magazines now carry a used-car price section, which can prove helpful, too.

Once you know your vehicle's value, give it a good clean. First impressions count. If it's grubby inside, a professional valet will bring it up spotless and it shouldn't cost more than £20. Then gather the registration document, MoT certificate, service book and all repairs and servicing bills, so you can present a good service history.

If you decide to part-exchange your car for a new model it's possible to get a very good

price, depending on the kind of car to which you are trading up. Generally speaking, the more expensive the new car, the better price you will get for your old model. Part-exchange is a convenient and hassle-free way to dispose of your old car.

However, many people prefer to sell privately through newspapers and magazines. If you take this route be prepared for time-wasters and canvassers as well as potential purchasers at call.

Keep your ad short, but with as much detail as possible, and include your telephone number, but no name. Inflate the asking price a little so you have room to haggle later.

When your potential buyer calls to look at the vehicle be careful not to leave him or her alone with the keys, no matter how trustworthy they seem. Ask if they are insured before you allow them to test-drive the car.

It's easiest if the buyer pays for the car in cash and it goes without saying that you shouldn't hand over the keys until you have checked it. However, many people prefer to pay by cheque. If this is the case, wait for the cheque to clear before allowing the buyer to take delivery of the car. Exercise the same caution even with banker's drafts or certified building society cheques.

Make out two invoices, each of which should be signed by both parties and fill in the form at the bottom of the registration document and send it off to the DVLA (see addresses page 439). The latter is particularly important if you don't want to receive the new owner's parking and speeding tickets.

If you fail to sell your car through the small ads, you could try offering it to local garages. An easier option might be the auction house. You can put a reserve price on it, so you need not let it go for a song. Auctions are particularly good for old, high-mileage, or damaged cars.

> **Green is still considered by some people as an unlucky colour and in parts of the West Country green cars just don't sell for that reason. Red is the most popular colour choice for British cars.**

Servicing and maintenance

As mentioned before, your car is one of your greatest assets, so you will want to look after it. Regular attention pays off and, fear not, doesn't take much technical skill or mechanical knowledge.

Of course, if you would like to know more about how your car works and would like to go further than just routine DIY servicing, some excellent manuals are available from motoring accessory shops. But all motorists, no matter how mechanically inept, should take a few minutes each week to carry out some simple checks.

Not only will regular checks lessen the likelihood of a large bill next time you take your car to the garage for a major service, but you are less likely to break down.

There are nine main areas to give the once-over each week; they may not need much attention on a weekly basis, but it's wise to look and see. The nine points are:

- ☞ Oil level
- ☞ Coolant level
- ☞ Brake fluid level
- ☞ Tyres
- ☞ Washer fluid level
- ☞ Battery
- ☞ Wipers and washers
- ☞ Lights and horn
- ☞ Fluid leaks

Oil level

Before you check the oil, make sure the car is on level ground, and, if the engine has been running, that it has been given a few minutes to cool down. Under the bonnet you will find an oil dipstick (it should be clearly marked). Pull this out and give it a wipe with a rag. You will see that it is engraved with two lines; one marked MAX, one marked MIN. Your oil level needs to fall between these two.

Return the dipstick fully and then slowly pull it out again; you will now have a true reading of the oil level. If it needs topping up, unscrew the oil filler cap – check it's the right one – and fill it up with a good-quality oil. Your car handbook will recommend the best oil for your model.

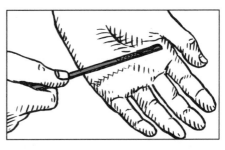

▲ **Wipe the oil dipstick with a rag, then reinsert. Pull it out slowly to get a true reading.**

Just how much you will need to get from MIN to MAX will vary from model to model – try half a litre first.

If you find that you are having to top up each week, it could be a symptom of a more serious problem. Check for any leaks and seek professional advice if necessary.

Coolant level

A glance at either the radiator filler neck or the expansion tank should tell you how much coolant you have.

If you need to top up, make sure the engine is cold before removing the filler cap. Then fill up with a mixture of water and antifreeze.

▼ **Ensure your engine is cold before removing the cap of your expansion (coolant) tank.**

Particularly in winter, it's a good idea to check on the level of antifreeze in the mixture. This can be done simply with a hydrometer – which costs about £2 from motoring accessory shops. One part anti-freeze to two parts water is about right. In extremely cold conditions a fifty/fifty mix may be required.

Again, if you find that each week more coolant is needed, there may be a more serious problem. If you can't find an obvious leak, pay a visit to your local garage for further investigation.

Brake fluid level

Although many cars now have a warning light to show when brake fluid levels are low, a visual inspection is a good precaution. Topping up should rarely be needed – so, if it is, check for a possible leak. For obvious reasons a brake fluid leak is very dangerous.

Check your car handbook for the correct type of fluid to use. Never use brake fluid that has been kept in an opened container, as this means it may have drawn moisture from the air, which will inhibit its efficiency.

Brake fluid should be changed every two years.

Tyres

Check your tyre pressures and look for any wear or damage. Your tyres are the only thing between you and the road – don't lose your grip.

▼ **The legal tread depth for tyres is 1.6 mm across the central three-quarters of the tyre.**

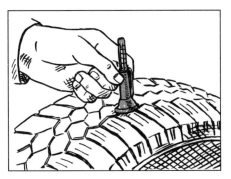

The ideal time to check tyre pressures is when the tyres are cold. After a journey or even when the weather is hot, the pressures will be distorted. If this is not possible, or you need to drive to a filling station to use their tyre pressure equipment, expect the pressures to be higher.

Look in your car handbook for the correct pressures and note if they need to be different when driving with a heavy load. Don't forget to check the spare – you never know when you might need it.

Look out for any objects imbedded in your tyres and pick them out, before they cause further damage. Any nails that have penetrated the surface of the tyre should be left there until professionally repaired or replaced. On pp. 361-2 you will find instructions on how to change a wheel.

The current legal tread depth for tyres is 1.6 mm across the central three-quarters of the tyre's width, along the full circumference of the tyre. However, for safety's sake, it is advisable to allow 2 mm. Tyres are expensive, but replacing them at 2 mm rather than 1.6 mm will only add about £8 to your annual motoring costs, and the extra tread could prove invaluable on a greasy road surface.

Washer fluid level

The reservoir for your washer fluid is under the bonnet along with the coolant reservoir and oil dipstick.

It's particularly likely that you'll need to top up in summer when dust and flies regularly need to be washed and wiped from your windscreen. Use water mixed with an additive to stop smears and freezing in winter.

Never use engine antifreeze instead of windscreen additive – it will ruin your washer system and quite likely your paintwork.

Battery

More and more batteries are the maintenance-free variety, which don't need topping up with distilled water. A quick glance at the indicator level on the top of the battery to see if it is still green is all that is required here.

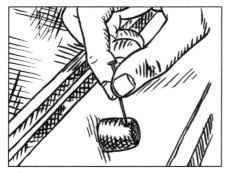

▲ **Unblock and redirect your washer fluid nozzle with a pin.**

But for standard batteries, topping up with distilled water may sometimes be required. Remove the cover from the top and add enough distilled water to cover the tops of the plates inside the battery, or alternatively the mark on the battery case. Don't use plain tap water which will reduce the life of your battery.

Wipers and washers

Wiper blades generally need replacing every year, a very easy job, but in between check for cracks in the rubber – a worn blade will cause smears on your windscreen.

Check the washers for blockages and the hoses for leaks. If required, adjust the washers using a pin inserted into the end of the nozzle.

Lights and horn

It's easiest to check your lights with the help of a friend, but if this is not possible, park up against a wall or window where you can see the reflected light. Try each of the lights in turn; side, dipped, full-beam, brakes, indicators, reversing and fog lamps. Replace any dead bulbs (see pp. 363-4).

Fluid leaks

Leaks can forewarn you of more serious problems, so always check the ground where your car is usually parked for signs of oil, water, petrol or other fluids. Look under the bonnet and check all the hoses and pipes. If you spot seeping fluid try and locate the source. If you suspect it may be petrol or brake fluid do not drive the car until you have sought professional advice.

Finding a garage

Apart from the above checks, your car should be given a full service at regular intervals. Your car handbook will advise of the manufacturer's recommended service intervals. If it does not, opt for a small service including oil change every 6000 miles or six months, and a full service every 12,000 or twelve months.

Finding a garage that is convenient to use, trustworthy, and not too expensive is a tricky business, and a personal recommendation can rarely be beaten. However, if you have yet to settle on a garage for your servicing needs, here are a few guidelines.

If you have a popular model vehicle it may be worth going to a fast-fit garage, where servicing is done on a menu basis. Here the items to be serviced are clearly written up and you can be sure of exactly what you are getting. This is good for people who don't know much about mechanics and fear their ignorance is sometimes exploited.

But if you have an unusual car, prefer personal service, or the option to have more specialist work carried out, it is better to find a local garage. The AA and RAC run approval schemes for the garage trade. Members of these schemes are subject to regular vetting. Garages approved by the Retail Motor Industry Federation or the Scottish Motor Trade Association must abide by a code of practice drawn up in consultation with the

▼ **Assessing the condition of your brake hoses is an important weekly check.**

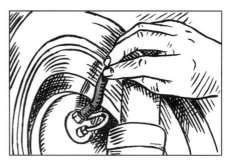

Used engine oil is a hazard to the environment and should be disposed of carefully. Never pour it down a drain or bury it underground. Most local authorities have special disposal sites for engine oil and used oil filters. Phone your council for details of where to go. Alternatively, your local garage may allow you to use their oil-disposal tank.

Office of Fair Trading. So if the garage sports an AA, RAC, RMI or SMTA logo, it should prove reputable.

When you take your car in for servicing, find out exactly what will be covered and how much it will cost. It is possible that while the mechanic is carrying out the service other items that require attention may come to light. Unless you are happy to be surprised by a bigger than expected bill, ask the garage to contact you before any other work is completed. Get them to explain exactly what needs doing and how much extra it will cost before allowing them to go ahead.

The MoT test

If you are lucky, the only other time you will need to go to the garage is for your MoT test. All cars over three years old (five years in Northern Ireland) are required by law to undergo an annual check to ensure they comply with basic safety and legal requirements. Without an MoT certificate you won't be able to tax and insure your car, but the test only costs about £25 (1995 prices).

In recent years there have been several additions to the test, including, in January 1993, the introduction of an emissions test. This is now applicable to both diesel and petrol-powered cars. Depending on the age of your vehicle, exhaust gas emissions must fall within certain limits. These are not excessively stringent and if your car is regularly serviced, should prove no problem at all.

Failing the MoT, and one in three cars does fail, can prove expensive. You will have to pay to have the necessary repairs or replacements and then fork out for a second test fee. Yet, with a little preparation, you can vastly improve your chances of passing first time, or at least reduce the cost of a re-take.

While it is impossible for all but the keenest of DIY mechanics to carry out a full dummy MoT test at home, the following are areas that everybody can check out.

Lighting and signalling equipment

Check that all your lights are working and don't flicker at all. See that pairs of lamps – headlights, for example – are of equal brightness. Check your dipped beam falls in the correct area, so that it lights up the road, but doesn't dazzle oncoming traffic.

Steering and suspension

Look out for any fluid leaks from the shock absorbers. Walk round your car and depress each corner in turn; it should rise and then settle. Make an objective assessment of your car's steering, looking out for any unusual free play.

Brakes

Check your handbrake; you should be able to engage it without having to yank it. Equally, check that it is not so loose that it can disengage of its own accord.

Try out the foot brake; when depressed it should be firm, rather than spongy.

Make sure there are no brake fluid leaks and look out for worn brake pads and shoes (your car manual will help you to locate these).

It's estimated that 50 per cent of vehicle pollution is caused by 10 per cent of cars. You can ensure your car isn't one of them by keeping it regularly serviced.

> **The old wives' tale that a pair of stockings will come in handy should the fan belt snap is, unfortunately, only that. It is doubtful that a pair of stockings would last very long at all. Besides, modern cars don't have a fan belt, but an alternator belt. Alternator belt failure is rare in all but the most neglected of cars.**

Finally, find a safe spot to carry out a brake test. Travelling at about 30 miles per hour (48 kph) apply the brakes firmly and progressively. The car should come to a halt in a straight line, without pulling to either side.

Tyres and wheels

If you check your tyres weekly (see page 358), they should be in tip-top condition. The MoT tester will check to see that there is 1.6mm of tread across the central three-quarters of the tyre width, along the full circumference of the tyre.

If there are cross-ply tyres fitted to your car, swap them for radials. Cross-ply tyres are not suitable for modern cars.

Seatbelts

Check that your seatbelts are working properly and are not frayed or worn. The mountings and locking mechanism should be secure and if you have inertia reel belts (the standard type of seatbelt fitted on all modern cards that 'lock' when you lurch forward, when the car brakes suddenly, for instance) they should lock and then release properly.

Other areas

There are a few other areas that are easy to check prior to an MoT test, some of which you will have covered in your weekly checks (see page 357).

The windscreen wipers and washers should be working properly, as should the horn, door handles and locks. Registration plates should be securely fitted, legible and clearly

displayed. The VIN (Vehicle Insurance Number) number should be displayed somewhere on the vehicle.

Finally, check your windscreen for cracks. On the driver's side cracks larger than 10mm are illegal. For the remainder of the swept area of the windscreen, cracks larger than 40mm are not allowed.

Even if you spot problems and are unable to rectify them yourself, carrying out these checks a few days before your MoT test is due will allow you to fix them in your own time at the garage of your choice, rather than having to pay up on the spot. It also saves having to pay excessive labour charges for a simple job that you could have done yourself in a few minutes.

Changing a wheel

When you first get your car, try changing a wheel. A rainy night at the side of a busy road is not the time to discover that you either have no jack, don't know where the jacking points are, or that your wheel nuts are so tight Arnold Schwarzenegger would have trouble getting them loose.

Read through your car handbook to discover where the spare wheel and jack are located, and where the jacking points are. Every car is different, so you cannot assume that the jacking points for your current car are the same as any previous model you may have used.

Try loosening the nuts. If they have been pneumatically tightened, you may have to add a piece of steel tubing to the end of the wheel brace for extra leverage. If you are still unable to loosen them, you'll probably have to pay a visit to your local garage to get them pneumatically loosened. At the end of your trial wheel change, tighten the nuts yourself, so that they are sufficiently tight but also reasonably easy to unscrew.

The correct procedure for a wheel change is as follows:
- Engage the handbrake and put the car in gear.
- Take off the hub cap – you may need a screwdriver to help prise it off.
- Loosen the wheel nuts.

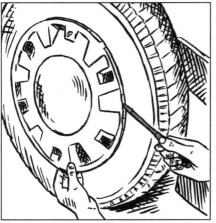

Prise off your hubcab with the help of a screwdriver.

Loosen your wheel nuts (see page 361).

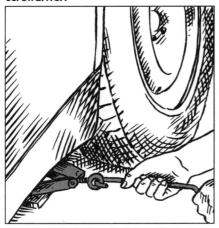

Place your jack directly below the jacking point (see page 363).

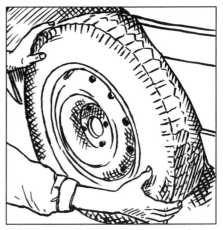

When the car is safely off the ground, remove the wheel nuts and wheel.

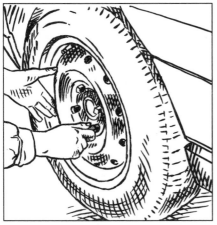

Fit the spare tyre and press firmly in place.

Tighten the wheel bolts, and lower the car carefully.

☞ Find the jacking points, selecting the one nearest to the wheel you are changing, if you have a choice.

☞ Slot the jack securely into the jacking point.

☞ Making sure the base of the jack is directly below the jacking point, slowly turn the jack handle so the car steadily begins to rise.

☞ When the wheel is clear of the ground, slide the spare under the car. This will break the car's fall should the jack collapse.

☞ Remove the wheel nuts and damaged wheel. Place it under the car.

☞ Fit the spare and tighten the wheel bolts.

☞ Lower the car as carefully as you raised it and place the damaged tyre in the spare wheel space for later repair or replacement.

If your car is fitted with a 'compact spare' (a small spare tyre suitable for driving only short distances until you can buy a replacement) it should be used only in an emergency and replaced at the earliest opportunity.

Never change a wheel on the hard shoulder of a motorway, or where you are unable to pull sufficiently to the side to avoid busy traffic. Some women may prefer to call breakdown assistance rather than tackle the job themselves – not because they are unable to, but because they may attract unwelcome attention.

Starting a car using jump leads

At some time or another you are bound to suffer a flat battery, either because it needs replacing or because you left your lights on. The best way to get going again is to use jump leads. Bump starting is not recommended, particularly for cars with catalytic converters.

You will need a pair of jump leads specifically designed for the job. These are not expensive and available from most motoring accessory shops. It is advisable to always carry a pair, particularly in winter.

The following procedure can be very dangerous, so follow each step carefully.

☞ Make sure the fully charged battery you are using to boost your own is of the same voltage (this should be clearly displayed on the top of the battery).

☞ Park the cars close together, so the leads will reach without straining, but be careful to ensure the two vehicles do not actually touch.

☞ Turn off all the electrics and put the car in neutral.

☞ Open both bonnets and connect the red jump lead to the positive terminals of each battery (marked with a 'plus' sign).

☞ Connect one end of the black lead to the negative terminal (marked with a 'minus' sign) of the booster battery, and the other to a suitable earth point on the car with the flat battery. The earth point should be a bare metal area on the engine block, about 45cm away from the battery.

☞ Make sure all the clips are secure.

☞ Start the engine of the car with the booster battery and let it run for a while. Then start the vehicle with the flat battery, depressing the clutch as the key is turned. It should now start normally.

☞ Allow the car with the re-charged battery to run for a short while, then remove the jump lead clips in reverse order.

☞ Never allow the ends of the two jump leads to touch at any point.

☞ Don't be surprised if your car stereo doesn't work after all this. Many modern cars have security-coded stereos that lock when the battery fails. If you don't know the correct code to punch in to get the unit working again, contact the local dealer for your car model.

Replacing bulbs

As with all light bulbs, those on your car only have a finite life. Paying a garage to replace blown bulbs is expensive – doing it yourself is easy.

Whenever you are renewing a bulb, disconnect the battery earth (the black lead) as a safety precaution.

Most headlight bulbs can be replaced from inside the engine compartment. Disconnect the wiring plug from the back of the light and remove the rubber cover. You will see the spring clip. Release the clips and take out the bulb. Fit the new bulb, ensuring the plugs fit into the housing securely. Replace the cover and plug.

The other exterior lights on your car follow the same principle, but your car handbook will give you details of how to reach the bulb and whether it is screw-fixed or spring-released.

Fuses and relays

Most electrical circuits in your car are protected by fuses. So, if you only know a few things about your car, knowing how to replace a fuse should be one of them.

A fuse will blow when that circuit becomes overloaded – a signal that an electrical component is faulty and will need repairing or replacing. Before replacing the fuse ensure the ignition and relevant circuit are switched off. Check your car manual to locate the fusebox and open it up. You will recognise

▼ You'll know a fuse is blown by the break in the wire between the two terminals.

the blown fuse by the break in the wire between the two terminals. Pull out the blown fuse and replace it with a fresh one of an identical rating. Fuses are colour-coded red, yellow and green for ratings of 10, 20 and 30 respectively. A fuse should never be replaced more than once without further investigation into the source of the fault.

Car security

The Eighties boom in car crime means that it now accounts for more than one-third of all reported crime. Car crime is theft of cars, theft from cars, so-called 'joy-riding', and car vandalism.

It's a particular problem for Britain where, in 1993, one in five motorists fell victim.

But car manufacturers and vehicle-accessory makers are now geared up to combat the scourge of modern motoring and security devices to deter the thieves are now effective and widely available. Of course, if a thief really wants your car, no security device will stop him from slipping it on to the back of a low loader. But being security conscious and using a security device will put off the casual thief.

Car security doesn't just mean buying an alarm. It's estimated one in five cars are left unlocked – an open invitation to theft. So just

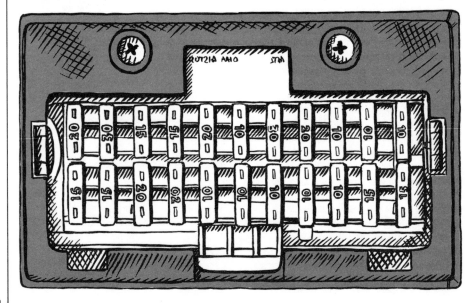

taking sensible precautions will drastically reduce the odds of your car being targeted by thieves.

☞ Always lock your car, whether you're just popping into the shop to buy a paper, or nipping across the road, or even when queueing to pay for your petrol. It only takes a few seconds to snatch a bag from the passenger seat. Don't forget the boot and petrol cap, too.

☞ All but very old cars have a steering-wheel lock, activated by the ignition key. If it's there, use it whenever you leave the car.

☞ Never leave valuables in the car, even in the boot. If this is not possible, at least keep possessions out of the sight of inquisitive eyes. If you can, cover or remove your car stereo. Similarly, if you have a car phone, carry it on your person if you can.

☞ Park in well-lit, busy areas, where a thief is more likely to be spotted.

☞ Get your windows etched with either the registration or VIN number of your vehicle. It doesn't cost much at your local garage, or you can buy a DIY kit.

It's worth considering buying a security device, particularly if you are unable to garage your car at night, or you have an expensive vehicle. Match the type of device to the value of your car. There's no point spending £500 on a sophisticated immobiliser if your means of transport is a battered Morris Minor.

Mechanical devices such as steering locks, which usually cost less than £50, are perfectly adequate for ordinary cars over four years old. Popular models less than four years old are more at risk and an alarm and/or immobiliser should be fitted.

Classic, sports and executive cars should be considered high-risk vehicles, as are convertibles, and should be treated accordingly. As well as a good-quality alarm and immobiliser system, a tracking device such as Tracker or Data Track should be considered.

This is only a general guide to car security and you should bear in mind that if your car has alloy wheels, expensive in-car entertainment or even fancy paintwork, it will appear more attractive to thieves. You should also consider how much your car means to you. It may only be worth £2000, but if it were stolen, would it disrupt your life to such an extent that spending £400 on an immobiliser is a reasonable investment?

Choosing a device isn't easy. There is a plethora of products available, but not all are good value. Some don't even work, and some could damage your car. However, in 1993, the Association of British Insurers set up a scheme with the Motor Insurance Repair Research Centre at Thatcham to evaluate security products.

There, rigorous tests are applied to mechanical devices, alarms and immobilisers to establish quality standards. There is now a fairly comprehensive list of approved products from which to choose. Buying a 'Thatcham-approved' device not only reassures you that yours is a reliable system, but it can also entitle you to discounts on your insurance. Your insurance broker will be able to advise you on the current list of approved products and the level of discount available.

Alarms

If you have considered buying a car alarm, you may be aware that there is something of a backlash against them, as people have grown tired of hearing them blaring, unattended and ignored in the street. Although the public might ignore car alarms, thieves don't. There is nothing more off-putting for a scavenging youth after your stereo than an incessant 130-decibel horn echoing round the multi-storey.

When shopping for an alarm, concentrate on the quality of the alarm, rather than the sensors. Sensors can be by-passed by most thieves, but a robust alarm is harder to crack. Units with their own alarm are better than those which use the car horn, as most thieves know how to disengage the horn.

Alarm systems are particularly good if you want to protect the contents of your car, but if you are more concerned about joyriders, or having the car itself stolen, an immobiliser is a better bet.

Plip keys

Many systems now come with a 'plip' key, which is linked to the central locking. Plip keys are small remote-control units which lock, immobilise and activate the alarm of your vehicle. These are ideal because they are easy to use – and what's easy to use, will be used.

If you have a plip-key system, get a spare key or a spare battery. Getting into a locked, immobilised car if you've lost your plip or it's battery is flat, is as difficult as you would hope!

Plip keys work by using either infrared or radio waves. Always buy a system that has rolling codes. Scanners and grabbers that can copy the codes of infrared and radio waves are now widely available. A plip key that uses a single code can be easily copied, allowing a thief to 'plip' his way into your car. Rolling codes defeat copying as the key uses a different code each time you lock and unlock your car.

In the event of crime

If the worst happens and your car is stolen or vandalised, you will probably feel distressed and may be temporarily stranded. Keep calm. If your car is not where you left it, report it to the police. They will want to know the make, model and registration of your car as well as where you left it and when you last saw it. Then get in touch with your insurance company. It can take a long time for policies to pay out, so the sooner you contact them, the better. Your insurance may provide a hire car in the interim.

If your car has been vandalised, do not attempt to drive it unless you are sure that doing so will not cause further damage. If you belong to a motoring organisation they may be able to help you. You should also report the matter to the police. Even if you live in a crime-ridden area, it is important that all incidents are reported. Again, contact your insurance company as soon as you can.

▼ Your VIN (Vehicle Identification Number) should be etched into each car window.

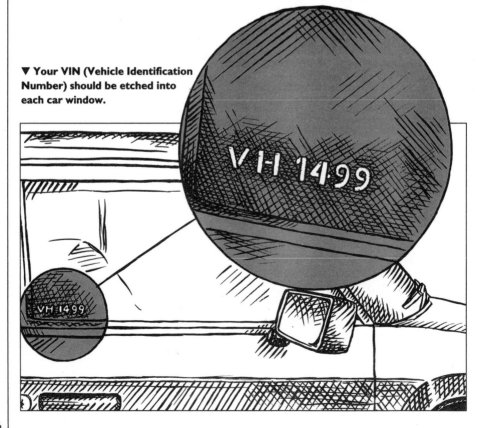

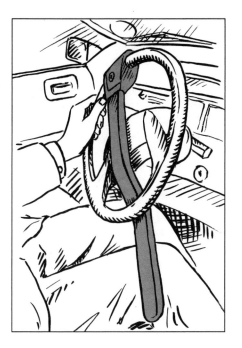

▲ **Fit a vehicle immobiliser device – one of the most common types consists of a metal bar which can be locked in place.**

Driver safety

These days it's not just cars that are at risk, but their drivers, too. Although the actual numbers of attacks are few, the big headlines these incidents attract have created fear among many drivers, particularly women.

However, taking a few sensible precautions will not only reduce the likelihood of attack, but will also boost your confidence.

☞ If you are planning a long journey on your own, plan your route in advance. Let a friend know when you are leaving, the route you are taking, and when you expect to arrive.

☞ Make sure your car is regularly serviced (see page 357) as this will reduce the likelihood of a breakdown and therefore the need to wait around for help. Learn how to change a wheel (see pages 361-3) and some mechanical 'first aid', so you can get yourself out of trouble.

☞ If you break down on the motorway use the emergency phones to call for assistance – there is always one less than a mile away.

☞ No matter how vulnerable you feel, don't wait inside your car on the hard shoulder of a motorway. The likelihood of your car being ploughed into by other traffic is far greater than the possibility of being attacked. Wait nearer the bank and leave the passenger door of your car unlocked, so you can hop in if you are approached.

☞ If someone stops to offer help, tell them you have already phoned the police. If you are approached while calling the police pass on the person's details to the operator.

☞ When help arrives always ask for identification before either getting out of the car, or giving your own details.

☞ If you are stopped by an unmarked police car, it will always be driven by a uniformed officer. If it is not, you have reason to be suspicious.

☞ When driving in urban areas, particularly in slow-moving traffic, lock your car doors and keep valuables out of sight.

☞ If you think you are being followed, pull over and slow down – but don't stop. If you still think you are being followed, drive to a well-lit, busy area. If necessary, blow your horn and flash your lights to attract attention.

☞ Make sure you also park in well-lit, busy areas. If you use a multi-storey, park near the exit and reverse into your space – so you can make a quick exit, if necessary.

☞ When returning to your car, have your keys ready, to avoid fumbling in a bag or briefcase. Check the car for anything suspicious before getting in.

If you see anything suspicious or you suspect a fellow motorist is in trouble, don't stop and become involved yourself, but do note some details and call the police – just as you hope somebody would do for you.

Try to remember that the likelihood of attack is small, and the pleasure and convenience of motoring are invaluable, so enjoy the freedom of the road.

USEFUL TELEPHONE NUMBERS	
AA Vehicle Inspections	**0345 500610**
RAC Vehicle Inspections	**0800 333660**
HPI Autodata	**0722 422422**

GARAGE TRADE JARGON

The garage trade is full of jargon and specialist terms. Here are a few explanations, to keep you up to speed with your mechanic.

ALTERNATOR — a device for converting rotating mechanical energy into electrical power.

BIG END — the end of a connecting rod, attached to the crankshaft

BRAKE FADE — a temporary loss of braking efficiency caused by overheating.

CROSS-PLY TYRE — a tyre constructed so that the weave of the fabric layers runs diagonally in alternately opposite directions.

EXPANSION TANK — a container used in cooling systems to collect overflowing coolant as it heats up and expands.

KERB WEIGHT — the weight of a car unladen, but ready to be driven.

OCTANE RATING — a scale for grading petrol.

PINKING — a metallic noise from the engine caused by pressure waves making the cylinder walls vibrate when ignited fuel/air mixture is compressed.

RUNNING ON — a tendency for an engine to keep running after the ignition has been switched off.

TORQUE — the turning force generated by a rotating component or wrench.

VISCOSITY — the fluidity of a liquid; i.e., oil.

Chapter Eight **Gardening**

Hazel Evans

Writes for the Sunday Mirror Magazine, Good Housekeeping and Sunday Supplement. Hazel is a specialist author on container gardening.

These are many decisions to make when planning a garden, and one of the first is how much time you will have to devote to it.
If the answer is 'not much', see the sections on 'The instant garden' (pp. 376-81) and 'The no-work garden' (pp. 381-6).
If your garden is going to be used by children, that dictates a completely different approach again (pp. 386-9).
There is a section of 100 plants that are easy to grow on pp. 389-96 and advice an window boxes (p. 396), hanging baskets (p. 397), ponds (p. 402) and houseplants (p. 407).

Planning your plot

Whether you're taking over an existing garden or starting from scratch, it pays to plan ahead before you plant so that you don't make expensive mistakes. If you want to make over a garden already planted by somebody else, don't be too hasty in tearing things out. If possible, go round it with the former owners and make a little map, with their help, of what is growing where. Try to live with the garden through the summer season at least. What looks like a bunch of dried twigs in winter or spring may be a stunning shrub that is covered in flowers come July. And what looks dull in summer may be a winter-flowerer giving you colour when you most need it in January and February.

Start off by asking some simple questions:

What sort of garden do you want?

Is it going to be a living picture, viewed mainly from your windows, or are you going to use it? Do you plan to sit out in it a lot? And to entertain out of doors – with a barbecue perhaps? Or is it going to be mainly a playground for the children during the next few years? And how much do you like gardening? Factors like this will help you decide how much lawn to have, if any, and how much of the area should be paved.

What size is it?

You need to be realistic about what you've got to work with. There's no point in trying to cram Versailles into a few square metres. Although we may all admire the traditional herbaceous border for instance, there's no doubt that it needs to be really deep – up to 1.50 m (5 ft) wide to get a really good show. If you're determined to have one, and your plot is small, site it on one side only, and have the garden path off-centre.

Which way does your garden face?

Aspect is very important; it determines what time of day that your plot gets the sun, which parts of the garden the sun reaches, and for how long each day. If your garden faces south, then you'll get the best of the summer sunshine for most of the day. If it faces east, you'll get sun in the morning but it will probably be shaded by the time the evening comes. If it faces west you'll get sunshine from the afternoon on, great for sitting out in the evening. If this is the case, plan to put in some scented flowers and climbers to make the most of it.

Is it in the shade?

It may be that your garden ought to have some sun but it is blotted out by buildings and trees. If yours is a mainly shady plot, don't despair, with a little bit of thought, planning and careful plant selection a shady garden can be every bit as lush as a sunny one – see the plant list on page 393. And bear in mind that you can brighten it up with bulbs and woodland plants, all of which thrive in shady conditions. In a case like this you might decide to make a sitting-out area away from the house, in the one spot that tends to get the sun. If your garden is heavily shaded by trees, never try to grow a lawn underneath them, it just won't work, for the trees' roots will have leeched out all the nutrients from the soil. It's better to put a paved area around them instead.

Is it exposed?

If yours is an exposed plot, then windbreaks in the form of fencing or shrubs and trees are going to be a number-one priority. And you may well decide to avoid plants that need staking, as they will tend to get blown over. You may want to build a brick wall or an overhead pergola too, to give shelter on the patio. In the short term – while a new hedge is growing, for instance – large mesh nylon netting stretched between posts will cut out a lot of the prevailing wind. Less obvious though just as destructive to gardens built in cities are the down-draughts and funnelling winds from nearby tall buildings. The best way to shield a garden from exposure of this kind is not, as you might think, to build a solid brick wall. Instead a pierced wall – decorative concrete blocks, trellises or even, again, nylon

netting will break the force of the wind but avoid the eddies that you get with a solid wall that might otherwise damage the plants beneath.

Are you overlooked?

Privacy is every bit as important as shelter, and you may want to put up some kind of screening from your neighbours, especially around a sitting-out area. Without it you may have the uneasy feeling that you are sitting out on a stage. Screening will also give you some shelter from the elements. The cheapest kind of permanent screen is a wooden fence but since that may not go with the general look of, say, a patio, it might be worthwhile to budget for bricks or concrete instead.

You may need screening for another purpose – to hide unsightly things like dustbins, a fuel tank or a neighbour's garage or shed. In this case it's best in the long run to use quick-growing trees or shrubs – Lawsons' Cypress, for instance, which gives a softer look than a wall. Or you might decide to put up a heavy-weight trellis and grow climbers over it. Be sure to include an evergreen like ivy to give cover in the winter time when others will have dropped their leaves.

How much time do you have?

If you are going to be hard-pressed to keep your garden under control, then plan it with time in mind (see pp. 381-6). Don't make it too labour intensive, with beds that need constant attention, and areas that need mowing unless you are going to have the time to keep it up.

What kind of soil have you got?

The important thing to find out is whether it is alkaline, acid, or somewhere in between. Ask around in your area – or have fun and buy a soil-testing kit which looks rather like a toy chemistry set. It will give you a reading in terms of pH. The lower the pH reading, the more acid your soil, the higher, the more alkaline. A pH reading of 7 means that your soil is neutral. One or two obliging trees and shrubs will put up with any conditions – acid

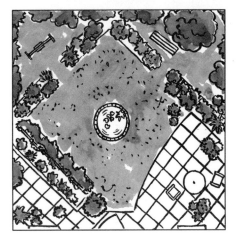

▲ If you inherit a fairly plain garden (top) and want to make it your own, there are hundreds of ideas to choose from. Add a patio, a pool, a trellis and a selection of mature trees and shrubs for instant transformation.

► Make an aerial plan (right) to work out where everything will go.

Take a photo of your garden from an upstairs window and sketch details on it,
or make a plan of your garden mapping out where all your essentials will go,
taking care to measure so they all fit! The plan above is for an intricately patterned
Tudor-style garden, should this be to your taste.

or alkaline. The birch (*Betula*) the hawthorn (*Crataegus*) and the yew (*Taxus*) are three examples: you can plant them almost anywhere. Others may be more fussy, especially plants that need a low pH reading.

An **acid soil** means you can grow anything in the rhododendron family with great success, many conifers and heathers will only grow in an acid soil, and plants like the hydrangea prefer it – only then will you get blue blooms. For further ideas see the plant list on pp. 394-5.

Many more trees and shrubs prefer a chalky, **alkaline soil** with lime in it. The Prunus and Acer families, for instance, and many decorative flowering shrubs – see the list on pp. 395-6. The lime content of a soil that is normally neutral or acid can be increased if there is builders' rubble in it that contains mortar. So remember this point if you are planting near newly built walls. Plant in containers, raised beds or troughs, of course, and you can choose your own custom-made soil, buying sacks of special compost from the garden centre.

Keep a garden notebook, write down ideas for plantings, the names of plants that you are attracted to in magazine illustrations. Visit some of the gardens open to the public while you're still at this planning stage. You'll be surprised how many ideas you will get, even from the gardens of stately homes.

Making your plan

Draw up your garden on graph paper, noting the scale at the bottom. Mark out paths beds and borders, and special areas for sitting out – measuring the projected patio to make sure it really is wide enough to take a table and four chairs and that there is room to stand up and pull a chair back without falling off the terrace. A patio that is to be used mainly for relaxing in the sun needs space for you to lie full-length when you want to – even if you only use fold-away sun beds rather than full-sized loungers.

Borrow a plant encyclopaedia from the library if you don't already have one, or use a plant catalogue to find out the eventual size of important plantings of trees and shrubs, then cut out a circle to scale and stick them in

place. If it is obvious that you have planned for too many trees, either cut down the numbers or choose something small like the miniature silver birch (*Betula nana*) and one of the flowering cherry family.

Once you are happy with the project on paper, try it out on site, using string or rope to mark out beds and paths, or sand dribbled from a bag with a hole in it. That way planning mistakes like a bed that's too wide, a path that's too narrow, will show up before you actually get down to work.

Give your garden a focal point if you can, something to feast the eye on. A statue, if it is carefully chosen, can lead the eye to an interesting corner. A sundial makes a good focal point in a paved garden or you could have a seat temptingly placed under a flowery bower.

Once you've worked out roughly what you want to do, it pays to take some photographs of the garden as it is, now, have several prints made, then try sketching in the trees you want to plant, where you plan to put features like a pond, items such as a shed, garden furniture.

Giving your garden a look

However small the space with which you're dealing, you can have fun by giving the area around the house a theme. The Mediterranean look is a good choice if you have a small space that is going to be used mainly as an outdoor room. You could plant the hardy hibiscus (*hibiscus syriacus*) for instance and perhaps a tall narrow cypress, and major on colourful geraniums in summer.

Or you could turn it into a traditional cottage garden, using perennial plants that will go on from year to year, tall spikes of hollyhocks and foxgloves mingling with well-loved favourites like michaelmas daisies and the hardy geranium.

If yours is a modern house, then you might like to go for architectural plants using the Yucca, the Chusan palm (*Trachycarpus fortunei*) and other plants with sword-like leaves – the Iris would grow well among alongside them.

If you're in an old house you might think about creating a 'period' garden. In Elizabethan times and again in the Victorian era, gardens were formally planned, the beds often edged with low-growing box. Knot gardens, where the edges form a pattern, look good all year round, even in the snow, and certainly suit a plot that is rectangular or square.

Or you may decide that you want the country look that is perfectly feasible even in town. Here the edges need to be blurred by a close planting of shrubs so that no one can see where the garden actually ends. Or you could use climbers lavishly to hide an all-too-solid fence – the Russian vine (*Polygonum baldschuanicum*) grows rapidly and can be trained up against a fence and clipped to make a fake one-dimensional hedge.

Using colour

Just as an artist chooses his palette of colours before starting to paint, so you need to think through the flowers you're going to use in your plot. If the garden is large enough, then you can go through the whole rainbow, but if it is very small a riot of different colours could become confusing, so try varying it from one season to another with pinks and reds at one time, oranges, and yellows another. Many seed companies offer special packets of all pink, yellow, blue flowers, graded according to their size.

You can use colour to create perspective and make your garden seem larger than it actually is. Dark green, grey or blue plants tend to recede when you look at them, as do mauve and silver ones. Warm colours like oranges, yellows and reds, on the other hand, seem to come towards you and should be reserved for planting right in front of your eyes. Very dark green foliage, too, tends to look further away from you than leaves in limes and sharp yellows.

Tools for the job

You'll need to buy a basic kit of tools to start with. It never pays to skimp when getting things for the garden; cheap forks and spades will snap, trowels bend and you end up throwing them away. Invest in the best you can afford. To get going you will need:

- ☞ A **spade.** This needs to be a heavy-duty item as it's going to do all your digging, but pick it up first and try it for balance before you buy. Make sure the top of the blade is comfortable for you to put the sole of your shoe on. Spades can be found in a lighter-weight 'ladies' version, too.
- ☞ A **fork.** Used to break up the surface of the soil and to lift and carry garden compost and mulching material. Buy the best that you can afford, so you don't end up with bent or snapped-off prongs. Try it for comfort and balance. It's available in a 'ladies' version, too.
- ☞ A **rake.** Choose a sturdy metal one to use for raking up vegetation from the surface of beds. Later you might want to invest in a spring-toothed version to get leaves off the lawn without damaging the grass. This has a fan-shaped set of slender metal ribs bent under at the ends.
- ☞ A **hoe.** You'll use this to chop the heads off annual surface weeds, and keep the flower beds looking trim. The best choice for this purpose is the Dutch hoe, which is stirrup-shaped.
- ☞ A **trowel** and **hand fork.** You'll need these to install bedding plants and transfer seedlings and cuttings. Those with wooden handles are the most comfortable to use.
- ☞ A **watering can** and **hose.** A plastic can is lighter to handle than a metal one, and the hose should be of the diameter that can take clip-on and -off items like a sprinkler, and a jet spray which can also be used for cleaning the car.

Gardening terms

Acid (soil) Lacking in lime. Most peaty and some very sandy soils are acid.

Alkaline (soil) Usually chalky soil, with a high lime content.

Alpine Strictly speaking a plant that grows above the tree line in mountainous regions. Now used to describe any small plant that is suitable for a rock garden.

Annual A plant that grows from seed and completes its life cycle in the space of one season.

Bedding plant A plant that is very often half-hardy, and is put into the ground for a short-term display. Usually discarded at the end of the season.

Biennial A plant that takes two years to complete its life cycle, starting from seed in the first year, producing flowers and seeds in the second.

Compost This can mean a bought-in medium, often a mixture of peat, sand and soil plus fertiliser, which is used for growing plants in pots or other containers. It also means a fertile substitute for manure, consisting of rotted-down vegetable matter and domestic scraps.

Deadheading Taking the faded blossom off a plant to stop seeds from forming and to encourage new flowers to appear.

Double A flower with more than the usual number of petals for its kind.

Half-hardy A plant that can stand an average winter out of doors as long as it is protected from frost. Or a plant from a warmer climate that can only be grown out of doors during the summer.

Hardy A garden plant that is capable of surviving frost anywhere in Great Britain.

Herbaceous A non-woody perennial plant that dies back to the ground at the end of the growing season and reappears the following spring.

Hybrid A plant that has been specially bred from crossing any two distinct parents.

Mulch A layer, usually of organic material, spread on top of the soil around plants to conserve moisture and deter weeds. Sometimes black plastic is used as a mulch to help delicate fledgling plants establish themselves.

Perennial A non-woody plant that lives for several years.

Shrub A woody plant, a perennial that has a number of stems springing up from the roots.

Tree A woody long-lived plant that springs normally from just one woody stem.

Tuber A thickened fleshy root or underground stem which provides food storage; e.g., potato, Jerusalem artichoke.

Latin names are useful for two reasons: because they tell us what family a plant belongs to and because you can identify it anywhere in the world. It is also useful because many plants may have conflicting common names, and you are not sure what you are getting. The Latin name often tells us more about the plant than might be obvious from the label; for example:

Alba means the plant has white foliage and/or flowers.

Aurea means that the plant has golden-yellow leaves.

Dentata means the foliage is toothed; i.e., with a jagged edge.

Fastigata, usually used to describe a tree, means that it has narrow upright growth.

Lanciata means the plant has deeply cut foliage.

Nana means that it is a dwarf or compact form of a plant.

Pendula means the plant has a weeping or pendulous form.

Purpurea means the plant has purple or bronze foliage.

Repens means it is a creeping rather than upright form of a plant.

Choosing a lawnmower

Your choice of a lawnmower depends on how much grass you have, how much energy you have and the shape and level of the lawn. You also need to decide whether you want a pristine 'bowling green' finish or simply want to cut the grass.

Then you also need to decide whether to go for a hand, power-driven or electric mower.

Hand mowers need the most muscle but are very cheap to buy. They're also easy to look after and make a good choice for a very small garden.

Petrol-driven mowers can be tricky to start and heavy to operate. But they may be your only choice if you have a very large, long garden.

Electric mowers are much safer than they used to be, thanks to things like circuit breakers, but they do have trailing cables that can get in the way.

Types of mower

The **rotary** and **orbital** mowers run on wheels with a single blade rotating horizontally under a protective cover, like a propeller slashing its way through the grass. They're best for long, rough grass or lawns where a close-cut finish is not necessary. They can be electric or petrol-driven.

The **hover** mower cuts in the same way as the rotary but has no wheels and glides over the surface of the lawn on a cushion of air. Fast and mobile, it is easier to use than other mowers, especially on slopes, and you can get a version with a disposable plastic blade that snaps if it hits a hard object – which could be your shoe. It can be petrol driven but is more usually electrically powered.

The **cylinder** mower is really your best choice if you want that pristine bowling-green finish. It works by a series of rotating blades which cut the grass as they roll along. The most simple version which is hand-operated has a grass collecting box but no roller at the back. To get that green stripe you need a petrol or electric version with the roller attachment.

More Tools

If you have patches of really rough grass to cut, especially in corners or around trees, posts and walls then it's worth while buying a **strimmer**. This has a fast-rotating nylon filament on the end of a long handle which goes at such a speed that it slashes through even the thickest grass. It can be electric but is more usually petrol-driven.

If your garden is any size at all, you'll want to invest in an **oscillating sprinkler** to attach to your hose and direct a fine spray of water over a large area.

Later you may want to add an **electric hedge trimmer**. The version that is operated by a rechargeable battery is more convenient than one that trails a flex, but it is heavier to use.

The instant garden

Whether you're faced with a brand new builder's plot or an old neglected garden, here are some ideas for quick fixes – tips to help you get it looking good in a minimum of time.

Nowadays when most plants, even trees, are raised and sold in containers it's perfectly possible to put in anything you choose at any time of year. But trees and shrubs still prefer to go in over the winter months when the soil is likely to be more moist – although they'll put down roots just as happily in summer as long as you keep them watered. So you could make a garden in the space of an afternoon if you had a cleared space to put it in – and unlimited cash.

Decide on your priorities

First of all, make a work plan. Decide what your eventual scheme is going to be, then make up a list of priorities. In the case of a brand new garden it will be the basic flooring – a lawn, paths, terrace that need going in. In the case of an old one you may find yourself spending the first few weeks pruning and cuttings things back to see what its basic skeleton shape is.

Start from the house

Cheer yourself up by getting in some colour right away. Any bright and beautiful plants placed near or in front of the windows not only give a welcoming look but very often help to hide the chaos beyond.

Window boxes and hanging baskets (see pp. 396-402) are quickly planted up with things bought from a barrow. You can even leave them in their pots on the windowsill.

Choose flowers that will keep going all summer – petunias are wonderful for this, so are fuchsias, geraniums, busy lizzies and begonias.

Dig the ends of flower beds that are nearest to the house and put in some quick-growing plants for near-instant colour. You can't go wrong with marigolds, lobelias, alyssum, nasturtiums. Sweet peas are good for quick colour too, and so are the cosmos with its huge cup-shaped flowers, the annual candytuft, primulas and pansies. You can grow them yourself from seed or pick them up as plants at the local garden centre.

Buy one big show-off item

Use it to distract the eye from a lawn that has yet to be laid, or overgrown flower beds. Buy one specimen tree that looks good all year round, for instance. Go for shape with a Japanese maple with foliage that turns deep red in autumn. Or pick a piece of furniture like a striking white-painted bench, and site it where it makes the most impact – later you can move it into a corner and build an arbour around it.

Instant screens

There may be something that you want to hide, in the short term, while a real long-term hedge is growing. Here you can use tall, quick-growing plants to give you a screen in the space of a summer.

Bamboo (Arundinaria)
This hardy evergreen will make a fast permanent screen and has the advantage of soundproofing as well, once it is established. It does however need plenty of space – allow 2 m (about 6 ft) between each plant and more space in front. The tallest variety, Arundinaria japonica, will soar to 3–4.5 m (10–15 ft) and turns itself into a thicket, so it's not suitable for a small garden. Choose instead Arundinaria murielae which is not so rampant, but nevertheless reaches 3 m (10 ft) or more.

Jerusalem artichoke (Helianthus tuberosus)
This is a relative of the sunflower, growing fast from tiny knobbly tubers which have a distinctive smoky taste and are used as a vegetable. They thrive in any kind of soil and will take sun or shade and go on from year to year. Plant the tubers in February or early March, and you'll have a screen of foliage 2.10–3.6 m (7–12 ft) high by the middle of the summer.

Plume Poppy (Macleaya)
This will grow up to 3.12 m (8 ft) in height. It puts out huge leaves like outstretched hands that are silver-green on top, silver-pink beneath, then tall sprays of flowers in mid-summer. It is strong and needs no staking except in very exposed places.

Rudbeckia (Rudbeckia nitida, laciniata)
Provided you buy the tall forms of this useful plant (see names above) they will make a striking screen. They have bold daisy-like flowers with dark centres and will grow up to 1.8–2.10 m (6–7 ft) high and go on from one year to another.

The lawn

If you are dealing with a new garden, your first task will probably be putting in a lawn. Even if you grow it from seed, it need not take as long as you think.

April or September are the best months for doing it. At these times the air is warm but without being too hot and drying, so there tends to be enough warmth and moisture in the soil to keep turf or seed from drying out.

You need to start with a level weed-free site. It pays to hire a cultivator to dig over the soil, and to borrow a roller if possible to level it. If you're moving into a brand new garden, then the builder might be able to prepare the ground roughly for you. Get the site ready then leave it, if you can, to settle for a week or two – after a while bumps and hollow may appear and can be levelled out. Rake it over to make it as smooth as possible. Remember that it's worth doing well because it's a once-and-only job. Once you're ready you've got two choices: turf or seed.

The instant lawn

If you want an instant lawn, then you're bound to choose one that's been grown for you. Turfing is like magic: a day's hard, satisfying work and a bare patch of soil is transformed into an emerald green carpet.

Buying turf

The quickest lawn of all is the one that is made from turf bought ready-grown on a fine-mesh backing in rolls, like carpeting. The turf is usually of the finest quality, and laying it is easy, but the cost is considerably more than that of the conventional kind of turf, so you need to weigh up the cost of both your time and the money involved. Having taken delivery of it, you simply roll it out like a carpet, staggering the joins, as if you were building a wall, and firm it down. Keep it well watered and it will 'wake' within a fortnight.

If you are buying the normal smaller turves remember that, as with other plants, the quality can vary considerably from meadow turf – field grass that has been treated with weed killer, to the more expensive specially grown kind, or turf stripped from parkland or downland. So make sure you inspect any grass that is sold as a 'bargain offer' before you buy. The turves should be of the same quality and thickness throughout and weed-free, or you'll end up with a lawn that looks like a patchwork quilt.

Although technically you can put down turf at any time of year, unless you are willing to put in a lot of effort on the watering front, it's best to lay turf in the spring or autumn.

Taking delivery

Have your turf delivered as close as possible to the day you intend to lay it. If you have to postpone the operation for a few days, keep it stacked in rolls, preferably out of direct sunlight. And if conditions are dry, water it well, using the finest possible spray or you may wash the soil away from the roots. In any case heavily sodden turves are very hard to handle and can break under their own weight.

Laying turf

Choose a day when the soil is reasonably dry, otherwise it may stick to your shoes and make working conditions more difficult than they need to be. To get the best results with small turves you'll need a tamping tool to press them down firmly into the soil. Make one for yourself by nailing together two 30cm (1ft) square boards, then fixing a broom handle into a block nailed on the top. If you've got only a very small area to do, you can use the head of a rake to press the turves into place.

Start at one side, slightly overlapping the final edge of the lawn with the first row of turves to allow for any shifting and readjusting.

> **The stars among plants that can take neglect are geraniums, which can stand almost any amount of drought, aubretia, pinks (dianthus), stocks and scabious. And, for winter, plant the universal pansy which goes on flowering without any attention.**

▶ Laying turf.
Start at one end, setting down a
row of turves that are slightly
overlapping.

▶ Unroll the turf carefully,
making sure it is level with any
hard surfaces.

▶ Angle the turf around walks,
and fill all empty patches with
pieces of turf slightly larger than
the hole to fill.

▶ The final result should look like
this – staggered rows to allow for
shifting.

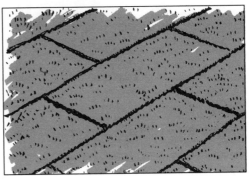

If your lawn butts on to a path or a patio it's very important the turf is laid so that it's above the level of the hard surface rather than flush with it, or even below. The lawn will inevitably 'settle' over the first year and end up at a lower level. And mowing the edge of a lawn that is lower than the path can wreak havoc on a lawn mower.

Press the first row of turves down well, then lay the second row, staggering the joins as you would with a row of bricks – this usually means cutting some of the end turves in half. Stand on a plank of wood on the laid turf, not on the soil, as you go. If you have a curve of any kind to negotiate, cut the turf with an edging tool rather than trying to bend it into shape.

If there is any kind of a gap between turves, fill it with a sliver of turf. If the gap is on an edge, don't fill it with a small piece or it will inevitably crumble away. Move the end turf out to the edge and fill the inner gap with the small pieces.

If you have, or can get your hands on, a garden roller, then use it once the lawn has been laid. If not, give it a light going-over with the roller of a cylinder mower, making sure that the blades are set high enough to clear the grass.

Your instant lawn can be walked on immediately, but it is best to leave it for a while to settle down, making sure you keep it watered if the weather is dry.

▲ Top: Sowing seeds. Mark the area needing to be seeded into squares and divide the seed accordingly.

▲ Above: Zigzag cotton across the ground to keep the birds off.

Starting from seed

The cheapest lawn is the one that you sow yourself. And it doesn't take as long to grow as you might think. Sow it in a warm spring and it could be sprouting within a week. It will certainly be growing away after three weeks. You also have more control over what you get, because you can choose special mixes of grass seed for shade, for hard wear, for the perfect green sward. The grass needs to be sown in spring or in the autumn, and the amount of seed you need is easy to calculate: Measure the length and width of your space and multiply it to get the number of square metres/yards. Allow 35–60 g per square metre (1¼–2oz per square yard), taking the higher figure if birds or weather conditions are likely to be a problem, or if you are using a tough heavy-duty mix. Buy a seed mix that has a bird repellent in it – otherwise you'll have to protect your lawn by zig-zagging black cotton just above the ground between sticks.

Sowing the seed

Choose a day when there is little or no wind, and make sure that the soil is not too wet. Give a final rake-over if necessary. To distribute the seed as evenly as possible, mark off the area into one metre (one yard) squares using bamboo canes or string stretched between pegs. Weigh the seed and divide it according to the number of squares to be sown. Starting at one end and working backwards, sow half the seed for each square in one direction, the remaining half at right-angles to it for perfect coverage.

After you've finished sowing, lightly rake the surface, first in one direction and then in another. 'Lightly' is the operative word here – if you cover the soil too deeply the seed will take a long time to come up. Finally, water it with a fine sprayer on the end of your hose so that you don't knock the seeds around or flood the area. Never allow a newly sown lawn to dry out. Give it its first mow when the grass is about 5 cm (2 in) high. Make sure the mower blades are sharp and at their highest setting – all you want to do is to take the tips off and encourage the grass to grow more thickly.

Fast paths

The quickest garden paths are those made from gravel or shingle, or from concrete poured straight on to the ground within the bounds of an edging made from wood placed on edge. This can be taken away, if you wish, by the time the concrete has set. You can

also put strips of wood in place at intervals before you pour, to give the appearance of paving stones. Or you can set pebbles in it to give a decorative look.

Gravel or shingle for paths is best put down on a narrow bed of sand that has been raked as level as possible. Keep it free from weeds by dosing it with a total weedkiller at intervals, but be careful that it does not leak on to nearby beds containing flowers.

The no-work garden

If you like to relax at weekends, if you'd rather be sailing or shopping than digging, if your job takes you away a great deal, then what you need is a garden that looks good but is easy to maintain.

It's all a matter of planning. You may have to invest a little money at first, buying more mature, larger-sized specimens, and you may have to put in some work for the first season, planting the good-natured plants, trees and shrubs that are going to make your life easier over the years ahead. But once the work is done, you'll be able to sit back and enjoy the scene.

Go with the flow

Stock your plot with plants that like living in your neighbourhood. That's easy to find out – just look at the things that are growing already in other gardens down the road. If you don't know their names, just ask – the owners might even give you some spare plants or cuttings. If those plants are happy at No.19 the chances are that they'll be happy with you and establish themselves fast. Look too at what's growing in the local parks, out in the wild. Remember: the right plant in the right location requires little or no work on it throughout the year.

Don't like mowing the lawn?

Then think of alternatives. A very small space could feature a camomile lawn instead – be sure to use the variety called 'treneague' which creeps along the ground, not the ordinary tall-growing version. Or you could make a tapestry of creeping thymes with a mix of bronze and bright green leaves and tiny colourful flowers. Alternative lawns take a while to get established but once they have knit together, they look good and can be trodden, though not played, upon.

Consider gravel, too – it's cheaper and easier to lay than paving and you can allow specimen plants to grow in it where you wish, or creep over the edges. You need to rake the area smooth and kill off all the weeds, then lay a sheet of plastic or some other membrane as an underlay to keep unwelcome things from growing up through it.

Choose easy-care trees

If you have a garden that is mainly lawn or paving, avoid deciduous trees that have large leaves. When they drop their leaves in autumn you'll feel obliged to sweep them up. Leave them in place and slugs, snails, earwigs – every pest you can think of will over-winter under them. The same goes for trees with messy fruits. Berries from the mulberry, for instance, will cover your patio with purple stains in no time at all.

Think in terms of evergreens

The ultimate easy-care garden is the one that has been planted with prostrate and low-growing evergreens like conifers. They don't all have to be dark green; they come in a whole range of tones from silvery-blue to bright gold, and in shapes that vary from pyramids to mounds, or small pencil-thin trees.

Architectural in their look, evergreens go particularly well with a modern house. Surround them with a chipped bark mulch and you'll have virtually nothing to do except to water them well while they settle in. If you want colour to go with them, invest in bulbs – see page 383.

Cut down weeding time

Use a mulch, a covering for the surface of the ground, until the plants you put in are large enough to suppress weeds. The most attractive kind is shredded bark, which is the colour of a rich dark soil. Buy it by the bagful and put it round the plants in your flower bed. It deters small annual weeds but allows things like bulbs to poke through.

Stop worrying about the watering

Buy an automatic watering kit with drip outlets to put among prized plants and a micro sprinkler, then link it up to a mini-computer fixed to your outside tap which turns the water on and off when you want. Look out for one in your local garden centre, it's surprisingly cheap – a complete set, including the computer programmer, costs well under £100.

Cut down on woodwork

Any wood that's used out of doors needs maintenance work on it. But now it's possible to own a gleaming white picket fence that stays that way indefinitely. It's made from moulded white polyethylene, the kind that is used for garden furniture, and the pieces fit together like a jigsaw. You can also get posts for chainlink fencing that are made in black or white, and nylon rather than metal chains to go between them.

Invest in all-weather garden furniture

Taking garden furniture inside for the winter is a chore, and you have to find somewhere to stow it. Go instead for tables and chairs that can be left out in all weathers, and that means avoiding untreated metals that can rust. The alternative is long-lasting cast iron which has been dipped in a white epoxy resin paint. Another expensive but enduring choice is furniture made from hardwoods such as teak and iroko. If you want something cheaper there is furniture made from lacquered moulded resin that can stay out too. It's stronger than ordinary plastic and is less likely to crack or blow over.

Sow your annuals the lazy way

Pick varieties that will seed themselves from year to year. You'll have a little hard work sowing the seed the first summer, but after that, let nature take over. Old favourites that you can depend on include candytuft, (Iberis), honesty, hollyhocks, marigolds, poppies. Be sure to leave the seed pods in place.

Climbers for the no-work garden

While many climbers need fixing in place, sometimes on trellis or netting, there are a chosen few that will clamber up the wall unaided.

Euonymus fortunei

This climbing evergreen can reach 4 m (13 ft) in a good soil, and has glossy dark green leaves. It supports itself against a wall.

Ivy (hedera)

Ivy does not pull mortar out of healthy brickwork despite its reputation for doing so, but it will attach itself to almost any surface with its aerial roots. One of the most rapid growing varieties is Canary Island ivy (*Hedera canariensis*) which has large heart-shaped leaves.

The Climbing Hydrangea

(*Hydrangea anomala petiolaris*)
This takes a while to get started but once it gets going it clings grimly to any surface, even a tree with rough bark.

The Virginia Creeper

(*Parthenocissus*)
This is one of the best-known climbers of all, with its foliage that turns crimson in autumn. It's best against a pale surface, rather than red brick to which it gives a rather florid look.

Bulbs for the no-work garden

Few things you can buy for the garden give you a better return for your money than bulbs, and nothing could be easier to grow. They're nature's convenience plants – just put them in the ground, forget about them, and they'll come up, year after year, giving you spot colour just when it's needed in early spring. They will also grow in tricky places – under the shade of trees, for instance, or in a dark corner. And many of them, daffodils and snowdrops in particular, increase in volume over the years to form large clumps. Apart from the most popular five – snowdrops, crocuses, daffodils, hyacinths and tulips – there are lots of delightful small bulbs to try,

like the grape hyacinth (*muscari*), with its cobalt blue flowers, or the sky-blue glory of the snow hyacinth (*Chionodoxa*). But that's not all; with a little planning, you can have a flower show all year round by choosing the right varieties of bulbs.

Choosing your bulbs

Decide, first, whether you are going to go for a rainbow mix of bright colours, or all pastels – which can look very pretty against a background of evergreens. Or you could go for a one-colour scheme which can be stunning in a town window box – a row of scarlet tulips, for instance. And if you are planning a mix of bulbs, take their height into account by putting, say, hyacinths and the taller tulips in the centre of a tub or at the back.

Buying

Since bulbs are an investment in the future, buy the best ones you can afford. It is safer to buy ones you can actually see – either loose in boxes or pre-packed in clear plastic, rather than something sealed up in a brown paper bag. Buying bulbs is rather like buying onions – you're looking for the same qualities in both. They should feel plump and firm, smooth-skinned and free from blemishes. And always buy from a reputable supplier, for if there are a lot of very small bulbs mixed in with those daffodils on sale at a ridiculously low price, they may be bulblets that won't flower in their first year.

Siting your bulbs

Bulbs look good everywhere in the garden. If money is tight, stick to one variety and mass them together, rather than spreading your cash over, say, a scattering of different kinds. To make a few go a long way, try them in a tub or a hanging basket, for a change. They grow well in stone sinks, too, provided there is enough depth for them. And bulbs go particularly well in a mixed border. They give you spot colour in spring, but then their dying foliage is hidden by the herbaceous plants as they grow and flower. In general, though, dense areas of closely planted bulbs look prettier and more natural than those strung out in single lines.

Planting your bulbs

Having bought your bulbs, handle them with care. If they are in a plastic packet, open it immediately to allow the air to circulate round them. If you are not planting them for a while, spread them in a single layer in a box or a tray in a cool, dry, airy place. Bulbs are not particularly fussy, but they do prefer a well-drained soil – if they remain in heavy wet earth they may rot.

Planting depths

Different bulbs need different planting depths. As a general rule, the larger the bulb the deeper it needs to go. However, one rule is common to all of them: they must be covered by a reasonable layer of soil or they won't flower. Most packets carry instructions on planting, but a good rule of thumb is to plant each bulb so that its top is two and a half times its length below the soil surface.

Daffodils should go in before the end of October. Plant them at least 10–15 cm (4–6 in) deep. Very small varieties, like the tiny Hoop Petticoat daffodil should be planted 7.5 cm (3 in) deep.

Crocuses should be planted 5 cm (2 in) deep and **snowdrops** 7.5–10 cm (3–4 in) deep, before the end of September. Wait a while before putting in **tulips**. They should be planted between October and the end of November, and go into the ground 10cm (4 in) deep.

Make sure that the bulb is set firmly on the base of the hole and that there are no air pockets beneath it; sprinkle a little sand or dry soil into the hold for it to sit on. How you space your bulbs depends on you – the spacing dimensions are usually suggested on the packet. If you are putting them close together, however, there must be a gap at least the width of a pencil between them.

Bulbs in lawns

Bulbs look particularly pretty growing in grass, so if you have an area of lawn that is difficult to mow – around a tree, perhaps, or in a

▲ **Forcing bulbs: set soil around with the tips of the bulbs just showing.**

corner, this is the place to put them. If you're planning to grow the larger bulbs like tulips or daffodils this way, go for shorter varieties like the Kaufmanniana tulips or for daffodils, the February Gold, or Jenny. The best way to arrange them for 'natural' planting is to toss the bulbs down on the grass, and dig them in where they land. If you are planting a number of bulbs this way, it is well worth buying a special bulb planter – a short cylinder with a sharpened edge and a wooden handle. With this you can simply dig out plugs of ground, put the bulbs in place, then replace the 'hats' of earth on top.

Flowers all year round

Having got your spring display organised – your daffodils and tulips – plant some more bulbs later on, to give you flowers right round the year. Strictly speaking, some of the plants we refer to as 'bulbs' have root systems that are more correctly called corms or tubers, but they all develop in the same way, and all go on from year to year.

In early summer you can enjoy the flowers of the **bluebells** (*Endymion nonscriptus*) and the **snake's head fritillary** (*Fritillaria meleagris*), the **lily of the valley** (*Convallaria*) and anemones. In summer, gladioli, montbretia and members of the lily family will give you long-lasting colour.

For autumn flowers plant the **autumn crocus** (*Colchicum*), with its large flowers on bare stems and the **autumn-flowering crocus** (*Crocus speciosus*), also sterbergia lutea with its bright yellow flowers. These need planting in July.

Finish the year with a flourish, with the beautiful pink blooms of the **South African lily** (*Nerine bowdenii*) in late October, November, from bulbs put in the ground at the end of this month.

▲ **Place bulbs in a dark container; a bin liner will do.**

Flowers for Christmas

Have a colourful Christmas and New Year by planting 'prepared' bulbs to bloom indoors over winter. Children love to join in the excitement of growing bulbs in this way. You will find the packs on sale at your local garden centre. They cost a little extra because the bulbs have been lifted early and specially treated to speed up their natural development.

You can plant indoor bulbs in compost, or in special bulb fibre, which is better for containers without drainage holes, but not for tall or heavyweight plants which will tend to topple over in it. For best results restrict each container to one type of plant.

Site your bulbs so that their tips poke out of the soil and just come level with the rim of the container, and fill them with compost up to 7.5 cm (3 in) below the rim of the pot to leave space for watering.

Next your Christmas bulbs need to develop a strong root system, so resist the temptation to put them somewhere warm to 'bring them on'. What they need at this stage are cool dark conditions. So put the pots in a black plastic bag and store them for the time being in the garage or plunged into a flower bed out in the garden. Leave them there for eight weeks, then check them from time to time. Once the tips show 7.5 cm (3 in) of new growth, bring them out into the light, then into the warm. They should flower anything between three to six weeks later.

So, to catch Christmas, plant hyacinths at the end of September and bring them in the first week in December. Daffodils, on the other hand, should be planted during the second week in October to be brought indoors on 1 December. Another plant well worth raising for this purpose is the amaryllis,

▲ **The bulbs should grow within a couple of weeks – move them inside if they seem to be slow starting off.**

which you will find specially packed for Christmas flowering. It has a huge bulb, and an equally huge flower which stays in bloom for weeks on end.

After care

Once your bulbs have flowered, indoors or out, resist the temptation to cut down their foliage. This is the most important time of year for them, and the leaves play a vital part in sending food down to the bulb, to be used next year. Wait until the leaves have turned brown before you cut them.

Your bulbs won't need any fertiliser in the first year, but after that a little bone meal worked into the topsoil will keep them looking good, especially 'greedy feeders' like dahlias, lilies and gladioli.

A garden for children

A garden that is going to be used by children and, possibly, pets, has got to work hard for its living. It needs to be good looking but also tough and childproof. And, quite apart from space for play, you may need to think in terms of outdoor storage for items like bicycles and large toys, as well as somewhere to hang out all the washing that children seem to generate.

The lawn

The grass in any garden that hosts children is bound to come in for punishment, so, if you are sowing from scratch, it's worth buying special mixed seed that includes a high percentage of tough rye grasses which will not wilt under the wheels of bicycles or an impromptu game of football. Later on, when the children grow up, you can re-seed the lawn if you want to acquire emerald-green smooth and perferction.

The patio

It pays to have a patio where children can play with small wheeled toys that can't be pulled around over grass. Make sure it is

> **Put some tough aromatic plants from the Mediterranean like rosemary and lavender into the family garden. They will give off a pleasant scent when a football hits them and can stand up to hard treatment.**

covered in smooth paving so that toddlers won't trip and hurt themselves. You could also put in a pergola, a framework of wooden poles that could take a roof of some sort – perhaps sheets of heavy duty fibreglass. Under this children will still be able to play out of doors on rainy days. The patio is a good place to build in storage – you could site some heavy-duty outdoor lockers that double as bench seats, a place where toys can be stowed out of site rather than lugged indoors.

The garden that grows up

If you're planning a family plot from scratch, think of it in terms of a two-tier garden that will grow up in time, remembering that the situation of the sandpit and the swing are as important for the children now as they are for your future garden.

Buy a **garden shed** now, paint it in bright colours and turn it into a children's **playhouse**. (Maybe you could keep tools in the garage, cellar or outdoor locker for the time being.) If the garden shed is large enough, you could partition off the far end for the storage of mower and tools, leaving the other half as a play area. Later on, when the children grow out of it, it would be simple to demolish the partition and take over the whole area for gardening equipment.

Use a small fibreglass **pre-formed pool** as the basis for a **sand pit**. Site it carefully where it looks attractive, but you can still keep an eye on small children from the house. You could even sink it into a corner of the patio. Make sure you have a heavy drop-on cover to slip in place when it's not in use, to keep out leaves, neighbourhood cats and rain. Then, as the children grow, it can be turned into a decorative pool that all the family will enjoy.

A swing is another piece of equipment that can lead a double life in a family garden. Site it over a pathway and then when it is no longer needed for play you could take out the swing seat, train roses and clematis over the frame and turn it into a **decorative arch**. Alternatively site it in a corner where a seat can be put under it eventually, and turn it into a rose-covered arbour. A climbing frame can be left in place, too, and turned into a support for large and vigorous climbers later on.

Plants

Plants for the family garden need to be resilient enough to survive footballs being flung at them and children chasing around them. The answer is to choose a framework of easily maintained evergreens and a mix of shrubs that will form a backdrop for the grown-up garden later on, You could add some low-growing perennial plants in front too – anything tall and spindly is likely to be easily snapped. Bedding plants are out, if you've got boisterous kids around, but you can still have flowers, using flowering shrubs instead.

The butterfly bush (*Buddleia*) can stand being knocked about; so can **escallonia** with its pretty white or red flowers in early summer. **Forsythia**, which brightens up the

▼ **A disused swing set can become a lovely rose-covered arbour.**

garden in spring with its showers of yellow flowers, is pretty well childproof, and so is **kerria**, which has golden pompom blooms on arching stems. Many fruit bushes like **flowering currants** and **gooseberries** can cope with being kicked around, as can **viburnum** and **spiraea**.

A child's own garden

Give children their own area to garden – a place where they can grow easy annuals and salad items like radishes. Growing something that you can eat always appeals to a small child. Buy pelleted seeds that small fingers find easier to handle (and the coating of nutrients gives the seed itself a better chance of survival) or mix the seed with plenty of sand first so that it is distributed properly.

Edge the beds with something imaginative – scallop shells, for instance, or giant pebbles – and make the beds narrow enough for children to reach over without trampling on other plants. Be inventive and make each one in the shape of the child's initial, marking them out with little stones.

Interest your children in gardening by giving them unusual things to grow. Look in the more unusual seed catalogues for ideas. There is the **giant Jersey cabbage**, for instance, that can be made into a walking stick. Get them to sow the seeds in the spring, and transplant them in the autumn – or they can be raised from seed in pots and then put in. Once the cabbage stem is about 45 cm (18 in) high, they need to pick off the lower leaves as they appear, then let the plant flower. With luck it will grow taller than they do and, when the stalk has become hard and woody it can be cut down, chopped to walking-stick length, dried and varnished.

Other plants well worth growing include the **sensitive plant** (mimosa pudica) which shrinks and folds its leaves when you touch it, and the **loofah** which comes from the cucumber family. Loofahs can be grown like a cucumber and then allowed to dry off to use in the bath.

Decorative gourds are another idea. The seeds need to be soaked overnight in warm (not hot) water to start them off, then they can be poked into the ground against a wall or fence with sticks to mark the spot. When the shoots come through they will wind themselves round the sticks, producing flowers and eventually bizarrely shaped fruits which can be picked and varnished.

Anything monster sized is bound to be a success so **sunflowers** are a must. Children will also enjoy growing a **giant marrow**, better still a **pumpkin**. Personalise it by cutting their names in the sides of the fruits, when they are quite small, taking care not to dig too deeply into the flesh. Then the children can watch their names grow, too.

Children can keep **cacti** out of doors in summer – plant up an old sink or shallow trough with sandy soil mixed with peat for the purpose, topped by a layer of sand to get that desert look. If they are spaced out properly in an old sink, they make a great site for games with miniature toys, like cowboys and Indians, for instance. The most exciting cacti to look for are spiny ones like the rock cactus (cereus peruvianus monstrosus) or those of the opuntia family which look like prickly pears. Just for fun they could have some of the woolly ones, the espostoas, which are covered in white fur, or the old man cactus (cephalocereus senilis) which has wild-looking silver hair all over it. Another fascinating family of cacti for children to own are the **living stones**, the lithops which do, indeed look just like pebbles rather than plants.

Birthday trees

It's a good idea for each child to have his or her own birthday fruit tree, planted on the day they were born. If you pick a 'family' tree you can have three different varieties of apples or pears grafted on to one rootstock. Take a photograph of your children standing beside their trees each year, to see how they are all growing. When the first fruits arrive, it is simple to cut out the child's initial in weather-proof surgical tape and stick it on the side of one fruit. Once it has ripened and coloured, take off the tape and see that the initials have remained green.

Poisonous plants

There are some plants that are dangerous to have in a garden where small children are around. Berries and pods can look deceptively attractive and may be highly poisonous – the pods of the laburnum for instance.

Plants to avoid are:

Box
Cotoneaster
Daphne mezereum
Ivy
Aconite
Aquilegia
Elder
Foxglove
Hellebores
Holly
Iris
Juniper
Lily of the Valley
Oleander
Polygonatum
Privet
Pulsatilla
Yew

100 plants that are easy to grow

20 plants for the flower border

All of the plants shown here are perennials, that is, once planted they will come up again and again each year. All of them produce flowers in midsummer and although they will look small at first, they will close ranks and produce a solid band of colour in the middle/back of the border in time. Plan your border for a mix of tall spires and rounded shapes. The heights given are for well-established plants that have been in place a year or so – bear them in mind when you are planting.

 Blanket flower (*Gaillardia*)
A good candidate for the back of any border with its large bright daisy-like blooms in yellow or red. It grows to 1 m (3 ft) tall in time.

 Bleeding heart (*Dicentra*)
A cottage plant with pretty pink and white heart-shaped flowers growing to 75 cm (2 ½ ft).

 Chinese lantern (*Physalis*)
An old-fashioned favourite that seeds itself generously. Grown for its lantern-like orange pods, it can reach to 1 m (3 ft) in height.

 Columbine (*Aquilegia*)
A deceptively delicate-looking plant with finely toothed leaves and long-spurred flowers in pink, white, purple, blue or yellow. A candidate for the middle of a border reaching 75 cm (2 ½ ft) in time.

 Cone flower (*Rudbeckia*)
A tall grower for the back of a border, its large yellow daisy flowers have black centres. It will grow up to 1 m (3 ft) high.

 Coreopsis (*Coreopsis grandiflora*)
Another plant with large daisy-like blooms, the golden yellow petals have ragged edges. It reaches 1 m (3 ft).

 Geranium
Not the pot-grown pelargonium but a hardy plant with attractive foliage and simple saucer-shaped flowers in pink, magenta, blue or white. For the middle of the border reaching 60 cm (2 ft) after a year or so.

Golden rod (*Solidago*)
An old-fashioned plant that gives you plumes of yellow flowers in midsummer. It can reach up to 1.8 m (6 ft) in height when established.

Hollyhock (*Althaea rosea*)
A striking plant for the back of a border with its funnel-shaped flowers on tall spikes. Hollyhocks come in yellow, pink, white or mauve and can reach up to 1.8 m (6 ft) tall.

✿ Iris

Best hidden in a border where its sword-like leaves contrast well with other foliage, irises come with yellow, white, mauve or blue flowers and reach up to 1.2 m (4 ft) tall.

✿ Lady's mantle (Alchemilla mollis)

A pretty plant all summer through with its delicate leaves that catch the morning dew and tiny star-shaped greeny-yellow flowers. It will reach up to 45 cm (1½ ft) tall.

✿ Lupin

This gives you tall flower spikes in a wide range of colours, especially pinks and mauves. Lupins can grow up to 90 cm (3 ft) tall.

✿ Michaelmas daisy (Aster novi-Belgii)

A good basic border plant with white, pink, blue, mauve or purple daisy flowers. It will reach 1.2 m (4 ft) in time.

✿ Phlox

Another tall grower with white, pink, purple or rose flower clusters. Expect it to reach 1.2 m (4 ft) in height.

✿ Red hot poker (Kniphofia)

A favourite plant with its poker-like red flower spikes graduating to yellow. It can reach 1.5 m (5 ft) in height.

✿ St John's wort (Hypericum)

Another useful plant which has yellow cup-shaped flowers and spreads quickly to fill gaps. It reaches 45 cm (1½ ft) in height.

✿ Scabious (Scabiosa)

A distinctive plant with its single blue or mauve flowers with 'pincushion' centres. It will reach 60 cm (2 ft).

✿ Shasta daisy (Chrysanthemum maximus)

An obliging member of the chrysanthemum family with single or double white daisy-like flowers with yellow centres. It grows to 1 m (3 ft) high.

✿ Solomon's seal (Polygonatum)

Grown for its attractive foliage, this plant has white pendant tubular flowers on arching stems and can reach up to 1.2 m (4 ft) in height.

✿ Yarrow (Achillea)

This plant produces clusters of flat-topped flowers in yellow, white or red. Expect it to grow 1.2 m (4 ft) high.

20 easy annuals

Raise your own cheap and cheerful plants from seed for quick colour to cover gaps in a new flower border. All the ones shown here can be sown straight into the ground in March to April. Don't forget to mark the spot where you put them, otherwise you may mistake the fledgling plants for weeds. Many of them will self-seed and come up in the same spot each year. The heights of the plants are given so you can choose where to site them.

✿ Baby blue eyes (Nemophila menziesii)

A bushy plant for the front of a border, it has sky-blue flowers like buttercups in shape. It'll grow to 22 cm (9 in).

✿ California poppy (Eschscholzia)

Grow this vigorous plant in full sun and it will give you a good display of vivid blooms in reds, orange and yellow. It will grow to about 23–37 cm (9–15 in).

✿ Convolvulus

A climber/crawler which produces funnel-like flowers in blues, pinks and crimson, with attractive markings on them. It likes the sun. Expect it to grow to about 37 cm (15 in).

✿ Cornflower (Centaurea cyanus)

A pretty cottagey plant with intense blue flowers from June through to September. It comes in a dwarf version now, too, but the original plant will grow to about 1 m (3 ft).

✿ Flax (Linum)

Usually grown for its cluster of blue funnel-shaped flowers, flax is now available in shades of white and red as well. It should reach 37–45 cm (15–18 in).

Godetia

A bushy plant that makes a profusion of saucer-shaped flowers in bright salmon pink, red, white and orange. It will grow to about 30–60 cm(1–2 ft).

Gypsophila

A delicate-looking bushy plant that produces masses of tiny white starry flowers. Grow it among other annuals. It should be about 37–45 cm (15–18 in) in height.

Larkspur (Delphinium ajacis)

This is the easy annual version of the tall growing delphinium, reaching only 1 m (3 ft). It has the same spikes of blooms in blues, red and white but on a smaller scale.

Love-in-a-mist (Nigella damascena)

A delicate-looking plant with fine feathery foliage and misty blue white or pink flowers, it should reach about 37–45 cm (15–18 in).

Love-lies-bleeding (Amaranthus caudatus)

A popular cottage plant, it has dark red tassels and stems that turn crimson in autumn. Expect to it reach 1m (3 ft).

Mallow (Lavatera)

A tall plant that quickly forms a bush up to 1 m (3 ft) high, with pretty pink trumpet-like flowers.

Mignonette (Reseda odorata)

An old-fashioned plant that is seldom seen these days. It has cones of sweetly scented flowers in red, tinged with yellow or green, and will grow to about 30–15 cm (1–2 ft).

Nasturtium (Tropaeolum majus)

Now available in a dwarf as well as a climbing version, this popular plant with trumpet-like flowers in bright yellows, oranges and reds keeps blooming all summer. It'll grow to between 20 and 37 cm (10–15 in).

Night-scented stock (Matthiola bicornis)

Grown for its heady scented flowers. The single lilac spikes look best mixed among other plants. It should grow to about 37 cm (15 in).

Poppy (Papaver)

The bright scarlet poppy also comes now in a double version and with flowers in pastel shades. It will seed itself well. Expect it to reach 30cm–1 m (1–3 ft).

Straw flower (Helichrysum)

A popular everlasting flower with bright double-daisylike flowers in mixed colours which have a texture like straw. Pick them to dry off for the winter. It should reach 1 m (3 ft) in height.

Sunflower (Helianthus annuus)

Grow one or two against the fence for fun. If it grows to a great height it may need supporting with a stake. It should grow up to 3 m (10 ft) in height.

Sweet pea (Lathrys odoratus)

This climber will hitch on to other plants with its leaf tendrils or it can be grown as a trailer in containers. It will make up to 2 m (6 ft) of growth.

Toad flax (Linaria)

Popularly known as 'bunny rabbits', this small bushy plant gives you small spikes of flowers in a variety of colours and is good for the front of a border. It should grow to about 20–37 cm (8–15 in).

Virginia stock (Malcomia maritima)

One of the easiest annuals to grow, it has clusters of flowers in mixed colours on slender stems. It will grow to 20 cm (8 in).

10 good plants for ground cover

All these plants can be relied upon to form a mat that, in time, keeps out the weeds. They also help to keep moisture in the soil.

Alpine strawberry (Fragaria vesca)

This edible ground cover blooms in early summer and produces delicious tiny fruits. It spreads quickly by runners, and thrives in the shade. It will reach about 20 cm (8 in) in height.

 Aubretia *(Aubretia deltoidea)*
This vigorous little plant will quickly give you a mat of evergreen foliage and masses of light purple flowers all summer through. It prefers a sunny position. Aubretia should reach 7.5–10 cm (3–4 in).

 Bugle *(Ajuga reptans)*
An attractive mat-forming plant which likes both sun and light shade. It has attractive blue flower spikes. Expect it to grow to 10–30 cm (4–12 in).

 Campanula *(Campanula portenschlagiana)*
Happy in sun or partial shade, it forms mats of heart-shaped leaves and has violet bell-shaped flowers in summer. It should grow to about 15 cm (6 in).

 Creeping Jenny *(Lysimachia mummularia 'Aurea')*
A ground cover plant for light shade, the buttercup-like flowers appear along the length of the trailing stems in summer, and grow to about 15 cm (6 in) tall.

 Lily of the valley *(Convallaria)*
This plant rapidly establishes itself in colonies and makes good ground cover in the shade under trees and shrubs. It is grown from crowns with multiply rapidly and produces the familiar highly scented white flower bells. It should grow to about 15–20 cm (6–8 in).

 Periwinkle *(Vinca minor)*
A fast grower that can spread over 1m (3ft) of ground or more after a year or so. You can buy a variegated kind with creamy leaf markings and mauve flowers. It grows to about 5–10 cm (2–4 in) in height.

 Prostrate thyme *(Thymus serpyllum)*
The low-grow versions of thyme like 'Annie Hall' form a mat-like cover that weeds find difficult to penetrate. All thymes prefer full sun. It should reach 7.5 cm (3–5 in).

 Stonecrop *(Sedum spathulifolium)*
Sedums do best in full sun and dry conditions and form rosettes of fleshy light grey leaves with bright yellow flowers in summer. It will grow to about 5-10 cm (2-4 in).

 Variegated ivy *(Hedera canariensis 'Variegata')*
This ivy has large leaves striped and edged in silvery grey and white. A tenacious kind of ground cover, it is fine for deep shade. It's height will be about 10 cm (4 in).

15 plants for a dry sunny bed

A flower bed in the sun that tends to dry out needs plants that can withstand summer drought. Many of these come from the Mediterranean where hot dry summers are the norm.

 Artemisia
A whole family of silver-leafed plants that thrive in a sunny border. Two of the best are 'Powis Castle' and 'Dusty Miller' which has almost white leaves. Artemisia should grow to about 1.3 m (3–4 t).

 Bear's breeches *(Acanthus)*
A handsome perennial plant with bold spikes of tubular flowers in lilac, white or purple. Good for a flower border, it will reach about 1 m (3 ft).

 Broom *(Cytisus)*
There are many different types of sun-loving broom ranging from dwarf types to those that grow to 5 m (15 ft) or more. Be sure to check the eventual size when you buy one from the garden centre. Most have yellow flowers but some versions come with red or purple blooms.

 Butterfly bush *(Buddleia davidii)*
An obliging shrub that survives on little water. It has grey-green leaves and, in summer, fragrant lilac-coloured flowers that attract butterflies. It'll grow to about 2.75 m (9 ft).

 Cotton lavender *(Santolina)*
A dwarf shrub with aromatic fine-cut silver leaves. Keep it clipped and it will make an

attractive mound, or it can be used as a low edging. In summer it has small yellow button-like flowers, and will grow to about 45–60 cm (18–24 in).

�֎ **Daisy bush** (Olearia x haastii)
This shrub has glossy green leaves with greyish-white felted undersides and white daisy-like flowers. A good-tempered grower, it does well in town conditions, and will grow to 2–2.6 m (6–8 ft).

✖ **Globe thistle** (Echinops ritro)
A handsome accent plant with deep grey-green leaves and globe-like steel-blue flowers. There are many other thistles that thrive in a sunny bed, but this one is more compact than most, reaching about 1–1.2 m (3–4 ft).

✖ **Oriental poppy** (Papaver orientale)
A tall showy poppy with large heads of ruffled flowers in pink or scarlet. It is a perennial plant and will go on from year to year in a border. Expect it to reach 60 cm–1 m (2–3 ft).

✖ **Lavender** (Lavandula)
This decorative shrubby plant with its blue-mauve flower spikes is well able to take care of itself, and also comes in a dwarf form 'Munstead'. Clip back in spring and again in the autumn, and it will grow to about 1–1.2 m (3–4 ft).

✖ **Mullein** (Verbascum)
A striking plant with its grey felt-like leaves and tall spikes in yellow, pink, or white. It will reach up to 1.8 m (6 ft) in height.

✖ **Potentilla** (Potentilla fruticosa)
A sun-loving shrub with small buttercup-yellow flowers. There is also a version, 'Red Ace' which has vermilion flowers splashed with yellow, and will grow to about 1.2–1.5 m (4–5 ft).

✖ **Sage** (Salvia)
Common garden sage can be found in three forms as well as the basic grey-blue: splashed with gold, with purple leaves and variegated tricolour sage which has leaves marked with white and pink. It should reach about 1 m (3 ft) in height.

✖ **Sweet Sultan** (Centaurea moschata)
An annual plant with narrow grey leaves and large scented flowers in yellow, white, pink or purple. Sow a few seeds each week from March to the end of May to ensure a succession of flowers all summer. It will grow to about 60 cm (2 ft).

✖ **Rosemary** (Rosmarinus officinalis)
An attractive Mediterranean shrub that can be used as an aromatic edging to a flower bed if you keep it clipped. There are versions available with white flowers as well as the traditional blue. Expect it to reach about 1m (3 ft).

✖ **Wallflower** (Cheiranthus cheiri)
Another sun-lover which gives you a splendid show of scented flowers in late spring. Choose from mixes of oranges, reds and yellows. It also comes in a dwarf form for the front of a bed – so can grow to between 20 cm (8in) and 60 cm (2ft).

15 plants for a damp shady bed

Damp shade need not be difficult to deal with if you choose plants that can stand the moisture. These are all happy in gloomy conditions. Their expected heights are listed in brackets.

✖ **Cornelian cherry** (Cornus mas)
A twiggy shrub with clusters of small golden-yellow flowers in early spring. It comes in several forms, some of them with leaves splashed with yellow or white. (2.4–3.6 m [8–12 ft])

✖ **Cyclamen** (Cyclamen coum)
A hardy version of a favourite indoor plant with attractive marbled leaves. It thrives in shade, and flowers during the winter months. (7.5 cm [3 in])

✖ **Elephant's ears** (Bergenia)
This plant has distinctive large evergreen leaves and gives you trusses of pink or white flowers on long stems. It is a good candidate for the centre of a shady bed. (37.5 cm [15 in])

Fatsia Japonica

An exotic evergreen with a tropical look that thrives in shade. It has glossy dark green leaves, and flowers that look like giant dandelion clocks which bloom in October. (2.4 m [8 ft])

Filipendula (Filipendula ulmaria)

This attractive plant with dark, deeply notched leaves thrives in a moist soil. It produces sprays of white flowers in summer. There is also another version, 'aurea', which has gold-green leaves. (60 cm–1m [2–3 ft])

Hellebore (Helleborus)

The whole hellebore family thrive in dark, damp places. The first to flower is H.niger, the Christmas rose, followed by 'Orientalis', the lenten rose in February. Then comes the stinking hellebore H.foetidus which produces handsome purple cup-shaped blooms from March to May. (30–60 cm [12–24 n])

Hound's tongue (Cynoglosum amabile)

This easily grown annual has flowers that look very much like forget-me-nots. Good for the front of a border, it likes damp soil but prefers the bed to be well drained, not boggy. (45–60 cm [18–24 in])

Mock orange (Philadelphus)

A useful, tall shrub that can take shade with oval, deeply veined leaves and showers of white flowers which are cup-shaped and smell strongly of orange-blossom – hence its name. (at least 1.8 m [6 ft])

Pachysandra

An amiable evergreen plant that appreciates plenty of shade and a moist soil. It makes large low mounds of dark green leaves with tiny purple-white flowers in spring. (30 cm [12 in])

Polyanthus (Primula vulgaris)

All the primrose family thrive in moist shade – in fact, they should never be allowed to dry out. Choose from a wide range of colourings – the Pacific strain has blooms in all colours of the rainbow, with yellow centres. (30 cm [12 in])

Purple loosestrife (Lythrium)

Here's a plant that really likes damp ground. It's a perennial and will form a clump in time with spires of tightly packed flowers in summer in pinks and purples. (60 cm–1.5 m [2–5 ft])

Osmanthus (Osmanrea x burkwoodii)

A compact evergreen shrub that likes at least partial shade. It has glossy dark-green leaves and clusters of scented white tubular flowers in spring. It can be used very successfully for a hedge. (1.8–3 m [6–10 ft])

Spirea (Spirea thunbergii)

Another shrub that can take moist shade, it has pale green leaves on slender branches and clusters of white blooms in spring. It can be used very successfully for a flowering hedge. (1.5–1.8 m [5–6 ft])

Viburnum (Viburnum Davidii)

A low-growing evergreen shrub with flat heads of white flowers, rather like those of the hydrangea, in early summer and berries in the autumn. (60–90 cm [2–3 ft])

10 plants that need an acid soil

If your soil is chalky and you really want to grow some of these plants, all is not lost: you can make a special raised bed and fit it with ericaceous compost bought from a garden centre, or grow a specimen plant in a pot. You'll find the expected height of each plant in brackets, following the description.

Azalea

A member of the rhododendron family that usually drops its leaves in autumn, this small-size shrub has flowers in pinks, yellows, mauves, some of them very sweetly scented. It prefers at least some shade. (1.5–3 m [3–10 ft])

Calico bush (Kalmia)

An evergreen shrub with glossy mid-green leaves and clusters of pretty pink flowers in early summer. This plant prefers at least partial shade. (1.8–3 m [6–10 ft])

Camellia (*Camellia japonica*)
A handsome plant all year round with its glossy dark leaves. It prefers to be somewhere sheltered, otherwise early morning sun after frost will tend to damage the large, attractive, rose-like flowers in pink or white. (1.8–3.6 m [6–12 ft])

Eucryphia (*Eucryphia glutinosa*)
An attractive but slow grower with glossy green leaves that turn orange-red in autumn. Attractive white flowers with yellow-tipped centres appear in July and August. (3 m [10 ft])

Heath (*Calluna vulgaris*)
An easy-to-grow plant for acid soils, it has small leaves and stiff branches and double flowers which appear for the whole of August and September. Choose from a whole colour range from white through to pinks and purples. (60 cm [2 ft])

Heather (*Erica*)
Almost the entire Erica family of plants need an acid soil – the one exception is the winter-flowering Erica carnea which can take chalk. A useful choice for an easy-care garden – they will give you greenery all year round and make good hedges or ground cover. The tiny bell-like flowers, which appear in the spring, are usually pink or white. (30–60 cm [12–24 in])

Pernettya (*Pernettya mucronata*)
This attractive evergreen shrub belongs to the heather family but has larger glossier leaves. It is grown mainly for its attractive fruits which form pink clusters on its branches in the autumn. (60–90 cm [2–3 ft])

Rhododendron
The most spectacular shrubs you can choose for an acid soil, rhododendrons can be found with flowers in almost every shade from white to purple. They prefer to be in sheltered semi-shady conditions as their shallow roots should not be allowed to dry out. (1.8–2.4 m [6–8 ft])

Skimmia (*Skimmia fortuneii*)
This particular variety of skimmia prefers a lime-free soil. It's a compact shrub with mid-green leaves and cones of tiny white flowers in early summer followed by crimson fruits in August. (90 cm–1.5 m [3–5 ft])

Vaccinium (*Vaccinium glaucoalbum*)
A relative of the cranberry family, this decorative shrub will only grow in an acid soil. It is evergreen with handsome leaves that are blue-grey on their undersides. White flowers, tinged with pink, bloom in early summer, followed by blue-black edible fruits. (90 cm–1.5 m [3–5 ft])

10 plants that like an alkaline soil

If your soil has a lot of chalk in it, then it is almost certainly alkaline. Fortunately there are many plants that suit it. Expected heights are in brackets.

Abutilon (*Abutilon vitifolium*)
Although most abutilons have to be grown indoors as house plants, this particular version will thrive in a sheltered garden. Its leaves are covered in white down, and it flowers all summer producing large lavender blooms. (2.4 m [8 ft])

Berberis
Here's a wall or hedging plant that really thrives in a chalky soil. It's grown mainly for its attractive scarlet berries, although the spring-flowering Berberis darwinii has berries that are blue. There are a large number of varieties to choose from, some of them dwarf in habit. (1.5–3 m [5–10 ft])

Daphne (*Daphne laureola*)
Grown mainly for its attractive foliage, it makes a small bush with shiny oval leaves. Its flowers, which are yellow-green, appear in very early spring. (60 cm–1.2 m [2–4 ft])

Deutzia (*Deutzia x hybrida*)
A good-tempered flowering shrub which produces showers of blooms in pink to rose-purple in early summer. It is a happy choice for a small garden. (1.2–1.8 m [4–6 ft])

�֍ **Eleagnus** (*Eleagnus angustifolia*)
A shrub that will cover a lot of ground – it is fast growing and tends to spread. It has silvery foliage, silver-white flowers and pale fruits and makes a good contrast to more colourful specimens. 3–4.5 m [10–15 ft])

✖ **Honeysuckle** (*Lonicera*)
Although they will grow almost anywhere, honeysuckles prefer a chalky soil. They are not all climbers – *Lonicera nitida* is a small evergreen shrub with insignificant flowers. It is used in place of box for small hedges and for topiary. (3–4.5 m [10–15 ft])

✖ **Japanese quince** (*Chaemoneles*)
Here's a wall shrub that is perfectly happy to grow in a chalky soil. Useful for giving colour in spring, its flushed pink flowers appear from March onwards, followed, if you are lucky, by handsome yellow fruits in the autumn. (1m [3 ft])

✖ **Kerria** (*Kerria japonica 'pleniflora'*)
A good shrub to grow against a wall, kerria produces masses of little yellow ruffled flowers against its new leaves in spring. Although it will grow in almost any garden soil, it prefers one that is chalky. (1.2–1.8 m [4–6 ft])

✖ **Spiraea** (*Spiraea japonica*)
Another useful shrub for a chalky soil, spiraea makes a good hedge, too. It produces pink, sometimes white, flowers in profusion in late summer. (1.8–2.4 m [6–8 ft])

✖ **Weigela** (*Weigela florida*)
One of the most popular of all flowering shrubs, weigela bears clusters of rose-pink flowers on short branches all summer through. One variety of this plant, 'variegata' has leaves that are edged with cream. (1.8 m [6 ft])

Gardening in window boxes and tubs

Putting plants in containers – to give a cheerful welcome at the front door, to decorate the patio or to augment permanent flower beds – has lots of advantages. You can switch them around as you wish, changing colour schemes from one month to another. You can plant on several different levels as well, if you choose a mix of low-standing troughs and higher tubs.

It's a way of getting more for your money, too, for plants in containers can be crammed in to give a luxurious profusion, a look that is expensive to achieve in a flower bed. Best of all, when things are past their peak and dying down – bulbs, for instance – it's easy to move them away out of sight.

Which container?

What's the right kind of container for your garden? It's important to pick something appropriate. Ornate old-fashioned urns may be attractive in their own right, but might look totally out of place in an ultra-modern setting. On the other hand, plain containers made from concrete or plastic need to be well planted, with plenty of trailers in front, if they are to avoid looking uninspiring and dull.

It always pays to get the biggest possible containers that the space will take, for they won't dry out too quickly in summer or require so much watering. But be warned, really large containers look good but can be very difficult to move, so they are best set on a mini-trolley made from a square of wood with casters. Alternatively, if you are only likely to want to move them around occasionally, you can tilt the container to one side, slip a stout piece of sacking or a strip of old carpet underneath and drag them along on that.

When siting a new container, always try it out first, empty, to make sure you've chosen the right spot. It's much easier to move around than when it's full.

Plastic has now overtaken terracotta as the most popular material for plant pots and tubs. It has many advantages: it is cheap, light, and holds water longer than clay or terracotta. It can be moulded into all kinds of interesting shapes including 'tower' pots which slot into one another, skyscraper fashion, with plants growing out of their sides. The main disadvantage of plastic is that it

> **One of the cheapest large containers you can use is a full-sized plastic bucket. Buy a plain black or white one, or paint it any colour you choose with outdoor emulsion. Leave the handle unobtrusively at the back – it will come in handy when you want to move the container.**

does not look particularly pretty and is best used with trailing plants over the sides. It also becomes brittle after a long time in the sun and will eventually start to crack.

Terracotta or **clay** pots look attractive but need careful handling because they break easily. Moisture evaporates through them too, so they need watering more frequently. Ordinary clay flowerpots are relatively cheap to buy but if you're going for anything really decorative it can be expensive.

Wood is often used for pots and window boxes that look good in country surroundings but need constant repainting to stop them from rotting. They have the advantage of keeping the roots of plants warmer in winter than other kinds of containers. If you are handy with a saw it is quite easy to make simple wood troughs, but you should choose a hardwood if they are to last at all.

Glass fibre pots are usually moulded to look like lead, stone, or some other traditional material. They are heavier than those made from plastic, and can cost a lot of money, but they are very convincing fakes.

Reconstituted stone is crushed stone mixed with cement. It is often used for decorative troughs and urns that look as though they are carved in stone. They are not cheap and they do occasionally crack in a hard frost.

Resin-bonded cellulose is one of the newer cheap container ideas. The pots look as if they have been moulded from compressed peat and they are often used to line hanging baskets and for short-term tubs on the terrace. Be warned, however: the largest sizes tend to be fragile when they are filled with soil – if you try to move one it may split.

Other ideas

Of course you don't have to buy containers that are made specially for plants. Be inventive: follow the Mediterranean fashion and save large tins and oil cans to use as planters. Group them together, paint them in bright colours with odds and ends left over from home decorating and they will make an attractive show – then you can throw them away at the end of the summer. Even a collection of empty baked bean tins, painted turquoise blue, can be grouped together to make a stunning show.

Look for other things around the house and garden: a broken wheelbarrow can be pressed into service to display a clutch of pots of geraniums, an old sink is excellent for alpines or miniature plants.

Hanging baskets

Hanging baskets and half baskets which you fix to the wall look very attractive and give you a chance to display colour at higher levels.

The most attractive versions are the wire baskets lined with spaghnum moss. To help conserve water, put inside an inner lining cut from black plastic. Or you could try a lining of cellulose mentioned above, cutting holes in it with kitchen scissors to put in trailing plants at intervals. It pays to buy special soil-less compost for hanging baskets because it is much lighter than ordinary garden soil. And invest in a watering lance, if you can, so you can reach your plants without taking down the basket. An alternative idea is to lash a piece of cane to the end of a hose for watering high baskets.

> **Be warned: hanging and half baskets need frequent watering – as often as twice a day in mid-summer– so make sure they are easy to reach and don't hang them over a sitting area or where people are likely to pass underneath them regularly.**

How to plant a hanging basket

1. Support the basket first by sitting it in the top of a bucket or, in the case of a half basket, across the top.

2. Put in the lining – kitchen foil, plastic sheeting or a bought cellulose liner – if you are using the latter, cut holes in strategic places to take trailing plants before you put it in place.

3. Make a hole in the bottom of the liner, lift the basket, and gently ease in a trailing plant, roots first from underneath. Cover it with 5–10cm (2–4in) of soil.

4. Make slits in the sides of the liner at intervals – all round or, in the case of half baskets, in front. Push in more trailers, roots first. Continue to fill the inside of the basket with compost, firming it with your hand as you go.

5. When you get to the top, stop short with the soil about 7.5cm (3 in) from the rim – you have to allow space for the main plants to go in. Put in more trailers round the side, siting them in diagonally so that they will grow in an outward direction. Make sure the roots are well covered, and peg down the stems with a hairpin to encourage them to grow out, and down, rather than up.

6. Now put in the main plants on top, firming them down well, covering the roots. Leave a small bowl-shaped depression in the soil in the centre, this will help keep the water in and stop it from splashing over the side when you fill it.

Finally, give your basket a good soak and leave it in the bucket to drain properly before you hang it up. Make sure that the bracket or hook on which it is to hang is secure – a fully planted basket is surprisingly heavy.

Filling your containers

Your containers are going to have to work hard all summer so don't skimp on soil. It pays to buy special compost to grow your plants in – making sure it is of the right texture and weed free. Hanging baskets and small pots in particular must have the best possible medium for the plants to grow in, to ensure you get a good display. If you are planting a very large tub, then you can half-fill it with ordinary garden soil to save cash, then top it up with compost. Always leave a gap of at least 5 cm (2 in) at the top of the container so that when you water it the soil will not spill over.

> **Look out for growing bags of compost which are often sold as cheap special offers in supermarkets. Use the contents to fill pots and tubs.**

Planting your containers

If your contained garden is part of a patio, then you'll need some basic evergreen plants to back up the display all year round. Once in place, they can be livened up with bulbs, spring flowers and in summer, showy, half-hardy plants and annuals.

5 evergreen plants to choose

These make a marvellous backdrop in containers tubs and window boxes.

Berberis

A small evergreen shrub that likes growing against walls and will reward you first of all with small yellow flowers and then with brilliant red berries.

Box (Buxus)

Keep it clipped into an attractive shape, and box will make a perfect background in even the smallest patio. Try a little topiary, turning it into a pyramid or a cone.

Dwarf juniper (Juniperus communis 'hibernica')

A perfect little plant for window boxes, it grows very slowly and never reaches more than 30 cm (1 ft).

Mexican orange blossom (Choisya ternata)

A very attractive evergreen for larger tubs that is grown mainly for its white star-like scented flowers in late spring. It grows very well sited up against a wall but can take some shade, too.

Ivy (Hedera)

Use it as a trailer spilling over the edge of a window box or as a climber up a frame – either way ivy is indispensable as a foil to your flowers. You can also purchase ivy in variegated forms; i.e., with leaves splashed with silver or gold.

15 flowers for pots and tubs

Here are some flowers you can pick up from a garden centre and simply put in – and they'll go on blooming all summer.

African marigold (Tagetes)

If you like vivid oranges and yellows, this is the flower to choose. It comes now with bigger, better blooms and gives you good value for money.

Busy Lizzie (Impatiens)

A good bushy plant that can take the shade, available in a mix of colours, mainly pinks and reds. It will give you colour all summer through.

Cherry pie (Heliotropium)

Go for scent and pick this compact plant with its rich blue-violet flowers against glossy green leaves.

Coleus

Grown mainly as a house plant, coleus, with its colourful leaves in scarlet edged with yellow, can be grown all summer in pots and hanging baskets.

Fuchsia

A perfect candidate for the centre of a tub or hanging basket, the fuchsia's elegant drooping bell-like flowers come in pinks, mauves and white, or a combination of all three.

Geranium (Pelargonium)

The best-natured container plant of them all. Choose between the ivy-leafed variety which will trail over the sides, or the upright versions. Both will give you a profusion of blooms.

Italian bellflower (Campanula isophylla)

A delicate trailer with blue or white star-shaped flowers, it goes well with other pastel shades, especially in a hanging basket.

Livingstone Daisy (Mesembryanthemum)

A dwarf plant that packs plenty of colour in its large starry flowers. Choose between brilliant pinks or yellows with dark centres. Ideal for putting around larger specimen plants.

 Lobelia

Take it in the trailing or upright version, in Oxford or Cambridge blue – the lobelia is an obliging edging plant for all kinds of containers.

 Monkey flower (*Mimulus*)

There are many new colourful hybrids of this bright busy plant. Its large flowers are like nasturtiums, spotted and blotched in colours ranging from oranges and reds through to ivory and yellow.

 Pansy (*Viola x wittrockiana*)

The large velvety blooms of the pansy guarantee a spectacular display and will keep on going if you take off the dead flower heads promptly.

 Petunia

One of the best tempered of all bedding plants, with blooms that keep on coming, petunias come in all shades of white, pinks and crimson. Look out, too, for those with ruffled double flowers.

 Senecio (*Cineraria maritima*)

Grown for its striking foliage – spreading sprays of deeply cut silver-grey leaves – senecio produces small bright yellow flowers, too.

 Slipper flower (*Calceolaria*)

Another plant that we often grow indoors, but which can be safely left out all summer, the slipper flower has distinctive pouch-shaped blooms in bright colours, mainly red splashed with yellow.

 Verbena

One of the prettiest plants you can choose for a container, the new verbena hybrids give you a choice of pinks, blue with a hint of violet, white, and peaches and cream. It has masses of small flowers with dark-green toothed foliage.

> **A polystyrene cup with a small hole in the bottom can be put on the top of a basket then filled with water to trickle feed moisture into it. A handful of ice-cubes put on the soil will do the same trick.**

Watering

Container plants, like house plants, rely on you to provide them with food and make sure they get enough to drink, depending on how wet the weather is. Check them regularly, a fingertip lightly dragged over the surface should feel moisture. Water until surplus runs out of the bottom of the container.

Be prepared to water your containers at least once, possibly twice, a day during the summer in a hot dry spell. If your hanging baskets or window boxes are placed up high, a special watering lance, which you can find at your garden centre, is a worthwhile investment, to save you having to take them down to water them.

Feeding

Plants need a complex cocktail of nutrients if they are to look their best – nitrogen for their leaves, phosphorus for flowers, potassium for good root growth. Other minerals are also necessary in smaller quantities, including essential trace elements which are in normal soil. A good shop-bought compost should contain everything your plants need for the first few weeks of their life, but these become absorbed as time goes by, and some tend to be flushed out by water, especially if you are in the habit of using a hose.

So, during the peak growing season, feed your plants at ten-day intervals to be sure of good flowers – weekly in the case of hanging baskets for a really superb display. You should water your plants first so that the chemical will spread evenly through the compost. Powder or granule fertilisers are spread on the surface and gradually penetrate the soil beneath. Liquid fertilisers are diluted and

▲ **Making a pond.**

watered in. Or look out for the newer slow-release fertilisers in the form of pills or 'match sticks' which you simply push into the soil.

Water in the garden

One of the most exciting features you can add to your garden is the element of water, used in some way or another. Whether it's a pool, a fountain or water trickling into a basin, it gives constant movement and interest and mirrors the sky. Add some lights, too, for an exotic after-dark scene.

Obviously it is not safe to have a pond if there are small children around, unless you are prepared to stretch a net across the surface, but that does not rule out the idea of having a water feature – a circle of pebbles with water trickling over it, a waterfall or a fountain.

> **If you take over a garden with an existing pond and there are toddlers around, make it safe by stretching strong wide-meshed nylon netting across it, just under the surface of the water.**

Ponds

At one time all garden ponds had to be made from concrete, a time-consuming business. Now it's perfectly possible with the help of plastics to make one in an afternoon.

▲ **Your finished pond can be any shape. If you want fish make sure you make it deep enough.**

There are two easy ways of creating a pond in your garden: with an off-the-peg pool in pre-formed fibreglass or plastic, or using a butyl heavy-duty lining. Either way, your first job is to excavate a hole large enough to take it.

Choosing a site

Don't put your pond in the shade if you want to grow water lilies for they must have adequate light to flower – ideally, they need at least six hours of sunlight each day. And don't put it under a deciduous shrub or tree unless you are prepared to clean it regularly to get rid of dead and decaying leaves. Vegetation left lying at the bottom of the water can build up over a long period and eventually poison your goldfish.

The pre-formed pool

Although the idea of having something completely and permanently watertight is a popular one, the problem with most pre-formed pond liners is that they tend to come in ugly shapes and in unnatural colours, like swimming pool blue. It is also surprisingly difficult to dig a hole of the right shape to hold one. The pool must be packed round carefully to stop it from rocking as you fill it. You're going to need a spirit level to make sure that it sits exactly right – for nothing looks worse than a tipsy pool with one side higher than the other, an ugly edge exposed. The easiest way to install a pool of this kind is with the aid of some sand – you can sprinkle it in dents and slopes that tilt the pool and then use it to fill in around the edges.

Homemade pools

A pool that you make yourself gives you endless scope for choosing the shape that you want, and makes it easier to incorporate it into an existing space between, say, a flower bed and a lawn. And if you choose a heavy-duty liner made from butyl rubber, rather than PVC, it will last for up to fifty years.

The easiest shape to choose is an oval or circular one. Cutting out an exact rectangle and keeping it that way while you are lining it is more difficult. Having said that, there is virtually no shape that you cannot make if you want to – you could even have a small fake stream.

Choosing a size

What size space should you dig? You can't really keep both plants and fish in anything less than 2.7 square metres (30 sq ft), and your pond should be at least 45 cm (1½ ft) deep if you are keeping fish in it, or if you want to grow a water-lily. A shallow pond tends to give fluctuating temperatures from near freezing to near boiling and is uncomfortable for pond life. Fish also need a minimum depth if they are to survive a hard winter. Even so, if ice forms on the pool you should break it.

Using a butyl liner

If you are doing a free-form shape, mark out the outline you want with a hosepipe or a length of rope, then cut out the silhouette carefully with a sharp spade and take off any turf that lies within it. If you are planning to edge the pool with paving – the easiest way to disguise the edge of the butyl – take out a further strip outside the marker that will allow the slabs to lie flush with the surrounding soil.

Once you start digging, make sure that the sides of the pond slope inward quite sharply; this will stop them from caving in, as time goes on. If you want to grow marginal plants such as sweet flag (*acorus*) or iris kaempferi, which grow only in shallow water, then you need to create a step about 30 cm (1 ft) wide, 23 cm (9 in) down from the top. This doesn't have to go all the way round the pool – it can just edge part of it.

As you finish digging, put a spirit level on a plank across the top of the pool and move it to all points of the compass to make sure that the edges are level. Otherwise you will have a terrible time disguising the butyl liner with overhanging slabs.

Calculating the liner size

How much liner do you need? To calculate the size, measure the length and the width of the whole, then add twice the depth to each measurement. In other words, if your pond is to be 60 cm (2 ft) wide, 90 cm (3 ft) long, and 45 cm (1½ ft) deep, you would add 45 cm (1½ ft) twice to the 60 cm (2 ft) width, then 45 cm (1½ ft) again to the 90 cm (3 ft) length, making the total 1.5 m x 1.8 m (5 ft x 6 ft). To this you need to add another 60 cm (2 ft) to each measurement to allow for tucking the edge of the liner under paving or burying it in the soil. So your final piece of butyl would need to be 2.10 m x 2.40 m (7 ft x 8 ft). If your pool is circular, the length and width will, of course, be the same. When you come to buy your liner, choose black, which gives an impression of depth, or beige, rather than blue. It will look more realistic once in place.

Lining your pool

Choose a warm day to line your pond; leave the butyl out in the sun for a while and it will be more flexible to handle, and to take to the shape you have made. Line the hole first, with an old piece of carpeting or underfelt if you have some, or sprinkle on some spadefuls of sand. This will prevent the risk of the odd sharp stone or severed root puncturing the lining.

Set the sheet of butyl carefully and centrally over the pond site making sure that it overhangs evenly all round – once the water is in it is impossible to adjust the lining. Anchor the cut edge round the side with bricks or heavy stones, allowing plenty of slack within the hole.

> **If you don't have an old piece of carpet, underfelt or sand to put under your liner, you can use large wads of newspaper instead.**

Now start filling the pond with a hose, easing the liner in place as it moulds itself to the shape you have made, adjusting the stones weighting the edge. You'll find that you will have to make some unobtrusive pleats in it – try to make them as neatly as you can.

Once the pond is full you can trim away any surplus butyl, leaving a good margin to bury in the surrounding soil or place flat to take the paving. Sprinkle any liner that shows with soil, then put the flagstones in place if you are using them. Make sure they overlap the pool by at least 5 cm (2 in); this not only disguises the liner but stops the sun from shining on it, which may make it rot.

Stocking your pool

To keep your pool in peak condition you'll need a hard-working team of aquatics – water plants – to clean and oxygenate it. Left to itself a pond soon becomes like a bowl of pea soup as sunlight on the water causes algae to form.

To tackle the problem you need pond plants – **oxygenators** – that will use up carbon dioxide given off by fish and decaying vegetable matter and return oxygen to the water. They also provide valuable shelter for fish, giving them somewhere to hide when they spawn. You need at least one to every square foot of water surface, and they don't need to be planted. They are usually sold with their roots weighted by a piece of zinc, and you simply drop them in the water. Oxygenators are available from most pet shops stocking fish, and from many garden centres.

Your main plants for display purposes will be **aquatics**, like water lilies. You can find them in almost all pastel colours and they usually like deep water – though there are dwarf versions which need less depth.

Deep-water plants like the water lily can be put directly into soil at the bottom of the pool, but since this tends to make the water murky, a container is normally used.

Be careful what soil you choose for your water plants – you want to give them a good start in life. Special potting compost is not a good choice in this case because it may contain chemical fertiliser or some form of

> **You can buy special plastic baskets for water plants, though an ordinary plastic flower pot will do equally well and generally keeps the soil in place more securely. If you do use a basket, line it first with a piece of sacking to help keep in the earth.**

mineral that could be poisonous to goldfish. A light, sandy or peat-based soil is unsuitable, too, for it may float away and make the pond unattractive. A heavy clay-like loam is best of all, and if your own garden soil is not suitable, you can buy packets of special pond soil from some garden centres that specialise in accessories for water gardens.

Once your aquatics are planted they will need extra help to stay in place underwater, so scatter some gravel or pebbles on the surface of the soil. If you do use gravel, make sure it is large grade, or the fish may move it.

Don't worry if your water lily disappears to the bottom of the pond when you plant it; it will grow a longer stem in an amazingly short time, to bring its leaves up to the surface of the water. Many people mistakenly believe that you have to set its container on something and gradually lower the plant to the bottom over a period of several weeks, but this is totally unnecessary.

If you want your pond to look well established in a very short time, do make a shelf for some **marginals** (see page 406) – plants that grow in just a few inches of water. One valuable task they perform is to hide hard edges as well as the evidence of butyl sheeting where it is most likely to show – just above the surface of the water. If you haven't planned for them, you can use any suitably shaped container – a rectangular plastic window box, for instance, placed on a brick or two to lift it to the surface of the water – and plant some marginals in that.

Finally, don't forget a few **floaters**, plants with roots that simply trail in the water. Drop one or two into a larger pool where they will add to its attractions.

Plants for your pond

Oxygenators

Canadian pondweed

(Elodea canadensis, Elodea crispa)
It has small semi-translucent leaves.
Plant it 15–48 cm (6–18 in) deep in the
water.

Water crowfoot *(Ranunculus aquatilis)*

This plant produces thin strip-like leaves
underwater, and floating ones like those of
the buttercup, with white flowers in spring.
Plant it in a depth of 15–35 cm (6–14 in).

Marginal Plants

Sweet Flag *(Acorus)*

This edging plant has aromatic iris-like leaves
and white horn-like flower spikes in summer.
It likes plenty of sun.

Flowering rush *(Butomus umbellatus)*

This marginal gives you better flowers if it is
planted only 5–15 cm (2–6 in) deep. It has
reed-like leaves and rose-pink blooms.

Marsh marigold *(Caltha palustris)*

A quick-growing marginal which gives you
masses of deep yellow cup-shaped flowers in
late spring, and lush green leaves. Plant it in
water up to 15 cm (6 in) deep.

Aquatics

Water hawthorn *(Aponogeton distachyus)*

This plant has fleshy leaves marked with
brown and creamy white flowers from late
summer, which appear just above the surface.

Water lily *(Nymphaea)*

This is the best-known pond plant of all with
its distinctive large flat leaves and large
flowers which, in some varieties, are scented.
Pick your lily to suit the depth of water you
can offer it.

Bog Plants

Royal fern *(Osmunda regalis)*

A distinctive plant, with its pea-green fronds,
which makes a perfect edging for a pond. It
needs damp conditions to thrive.

Astilbe *(Astilbe x arensii)*

A delicate-looking perennial plant with deep-
green fern-like foliage and minute flowers in
pink, red or white.

Floaters

Water soldier *(Stratiotes aloides)*

The sword-shaped leaves of this plant
normally lie just below the surface, but rise up
above it when it produces its white flowers in
late summer. It produces plenty of plantlets.

Water hyacinth *(Eichornia crassipes)*

This floating plant has rounded glossy green
leaves and produces short spikes of lavender-
blue flowers from mid-summer onwards. Fish
like to lay their eggs on the dangling roots of
this plant.

Maintaining your pond

Remember that your pond is going to need
maintenance, as does any other part of the
garden. It will quickly look drab and neglected,
especially if you allow autumn leaves, grass
cuttings and other vegetation to float on the
surface. Remember, too, to remove the
heads of water lilies and other pond flowers
as soon as they have died off, or they will also
decay in the water.

Clean your pond by drawing a rake across
the surface of the water – use a wooden rake
if you can find one. And give flowering plants
a feed every summer once they are
established. They thrive on bone meal – mix
some with a little heavy soil and water into a
pellet and press it into the soil of the plants'
containers.

From time to time you will find your pond
is beginning to look rather overgrown. Tackle
this problem just the way you would with
perennials in the flower bed – rake up
submerged aquatics and divide them, and do
the same for marginal plants.

Winter care

Once the first frosts arrive, cut down dead or
dying growth from plants around the edge to
stop pests from wintering among them. If
there are fish in the pond, don't let it ice over.

If it does, the ice should be broken gently – hacking at it causes shock waves that can damage the fish.

> **To prevent ice forming all over, float a rubber ball on the surface – more than one if the pond is large. If ice forms underneath, pour hot water over the ball and lift it out temporarily. This will leave a hole through which the fish can get air. Replace the ball at night.**

Fountains

Fountains are fine and fairly easy to install, provided you get the right size for your pond. One with too fierce a pump will shower everyone with spray no matter how hard you try to turn it down, and drain the pond of its water in time. Bear in mind, however, that water lilies prefer to grow in still water, so if you are combining the two, put the fountain up one end of the pond rather than in the middle. Even so, if it sprays a nearby flower bed constantly, consider putting some bog plants in it for an attractive display: dig out some of the soil, put down a layer of plastic to conserve moisture, then replace it.

Remember that anything like a fountain that needs electricity to work it must have a safe heavily insulated supply to plug into, and a waterproof plug.

Other ways with water

There are plenty of other ways of using water in the garden. An ornamental mask, mounted on the wall, can trickle water down into a basin. And if space is limited, water rippling over a base of cobblestones looks equally good, especially on a terrace. Both these ideas can easily be achieved using a pump. Streams and waterfalls, any kind of moving water other than a fountain, need to be thought out carefully if the mechanics are not to show, including bird baths. But the most effective requires a pump.

Making a stream

A 'stream' can be made quite simply by excavating a long sloping trough and lining it with butyl. The trough needs to be deeper at one end than the other, and this is where the pump goes. It will then 'lift' the water back up to its source by pumping it along a concealed piece of hose buried beside the 'stream'. To make it look more attractive, fill it with pebbles and allow the water to trickle through them.

Anything that can hold water can be used as a smaller alternative to a pond, an urn, for instance, which could be planted with miniature water lilies. Or an old stone sink can be plugged and pressed into service as a shallow pool for marginal plants.

The garden indoors

Decorating with houseplants is the quickest way to brighten up your home. They bring the garden indoors and may well cost less than a bunch of flowers, which won't last much more than a week.

Use plants around the house to hide an ugly view, as room dividers, to liven up a dull corner, and most importantly, to soften hard lines such as a blank wall, a bookcase or a bare window. Many of them are actually trees in their native setting and plants like the **parlour palm** and the **weeping fig** make splendid specimens grown in display tubs on their own. Switch around from time to time to give your rooms a fresh look.

There are so many textures and shapes to choose between, from the furry-leafed **Africa violets**, for instance, to the sharp reed-like fronds of the **umbrella plant**, or the plump quilted cushions of **peperomia**. Then, to cheer up the house in mid-winter there's the **poinsettia** with its bright red bracts, the **cyclamen**, the **Jerusalem cherry**, and the little indoor **azalea**.

Mass your smaller plants together as much as possible to make life easier for yourself and them when you water and feed, and to make more impact – they make much more of an impression if you put several in a large containers. All house plants do better when they are put near to one another because they create their own moist micro-climate. You'll find that they need watering less, too. If you are going for foliage rather than flowers try growing them in a white ceramic pot or trough – the green against white is startlingly beautiful.

Choosing your plants

If you're planning an indoor garden it's important to their survival to pick the right plants for the conditions they are going to encounter. As a rough rule of thumb, north-facing rooms have the lowest light level; east-facing rooms are the coolest; south-facing rooms usually have the most light; and west-facing rooms are the warmest of all in summer.

There are some people who claim that they are so inept with houseplants that they practically kill them on sight. But toughies like **mother in law's tongue** or **cactus** will survive virtually anything. **Sweetheart vines** are easy-care plants, too – so is **devil's ivy** – and easiest of all are the **dumb cane** and the **spider plant**.

Anyone who is busy or away a great deal should invest in the **aspidistra**. Its nickname 'cast iron plant' gives a good clue to the way that it will survive almost any amount of neglect. The **Swiss cheese plant** and the **rubber plant** will also cope with being left unattended for a while, and are both great 'architectural' plants, like living sculptures.

Light is an important factor to take into consideration when choosing a plant. Few flowering plants can cope with gloomy conditions but those with handsome foliage like the **asparagus fern**, **caladiums**, **Chinese evergreens** and **dracaenas** can take low light, – so can the **sweetheart vine**, **marantas** and the ubiquitous **spider plant** once again. If your plant is going to an unheated home, stick to **ivies**, **fatshedera**, the **castor oil** plant and the cyclamen, which will all be able to grow happily in coolish conditions, as will bulbs grown indoors.

> By all means put sun-lovers on the windowsill but mind their leaves don't scorch if they actually touch the window pane. And in winter, keep them on the inside of the curtain or they could be damaged by a sharp frost.

15 foliage plants for beginners

�֎ **Asparagus fern** (Asparagus setaceus)
Not a true fern, it looks delicate but is surprisingly tough. Pretty to use as a trailer, it prefers some humidity and indirect sunlight.

✖ **Aspidistra** (Aspidistra elatior)
The Victorians really knew what they were doing when they used its shining green spikes in their gloomy rooms. It is not called the cast iron plant for nothing – it can cope with almost any conditions, especially cool and shady ones.

✖ **Castor oil plant** (Fatsia Japonica)
Fast-growing – with big sycamore tree-like leaves – it will soon reach 1m (3 ft), but you can cut back the top to keep it looking bushy.

✖ **Chinese evergreen** (Aglaonema)
This is a good plant for dim light, and has attractive two-tone green leaves.

✖ **Grape ivy** (Rhoicissus rhomboidea)
Another useful climber/trailer which will thrive even in badly lit rooms. It looks good growing up a bamboo frame.

✖ **Ivy** (Hedera)
Good for cool rooms and for underplanting among showier items, it can be used as a trailer or climber and for indoor topiary

✖ **Ivy tree** (Fatshedera lizei)
This is an easy plant to grow in cool rooms. It can take shade, too, but it needs regular watering.

✖ **Kangaroo vine** (Cissus antarctica)
A cousin of the Virginia creeper, it's a good basic indoor climber with saw-edged shiny leaves.

✽ **Madagascar dragon tree**
(Dracaena marginata)
A fountain of dark-green sword-like leaves edged with red makes this foliage plant a good accent piece. It appreciates good drainage but will stand neglect.

✽ **Mother in law's tongue** *(Sanseviera)*
The most indestructible plant of all time, it will stand any conditions – even on top of a radiator – and is easy to propagate. Just cut off a piece of leaf and stick it in the soil.

✽ **Pick-a-back plant** *(Tolmiea menziesii)*
A prolific grower which produces new plantlets on its leaves and is very easy to grow in the poorest conditions.

✽ **Prayer plant** *(Maranta)*
A good mixer with distinctive dark markings on its leaves, the markings on this plant actually improve with low light levels.

✽ **Spider plant** *(Chlorophytum)*
It is good-natured, taking bright sun and shade with equal grace. Once it starts its production of plantlets on the end of those thin runners, there's no stopping it. The spider plant has dainty white flowers, too.

✽ **Sweetheart vine**
(Philodendron scandens)
Easy-going and amiable, it's a good climber to dress up a room and has tough glossy leaves.

✽ **Wandering sailor** *(Tradescantia)*
A cheap and cheerful plant which roots new cuttings easily in water. Keep it trimmed to stop it getting brown and stringy at the ends.

6 flowering plants to choose

✽ **African violet** *(Saintpaulia)*
This pretty little plant comes into flower all year round and is now available in a wide variety of colours from white to deepest mauve. It needs bright conditions, but will grow well if there is fluorescent lighting around, and prefers a slightly humid situation.

✽ **Gloxinia** *(Sinningia speciosa)*
A plant with large velvety blooms which likes plenty of light but should be kept away from direct sun. When it finishes flowering and the leaves turn yellow, dry it off, store it and re-start it by watering in the spring.

✽ **Hippeastrum** *(Amaryllis)*
Grow the huge bulb of this magnificent lily-like flower in a decorative container; it blooms in the spring.

✽ **Christmas cactus** *(Zygocactus)*
You can't miss this distinctive plant with its flat jointed stems and vivid carmine flowers. It likes a warm temperature in winter but prefers cooler conditions in summer.

✽ **Cyclamen** *(Cyclamen persicum)*
On sale everywhere in the shops, it has much larger flowers than the hardy outdoor variety. It prefers cool airy conditions, but it hates draughts or sudden temperature changes.

✽ **Bush violet** *(Browallia)*
A bushy plant with dark green leaves and deep violet tubular flowers which have white centres. It likes its soil to be moist at all times, and should be given fertiliser when it is flowering.

Buying your plants

The plant you choose should look fresh and well groomed, and should have an identification label with care instructions on it. Avoid anything with yellowing or limp leaves, mossy soil, or leaves covered in dust. Choose something that is compact and sturdy.

Don't be tempted to go for the tallest, picking something that is thin and weak with long stretches of bare stem between the leaves. This is a sure sign that the plant has been badly grown at a low light level. The foliage of a well-grown pot plant should tend to overlap the edge of its container, while tall thin specimens like mother in law's tongue should be twice as tall as their pot. If you are buying a plant in flower, go for an abundance of buds rather than blooms, which may well have dropped by the time the plant reaches home.

Plants for particular places

The Bedroom

Go for flowering plants, bring them in to your bedroom windowsill while they are in bloom, then mix them in with massed plantings in other rooms during their resting seasons:

African violet *(Saintpaulia)*
Bush violet *(Browallia)*
Gloxinia *(Sinningia speciosa)*
Primula
Jasmine *(Jasminum polyanum)*
Geranium *(Pelargonium)*
Fuchsia
Hibiscus *(Hibiscus rosa-sinensis)*
Passion Flower *(Passiflora)*
Plumbago

The Hall and Stairs

Lighten up a dull vista with a house plant or two in the hall. If you've a staircase window, then place some there as well.

Cacti
Cape heath *(Erica gracilis)*
Castor oil plant *(Fatsia japonica)*
Christmas pepper *(Capsicum annuum)*
Mock orange *(Pittosporum tobira)*
Poinsettia *(Euphorbia pulcherrima)*
Winter cherry *(Solanum capistratum)*

The Living Room

This is the place to display large foliage plants, some of which can happily take quite low light levels – in a corner, for instance.

Angel's wings *(Caladium)*
Bird's nest fern *(Asplenium nidus)*
Boston fern *(Nephrolepis exaltata bostoniensis)*
Crown of thorn *(Euphorbia milii)*
Fiddle leaf fig *(Ficus lyrata)*
Flowering maple *(Abutilon hybridum)*
Ivy *(Hedera)*
Parlour palm *(Chamaedora elegans)*

Ribbon plant *(Dracaena sanderiana)*
Rubber plant *(Ficus elastica)*
Sweetheart vine *(Philodendron scandens)*
Swiss cheese plant *(Monstera deliciosa)*
Wandering Jew *(Zebrina pendula)*
Weeping fig *(Ficus benjamina)*

The Kitchen

Go for herbs here – many of them grow well in pots – and one or two bright flowers to brighten the windowsill:

Basil *(Ocinum basilicum)*
Busy Lizzie *(Impatiens)*
Chives *(Allium schoenoprasum)*
Geranium *(Pelargonium)*
Marjoram *(Origanum)*
Mint *(Menta spicata)*
Parsley *(Petroselium crispum)*
Sage *(Salvia officinalis)*
Tarragon *(Artemisia dracunculus)*
Thyme *(Thymus)*

The Bathroom

The humid atmosphere of the average bathroom is an ideal place to grow some plants, but remember that the temperature is likely to go up and down, too.

Kangaroo vine *(Cissus antarctica)*
Maranta
Goosefoot plant *(Syngonium)*
Snakeskin plant *(Fittonia argyoneura)*
Peperomia
Parasol plant *(Heptapleurum ajubricola)*
Umbrella plant *(Cyperus)*
Ferns including the maidenhair fern *(Adiantum)*
Spider plant *(Chlorophytum)*
Ivy tree *(Fatshedera lizei)*
Mother of thousands *(Tolmiea menziesii)*

Beware of buying houseplants from a street market stall in winter. As most houseplants originate in the tropics, exposure to the cold, even if only for a few hours, will almost certainly make them drop their leaves, and possibly die off. Any houseplant purchases should be securely wrapped and taken home as quickly as possible, for any change disturbs them.

When you are planting up a container, be sure to stick to varieties that need the same amount of water. Geraniums, for instance, would soon turn sickly and rot if their bed-fellows were plants that need a great deal of moisture, like the umbrella plant; similarly, cacti and succulents are better grouped together, rather than mixed in with moisture lovers.

How to keep your houseplants happy

Remember that houseplants they rely on you entirely for food and drink. See pp. 434-5 for trouble shooting tips.

Don't over-water them

More houseplants are killed by kindness than by neglect. Remember that their roots need air just as the leaves do, and if there isn't any left between the particles of compost in

▲ **For a topiary animal, wind your ivy around a styrofoam or metal frame, pinning it as you go with hairpins.**

which they are growing, they will drown. The first sign that your plant has been over-watered is when it keels over suddenly and dies – then it's too late.

The surface of the compost should be as damp as a well-wrung flannel. If you know you're inclined to overwater, either buy a

(Continued on page 415)

Repotting your plants

Does your plant need repotting? These are the signs to look for:

- ☞ There are tips of roots poking out of the drainage holes in the bottom of the pot.
- ☞ The soil seems to dry out very quickly – probably because the roots can't get enough moisture.
- ☞ The plant looks top-heavy in its container. It may also tend to topple over as the soil dries out.
- ☞ Growth seems to have slowed up.

How to repot

Water the plant then leave it for an hour for the moisture to drain thoroughly. Then take a new pot that is no more than two sizes larger than the old one. Put a layer of compost in the bottom.

Slide your hand around the base of the plant, palm downwards, fingers either side of the stem. Tip its pot upside down, and give the bottom a light tap with your other hand. It should now slide out easily with the rootball intact.

Put the plant, complete with rootball, in the centre of the new pot you have chosen, sitting it on the compost you put in, adding more if necessary to get the base of the plant just below the top of the rim. Now fill in the gap in the sides with dry compost.

Tap the pot from time to time to let it settle. Then water, and firm it down gently. After few hours, firm it again and add more compost if necessary.

It now needs a little time for convalescence. Leave a re-potted plant out of strong sunlight for a day or two, to let it settle into its new home. Mist its leaves, too.

> **Save tea-leaves from the pot and scatter them around the surface of your foliage plants. They are rich in nitrogen and will increase their growth. You can do the same thing with outdoor plants, too.**

◀ **Making a standard plant.**
Clip off branches to encourage bushier growth at the top.

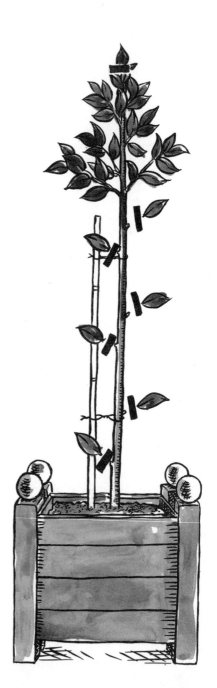

▶ **Ensure that the top leaves are cut regularly.**

stick-in-the-soil watering indicator which will tell you what the situation is, or grow your plants in a compost that is mixed with tiny white polystyrene granules.

Some plants really need a humid atmosphere to thrive – African violets, for instance. In this case set their pots in a saucer of pebbles which you keep moist at all times – the air around them will take up the moisture and give them just the kind of climate they need.

Groom their foliage

Dust them regularly, take off dead leaves, trim off brown tips and take off dead flowers. And if they are beginning to look spindly, pinch out the top growing tips and they will bush out. Dust large leathery-leafed plants and mist the leaves of those, such as ferns, which have feathery fronds.

Feed them regularly

A houseplant should be given a liquid feed every ten days during the growing season, which is normally from spring, when the first green shoots appear, through till autumn.

Check them over for pests

The dry hot atmosphere of a centrally heated house spells trouble for most houseplants and encourages things like the red spider mite to lurk among their leaves. Whitefly are another nuisance and rise up like clouds of cigarette ash when you move a plant. Check your charges regularly, especially the undersides of the leaves where pests often hide. If you suspect something is wrong, isolate the plant at once. Spray it with malathion, then cover it quickly with an up-turned bucket or binliner to make sure the insecticide does its work.

Put them out for a spell in summer

Indoor plants really appreciate a summer holiday. For one thing, they are able to have

▶ **A standard plant will require a stake to hold its stem until it's strong enough to stand on its own.**

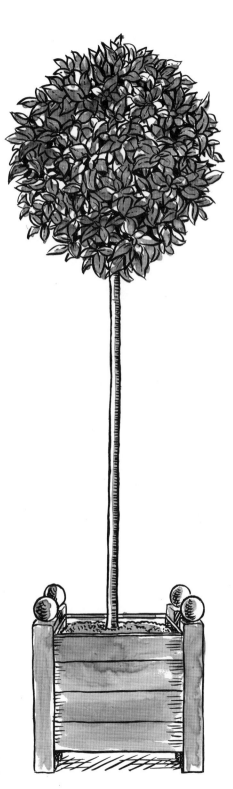

light all around them instead of coming from one direction only, as it usually is in a room. Put the pots out on the patio any time during July and August, and you'll be amazed at the amount of growth they make in that time. They'll make a decorative addition to the patio, too.

Raising your standards

Raise your own small standard trees from plants like lavender, rosemary, geraniums. Start with a plant that has a single good strong stem – a rooted cutting would be ideal. Pot it up and stake it to a chopstick or a sliver of bamboo, tying it in place loosely with a piece of knitting wool. Once it has settled into its new pot, pinch out any side shoots, just leaving those at the top, but leave one or two leaves on the stem for the time being. Feed your plant well, and when it has grown to the height you want it to be, nip off the top growing tip to encourage it to bush out

and produce a mass of side shoots, and take the remaining leaves off the stem. As the top side shoots grow, trim them back with nail scissors to form a mop-head shape.

Indoor topiary

Have fun with some indoor topiary. Cut out the shape of an animal, a pyramid or a sphere from an oasis, the flower-arranging foam, then plant small-leafed ivy around it. As it grows, tether it to the shape with small hairpins.

**To shine leathery-leafed plants like the Swiss cheese plant, and the rubber plant, wipe over their foliage with a half-and-half mixture of milk and water.
Use a feed that is high in nitrogen for foliage plants, high in phosphorous for flowering plants.**

CHAPTER NINE **Pets**

Claire Bessant

Editor and Chief Executive of the Feline Advisory Bureau, and author of How to Talk to Your Cat, The Ultra-fit Older Cat (with Bradley Viner) and How to Give Your Dog a Longer and Healthier Life (with Bradley Viner and Peter Neville). Claire is also the owner of three cats, one dog and five geese.

Keeping pets should be fun – they can make great companions providing years of enjoyment and friendship that usually outweigh the responsibility and care necessary for their upkeep. Owning a pet can teach children about the responsibility that goes with it, and the special needs of different animals. However, taking on a pet is not something which should be done on impulse. Children may tire of an animal in a few short weeks, so unless there is someone else in the family who is really interested and willing to take on the caring role, it is better not to get a pet at all. Even the 'small and furries' such as rats, mice, gerbils or hamsters can live for two years or more and need regular care and attention. Dogs live an average of twelve years but can go on to late teens, depending on the breed; and cats live even longer, usually to about fourteen, but can survive into their twenties!

Deciding on a pet

The general principles of choosing and keeping a pet are the same for all species.

Do your research well beforehand to find out exactly what type of pet will suit your family and lifestyle. If it's a dog, cat or even rabbit, learn about the different needs of the various breeds. In all cases, some require less grooming than others, some have more amenable temperaments, and others are easier to train.

Find out about the care the chosen animal will need, the type of housing it will require, its nutritional needs, exercise demands, and veterinary needs such as vaccinations, anti-worming treatments etc.

Discuss the matter carefully with all the family and agree on individual responsibilities such as who will feed, clean out or exercise the new pet,

Find out the best place to get the animal you want – usually this will mean locating a breeder, rather than a pet shop or 'dealer'. You will need to know where your local

veterinary surgery is and would be well advised to seek some advice from them about the type or breed of pet you choose. They might even be able to point you in the direction of a good local breeder. Although the pet shop may be the most obvious place to purchase animals, especially the small and furred or feathered, it is not always the best. Find a good local breeder who is keeping his or her animals in the best surroundings for their behavioural needs, feeding them correctly, and with a range of animals to choose from. Here you'll also be able to see the mother of the larger species, such as cats or dogs, and the breeder may also be able to give you expert advice on any special needs or breed-specific behaviour of that particular type of pet. You will then also have a contact to help, should you have any difficulties or worries later on.

Be creative

Remember too that you should be trying to keep your pet, especially if it is confined to a

417

cage or terrarium, in conditions that are as natural as possible.

Look at things from your pet's point of view, find out about how it lives in the wild and be creative so it does not become bored and miserable. There are many types of cages and pet homes on the market – many are too small or not suited to certain types of animals, so find out exactly what you want or perhaps make or adapt something youself rather than buy the first one you see.

Start young

If you want to handle a small pet, such as a hamster, guinea pig, mouse, rat, etc., and have a relaxed and friendly relationship with it, then you must get a young animal and handle it in short, frequent and, most importantly, gentle sessions. It will then see you as part of its normal life and not become stressed or frightened by the attention. Young animals have much less fear than mature ones and are inquisitive about everything around them. If handled carefully at an early age they will make very good pets as adults. Children must be watched to make sure they don't hurt or frighten the pet by being clumsy.

Do your research

There are many ways in which you can find out about the different types of pet and their specific needs. Information is available from your vet, RSPCA booklets, general books from libraries or pet shops. Specialist pet and breed clubs and organisations will also usually have literature that they can send you. The list of addresses at the end of the chapter covers most of the more common pets and a few exotic species.

Dogs

Dogs require the most effort from their owners in terms of time – they need attention and exercise, without which they can become a nuisance, especially when young and full of energy.

You may want to give a home to a mongrel but unless both parents are known there is no guarantee of how large the puppy will become. You may want to give a home to a dog from an animal welfare rescue home, but again be careful about your choice – often they have been abandoned because they did not fit into their previous home. This does not mean that you cannot get an excellent dog, but you should find out as much as possible about its background, be assured of ongoing backup from the rescue centre and ensure that you are able to return the dog after a trial period if things do not work out. Do not be forced to keep it by feelings of guilt, and struggle along with a dog which is giving no joy at all, or one which is dangerous, especially if there are children in the house.

There are over 150 common breeds of dog to choose from and the range of sizes, coat lengths and breed characteristics is almost endless.

Do not simply decide on a breed because you like the look of it – find out what that breed has been bred for. Collies may look good and behave impecably on 'One Man and His

Pet	Average Lifespan (yrs)	Work (average)	Petability* attention	Initial cost	Running costs
Dog	12	★★★★★	★★★★★	★ – ★★★★	★★★★
Cat	14	★★★★	★★★★★	★ – ★★★	★★★
Guinea pig	7	★★	★★★★*	★★	★
Rat	2	★★★	★★★★*	★★	★
Mouse	1-2	★★	★★	★★	★
Rabbit	7	★★★	★★★★*	★★	★
Hamster	1 – 2	★★	★★	★★	★
Gerbil	2 -3	★	★*	★★	★
Budgie	8	★★	★★	★★	★
Parrot	30	★★★★	★★★	★★★★	★★
Tortoise	30	★★	★★	★★★	★
Fish	–	★	★	★ – ★★★	★

Initial costs include cost of animal plus cage, hutch, etc. – **Running costs** include food and veterinary care – * good for children

Dog', but kept in a town house with little exercise they may prove disastrous as a pet. The intelligent working breeds usually need to work and frustrations and untapped energy can cause problems if they don't. Nor is size an indication of exercise needs. Some larger dogs, such as bulldogs or Great Danes are happier to lie around the house than an energetic terrier might be.

If you have children you may prefer to have a bitch which will usually be more patient and willing to please than a male dog, especially during its adolescent period! You may want to talk to your vet or a pet behaviourist (see below for the address) about the breed which would suit you best.

Whatever you decide on make sure you find a reputable breeder, visit and see the puppies with their mother, take note of her temperament and disposition and come away if you are not happy. A dog lives for a long time, so choosing the right one for you and your circumstances is vital. Avoid shops or anywhere which might be selling pups from a puppy farm – these will not be with their mother and may have become stressed and picked up diseases. They will not have been carefully bred to minimise genetic problems, such as poor hip joints. Interbreeding can also cause health problems.

When you choose a pup, visit your vet for vaccinations and information about worming. The pup shouldn't mix with other dogs until protected. Find out if there are puppy parties or classes in your area – these are invaluable as an early education for both you and your pup. They are aimed at socialising the pup and helping it learn to mix with other dogs, adults and children, as well as teaching it simple basic commands when it is still young.

You and the pup will learn that examining its eyes, mouth skin, etc. can be fun and part of normal day-to-day life. This in turn makes treatment and veterinary visits much easier in later life. You must be able to take its food bowl away without it snapping, and teach it the simple commands of 'sit' and 'stay'. If the pup learns the basics early on there will be less need to visit training classes later, unless you want to go more deeply into agility or obedience. It's all about common sense, learning to communicate, and having fun and it's well worth the effort – you'll probably meet some other nice dog owners there, too.

Responsible ownership

Owning a dog can affect many people, not just those within the family. During exercise or during day-to-day outings it will meet with many other types of people, dogs and animals and it is the owner's legal responsibility to prevent harm coming to any of these because of the dog's behaviour. This does not merely mean aggression problems but also covers the nuisance of barking or howling when the dog is left alone in the house, parasite control, neutering to prevent the birth of unwanted puppies and cleaning up after your dog if you walk it in the local town park or recreation areas – a poop scoop is a must! If your pet has a behaviour problem ask your vet to refer you to your nearest animal behaviourist or contact the **ASSOCIATION OF PET BEHAVIOUR COUNSELLORS** at 257 Royal College Street, London NW1 9LU.

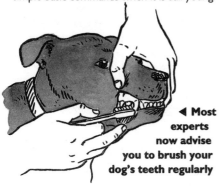

◀ **Most experts now advise you to brush your dog's teeth regularly**

Things you'll need	☞ Bowls
☞ Basket or bean bag	☞ Brush and comb
☞ Lead	☞ Toothbrush and doggy toothpaste
☞ Collar (not a choke chain – these are cruel, potentially dangerous and very old fashioned) or headcollar	For you, ☞ Walking shoes ☞ Wellingtons ☞ Wet-weather clothing

Feeding

There is a huge range of dog foods available, from canned and semi-moist diet to all-in-one 'complete' dry diets. A growing puppy will need a slightly different diet from a mature dog and this will be marked on the food – if in doubt ask your vet. Always make sure that fresh drinking water is available.

Veterinary care

You will need to worm your dog regularly and combat fleas during most of the year, but especially in the summer. Dogs can be protected from just about all of the canine infectious diseases by vaccination. This should begin as early as possible in puppyhood (ask your vet for details) and your dog should have annual boosters. If you have a female dog, it is likely you will want to have her neutered (spayed), you may also want to neuter your male animal (castration). Talk to your vet about behavioural changes, weight gain, etc. It is well worth insuring your dog to cover unforseen veterinary costs. There are several companies which specialise in pet insurance and your vet will have leaflets in the surgery. Pet insurance usually also provides third party liability cover should your dog cause an accident or injury to a person or another animal.

At holiday time, unless you have friends or family willing to feed, walk and groom your dog, you will have the considerable expense of kenneling to bear in mind. However, there are many lovely places in Britain where you can holiday with your pet – and no doubt he'll enjoy the break, too!

roughly the same size. There are breed differences in behaviour but whether moggie or pedigree, they have basically the same needs. If you want a pedigree cat, you should acquire your kitten from a reputable breeder where you can see it with its mother. If you want a moggie you can usually take it from its mother shortly after weaning, at about six weeks old. If you do choose a particular breed you will find that breeders will not sell the kitten to you until it is twelve weeks old and had its vaccinations – this is a ruling of the Governing Council of the Cat Fancy. Choose a confident outgoing kitten – or perhaps two, so that it has company if you are away from home a lot. If you live in a 'mad house' of children, other animals and continual comings and goings, make sure the kitten you choose also comes from a busy household and has not spent the first twelve weeks of its life in a clinical environment of a breeding shed at the bottom of the garden. The younger a kitten becomes used to the hurly burly of life the more normal it will seem and the cat will cope with your lifestyle without difficulty. If it has never explored or faced a challenge until it is over three months old, it may become nervous and withdrawn – not the best pet.

Feeding

Look at your supermarket shelves and you will find an enormous display of canned food for cats! There are also complete dry diets which are available from vets and pet shops. The growing kitten will need a different food to the adult cat so look out for this when you buy a certain food. If in doubt, ask your vet.

Cats

Cats are usually a lot easier to keep than dogs although they too need their share of love and attention. There are a wide range of breeds to choose from but, unlike the dog, they are all of

Things you will need

☞ Cat bed (however the cat may not choose this to sleep on!)

☞ Sturdy cat carrier – useful for collecting kitten and trips to the vet

☞ Litter tray and litter – even if is only for the first couple of weeks before the cat has been fully vaccinated; after this, your cat can go out

☞ Bowls

☞ Brushes, especially if your cat is long haired

☞ Toys – make sure you choose safe toys with no detachable 'eyes' or bits that could get caught in the teeth

Veterinary care

As with dogs, cats need regular worming and flea control. Both male and female cats are usually neutered at around six months of age. This prevents the birth of unwanted kittens and some of the more antisocial behaviour of entire males. While cats can be vaccinated against most feline infectious diseases, there a still some for which no vaccine has yet been developed. It is worth considering insuring your cat against unforseen veterinary bills – they can get into all sorts of trouble, especially in the first year of life.

Cats will always hunt – millions of years of evolution which have produced a near-perfect hunter cannot be undone by owners wanting to protect the wildlife in the garden! Keeping cats in at dawn and dusk, the preferred hunting time of cats, can help cut down on the carnage.

Guinea pigs

Guinea pigs, or cavies as they are correctly known, make good pets for children – they are good natured and seldom bite. They squeak and chatter to each other and their owners in a very pleasing manner. When fully grown they weigh about 2 kg (about the same as a bag of sugar) and therefore they are large enough for children to handle with ease. Guinea pigs have a variety of coat colours and lengths and can live for up to eight years.

Because they are social animals cavies are happiest kept in groups of females (males tend to fight), unless of course you wish to breed from them. They can be housed in a hutch with a three-sided solid compartment to sleep in and wire mesh over the other side. Guinea pigs are affected by extremes of temperature and so the hutch should be moved into a shed in the winter. An outdoor run is essential for both exercise and grazing in nice weather.

Feeding

Feed should consist of grass, hay, vegetables, bran, oats, barley and maize, remembering to add fresh vegetables for Vitamin C.

Guinea pigs do not make their own Vitamin C and so need it in the diet in cabbage, broccoli, spinach, carrots and beetroot.

Good cavy feeds have added vitamin C, so ensure you choose one specifically for cavies and not just a rabbit mix. Fresh water should always be available.

Veterinary care

The most common reason for a guinea pig to require veterinary care is to have their teeth and nails clipped. The teeth of rodents grow continually and unless they are worn down by gnawing hard substances, such as wood, they can become overgrown and can cause problems eating. Itching caused by mites can also be a problem but guinea pigs are usually fairly healthy creatures.

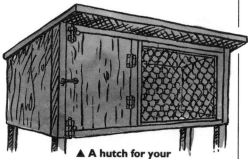

▲ **A hutch for your guinea pig can be made or purchased. Make sure it's well ventilated.**

Rats and mice

Rats often have a very bad press and many people dismiss them as dirty and disease-ridden animals. However, pet rats are specially bred free of disease and because of their size, intelligence and willingness to interact with people, they make excellent pets. They are friendly and very responsive to kind treatment. Fancy rats come in all sorts of colours, from silver grey to agouti, all with a similar short coat. Two years is the average lifespan.

In the wild, rats live in large family groups and enjoy company. Keep several of the same sex together and they will groom each other and sleep together. Handled regularly from a young age they soon come to enjoy this attention and will climb on to people with confidence.

Feeding

Rats will eat anything! However, a balanced diet of grain and vegetables will keep them happy and they may even appreciate an occasional portion of meat. Although rats love sweet things, these are best avoided as they can become overweight. Clean water should always be available.

Because they are quite large animals, rats need a lot of space. A cage or aquarium for one or two adult rats should be at least 38 by 60 cm (15 in by 2 ft), and at least 30 cm (12 in) high. Furnish with shelves, ramps, boxes and wood, wood shavings and paper, and let them have some fun.

Veterinary care

If cared for correctly, rats are tough and have few ailments. They are prone to lumps and bumps – some of which are abscesses if males kept together have had a scrap. But they can also be tumours, especially in older animals. These are seldom malignant, do not appear to be painful and can be removed surgically by the vet if necessary. Rats may also suffer from respiratory problems and itch because of mite infestation – aways check with your vet if your rat is unwell.

Mice don't mix with humans quite as readily as rats but need similar care. The males cannot usually be kept together. The lifespan of a mouse is between one and two years.

Rabbits

Rabbits come in all shapes and sizes and can become very large, so choose one for which you have room. They live for about eight years, and handled early they can make good pets, although males may be more aggressive than females unless handled a lot or neutered. Rabbits are social animals and prefer company and two or more does will live happily together. Different breeds may also be more suitable as family pets, being

more amenable to handling or easier to housetrain. Breeders will advise you on this.

Most rabbits are kept in hutches but will need also exercise in a run or enclosed yard. Some owners litter train their rabbits so they can have free run of the house, too. The hutch needs to be sturdy and have two compartments, one for sleeping and the other for eating, exercise and toilet. If there are predators, such as foxes or cats, about then the run must also be very secure.

Feeding

Rabbits eat grass in the wild and fruit, cereals, vegetables and seeds, and hay can also be offered. Fresh water must be available.

A piece of applewood for gnawing may help prevent overgrown teeth.

Veterinary care

As with guinea pigs, rabbits are prone to overgrown nails and teeth when kept as pets and sometimes suffer from stomach upsets, which can become very serious. Always contact your vet as soon as possible in the event of illness. Rabbits may also suffer from tumours and respiratory problems. Pet rabbits can catch myxomatosis, a contagious and usually fatal viral disease which is very prevalent in the wild, so it is worth vaccinating against it. Ask your vet for details.

Hamsters

Hamsters, which are commonly kept as children's pets, live for about eighteen months to two years. However, they are not the best choice of 'small and furry' because they are nocturnal and so are active during the night and asleep during the day when they may bite if disturbed. In the wild they live in the desert and have adapted to survive in harsh conditions. They sleep in deep burrows and carry food in the cheek pouches back to their store.

There are now several types of hamster available – the one most of us know is the golden or Syrian hamster. They now come in various colours and coat types, including long-coated or 'teddy bear' hamsters.

Syrian hamsters need to be kept alone as they fight, so try and provide a large interesting home for them which can incorporate their burrowing and hoarding activities. There are novel cages with plastic interconnecting tube housing available. Hamsters will gnaw through hardwood so take care with homemade cages. Gnawing blocks or whole brazil nuts help to keep their teeth worn down and plenty of handling, and when they are awake in the evening, will help keep them friendly and occupied.

Other types of hamster, such as the Russian, are now available in the UK and can be kept in groups – find out about them by contacting one of the hamster clubs (see addresses page 439).

Feeding

Hamsters need a diet of mixed seeds, grains and nuts as well as a little dog meal and porridge oats, and fresh fruit and vegetables such as apples and carrots. Ensure that the cages are cleaned regularly so that uneaten fresh food does not go off.

Veterinary care

Hamsters can suffer from respiratory problems and need nail and teeth clipping. Known as 'wet tail', diarrhoea can lead to serious health problems. Keeping the cages scrupulously clean and dry can help prevent this condition. Hamsters naturally stuff their cheek pouches with food but these can occasionally become impacted and require veterinary treatment.

Gerbils

Gerbils are desert animals which live deep in burrows in the wild. The are awake and active during the day and are usually not aggressive. They normally live in groups so it is best to keep several female littermates together. Gerbils live for two to three years.

Gerbils can be kept in a gerbilarium – an aquarium with alternate layers of moist peat and straw in which they can burrow. Do not let this come higher than halfway up the

aquarium as they can jump out. Always fit a secure lid. This type of housing does not have to be cleaned out too often as long as any excess food is removed.

Feeding

A varied diet includes seeds and grains, perhaps available from your pet store as 'gerbil' mix, and some fruit and vegetables.

Veterinary care

These burrowing creatures can develop sore noses and eyes because of their vigorous activities. Again, teeth and claws may need attention.

Birds

Birds, especially budgies and canaries, are very popular pets. As they are bred in this country their status in the wild is not threatened. This is not so true for the more exotic birds, especially some of the parrots.

If you are thinking of getting a parrot then do buy from a reputable breeder in this country – so that you will not be encouraging the capture of the birds from the wild and the illegal shipment during which so many birds die.

Parrots are not cheap but, if looked after correctly, may live for fifty to eighty years. It is said that keeping a parrot is like looking after a young baby in terms of attention required! They are highly intelligent and can easily become bored and stressed. This often manifests itself as feather-plucking: resulting in a bald bird! All caged birds need as large a cage as possible and, if possible, to be let out to fly around the room for exercise. Provide a varied diet of seed and fruit etc., and find out about the needs of your particular species from the appropriate society listed at the end of this chapter before you take on a bird.

> **Keep birds away from the kitchen if there is any danger of burning a non-stick pan – they are highly susceptible to the fumes produced by overheated coating.**

Fish

Millions of households across the country keep fish, from the common goldfish to carefully maintained marine aquaria with corals and colourful fish from warm exotic waters. Just how much you want to spend and the time you need to put into their care depends on the type of fish you keep. Most beginners are better off with the tough freshwater fish such as carp (goldfish). However, whichever you choose you must try to give the fish a clean natural habitat with things to hide behind and enough room to swim around – the days of the round goldfish bowl are long past! Do your research before you start and buy fish from a shop where the stock looks healthy and aquaria are clean. With marine or tropical fish, try to buy only home-bred stock so that you are not perpetuating the trade and transport losses of wild caught fish from far away.

Tortoises and terrapins

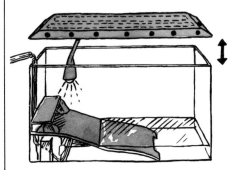

▲ **An aquarium should have a tightly fitting lid, but one that supplies adequate ventilation.**

In years past when tortoises and terrapins were imported in their hundreds of thousands, it was very easy to get hold of these reptiles. Huge numbers died during importation and numbers in the wild dwindled. The majority of pet tortoises also died, usually because of ignorance of their need for hibernation. Now it illegal to import tortoises (and many of the terrapins) for sale as pets. They are being bred in this country,

but because of their rarity, are expensive. If you are taking on a re-homed tortoise you will need a licence, and be able to prove it came into the country before 1984 when importation was banned. It is best to contact the specialist Chelonia groups (see addresses, page 439) for information on keeping tortoises and terrapins correctly and where to obtain them legally. They will also be able to tell you the adult size of some terrapins and the size of aquarium you will need – some species grow very large. The British Chelonia Group has even collated information on how to bequeath a tortoise in your will, as they can live for over sixty years!

Exotic pets

There are now a wide range of the more exotic pets available as 'pets'. Many do not interact with their owners as we would normally define 'pets' but enthusiasts keep them for interest and the challenge of looking after an interesting animal and keeping it healthy. There are now many types of snake, frog, insect, spider, etc. available; however, it is not wise even to consider getting an exotic pet until you know if you can keep it correctly. Contact the specialist clubs and organisations which will have information. The welfare of the animal must come first.

General care

In general, cages and hutches need to be cleaned out regularly, once or twice a week, and more in the summer when bacteria and flies readily multiply and can cause distress. A supply of clean water should always be available. If you are buying proprietary food from a pet shop make sure it is fresh and keep it in an airtight container so that it does not become mouldy. If your pet shows any signs of skin disease, snuffles, etc., contact your vet immediately. To delay, particularly with cage animals, birds and exotics, can be fatal. The above outlines are brief and are by no means everything you need to find out before getting a small pet which needs to be kept in a cage, hutch or aquarium.

Useful information

Conversion tables

Weights and measures

(To go from units on left to units on right, multiply; to go from units on right to units on left, divide)

Metric	Imperial	Multiply/ divide by
millimetres	inches	0.03937
centimetres	inches	0.3937
centimetres	feet	0.03281
metres	inches	39.3701
metres	feet	3.2808
metres	yards	1.0936
kilometres	miles	0.62137
sq cm	sq inches	0.155
sq metres	sq feet	10.7639
sq metres	sq yards	1.19599
hectares	acres	2.47105
sq kilometres	sq miles	0.3861
litres	pints	1.7598
litres	gallons	0.21997
cu metres	cu feet	35.3147
grammes	ounces	0.03527
kilogrammes	pounds	2.20462

Approximate equivalents at a glance:

Metric	Imperial
1 centimetre	0.4 inches
1 metre	3.3 feet/1.1 yards
1 square metre	10.7 square feet/ 1.2 square yards
1 kilometre	0.6 miles
1 litre	1.8 pints/0.22 gallons
1 cubic metre	35 cubic feet
1 gramme	0.03 ounces
1 kilogramme	2.2 pounds

Imperial	Metric
1 inch	25.5 millimetres/2.5 centimetres
1 foot	30 centimetres/0.3 metres
1 yard	90 centimetres/0.9 metres
1 square foot	0.09 square metres
1 square yard	0.8 square metres
1 mile	1.6 kilometres
1 pint	0.6 litres
1 gallon	4.5 litres
1 cubic foot	0.03 cubic metres
1 ounce	28 grams
1 pound	0.45 kilograms

Speed and distance

Quick conversions
Kilometres to miles (or km/h to mph)
multiply by 5 then divide by 8
Miles to kilometres (or mph to km/h)
multiply by 8 then divide by 5

Approximate Equivalents at a glance

miles/ miles per hour	kilometres/ kilometre per hour
20	32
30	48
40	64
50	80
60	96
70	112
80	128
90	144
100	160

Temperatures

Quick conversions
Centigrade to Fahrenheit
multiply by 9, divide by 5 and add 32
Fahrenheit to Centigrade
subtract 32, multiply by 5 and divide by 9

Approximate Equivalents at a glance

40°F	4°C
50°F	10°C
60°F	15°C
70°F	20°C
80°F	26°C
90°F	32°C
100°F	38°C

Paper sizes

Size	Inches	Millimetres
A7	$2\frac{7}{8} \times 4\frac{1}{8}$	74 × 105
A6	$4\frac{1}{8} \times 5\frac{7}{8}$	105 × 148
A5	$5\frac{7}{8} \times 8\frac{1}{4}$	148 × 210
A4	$8\frac{1}{4} \times 11\frac{3}{4}$	210 × 297
A3	$11\frac{3}{4} \times 16\frac{1}{2}$	297 × 420
A2	$16\frac{1}{2} \times 23\frac{3}{8}$	420 × 594
A1	$23\frac{3}{8} \times 33\frac{1}{8}$	594 × 841
A0	$33\frac{1}{8} \times 46\frac{3}{4}$	841 × 1189

Clothing sizes

Women's suits & dresses

British	American	European
8	10	36
10	8	38
12	10	40
14	12	42
16	14	44
18	16	46
20	18	48

Women's shoes

British	American	European
$4^1/_2$	6	38
5	$6^1/_2$	38
$5^1/_2$	7	39
6	$7^1/_2$	39
$6^1/_2$	8	40
7	$8^1/_2$	41

Men's suits & coats

British	American	European
36	36	46
38	38	48
40	40	50
42	42	52
44	44	54
46	46	56

Men's shirts

British	American	European
14	14	36
$14^1/_2$	$14^1/_2$	37
15	15	38
$15^1/_2$	$15^1/_2$	39
16	16	41
$16^1/_2$	$16^1/_2$	42
17	17	43

Men's shoes

British	American	European
7	8	41
$7^1/_2$	$8^1/_2$	42
$8^1/_2$	$9^1/_2$	43
$9^1/_2$	$10^1/_2$	44
$10^1/_2$	$11^1/_2$	45
11	12	46

Children's clothes

height (in.)	height (cm)	
British	American	European
43	4	125
48	6	135
55	8	150
58	10	155
60	12	160
62	14	165

Timber-buying guide

Quick-reference

Wood is sold in METRIC FEET
(1 metric foot = 300mm).
FINISHED SIZE is the best way to order softwood so that it is planed to an exact width and thickness.

Hardwood

WIDTHS are usually $1/_2$–1 metric foot.
THICKNESS is usually $1/_4$–$3/_4$ in.

Manufactured board

STANDARD SHEET SIZE is 8 ft x 4 ft.

Softwood

STANDARD LENGTHS AVAILABLE range from 6 metric feet (5 ft 11 in) to 21 metric feet (20 ft 8 in).
WIDTH AND THICKNESS will depend on whether the wood is planed.
ROUGH SAWN (unplaned) softwood is only suitable if the wood will not be seen.
PLANED TIMBER can be either PAR (planed all round) or PBS (planed both sides). Planing removes about 3mm ($1/_8$ in) from the width or thickness.

Freezer life

Fruit

Apples	12 months (slices), 6 months (purée), 3 months (baked)
Apple juice	6 months
Apricots	9–12 months (in syrup), 6–8 months (purée)
Avocado	2 months
Blackberries	8–12 months (in syrup/sugar), 6–8 months (purée)
Blackcurrants	1 year
Blueberries	1 year
Cherries	1 year (loose), 9–12 months (in syrup)
Gooseberry	1 year
Grapes	1 year (seedless)
Grapefruit juice	4–6 months
Kiwi fruit	1 year
Peaches	9–12 months (in syrup)
Pears	8 months
Pineapple	1 year (in syrup)
Plums	1 year
Redcurrants	1 year
Rhubarb	1 year (purée), 6–8 months (uncooked)
Strawberries	1 year

Vegetables (blanched)

Asparagus	9 months
Aubergine	1 year (peeled and blanched)
Broccoli	1 year
Brussels sprouts	1 year
Cabbage	6 months
Carrot	1 year hed)
Cauliflower	6–8 months
Cauliflower cheese	6 months
Courgettes	1 year

Meat and fish

Bacon	3 months (vacuum-packed), 2 months (smoked rashers, gammon steaks), 1 month (unsmoked rashers)
Beef	8 months (joints), 6 months (steaks), 3 months (mince)
Casseroles	4 months (beef, chicken or lamb), 6 weeks (bacon, ham or pork)
Chicken	1 year (uncooked), 2–3 months (cooked)
Cod	3 months
Crab	1 month (cooked)
Curry	2 months
Duck	6 months
Gravy	3 months
Ham	2 months (raw), 1 month (cooked)
Herring	3 months
Kidneys	3 months
Lamb	6 months (raw), 3 months (cooked)
Liver	3 months (raw), 2 months (cooked)
Mackerel	2 months (fresh or smoked)
Paté	3 months (1 month if it contains bacon)
Pork	6 months (uncooked)
Prawns	1 month
Salmon	2 months
Sausages	2 months
Scampi	1 month
Shrimps	1 month (raw, cooked or potted)
Sole	3 months
Trout	2 months
Turkey	6 months (uncooked), 1 month (cooked)

Staples

Bread	6 months (wrapped), 6 weeks (unwrapped)
Breadcrumbs	3 months (fresh), 1 month (fried)
Butter	9–12 months (unsalted), 6 months (salted)
Cake	4–6 months (plain), 2 months (iced or filled)
Cheese	3–6 months
Chocolate	2 months
Christmas pudding	4 months
Cream	1 year (clotted), 3 months (double and whipping)
Custard	3 months
Ice cream	1 months
Margarine	5 months
Milk	1 month
Mince pies	3 months
Pasta	2–3 months (pasta dishes), 1 month (cooked pasta)
Pastry	6 months (baked), 3 months (unbaked)
Pies (baked)	6 months (fruit), 3–4 months (meat)
Pizzas	3 months (cooked), 1 month (uncooked)
Quiches	2 months

Microwave cooking times

Fruit
(for 1lb/450g unless otherwise stated)

Apples, sliced	5–6 mins
Apples, whole	2–3 mins (for 1), 4–5 mins (for 2)
Berries	4–5 mins
Pears	5–7 mins
Rhubarb, fresh	7–8 mins, stand 3 mins
Rhubarb, frozen	9–10 mins
Soft fruit	4–5 mins

Vegetables (for 1lb/450g fresh vegetables, unless otherwise stated)

Asparagus	7–9 mins
Asparagus (frozen)	11–12 mins
Aubergine	5–7 mins, stand 3–4 mins
Broccoli	7–8 mins, stand 2 mins
Brussels sprouts	7–8 mins, stand 2 mins
Cabbage	5–7 mins
Carrots	6–8 mins
Cauliflower	6–8 mins
Corn on the cob	7–8 mins (for 2)
Courgettes	6–7 mins
Mangetout	3–4 mins
Marrow	5–7 mins
Potatoes (new)	8–10 mins
Potatoes (jacket)	5 mins (1 x 150g), 6–8 mins (2 x 150g)
Spinach	3–4 mins

Meat and fish
(for 1lb/450g unless otherwise stated)

Bacon joint	13–15 mins
Bacon rashers	30–45 secs (1 rasher), 2–2½ mins (4 rashers)
Beef joint	15 mins, stand 15 mins
Beef, minced	7–8 mins
Chicken	7–9 mins, stand 15 mins
Kidney	6–8 mins, stand 3 mins
Kipper (225g)	3–4 mins, stand 2 mins
Lamb joint	6–10 mins, stand 15 mins
Lamb chops	5–6 mins, stand 4–5 mins
Liver	6–7 mins, stand 3 mins
Plaice, sole	2–3 mins, stand 2 mins
Pork joint	9–12 mins, stand 15–20 mins
Prawns, shrimps	3–4 mins
Sausages	6–7 mins
Steak, braising	50 mins, stand 10 mins
Turkey	8–9 mins, stand 15–20 mins

Microwave defrosting times
(setting: Low)
(for 1lb/450g unless otherwise stated)

Bacon rashers	3 mins, stand 5–10 mins
Beef joint	10–12 mins, stand 1 hour
Beef, minced	6–8 mins, stand 10 mins
Bread (large loaf)	6–8 mins, stand 5–15 mins
Bread roll	15–20 secs (for 2), stand 2–3 mins
Chicken	6–8 mins, stand 30 mins
Lamb joint	5–6 mins, stand 30–45 mins
Lamb chops	8–10 mins, stand 10 mins
Pastry	2 mins, stand 20–30 mins
Pork joint	7–8 mins, stand 1 hour
Pork chops	8–10 mins, stand 10 mins
Sausages	3–5 mins, stand 15 mins
Steak	7–9 mins, stand 10 mins
Turkey	10–12 mins, stand 30 mins

Oven temperatures

Gas	Celsius	Fahrenheit
¼	120	250
1	140	275
2	150	300
3	160	325
4	180	350
5	190	375
6	200	400
7	220	425
8	230	450
9	240	475

Commonly used E numbers

Number	Name	Risk/No risk
E101	Vitamin B2 (riboflavin)	N
E102	Tartrazine	R
E104	Quinoline	R
E110	Aunset yellow FCF	R
E120	Cochineal red	R
E122	Carmoisine	R
E123	Amaranth	R
E124	Ponceau 4R	R
E127	Erythrosine	R
E131	Patent blue V	R
E132	Indigo carmine	R
E133	Brilliant blue FCF	R
E140	Chlorophyll	N
E141	Chlorophyllins	N
E150	Caramel	R
E151	Black PN	R
E153	Carbon black	R
E160 a, c, e, f	Extracts of plant colourings	N
E170	Calcium carbonate	N
E172	Iron oxides and hydroxides	N
E210	Benzoic acid	R
E211–219	Benzoates	R
E220	Sulphur dioxide	R
E221–227	Sulphites	R
E230–232	Nitrites & nitrates	R

E260	Acetic acid	N
E261	Potassium acetate	N
E300	Vitamin C & ascorbic acid	N
E301	Sodium ascorbate	N
E302	Calcium ascorbate	N
E306–309	Vitamin E	N
E310–312	Gallates	R
E320	Butylated hydroxyamisole (BHA)	R
E321	Butylated hydroxytoluene	R
E322	Lecithin	N
E330	Citric acid	N
E331–333	Citrates	N
E334	Tartaric acids	N
E335–337	Salts of tartaric acids	N
E339–340	Derivatives of phosphoric acid	N
E350–352	Derivatives of malic acid	N
E353	Metatartaric acid	N
E355	Adipic acid	N
E375	Niacin	N
E400	Alginic acid	N
E401	Sodium alginate	N
E406	Agar	N
E407	Carrageenan	R
E410	Carob gum	N
E415	Corn sugar gum	N
E420, 421	Sorbitol	R
E430, 431	Stearates	R
E432–435	Sorbitol derivatives	R
E440	Pectin	N
E450	Phosphates	R

BSI (British Standards Institute) Symbols

The kitemark shows the product meets the general standards set by the BSI, and that production has also been checked.

The BSI safety mark, indicating that the goods have reached a level of safety required by the inspectors.

This label shows that electrical appliances have been tested by and meet the approval of the British Electrotechnical Approvals Board, and meet standards for safety and durablility set out by the BSI.

Distances between British cities

KILOMETRES (upper right) · MILES (lower left)

	Aberdeen	Aberystwyth	Birmingham	Brighton	Bristol	Cambridge	Cardiff	Dover	Edinburgh	Exeter	Glasgow	Hull	Leeds	Leicester	Liverpool	London	Manchester	Newcastle	Nottingham	Oxford	Penzance	Sheffield	Southampton
Aberdeen	—	724	658	895	789	742	792	924	198	911	241	560	518	671	538	806	534	370	624	747	1099	576	853
Aberystwyth	450	—	193	425	206	267	177	459	526	259	525	369	278	243	167	341	214	435	248	253	504	254	325
Birmingham	409	120	—	267	142	161	177	322	467	275	459	230	180	64	151	190	130	336	80	100	431	121	206
Brighton	556	264	166	—	217	180	288	130	697	275	723	359	404	246	418	89	398	525	286	159	433	349	97
Bristol	490	128	88	135	—	233	71	314	591	121	589	364	332	180	264	183	269	475	212	106	299	262	121
Cambridge	461	166	100	112	145	—	288	204	544	351	566	200	238	109	296	84	248	372	135	127	529	200	219
Cardiff	492	110	110	179	44	179	—	385	587	192	608	393	341	224	264	249	277	499	245	172	370	283	192
Dover	574	285	200	81	195	127	239	—	726	391	752	404	433	275	447	117	426	554	315	208	570	378	240
Edinburgh	123	327	290	433	367	338	365	451	—	723	72	362	320	473	338	608	336	172	426	549	901	378	669
Exeter	566	161	171	171	75	218	119	243	449	—	721	484	431	301	385	275	389	595	333	224	179	399	179
Glasgow	150	326	285	449	366	352	378	467	45	448	—	402	338	484	340	634	338	230	447	547	900	386	668
Hull	348	229	143	223	226	124	244	251	225	301	250	—	90	145	196	270	151	190	148	262	663	103	412
Leeds	322	173	112	251	206	148	212	269	199	268	210	56	—	158	119	306	64	148	116	272	613	58	378
Leicester	417	151	40	153	112	68	139	171	294	187	301	90	98	—	187	158	138	301	42	119	480	105	225
Liverpool	334	104	94	260	164	184	164	278	210	239	211	122	74	116	—	330	55	253	167	251	563	119	357
London	501	212	118	55	114	52	155	73	378	171	394	168	190	98	205	—	309	436	198	90	454	261	127
Manchester	332	133	81	247	167	154	172	265	209	242	210	94	40	86	34	192	—	212	119	230	568	64	325
Newcastle	230	270	209	326	295	231	310	344	107	370	143	118	92	187	157	271	132	—	254	412	774	206	518
Nottingham	388	154	50	178	132	84	152	196	265	207	278	92	72	26	104	123	74	158	—	156	512	64	262
Oxford	464	157	63	99	66	79	107	129	341	139	340	163	169	74	156	56	143	256	97	—	402	217	106
Penzance	683	313	268	269	186	329	230	354	560	111	559	412	381	298	350	282	353	481	318	250	—	560	357
Sheffield	358	158	75	217	163	124	176	235	235	248	240	64	36	65	74	162	40	128	40	135	348	—	323
Southampton	530	202	128	60	75	136	119	149	416	111	415	256	235	140	222	79	202	322	163	66	222	201	—

International dialling codes

Australia	00 61
Austria	00 43
Belgium	00 32
Canada	00 1
Cyprus	00 357
Denmark	00 45
Egypt	00 20
France	00 33
Germany	00 49
Gibraltar	00 350
Greece	00 30
India	00 91
Ireland	00 353
Israel	00 972
Italy	00 39
Japan	00 81
Netherlands	00 31
New Zealand	00 64
Norway	00 47
Pakistan	00 92
Poland	00 48
Portugal	00 351
South Africa	00 27
Spain	00 34
Sweden	00 46
Switzerland	00 41
Turkey	00 90
USA	00 1

Telephone services (BT)

Operator
100
International operator
155
Directory enquiries
192
International directory enquiries
153
Customer service
150
Fault reporting
152

How to show your telephone number and national code

Always show your number in full on personal stationery, letterheadings, advertisements etc., in the following form:
Telephone numbers in and around certain major cities including London, are all-figure numbers, e.g. 0171-356 5000 which do not have exchange names.
In any other areas, always show the exchange name (national code) local number.
e.g. Bristol (0117 9) 12345

Helping people abroad to dial you

If you have correspondents abroad, it will help them to dial you if you use the internationally agreed format for showing international numbers, e.g.

National	0171-246 8071
International	+44 71-246 8071

+ tells callers to dial their own international prefix which varies from country to country. 44 is the 'country code' to reach the UK. The '01' of the national code is not dialled by callers abroad.

Starting your own business

If you are starting your own business, the more homework you can do first, the better your chances of success. And the better thought-out your business plan, the better your chances of getting the right financial backing.

A good port of call for help in getting your business on to the right track with the right plan is your local Training and Enterprise Council (TEC) or, in Scotland, Local Enterprise Council (LEC). These can also provide you with a lot of useful information about setting up in business, and free or low-cost business training plans.

If you are unemployed at the time you decide to take the plunge into your own business, you may qualify for a business start-up allowance. But it's important that you apply for one of these before you start the business running, or you may no longer qualify. Talk to your local Job Centre, TEC or LEC about these allowances as soon as possible.

If you need financial support from a bank – such as an overdraft or loan facility – local bank managers can tell you about their own banks' special financial packages for small businesses. Shop around before you decide which one best suits your plans. When you are ready to approach one of the banks with your idea, remember that the bank manager will need to see your business plan before agreeing to support you, so take it with you. Make sure that you understand exactly what loan or overdraft terms are offered, what the interest rate will be, and how it is levied, as well as any other bank charges. The bank should give you a list of its tariffs and charges. Always check your bank statements – errors can occur – and if you don't understand them, or the interest bill, query it. You will also need to keep your own books and records up to date and, depending on your level of turnover, you may need to register for Value Added Tax (VAT). This means you will have to charge VAT on your services to customers, and pass it on to Customs & Excise at regular intervals. It is a good idea to open a separate account and put the VAT you collect into it. That way it's kept separate from the business's own money and is always there to pay the VAT bill on time! You can also reclaim VAT on goods and services bought by your business, netting it out of the VAT you have collected.

Failing to register for VAT, and doing your VAT returns late, can result in hefty fines so do check the current rules with the local VAT office (you'll find their address in the phone book). There is very little leeway for paying VAT (or fines) late. You will also need to fill in a regular tax return. You can offset certain expenses against the business's income before calculating the taxable profit. The Inland Revenue publishes useful leaflets on self-employment, starting a business, and tax matters which will help you with all this.

In the Nineties, the tax system is moving from levying tax on your accounts a year in arrears, towards a system of collecting tax on a self-assessed basis during the current year of trading – so don't expect a year's grace before the first tax bill is due for payment! Your local tax office, or your accountant, will help you cope with the changes. Set money aside regularly for tax, in a separate account, and you should avoid cash crises when the bills are due. You will also earn a little extra interest in the meantime.

If you do find the paperwork hard going, it may be cheaper to hire an accountant or book-keeper to do it for you. That way things are kept up to date while you can spend more of your own time organising and fulfilling profitable business. And your accountant can resolve any hiccups with the taxman or VATman for you.

Keeping your accounts and your tax and VAT matters up-to-date are just as much part of running a business as getting and meeting orders for your goods or services. So are chasing up payment from your customers, and meeting your own bills! Don't neglect any of these or fall behind with them. Set aside a regular day a week or month to keep up to date and you will have a much clearer idea of how things are going.

Houseplants

The essential elements for healthy houseplants are light, water, warmth, humidity and food. An imbalance in any one of these factors can cause flower, leaf, or stem problems.

Water

Overwatering – signs to look out for
– Mouldy flowers
– Poor leaf growth
– Limp, soft leaves
– Rotten patches on leaves
– Wilting yellow leaves
– Brown leaf tips
– Mushy, brown roots
– Old and new leaves fall at same time
Underwatering – signs to look out for
– Wilting leaves with little or no growth
– Curled, yellow lower leaves
– Leaf edges brown and dry
– Oldest leaves fall first
– Quickly fading flowers

Light

Too little light – signs to look out for
– Lower leaves turning yellow, drying up and falling
– Variegated leaves turn completely green
– Growth spindly or absent and abnormal length between leaves
– Leaves smaller and paler than normal
– Flowers poor or absent

Too much light – signs to look out for
– Pale, washed-out looking leaves
– Shrivelled leaves
– Leaves wilt at midday
– Scorch patches on leaves

Temperature

Excess warmth
– Wilting lower leaves
– Brown leaf edges
– Bottom leaves fall
– Spindly growth

Excess cold
– Leaves curl, turn brown and fall
Leaves falling after rapidly turning yellow is often caused by sudden extreme change in temperature.

Humidity

Too much humidity
– Grey mould patches on leaves
– Grey mould on flowers
– Patches of rot on leaves or stems

Too little humidity
– Brown, shrivelled leaf tips
– Yellow leaf edges
– Leaves, buds and flowers may fall

Fertilizer

Too much fertilizer
– Crisp brown spots on leaves
– Scorched edges on leaves
– Leaves wilt
– White crust on surface of composts and clay pot in soft water area
– Summer growth stunted
– Winter growth lanky and feeble

Too little fertilizer
– Slow growth
– Low resistance to pests and diseases
– Flowers are smaller and paler than normal or may be absent altogether
– Weak stems
– Lower leaves drop prematurely

Pot-bound plants

The following symptoms are indications of pot-bound plants:
– Roots growing through drainage hole in bottom of pot
– Stem and leaf growth slow even when plant is fed regularly
– Soil dries out quickly necessitating very frequent watering
– Matted mass of roots at bottom of soil when plant removed from pot

Caring for your houseplant

Indoor plants require a cooler, moister atmosphere than might be expected. During the growing season plants provide plants with a constant, moderate temperature and during the resting season with a cooler atmosphere.

Never use unsterilized soil. To avoid pest and disease either buy specially prepared compost or sterilise soil if you wish to prepare homemade compost.

Inspect new plants carefully for pest or disease
Never put plants . . .
– between an open window and a door
– near an air-conditioning/heating duct
– on top of a television or radiator unless providing excess humidity

– on a windowsill with badly-fitting frames
– in an unlit corner or dark passageway
– between closed curtains and the window during cold weather

Make sure that leaves are kept clean as dirt and dust on plants can prevent them from being able to "breathe". Gently dust smooth-leaved plants with a brush, duster or damp cloth or rinse leaves in tepid water. Cacti, succulents or hairy-leaved plants can be brushed with a soft brush such as a paintbrush.

Cacti can be washed with clean water.

Most plants can be watered from above or below, some species such as African Violets and gloxinias do not like the top of the soil to be wet. The majority of plants like the soil to be just moist but some species (such as azaleas) prefer wetter soil and others (such as cheese plants) require the soil to dry out slightly between waterings. Always use water that is at room temperature.

Common problems with houseplants

SYMPTOM	POSSIBLE CAUSE
Wilting leaves	Both overwatering and underwatering can cause leaves to wilt. Shrivelling and browning of the leaves usually indicates dryness, whereas yellowing leaves would be due to excess water. Wilting may also be caused by too much heat, too much sunlight, too dry an atmosphere, lack of drainage, pot-bound roots or even pest damage.
Brown leaf-tips or edges	Too dry an atmosphere, bruising overwatering, underwatering, too much or too little heat, overfeeding or draughts.
Leaves falling suddenly	Shock caused by plant being moved, sudden change of temperature, sudden change in light intensity or excessive dryness at the roots
Falling leaves on new plants	Loss of one or two leaves is common in newly purchased plants or plants that have been moved or repotted.
Dry and falling lower leaves	Too little light, underwatering or too much heat.
Pale, weak foliage	Poor light conditions, dirt on leaves, red spider mite.
Leaves, firm but yellow	Usually occurs in plants which dislike lime, particularly in hard-water areas or where compost containing calcium has been used. Falling leaves may be caused by overwatering or even simply due to old age.
Variegated leaves turning green	Lack of light.
Rotting leaves and stem	Often caused by disease but may also be due to overwatering in winter or leaving water on leaves at night.
Leaf spots	Crisp, brown leaf spots are often the result of underwatering; soft, dark brown spots are the result of overwatering; white or pale spots may be caused by watering with cold water or water splashes; blisters or sunken, dry spots indicate disease.
Slow or absent plant growth	Normal in winter for most plants. In summer this may be due to underfeeding, too little light, overwatering or even pot-bound roots.
Small, pale leaves spindly growth	In winter and spring often a symptom of excess warmth and overwatering. May also be caused by underfeeding or too little light.
Holes in leaves	Probably pet damage or insect damage
Falling flower buds	Usually caused by moving the plant, too little light, underwatering or dry air.
Quickly-fading flowers	Underwatering, dry air, too much heat or too little light
No flowers	The possible causes are too little light, overfeeding, dry air, repotting or inappropriate daylength
Green slime on pot	Overwatering or blocked drainage.
White crust on pot	Hard water or overfeeding.

Pests and diseases

A simple method to get rid of pests is to secure a plastic bag over the soil to hold plant in its pot, and then rinse the leaves in cool soapy water. When using insecticide always spray plant out of doors.

Common problems

SYMPTOM	POSSIBLE CAUSE	SUGGESTED TREATMENT
Plant weakened and with sticky honeydew deposit	Aphid (Greenfly) – usually green in colour, but may be black, grey or orange	Spray with insecticide, malathion or derris
Leaves turn yellow and drop, sticky deposit on underside of leaves.	Whitefly – tiny white moth-like insects	Spray with insecticide at three-day intervals.
Spotted, distorted flowers, stunted growth, silvery streaks on plant	Thrips – tiny black insects	Spray with insecticide
Ragged holes on leaves	Earwig – dark brown body and pincer-like tail	Insect not usually seen on the plant as it feeds at night and hides during daylight hours. Pick off the insects, check leaves and flowers thoroughly. Spraying is not necessary.
Speckled yellow blotches on leaves; prematurely falling leaves; white webbing sometimes detected between leaves and stems	Red spider mite	Spray with insecticide. Daily misting will help prevent attacks.
Yellowing, wilting and falling leaves.	Mealy bug – small, fluff covered pests, usually visible in clusters on stems and under leaves	Wipe off with damp cloth. In the case of severe attacks treat weekly with insecticide.
Small brown discs attached to underside of leaves. Leaves may turn yellow with sticky deposit	Scale	Wipe with damp cloth and spray plant with insecticide. Once leaves have turned yellow plant may be difficult to save.
Brown moist spots on leaves –spots may enlarge and merge in severe attacks	Leaf spot	Remove affected leaves and spray plant. Keep plant dry for several weeks.
Brown rings on underside of leaves	Rust	Remove affected leaves, improve ventilation around plant and use appropriate spray
Stem of cutting turns black	Black leg – fungus	May be caused by overwatering, inadequate drainage or overcompact soil. Remove infected cutting.
Stem or crown turns soft and rotten	Crown and stem rot	This fungus spreads rapidly therefore unless catching disease very early plant, compost and pot should be thrown away. In early stages remove affected parts and avoid overwatering and underventilating.
Patches of grey, fluffy mould on leaf, stems or flowers, particularly common in cool, humid atmosphere	Grey mould (Botrytis)	Cut away affected parts and remove mouldy compost. Spray. Reduce watering and misting and increase ventilation.
Yellowing and wilting leaves, followed by browning and falling. Tends to occur in cacti, succulents, begnias and palms.	Root or Tubor Rot – fungus	Caused by waterlogged roots. Needs to be dealt with in the early stages. Remove all soil from roots and cut away any roots, stem or leaves that have been affected. Repot in fresh compost and avoid overwatering.
Brown, crumbly growth on underside of leaves	Cork Scab (Oedema)	Remove badly affected leaves and transfer the plant to better lit position and reduce watering. No further treatment is necessary as this is simply the plant's response to waterlogged compost and insufficient light.
White, powdery spots or coating on leaves, may spread to flowers and stem	Powdery mildew	Spray the plant or dust with sulphur, removing any badly-affected leaves. Increase ventilation

Useful addresses

A New Home

The Association of Manufacturers of Domestic Electrical Appliances
AMDEA House
593 Hitchin Road
Stopsley
Luton LU2 7UN

British Association of Removers (BAR)
277 Grays Inn Road
London WC1X 8SY

British Standards Institution
Certification and Assessment Department
Linford Wood
Milton Keynes MK14 6LE

Child Accident Prevention Trust
28 Portland Place
London W1N 4DE

The Consumers' Association
Freepost
24 Buckingham Street
London WC2N 6BR

Decorative Lighting Association
Bryn
Bishop's Castle
Shropshire SY6 5LE

The Home and Contract Furnishing Textile Association
Manchester Chamber of Commerce
Third Floor
56 Oxford Street
Manchester M60 7HJ

Master Locksmiths Association
13 Parkfield Road
Northolt, Middlesex UB5 5NN

National Association of Retail Furnishers
17-21 George Street
Croydon CR9 1TQ

The National Bedding Federation
251 Brompton Road
London SW3 2EZ

National Institute of Carpet Fitters
Wira House
West Park Ring Road
Leeds LS16 6QL

The National Supervisory Council for Intruder Alarms
Queensgate House
14 Cookham Road
Maidenhead, Berks SL6 8AJ

Radio, Electrical and Television Retailers' Association
100 St Martin's Lane
London WC2N 4BD

The Royal Society for the Prevention of Accidents
Cannon House
The Priory Queensway
Birmingham B4 6BS

Basic DIY

Black and Decker
Westpoint
The Grove, Slough, Berks SI1 1QQ

Confederation for the Registration of Gas Installers (CORGI)
St Martin's House
140 Tottenham Court Road
London W1P 9LN

Draught Proofing Advisory Association
External Wall Insulation Association
National Association of Loft Insulation Contractors
National Cavity Insulation Association
all at PO Box 12
Haslemere, Surrey GU27 3AN

Electricity Consumers' Council
Brook House
2/16 Torrington Place
London WC1D 7LL

Electricity Council
30 Millbank
London SW1P 4RD

Federation of Master Builders
14 Great James Street
London WC1N 3PD

Gas Consumers' Council
Sixth Floor
Abford House
15 Wilton Road
London SW1V 1LT

Glass and Glazing Federation
44-48 Borough Heath
London SE1 1XB

The Institute of Electrical Engineers
Savoy Place
London WC2R 0BL

The Institute of Plumbing
64 Station Lane
Hornchurch, Essex RM12 6NB

The National Association of Plumbing, Heating and Mechanical Services Contractors
6 Gate Street
London WC2A 3HX

National Federation of Roofing Contractors
15 Soho Square
London W1V 5FB

The National Inspection Council for Electrical Installation
Vintage House
36-7 Albert Embankment
London SE1 7UJ

The Royal Institution of Chartered Surveyors
12 Great George Street
Parliament Square
London SW1P 3AD

The Scottish and Northern Ireland Plumbing Employers Federation
4 Walker Street
Edinburgh EH3 7LB

Timber Research and Development Association
Stocking Lane
Hughenden Valley
High Wycombe, Bucks HP14 4ND

Water Authorities Association
1 Queen Anne's Gate
London SW1H 9BT

Homecare

ARCO
PO Box 21
Waverley Street
Hull HU1 2BJ

The Association of British Laundry, Cleaning and Rental Services Ltd
Lancaster Gate House
319 Pinner Road
Harrow, Middlesex HA1 4HX

British Pest Control Association
Alembic House
93 Albert Embankment
London SE1 7TU

Carpet Cleaners Association
126 New Walk
De Montfort Street
Leics LE1 7JA

Dylon International Ltd
Worsley Bridge Road
Lower Sydenham
London SE26 5HD

Home Laundering Consultative Council
7 Swallow Place
London W1R 7AA

Lever Brothers Ltd
Consumer Advice Service
Lever House
3 St James's Road
Kingston upon Thames
Surrey KT1 2BA

Rentokil Ltd
Felcourt House
East Grinstead
West Sussex RH19 2JY

The Royal School of Needlework
12 A Hampton Court Palace
East Molesey KT8 9AU

Food and drink

Friends of the Earth
26 Underwood Street
London N1 7JQ

Kitchen Specialists Association
PO Box 123
Horsham, West Sussex RH13 8YU

The Meat and Livestock Commission
5 St John's Square
London EC1M 4DE

Microwave Association
Lansdowne House
Lansdowne Road
London W11 3LP

National Dairy Council
5 John Prince's Street
London W1M 0AP

The Vegetarian Society of the United
Kingdom Ltd
Parkdale
Dunham Road, Altrincham
Cheshire WA14 4QG

Healthcare

Alcoholics Anonymous
PO Box 514
11 Redcliffe Gardens
London SW10 9BQ

Alcohol Concern
305 Gray's Inn Road
London WC1 8QF

ASH (Action on Smoking and Health)
5-11 Mortimer Street
London W1N 7RH

British Airways Medical Centre
75 Regent Street
London W1

British Epilepsy Association
Anstey House
40 Hanover Square
Leeds LS3 1BE

The British Heart Foundation
102 Gloucester Place
London S1H 4DH

The British Medical Association
BMA House
Tavistock Square
London WC1H 9JP

British Migraine Association
1778A High Road
Byfleet, Surrey KT14 7ED

The British Nutrition Foundation
15 Belgrave Square
London SW1X 8PS

The British Red Cross Society
9 Grosvenor Crescent
London SW1X 7EJ

Brook Advisory Centres
153A East Street
London SE1 2SD

Families Anonymous
5–7 Parsons Green
London SW6 4VL

Family Planning Association Information
Service
27–35 Mortimer Street
London W1N 7RJ

Foresight (The Association for
Preconceptual Care)
The Old Vicarage
Church Lane
Witley, Godalming, Surrey GU8 5PN

Health Education Authority
78 New Oxford Street
London WC1A 1AH

The Herpes Association
41 North Road
London N7 9DP

La Leche League
BM3424
London WC1N 3XX

The London Food Commission
80 Old Street
London EC1V 9AR

MASTA
(The London School of Hygiene and
Tropical Medicine)
Keppel Street
London WC1 7HT

The Maternity Alliance
15 Britannia Street
London WC1X 9JP

Medical Advisory Service
10 Barley Mow Passage
London W4 4PH

Miscarriage Association
18 Stoneybrook Close
West Bretton
Wakefield
West Yorkshire WF4 4TP

Narcotics Anonymous
PO Box 417
47 Milman Street, London SW10

National Childbirth Trust
Alexandra House
Oldham Terrace
London W3 6NH

The National Eczema Society
Tavistock House North
Tavistock Square
London WC1H 9SR

Patients' Association
Room 33
18 Charing Cross Road
London WC2H 0HR

PPP Immunisation Clinic
99 New Cavendish Street
London W1M 7FQ

Relate (National Marriage Guidance
Council)
Herbert Gray College
Little Church Street
Rugby CV21 3AP

St Andrew's Ambulance Association
48 Milton Street
Glasgow G4 0HR

St John Ambulance Association
1 Grosvenor Crescent
London SW1X 7EF

Terrence Higgins Trust
BM/AIDS
London WC1N 3XX

Thomas Cook Ltd
45 Berkeley Street
London W1A 1EB

Personal finance and legal matters

The Association of British Insurers (ABI)
Aldermary House
10-15 Queen Street
London EC4N 1TT

Board of Inland Revenue
Somerset House
The Strand, London WC2R 1LB

British Insurance Brokers Association
(BIBA)
14 Bevis Marks, London EC3A 7NT

Building Societies Association
3 Savile Row
London W1X 1AF

Family Law Bar Association
4 Paper Building, Temple
London EC4Y 7EY

Federation of Independent Advice
Centres
13 Stockwell Road
London SW9 9AU

Financial Intermediaries Managers and
Brokers' Regulatory Association (FIMBRA)
22 Great Tower Street
London EC3R 5AQ

Institute of Loss Assessors
14 Red Lion Street
Chesham, Bucks HP5 1HB

The Insurance Ombudsman Bureau
3a Southampton Row
London WC1B 5HJ

Land Registry
32 Lincoln's Inn Fields
London WC2A 3PH

The Law Society
113 Chancery Lane
London WC2A 1PL

Life Assurance and Unit Trust Regulatory
Organisation (LAUTRO)
Centrepoint
103 New Oxford Street
London WC1A 1QH

National Association of Citizens Advice
Bureaux
Myddelton House
115/123 Pentonville Road
London N1 9LZ

National Consumer Council
20 Grosvenor Gardens
London SW1W 0DH

Office of Fair Trading
Field House
Bream Buildings, London EC4A 1PR

Pension Appeals Tribunal
48-49 Chancery Lane
London WC2A IJR

Solicitors Complaints Bureau
Portland House
Stag Place, London SWIE 5BL

Basic car maintenance

HPI
(Hire Purchase Information)
Dolphin House
PO Box 61
New Street
Salisbury, Wiltshire SPI 2TB

DVLA
Swansea SA6 7JL

AA
Norfolk House
Basingstoke RG24 9NY

RAC
RAC House
MI Cros, Brent Terrace
London NW2 ILT

Retail Motor Industry Federation
201 Great Portland Street
London WIN 6AB

Gardening

Seeds
Samuel Dobie & Sons
Broomhill Way
Torquay – Devon TQ 76W
Tel: 0803 616281

W.W. Johnson & Son Ltd
Boston
Lincolnshire PE31 8AD
Tel: 0205 365051

Thompson & Morgan (Ipswich) Ltd
Poplar Lane
Ipswich, Suffolk IP8 3BU
Tel: 0743 688588
(unusual seeds)

Mr. Fothergill's Seeds Ltd.
Gazeley Road
Kentford
Newmarket, Suffolk CB8 7QB
Tel: 0638 751161

Chiltern Seeds
Bortree Stile
Ulverston, Cumbria LA12 7QB
Tel: 0229 581137
(unusual seeds)

Samuel Dobie & Son Ltd (D)
Broomhell Way
Torquay, Devon TQ2 7QW
Tel: 0803 612011

Sutton Seeds
Hele Road,
Torquay, Devon TQ2 7QJ
Tel: 0803 612011
(special grass seeds)

Unwins Seeds Ltd.
Histon, Cambridge CB4 4ZZ
Tel: 0945 588522

Fruit
Higfield Nurseries
Whitminster, Gloucester GL2 7PL
Tel: 0452 740266

Ken Muir
Honeypot Fruit Farm
Clacton, Essex
Tel: 0255 830181

Roses
R Harkness & Co
The Rose Gardens
Cambridge Road
Hitchin, Herts SG4 OJT
Tel: 0462 420402

Herbs
Suffolk Herbs
Sawyers Farm
Little Cornard
Sudbury, Suffolk CO10 ONY
Tel: 0787 227247

Hollington Nurseries
Woolton Hill
Newbury
Berks RG15 9XT
Tel: 0635 253908

Trees and shrubs
Notcutts Nurseries Ltd.
Head Office
Woodbridge
Suffolk IP12 4AF
Tel: 03943 83344

Pets

Most of the Clubs and Societies below
are self-funded and would appreciate a
large (A4) stamped, addressed
envelope with your query.

Cats
Governing Council of the Cat Fancy
4 - 6 Penel Orlieu
Bridgewater, Somerset TA6 3PG

Feline Advisory Bureau
235 Upper Richmond Road
Putney, London SW15 6TL

Dogs
Kennel Club
1 Clarges Street, London WIY 8AB

Guinea pigs
National Cavy Club
Mrs E B van Lliet
Olney Park Cottage
Yardley Road
Olney, Bucks MK46 5EJ

Rats
National Fancy Rat Society
6 Kemps Way
Salehurst
Robertsbridge
East Sussex TN32 5PD

Mice
National Mouse Club
Mr and Mrs R Wilson
29 Manor Close
Tunstead
Norwich NR12 8EP

Rabbits
British Rabbit Council
Purefoy House
7 Kirkgate
Newark
Nottinghamshire NG24 IAD

Hamsters
British Hamster Association
PO Box 825
Sheffield S17 3RU

Parrots
The Parrot Society
108b Fenlake Road
Bedford MK42 0EU

Budgerigars
The Budgerigar Society
49 - 53 Hazelwood Road
Northampton NNI ILG

Fish
Aquarian Advisory Service
Dr David Ford
PO Box 67
Elland
West Yorkshire HX5 0SJ

Tortoises and terrapins
The British Chelonia Group
⅝ Dr R Avery
School of Biological Sciences
The University
Bristol BS8 IUG

The Tortoise Trust
BM Tortoise
London WCIN 3XX

Spiders
British Tarantula Society
81 Phillimore Place
Radlett – Herts WD7 8NJ

Snakes
British Herpetological Society
⅝ Zoological Society of London
Regent's Park
London NWI 4RY

General
RSPCA
Causeway
Horsham
West Sussex RH12 IHG

PDSA
Unit 6B
Ketley Business Park
Telford, Shropshire TF1 4JD

Universities Federation
for Animal Welfare
8 Hamilton Close
South Mimms
Potters Bar
Hertfordshire EN6 3QD

Index